T0319148

Routledge Handbook of Tourism in Africa

This book provides a comprehensive and readable overview of the critical debates and controversies around tourism in Africa, and the major factors that are affecting tourism development now and in the future.

Drawing upon research emerging from collaborations between a growing number of African academics and practitioners based in the continent and in the African diaspora as well as international colleagues, the *Handbook* offers key critical insights into the issues, challenges and trends that Africa and African tourism is facing. Part I covers continent-wide issues such as climate change, ICT, heritage and development. The remaining parts are organised along geographic lines, with each chapter covering the development of tourism, current trends and discussion of critical issues such as community participation, gender, backpacking, urban tourism, wildlife tourism and conservation.

Combining an overview of key theories, concepts, contemporary issues and debates, this book will be a valuable resource for students, academics and practitioners investigating the role of tourism in Africa.

Marina Novelli is Professor of Tourism and International Development at the University of Brighton, UK.

Emmanuel Akwasi Adu-Ampong is an Assistant Professor in the Cultural Geography Chair Group at Wageningen University and Research, the Netherlands, and a Research Associate at the School of Tourism and Hospitality, University of Johannesburg, South Africa.

Manuel Alector Ribeiro is a Lecturer in Tourism Management at the University of Surrey, UK, and a Senior Research Associate at the School of Tourism and Hospitality, University of Johannesburg, South Africa.

Routledge Handbook of Tourism in Africa

Edited by Marina Novelli, Emmanuel Akwasi Adu-Ampong and Manuel Alector Ribeiro

LONDON AND NEW YORK

First published 2021
by Routledge
2 Park Square, Milton Park, Abingdon, Oxon OX14 4RN

and by Routledge
52 Vanderbilt Avenue, New York, NY 10017

Routledge is an imprint of the Taylor & Francis Group, an informa business

British Library Cataloguing-in-Publication Data
A catalogue record for this book is available from the British Library

Library of Congress Cataloging-in-Publication Data
A catalog record has been requested for this book

ISBN: 978-1-138-49608-8 (hbk)
ISBN: 978-0-367-62272-5 (ebk)

Typeset in Bembo
by codeMantra

Contents

Contents

Illustrations

FIGURES

TABLES

Editors and contributors

Editors

Marina Novelli (PhD) is a Professor of Tourism and International Development at the University of Brighton, where she also leads the Responsible Futures' Research and Enterprise Agenda. She has a background in economics and a keen interest in international development. A native of Italy and African by 'professional adoption', she has written and advised extensively in the field of tourism policy, planning, development and management in 20 African destinations to date. She is known for her collaborations with The World Bank Group, the EU, the UN, the Commonwealth Secretariat, National Ministries and Tourism Boards, Regional Development Agencies and NGOs and research that has impact beyond tourism, by contributing to more sustainable economic development, improved environments and more inclusive societies. Her most recent volume *Tourism and Development in Sub-Sahara Africa: Current Issues and Local Realities* (2015, Oxford: Routledge) conveys her extensive empirically grounded research and consultancy engagements in the continent.

Emmanuel Akwasi Adu-Ampong is an Assistant Professor in the Cultural Geography Chair Group at Wageningen University and Research, the Netherlands, and a Research Associate at the School of Tourism and Hospitality, University of Johannesburg, South Africa. He is co-editor of *Tourism Planning and Development* journal. He obtained his PhD from the Department of Urban Studies and Planning at the University of Sheffield, UK. He has previously been a Senior Lecturer in Tourism Management at Sheffield Hallam University and a Lecturer in Tourism Management at the University of Lincoln both in the UK. His interdisciplinary research interests lie mainly in tourism policy and planning, cultural heritage management and international development planning. His work is published in leading international journals in the field of tourism and international development such as *Annals of Tourism Research, Current Issues in Tourism, Tourism Planning and Development, International Development Planning Review* and *Development Policy Review*.

Manuel Alector Ribeiro is a Lecturer in Tourism Management at the University of Surrey, UK, and a Senior Research Associate at the School of Tourism and Hospitality at the University of Johannesburg, South Africa. He holds a Master's degree in Tourism Management and Development and a PhD in Tourism Studies at the University of Algarve, Portugal. He has research interests in applied quantitative methods and modelling to community support for sustainable tourism development, pro-environmental behaviour, place attachment, the political economy of tourism, public trust in tourism institutions, emotional aspect of consumption and gender and entrepreneurship in tourism. His work is published in leading international journals such as *Tourism Management, Journal of Travel Research, Journal of Sustainable Tourism, Journal of Hospitality Marketing and Management or International Journal of Tourism Research*. He serves in the editorial board of the *Journal of Travel Research*.

Contributors

Mariamo Abdula holds a five-year degree in Geography from the Eduardo Mondlane University (UEM), Mozambique, and an MA in International Business from the University of Newcastle, Australia. She is currently a PhD candidate in Tourism at the University of Aveiro (Portugal), being awarded a scholarship from the Calouste Gulbenkian Foundation. Her provisional thesis title is "Image (re)construction of (un)safe tourism destinations: Implications of risk perception in the image of Mozambique". She began her professional career in research at the UEM in 1997 as an assistant researcher at the Center for Population Studies and, later, at the Center for Research in Social Sciences and Health Systems. In 2005 she moved to a teaching career at the Inhambane School of Hospitality and Tourism, teaching courses of Tourism Marketing, Market Studies and Research Methodology. From 2007 to 2016 she also served as Head of the internship department and as Vice-Dean for administration.

Ogechi Adeola teaches Marketing Management at the Lagos Business School (LBS) at Pan-Atlantic University, Nigeria. She is the Academic Director of LBS Sales & Marketing Academy. Her research interests include financial inclusion, tourism and hospitality marketing, strategic marketing and export marketing strategies in sub-Saharan Africa. She has published academic papers in top scholarly journals. Her co-authored papers won Best Paper Awards at conferences in 2016, 2017 and 2018. She holds a Doctorate in Business Administration (DBA) from Manchester Business School, United Kingdom, and started her career at Citibank Nigeria, spending approximately 14 years in the financial sector before moving into academia.

Olayemi Akinoshun is a Technical Instructor at Landover Company where he currently facilitates training of various aviation technical courses including Basic Aircraft Technician Course (BATCO). Prior to joining Landover Company, he was a Cadet Aircraft Engineer with Bristow Group as part of the 20 graduate engineers selected in Nigeria to undergo engineering apprenticeship program and acquisition of aircraft maintenance engineering license (AMEL). Olayemi is a volunteer at *Aviators Africa* where he is facilitating Aviators Africa Academy, a programme aimed at inspiring the next generation of aviation professionals. He is also the online editor of *Aviators Africa* magazine.

Fernando Almeida-García is an Associate Professor at the Department of Geography in the Faculty of Tourism at the University of Malaga, Spain. His research is focused on tourism and residents' attitudes, sustainable development, economic development and tourism policy. He is the Director of the research group "Territory and Tourism" (SEJ-402). He has published many papers on these subjects. He has collaborated in several international projects with European and Latin American universities and taught in these places. Also, he worked professionally for the tourism government in Santiago de Compostela and Melilla (Spain).

Lucy Atieno is a tourism researcher, trained in sustainable tourism and communication studies. She currently works with Sustainable Travel and Tourism Agenda (STTA, Kenya), where she enriched her understanding about creating shared value in tourism. Lucy is passionate about driving sustainability initiatives in tourism and profoundly appreciates seeing how sustainability can make life better in destination communities.

Sisco Auala is a volunteer at Hatika Adult Education Centre where she trains women on community tourism development, tourism product development and entrepreneurship skills. She was awarded a Doctor of Philosophy in Tourism Management (PhD) from the Nelson Mandela University, South Africa, in April 2019. Her research interest lies in sustainable tourism, with a special focus on community tourism development. She is passionate about the transformation of the tourism sector, both in Africa and elsewhere in the world. She believes that tourism has the potential to transform our world by fostering understanding and mutual respect among people, even from disparate backgrounds, and ensuring that tourism benefits all. She recently joined the International University of Management (IUM) in Namibia, Windhoek as a lecturer, as of 1 October 2019.

Julian K. Ayeh teaches at the Department of Tourism and Heritage in the College of Humanities and Social Sciences at United Arab Emirates University. His principal research interests lie within the fields of innovation and technology management, travel consumer behaviour and marketing communications. He received his PhD. in Hotel and Tourism Management from the Hong Kong Polytechnic University. He has worked over the last decade with various universities across continents and authored several publications in top-tier international journals in Hospitality, Tourism and related fields. His current research focuses on strategic management issues in hospitality and tourism organizations as well as the influence of innovation and emergent technological trends on travel consumer behaviour.

Greg Bakunzi has over the past years gained experience working as a Rwandan tour organizer and guide for various international tour operators. His professionalism and reliability, along with an exceptional understanding of the needs and desires of international visitors, have gained him renown among clients and respect among the members of local communities. He relies on a network of contacts in the area, all of whom are happy to take part in his projects. With his experience, know-how and contacts, he is able to make bespoke visitor experience memorable, while also benefiting the locals as much as possible.

Zélia Breda holds a PhD in Tourism, an MA in Chinese Studies (Business and International Relations) and a five-year Degree in Tourism Management and Planning from the University of Aveiro (UAVR) (Portugal). She is an Assistant Professor at the Department of Economics, Management, Industrial Engineering and Tourism (DEGEIT), holding the position of Director of the Master's Degree in Tourism Management and Planning. She is a full researcher of the Research Unit on 'Governance, Competitiveness and Public Policies' (GOVCOPP) of the UAVR, a Vice-President of the Observatory of China and a senior researcher of the Research & Development spin-off tourism company Idtour. She is a member of the editorial, scientific and review boards of a few academic national and international journals, as well as a member of the organizing and scientific committees of international tourism conferences.

Brígida Rocha Brito is an Associate Professor and a scientific coordinator of the BSc in International Relations at the Universidade Autónoma de Lisboa, Portgual. She is an integrated researcher and member of the Board in OBSERVARE, and the Deputy Director of the scientific e-journal indexed in Scopus, JANUS.NET. She holds a Master's degree with dissertation on local development and participatory strategies in Africa and a PhD in African Studies with thesis on ecological tourism and sustainable development in Sao Tome and Principe. She completed postdoctoral research on sustainable local development in African islands as a fellow of FCT. She coordinated a research team project on the impacts of tourism on community development in African islands, funded by FCT. She collaborates with NGOs as an external consultant in development cooperation projects in Africa funded by the European Union. She organizes and participates in scientific meetings and publishes articles, proceedings, books and chapters.

Desmond O. Brown is a native of Sierra Leone and obtained his PhD from Virginia Tech University, USA. He currently serves as a Professor and Chair of the Bob Billingslea School of Hospitality Management at Bethune Cookman University in Daytona Beach, Florida. He previously served as an Associate Professor of Hospitality & Tourism at the University of Kentucky. His research interests include poverty alleviation in developing countries through sustainable tourism. He has published in major industry journals including *International Journal of Hospitality and Event Management; Journal of the Hospitality & Tourism Research; Journal of Vacation Marketing; Journal of Hospitality and Tourism Research; Tourism Management; Journal of Sustainable Tourism* and *International Journal of Hospitality Management.*

Oliver Chikuta is the Executive Dean of the School of Hospitality and Tourism at the Chinhoyi University of Technology, Zimbabwe. His research interests include accessible tourism and nature-based tourism.

Isabelle Cloquet is an Associate Professor in the Department of Geoscience, Environment and Society in the Université Libre de Bruxelles, Belgium. Parts of her research centre around the conceptualization of tourism destination development, including in Africa. Her research on Gabon was conducted as part of her PhD, which was awarded to her in 2015. Since then, she has been involved in several research projects and teaching programmes relating to tourism and sustainable community development in Guinea, Uganda and Madagascar. Aside from her work on Africa, she has additional research interests including the relationships between tourism, social inclusion and well-being; the role of the third sector in the tourism industry; and, more recently, the adoption of smart technologies by tourism organizations, and its effects on employees, the labour market and the structure of the industry.

Jon Danks has over 20 years of senior leadership experience in integrated Digital, Marketing, Communications and Distribution and has travelled extensively across Africa. He held senior roles at British Airways where he took charge of the brand's ancillary market entry, and established the CRM strategy behind their step change in direct performance before leading a new division responsible for integrated communication. He switched sectors into financial services with Aviva to lead distribution and pricing at the UK's most established motoring organization. He was then brought in by the Government ahead of the London 2012 Olympics to restructure its marketing division to drive a strategic skills legacy, before joining The Times Ed as CMO for the world's largest online teaching community. He moved back into aviation with South African Airways to oversee a radical overhaul of digital, marketing and communications, and recently held the Marketing Chair responsibility for the world's largest global aviation alliance.

Frederick Dayour is a Lecturer in Hospitality and Tourism Management at the University for Development Studies, Ghana. He obtained his Bachelor's and Master of Philosophy degrees in tourism management from the University of Cape Coast and PhD from the University of Surrey, the United Kingdom. His research interests comprise ICTs in tourism, tourist risk perception and travel motivations as well as climate change research. He has published in many star-rated journals including *Annals of Tourism Research*, *Tourism Management* and *Tourism Management Perspectives*.

Kwakye Donkor is CEO of Africa Tourism Partners, a South African-based International Tourism, Strategic Marketing and Advisory agency with offices and alliances partners in Botswana, China, Ghana, Nigeria, Tanzania, Kenya, Rwanda, Singapore, Scotland, the United Kingdom, the United States and Zimbabwe. He is convener of the Africa Tourism Leadership Forum and Africa Business & MICE Tourism Master Classes (Africa MICE Academy), Africa Women in Tourism Summit and Youth in Tourism Initiatives. He is an international tourism and destination marketing expert, with a global reputation in leading and working with key stakeholders and teams in research, destination strategy formulation and implementation, marketing and Business and MICE Tourism development in Africa. He's a Guest Lecturer at TUT Business School, South Africa.

Oserere Eigbe is currently a Private Research Assistant to a Faculty Member at the Lagos Business School at Pan Atlantic University, Lagos, Nigeria. She holds a Master's degree in Information Science and a Bachelor's degree in Economics, both from the University of Ibadan, Nigeria. Her areas of research interest include but not limited to teaching, technology and innovation.

Maria Celeste Eusébio is an Assistant Professor at the Department of Economics, Management, Industrial Engineering and Tourism (DEGEIT) of the University of Aveiro (UAVR) (Portugal) and full researcher of the Research Unit on 'Governance, Competitiveness and Public Policies' (GOVCOPP) of the UAVR. She holds a PhD in Tourism from the UAVR, an MSc in Economics from the University of Coimbra and a five-year Degree in Tourism Management and Planning from the UAVR. She has held several coordinating positions regarding the first and second cycle of studies in Tourism, being currently the Director of the BSc in Tourism. She has been involved in several research projects, and has authored and edited several works in international relevant publications. She has also participated in the organizing and scientific committees of several national and international conferences, being a member of editorial committees and review boards of national and international journals. Her research interests include tourism and economic development.

Sarah Gafarou has experience working in the realm of international development for NGOs and international organizations. She specializes in promoting tourism as a tool for development. She currently works as a regional project specialist for the Regional Africa Department at UNWTO in Madrid, Spain, and holds a MSc Environment and Development from King's College, London. Prior to this experience, she conducted field research in Niger, delving into the specifics of tourism there and investigating the constraints and opportunities of its use for conservation in the context of W National Park, a transboundary-protected area shared with Benin and Burkina Faso.

Edson Gandiwa is a Professor and Dean of the School of Wildlife, Ecology and Conservation at Chinhoyi University of Technology, Zimbabwe. His research interests include media framing of wildlife conservation and biodiversity conservation.

Julia Kathryn Giddy is a Lecturer in Geography at the University of Mpumalanga and a Research Associate at the University of Johannesburg. The majority of her research has focused on human-environment interaction in the tourism sector, with a specialization in adventure tourism. She has also published work on the influence of extreme weather and climate change on South Africa's tourism industry. She is currently involved in a long-term project analysing linkages between state-owned tourism assets and SMME development in large state-owned wildlife parks throughout South Africa. Her more recent research, however, has focused largely on the tourism-poverty nexus, including tourism in inner city Johannesburg and examining tourism and the gig economy within a decent work framework.

Judy Kepher Gona is the Founder of Sustainable Travel & Tourism Agenda, an organization that uses education, research, advocacy and training to promote sustainable tourism as a quality management system. She has over 20 years' experience working with the tourism sector, community-based tourism and community conservation. She holds an MA in Rural Sociology & Community Development from the University of Nairobi, Kenya. She has built her career in tourism around community-based tourism and conservation, certification and sustainability assessment and social impact assessment. Judy has served as a judge of WTTC Tourism for Tomorrow Awards, onsite evaluator for Nat Geo Unique Lodges of the World and World Legacy Awards, as a judge for IIPT Awards and co-chair of Africa Tourism Leadership Awards. She has previously served in TIES and GSTC boards and is current board member of Fair-Trade Tourism. In 2019, she was awarded the Sustainable Citizen Award by Forbes Woman Africa.

Marie-Alise Elcia Grandcourt is the Director of the Africa Programme at the UNWTO. She is an experienced Regional Program Director with a demonstrated history of working in the international trade and development industry. Skilled in Sustainable Development, Front Office, Travel Planning, Business Travel, and Incentive Travel, she is a strong business development professional. She is a graduate from the Singapore Hotel and Tourism Education Centre (SHATEC).

Wame L. Hambira is a Senior Research Scholar and Coordinator of the Climate Change Research Programme at the Okavango Research Institute at the University of Botswana. Her research entails determining the effects of climate change on livelihoods and businesses as well as identifying potential response trajectories across the Okavango River Basin. This includes analysing national and sub-regional policy frameworks to identify gaps with the view of mainstreaming sustainable development and the green economy. She holds a PhD in Geography (Tourism & Climate change) from the University of Oulu, Finland, and an MSc in Environmental Economics at the University of York (UK).

Vyasha Harilal is a Lecturer in the Tourism Department at the School of Tourism and Hospitality at the College of Business and Economics at the University of Johannesburg.

She holds a Master of Social Science in Geography and Environmental Management, and also holds her Honours and Bachelor degree's in the same field, all from the University of KwaZulu Natal. She is currently registered for a PhD in Tourism and Hospitality Management at the School of Tourism and Hospitality. She has been lecturing in the fields of human geography and tourism since 2011, and is involved in research related to these domains, including community development, eco-tourism and policy-related issues. She is the author of various works, including journal articles and a book chapter, on the aforementioned topics.

Heather Jeffrey is a Senior Lecturer in the Social Sciences at Middlesex University, Dubai. She completed her PhD in 2017 on the topic of discourse, gender and tourism within the context of Tunisia, and her main research interests are women's rights, genders and feminism within the context of tourism. She is a Marie-Curie alumnus, an associate at the charity Equality in Tourism, and was nominated for an emerging scholar profile in the *e-Review of Tourism Research* where she is now managing editor. Her first co-edited book on gender-based violence and tourism was published in 2020 with CABI.

Bénédicte Joan has dedicated over ten years of management experience in human resources development and tourism across humanitarian field in sub-Saharan Africa and Asia to create a non-profit that trains women in sustainable tourism. She is a Congolese (Brazzaville) young leader and the Founder and Board Member of Train & Travel, a Community Tourism Non-Profit based in Abidjan, Côte d'Ivoire. She focuses on strategic partnerships and digital branding for solidarity tourism and training for disadvantaged women. She is an experienced traveller, having been to over 60 countries on a shoestring. She is passionate about exchanging skills with youth and women when visiting a new country. Her passion for sustainable tourism led her to be recognized as a Young African Leader 2018, a programme initiated by President Barack Obama. Her vision is to encourage women in her community to work and believe in tourism using the 17 Sustainable Development Goals as a tool.

Forbes Kabote is a Lecturer in the School of Hospitality and Tourism at the Chinhoyi University of Technology, Zimbabwe. His research interests include sustainable tourism, domestic tourism and tourism economics.

Tatenda W. Kaswaurere is a Travel Consultant at Chirorodziva Travel and Tours in the School of Hospitality and Tourism at the Chinhoyi University of Technology, Zimbabwe.

Nana Osei Kwadwo is a Journalist and a curator based in Accra Ghana. He holds a BA in Communication Studies from the Ghana Institute of Journalism. He has worked as a new media strategist for UNICEF Ghana and Gallery 1957. For the past year, he's been researching and documenting Ghana's public transport system called the "Trotro" and collaborating with Prof. Marina Novelli and her team from the University of Brighton researching on the role of contemporary arts in community development and well-being.

Noel Biseko Lwoga is a Lecturer and Head of the Department of Archaeology and Heritage Studies at the University of Dar es Salaam in Tanzania, and a postdoctoral fellow in the Department of Tourism at the University of Johannesburg in South Africa. He obtained Bachelor and Master's degrees in Tourism and Heritage at Makerere University in Uganda and Open University of Tanzania. He also completed a Master's degree in Archaeology and a PhD in Business Administration at the University of Dar es Salaam, Tanzania. His research focuses on integrating socio-cultural and tourism-based economic approaches – putting the local communities at the centre – in analysing heritage and its value, and in bringing the link between conservation and development of heritage resources. He also investigates issues on heritage consumer behaviour, local resident's sustainable behaviours, local stakeholder participation in tourism and conservation and heritage marketing and entrepreneurship.

Joseph E. Mbaiwa is a Professor of Tourism Studies and the Director at the Okavango Research Institute (ORI) at the University of Botswana. He graduated with a PhD in Recreation, Park & Tourism Sciences at Texas A&M University (USA) in 2008. He also holds MSc Environmental Science, postgraduate Diploma in Education (PGDE) and Bachelor degree in Environmental Science all from the University of Botswana. He has close to 20 years' experience in tourism and natural resource management research and consultancy experience in Botswana. He has widely published on issues of tourism development, rural livelihoods and biodiversity conservation issues with focus on the Okavango Delta Botswana. He was a task force member appointed by the Ministry of Environment, Natural Resource Conservation and Tourism to prepare a proposal dossier that resulted in the Okavango Delta being listed as the 1000th UNESCO World Heritage Site.

Huda Abdullah Megeirhi holds a PhD in Tourism Management, and she is a senior researcher at the University of Benghazi, Libya. Her main research interest lies in the field of cultural heritage preservation at UNESCO world heritage sites and resident behaviour at tourist destinations. She also has research interested in other areas such as organizational behaviour and positive physiological capital. Her research outputs were presented in several international conferences and published in several *SSCI* journals.

John Thomas Mgonja is a native of Tanzania and obtained his doctorate degree from the Department of Parks, Recreation and Tourism Management (PRTM) at Clemson University, South Carolina, the USA in 2015. He received his BSc in Food Science and Technology from the Sokoine University of Agriculture and MSc degree in Food Quality Management specializing in food safety and supply net-chains from Wageningen University in the Netherlands. Between 1999 and 2005, he worked as a Quality Assurance Manager in two food processing companies before making the transition into academia at the Sokoine University of Agriculture in Morogoro, Tanzania, where he was appointed as an Assistant Lecturer in the Department of Tourism and Recreation. His research interests lie in sustainable tourism development and poverty alleviation, community development, community-based tourism/ecotourism, local food and food tourism, conservation, as well as visitors' management. He has also worked as a Project Manager for a now-profit organization known as KWIECO/APT, a project which focused on empowering rural destitute women in Kilimanjaro region.

Never Muboko is the Chair of the Department of Wildlife Ecology and Conservation at the Chinhoyi University of Technology, Zimbabwe. His research interests include social ecology and community-based natural resource conservation.

Thomas Muller is an entrepreneur with more than 37 years of experience in IT and more than 16 years in digital marketing and technology in the global hospitality and tourism industry. While working for companies such as IBM, Vodafone, TUI, Thomas Cook, amongst others, he was part of opening four Hotels, turning around Hotels and other tourism businesses and started rainmaker digital as a social enterprise TravelTech company in Namibia in 2016. Thomas had the opportunity of working and living in eight countries around the globe and Southern Africa is his home for more than 10 years. It is his passion to democratize technology for African destinations and its hospitality and tourism businesses to keep more tourism spend in the destination for sustainable tourism development. For the achievements of the 5 Stages of Success and the VISTA Destination Network, Thomas and rainmaker were honoured with several awards in Europe, the United States, and Africa.

Ian E. Munanura is an Assistant Professor in the Department of Forest Ecosystems and Society at Oregon State University, USA. His research seeks to identify factors that affect rural household's resilience and well-being, which impede the coexistence of humans and natural systems in globally important ecoregions, and the mitigation potential of tourism. He also teaches courses on sustainable tourism planning, and applied experiences of ecotourism and human ecology. His geographical area of scholarship interest is the Pacific Northwest, Southeast Asia and East Africa.

Omotayo Muritala is a Research Manager at the Lagos Business School. He obtained a Master's degree in Economics from the University of Ibadan with a special interest in Development Economics. Before joining Lagos Business School, he worked as a Deputy Research Executive at Value Fronteira Ltd where he was engaged in consulting studies for USAID, NESG/World Bank and private organizations in Nigeria. In 2014/15 he was a member of the team that produced technical requirements for "Strengthening Advocacy and Civic Engagement": a nation-wide study that examined media strategies for strengthening advocacy programs and public policy reforms in Nigeria. He is a passionate economist and was a Development Knowledge Facilitator (DKF) on Millennium Development Goal. He is exploring studies in behavioural economics.

Chiedza Ngonidzashe Mutanga is a Senior Lecturer in the School of Hospitality and Tourism at the Chinhoyi University of Technology, Zimbabwe. Her research interests include sustainable tourism and wildlife tourism management.

Rayviscic Mutinda Ndivo holds a PhD in Tourism and Hospitality Management obtained from Kenyatta University and a postdoctorate in Tourism Planning and Development from Switzerland. His areas of research interests are in tourism development and planning, destination competitiveness, tourism product development and tourism investment. He is currently a tourism planning consultant with the UN Economic Commission for Africa (UNECA) and a Senior Lecturer at the Mount Kenya University's School of Hospitality, Travel & Hospitality Management. Key among his past experiences include formulation of the National Tourism Master Plan for Ethiopia and a policy research on the convergence of the Tourism and Aviation sector in Africa. Currently, he is the consultant in the formulation of the African Tourism Strategy Framework.

Ben Ohene-Ayeh is communication and PR consultant with three decades of experience with Ghana Tourism Authority, New Times Corporation and many other news outlets in Ghana. He is currently Consulting Editor for VoyagesAfric Travel Magazine.

Haywantee Ramkissoon is a Professor based at the College of Business, Law and Social Sciences at the University of Derby in the UK, and at the School of Business and Economics at UiT at The Arctic University of Norway. She also holds a Senior Research Associate position at Johannesburg Business School at the University of Johannesburg, South Africa. Her previous teaching and research experience were at Monash and Curtin University, Australia. She has been honoured for Research Excellence including Australia's best 5 performers from Business, Economics & Management and in top 40 researchers with a career of less than 10 years in Australia and the prestigious 2017 Emerging Scholar of Distinction award from the International Academy for the Study of Tourism for her substantial contribution to ground-breaking and innovative research in tourism. She also received the 'distinguished educator and scholar' award for her contributions. Haywantee has published widely and serves on several editorial boards of prestigious journals and international scientific committees. She is the book review editor for *Current Issues in Tourism,* and serves as *Research Note/Associate Editor* for the *Journal of Hospitality Marketing & Management.* Her current research focuses on behaviour change, public health, sustainable tourism, pro-environmental behaviour, place attachment, health tourism, corporate social responsibility and cultural heritage management. She works closely with industry partners and academic institutions and organizations, and disseminates her work through conferences, workshops and seminars.

Christian M. Rogerson is Research Professor in the School of Tourism and Hospitality at the College of Business & Economics at the University of Johannesburg. His research interests are in the tourism-development nexus, small business development and local economic development.

Jayne M. Rogerson is an Associate Professor in the School of Tourism and Hospitality at the College of Business & Economics at the University of Johannesburg. Her research interests are in urban tourism, greening of tourism, historical aspects of tourism and hotel geographies.

Nick Rumens is a Professor of Business and Management at Oxford Brookes University, UK. His main research interests are lesbian, gay, bisexual, transgender and queer (LGBTQ) sexualities and genders in organizations, workplace friendships and queer and feminist theories. He has published on these topics in journals including *Human Relations, Organization Studies, British Journal of Management, Organization, International Journal of Human Resource Management, Journal of Personal and Social Relationships, Sociological Review and Gender, Work & Organization.* He has also (co)authored and (co)edited books including *Contemporary perspectives on ecofeminism* (Routledge, 2016); *Sexual Orientation at Work: International issues and perspectives* (Routledge, 2014); *Queer Company: Friendship in the work lives of gay men* (Ashgate, 2011). His latest single-authored book is *Queer Business: Queering organisation sexualities* (Routledge, 2018).

Andrea Saayman is a Professor in Economics and research program leader at the School of Economic Sciences as well as a researcher for Tourism Research in Economic, Environs and Society (TREES) at the North-West University. She is an applied econometrician, and her research interests include topics such as tourism economics and forecasting, financial and exchange rate economics. She was recently elected as President of the International Association for Tourism Economics for the term 2019–2021. She is also on the editorial boards of a number of international journals.

Melville Saayman was a Professor and Research Director for Tourism Research in Economic, Environs and Society (TREES) at the North-West University. He was active in the field of tourism and leisure economics and development with a clear focus on poverty alleviation. He has done significant research in the field of event economies, nature-based tourism, marine tourism and how these types of tourism alleviate poverty. He served on numerous international editorial boards and has published in the majority of national and international tourism journals. He sadly passed away in March of 2019.

Edwin Sabuhoro is an Affiliate Professor in the Human Dimensions of Natural Resources Department at the Warner College of Natural Resources of the Colorado State University, USA. He is the former Chairman of Rwanda Chamber of Tourism. He leads community outreach programs in East Africa, which engage and support wildlife poachers to improve livelihoods through integrated and community-based human development and wildlife conservation programs.

Dagnachew Leta Senbeto is a Research Assistant Professor at Lee Shau Kee School of Business and Administration at The Open University of Hong Kong. He was previously a Lecturer and researcher at Arba Minch University, Ethiopia. He has completed his PhD at The School of Hotel and Tourism Management at The Hong Kong Polytechnic University. His research interests include crisis, sustainability, seasonality and workforce in tourism and hospitality.

Aby Sene-Harper is a faculty in the Department of Parks, Recreation and Tourism Management at Clemson University, USA. Her research areas include sustainable tourism, rural development and parks and protected areas management. Her work seeks to inform strategy and policy development to integrate rural and historically marginalized communities in development and conservation programs in sub-Saharan Africa and the United States. She has been involved in major research studies including the evaluation of the integrated management plans in two national parks, one in Senegal and another in Mauritania, and the impact of tourism development on the Gullah-Geechee community of South Carolina. More recently, she's been involved in studies funded by the US National Park Service and designed to increase national park visitation by African American tourists. She has written several technical reports and published numerous journal articles on topics of community-based tourism, diversity and inclusion in US national parks, and rural livelihoods within the context of conservation.

Doaa Shohaieb is currently a Lecturer of Marketing at Portsmouth University, UK. She graduated from Menoufia University, Egypt, in 2006 and held a position there as a Lecturer Associate for nearly six years. She received her PhD from the University of York, UK, which focused on the marketing strategies used in the tourism industry in Egypt during political crises. She has since been interested in the history of the Egyptian tourism sector and keen to learn more about current topics in the field of tourism. Her research interests are relatively broad, but through the last few years she has been focusing on marketing strategies, tourism and business history. Her dream is to be able to play a role in this industry in the future especially when it faces unexpected circumstances. She now teaches courses in marketing and tourism.

Vishnee Sowamber is PhD researcher in Tourism and Socio-economic Development at Coventry University, UK (Centre for Financial and Corporate Integrity, Faculty of Business and Law). She has co-authored book chapters on tourism, environment and sustainable development. Vishnee has over a decade of experience as a sustainable development strategist who has worked with resorts present in Mauritius, Reunion Is., Maldives, China, Turkey and different stakeholders in South Africa, Europe, the United States, Asia, among others, gearing projects in line with international Sustainability Frameworks [UN Global Compact, UN SDGs, Global Reporting Initiative, Montreal Greenhouse Gas Protocol, DEFRA UK

(Department of Environment, Food & Rural Affairs), HCMI (Hotel Carbon Management Initiative)], all while contributing to the GRI Stakeholder Council. Vishnee also holds a LLB, a MBA and a BSc in Tourism, with various academic and professional awards, both nationally and internationally.

Tembi Tichaawa is the Academic Head of the Tourism Department and an Associate Professor in Tourism at the School of Tourism and Hospitality at the University of Johannesburg. He holds a PhD in Geography and Environmental Management from the University of KwaZulu-Natal, and a Master's degree in Tourism and Hospitality Management (Cum Laude) from the Cape Peninsula University of Technology. He has a combined 19 years' industry and academic experience in the domain of tourism, events and hospitality management. He is a passionate lecturer and researcher; he lectures a number of modules in the tourism discipline including Tourism Development, Management and Research Methodology. He conducts research on a range of developmental issues linked to tourism, hospitality and events management with specific focus on the developing country context. He is the author of over 65 published scholarly works including journal articles and book chapters.

Toni Ukachukwu is the Publisher and CEO of *Aviators Africa*, a media and integrated marketing company that provides services for the travel and tourism industry. He also founded Aviators Africa Academy, a social enterprise that seeks to inspire and engage the next generation in aviation and Aerospace in Africa. Toni is the Aviation Development Director, Africa, at AviaDev. This premier route development event dedicated to improving air connectivity to, from and within the African continent. He is the Regional Manager at African Business Travel Association (ABTA)and partner at Nigeria Travel Week.

Armand Viljoen is a researcher for TREES at the North-West University. He obtained his PhD in May 2018 and has to date co-authored 13 articles in national and international journals. His research interests include the management and segmentation of niche tourism experiences. This is applied in various tourism contexts such as national park and wildlife tourism, national arts festivals and events and culinary tourism experiences.

Kojo Bentum Williams is Managing Editor and CEO of VoyagesAfriq Media Limited, a pan African travel media company, which publishes VoyagesAfriq Travel Magazine Quarterly and operates the online portal VoyagesAfriq.com. In 2019, he was appointed as the UN World Tourism Organization's (UNWTO) Senior Expert for Communications in Africa, with the aim to grow visibility about the UNWTO's ten-point Africa agenda and reach out to members of the African media and hold clinics to further train and inform travel media on the continent.

Kyle Maurice Woosnam is an Associate Professor of Parks, Recreation, and Tourism Management within the Warnell School of Forestry and Natural Resources at the University of Georgia. He is also a Senior Research Fellow in the School of Tourism and Hospitality Management at the University of Johannesburg. His research centres on community and sustainable tourism research – primarily focused on resident and tourist interactions. In his spare time, he enjoys watching his Alma Mater, Clemson University, own the NCAA during the football season. His research has appeared in *Tourism Management, Journal of Travel Research, Annals of Tourism Research, Journal of Sustainable Tourism, Journal of Hospitality and Tourism Research, Tourism Geographies, the International Journal of Tourism Research*. Throughout the last 15 years, he has conducted research in over 25 countries on six continents.

Foreword

On behalf of the World Tourism Organization (UNWTO), it is my great pleasure and privilege to share a message on the importance of sustainable tourism development for the Africa region. 2018 was a year of immense growth for African tourism. Outgrowing the world average, international tourist arrivals were up around 8%, adding around 63 million people crossing borders for tourism purposes, and continuing to make the sector more important than ever for African economies and societies. These strong results show the potential of tourism in the continent. They are a proof that today many African countries are:

- prioritizing tourism in their development agendas,
- improving the business climate for tourism, and
- encouraging investment in infrastructure and hospitality.

UNWTO forecasts that tourism growth in Africa will more than triple to 134 million international arrivals by 2030, thanks to sustained annual growth of 4%–5%. UNWTO expresses its support and commitment to ongoing collaboration with our African Member States, and the private and public sector stakeholders in their continued efforts to maximize this potential and make tourism a force for positive change in Africa.

Tourism is a people's sector. One in ten people in the world is directly or indirectly employed by tourism. Ours is the responsibility to ensure that tourism benefits each and every community, leaving no one behind. If well managed, tourism's sustained growth brings immense opportunities for economic welfare and lasting development. Yet, it also represents many challenges. Adapting our sector to safety and security, constant market changes, digitalization or to the limits of our natural resources should be among the priorities in our common action. As we move towards a future guided by the universal 17 Sustainable Development Goals (SDGs), I take upon me to lead UNWTO with a strong focus on building partnerships with the public and private sector, fostering jobs and opportunities for all, mastering technology and innovation and advancing sustainability as well as the fight against climate change.

Tourism has an undisputed positive impact on reducing poverty and inequality around the world. International tourism moved over 1.4 billion people in 2018 alone. It contributes to economies, enriches societies and impacts lives. Hence, tourism can be a pillar of Africa's structural transformation and socioeconomic reform and an essential tool for Africa to reach the SDGs and the objectives set in the Africa Union Agenda 2063. This needs closer and stronger collaboration. We need to ensure innovative ways of financing, to foster the collaboration with the private sector along the tourism value chain and to better support small and medium enterprises. We need to promote the sustainable management of resources, and we need to share the good news coming out of Africa with the world. These are important steps along the way to creating more and better quality jobs and business opportunities, especially for the women and the youth which will spearhead Africa towards a better future. This is the key goal and focus behind the work of UNWTO in Africa and features among the top priorities of my mandate that have been formed by listening to the needs of our Member States. Creating more and better tourism jobs, improving tourism education and fostering innovation are among the crucial ones, because the competitiveness of our sector, and of African economies, depends on how much we invest in delivering them.

Our Agenda for Africa is based on listening to Member State needs, the specific needs of Africa. We are certain to have built a truly common action plan to serve the common objectives. The central priorities of the agenda are:

- to alleviate poverty through tourism projects,
- to find innovative approaches to developing tourism in the region, and
- to find and foster new partnerships and resources.

It is important for us to frame these priorities to Africa, as this region will be one of the fastest-growing in tourism terms between now and 2030, with research that support these being highly welcomed.

ZURAB POLOLIKASHVILI
SECRETARY-GENERAL,
United Nations World Tourism Organization (UNWTO)
Madrid, Spain

Preface

In recent times, the "Africa Rising" chorus is being heard across multiple socio-economic, political and cultural arenas. The tourism sector is one of such arenas in which much has been written about the promise, potential and pitfalls of tourism in transforming communities across the continent. Much of this "Africa Rising" related narratives within the tourism sector, however, tend to be written by those with only a passing knowledge of a vastly complex continent. Tourism, while a global phenomenon, is mediated by local specificities. There is an urgent need to pay attention to the nuances this entail instead of relying on unexamined categories and stereotypes. It is this commitment to nuance, specificity and local perspectives that has drawn the three editors together for this project. When the invitation came to develop this *Routledge Handbook of Tourism in Africa*, we enthusiastically signed up, as we envisaged the potential opportunities it represented – although we underestimated the challenges this would also pose.

This *Handbook of Tourism in Africa* was conceived out of a commitment to a collaborative project that showcases critical research grounded in local thinking and nuance, the wisdom and empirically grounded writings, primarily by African academics and practitioners about Africa. We sought to make this *Handbook* a dialogue between academics and industry practitioners. Our attempt has been to allow those at the forefront of the day-to-day workings of the tourism sector on the African continent to provide the perspectives paramount to a critical study of the sector. We have endeavoured to balk the trend of distinguishing North Africa from sub Saharan Africa by viewing the continent as a whole. Using the United Nations Geoscheme for Africa as a guide, we have included Chapters and InFocus sections from Eastern Africa, Middle Africa, Northern Africa, Southern Africa and Western Africa.

Our ambition from the onset was to have a comprehensive representation of countries across the continent, especially countries that are poorly represented within the tourism literature. In the end, our ambition met with the reality of the availability of research and willingness of authors to contribute to this project. We believe that the results of our approach have been the assembly of Chapters and InFocus sections by a distinguished array of scholars in various stages of their academic careers and industry practitioners. We have made considerable efforts to have contributions from non-English speaking countries on the continent. We believe that the contributors to this *Handbook* have presented what collectively comes together as an extensive overview of some of the challenging, changing and innovative areas of tourism research and practice across the continent. The geographic spread of cases and topics covered in this *Handbook* is especially gratifying, as they are at the interface of academic research and the concerns of industry practitioners. We see our role in this regard as providing an avenue that stimulates further critical reflection on the dynamism and complexity of tourism on the continent by curating research which is representative of academics, practitioners and community members from as many walks of life possible.

As with a book of this nature, there are many people who have to be acknowledged and thanked for their support. We would like to first thank all our contributors, both scholars and practitioners who have contributed a Chapter or an InFocus piece. We are immensely grateful for their willingness and commitment.

Marina would like to acknowledge the critical eyes and inspirational presence of her two co-editors of this volume: Dr Adu-Ampong to whom she will be forever grateful for taking over the bulk of the editorial work at a rather difficult time of her life and Dr Ribeiro for working tirelessly to complete this collection. There are very special people which we encounter during our professional life and those two are undoubtedly a reflection of that. In addition to this, she would like to acknowledge the importance of the continued support received by her family, friends and colleagues and the immense value of the inspiring encounters during her travel throughout the continent. Emmanuel would like to thank his fellow editors for the conviviality and discussions throughout this project; his children, Zoë, Joshua and Daniel for allowing their Papa the space to 'work-from-home' and for providing him respite through their *"Buurman & Buurman"* antics; and – above all – he would like to acknowledge the devoted and constant support of his wife, Marre, who makes it possible for him to maintain an academic life and a thriving family life. Alector would like to thank his fellow editors Marina and Emmanuel for their encouragement to embrace this project, ongoing camaraderie and their passion for studying tourism in Africa. He would also like to thank his parents Artur and Maria Antónia, for their continuous support and love. Finally, Alector would like to extend the most sincere gratitude to Montserrat for her extraordinary love and support throughout the years.

We hope this *Routledge Handbook of Tourism in Africa* will be the first of many collections sharing what African tourism is all about. Despite the obvious challenges associated with the sector and the fast-evolving continental socio-economic context, we hope that some of the lesson learnt here may serve to make a better future for the continent.

Marina Novelli, University of Brighton, UK
Emmanuel Akwasi Adu-Ampong, Wageningen University, the Netherlands
Manuel Alector Ribeiro, University of Surrey, UK
January, 2020

COVID-19 Notice

By the time you will be reading this book, the changing effects of the COVID-19 global health pandemic will be ongoing and will have triggered an unprecedented crisis in the global tourism economy. Most tourism destinations around the world have been deeply suffering from the economic consequences of the widespread lockdown policies and borders' closure. The COVID-19-induced tourism crisis has touched all aspects of the sector with consequences on conservation, heritage and livelihoods at large, to name just a few. Many have lost their jobs while several tourism businesses have folded up indefinitely, leaving many communities in general economic hardship. In Africa, the situation is having catastrophic consequences due to the high dependence on international travel and tourism.

Given that this book was put together prior to the onset of COVID-19, it not only provides a useful state of the art collection related to the pre-COVID-19 period, but the results, discussion and conclusions will be extremely useful as terms of reference to reflect and act while the COVID-19 crisis unfolds and hopefully will end. Several have been the measures put in place to save tourism, but the challenges that COVID-19 has brought to Africa's tourism will be felt for many years to come. Having said this, it has provided an opportunity for novel ways to rethink the sector in a more resilient fashion. Like in many other parts of the world, the attention has shifted to domestic and regional tourism patterns and great efforts are being made to encourage and expand health and safety measures.

The recovery of tourism post-COVID-19 is being treated like 'a wild beast' that nobody knows how to fully tame, but the issues, challenges and opportunities discussed in this *Routledge Handbook of Tourism in Africa* remain relevant more than ever, as any future rethinking and resetting process of Africa's tourism require clear insights into what the sector has been like for the past few decades and what it will need to be in the future. The tourism sector is one of the most resilient and is likely to bounce back post-COVID-19, but robust strategy for recovery and stronger global collaborations will be paramount for the future of tourism globally and in the African continent.

Given the centrality of further understanding tourism at such a complex historical time, this book provide insights into core issues of great interest to practitioners, students, academics and the general public.

Emmanuel (Wageningen, the Netherlands),
Alector (Algarve, Portugal) & Marina (Bari, Italy)
August, 2020

Introduction

Tourism in Africa – continental issues and regional contexts

Emmanuel Akwasi Adu-Ampong,
Marina Novelli and Manuel Alector Ribeiro

Introduction

A consensus seems to have been reached between academics and practitioners regarding the potential of tourism as a vehicle for economic growth, job creation, environmental conservation and poverty alleviation in both developed and developing countries. At the global level, the United Nations World Tourism Organisation (UNWTO, 2019) estimates that tourism is the world's third largest export category after chemicals and fuels, and ahead of automotive products and food. Notwithstanding the occasional shocks, tourism has demonstrated strength and resilience over the past years contributing to 10% of global GDP and representing one out of ten jobs. The sector makes up 30% of all services export and contributes to USD 1.4 trillion or 7% of the world's exports (UNWTO, 2018). The tourism sector has enjoyed continued expansion with international arrivals and receipts reaching 1.4 billion and USD 1.4 billion, respectively, in 2018 (UNWTO, 2019). Much of this continued growth is to be found in emerging economies in Asia and the Pacific as the fastest-growing tourism region in 2018 followed by Africa.

Indeed, that travel and tourism is a potential major contributor to Africa's economy is an increasingly discussed topic (Christie et al., 2014; Novelli, 2015; UNCTAD, 2017). However, in an era of growing tourist arrivals at global level and especially on the African continent, the phenomenon of tourism in Africa requires deeper consideration in terms of its potential and challenges, as much as its inconsistent and questionable implications for development at the regional and local level (Novelli, 2015). Given the economic, social and environmental importance of tourism in Africa, there is a need for a comprehensive and readable overview of the critical debates and controversies in tourism at regional level and the major factors that are affecting tourism development now and in the foreseeable future. It is thus these inherent arguments and paradoxes regarding the under-utilising of tourism's potential in Africa that this book attempts to address.

This chapter offers a brief introduction to a number of theoretical perspectives on the relationship between tourism and development and provides a critical account of the state of tourism in Africa. The chapter provides a broad examination of current issues and stumbling blocks to sustainable tourism development in Africa, many of which will be specifically addressed in the chapters that follow.

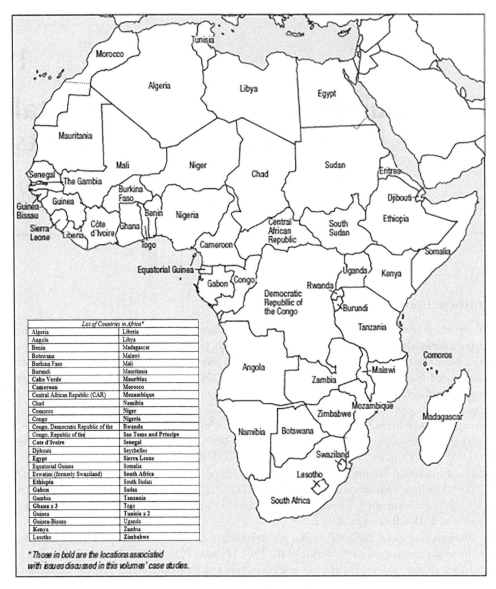

The following table appears within the map image:

List of Countries in Africa*	
Algeria	Liberia
Angola	Libya
Benin	Madagascar
Botswana	Malawi
Burkina Faso	Mali
Burundi	Mauritania
Cabo Verde	Mauritius
Cameroon	Morocco
Central African Republic (CAR)	Mozambique
Chad	Namibia
Comoros	Niger
Congo	Nigeria
Congo, Democratic Republic of the	Rwanda
Congo, Republic of the	Sao Tome and Principe
Cote d'Ivoire	Senegal
Djibouti	Seychelles
Egypt	Sierra Leone
Equatorial Guinea	Somalia
Eswatini (formerly Swaziland)	South Africa
Ethiopia	South Sudan
Gabon	Sudan
Gambia	Tanzania
Ghana x 3	Togo
Guinea	Tunisia x 2
Guinea-Bissau	Uganda
Kenya	Zambia
Lesotho	Zimbabwe

Those in bold are the locations associated with issues discussed in this volume's case studies.

Figure 1.1 Map of Africa and list of countries in Africa
Source: http://worldmap.harvard.edu/africamap.

Tourism and development – theoretical perspectives and outstanding issues

One of the myths surrounding the relationship between tourism and development has been the assumption that "initiatives, projects, and investments in this activity systematically result in strong and sustainable development effects for the countries and regions involved" (Fayos-Solà et al., 2014: ix). This myth about a straightforward relationship between developing the tourism sector and corresponding effects on national development has been fostered and echoed by stakeholders including businesses, governments and local and international organisations with varying vested interests in the tourism sector. Given the growing size and importance of tourism to the global economy, one of the greatest challenges is how to utilise the potentials for improved development outcomes of tourist destination. Currently, the call in the tourism and development literature has been for a deeper understanding of the nature of tourism as a powerful social force, the end product of which is shaped by a variety of factors (Spenceley and Meyer, 2012). Thus, while tourism as a socio-economic and political phenomenon can no longer be ignored in the context of development efforts, outcomes are anything but systematically guaranteed. Consequently, a renewed focus on understanding the nature of tourism's relationship with development is a critical first step.

It is following the end of the Second World War that tourism began to be linked to economic development with the development of the jumbo jet, the growing affluence of Western countries and the rise of charter tours in the 1960s marking this optimism. The rise in travel was perceived as an opportunity for newly decolonising countries to gain needed foreign currency, generate employment and income and to generally stimulate economic development – ultimately leading to poverty reduction (Harrison, 2001). Initially, tourism was considered as being functional to development in line with modernisation theory. It was generally believed that the benefits of tourism would result in a greater multiplier effect that would stimulate local economies. During this period of the late 1960s and 1970s, the economic case for tourism was overstated and the sociocultural cost almost completely neglected (Boissevain, 1977). This view meant that the state's role was reduced to essentially one of enacting incentive-based policies to promote foreign investment in the tourism sector and to then allow market forces to bring about the expected benefits to the economy.

Low multiplier effects, high rates of leakages and perceived widening of inequalities in tourism communities led to the questioning of the economic case for tourism. In what is considered a seminal article in tourism studies, Britton's work on the political economy of tourism in the South Pacific found that up to that point, "discussion of tourism is typically divorced from the historical and political processes that determine development" (1982: 332). Using the idea of centre-periphery as a critique to the functionalism of modernisation theory, Britton argued that tourism companies from the metropolitan countries dominate "Third World tourist destinations" (1982: 331). Metropolitan companies have direct contact with tourists, control the means of travel and have the capital resources that provide them with a competitive advantage over companies in the periphery of the international tourist system. His conclusion was that this situation results in peripheral destinations in developing countries having a development mode, which reinforces dependency on, and vulnerability to, the core developed countries. Unlike the laissez-faire role for governments advocated by modernisation theory, Britton suggested that governments in developing countries take up a deliberately central redistributive role in the organisation of the tourism industry and the benefits accruing thereof.

The need for the state to play a critical role through deliberate governing and institutional design of the tourism sector had earlier been articulated in a seminal volume edited by de Kadt in 1979. The title of this volume "Tourism: Passport to Development? Perspectives on the Social and Cultural Effects of Tourism in Developing Countries" reflects the uncertainty felt of the relationship between tourism and development even at this time. The various contributors to the volume highlighted the positive contribution tourism can make to employment and income, as well as the negative tendency of the sector to worsen existing inequalities. Although no consensus was reached on the role of tourism in economic development in these early debates, what became clear was that the state had a critical role to play in order to minimise the negative impacts of the sector, while encouraging the positive impacts. This was considered most significant for developing countries, in order not to fall in the trap of dependency.

The evolving debates in the 1970s and 1980s centred on tourism as a developmental tool without specifying exactly how this was to benefit the poor. Harrison (2008) contends that the critical question of how tourism specifically affects poverty in a significant way was deflected through the broadening of the debates to include community participation. Up to the 1990s, there were rarely empirical assessments of tourism's impact on poverty reduction, and what little evidence there was offered contradictory conclusions. However, the debates were moved forward in the late 1990s, when it became focused on how tourism as a developmental tool can specifically bring benefits to the poor (Harrison and Schipani, 2007). It was in this context of moving the debates forward that the idea and movement of 'pro-poor tourism' emerged at the turn of the millennium (Bennett et al., 1999). Since then, tourism continues to be touted as having the potential to turn around the economic fortunes of countries. In some cases, tourism is regarded as *a* vehicle, if not *the* vehicle for socio-economic development and poverty reduction. It is however important to situate the changing view of tourism's potential for economic development within the wider evolution of development theory and practice.

Notwithstanding the increasing attention being paid to tourism as potentially a vehicle for economic development and poverty reduction, there has been relatively few attempts in the tourism literature and the wider development literature to situate this view of tourism vis-à-vis the evolution of development theory and thought (Sharpley, 2000). There have of course being very notable exceptions to this critique – Britton (1982), Lea (1988), Dieke (1995, 2000), Harrison (2001), Konadu-Agyemang (2001), Sharpley (2003), Scheyvens (2007), Scheyvens (2011), Holden (2013), Sharpley and Telfer (2002, 2015). Many other studies of tourism's role in development tend to gloss over how this is situated in the wider ongoing development context. To assess tourism's potential role as a vehicle for development, it has to be held up and viewed in the light of broader developmental context in which it is to contribute.

The term development is characterised by a lot of ambiguities and thus appear to be beyond definition. Thus development in the words of Cowen and Shenton (1996: 2) "seems to defy definition, although not for a want of definitions on offer". Much has been written on the meanings of development since the post-war era when development studies as a field of inquiry emerge with the dawn of development economics. Whether in descriptive and/or normative terms, development is used to characterise the socio-economic condition of a given society. On a most basic level, "development means making a better life for everyone" (Peet and Hartwick, 2009: 1). This definition, which on first reading appears simple and appealing to all, masks over the contentious and bitter arguments surrounding how to interpret this idea of development and the approach required to make this idea a reality. Development theories and thoughts have evolved over time to reflect both academic debates and, but most importantly, the empirical evidence of the development conditions of various societies around the world. Thus "from the economic development theories of the 1950s to the 'basic human needs approach' of the 1970s – which emphasized not only economic growth per se as in earlier decades but also the distribution of the benefits of growth" – (Escobar, 1995: 5), through to the human development approach and the current UN Agenda 2030 for Sustainable Development and related Sustainable development Goals (SDGs), the development enterprise has been concerned with improving a lot of societies in both advanced and less advanced economies.

Since the emergence of the development enterprise in the aftermath of the Second World War, a number of complex development thought has been put forward. Paradigms of different variants continue to appear and recede. It has been noted that the various development theory and paradigms never totally disappear, even as their prominence is usurped by new paradigms. Ideas in old paradigms get recycled and recast to meet the needs of emerging paradigms (Cowan and Shenton, 1996; Craig and Porter, 2006; Rapley, 2002). The idea of development has evolved beyond simple economic criteria, to include other measures such as sustainability and cultural and human development. However, there remains a preoccupation with economic growth as a significant means to poverty alleviation (Sharpley, 2000). Consequently, a number of economic sectors have been prioritised as being essential for overall economic growth and development. Tourism is one such sector, which for a long time has been considered to have the potential to serve as a catalyst for development. Despite years of tourism-focused development interventions, the results have been anything but certain. The literature on tourism's role in development reveals a surprisingly inadequate attention to the issues of governance and political analysis. Moreover, the questions of why many tourism centred development interventions have failed to yield expected results remain unresolved and few analytic tools are available for examining the governance context within which tourism centred development interventions take place.

Scheyvens (2011) makes a distinction between liberal, critical, alternative, neoliberal and post-development perspectives to development theories, with differing effects on tourism's perceived role in economic development. The first major theory in international development came from within the liberal tradition of linearity and evolution (Holden, 2013) and is commonly referred to as modernisation theory. In its most basic essence, modernisation theory posits that the path to a society's socio-economic development is an evolutionary and linear one, propelling traditional societies into modern societies. Adherents of the idea of stages of economic growth see development as being synonymous with economic growth. From the late 1960s, modernisation was challenged and critiqued on several fronts – especially with the emergence of the neo-Marxist school of dependency theory of mainly Latin American writers. Dependency theorists for one have pointed out that modernisation theory is a camouflage ideology used by the West to justify their domination of developing countries. Moreover, the unidirectional development path advocated by Rostow was critiqued as being incorrect, as was the inherent assumption in the model that traditional values were incompatible with modernity (So, 1990).

Many tourism studies in developing countries are implicitly based on modernisation theory (Telfer, 2015). Tourism is continually touted as a means of achieving development through employment creation, foreign exchange generation, technology transfer and the promotion of a modern way of life based on Western values (Ashley et al., 2000; Goodwin, 2008; Mitchell and Ashley, 2010). In the 1960s and 1970s, several tourism research works explicitly drew on Rostow's work. For instance, Krapf (1961, cited in Pearce, 1989: 11) worked on the economic growth of tourism drawing heavily on the modernisation model of Rostow. The argument was also made by Van Doorn (1979, cited in Pearce, 1989: 12) that "tourism cannot be considered outside the context of the different stages of development countries have reached". He therefore proposed a typology linking levels of socio-economic development with the stage of tourist development. The Tourism Area Life Cycle (TALC) as outlined by Butler (1980) is widely considered to be synonymous with tourism research with an implicit basis on modernisation theory. The TALC is based on a product life cycle and traces the evolution of tourist resorts through six stages – exploration, involvement, development, consolidation, stagnation and decline/rejuvenation stages. In more recent times, Sharpley's study of tourism development in Cyprus provided evidence that "tourism has proved to be an effective growth pole, underpinning both dramatic economic growth and also the *fundamental structural modernisation of the economy*" (2003: 254, emphasis added). In contemporary times travel and tourism are now ubiquitous to the modern way of life, with places and people being commoditised and consumed under the tourist gaze (Urry and Larsen, 2011).

Initially, much of the research influenced by modernisation theory focused on the positive impacts of tourism. Tourism was seen as being functional for the socio-economic development of countries. It was generally believed that the benefits of tourism would result in a greater multiplier effect that would stimulate local economies. However, as the expected trickle-down effect failed to materialised, attention was turned to questioning the value of tourism with its associated environmental issues (Britton, 1982; Brohman, 1996; de Kadt, 1979).

Critical perspectives and tourism

When the expected 'trickle-down' of development to the poor promised in modernisation theory failed to materialise, a number of critiques emerged against the then prevailing liberal development thought. A basic primer of dependency theory is that developing countries are kept in a dependent and exploitative relationship with developed countries due to internal and external political, institutional and political structures. Thus, while development was taking place in developed countries, developing countries were being simultaneously underdeveloped. Underdevelopment and development were considered by Andre Gunder Frank to be a simultaneous process rather than sequential – the 'development of underdevelopment' (Cowen and Shenton, 1996: 58–59). Although many nuances and variants emerged, including work by postcolonial writers, the overriding thrust of dependency theorist remained that "as long as third-world economies were linked to the first world they could never break free of their dependence and poverty" (Rapley, 2002: 18). It was argued that a way to sever these ties was for the State to actively partake in development through autonomous national-development strategies.

In tourism research, dependency theory has been one of the dominant paradigms that have underlined a number of studies (Akama, 2004; Bianchi, 2002; Britton, 1982; Chaperon and Bramwell, 2013; Lea, 1988; Mbaiwa, 2005; Mowforth and Munt, 2009). Inspired by the critical perspectives of dependency theory, postcolonial writers have also highlighted how international tourism in many cases leads to exploitation and entrenchment of poverty and inequalities. There was a shift from the 1970s away from the earlier modernisation idea that tourism de facto will lead to poverty alleviation (see for example de Kadt, 1979). Postcolonial writers such as Wels (2004) have shown how contemporary tourism is still rooted in colonial and postcolonial relationships with tourism marketing infused with neo-colonial ideas of the 'exotic other' (see Said, 1978). The taken for granted power relations within international tourism has also been questioned by for example Akama (2004). Furthermore, it has been noted that the structure of international tourism is a new form of plantation economy (Hall and Tucker, 2004: 5; Telfer, 2015: 46) in which tourist destinations in developing countries as the periphery – especially island nations – are no more than a production location within a trade and production system in which power and control are held in the core developed countries.

Alternative perspectives and tourism

From the 1970s onwards, there was a widespread dissatisfaction with mainstream development models – be they based on modernisation theory or dependency theory – within the international development community. This dissatisfaction led to the critique of the mainstream theories and a search for alternatives which tended to be mainly people-oriented approaches (Pieterse, 2010). In practical terms, alternative development has been primarily centred on the needs of people and the environment. The key point in alternative development is that it is about development from 'below', particularly in reference to communities and NGOs' involvement. In many discussions, alternative development has come to be associated with and reinforced through issues and processes such as the peasant movement, new social movements, green thinking, feminism, anti-capitalism, empowerment, indigenous knowledge, endogenous development, agency, local control over development policies, participatory approaches and other grassroots approaches emphasising a bottom-up approach to development (Escobar, 1995; Peet and Hartwick, 2009; Pieterse, 2010). Concepts such as sustainable development, human development, Agenda 21 and international environmental conferences like Rio '92 and Rio+20 have all come under the umbrella of alternative development. Furthermore, the rise of national and international NGOs in various fields of development and environment represents a key defining feature of alternative development.

In line with the dissatisfaction of mainstream development theory, the disillusionment with mainstream or mass tourism and its many problems led to many tourism researchers advocating for 'alternative tourism' development. In an edited book by Eadington and Smith (1992) – *Tourism Alternatives: Potentials and Problem in the Development of Tourism* – the authors acknowledge the existence of critical perspectives on tourism. Nonetheless, the point was put forward that tourism can contribute to development when it is approached in an alternative way. After years of rapid mass tourism development, many locals and tourists alike experienced a retrospective disappointment about the ultimate outcomes of tourism developments. A key source of this disappointment was how tourism development created 'winners' and 'losers' in the local communities without a commonly agreed way of ensuring equitable redistribution (Eadington and Smith, 1992). The turn to alternative tourism however did not come with precision as Butler (1992: 31) was quick to note that,

> alternative tourism has emerged as one of the most widely used and abused phrases of the last decade. Like sustainable development it sounds attractive, it suggests concern and thought, a new approach and a philosophy toward an old problem, and it is hard to disagree with…[but] the phrase can mean almost anything to anyone.

Notwithstanding the imprecision of alternative tourism development, Brohman (1996: 65) identifies several key characteristics and recurring themes that see alternative tourism development as being small-scale community organised tourism, that encourages community participation and local ownership of businesses, in a way that does not denigrate host culture. Some of the alternative tourism that have been advocated include 'ecotourism/green tourism', 'volunteer tourism' and 'justice tourism'. Tourism researchers have therefore built on the alternative development perspectives on empowerment, gender-sensitivity, participation and grassroots development in their analysis. Community-based tourism (CBT) emerged strongly during this period and the literature has noted how these initiatives were often led by foreign interests (Mowforth and Munt, 2009; Tosun, 2000) rather than local priorities, more often than not leading to implementation challenges, in terms of empowering the 'poor' as actors rather than spectators, generally associated with the lack of local capacity and CBT's controversial, mainly top-down and tokenistic development approaches (Moscardo, 2008; Novelli and Gebhardt, 2007; Novelli and Tisch-Rottensteiner, 2011; Tosun, 2000). The need for community participation in tourism planning continues to be stressed within the literature (Adu-Ampong, 2016, 2017; Bramwell and Lane, 2000; Jamal and Getz, 1995; Melubo and Lovelock, 2019; Tosun, 2000, 2005). There are however some institutional challenges that make it difficult for increased community participation and empowerment within the tourism planning process.

Neoliberal perspective and tourism

From the 1970s onwards, the liberal perspectives of development theory discussed earlier were usurped through a surge of support for neoliberalism. The exact definition of neoliberalism remains contested and elusive (Peck, 2013). However, there are certain socio-economic and political features that are associated with it. Öniş and Şenses (2005) argue that neoliberalism was a counter-revolution in development theory and a direct assault on state-led national developmentalism practiced by many postcolonial and post-independent countries of Africa, Asia and Latin America. As a theory of political economic practices, neoliberalism

> proposes that human well-being can best be advanced by liberating individual entrepreneurial freedoms and skills within an institutional framework characterised by strong private property rights, free markets and free trade. The role of the state is to create and preserve an institutional framework appropriate to such practices.
>
> *(Harvey, 2005: 2)*

Thus, neoliberalism as a new mode of development centres on privatisation, deregulation, trade liberalisation, the primacy of individualism and a retraction of state involvement to allow a market-led development process among other things. These and other characteristics underlined by an unquestionable belief in and acceptable of free market and less state involvement came to be termed as the 'Washington Consensus' (Williamson, 2009).

Surprisingly, it was under the upsurge of neoliberalism that a strong focus on poverty and poverty alleviation came to the fore. This was however after the realisation that the structural adjustment programmes (SAPs) initiated by the World Bank and IMF and implemented in many development countries failed to achieve the intended goals (Owusu, 2003). The socio-economic policies were implemented under the SAPs have also come in for severe criticism. The SAPs focused on short-term economic measures at the expense of more structural transformation resulting in a high social cost. These dire social conditions included falling wages, cuts in social welfare, increasing the cost of basic items and a general shrinking of national economies. In effect the SAPs ironically contributed to the growth of poverty and threatened the long-term development prospects of countries – especially in sub-Saharan Africa (Owusu, 2003). The paradox of neoliberalism's focus on the poor is that the very pro-poor policies that are to increase equity and reduce inequalities within countries are dependent on policy strategies requiring strong state interventionism and protectionism. These policy strategies are however the very opposite of neoliberal strategies of free market, trade liberalisation and a limited state role focusing on macroeconomic stability and spending conducive to private sector growth (Frenzel, 2013).

Tourism development under a neoliberal perspective continues to represent the biggest proportion of tourism product development around the world. International and regional level financial institutions like the World Bank, the Inter-America Development Bank (IDB), the Asian Development Bank (ADB) and the African Development Bank (AfDB) continue to fund tourism projects as a development strategy and pathways to economic growth. Development agencies such as the Netherlands' Development Agency (SNV), the UK Department for International Development (DFID) and the Overseas Development Institute (ODI) have also played a leading role in tourism development under a neoliberal perspective. Tourism research under the liberal/neoliberal perspective focused on the propensity of tourism to contribute to foreign exchange earnings, job creation and income generation. Schilcher (2007: 168) shows that while on one hand, international tourism directly benefits from the neoliberalism's facilitation of free movement of capital, labour and consumers under an open economic environment, on the other hand, notwithstanding the high degree of volatility associated with it, tourism represents a viable option for economic development in destinations, like small island states that lack alternative means of accelerated economic development. Thus, in some respect, tourism within the (neo) liberal perspective was held up as a panacea for economic development prior to the emergence of criticisms about the environmental costs and issues of sustainability.

In a study of how the implementation of the World Bank and IMF's SAPs affected tourism development in Africa countries, Dieke (1995) shows that the liberalisation of the economy made way for local private sector and foreign investment in the tourism sector. The impact of the SAPs was to consign the role of the state to that of an enabler rather than an operator for the tourism sector. Konadu-Agyemang (2001), however, contends that in Ghana, for example, the implementation of SAPs resulted in higher leakages of tourism revenues due to increased rates of foreign and private sector involvement. Moreover, SAPs brought about increased and entrenched socio-economic and spatial disparities some of which persist to date. This is because tourism development for instance focused on areas in the south of the country that had the potential for a quick return on investment at the expense of areas with sufficient tourist attraction but lacking needed infrastructure. Thus, while the SAPs enabled tourism to be positioned as a development strategy, the lack of active state control resulted in uneven development and sharing of benefits because the SAPs lacked a humane face (Dieke, 1995; Konadu-Agyemang, 2001).

Post-development and tourism

As an umbrella term that covers the diverse reactions to the development dilemmas at the end of the 20th century, post-development thinking includes among others, postmodernist, postcolonialist and post-structuralist thought (Scheyvens, 2011: 42). As Pieterse (2010: 110) puts it, the starting point of post-development is the basic realisation "that attaining a middle-class lifestyle for the majority of the world's population is impossible". The possibilities promised by development were seen as achievable by only a few, while everyone was made to pay the price in terms of environmental degradation and breakdown of social cohesion. Upon this realisation, post-development critique is centred on questioning 'development' and contesting the grand development theories. Post-development thinking tends to reject reductionist view of the world. While some variants of post-development thinking proclaimed the death of 'development' noting that the idea has become outdated and has grown obsolete, other variants reject the reductionist perception of 'development' as either a force for good or for evil. In this respect, post-development critique shares overlap with critical theory and ecological movements (Pieterse, 2010: 110).

Given the variety of perspectives within post-development thinking, the counter-critiques tend to be varied. For detailed counter-critiques to the various strands of post-development thinking see for example Peet and Hartwick (2009: chapter 6) and Pieterse (2010: chapter 7). The basic counter-critique to post-developmentalists' rejection of 'development' is the question of: 'what do you propose?' Three main positions emerge from post-developmentalist in response to this question. According to Rahnema (1997, cited in Peet and Hartwick, 2009: 228–230) these three are (1) radical pluralism – the need for local actions to make a difference rather than grandiose global action, (2) simple living – life centred on both ecological and spiritual harmony and (3) reappraisal of non-capitalist societies – the idea that social and economic life in 'non-developed' societies was not too bad because, although they did not have modern consumer materials, they had "effective personal and collective moral obligations" that ensured they had their basic needs fulfilled. Thus, post-development thinking rejects current ways of thinking about modern development and instead calls for revitalised non-modern (non-Western) perspectives.

Post-development thinking within tourism research basically rejects the reductionist perspective of seeing tourism as either a force of good or a force of evil. Tourism is seen as a system that involves a range of actors (e.g. public sector, private sector, civil society and communities) across multiple and varying scales (Adu-Ampong, 2017, 2019; Dredge and Jamal, 2015). Post-development thinking in tourism attempts a holistic study of tourism – both as an industry and as a system. The interest is therefore to understand how tourism systems and processes work and how these shape the interactions between people and places (Cornelissen, 2005). Importantly, the interest is to understand the role of culture and power in shaping the actions and inactions of tourism stakeholders in a given destination (Bramwell and Meyer, 2007; Cheong and Miller, 2000; Church and Coles, 2006). Within such a perspective, research considerations can be given to how communities based on their own interests and that of other stakeholders engage in tourism. Communities are not to be cast as simply powerless victims of tourism, but rather they are seen as powerful actors who adapt, embrace or reject tourism (Beeton, 2006; Scheyvens, 2002, 2011).

Tourism research rooted in post-development thinking offers a nuanced understanding of the shaping effects of the tourism phenomena on both communities and tourists. Within this perspective, tourism is seen neither as a panacea nor the sources of all negative issues in a destination (Scheyvens, 2011). Since tourism involves multiple stakeholders across various scales of interactions, tourism acts as a social force that is shaped by various interests – sometimes for good, sometimes for bad. Informed by alternative theoretical and philosophical perspectives that include ecocentrism, community development and post-structuralism, Wearing et al. (2005) have argued for a 'decommodified research paradigm' in which neoliberal thinking in terms of profitability no longer takes precedence at the expense of social and environmental consequences. Indeed, for Higgins-Desbiolles (2006: 1192) "tourism is in fact a powerful social force that can achieve many important ends when its capacities are unfettered from the market fundamentalism of neoliberalism and instead are harnessed to meet human development imperatives and the wider public good". Unfettering tourism from the market fundamentalism means questioning and examining actors – local and international – in the tourism process, their power differentials and how these shape interactions and outcomes.

As a highly contested concept, the nature of development and its outcome is shaped by a range of socio-economic, political and environmental considerations, each with sometimes compatible, most times incompatible value sets. What has been made clear so far is the contentious relationship between tourism and development over the years. Table 1.1 provides an overview of this.

Table 1.1 A historical overview of theoretical perspectives on tourism and development

Historical evolution

	[1950s–1960s]	[1970s onwards]	[1980s onwards]	[late 1990s onwards]	[2000s]	[2010s+]
Modernisation	Tourism can contribute to modernisation thorough economic growth, employment generation and the exchange of ideas. Benefits will trickle down to the poor.					
Economic Neoliberalism	Initial symptoms of neo-colonial approaches to tourism development, exploiting natural resources by developing countries.	Foreign direct investment is seen as the way to stimulate stagnating economies and investment in tourism adds a possible dimension attracting foreign exchange.	Tourism offers a way out of indebtedness; 'trade your way out of poverty'. It encourages foreign investment and private sector development while providing employment and generating foreign exchange earnings.	Tourism is promoted hand-in-hand with free trade, democratisation and anti-poverty agendas. Investment in tourism in third world countries gives foreign companies a presence in major or growing markets. Poverty Reduction Strategy Papers identify tourism as an economic sector that can contribute to poverty reduction. Public–private partnerships encouraged. Tourism is seen as a mean of helping to overcome poverty and inequality, which can breed terrorism.	Under the UN Millennium Development Goals, various organisations such as the UNWTO set aside actions to make tourism an effective contributor to development. Tourism is at the core of economic development debates, with dilemmas concerning the issues related to climate change and the Rio+ Agenda.	Agenda 2030 for Sustainable Development spans across nations as the panacea for the future. Seventeen Sustainable Development Goals are agreed and launched for implementation. Tourism becomes increasingly core subject of sustainable development debates, with specific SDGs – 8, 12 and 14, for the very first time recognising tourism as a key economic sector.

(*Continued*)

Historical evolution

Critical	[1970s–1980s]	[1980s onwards]	[late 1990s onwards]	[2000s]	[2010s+]
	Tourism is associated with enclave development, dependence on foreign capital and expertise, growing social and economic disparities and repatriation of profits (leakages). It often undermines local cultures, social networks and traditional livelihoods (i.e. people's relocation to give space to national parks establishment).	Post-development writers view 'local culture and knowledge' as the base for any tourism development. The concept of tourism is based around solidarity and reciprocity came to the fore. Tourism policy must focus on direct democratic processes and on traditional knowledge systems, or at least a combination of modern and traditional knowledge.	Anti-globalisation lobby sees tourism as a way of advancing the forces of capitalism into more remote places and cultures. Postcolonial writers comment on the allure of the 'other' – poverty attracts tourists, as poor places are associated with 'authentic' experiences of culture and nature. Strong class differences between 'hosts' and 'guests' are noted.	There is a struggle in the determination of guidelines and parameters to establish tourism success in contributing to poverty reduction. The notion of tokenistic involvement of communities is introduced. The failure of numerous ventures is a symptom of a failing global development agenda, which has at times been worsened by a 'poorism' mentality.	There is still a struggle in the understanding of how to measure success, for instance, what needs to be done to achieve the set of 17 SDGs and related targets, making this potentially another utopian project. Although the inclusion of tourism in the Agenda 2030 for Sustainable Development and related SDGs is seen as a positive improvement in the recognition of the importance of tourism, many argue that tourism has the potential to contribute, directly or indirectly to all the 17 goals and this should be better articulated to enable a clearer and more effective way forward. The UNWTO increases its campaign to promote ways to achieve the SDGs and a number of international development agencies such as the World Bank commit funds to support developments in this direction,

Alternative	[late 1970s onwards]	[1980s onwards]	[late 1990s onwards]	[2000s]	[2010s+]
	Alternative forms of tourism that are small-scale, involve education of tourists and more local control over tourism, are seen as worthy of support (i.e. justice tours, conservation tours).	The 'green agenda' of the 1980s leading to the 1992 UN Summit in Rio de Janeiro renews the emphasis on the environment including ecological and social sustainability. Ecotourism comes to the fore.	Tourism offers poor communities a way of diversifying their livelihood options. Communities can actively participate in tourism and be empowered through their experiences.	The main barriers to tourism and development emerge, which are linked to broader grievances about socio-economic development.	Climate change is declared a global emergency. Aviation takes centre stage in the blame game. Undoubtedly adaptation actions are urgently required, however, those who have worked to develop tourism in remote destinations and those destination communities that have tourism as one of their few economic options feel under threat. Alternative markets are explored as alternative to the traditional ones.

	Capacity building emerges as one of the key required action to enable tourism to truly contribute to community development and empowerment.	Plastic and waste becomes of increased concern not only for the wellbeing of and attractiveness of tourism destinations, but most importantly as a global health issues. The tourism sector starts using alternative materials and exploring circular economy adaptation strategies, but the move remans negligible.
Post-development	The possibilities promised by development were seen as achievable by only a few, while everyone was made to pay the price in terms of environmental degradation and breakdown of social cohesion. Upon this realisation post-development critique emerged as centred on questioning 'development' and contesting the grand development theories.	Post-development thinking within tourism research rejects the reductionist perspective of seeing tourism as either a force of good or a force of evil. Tourism is seen as a system that involves a range of actors (public sector, private sector and civil society) across multiple and varying scales. Transforming the traditional tourism growth paradigm takes centre stage. Both academics and practitioners advance solutions to well-traversed issues such as the excessive growth of tourism and the effect of overtourism that affects certain destinations. Conscious travel behaviour emerges from a desire to ground any travel and tourism activities in line with the on-going global crisis.

Source: Adapted from Novelli (2015).

Recognition of the complexities of development offers a lens through which to understand the complexities of using tourism as a tool for local economic development and poverty reduction – an aspiration for many African countries. What has been clear so far is that, given the complexities of the tourism-development nexus, there is a need for state intervention in tourism development planning in order to harness the potentials of tourism while offsetting the negative impacts. Undoubtedly, there is a role for the state to play in tourism and economic development planning, but the extent to which this happens effectively in the African and other developing contexts remains debatable.

The current state of tourism and development (research) in Africa

Beginning from the pre-colonial through the colonial periods to the current postcolonial era, certain stereotypes and myths about African countries have built up. These stereotypes have proven difficult to discount and/or eradicate, as they are constantly portrayed and shared across the global media. It is undeniable that African countries exist within a complex socio-economic state of affairs that calls for economic diversification. In such context, however, tourism has increasingly emerged as an avenue for such diversification, growth and ultimately development.

Agenda 2030 for Sustainable Development and the SDGs, the challenge of climate change and the integrity of the destinations in Africa have become paramount, both in terms of its long-term survival and the responsibility we have to take action for the preservation of the very resources – natural and human, that attracted tourists in the first place (see Boluk et al., 2019). Tourism aspires to be a more stable, higher-yielding, responsible and sustainable, delivering tangible and equitable benefits to communities, preserving the natural environment, fostering inclusive growth, peace and stability, and ultimately achieving the SDGs. However, there is an increasing danger in approaching tourism only from a commercially focussed perspective and reacting purely to shifting market demands, which will not deliver the aspired responsible forms of tourism that promote and enhance long-term inclusive growth and sustainable development in Africa (Novelli, 2015).

In relation to Northern Africa, the *2017 World Economic Forum Travel and Tourism Competitiveness Report* highlighted that the "natural and cultural resources remain mostly underexploited, international openness is still limited, and security perceptions remain the biggest hurdle" (WEF, 2017: 17). For sub-Saharan Africa, the report highlights that, on aggregate,

> it remains the region where travel and tourism competitiveness is the least developed. Although regional performance has increased, it has improved less compared to other parts of the world. Southern Africa remains the strongest sub-region, followed by Eastern Africa and then Western Africa. Yet, on average, Eastern Africa is the most improved region, while Southern Africa has experienced a slight decline.
>
> *(WEF, 2017: 18)*

Air connectivity and travel costs remain challenging as well as visa policies and infrastructure. While tourism in the region is mainly driven by nature-based tourism, there is significant room for improvement in protecting, valuing and communicating cultural resources (WEF, 2017).

The *Economic Development in Africa Report 2017: Tourism for Transformative and Inclusive Growth* (UNCTAD, 2017) examines the role that tourism can play in Africa's development process. It argues that tourism can be an engine for inclusive growth and economic development as well as being complementary to development strategies, aimed at fostering economic diversification and structural transformation within the right policy context.

> To unlock the potential of intersectoral linkages to contribute to structural transformation, cross-sectoral issues need to be aligned with, and integrated into, policy frameworks at the national, regional and continental levels… Beyond generating economic benefits and boosting productive capacities, tourism has the potential to foster inclusion by creating employment opportunities among vulnerable groups such as the poor, women and youth.
>
> *(UNCTAD, 2017: 6)*

African destinations have primarily concentrated on attracting international tourism and what is also of key relevance is the reference made by the UNCTAD (2017) report to the increase of continental and intraregional tourism in Africa and the opportunities associated with this phenomenon, for economic and export diversification.

> African countries would benefit if they made further progress with the free movement of persons, currency convertibility and liberalizing air transport services. This would facilitate greater access to tourism destinations and boost the competitiveness of destinations. It also requires regional economic communities and countries to comprehensively plan for intraregional and continental tourism.
>
> *(UNCTAD, 2017: 6)*

While tourism's potential for driving inclusive economic growth and development across Africa is undeniable, there are several challenges and key issues that continuously confront the sector on the continent. A summary of these is provided in Table 1.2.

While the region's situation has improved since the 2017 edition of the *World Economic Forum Competitiveness Report*, sub-Saharan Africa ranks at the bottom of the Travel and Tourism Competitiveness Index (TTCI), lagging behind the rest of the world across all parameters, with only Mauritius, South Africa and Seychelles scoring above the global average on the index. Concurrently, however, the region continues to outperform the global average in international tourism arrivals and receipts growth, with the World Travel and Tourism Council (WTTC) forecasting that those Africa economies covered by the 2019s TTCI will have the second highest rate of growth in travel and tourism GDP between 2019 and 2029 (see Figure 1.2). As a result, it is envisaged that if SSA manages to maintain the level of improvement, investors will more likely view the region as an attractive investment opportunity to diversify from other more mature destinations (WEF, 2019a, 2019b).

According to the 2019 *World Economic Forum Competitiveness Report*, SSA's travel and tourism market is still very small. In 2018, the travel and tourism industry's GDP of African countries covered in the 2019 report totalled approximately $42.1 billion, with 37.4 million tourist arrivals in 2017, about 1.6% and 3.0% of the global total, respectively. The 2019 Report also highlights that,

> with the majority of the region's economies classified as low or lower-middle income, SSA lacks the robust middle class and economic resources required to generate intra-regional travel and tourism investment at the same scale as other parts of

Table 1.2 Tourism in Africa – current situation and development perspectives

Key issues	Current situation	Development perspectives
Governance and policy	Governments increasingly recognise the benefits and income that tourism can bring to their countries and the need to develop initiatives to support the sector. However, the destructive style of political and economic leadership worsens the weak business environment. Lack of funding is very often a barrier to effective tourism development. Foreign and Direct Investment remains the main focus of Africa development policies, however increasing attention is placed on diasporas and newly emerging African middle classes (i.e. South Africa, Nigeria, Angola). The increasing influence of China in Africa is well debated and recognised by a number of Africa governments.	With many nations having unique attractions, in order to attract investors, governments have instigated policies to promote and manage the growth and created incentives, such as tax advantages, land concessions, marketing assistance, cash subsidies, business financing and skills development incentives. The dynamics associated with attracting BRIC countries need to be fully recognised. For example, in order to promote Africa to Chinese visitors, Approved Destination Status (ADS) is required. ADS countries are only granted to overseas destinations by the Chinese government through a bilateral government agreement. It is only concerned with tourism groups of specific Chinese travel retailers and excludes business and official travel abroad. The increased presence of Chinese investors emerging from bilateral agreements has evolved in the growth of interventions in the tourism sector particularly linked to grand infrastructural such as new airports constructions and expansions of existing ones.
Socio-economic sustainability	Tourism help diversifies exports as many Africa economies are narrowly focused on agriculture, mining, and, more recently, telecommunications. Export diversification is a key concern. Across Africa, a growing number of traditional and non-traditional investors are looking at hotels, restaurants, second homes, and passenger transportation as business opportunities. Tourism has accelerated change by encouraging pro-business policies and reforms that can help SME development and stimulate foreign investment. Tourism can benefit all layers of society, genders and age as well as geographical areas of a country. Tourism creates demand for non-tourism goods and services (i.e. transport, petrol, retailing, finance, real estate, agriculture, and communications).	Diversification makes economies less vulnerable to fluctuations in demand, more dynamic, and more agile in the face of change. By stimulating business investment in rural and peripheral areas, tourism has the potential to contribute to poverty alleviation and community empowerment, offering an alternative viable sector. By bringing foreign consumers to a destination, tourism provides an ideal opportunity for market-testing new products and diversifying exports. Success in tourism has a cascading effect on other areas of economic activity and contributes to increases in domestic consumption. By providing jobs for women, tourism can improve the non-monetary aspects of poor people's lives such as health, security, social mobility, and empowerment. By engaging young people in productive employment, tourism can provide an alternative to out-migration, urban poverty, and armed conflict.

Environmental sustainability	Africa's unique environments are benefiting from a growing awareness amongst government officials and visitors of the importance of responsible practices. Tourism generates income for biodiversity conservation and cultural heritage protection. Conservation International, the World Wildlife Fund for Nature (WWF), United Nations Environmental Programme (UNEP), and the Global Environment Facility (GEF) increasingly support tourism projects.	Despite the increasing number of organisations and individual committing to responsible tourism practices, it is evident that travellers are not yet willing to pay extra for green options, pushing the onus onto tourism professionals. Environmental incentives and initiatives are broadly linked to the issues of climate change and environmental management, a topic at the fore of many international organisations, national governments and civil society organisations. Funding to support these are limited, but yet available.
Inter-regional development	Many neighbouring countries are establishing close co-operation in tourism activities, building on visitors who wish to see more than just one country in a trip, as well as learning from more experienced destinations. Peace Parks, otherwise known as trans-frontier conservation areas, are parks that straddle frontiers and require joint management by the governments concerned. However, a number of complexities are associated with the nature of the initiative (i.e. cross-border poaching, illegal migration of people and goods).	Learning from the Schengen Visa experience, the current plans to implement a common visa scheme in East and Southern Africa is seen as a way to enable a significant increase in tourist arrivals in the region. The World Bank provides loans to assist in maintenance, and tourism is encouraged to the areas. Animals and people are allowed to migrate unhindered across the parks, which may have a boundary around them to prevent any unauthorised migration.
Destination image and ICT	Successful tourism can change perceptions of a country and create a positive national image. Online services in Africa are lagging behind the rest of the world, with internet access available to only a very small section of the population. An estimated 6.2% of the population has internet access, although the percentage varies enormously according to country. The services available vary, with online users in some countries only able to access information and not make payments.	Africa has a long way to go to capitalise fully on the continent's tourism potential. Despite its unique attractions, poverty, security concerns, political instability and poor infrastructure hinder the development of tourism. Online sales have yet to make a significant impact on tourism and online services are primarily for marketing and information purposes. For many potential European and North American visitors, these can be the major source of data and research for their travel choice. Review sites, such as Trip Advisor and Virtual Tourist are remarkably useful, and tourism professionals need to ensure an up-to-date and accurate web presence to entice visitors.

(Continued)

Key issues	Current situation	Development perspectives
Safety and security - health and hygiene	The importance of 'safety and security' as well as 'health and hygiene' conditions is a well-understood determinant for a country's tourism competitiveness. Security remains a concern for many tourists travelling in Africa, with the region having a perceived weak track record for safety and security. Safe and secure countries often suffer due to poor comprehension of an unrelated conflict in a neighbouring country. What is more of a travellers' concern is the risk of contracting malaria and other tropical diseases. This may deter some travellers from considering Africa as a holiday destination.	Governments' actions to ensure 'safety and security' and 'health and hygiene' are being increasingly being addressed. The lingering fears regarding countries, which have previously seen conflict (i.e. Rwanda and Uganda), are to be addressed by increasing the visibility of those increasingly safe to visit. Access within the country to improved drinking water and sanitation is important for the comfort and health of travellers. In the event that tourists do become ill, the country's health sector must be able to ensure they are properly cared for, as measured by the availability of physicians and hospital beds.
Human resources	The importance of addressing health and education issues in Africa is not a new subject. A number of initiatives are being implemented to improve human resources in all sectors including tourism. Formal education and training (primary and secondary) and informal private-sector involvement in human resources development are increasingly addressing the need for a qualified labour force. Flocks of international experts and volunteers travel to Africa on a daily basis to 'help' address a number of issues. Despite recognising the value of this, there is a need for a better-coordinated process addressing local problems rather than being international organisations agendas' focused.	Quality human resources in the economy ensure that the industry has access to the collaborators it needs to develop and grow. Human resources development plays a pivotal role in stimulating employees' 'sense of belonging' to their work place, which is one of the most important employees' motivation factors in providing better on job performance. Train-the-trainers programme is amongst those capacity building initiatives enabling the creation of a body of locally available educators and trainers, rather than depending upon international experts and volunteers.
Destination access and visa regimes	*Land transportation* is the most popular form of transportation in Africa, despite the growth of the air industry. However, it remains a slow and often difficult way to get around, as infrastructure is poor across the region and in need of investment. For many Africans with limited disposable income, land transport is the only possible way of travel, either by shared car, bus or taxi services.	*Land transportation* A number of roads are being built and improved across this region. The African Development Bank has a number of projects in this area, along with many foreign investors, which often improve infrastructure as a by-product of their main project goals. *Air transportation* Air traffic control requires major upgrades to improve the continent's baleful safety record. Policy challenges include strengthening regulatory oversight and achieving full liberalisation of the air transport sector.

Air transportation is the second most popular method of transportation. Due to the vast size of the continent, air travel is by far the quickest way of getting around, but remains expensive in most countries, with safety and security not always meeting international standards. Landing charges are high owing to the absence of support from concessions enjoyed in many parts of the world. Operating costs have soared with fuel prices, choking off air connections in many countries.

Rail transportation is limited and travelling by train remains a difficult and therefore limited option for tourists. Lines are not comprehensive across the region, and services are slow, with unreliable schedules. Following economic liberalisation in many African countries and major improvements to the region's road network, most of the continent's railways lost their economic edge. A few classic train journeys have had their infrastructure restored and maintained to their former glory, such as the steam railway in Eritrea, as well as luxury journeys on the Blue Train in South Africa, and the Shongololo Express in Namibia.

Road System has improved in most African countries in recent years, as governments have strived to increase the density of their road networks and carry out institutional reforms. In cities, road construction has not kept pace with urbanisation. In many countries, road maintenance remains inadequate. Even the Trans-African Highway, the symbol of modern Africa, has long gaps.

Waterways transportation is possible, but remains a limited option for countries with a coastline over the sea or the African Great Lakes, as there are only few organised official ferry services. Private boat trips have diminished around the Horn of Africa, due to increased piracy.

Visa Regimes are viewed as one of the major hindering factors in destination accessibility and remains.

Rail transportation The standard policy response has been to concession many of Africa's railways. But while concessions have led to significant service improvements and helped to reverse the decline in traffic, they have not generated enough revenue to finance much-needed track rehabilitation.

Road system Tremendous progress has been made in establishing institutions to manage and maintain Africa's roads, for example, but still only one in three rural Africans has access to an all-season road. Unable to reach urban markets, millions are trapped in subsistence agriculture and tourism certainly suffers from this as the lack of accessibility to a number of sites remains one of the determinants of the sector seasonality.

Waterways transportation There is an increased interest in developing the cruise sector in areas like the Indian Ocean, but piracy remains a constraint. Popular routes include travel to and from islands such as Cape Verde and Zanzibar (Tanzania), with an increased interest emerging in developing the waterways over Lake Victoria and Lake Tanganyika.

Multimodal transport, whereby roads, railways, airlines, and shipping operate in harmony, can contribute significantly to growth and productivity if the modalities are well integrated. In Africa, unfortunately, integration is not the rule. Corrupt customs administration and restrictions on entry into transport markets are blocking the development of multimodal transport. These and other impediments delay freight, raise the costs of moving international freight, and compromise the logistical systems on which global trade depends. Transportation costs increase the prices of African goods by a whopping 75%.

Visa regimes are under review in several African nations, with an increasing number of destinations looking at visa on arrival agreements as the way forward. While this is a progressing strategy across destinations in the continent, changing visa regimes remains a complex issue to resolve.

(Continued)

Key issues	Current situation	Development perspectives
Accommodation	Independent hotels dominate the accommodation sector, with international chain outlets only present in significant numbers in key tourism hotspots such as South Africa, Mauritius, Kenya and Tanzania. Lodges are a traditional safari option and can range from basic facilities to the ultimate luxury stay. Hostels are a popular option amongst budget travellers, as are guesthouses, which are also seen as an economical choice. Home-stay accommodation both in rural and urban locations is a growing niche in the region. It is a relatively inexpensive option, and one where visitors can gain a more traditional African experience.	By 2011, Accor had outlets in 17 countries across the region, mainly the mid-range Ibis and Novotel brands. Starwood is also present in Africa, with its Sheraton brand present in Gambia, Nigeria, Djibouti and South Africa. South African group Protea has expanded throughout the region, with outlets in eight countries. A number of other international brands are making their way into the growing economies of Rwanda and Nigeria. In destinations like Kenya, global brands have increasingly taken business away from locally owned businesses, hindering their ability to survive on the market. The desire for increased foreign and direct investment in the sector to serve an assumed growing market has not been coupled with the need to guarantee equitable and inclusive access to the tourism market. High prices and service standards remain problematic across the continent, with only a few pockets of excellence. A number of initiatives to improve service standards are needed and are currently taking place even in some of the most seasoned destinations like South Africa, The Gambia and Namibia. Despite recognising the challenges imposed by the high cost of running businesses in Africa, a full recalibration of accommodations' prices is required to guarantee destination competitiveness.
Traditional and niche products	Safari Tourism is the quintessential African travel retail product focused on 'big five' of elephant, lion, leopard, rhino and cape buffalo, with the key destinations being Kenya, Tanzania, Botswana, Namibia, South Africa, Zimbabwe and Zambia. A growing number of other types of safaris are also emerging - i.e. gorilla tracking in Rwanda and Uganda, bird watching in The Gambia. Beach tourism is an important secondary product in East Africa and West Africa and, to a lesser extent, in Southern Africa. Nature/Adventure tourism is a growth area for Africa. The continent's varied terrain and remote locations make it an ideal location for many nature-based adventure sports, such as dune-boarding in Namibia and lemur tracking in Madagascar.	Product diversification remains the greatest concern for any tourism destination. Safari tourism is increasingly packaged in conjunction with other activities, and this is used as a strategy to extend stay in the destination and increasingly as a strategy to encourage visitors to visit more than one destination. Beach tourism is highly competitive and environmentally sensitive and actions are required to maintain Africa beach resorts' comparative advantage mainly associated with the integrated product which is offered on the market – i.e. safari + beach experience. Nature/Adventure tourism offers development opportunities for some of the most remote and less known Africa destinations. There are a growing number of products for the most seasoned travellers, which travel to fulfil specific nature-based – i.e. geology, wildlife and/or adventure interests – i.e. extreme sports.

Cultural heritage tourism is one of the fastest-growing segments of the tourism industry worldwide. Forty per cent of all international leisure tourism has a cultural component. Cultural heritage in Ethiopia, music in Cape Verde, and architecture in Pays Dogon in Mali are some of the attractions for cultural tourists to Africa.

Eco-tourism, community-based tourism and agritourism are growth sectors for Africa, attracting city dwellers wishing to experience rural life. Visitors are often hosted in eco-resorts, community camps, homestays and working farms, or spend time exploring community life, the development of crafts and food products, ranging from fish, meat, coffee and tea to cereal, fruit and vegetable crops. Ecotourism has become a buzzword across Africa, with almost every country claiming to offer holidays catering to this demand.

Volunteerism is an increasingly common form of philanthropic travel. A popular choice amongst young travellers, in particular those from Europe and North America, it entails participating and working within a local community, with board and lodging provided from the fee paid.

Business travel is an important growth area for Africa. Unlike leisure travel, business travel flows depend on the dynamism of economic activity in the destination.

Diaspora tourism to Africa includes city tours, visits to historic sites, arts and crafts shopping, and trips to slave trade memorials. The continent contains many landmarks, build and relics connected with the trans-Atlantic slave trade, most of which are located in West African countries such as Ghana, Nigeria, Gambia and Senegal.

Intra-regional and domestic tourism may be the sleeping giant of Africa tourism. Already more than 10 million people are travelling across international borders every year within Africa for shopping, medical reasons, sport trips, religious journeys, business meetings and conferences, and visiting friends and relatives. Under the right conditions, the tourism sector can tap this growing wealth.

Cultural heritage tourism has great potential for Africa due to the continent's rich traditions in music, art, dance, literature, and culture. Cultural tourism generates economic activity and an enhanced sense of pride for residents. It also can generate resources for the conservation of historic sites and traditional activities.

Eco-tourism community-based tourism and agritourism very often, address the needs and requirements for many developing countries seeking sustainable economic development. However, while community-based tourism remains generally a western conceived concept highly dependent on external funding, agritourism provides an alternative to the main resort for those with a specific interest in rural life.

Volunteerism - Although in parts recognising the value of this form of tourism, this is a sector that needs careful consideration and regulations as the good intention of those engaging in volunteering activities is not always matched by positive impacts on the ground.

Business travel – Global hotel groups such as Accor, Starwood, Intercontinental, and Kempinski are planning for growth in the business travel market. Business tourists tend to have a higher average daily spend and are less seasonal than leisure tourists. The development of high quality business hotels creates a large network of downstream benefits for the destination.

Diaspora tourism has great promise for further growth with visitors from Europe and the United States as product development is enhanced and value chains strengthened. There is a growing segment associated with what is known as dark tourism - i.e. slave trade in West Africa, genocide sites in Rwanda.

Intra-regional and domestic tourism - As the size of the middle class increases, the number of intra-regional tourists is likely to rise. Intra-regional travel in East Africa is already significant. Nigeria is a potential regional tourism powerhouse in West Africa. Zimbabwe and Angola also have potential as a large source market for intra-regional travel. Domestic travel in South Africa is driving growth. Kenya has already prioritised domestic travel. Zimbabwe, Ghana and Nigeria are starting to do the same.

Source: Adapted from Novelli (2015).

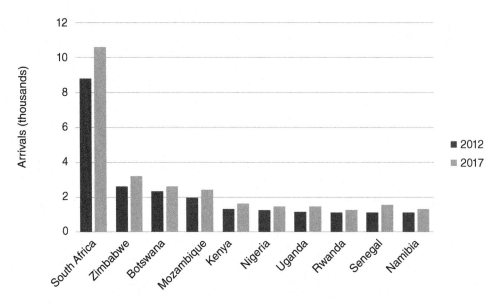

Figure 1.2 Sub-Saharan Africa's international arrivals by key destinations 2012–2017

the world, although both aspects are demonstrating steady growth. In particular, the current lack of investment means that the region has the least-developed infrastructure in the world, clogging up the vital arteries of travel and tourism. The region's air transport —infrastructure—defined by a weak domestic airline industry and a lack of airport density—greatly undermines local economies' ability to facilitate tourist and business travel, which are already hampered by the vast size and geographic barriers of Africa. Below-average international openness contributes to this issue.

(WEF, 2019a: 54)

In addition to this, the 2019 Report denounces "a pronounced lack of ICT adoption, [as] a vital requirement to attract visitors when travellers and industry players increasingly rely on technology" as well as the recurring health and hygiene concerns, which is SSA's most substantial gap with global averages. Despite the widely acknowledged attractiveness of SSA's nature (Soshkin, 2019), the combination of all these barriers may be behind the region's poor competitiveness performance also on TTCI indicators related to natural and cultural resources. Notwithstanding these broad issues, many sub-Saharan African and North African economies have made great efforts to improve their competitiveness. Table 1.3 provides further details on the continental conditions highlighted in the WEF (2019a).

Having analysed some of the key tourism issues in Africa and despite recognising the enormous potential of tourism development at continental level, five main interrelated constraints highlighted by Novelli (2015) to the fulfilment of the 'African tourism dream' remain. These are organised according to the World Bank terminology, as: (a) unpredictable and weak business environments; (b) institutional weaknesses; (c) inadequate access; (d) low level of linkages; and (e) price/value mismatch (see Table 1.4).

The chapters that follow provide a useful set of accounts to analyse those challenges and identify possible ways forward for the future.

Table 1.3 WEF 2019 summary of continental conditions

WEF 2019 regional overview	WEF 2019 countries' specific highlights
North Africa scores lower than the Middle East, but demonstrates far greater improvement in overall competitiveness. The subregion outscores the Middle East on five pillars and bests the global average on four. North Africa is the most price competitive subregion in the world, with three out of its four members among the 12 least-expensive economies covered in the report. North Africa's greatest advantage relative to the Middle East is its natural and cultural resources – although it still underperforms the world on both the Natural Resources and Cultural and Business Travel pillars. The subregion also bests the MENA average in prioritisation of T&T and environmental sustainability, areas where it has improved since 2017. On the other hand, North Africa has underdeveloped infrastructure and T&T enabling environment, contrasting some of the high performers in the Middle East subregion. In particular, North Africa trails when it comes to tourist service infrastructure and ICT readiness. The subregion's strong rate of improvement is due to enhanced safety and security, overall T&T policy and enabling conditions and air transport and ground infrastructure.	All four members of the North Africa subregion increased their TTCI scores over 2017. **Egypt** (65th) is the subregion's top scorer and its largest T&T economy. The country is also MENA's most improved scorer. Egypt is price competitive (3rd) and has MENA's highest score for cultural resources (22nd). Its improvement comes from increases on 11 pillar scores. These include the world's second-best enhancement of safety and security (130th to 112th), albeit from a low starting base. **Morocco** (66th) demonstrates North Africa's slowest improvement in TTCI performance. The country is a close second to Egypt when it comes to *overall* competitiveness, boasting the MENA region's top TTCI scores on natural resources (63rd) and North Africa's best enabling environment (71st) and infrastructure (69th). However, TTCI performance improvement is tempered by declining safety and security (20th–28th), which remains well above the subregion's average, and a deteriorating combination of natural and cultural (41st–54th) resources. **Algeria** (116th), is the lowest scoring in North Africa, but nonetheless did move up two ranks globally. The country ranks low on business environment (118th), T&T prioritisation (132nd), tourist services infrastructure (136th), environmental sustainability (133rd), natural resources (126th) and international openness (139th). On the other hand, Algeria is one of the most price-competitive countries in the world (8th).
Eastern Africa is a close second to Southern Africa in terms of competitiveness but did experience stagnation since the last edition of the report. Overall, Eastern Africa tops the broader sub-Saharan Africa subregion on nine pillars, ties on three, and is the top-ranked subregion on seven. Compared to the sub-Saharan Africa average, it maintains a minor disadvantage regarding price competitiveness, which is still its highest-scoring pillar, and a larger gap on ICT readiness. Eastern Africa's most significant advantages over Southern and Western Africa comes from better ground and port infrastructure. However, it is on natural resources where the subregion outperforms the global average. Eastern Africa lost competitiveness on seven pillars. The biggest declines came from cultural resources and business travel, health and hygiene and tourist service infrastructure. However, these losses were offset by strong growth in price competitiveness and enhancements to air and ground infrastructure.	Of the ten economies ranked in 2017, five decreased in competitiveness and all but one dropped in ranking. For example, **Rwanda** (107th) experienced the biggest decline, dropping ten places, due mainly to worsening health conditions (112th–129th) that were caused primarily by a spike in malaria (118th–140th). **Burundi** (137th) is the lowest-ranked economy in Eastern Africa but had the highest percentage increase in competitiveness. Globally, it ranks last in terms of tourist service infrastructure and, in value terms, lags behind the Eastern Africa average in terms of T&T prioritisation (134th). Burundi's increased competitiveness came from improved T&T enabling conditions and, in particular, price competitiveness, where it moved up seven places to 75th. The highest-scoring country in the subregion is **Mauritius** (54th), which is also the highest scorer in entire sub-Saharan Africa. The country is sub-Saharan Africa's top scorer when it comes to T&T prioritisation – where it ranks fifth globally – due to government focus on the industry including relatively high government expenditure (fourth) in the sector. Regarding T&T GDP size, Eastern Africa is dominated by **Ethiopia**, **Kenya** and **Tanzania**, with Ethiopia (122nd) the largest of the three. The country has the subregion's largest population but lags behind Eastern Africa's average on the majority of the 14 TTCI pillars. Most notably, Ethiopia has an underdeveloped overall T&T infrastructure (128th).

(Continued)

Western Africa enjoyed the greatest increase in competitiveness in the region, yet it also ranks the lowest on the global TTCI. The subregion lags behind Southern and Eastern Africa in all areas apart from environmental sustainability, where it has a slight edge, and ICT readiness, where it ranks higher than Eastern Africa. Like the other African subregions, Western Africa scores highest on price competitiveness and lowest on cultural and business travel. Its greatest disadvantages, relative to the rest of sub-Saharan Africa, come from lower prioritisation of T&T, tourist services infrastructure and natural resources. Western Africa's competitiveness improvements from 2017 to 2019 are concentrated in nine pillars, with the most considerable improvement coming from increased international openness and ICT readiness. Moreover, Western Africa was the only subregion to show an overall improvement in the Health and Hygiene pillar. However, subregional economies experienced further decreased competitiveness on natural and cultural resources and tourist service infrastructure.

Southern Africa is the most competitive of the three subregions but experienced slow growth in competitiveness over the past two years. In 2019, it outperforms the broader regional average on 11 pillars. The subregion is also the most price-competitive in sub-Saharan Africa, which is also its highest-ranking pillar. However, Southern Africa's biggest advantages over the other two subregions come from tourist services infrastructure and prioritisation of travel and tourism, though the subregion does perform below the *global* average in both areas. Southern Africa's growth over its 2017 performance consisted of broad improvement in T&T-related policies and enabling conditions, especially price competitiveness and international openness. ICT readiness and tourist service infrastructure also improved, but this subregion's traditional lead in overall enabling environment and natural and cultural resources deteriorated. In particular, Southern Africa's Health and Hygiene pillar worsened, reinforcing the subregion's greatest disadvantage compared to the global average.

Eight of the 12 economies in the subregion covered in both the previous and current edition of the TTCI improved their competitiveness. Yet only four of them rose in the rankings, demonstrating that there is still a long way to go for the area to become genuinely competitive.

Nigeria (129th) accounts for nearly half of the subregion's T&T GDP and is also its largest economy. However, it ranks in the middle of the pack regarding competitiveness and has the worst safety and security ranking (139th) in entire Sub-Saharan Africa.

Cape Verde (global rank of 88th) is Western Africa's highest-ranking member on the global index and sixth-highest in sub-Saharan Africa. The country is more competitive than its sub-regional counterparts in all areas except the cultural (128th) and natural (136th) resources indicators.

Benin experienced the largest growth in the subregion, moving up four spots to 123rd. The country drastically reduced its visa requirements, where it has risen to seventh globally.

Côte d'Ivoire had the sharpest decline, dropping ten spots on the index to 119th, due primarily to deteriorating road and port infrastructure (67th–98th).

Chad (139th) ranks the lowest in the subregion due in part to the worst performance in the world and second to last performance in infrastructure.

Southern Africa's growth is primarily due to the performance of **Lesotho**, which moved up four places in 2019 to a global rank of 124th. The country experienced jumps in price competitiveness (57th to 10th) and international openness (129th to 107th), caused by the lowest ticket and airport charges in the world as well as reduced visa requirements (110th to 28th). Three of the five other countries in Southern Africa that were ranked in 2017 lost places on the TTCI.

Botswana experienced the subregion's largest decline, dropping seven places to rank 92nd globally due to a worsened enabling environment (83rd to 99th), infrastructure (89th to 99rd) and natural and cultural resources (70th to 67th).

Angola (134th) is the lowest ranking member of Southern Africa, ranking near the bottom on most pillars.

South Africa (61st) currently accounts for approximately 70% of Southern Africa's T&T GDP and is the subregion's highest scorer on the TTCI, with a particularly strong lead over the countries in the rest of the region in areas related to cultural resources and business travel (23rd).

Table 1.4 Constraints to tourism growth in Africa

	Constraints	Examples	Possible solution
Unpredictable & weak business environment	Political instability, high crime rates, restrictive visa restrictions, unsafe roads, inadequate water, poor sanitation, high cost of electricity, poor construction practices, insufficient infrastructure and lack of health facilities result in unpredictable business environments.	Even in developed destinations such as Kenya and The Gambia, roads are limited. In Cape Verde and Ghana, water and sanitation services are serious constraints. The price of electricity and fluctuations in supply in Senegal and Uganda increases the cost of doing business and going on holiday in these destinations.	Policy reforms, prioritisation of basic infrastructural improvements, streamlined immigration and visa processing are crucial for tourism. Increased regional integration and the growth of regional trading blocs provide opportunities for greater ease in trans-border activity. Create institutional frameworks and mechanisms that bring together governments and private entrepreneurs.
Institutional weaknesses	Tourism is a complex phenomenon. It requires coordination between multiple government agencies, private sector bodies, civil society organisations and community stakeholders.	Transportation, communications, finance, education, sanitation and immigration are just a few of the many areas where greater coordination is required. When tourism growth goes unmanaged, the natural, cultural, and social asset base on which tourism depends becomes vulnerable.	Support services for tourism such as planning, marketing, regulatory frameworks, and monitoring are required to develop a sustainable tourism sector. Inter-ministerial and public-private collaborations and needed to formulate appropriate policies and strategies for human resource development in tourism.
Inadequate access	Africa distance from generating international and intra-regional markets creates an acute need for higher quality and more competitive air access both to and within Africa. Access requires attention not only for the development of the T&T industry, but also for the efficient movement of people and goods for the proper functioning of market economies.	Air service within Africa is characterised by expensive, infrequent services and multi-stop itineraries. Average one-way fares in Africa are twice as expensive as those in Latin America and four times as expensive as domestic flights in the United States. The seasonal nature of tourism in some areas further exacerbates this problem.	Investment in air transport represents a valuable opportunity throughout much of Africa. Vital for the ease of movement within the country is the extensiveness and quality of the country's ground transport infrastructure. Investment in air and land based transportation and infrastructure are essential.

(Continued)

	Constraints	Examples	Possible solution
Low level linkages	Despite increasing evidence of the multi-sector benefits from tourism, the sector is often regarded as elitist and dominated by foreign firms. Constraints to tourism value-chain development in Africa include poor quality products, lack of tourism awareness, and a problematic business environment.	In many cases local products (e.g. horticulture, produce, crafts, entertainment, transportation) are not sufficiently developed or are not of high enough quality to supply the tourism industry. In many destinations, sectors such as manufacturing, mining and agriculture fail to fully consider tourism sector demand. Further constraints to effective value chain development are lack of business knowhow and the difficulty that many MSMEs have in accessing loans.	Improve the quality of products and the value chain linkages. Increase the capacity of those working both in the formal and informal sectors directly and indirectly linked to tourism to improve the pro-poor effects of tourism. Create mechanisms that encourage private entrepreneurs to improve the quality of their performance and actively engage with tourism.
Price/Value mismatch	T&T services can be expensive and not necessarily matched by adequate services. Air transport, utilities, and access to land and to finance are constrained by the high cost of doing business in Africa. The reasons for elevated prices are the high cost of airfares and utilities, the need for imported goods and services, and high import duties. There is a lack of differentiation between business and leisure tourism markets at times leading to a disappointing experience.	T&T prices can be 25–35% higher than tours in other parts of the world. Accommodation in star-rated hotels can be as or more expensive than any hotel of similar rating located in Europe or the United States. Star rating and service delivery often do not reflect international standards. Staff poaching by global hotel brands is often reported as a hindering factor to the improvement of the sector service delivery in MSMEs operations.	Enable the production of good locally to avoid importing them. Create institutional mechanisms that bring together governments and private entrepreneurs and initiatives incentivising investments and capacity building. Product diversification and service quality should address different market needs (business vs. leisure travellers) and international level of service providing a better quality-value experience. Restructure formal tourism and hospitality training to match market needs.

Source: Adapted from Novelli (2015).

Conclusion

This *Handbook of Tourism in Africa* aims at advancing the existing, but yet limited, body of knowledge about tourism in Africa, including chapters that offer both practical and theoretical perspectives, authored primarily by a growing number of African scholars and practitioners.

For organisational purpose and ease of reading, this *Handbook* comprises six parts which follows the United Nation's geoscheme for Africa in terms of regional division – *Northern Africa, Western Africa, Middle Africa, Eastern Africa* and *Southern Africa*. This introduction section has discussed some of the continental issues and regional context of tourism development in Africa. Part I is focused on "Africa and Tourism" and covers continent-wide issues more broadly. Part II on "Tourism in North Africa" focuses on several aspects related to gender, cultural heritage preservations and current issues of tourism in that region. Part III on "Tourism in West Africa" deals with topics associated with the political economy of tourism, community-based tourism, backpacking and sustainable growth. Part IV on "Tourism in Middle Africa" offers perspectives and case studies from that region on community participation and stakeholder's engagement in tourism development. In Part V on "Tourism in Eastern Africa", the chapters address issues related to conservation, cultural heritage and development. Finally, in Part VI on "Tourism in Southern Africa", there are discussion on urban tourism and wildlife tourism and conservation which are pertinent to that region.

The diversity of topics and countries covered in this *Handbook*'s 30 chapters and the 10 InFocus contributions (short practitioners' pieces) offers the readers a rare opportunity to understand the challenges and issues of tourism and development in Africa. Undoubtedly, there are many other topics, themes and countries that are not covered in this volume. However, what is here provides a useful set of key critical insights into the issues, challenges and trends that Africa and African tourism is facing. By drawing upon research emerging from collaborations between a growing number of African academics and practitioners based in the continent and in the African diaspora as well as international colleagues, this *Handbook* is interdisciplinary in nature and diverse in content. This makes it appropriate not only to undergraduate, master and research students but also to consultants, industry experts and policy-makers. In a nutshell, we believe, as editors, that this volume will provide a valuable addition to the current body of knowledge on tourism in Africa.

References

Adu-Ampong, E. A. (2019). The tourism-development nexus from a governance perspective: A research agenda. In R. Sharpley and D. Harrison (Eds.), *A research agenda for tourism and development* (pp. 53–70). Cheltenham: Edward Elgar Publishing.

Adu-Ampong, E. A. (2017). Divided we stand: Institutional collaboration in tourism planning and development in the Central Region of Ghana. *Current Issues in Tourism, 20*(3), 295–314.

Adu-Ampong, E. A. (2016). *Governing tourism-led local economic development planning: An interactive tourism governance perspective on the Elmina 2015 Strategy in Ghana.* (Unpublished doctoral dissertation), University of Sheffield, Sheffield, UK.

Akama, J. S. (2004). Neo-colonialism, dependency and external control of Africa's tourism industry. In C. M. Hall and H. Tucker (Eds.), *Tourism and postcolonialism: Contested discourses, identities and representations* (pp. 140–152). London: Taylor & Francis.

Ashley, C., Boyd, C., & Goodwin, H. (2000). Pro-poor tourism: Putting poverty at the heart of the tourism agenda. *Natural Resource Perspectives, 51*, 1–12.

Beeton, S. (2006). *Community development through tourism.* Australia: Landlinks Press.

Bennett, O., Roe, D., & Ashley, C. (1999). *Sustainable tourism and poverty elimination study* (pp. 1–94). London: Department for International Development.

Bianchi, R. V. (2002). Towards a new political economy of global tourism. In R. Sharpley and D. J. Telfer (Eds.), *Tourism and development: Concepts and issues* (pp. 265–299). Clevedon: Channel View Publications.

Boissevain, J. (1977). Tourism and development in Malta. *Development and Change, 8*(4), 523–538.

Boluk, K. A., Cavaliere, C. T., & Higgins-Desbiolles, F. (2019). A critical framework for interrogating the United Nations Sustainable Development Goals 2030 Agenda in tourism. *Journal of Sustainable Tourism, 27*(7), 847–864.

Bramwell, B., & Lane, B. (Eds.) (2000). *Tourism collaboration and partnerships: Politics, practice and sustainability* (Vol. 2). Clevedon: Channel View Publications.

Bramwell, B., & Meyer, D. (2007). Power and tourism policy relations in transition. *Annals of Tourism Research, 34*(3), 766–788.

Britton, S. G. (1982). The political economy of tourism in the third world. *Annals of Tourism Research, 9*(3), 331–358.

Brohman, J. (1996). New directions in tourism for third world development. *Annals of Tourism Research, 23*(1), 48–70.

Butler, R. (1992). Alternative tourism: The thin edge of the wedge. In V. Smith and W. Eadington (Eds.), *Tourism alternatives potentials and problems in the development of tourism* (pp. 31–46). Philadelphia: University of Pennsylvania Press.

Butler, R. (1980). The concept of a tourist area cycle of evolution: Implications for management of resources. *Canadian Geographer, 24*, 5–12.

Chaperon, S., & Bramwell, B. (2013). Dependency and agency in peripheral tourism development. *Annals of Tourism Research, 40*, 132–154.

Cheong, S. M., & Miller, M. L. (2000). Power and tourism: A Foucauldian observation. *Annals of Tourism Research, 27*(2), 371–390.

Christie, I., Christie, I. T., Fernandes, E., Messerli, H., & Twining-Ward, L. (2014). *Tourism in Africa: Harnessing tourism for growth and improved livelihoods*. Washington, DC: World Bank Publications.

Church, A., & Coles, T. (Eds.) (2006). *Tourism, power and space*. London: Routledge.

Cornelissen, S. (2005). *The global tourism system: Governance, development and lessons from South Africa*. Aldershot: Ashgate.

Cowen, M., & Shenton, R. (1996). *Doctrines of development*. London: Routledge.

Craig, D. A., & Porter, D. (2006). *Development beyond neoliberalism? Governance, poverty reduction and political economy*. London: Routledge.

de Kadt, E. (Ed.). (1979). *Tourism: Passport to development? Perspectives on the social and cultural effects of tourism in developing countries*. Oxford: Oxford University Press.

Dieke, P. U. (2000). *The political economy of tourism development in Africa*. New York: Cognizant Communication Corp.

Dieke, P. U. (1995). Tourism and structural adjustment programmes in the African economy. *Tourism Economics, 1*(1), 71–93.

Dredge, D., & Jamal, T. (2015). Progress in tourism planning and policy: A post-structural perspective on knowledge production. *Tourism Management, 51*, 285–297.

Eadington, W. R., & Smith, V. L. (Eds.) (1992). *Tourism alternatives: Potentials and problems in the development of tourism*. Philadelphia: University of Pennsylvania Press.

Escobar, A. (1995). *Encountering development: The making and unmaking of the third world*. Princeton, NJ: Princeton University Press.

Fayos-Solà, E., Alvarez, M. D., & Cooper, C. (2014). *Tourism as an instrument for development* (Vol. 5). Bingley: Emerald Group Publishing.

Frenzel, F. (2013). Slum tourism in the context of the tourism and poverty (relief) debate. *DIE ERDE– Journal of the Geographical Society of Berlin, 144*(2), 117–128.

Goodwin, H. (2008). Pro-poor tourism: A response. *Third World Quarterly, 29*(5), 869–871.

Hall, C. M., & Tucker, H. (Eds.) (2004) *Tourism and postcolonialism: Contested discourses, identities and representations*. London: Taylor & Francis.

Harrison, D. (2008). Pro-poor tourism: A critique. *Third World Quarterly, 29*(5), 851–868.

Harrison, D. (Ed.) (2001). *Tourism and the less developed world: Issues and case studies*. Wallingford: CAB International.

Harrison, D., & Schipani, S. (2007). Lao tourism and poverty alleviation: Community-based tourism and the private sector. *Current Issues in Tourism, 10*(2–3), 194–230.

Harvey, D. (2005). *The new imperialism*. Oxford: Oxford University Press.

Higgins-Desbiolles, F. (2006). More than an "industry": The forgotten power of tourism as a social force. *Tourism Management*, *27*(6), 1192–1208.

Holden, A. (2013). *Tourism, poverty and development*. Oxon: Routledge.

Jamal, T. B., & Getz, D. (1995). Collaboration theory and community tourism planning. *Annals of Tourism Research*, *22*(1), 186–204.

Konadu-Agyemang, K. (2001). Structural adjustment programmes and the international tourism trade in Ghana, 1983–99: Some socio-spatial implications. *Tourism Geographies*, *3*(2), 187–206.

Lea, J. (1988). *Tourism and development in the third world*. Oxon: Routledge.

Mbaiwa, J. E. (2005). Enclave tourism and its socio-economic impacts in the Okavango Delta, Botswana. *Tourism Management*, *26*(2), 157–172.

Melubo, K., & Lovelock, B. (2019). Living inside a UNESCO world heritage site: The perspective of the Maasai community in Tanzania. *Tourism Planning & Development*, *16*(2), 197–216.

Mitchell, J., & Ashley, C. (2010). *Tourism and poverty reduction: Pathways to prosperity*. London: Earthscan.

Moscardo, G. (Ed.) (2008). *Building community capacity for tourism development*. Cambridge, MA: CABI Publishing.

Mowforth, M., & Munt, I. (2009). *Tourism and sustainability: Development globalisation and new tourism in the third world* (3rd ed.). London: Routledge.

Novelli, M. (2015). *Tourism and development in Sub-Saharan Africa: Current issues and local realities*. Oxon: Routledge.

Novelli, M., & Gebhardt, K. (2007). Community based tourism in Namibia: 'Reality show' or 'window dressing'? *Current Issues in Tourism*, *10*(5), 443–479.

Novelli, M., & Tisch-Rottensteiner, A. (2011). Authenticity vs development – Tourism to the hill tribes of Thailand. In O. Moukaffir, and P. Burns (Eds.), *Controversies in tourism* (pp. 54–73). Wallingford: CABI.

Öniş, Z., & Şenses, F. (2005). Rethinking the emerging post-Washington consensus. *Development and Change*, *36*(2), 263–290.

Owusu, F. (2003). Pragmatism and the gradual shift from dependency to neoliberalism: The World Bank, African leaders and development policy in Africa. *World Development*, *31*(10), 1655–1672.

Pearce, R. (1989). *Tourist development* (2nd ed.). Essex: Longman Group Limited.

Peck, J. (2013). Explaining (with) neoliberalism. *Territory, Politics, Governance*, *1*(2), 132–157.

Peet, R., & Hartwick, E. (2009). *Theories of development: Contentions, arguments, alternatives* (2nd ed.). New York: Guilford Press.

Pieterse, J. N. (2010). *Development theory*. London: Sage.

Rapley, J. (2002). *Understanding development theory and practice in the third world*. London: Lynne Rienner Publishers.

Said, E. (1978). *Orientalism*. New York: Pantheon Books.

Schilcher, D. (2007). Growth versus equity: The continuum of pro-poor tourism and neoliberal governance. *Current Issues in Tourism*, *10*(2), 166–193.

Scheyvens, R. (2011). *Tourism and poverty*. Oxon: Routledge.

Scheyvens, R. (2007). Exploring the tourism-poverty nexus. *Current Issues in Tourism*, *10*(2–3), 231–254.

Scheyvens, R. (2002). *Tourism for development: Empowering communities*. London: Pearson Education.

Sharpley, R. (2003). Tourism, modernisation and development on the island of Cyprus: Challenges and policy responses. *Journal of Sustainable Tourism*, *11*(2–3), 246–265.

Sharpley, R. (2000). Tourism and sustainable development: Exploring the theoretical divide. *Journal of Sustainable Tourism*, *8*(1), 1–19.

Sharpley, R., & Telfer, D. J. (Eds.) (2015). *Tourism and development: Concepts and issues* (2nd ed.). Bristol: Channel View Publications.

Sharpley, R., & Telfer, D. J. (Eds.) (2002). *Tourism and development: Concepts and issues*. Clevedon: Channel View Publications.

So, A. (1990). *Social change and development modernisation, dependency, and world-system theory*. London: Sage Publications.

Soshkin, M. (2019). *Sub-Saharan Africa has all the natural capital it needs to grow its tourism industry*. Available at: https://www.weforum.org/agenda/2019/09/travel-and-tourism-africa-2019/ [Accessed: 12/01/2020].

Spenceley, A., & Meyer, D. (2012). Tourism and poverty reduction: Theory and practice in less economically developed countries. *Journal of Sustainable Tourism*, *20*(3), 297–317.

Telfer, D. J. (2015). The evolution of development theory and tourism. In R. Sharpley and D. J. Telfer (Eds.), *Tourism and development: Concepts and issues* (pp. 31–73). Bristol: Channel View Publications.

Tosun, C. (2005). Stages in the emergence of a participatory tourism development approach in the developing world. *Geoforum*, *36*(3), 333–352.

Tosun, C. (2000). Limits to community participation in the tourism development process in developing countries. *Tourism Management*, *21*(6), 613–633.

UNCTAD. (2017). *Economic development in Africa Report 2017: Tourism for transformative and inclusive growth*. New York: United Nations Publication.

United Nations World Tourism Organization [UNWTO]. (2019). *Tourism highlights, 2019 edition*. Madrid: UNWTO.

United Nations World Tourism Organization [UNWTO]. (2018). *Tourism highlights, 2018 edition*. Madrid: UNWTO.

Urry, J., & Larsen, J. (2011). *The tourist gaze 3.0*. London: Sage.

Wearing, S., McDonald, M., & Ponting, J. (2005). Building a decommodified research paradigm in tourism: The contribution of NGOs. *Journal of Sustainable Tourism*, *13*(5), 424–439.

Wels, H. (2004) About romance and reality: Popular European imagery in postcolonial tourism in southern Africa. In C. M. Hall and H. Tucker (Eds.), *Tourism and postcolonialism: Contested discourses, identities and representations* (pp. 76–94). London: Routledge.

Williamson, J. (2009). A short history of the Washington Consensus. *Law & Bus. Rev. Am.*, *15*, 7.

World Economic Forum. (2019a). *Sub-Saharan Africa report*. Available at: http://reports.weforum.org/travel-and-tourism-competitiveness-report-2019/wp-content/blogs.dir/144/mp/files/pages/files/ssa3.pdf [Accessed: 12/01/2020].

World Economic Forum. (2019b). *Middle East and North Africa report*. Available at: http://reports.weforum.org/travel-and-tourism-competitiveness-report-2019/regional-profiles/middle-east-and-north-africa/?doing_wp_cron=1578846119.3198719024658203125000 [Accessed: 12/01/2020].

World Economic Forum. (2017). *The Travel and Tourism Competitiveness Report 2017*. Available at: http://www3.weforum.org/docs/WEF_TTCR_2017_web_0401.pdf, [Accessed: 12/01/2020].

Part I
Africa and tourism

2

The changing nature of Africa as a competitive tourism role-player

Andrea Saayman, Melville Saayman and Armand Viljoen

Introduction

Unavoidably, Africa's pre- and post-colonial history is still observed throughout many in-dependent African states. During pre-colonisation, many Africans were sold into slave trade from West and East Africa, resulting in mass extradition of human resources to fuel growing labour demands across the Atlantic. After anti-slave trade legislation passed, the exports from Africa had to adapt from labour exports to resource exports. This is especially noticeable after the Berlin conference of 1884/1885. Dawning into the era of post-colonisation and independence, many African countries and governments were unable to transition from export-led economies to industrialised economies with averages of industrialisation remaining around 10%, the same as in the 1970s (Page, 2014). The industrialisation growth in Africa is disappointing, with manufacturing output per person in Africa only about a third compared to other developing countries. While manufacturing might be considered an avenue to reduce unemployment on the continent, another prominent employment sector in Africa is tourism, employing on average 1 in every 14[1] or 7% of Africans (UNCTAD, 2017). However, certain challenges still outweigh the future prospects of post-industrialised industries and sectors such as tourism. Tourism has been identified as a catalyst for economic growth for Africa; however, tourism is such a multi-sector industry that many development challenges constrain Africa's tourism potential.

Africa's challenges are further enhanced by political, social and economic dimensions. Politically, Africa has experienced much tension from the slave trade and conquest of Africa (15th century), Africa's colonisation (19th century) to independence (1960s) and present-day conflicts (Curtin et al., 1995:17; Falola, 2002:189; Worger, Clark & Alpers, 2010:14). Socially, Africa is still lagging behind mainly due to poverty, lack of education, lack of social equality and diminished safety and security (Torres & Momsen, 2004:297). Economically, the majority of least developed countries (LDCs) are African countries, which fuels the other issues burdening the continent due to slower or stagnated economic growth, subsequently resulting in less tourism development (Bardy, Drew & Kennedy, 2012:278). However, Africa's potential for tourism is indisputable, especially considering the challenges faced by many African countries.

The advantages that Africa possesses to compete more efficiently in the global market include Africa's *price competitiveness, affinity for tourism, abundant natural resources,* and *efforts towards environmental sustainability.* However, the challenges that deter tourism development are obstacles related to safety and security, health and hygiene, poor infrastructure, and the need for skilled human capital. The opportunities for the African tourism industry include improved visa schemes, community-based tourism, utilising natural resources to benefit the poor and leveraging Africa's cultural assets (African Development Bank [AFDB], 2015:6).

The United Nations Conference on Trade and Development (UNCTAD, 2014:36) confirms that over the past two decades most African countries have shown significant growth and stabilisation of their economies, increased government spending on education reform and feeding schemes. What is more, African countries have improved access to healthcare and have devised policies and procedures to ensure their success in future. Nonetheless, it is still detrimental to investigate whether these developments and improvements will result in larger market shares of domestic, regional and international tourism, and if so, which of those improvements would have the most satisfactory results.

This chapter investigates the current state of Africa's tourism industry, identifying the persistent trends within inbound (international tourists from outside Africa), outbound (Africans travelling abroad outside of Africa) and intra-African travel (Africans travelling within Africa), as well as observing a more holistic image of what Africa has to offer within the global tourism marketplace.

Inbound tourism to Africa

Current situation

Most reports[2] indicate that Africa attracts around 5–6% of global tourism arrivals, making Africa one of the least visited regions in the world. According to the UNWTO (2018), the 2017 tourism growth numbers were 8% for both Europe and Africa, 6% for Asia and the Pacific, 5% for the Middle East and 3% for the Americas. When one delves deeper into the African tourism arrival numbers, consistent growth has led to 63 million arrivals in 2017, compared to 14.8 million in 1990. In terms of arrivals per region, in order of prominence, Northern, Southern, and Eastern Africa lead the way, followed by Western Africa and lastly Central/middle Africa, with the least number of arrivals. The increase in arrivals is also very prominent to selected countries with Egypt, Morocco, South Africa, and Tunisia recording the highest numbers of arrivals on average from 2011 to 2014 (UNCTAD, 2017). The 2011–2014 arrivals to these four countries account for 64% of arrivals to Africa. During the period 2014–2017, South Africa attracted the most international tourist arrivals, followed by Morocco and Egypt. South Africa, on average attracted 25% of arrivals to Africa, followed by Morocco (19%) and Egypt (14%). Cumulatively, these three countries still attract around 60% of African arrivals (UNWTO, 2019). These arrivals are also vital economic contributors, especially since tourism can be viewed as a service export and an important foreign exchange earner. During 2016, South Africa banked the most on inbound tourism receipts (US$ 8.7 billion), followed by Morocco (US$ 7.8 billion) and Egypt (US$ 3 billion) and Tanzania (US$ 2.4 billion) (World Travel and Tourism Council [WTTC], 2018). However, how much of this success is still backed by the traditional source markets and investors in Africa?

The traditional source markets have strong colonial ties within Africa, especially France, Britain, Portugal, Belgium, Germany, Spain and The Netherlands. These Western European countries and the United States are not only the traditional source markets to Africa but have also historically been the greatest investors in Africa. However, new markets are also interested in Africa, with growth in tourism from Middle and Eastern Europe, South America and Asia, especially China.

Figure 2.1 indicates the inbound arrivals (averaged from 2014 to 2017) per region to Africa. It is clear that the vast majority of arrivals are European, followed by arrivals from Asia, North America, Oceania and South America. Considering that emerging markets in Asia (Russia, India, China) and South America (Brazil), which have trade ties within Africa (especially South Africa), are becoming new source markets to Africa, it is understandable that emerging markets' international tourism share worldwide has risen prominently since the 1980s (30%) to 2016 (45%) and is projected to reach 57% by 2030 (UNWTO, 2017:3).

As seen in Figure 2.2, international arrivals from Europe are still considered the most prominent to Africa; however, there seems to be cyclical patterns in arrivals from European countries. Similar trends are evident for Asia, although here the decline during the last cycle

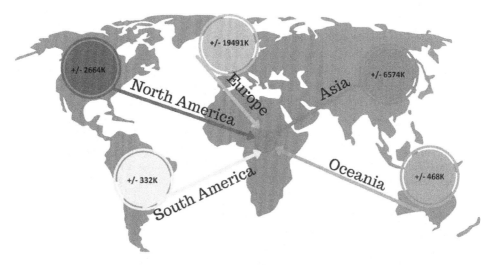

Figure 2.1 Arrivals to Africa (averages from 2014 to 2017)
Source: Compiled from UNWTO data.

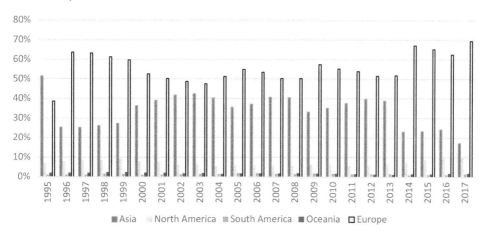

Figure 2.2 Percentage market share of arrivals to Africa (1995–2017)
Source: Compiled from UNWTO data.

is far more rapid and volatile. Both the Americas and Oceania exhibit stable arrival numbers, with little fluctuations and arrivals from North America showing a slight increasing trend.

What drives international tourism to Africa?

It is widely accepted that tourism has a catalyst effect on employment, exports, tax income generation and the stimulation of infrastructure, making it an attractive sector for developing countries. These economic and social development benefits of tourism are often relied upon by emerging economies, small island nations, and deindustrialised countries. The demand for a destination is often analysed from an economic perspective, and therefore the main traditional factors driving tourism demand include income, price, travel cost, exchange rates, competitor country prices, and marketing expenditure (Lim, 1997). It is important to contextualise the evolution of the research. During the 1990s, much scholarly attention on the economic drivers of tourism was investigated, while in the early 2000s, alternatives beyond economic drivers became popular in determining arrivals.

While there is a wealth of knowledge concerning tourism demand for Europe, the US and Asia and Australasia, few authors have investigated the demand for Africa as a tourism destination. This might also be due to the lack of available data on Africa and also the fact that Africa was never viewed as one of the top tourism destinations. Only after the year 2000, some research on the drivers of tourism demand in Africa became available, coinciding with the fast growth rates in tourism to the continent shown in Figure 2.2. Most of these research efforts were focused on country case studies, with destinations such as South Africa (see for example Saayman & Saayman, 2008; Seetanah, Durbarry & Ragodoo, 2010), Kenya (see for example Buigut & Amendah, 2016; Chabari, 2014), Zimbabwe (see Muchapondwa & Pimhidzai, 2011; Vutete & Chigora, 2015) and Nigeria (see Bankole & Babatunde, 2010; Okon, 2014) attracting attention.

Research related to the African continent and determinants of tourist arrivals is scarce, with the exception of Naudé and Saayman (2005), Kareem (2008), Fourie and Santana-Gallego (2013), and Viljoen (2018). A summary of this research is provided in Table 2.1; some of the studies have produced similar results in terms of the determinants that influence tourism arrivals to Africa and it is especially encouraging to see that previous arrivals tend to be positive and significant, indicating habit formation and persistence in tourism to Africa as a whole.

It is clear from Table 2.1 that there are more than traditional economic factors that influence the demand for Africa as a tourism destination, and although the traditional economic factors remain important, Africa is facing obstacles such as health risks, safety and security issues, development challenges and lack of infrastructure that make Africa a less sought-after destination. However, it also signals areas that can be addressed to improve the situation, such as improved conservation and infrastructure development, as well as policing of tourist hubs.

While the studies in Table 2.1 reviewed tourism demand for Africa as a continent, recent research by Viljoen (2018) also investigated different drivers of tourism arrivals for each region of Africa, as indicated in Figure 2.3. As indicated in the figure, it is clear that determinants to Africa's regions differ from one region to another. With the exception of Central Africa, all regions indicate persistence in tourism arrivals. Income is especially important in Northern and Western Africa, while health is observed in both Central and Southern Africa.

Table 2.1 Summary of previous research on inbound tourism to Africa

Author(s)	Determinants of inbound tourism to Africa
Naudé and Saayman (2005)	Political stability (positive effect)
	Communication infrastructure and marketing (internet usage) (positive effect)
	Level of development (urbanisation rate) (positive effect)
	Tourism infrastructure (hotel capacity) (positive effect)
	Health risk (malaria) (negative effect)
	Sharing a border with South Africa (positive effect)
Kareem (2008)	Political instability (ambiguous effect)
	Crime rate (negative effect)
	Exchange rate (negative effect)
	Prices (negative effect)
	Previous tourist arrivals (positive effect)
	Infrastructure (number of telephone lines) (positive effect)
	World income (positive, but not significant)
Fourie and Santana-Gallego (2013)	Previous tourist arrivals (positive effect)
	Income (origin and destination countries) (positive effect)
	Land size (positive effect)
	Sharing a common language or religion (positive effect)
	Colonial ties (positive effect)
	Distance (negative effect)
Viljoen (2018)	Previous tourist arrivals (positive effect)
	Income (advanced economies) (positive effect)
	Relative prices (negative effect)
	Health risks (TB) (ambiguous and regional specific)
	Safety and rule of law (prevalence of crime) (ambiguous and regional specific)
	Tourism communication infrastructure (internet users) (positive effect)
	Level of development (death rate) (positive effect)
	Tourism conservation (terrestrial and marine protected areas) (positive effect)

Source: Authors.

What does it imply for the future?

Estimates indicate that Africa's tourism market share will increase from 5.3% (2010) to 7.4% by 2030 (UNWTO, 2017:15). This increase seems small, but it would account for more than a 100% growth in arrivals to Africa, from 50 million to 134 million. In order to cater for the amount of tourism activity, African countries, states and regional blocks have to be prepared to ensure the attractiveness of the continent and to reap the economic and social development benefits that increased tourism activity may bring.

It is imperative that infra- and suprastructure projects and developments are aligned with national/regional strategies to increase and foster tourism. It is also necessary to ensure that air transport linkages are available to all African countries since accessibility remains a concern. While Africa with its tropical climate is prone to health risks, such as malaria and the Ebola virus, improving health infrastructure on the continent to control disease breakouts

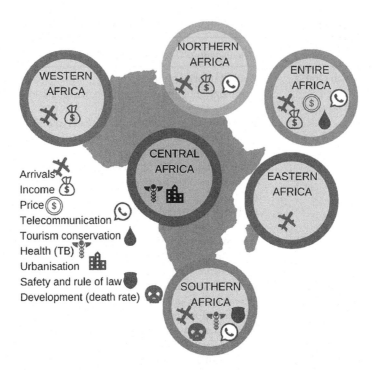

Figure 2.3 Dynamic determinants for Africa and regions
Source: Adapted from Viljoen (2018).

would benefit tourism positively. Much can also be achieved through a political will to stabilise the African continent and to enhance the safety of tourists visiting the continent.

Intra-African tourism

Current situation

Around the world, domestic and regional travel is considered the backbone of the tourism industry, with as much as 80% of international visitors travelling within the same region, or every four out of five visitors (Manyara, 2017; UNWTO, 2016). This is, however, dependent on various factors that permit travellers to freely move around a particular region without too much bureaucracy or red-tape. As indicated in Figure 2.4, nearly 21 million arrivals on the African continent are considered intra-African.

Tourism and trade have a bilateral relationship. This is rooted in the theoretical links introduced by Santana-Gallego, Ledesma-Rodríguez and Pérez-Rodríguez (2011:93). On the tourism promoting trade argument, tourism is seen as a vital source of investment, foreign exchange earnings, employment as well as business opportunity. The multiple links that tourism shares with other economic sectors position it as a catalyst for development, especially in developing countries. However, tourism is 'trade', specifically trade in services, making traditional trade theory somewhat complex when applied to tourism scenarios (UNWTO, 2015:3). The benefits associated with 'tourism trade' are numerous, from the spillover effect in other sectors to building resilience, developing communities and contributing to partnerships. However, tourism's potential is not fully recognised and supported in trade, investment and business development policies (UNWTO, 2015:5).

Since trade can promote tourism in Africa, it implies that regional integration is necessary to foster regional tourism. When comparing trade within Africa to that of other regions, the total intra-African exports (2007–2011) accounted for 11% compared to intra-European (70%) and intra-Asian (50%) exports (UNCTAD, 2013:13). More recently, during 2017 intra-African exports accounted for 17% of total African exports; still low compared to Europe (69%), Asia (59%) and North America (31%) (UNECA, 2019). Some assign the low growth in intra-regional trade to historical causes of colonisation, inadequate infrastructure, non-tariff barriers, low investment and low competitiveness between African countries, economic vulnerability due to external shocks, lagged growth and development opportunities, and limited participation in global value chains.

Infrastructure, especially electricity, transport (ports) and the internet, has an influence on African trade. Only 30% of Africans have access to electricity, creating industrialisation difficulties. Furthermore, 90% of African trade occurs by sea, and therefore ports need to be upgraded and modernised. Africa's average internet penetration is 28.6%, with the global average being 50%. This affects trade, telecommunication, and tourism (WEF, 2016).

Evaluating the role of trade and exports within Africa relies on investigating Africa's regional economic communities (RECs) in order to explore the potential of creating intra-African tourism coordination. Africa's eight regional economic communities are indicated in Figure 2.4 and make up the African Economic Community spanning across the continent to include 54 countries.

Due to Africa's size and scale, the Regional Economic Communities (RECs) aim for economic integration on the continent for economic development The African Economic Community (AEC) facilitates the interaction between the RECs to create free trade areas, customs unions, a single market, a common central bank, and a common currency to establish an economic and monetary union similar to the European Union. RECs, or 'trading blocs', are not only responsible for economic integration between the member states, but also facilitate the movement of people between countries and across borders. Economic and political integration complements and functions symbiotically due to the improved financial performance and increased competition from all participating countries (Brou & Ruta, 2006:192).

Given the number of regional trade agreements in Africa, it is surprising that Africans are also subjected to this lack of visa openness, making Africa inaccessible to Africans. Nearly 55% of all Africans require visas to travel within Africa (African Development Bank [AFDB], 2016:1). The associated cost and time to procure a visa discourage Africans to travel within Africa, as only 13 countries offer visa-free or visa on arrival entry (AFDB, 2016:13). Business visas are also more difficult to procure, causing an almost impossibility for Africans to work across Africa's 600 borders.

The benefits associated with 'tourism trade' are numerous, from the spill-over effect in other sectors to building resilience, developing communities and contributing to partnerships. However, tourism's potential is not fully recognised and supported in trade, investment and business development policies (UNWTO, 2015:5). These benefits are well documented, and many can be associated with international tourism.

What drives tourism between Africa countries?

Since the argument for trade promoting tourism is invaluable to understanding tourism flows, it is not surprising that intra-regional tourism is often investigated using trade theoretical models. According to Morley, Rosselló and Santana-Gallego (2014), gravity specifications

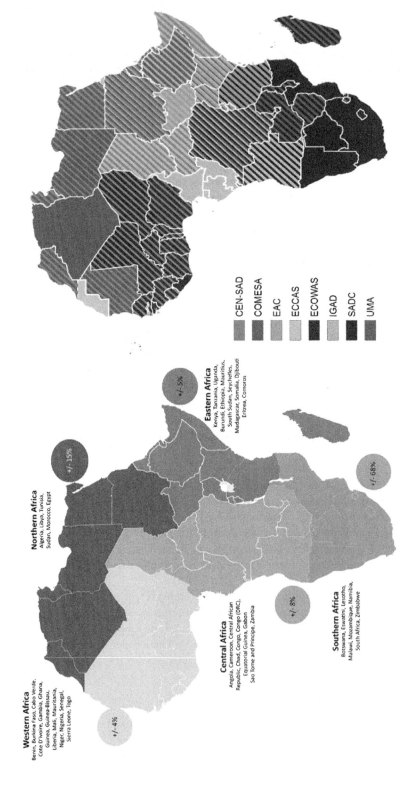

Figure 2.4 Intra-African arrivals (2014–2017) and RECs

Source: Compiled from UNWTO data; UNECA (2013).

have been neglected by the tourism demand literature for the past decades; yet, have re-emerged as a way to model tourism demand when the role of structural factors on tourism has to be evaluated. Gravity models are appropriately named as the determinations considering the impact that 'gravity' factors, for example economic size and distance, play in explaining trade between nations (Blanchard, Gaigné & Mathieu, 2008:669).

Research using the gravity model and Linder's model in tourism by Keum (2010) indicates that the tourism flows in Asia can be better explained using the gravity model compared to Linder's hypothesis. Santana-Gallego, Ledesma-Rodríguez and Pérez-Rodríguez (2016) used a gravity specification and indicated that tourism might reduce fixed and variable trade costs due to new information provided by visits, improved tourism infrastructure facilitating trade and reducing cultural distance.

Investigating intra-African tourism flows has also attracted some research attention, with Saayman and Saayman (2012) revealing that South Africa is a retail destination for many other African countries and that Africans travel to South Africa for shopping-related activities. Most of the countries they investigated fall within the same regional economic community (REC), namely Southern African Development Community (SADC).

Using a gravity specification, Fourie and Santana-Gallego (2013) also investigated intra-African flows. They found strong evidence for persistence and habit-formation in intra-African tourism and that distance is a deterrent of tourism flows, also between African countries. Income (origin and destination countries), land size and sharing a common border, language, religion or former colonial ties all increase tourist arrivals between African countries. While shared religion as a determinant of intra-African tourism flows is unique to African countries, they postulate that this probably proxies for other historical and cultural linkages not already captured in the explanatory variables. Their research results also highlight the link between intra-African tourism and trade with both the magnitude of trade as well as a dummy variable indicating regional trade agreements, significant predictors of intra-African tourism.

Recently, Viljoen (2018) investigated the determinants of intra-African tourism using an array of trade theories, namely (a) the Heckscher-Ohlin (HO) model of resource endowment, together with the Ricardian comparative advantage theory; (b) Linder's country similarity model; and (c) The gravity model. In addition, the five regions, namely Northern-, Eastern-, Southern-, Western-, and Central Africa, were also investigated and not only Africa in total.

The Ricardian theory of comparative advantage is based on labour productivity differences, and the subsequent theory of Heckscher-Ohlin ascribed the differences in productivity as a result of differences in factor endowments. Both these theories therefore focus on the competitiveness of a country, but from different perspectives. Linder (1961) takes a demand-side view and postulates that trade between countries with similar demand structures (income per capita) would be most intensive. As already mentioned, the basic assumption of the gravity model is that a country will experience a higher degree of trade with another country if they share common characteristics. Distance, both geographically and culturally, based on similar language, currency, colonial connections and political history therefore enhances trade and tourism according to the gravity model.

The findings of Viljoen (2018) indicate that the gravity results confirm that mass variables (GDP per capita and total population) and distance (travel costs) explain tourism flows. This is consistent with economic theory concerning the gravity model. Contrary to the results of Fourie and Santana-Gallego (2013), trade was insignificant in explaining tourism flows, which could be due to Africa's lack of economic integration and intra-regional trade.

Viljoen (2018) also found that countries that have decreased cultural distance experience enhanced tourism flows – a result that confirms the research of Fourie and Santana-Gallego (2013). This is greatly beneficial for the tourism industry, as one country may evaluate the tourism demand of the domestic market, which could then, with little alteration, attract similar African tourists who share the same ethnic language and who border the host country. Contrary to trade models, landlocked destinations experience increased tourism flows in Africa, while East African countries are the major gainers and West African countries presenting mainly deterioration in tourism (Viljoen, 2018). This could be due to the East African region's open-border policies within the trade bloc.

Similar to the findings of Kuem (2010) for South Korea, Viljoen (2018) could not find any support for the notion that African countries with similar characteristics travel more to one another. The opposite is rather shown, namely that Africans are inclined to travel to countries that have a much higher GDP per capita than their home country and that are more urbanised. It therefore indicates that countries with vastly different demand structures experience increased tourism flows, with larger and more advanced African economies attracting more African arrivals.

The comparative advantage theory states that countries that specialise in producing a product more (cost) efficiently will increase economic welfare by focusing production on that product and exporting it to other countries. The results also indicate that countries already benefiting from tourism are also more popular destinations for Africans (Viljoen, 2018). Tourism-oriented countries are successful due to the existing tourism development, indicating economies of scale. The results for resource endowment differences between countries that explain tourism flows contradict the HO theory (Viljoen, 2018). The results were mainly insignificant, finding no support that African tourists travel to other African countries that offer different resources than their home country. This result may be driven by a lack of quality data, or that the African countries were too similar in size (population) and resource endowment.

What does it imply for the future?

Similar to other regions worldwide, intra-African arrivals are a major contributor to the African tourism industry. Its scale and size are, however, still not comparable to that of other regions – not only in terms of tourism but also in terms of trade. Using theoretical trade models, intra-African trade can best be explained by the gravity model. The similarities between African countries, such as having been colonised by the same country, speaking a common language and sharing a common border, lead to increased tourism flows between African countries. This indicates that intra-African arrivals are most likely to be evident in regional economic communities and that regional African tourism is a viable avenue to increase intra-African arrivals. Since distance reduces bilateral tourism arrivals, the importance of regional African tourism is again reinforced.

In terms of the various regions, the regional analysis done by Viljoen (2018) shows that Eastern Africa is expected to experience increased arrivals and the region's visa-openness policy may be a driving factor behind this result. The drive for regional integration in Eastern Africa therefore not only benefits trade in goods but also tourism flows within the region. Northern and Western African states are expected to experience decreased arrivals, mainly due to political instability in the north, and health threats (such as Ebola) in the west.

Within Africa, tourists from less urbanised countries tend to travel to more urbanised countries. This is due to the benefits from more advanced services and availability of goods in more urbanised and advanced economies. The notion that a large proportion of African tourism is for shopping purposes is therefore supported by recent research, and African countries that have the infrastructure for tourism therefore experience economies of scale.

Outbound African tourism

Current situation

Where and why Africans travel has not received much attention to date. This is not surprising, since only around 3% of Africans travel outbound to the rest of the world. As previously stated, the vast majority of Africans travel within Africa, with travel to the other five regions – Asia, Europe, North-America, South-America, and Oceania – lagging substantially behind intra-African travel. Figure 2.5 indicates how this 3.15% is divided into five other global regions and popular destination countries within each region. The size of the circle approximates the popularity of the region in for the averages between 2014 and 2017.

However, outbound tourism from Africa is not stagnant and, in order to illustrate the changes in destination preferences, Table 2.2 provides a snapshot of outbound African travel to the five global regions over five-year intervals. The destination preference changes are noticeable, and for the last couple of years, Europe has been the main destination of choice.

A brief review of the important countries in each region also sheds light on the changing travel patterns of African tourists. In Asia, the prominent destinations include Saudi Arabia, the UAE, China (Mainland, Hong Kong and Macao), Turkey and India. China and India as destinations are becoming increasingly popular with African tourists. This could be due to increased trade agreements and investments by Chinese companies within Africa. However, Saudi Arabia remains the largest destination within Asia, which may be ascribed to Mecca and Medina as well as the hajj pilgrimage that takes place in this country. North African countries are nearly completely Muslim, with 93% of the population affiliated with Islam (Pew Research Centre, 2017:online).

Within Europe, the most popular destinations for African tourists are France and Spain. This is followed by the United Kingdom, Italy and Germany. All of the destinations were colonial powers in Africa, and are also known as traditional source markets of inbound tourism to Africa.

Although North America is not nearly as popular among African tourists as Asia and Europe, on average (±78%) of Africans who visit the North American region, visit the United States. Among the Oceania region, the two most visited countries for African tourists are

Table 2.2 African outbound arrivals

Year	Asia (%)	Europe (%)	North America (%)	South America (%)	Oceania (%)
1995	51	39	7	1	2
2000	36	53	8	1	2
2005	35	55	6	2	2
2010	35	55	6	2	2
2015	41	50	7	1	1

Source: Compiled using UNWTO data (1995–2015).

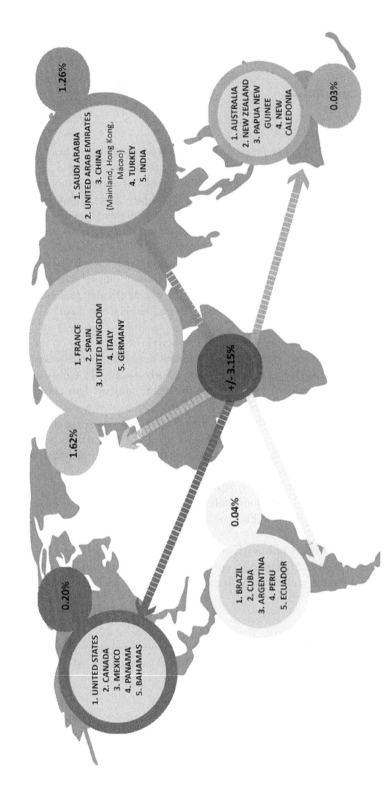

Figure 2.5 Outbound African arrival countries

Source: Compiled using UNWTO data (2014–2017).

Australia (±78%) and New Zealand (±20%). Similarly, tourism to Brazil (±67%) dominates African tourism to South America, with Cuba (±11%) the next popular destination.

What drives African outbound tourism?

Very little research has been conducted on African travel behaviour outside of Africa. Recently though, Saayman, Viljoen and Saayman (2018) analysed African outbound travel to the various regions of the world. To determine the tourism demand of African countries for other international destinations, as well as the role of price and expenditure elasticity in the country of reference, the Almost Ideal Demand System (AIDS) is the preferred methodology in the tourism demand literature. The AIDS model is a very effective tool in assessing the economics of tourism as it examines the entire set of price and expenditure elasticities while addressing the sensitive nature of tourism demand (Durbarry & Sinclair, 2003:927). This approach was therefore also preferred in the research on African outbound tourism.

The majority of tourism-related AIDS model research is based on the Western European travel market (Li, Song & Witt, 2004; Mangion et al., 2012; Mello, Pack & Sinclair, 2002) to various European destinations (Spain, France, Greece, Italy, Portugal, Malta, and Cyprus) making use of linear and dynamic AIDS models. Mello, Pack and Sinclair (2002:518) state that the AIDS model results are "consistent with the properties of homogeneity and symmetry". This is in accord with the micro-foundations of the AIDS model approach and increases the credibility of the elasticity values. Because of this, Mangion et al. (2012:1270) find that the AIDS model is useful in quantifying tourism policy to strengthen public policymaking.

Within the African context, the model has been applied by Saayman and Cortés-Jiménez (2013), who investigated long-haul tourism consumption from France, Germany, the United Kingdomand the United States in South Africa. Furthermore, Botha and Saayman (2013) investigated United Kingdom and United States outbound travel behaviour using an AIDS specification and including South Africa as one of the destinations in order to determine the elasticity and cross-elasticities of South Africa as a tourist destination for these countries.

Using a linear static and dynamic AIDS specification, Saayman, Viljoen and Saayman (2018) modelled African outbound tourism to the various regions of the world and the resulting expenditure and income elasticities that they found are summarised in Table 2.3. They found that African tourism to Oceania and Africa is relatively expenditure elastic, with elasticities greater than unity, while all other destinations are expenditure inelastic. This implies that an

Table 2.3 Summary of the AIDS model elasticities for African outbound tourism

	Expenditure elasticities	Own price elasticity	Asia	Europe	North America	Oceania	South America	Africa
Asia	Inelastic	Inelastic		S	C	C	C	S
Europe	Inelastic	Inelastic	S		S	S	C	S
North America	Inelastic	Elastic	C	S		S	S	S
Oceania	Elastic	Elastic	C	S	S		S	S
South America	Inelastic	Elastic*	C	C	S	S		S
Africa	Elastic	Inelastic	S	S	S	S	S	

Note: S = substitute destinations; C = complementary destinations; * = cannot be confirmed in the static model
Source: Saayman, Viljoen and Saayman (2018).

increase in African income might benefit Oceania and other African destinations more than destinations in Asia, Europe, North or South America. However, Oceania and Africa will be hit more severely with declining tourism numbers in the event of a decline in African income.

Furthermore, African tourists are more sensitive to price changes in North America, South America and Oceania than in Asia, Europe and the rest of Africa (Saayman, Viljoen & Saayman, 2018). The more popular destinations for African tourists are therefore also the ones for which they have lower sensitivity to price changes, which might indicate some form of loyalty.

In terms of the cross-price elasticities, the AIDS model allows the identification of substitute and complementary destinations. Quite noticeable is the fact that Africa is a substitute for all other continents, and increased prices worldwide, or weakening African currencies would therefore benefit tourism to other African countries at the expense of all other continents (Saayman, Viljoen & Saayman, 2018). While most destinations are substitutes, as would be expected in international tourism, some complementary destinations were also identified. These include Asia and North America, North and South America, Asia and Oceania, and Asia and South America. Most of these complementary pairs can be explained by flight routes and flight hubs (for example in Qatar, the UAE and Singapore), which makes the rest of the world accessible to African tourists (Saayman, Viljoen & Saayman, 2018).

What does it imply for the future?

African outbound travel to the rest of the world has not been researched extensively and the understanding of African travel patterns, their needs and desires, is still in its infancy. With the rapid economic growth that large parts of the continent have experienced in the past decade or two, a new source market for international tourists is emerging. Understanding African travel behaviour is therefore an area that needs additional research and some continents and destinations are starting to position themselves to reap the benefits of this new and growing source market.

Recent research by Saayman, Viljoen and Saayman (2018) shows that although intra-African tourism is still the main form of African tourism, there is a growing demand for other international destinations. The increase in African income has seen a growth in demand for all international regions, although it is noteworthy that Europe is a destination that is rapidly growing in popularity for African tourists. The results of Saayman, Viljoen and Saayman (2018) show that the costs of travel are still an influential factor in destination choice for Africans and African outbound tourism can be enhanced through increased accessibility, such as the creation of travel hubs and flight routes to and from African countries.

Challenges for the future

With arrivals to Africa growing at a fast pace and more and more Africans travelling abroad, the continent is starting to become a more competitive role player in the international tourism arena. Given the research to date, what are the challenges that African countries face in developing tourism to its full potential and to reap the benefits in terms of economic growth and development?

First, African countries need to acknowledge that tourism development needs to be coordinated and planned. The enhancement of Africa's tourism competitiveness is now a main objective within the African Union, and already saw the establishment of a specialised technical committee on transport, intercontinental and interregional infrastructure, energy and tourism. This is a step in the right direction and will potentially urge African countries to prioritise tourism development.

Infrastructure remains a key concern and especially transport infrastructure. Not only are there few transport hubs on the continent, but travelling between countries and to rural areas where tourism can especially aid in poverty alleviation, is in many cases impossible. Airport, rail, road and communication infrastructure therefore has to be prioritised. While cities are always an initial starting point for tourism development, it is also paramount that rural tourism developments should not be neglected.

In this regard, one also has to recognise the importance of regional integration and the role that trade infrastructure development can play in facilitating tourism development. In addition, integration also ensures more social cohesion within regions and provides opportunities to reduce cultural distance and intra-African tourism.

One also has to acknowledge that Africa is a popular destination due to its variety of wildlife and unspoiled beauty. Over-development should therefore be guarded against in the interest of sustainable tourism. Choosing the right types of tourism developments is also crucial within this context and ensuring that local communities benefit through tourism development must remain a key focus. Support for small- and medium-sized tourism enterprises must therefore not be underestimated, rather than the all-inclusive resort type of developments.

Outbound travel from Africa is currently still in its infancy; it does, however, indicate ample opportunity for growth. Several factors are shaping this new consuming class. Africa's population, the fastest growing and youngest in the world, is concentrated in urban areas (McKinsey & Co., 2018). It is projected that by 2020 the African consumer market will be the single largest business opportunity. In addition, as economic prosperity increases across Africa, and social and political stability is ensured, the African traveller might become the 'emerging tourist', with destinations worldwide, but especially in Europe and Asia that will benefit most.

Conclusion

In an attempt to illustrate the changing nature of tourism to, in and from Africa, this chapter highlights and describes aspects to consider when thinking about tourism potential on the continent. The potential for Africa increases due to economic, social and political stability, and increased investment from both traditional markets (Europe and the United States) and emerging economies (China). However, Africa is still largely affected by external shocks such as the impending 'Brexit' negotiations and the withdrawal of Britain from the European Union, the increased infra- and suprastructure investments from, among others, China, as well as internal struggles related to weak institutional support for tourism and even weaker intra-African trade. Amidst these challenges and addressing the subsequent events and implications thereof, Africa is in an extremely fortunate position to capitalise on the continent's potential for increased tourism.

Notes

1 Average from 2011 to 2014.
2 UNWTO, World Economic Forum, World Bank Group.

References

AFDB. 2015. *African tourism monitor.* Available online: http://www.afdb.org/fileadmin/uploads/afdb/Documents/Publications/Africa_Tourism_Monitor_Unlocking_Africa%E2%80%99s_Tourism_Potential_%E2%80%93_Vol_3_%E2%80%93_Issue_1.pdf

AFDB. 2016. *Africa visa openness report, 2016.* Available online: http://www.afdb.org/fileadmin/uploads/afdb/Documents/GenericDocuments/Africa_Visa_Openness_Report_2016.pdf

Bankole, A. S. & Babatunde, M. A. (2010). Elasticities of demand for tourism in Nigeria: An ARDL approach. *Tourism Analysis, 15*(4), 489–496.

Bardy, R., Drew, S. & Kennedy, T. F. 2012. Foreign investment and ethics: How to contribute to social responsibility by doing business in less-developed countries. *Journal of Business Ethics, 106*(3), 267–282.

Blanchard, P., Gaigné, C. & Mathieu, C. 2008. Foreign direct investment: lessons from panel data. In Mathyas, L. & Sevestre, P., eds. *The econometrics of panel data: Fundamentals and recent developments in theory and practice.* Berlin, Heidelberg: Springer-Verlag, pp. 663–696.

Botha, A. & Saayman, A. 2013. Modelling tourism demand for South Africa: An almost ideal demand system approach. *Journal of Economic and Financial Sciences, 6*(3), 683–706.

Brou, D. & Ruta, M. 2006. Special interests and the gains from political integration. *Economics and Politics, 18*(2), 191–218.

Buigut, S. & Amendah, D. D. 2016. Effect of terrorism on demand for tourism in Kenya. *Tourism Economics, 22*(5), 928–938.

Chabari, P. K. 2014. Determinants of inbound tourism to Kenya (Doctoral dissertation, School of Economics, University of Nairobi).

Curtin, P., Feierman, S., Thompson, L. & Vansina, J. 1995. *African history from earliest times to independence.* 2nd ed. London: Longman.

Durbarry, R. & Sinclair, M. T. 2003. Market shares analysis: The case of French tourism demand. *Annals of Tourism Research, 30*(4), 927–941.

Falola, T. 2002. *Africa: Volume 4: The end of colonial rule: Nationalism and decolonization.* Durham, NC: Carolina Academic Press.

Fourie, J. & Santana-Gallego, M. 2013. The determinants of African tourism. *Development Southern Africa, 30*(3), 347–366.

Kareem, O. I. (2008). A panel data analysis of demand for tourism in Africa. Paper presented at the 14th African Econometric Society, Annual Conference, Cape Town, South Africa.

Keum, K. 2010. Tourism flows and trade theory: A panel data analysis with the gravity model. *The Annals of Regional Science, 44*(3), 541–557.

Li, G., Song, H. & Witt, S. F. 2004. Modeling tourism demand: A dynamic linear AIDS approach. *Journal of Travel Research, 43*(2), 141–150.

Lim, C. 1997. Review of international tourism demand models. *Annals of Tourism Research, 24*(4), 835–849.

Linder, S. B. 1961. *An essay on trade and transformation.* Stockholm: Almqvist & Wiksell, pp. 82–109. Available online: https://ex.hhs.se/dissertations/221624-FULLTEXT01.pdf

Mangion, M., Cooper, C., Cortéz-Jimenez, I. & Durbarry, R. 2012. Measuring the effect of subsidization on tourism demand and destination competitiveness through the AIDS model: An Evidence-based approach to tourism policymaking. *Tourism Economics, 18*(6), 1251–1272.

Manyara, G. 2017. *Developing regional and domestic tourism in Africa.* Available online: https://au.int/sites/default/files/documents/32251-doc-domestic_and_regional_tourism_development.pdf

Mello, M. D., Pack, A. & Sinclair, M. T. 2002. A system of equations model of UK tourism demand in neighbouring countries. *Applied Economics, 34*(4), 509–521.

McKinsey & Co. 2018. *The rise of the African consumer.* Available online: https://www.mckinsey.com/industries/retail/our-insights/the-rise-of-the-african-consumer

Morley, C., Rosselló, J. & Santana-Gallego, M. 2014. Gravity models for tourism demand: Theory and use. *Annals of Tourism Research, 48*(2014), 1–10.

Muchapondwa, E., & Pimhidzai, O. (2011). Modelling international tourism demand for Zimbabwe. *International journal of business and social science, 2*(2): 71-81

Naudé, W. & Saayman, A. 2005. Determinants of tourist arrivals in Africa: A panel data regression analysis. *Tourism Economics, 11*(3), 365–391.

Okon, E. O. 2014. Inbound tourism and social factors in Nigeria: Evidence from an Ardl-Ecm Model. *Asian Journal of Economics and Empirical Research, 1*(2), 40–47.

Page, J. 2014. *Africa's failure to industrialize: Bad luck or bad policy?* Available online: https://www.brookings.edu/blog/africa-in-focus/2014/11/20/africas-failure-to-industrialize-bad-luck-or-bad-policy/

Pew Research Centre. 2017. *World's Muslim population more widespread than you might think.* Available online: http://www.pewresearch.org/fact-tank/2017/01/31/worlds-muslim-population-more-widespread-than-you-might-think/

Saayman, A. & Cortés-Jiménez, I. 2013. Modelling intercontinental tourism consumption in South Africa: A systems-of-equations approach. *South African Journal of Economics, 81*(4), 538–560.

Saayman, A. & Saayman, M. 2008. Determinants of inbound tourism to South Africa. *Tourism Economics, 14*(1), 81–96.

Saayman, M. & Saayman, A. 2012. Shopping tourism or tourists shopping? A case study of South Africa's African tourism market. *Tourism Economics, 18*(6), 1313–1329.

Saayman, A., Viljoen, A. & Saayman, M. (2018). Africa's outbound tourism: An almost ideal demand system perspective. *Annals of Tourism Research, 73*, 141–158. https://doi.org/10.1016/j. annals.2018.06.005

Santana-Gallego, M., Ledesma-Rodríguez, F. & Pérez-Rodríguez, J. 2011. Tourism and trade in small island regions: The case of the Canary Islands. *Tourism Economics, 17*(1):107–125.

Santana-Gallego, M., Ledesma-Rodríguez, F. J. & Pérez-Rodríguez, J. V. 2016. International trade and tourism flows: An extension of the gravity model. *Economic Modelling, 52*(1), 1026–1033.

Seetanah, B., Durbarry, R. & Ragodoo, J. N. (2010). Using the panel cointegration approach to analyse the determinants of tourism demand in South Africa. *Tourism Economics, 16*(3), 715–729.

Torres, R. & Momsen, J. H. 2004. Challenges and potential for linking tourism and agriculture to achieve pro-poor tourism objectives. *Progress in Development Studies, 4*(4), 294–318.

UNCTAD. 2013. *Economic development in Africa. Report 2013. Intra-African trade: Unlocking private sector dynamism.* Available online: https://unctad.org/en/PublicationsLibrary/aldcafrica2013_en.pdf

UNCTAD. 2014. *Economic development in Africa. Report 2014. Catalysing investment for transformative growth in Africa.* Available online: http://unctad.org/en/PublicationsLibrary/aldcafrica2014_en.pdf

UNCTAD. 2017. *Economic development in Africa: Tourism for transformative and inclusive growth.* Available online: http://unctad.org/en/PublicationsLibrary/aldcafrica2017_en.pdf

UNECA. 2019. *Boosting trade and investment: A new agenda for regional and international engagement.* Available online: https://www.brookings.edu/wp-content/uploads/2019/01/BLS18234_BRO_book_006.1_CH6.pdf

UNWTO. 2015. *Tourism driving trade, fostering development and connecting people.* Available online: http://cf.cdn.unwto.org/sites/all/files/pdf/tourism_driving_trade_fostering_development_connecting_people.pdf

UNWTO. 2016. *Supporting tourism for development in least developed countries.* Available online: http://www.intracen.org/uploadedFiles/intracenorg/Content/Exporters/Sectors/Service_exports/Trade_in_services/Supporting_Tourism_Development_v3.pdf

UNWTO. 2017. *Tourism highlights, 2017 edition.* Available online: https://www.e-unwto.org/doi/pdf/10.18111/9789284419029

UNWTO. 2018. *International tourism results: The highest in 7 years.* Available online: http://cf.cdn.unwto.org/sites/all/files/pdf/unwto_barom18_01_january_excerpt_hr.pdf

UNWTO. 2019. *Compendium of Tourism Statistics dataset [Electronic].* Madrid: UNWTO, data updated on 11/01/2019.

Viljoen, A. H. 2018. A critical assessment of Africa's growth potential as a global competitive tourism role-player. PhD thesis, North-West University, Potchefstroom, South Africa.

Vutete, C. & Chigora, F. 2015. Rebranding Zimbabwe through tourism and hospitality variables: The reality of nation branding. *International Open and Distance Learning Journal, 1*(3), 18–32

WEF. 2016. *Africa needs to trade with itself – Here's how.* Available online: https://www.weforum.org/agenda/2016/04/africa-needs-to-trade-with-itself/

Worger, W. H., Clark, N. L. & Alpers, E. A. 2010. *Africa and the west: A documentary history. Volume 1: Africa and the West: From the slave trade to conquest, 1441–1905.* Oxford: Oxford University Press.

WTTC. 2018. *Visitor Exports.* Available online: https://docs.google.com/spreadsheets/d/1ssCcIcVUox80Rufg-yEblk6r30zfjSbpSOclghkfbu4/edit#gid=0

3

Information communication technology (ICT) and tourism promotion in Africa

Julian K. Ayeh

Introduction

Unquestionably, technology has revolutionised travel and tourism industries around the globe. From the humble beginnings of jet planes and SABRE CRS in the 20th century to the present use of smart technologies and the application of artificial intelligence in offering robotic services in hotels, restaurants and airports, to an anticipated future of windowless airplanes, the evolution and transformative impact of technology are evident in every area of the tourism sector. The World Travel and Tourism Council ([WTTC] 2018a) estimates that in every 24-hour cycle, there are 11.2 million air passengers, 15 million Uber rides, over 2 billion transactions on global distribution systems (GDS), over a billion credit card transactions, over 5 billion travel-related searches on Google, 15.2 million visits to TripAdvisor, 22.5 million visitors on Expedia, 14 million hotel bookings, 100,000 flights and 22.7 million people passing through airports around the world.

Though many African countries have traditionally been laggards in technology adoption, the continent has not been left untouched by the increasing digitisation and transformation generated by information and communication technologies (ICTs) revolution. ICTs broadly refer to multiple communication technologies, ranging from simple to complex applications including Cell Phone applications (SMS), Digital Cameras, Internet, Wireless (Wi-Fi and WiMAN), Voice over Internet Protocol (VoIP), Global Positioning System (GPS), Geographic Information System (GIS), Convergence (data, voice, media), Digital radio, and other emerging technologies (Shanker 2008). Technology has broken new frontiers on the continent with some African countries at the forefront of certain genres of innovation adoption. Nonetheless, a lot of unexplored grounds remain, and ICT is still underutilised in many of the continent's geographic regions and subsectors. Africa has been at the core of the "digital divide" – i.e. "the gap between individuals, households, businesses and geographic areas at different socio-economic levels with regard both to their opportunities to access ICTs and to their use of the Internet for a wide variety of activities" (OECD 2001, 4). Nonetheless, limited attention has been given to the implications of the digital divide for the tourism sector (Minghetti and Buhalis 2010). Besides, the literature on the ICT and Tourism nexus reveals inadequate focus on countries in the global south and particularly in Africa. Yet examining

ICT role in tourism from developing countries' perspective is even more crucial in view of the contribution of tourism to economic development and the potential of technology in providing competitive advantage and in accelerating tourism benefits. This chapter discusses how the continent could harness ICT to competitively market its tourism potentials and the critical issues demanding attention.

ICT and tourism nexus

The impact of ICT on various industries within the tourism sector cannot be overemphasised as ICTs have transformed the structure and organisation of the tourism system (Minghetti and Buhalis 2010; Sheldon 1997). Information technology offers a wide range of opportunities for numerous sub-sectors including transportation, lodging, food service, travel agencies, tour operators, attractions and entertainment services in a globalised milieu (Buhalis and Law 2008; Tichaawa, Mhlanga and Sicwebu 2017). Several scholars have underscored how ICTs have led to a new paradigm shift, altered the structure of tourism industries and generated a vast range of opportunities (Buhalis 2003; Buhalis and Kaldis 2008; Buhalis and Law 2008; Rihova et al. 2018; Sheldon 1997; Sigala 2003; Werthner and Klein 1999a).

The intricate relationship between ICT and tourism is likewise conspicuous on the African continent. The tourism sector in Africa has experienced critical changes stemming from ICT generated innovations. Emerging technologies continue to transform tourism-related industries and the entire process of tourism service development, delivery, management and marketing (Opara and Onyije 2013; Tichaawa, Mhlanga and Sicwebu 2017). For African countries, ICT could represent a powerful tool for generating boundless gains in promoting and strengthening the strategy and operations of the tourism sector as a whole (Tichaawa, Mhlanga and Sicwebu 2017, 2). It also represents a critical instrument in determining the capabilities of African destinations and tourism organisations for survival and competitiveness in our highly digitised and globalised economy (Parsons and Oja 2013). Notwithstanding, most African countries are yet to fully tap into the potential of ICT to maximise tourism gains.

ICT potential for Africa's tourism promotion

At the global stage, African countries have often received the least share in tourism benefits. In 2017, for instance, the United Nations World Tourism Organisation (UNWTO 2018) reports that Africa earned merely 5% (63 million) of the global share in international tourist arrivals. In contrast, the shares of Europe, Asia-Pacific and the Americas' were 51% (672 million), 24% (323 million) and 15% (211 million), respectively. The situation is even more worrying with regards to the economic revenues from tourism. Out of a total US$ 1.3 trillion global earnings in tourism, Africa's share was a meagre 3% (US$37 billion), in contrast to Europe's 39% (US$519 billion), Asia and the Pacific's 29% (US$390 billion) and America's 24% (US$326 billion) of international tourism receipts. A closer look at the distribution of Africa's share reveals another disturbing picture: the greater share of international tourist arrivals and receipts is concentrated on a few countries (e.g. South Africa, Egypt, Morocco, Kenya, Tunisia, Tanzania) with the majority of the 54 African countries receiving very little in tourism earnings. Giving the significant role of tourism in cultural preservation, environmental protection, job creation, peace and security, and economic growth and development, it goes without saying that the African continent is in dire need of tourism promotion. There are several political, social and economic factors that account for this poor performance.

Nevertheless, information and communication technologies offer immense potential for addressing some of these setbacks, as well as in offering opportunities for bridging the gap and maximising tourism gains for the continent. With ICTs, African tourism destinations have more opportunities and possibilities than ever before.

In the framework of the extended marketing mix paradigm (Booms and Bitner 1981; McCarthy 1964), ways in which technology could be harnessed to market Africa's tourism potential are discussed below. The marketing mix paradigm represents one of the core concepts of marketing theory. The extended marketing mix embodies a combination of elements (i.e. product, price, place, promotion, people, process and physical evidence) that could be employed by tourism destinations and businesses to meet the needs and expectations of both existing and potential tourists (Figure 3.1).

Product: Most African countries have traditionally relied on their raw natural and cultural heritage assets as tourism products. Not only do emerging technologies offer opportunities to enhance the existing stock of tourism products but also the chance to develop new and competitive tourism offerings and to provide more diversified products. The Internet, Big Data

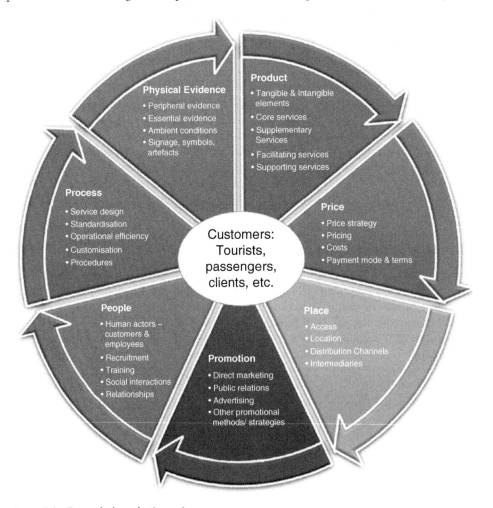

Figure 3.1 Extended marketing mix
Source: Adaption of Booms and Bitner, 1981; McCarthy 1964.

Analytics and Artificial Intelligence among others now offer unimaginable opportunities to ascertain tourists' needs and to develop the right products to meet those needs. ICT further offers opportunities for value co-creation of tourism experiences (Cabiddu, Lui and Piccoli 2013; Campos et al. 2018; Rihova et al. 2018) in response to the growing demand for more participative and interactive experiences (Scott, Laws and Boksberger 2009). Geographic Information Systems (GIS) are now used for identifying tourist sites and destinations. GIS, GPS, drones and other emerging technologies further help to monitor and manage tourist sites to ensure sustainability. Museums and other heritage sites are utilising audio guide, electronic multi-media guide, GPS tours, automatically triggered devices, virtual-reality tour, mobile apps and cell phone tours to enhance interpretation and tour guiding. Others are experimenting with emerging technologies like iBeacon and augmented reality to improve product features and add value to existing attractions.

From the tourist point of view, ICT helps to minimise the uncertainties associated with the tourism product. The Internet, social media/consumer-generated media and new technologies like augmented reality facilitate the 'tangibilization' of tourism offerings and address several uncertainties and concerns concomitant with the intangible tourism service.

Price: ICTs make it easier to determine how much tourists are willing to pay for travel products and services. ICT can also be employed for cost reduction and consequently price decreases. At present, many African countries are perceived as expensive destinations. Air travel fares to and within the continent are among the most expensive compared to other regions of the world. Hotel services are overpriced in some destinations and often the cost of doing business is high due to limited ICT infrastructure, perceived risks, unfair trade policies and political situations among others; thus, making it difficult for African destinations to compete favourably at the global stage. Advance use of ICT could help bring costs down and enable tourism businesses on the continent to offer more competitive prices to international tourists. ICT does so by minimising the cost of production. Technology makes it possible to produce, transmit, access and share knowledge at the least cost. Mobile payments, for instance, has the advantage of lower processing fees compared with traditional alternatives. This decrease in transactional costs also comes along with reduction in inefficiencies and price offerings. On the demand side, the Internet empowers consumers to compare alternatives regarding product attributes and prices and to build customised itineraries that fit their financial situations (Buhalis 2003; Rihova et al. 2018).

Place: Perhaps, among the most significant transformation brought by ICT into the tourism sector regards how tourism products are distributed to consumers. Unlike traditional products where products are transported to where the consumer is, with tourism, it is the other way around – the tourist has to move spatially to where the product is. As a result, decision making and consumption are separated in time and space (Werthner and Klein 1999a). This makes the distribution of tourism particularly disadvantageous to African destinations which are often plagued with negative media publicity about political turmoil and issues that raise safety concerns. As a result, the continent is frequently perceived by many potential tourists as exotic and unsafe. ICT could help address these challenges through innovative applications of the Internet and mobile apps, smart technologies and emerging technologies like augmented reality. The Internet and the convergence among informatics, communication and multimedia offer destinations, tourism businesses as well as tourists with new channels through which to augment their communication process while minimising distribution costs and search (Buhalis and Law 2008; Minghetti and Buhalis 2010; Werthner and Klein 1999b).

Compared with traditional channels, the Internet is especially noted for enriching and easing the search for destinations, hospitality and tourism services. It makes it possible to bypass both external online and offline intermediaries and enhances opportunities for building direct relationships between consumers and suppliers (Minghetti and Buhalis 2010; Werthner and Klein 1999b).

Usually tourist destinations in Africa are considered to be in the peripherals or in less developed regions. These destinations are often less accessible from the main tourist generating regions, both physically and electronically (Hall and Page 2006; Minghetti and Buhalis 2010; Nash and Martin 2003). Nonetheless, as Minghetti and Buhalis (2010, 267) observed:

> the evolution of tourism demand, the emergence of a more skilled and demanding traveller who wishes to explore new destinations and live new experiences, supported by transport developments (low-cost carriers, fast trains, and the proliferation of private cars) and the Internet, make all these destinations close to their potential markets.

The Internet, e-commerce, global distributions systems, e-businesses (e.g. online travel agencies), and other technological applications make it possible to overcome the constraints of distance and geography by connecting across geographic boundaries of nation states. Service providers and potential tourists can share information, specifications and service processes globally. In other words, ICT facilitates multichannel distribution and provides opportunities for tourism businesses to promote and sell services on a global market, enabling direct rapport with prospective consumers, and bypassing intermediaries (Buhalis 2003; Minghetti and Buhalis 2010).

For instance, a study by Tichaawa's, Mhlanga and Sicwebu (2017) found ICT in the hotel sector to be most influential in increasing market share. This is often realised through successful implementation of Customer Relationship Management (CRM) software solutions that improve business relationships and interactions with both existing and potential customers. Internet and social media further make it possible to reach market segments that were previously inaccessible due to geographic or financial constraints. As Shanker (2008) observed, the capacity to reach a global audience, acquire instant market information and carry out electronic business transactions have increased efficiency and opened markets for tourism products and services from the developing world.

Promotion: ICT has presented tremendous opportunities for informing and persuading potential visitors from across the globe to book and visit destinations. ICT tools could provide African destination marketing organisations (DMOs) and service providers with incredible opportunities for communicating offerings, improving market visibility and augmenting competitiveness (Gretzel, Yuan and Fesenmaier 2000). Online survey tools, big data analytics (e.g. Google search trends) and other Internet applications allow for the collection of consumer metrics for effective market segmentation, targeting, advertisement and other promotional activities.

Information is regarded as the "lifeblood" of tourism (Buhalis 2003; Minghetti and Buhalis 2010; Sheldon 1997). A vital gain from ICTs is the upsurge in the supply of information. Since travel decision making and consumption are separated by time and space, the tourism product is largely based on confidence – as opposed to uncertainty – and hence information and communication (Werthner and Klein 1999a). Internet applications facilitate the sharing and dissemination of information to larger audiences/markets that weren't previously possible. It could offer African tourism destinations and businesses cheaper but far-reaching communication channels and a degree of control over content. Though more effective in reaching global audience, it is usually less expensive and offers an equitable platform to compete.

The Internet, Web 2.0 and social media have utterly transformed the marketing field. To an extent, ICT levels the playing field. Even smaller and less-resourced service providers, with the requisite skills, could employ affordable and simple solutions, and a variety of distribution solutions to partake in the emerging marketplace (Minghetti and Buhalis 2010; Paraskevas and Buhalis 2002). The misrepresentation of Africa continues to hurt the economies of African countries (WTTC 2018b). By providing a certain degree of control over content, ICT empowers African destinations to take charge of their own narratives and offers effective communication channels for addressing stereotypes, prejudices, fears and concerns about safety, etc. Giving the growing use of smartphones and social media, African destinations and service providers could as well tap into the power of viral videos and user-generated content in general to promote destinations and services (Osei, Mensah and Amenumey 2018). The success of innovative promotional strategies could as well be amplified by ICT, as evidenced in successful Australia's "Best Job in the World" youth campaign (Tourism Australia 2019).

People: The critical role of the people who make contact with tourists in delivering tourism services cannot be overemphasised. Since services are inseparable from those who deliver it, human resource is a defining factor in the service delivery process. Therefore, service training for staff is of the utmost priority for hospitality and tourism service organisations and ICT facilitates more effective and efficient delivery of this.

E-learning makes it possible for many Africans in remote regions to receive state-of-the-art training in hospitality and tourism management from some of world's best training institutions. Massive Open Online Courses (MOOCs) are free online courses available for anybody to enrol. MOOCs could offer service personnel in Africa affordable and flexible ways to learn new skills and advance careers in hospitality and tourism. Hospitality and tourism businesses on the continent could also leverage online courses to educate and train their workforce. A list of the MOOCs in Tourism and Hospitality is available at the website of the International Federation for IT and Travel and Tourism (IFITT) [https://www.ifitt.org/hospitality-and-tourismmoocs/]. Most exciting is that many MOOCs are free and easily accessible.

Training institutions could also apply AR/VR (Augmented Reality/Virtual Reality) technologies, including the use of virtual hotels and restaurants (using *Second Life* [https://secondlife.com] for example) to augment practical training for hospitality and tourism students. Content Management Systems, Voice over Internet Protocol (VoIPs) applications and other emerging communication technologies offer opportunities for hospitality and tourism institutions on the continent to collaborate with the world's best in delivering effective and efficient education and training to improve the skills and knowledge of the tourism workforce (Ayeh 2008a).

Process: ICTs have served to transform the systems and processes that deliver products to the customer. In the tourism sector, this has led to the generation of new systems and processes, including the use of global distribution systems (GDS), e-commerce (including online bookings and digital payment systems), personal digital assistants (PDAs), Point of Sale (POS) systems, mobile apps and smart applications among others. For instance, some restaurants and cafeterias are now using tablets (iPads) and smartphones to take orders from customers instead of the traditional menu cards. Travellers are using mobile apps to book and to digitally pay for transportation, accommodation, food and other travel-related services. The swipe-to-book action of mobile payments for example simplifies the payment process. Others are employing mobile devices to obtain electronic boarding pass, access in-flight entertainment and unlock hotel rooms among others (WTTC 2019).

Biometric technology – which offers the ability to identify a person on the basis of unique personal characteristics like eyes (iris), fingerprints, face, etc. – is still evolving. Nonetheless, it is transforming service processes in travel, hospitality and tourism sectors at an extraordinary speed (WTTC 2018c). For instance, by eliminating various forms of documentation. Some airports are employing biometric technology to identify travellers and speed up passenger journeys through e-Gates. Hotels (e.g. Marriot Hotels) are testing facial recognition for check-in. Facial recognition is also reported to have decreased processing time for disembarking cruise passengers by 40% (SecureIDNews 2017). In many ways, biometric technology can help African businesses to manage and track staff, ensure safety and security, as well as manage customers' preferences or personalisation. For example, staff in several hotels and restaurants are now clocking into work using biometric fingerprint terminals, keys are being replaced with biometric readers, and webcams are being used to assess travellers' responses to stimuli like images and sounds to determine their travel preferences, among others.

In essence, ICT leads to more efficient and effective product delivery. By digitising the service process, ICT could help African tourism businesses to improve their service delivery processes. It facilitates greater transparency in service delivery. Networking and information sharing ensure more openness and transparency.

Physical evidence: In no small ways, technology is reshaping elements of the physical environment within which consumers experience tourism. Giving that tourism services and experiences are essentially intangible in nature, ICT empowers destination marketers and service providers to integrate tangible elements into their offerings to augment tourists' experiences. For example, interactive tools, gaming applications and other visual technologies are been utilised in the lobbies of hotels, restaurants, airports, tourist sites, etc. to engage clients, and help them to relax while they await their turn for services. Likewise, African tourism service providers can employ various ICT applications to offer tangible and unique experiences to guests/ customers. ICT also facilitates virtual ways to experience the tourism product. Augmented reality and virtual reality technologies can be employed to enhance the visual effects of tourist sites and facilities. 3D-Modelling technology is helping in resurrecting the past and recreating extinct or ruined heritage resources that tourists can interact with.

Critical issues facing the adoption of ICT in the tourism sector

Laying out the challenge

Despite the immense potential of ICT for the promotion of Africa's tourism, significant disparities still exist in access, skills, use of the Internet and other ICT services (Minghetti and Buhalis 2010). Africa needs to overcome many infrastructural and knowledge barriers to support the wide usage of ICT. Others may have access but are not able to use it effectively due to varied factors including lack of knowledge, trust, literacy, language skills and content availability, credit card and low bandwidth (Minghetti and Buhalis 2010).

Though significant gains have been made over the last decade, the continent still lags considerably behind the rest of the world when it comes to Internet penetration. There are over 465 million Internet users in Africa, constituting 11% of global Internet users (Internet World Stats 2018a). While this represents the third largest in the world (after Asia and Europe), when it comes to Internet penetration (% of population with Internet access), the continent has the least penetration rate (36.1%), compared with the world's average of 55.1% or North America's 95%, Europe's 85.2%, Oceania/Australia's 68.9%, Latin America/Caribbean's 67.2% and Asia's 49% (see Figure 3.2 below). There is however a promising future outlook in this area. Since 2000, the African continent has experienced the world's fastest growth rate (10.199%) in Internet users.

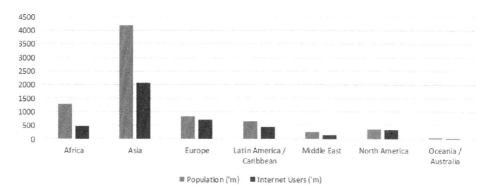

Figure 3.2 World Internet users and 2018 population stats by region
Source: Data culled from Internet World Stats, 2018a.

Table 3.1 summarises international tourism statistics and key Internet indicators of African countries. Among the countries with the highest number of Internet users are Nigeria (98.4 m), Egypt (49.2 m), Kenya (43.3 m) South Africa (30.8 m), Tanzania (23 m), Morocco (22.6 m), Uganda (19 m), Algeria (18), Ethiopia (16.4 m), Mali (12.5 m), Sudan (11.8 m) and Ghana (10.1 m). The highest Internet penetration rates can be found in Kenya (85.0%), Seychelles (70.5%), Tunisia (67.7%), Mali (65.3%), Mauritius (63.4%), Morocco (62.4%), Senegal (59.8%), Libya (58.7%) and South Africa (53.7%). Sadly, more than half of the population in each of the remaining 45 countries have no Internet access with countries such as Burundi, Central African Republic, Chad, Democratic Republic of Congo, Eritrea, Guinea-Bissau, Liberia, Madagascar, Malawi, Niger, Somalia and Western Sahara recording penetration levels of less than 10%. The use of social media mirrors a similar trend with most users in Egypt (35 m), Algeria (19 m), Nigeria (17 m), South Africa (16 m), Morocco (15 m) Kenya (7 m), Tunisia (6.4 m), Tanzania (6.1 m), Ghana (4.9 m) and Ethiopia (4.5 m).

Critical to the problem of access is the issue of cost and affordability. The challenge is that though the continent is somewhat perceived as poor, Internet access is quite expensive compared to other regions of the world. Internet services in some parts of the continent are also the slowest and least efficient due to bandwidth limitations. Much of the opportunities offered by ICT in e-Learning, e-Marketing and e-Tourism cannot be appropriately realised if Internet infrastructure on the continent is not extensively improved.

By its very nature, tourism is a highly information-rich sector and hence the availability of Internet resources offers the sector opportunities to provide wider, deeper and more custom-ised and competitive offerings. This implies that limited Internet resources in certain African countries represent a huge setback to tourism promotion in such countries. Hardly, would a contemporary tourist book a trip without looking up the destination on the Internet, check-ing out the online reviews for the hotels and other service providers or exploring the possible tourist activities online. Others may want to share their experiences in cyberspace using social media and consumer-generated review websites like TripAdvisor, Virtual Tourist, and WAYN among others.

Besides access, another challenge is knowledge and skills. Warschauser (2004) observed that the most critical issue about ICT is not so much of availability but instead people's ability to make meaningful use of the technology. Currently, many travel agents on the continent still rely on the traditional approach to marketing, operations and management.

Table 3.1 International tourism flows and Internet users statistics for Africa

Countries	International tourist arrivals (1,000)		International tourist receipts (US$ million)		Internet users (31-Dec-2017)	Penetration (% population)	Internet growth (% 2000–2017)	Facebook subscribers (31-Dec-2017)
	2010	2017	2010	2017				
Algeria	2,070	2,451	220	–	18,580,000	44.2	37,060	19,000,000
Angola	425	–	719	–	5,951,453	19.3	19,738	3,800,000
Benin	199	–	149	–.	3,801,758	33.1	25,245	920,000
Botswana	1,973	–	510	704	923,528	39.6	6,057	830,000
Burkina Faso	274	143	72	–	3,704,265	18.8	36,942	840,000
Burundi	142	–	2	–	617,116	5.5	20,470	450,000
Cabo Verde	336	668	278	436	265,972	48.1	3,225	240,000
Cameroon	569	–	159	–	6,128,422	24.8	30,542	2,700,000
Central African Rep.	54	–	11	–	256,432	5.4	16,995	96,000
Chad	71	–	–	–	768,274	5.0	76,727	260,000
Comoros	15	28	35	–	130,578	15.7	8,605	120,000
Congo	194	–	27	–	650,000	12.0	129,900	600,000
Congo, Dem. Rep.	81	–	–	–	5,137,271	6.1	1,027,354	2,100,000
Cote d'Ivoire	252	1800	201	–	6,318,355	26.3	16,246	3,800,000
Djibouti	51	–	18	–	180,000	18.5	12,757	180,000
Egypt	14,051	8,157	12,528	1,775	49,231,493	49.5	10,840	35,000,000
Equatorial Guinea	–	–	–	–	312,704	23.8	62,441	67,000
Eritrea	84	–	–	–	71,000	1.4	1,320	63,000

Ethiopia	468	–	522	434	16,437,811	15.3	164,278	4,500,000
Gabon	–	–	–	–	985,492	47.7	6,470	620,000
Gambia	91	–	74	–	392,277	18.1	9,707	310,000
Ghana	931	–	620	850	10,110,000	34.3	33,600	4,900,000
Guinea	12	–	2	–	1,602,485	12.3	19,931	1,500,000
Guinea-Bissau	22	–	13	–	120,000	6.3	7,900	110,000
Kenya	1,470	1,364	800	926	43,329,434	85.0	21,564	7,000,000
Lesotho	414	–	23	23	627,860	27.7	15,596	310,000
Liberia	–	–	12	–	395,063	8.1	78,912	330,000
Libya	–	–	60	–	3,800,000	58.7	37,900	3,500,000
Madagascar	196	255	309	–	1,900,000	7.2	6,233	1,700,000
Malawi	746	–	31	31	1,828,503	9.5	12,090	720,000
Mali	169	193	205	–	12,480,176	65.3	66,283	1,500,000
Mauritania	–	–	–	23	810,000	17.8	16,100	770,000
Mauritius	935	1,342	1,282	1,748	803,896	63.4	824	700,000
Mayotte (FR)	–	–	–	–	107,940	41.6	n/a	71,000
Mozambique	1,718	–	108	151	5,279,135	17.3	17,497	1,800,000
Namibia	984	–	438	188	797,027	30.8	2,557	570,000
Niger	74	–	105	–	951,548	4.3	18,931	440,000
Nigeria	1,555	–	576	2,549	98,391,456	50.2	49,096	17,000,000
Reunion (FR)	421	508	392	401	480,000	54.3	269	420,000
Rwanda	504	932	202	438	3,724,678	29.8	74,393	490,000
Saint Helena (UK)	–	–	–	–	2,200	54.3	n/a	1,700
Sao Tome & Principe	8	–	11	66	57,875	27.7	790	52,000
Senegal	900	–	453	–	9,749,527	59.8	24,274	2,900,000
Seychelles	175	350	343	483	67,119	70.5	1,018	61,000
Sierra Leone	39	–	26	–	902,462	11.7	17,949	450,000

(Continued)

61

Countries	International tourist arrivals (1,000)		International tourist receipts (US$ million)		Internet users (31-Dec-2017)	Penetration (% population)	Internet growth (% 2000–2017)	Facebook subscribers (31-Dec-2017)
	2010	2017	2010	2017				
Somalia	–	–	–	–	1,200,000	7.9	599,900	1,100,000
South Africa	8,074	10,285	9,070	8,818	30,815,634	53.7	1,184	16,000,000
South Sudan					2,229,963	17.3	n/a	180,000
Sudan	495	–	94	1,029	11,816,570	28.5	39,288	2,600,000
Swaziland	868	921	51	–	446,051	32.1	4,360	170,000
Tanzania	754	–	1,255	2,339	23,000,000	38.9	19,900	6,100,000
Togo	202	496	66	–	899,956	11.3	800	560,000
Tunisia	7,828	7,052	2,645	1,299	7,898,534	67.7	7,798	6,400,000
Uganda	946	–	784	918	19,000,000	42.9	47,400	2,600,000
Western Sahara					28,000	5.0	n/a	24,000
Zambia	815	–	492	653	7,248,773	41.2	36,144	1,600,000
Zimbabwe	2,239	2,423	634	–	6,796,314	40.2	13,492	880,000
Total Africa	50,400	62,700		37,300	453,329,534	35.2	9,942	177,005,700
Rest of World	901,600	1,263,300		1,302,700	3,703,602,606	58.4	89.1	1,942,054,452
World total	952,000	1,326,000		1,340,000	4,156,932,140	54.4	100.0	2,119,060,152

Sources: UNWTO (2018); Internet World Stats (2018b).

Traditional offline intermediaries continue to play a prominent role in travel distribution in most African countries. Inadequate online information, low-tech interactions and necessity for offline transactions usually compels many tourism consumers to rely on online travel agencies (OTAs), tour operators and international travel agencies, thus making the planning process less attractive and more complex. However, as the information society advances and a new generation of high-tech tourists emerges, less developed destinations risk to be progressively excluded from the decision set of international tourists.

Giving what happened to some travel agencies in developed countries in the aftermath of the Internet revolution when online travel agencies transformed the then structure of intermediaries, African tourism intermediaries risk losing their existing market share if they don't quickly adapt to emerging ICT and structural changes. Unlike their counterparts in developed countries, they have only been able to survive because the greater share of their domestic markets is still less reliant on the Internet or represents what Minghetti and Buhalis (2010) termed as *low-digital-access tourists*. But this is changing – a growing number of people in Africa (particularly the younger generation) now fall into the category of *upper-digital-access tourists*. It is not surprising many tech start-up ventures in Africa have become a resounding success.

Another key concern is inadequate online presence. Several destinations as well as service providers in Africa have limited, dysfunctional, and – in some cases – no websites. Furthermore, despite the wide and growing usage of mobile phones within and outside the continent (Dayour, Park and Kimbu 2019), the mobile version of various tourism-related websites in Africa still perform poorly.

Online presence of destinations is usually contingent upon the size, expertise, vision, resources, and structure of local tourism organisations and private operators like DMOs, information bureaus, and tourism SMEs (Buhalis 2003; Minghetti and Buhalis 2010). This implies that most small and medium sized tourism enterprises may struggle to compete at the global stage. Another challenge for African tourism businesses is that online presence frequently mirrors the degree of ICT deployment in their respective locations instead of the level of use anticipated by their prospective customers (Minghetti and Buhalis 2010). These potential clients or tourists usually operates in high-digital-access regions and

> live in countries that are at the top of the "information society" (e.g., high Internet penetration and usage as well as high online transaction conversion rates), show a high acceptance of ICTs (motivational access), and a good level of digital skills and ICT use.
>
> *(Minghetti and Buhalis 2010, 275)*

For instance, the Internet penetration rates for most of the world's major traveller generating regions range from 85.2% to 95% (Internet World Stats 2018a). In addition, many African countries heavily rely on backpackers and students for inbound tourism. These groups often fall into the categories of *high-digital-access* tourists and *upper-digital-access* tourists.

Tourism businesses in Africa can no longer survive if they continue to rely on the traditional approach to marketing. As Buhalis and Kaldis (2008) warned, tourism businesses and DMOs that ignore ICT use are cut off from electronic distribution channels and e-commerce. African destinations and service providers cannot risk continuing to be invisible to this fast growing segment of the market that increasingly depends on the Internet for travel search, decision making and purchase. In addition to being cut off from a substantial set of potential tourists, many African destinations continue to tussle with access to expertise, capital, and technologies that could empower them to promote their products and cultivate the appropriate tools for appealing to new markets. As a result, numerous African destinations and businesses depend highly on external traditional intermediaries for putting their offerings forward to the marketplace (Bastakis, Buhalis and Butler 2004; Minghetti and Buhalis 2010). Sadly, this leads to economic leakages, limiting the multiplier effect of tourism revenues in the local economy.

Another concern is inadequate digital payment options in some African destinations. While this may be as a result of security concerns, regulatory setbacks and inertia among others, service providers and governments need to recognise that online and mobile payment options are now required by international as well as domestic travellers. Maximising opportunities from digital payment systems for African economies would require concerted efforts from both public and private stakeholders. Regulatory policies, interoperable systems and a commitment to address infrastructural challenges among other setbacks are crucial.

At the core of these issues is the absence of an effective digital strategy for many African destinations. Often NTOs/DMOs merely copy promotional activities from other destinations without any clear strategy driving such efforts. Besides, public and private stakeholders hardly work together to present a unified strategic approach to e-destination marketing. Yet scholars have cautioned that "a more inclusive approach that allows for successful strategy development is extremely important" (Mistilis, Buhalis and Gretzel 2014, 788). In this regard, leadership at every level (Spencer, Buhalis and Moital 2012) and an understanding of the smartness concept as a means for competitiveness in tourism destinations (Boes, Buhalis and Inversini 2016) are key. Evidently, a successful digital strategy is an unqualified necessity for the future of African tourism destinations.

Areas in need of research attention

Though the nexus between tourism and ICT has gained significant attention in the global context over the last couple of decades, research on this theme from an African perspective is nonetheless lamentably rare. The few studies in this regard tend to focus on technology adoption by the industry in relation to rudimentary ICT applications (e.g. Ayeh 2007, 2008b; Migiro, and Ocholla 2005; Mpofu and Watkins-Mathys 2011). Others have also explored the impact of ICT on tourism businesses in Africa (e.g. Tichaawa, Mhlanga and Sicwebu 2017; Uwamariya, Cremer and Loebbecke 2015). More recently, attention has been drawn to the use of social media (e.g. Osei, Mensah and Amenumey 2018); smartphones (e.g. Dayour, Park and Kimbu 2019), online destination marketing (e.g. Kotoua and Ilkan 2017) and Internet use for co-creation of tourist experiences (e.g. Berrada 2017) in African contexts.

The digital divide continues to raise concern globally and as a consequence, there has been an upsurge of the digital divide literature (Antonelli 2003; van Dijk 2005, 2006; Warschauser 2004). At the global level, extant literature indicates this is often caused by disparities in income, GDP, human capital and digital skills, ICT infrastructure, connectivity, policy and regulatory mechanisms as well as sociodemographic factors (Minghetti and Buhalis 2010; van Dijk 2005, 2006). Nevertheless, it is critical for research to examine the current idiosyncrasies within Africa concerning this divide. Research is particularly vital for less technologically advanced countries in Africa if ICT usage is to be extended to facilitate the successful promotion of tourism offerings, effective interaction with consumers from the world's major source markets and consequently, minimise the dependency on offline intermediaries (Minghetti and Buhalis 2010). Research could as well consider why some countries have so quickly bridged the gap within the last decade while the divide continues to widen and deepen for many other African countries.

The digitised world is advancing very fast and yet studies are lacking in many critical areas in the African context. Scholars may want to examine how African hospitality and tourism enterprises are responding to the opportunities offered by the platform economy, augmented and virtual reality technologies, robotics and automation, digital marketing and social media tools as well as gaming applications. Giving the current state of many African destination websites, it is imperative for scholars to study website design and evaluation, digital distribution and social selling, consumer behaviour in digital space as well as e-strategy and e-business models.

The role of ICT in tourism governance, sustainability and education cannot be over-emphasised. The research could explore how ICT is being deployed on the continent for regional tourism development and sustainability, partnership and collaboration, e-learning, e-Governance and public policy. Recent concerns about data security also call for research on privacy and Internet security as well as on the legal and ethical aspects of ICT deployment within the tourism sector.

Emergent technologies necessitate tourism-related research into big data, data mining and analytics; artificial intelligence, machine learning and deep learning; sentiment analysis, emotions and personality-based systems; location-based services and context-aware systems; mobile services and wearable technologies; semantic web and tourism ontologies; Internet-of-Things; smart destinations; travel chatbots and blockchain among other emerging technologies.

Conclusion

It is indisputable that ICT has transformed the entire value of tourism production, marketing, distribution and consumption (Buhalis 1998). The challenge is that many African countries have failed to fully exploit the numerous opportunities offered by these technologies in the tourism sector. Internet penetration rate on the continent is the lowest of all the world's regions and over 823 million people still lack access. The digital divide has not only led to both digital and social exclusion (Selwyn 2004) but also economic marginalisation in tourism earnings. Disparities in access, control, process, communication and distribution of information wield much stronger impact on tourism creation and consumption than in other sectors (Minghetti and Buhalis 2010).

Some scholars have argued that these disparities are fashioned by the availability of technological tools for the provision and broader distribution of accurate information as well as the ability to employ these tools effectively (Minghetti and Buhalis 2010; Warschauser 2004). For African destinations, this implies being unable to fully participate in the growing digital market and the gains arising from emerging opportunities. No wonder countries with high ICT infrastructure are among the leaders in tourism flows. Hence African countries that fail to keep up with the pace of new ICT developments in our ever-increasing digitised world may lag in tourism growth compared with those that have significant ICT infrastructure. This would require effective leadership (Spencer, Buhalis and Moital 2012) and tourism digital strategies that offer mechanisms for uniting disconnected key stakeholders into networks that augment the process of development and implementation (Mistilis, Buhalis and Gretzel 2014).

Notwithstanding, there is great optimism for the future as the continent has made significant gains over the last two decades – including recording the world's fastest Internet growth rate. Increasing access to the Internet and the wide usage of mobile phone technology even in very remote regions in Africa present unique opportunities for Africa's tourism sector.

The WTTC (2018b) estimates that 30–45 million jobs can be created by 2028 in Africa's travel and tourism sector. New and emerging technologies could further empower destinations and tourism businesses on the continent to overcome the age-old challenges and maximise economic, socio-cultural and environmental gains from tourism.

References

Antonelli, C. 2003. "The Digital Divide: Understanding the Economics of New Digital Information and Communication in the Global Economy." *Information Economics and Policy*, 15(2): 173–199.

Ayeh, J. K. 2007. "Determinants of Internet Usage in Ghanaian Hotels: The Case of Greater Accra Region." *Journal for Hospitality Marketing and Management*, 15(3): 87–109.

Ayeh, J. K. 2008a. "ICT and Global Education: The Challenges of the African Virtual University Learning Centres in Ghana." *Journal of Information Development*, 24(4): 266–274.

Ayeh, J. K. 2008b. "Adoption of Information and Communication Technologies in Hotels: A Case Study of Greater Accra Region." In *Tourism in Ghana: A Modern Synthesis*, edited by O. Akyeampong, and A. B. Asiedu, 177–195. Accra: AGLC.

Bastakis, C., D. Buhalis, and R. Butler. 2004. "The Impact of Tour Operator's Power on Small and Medium Sized Tourism Accommodation Enterprises on the Mediterranean Islands." *Tourism Management*, 25(2): 151–170.

Berrada, M. 2017. "Co-Creation of the Tourist Experience via Internet: Towards Exploring a New Practice." *Journal of International Business Research and Marketing*, 2(5): 18–23.

Boes, K., D. Buhalis, and A. Inversini. 2016. "Smart Tourism Destinations: Ecosystems for Tourism Destination Competitiveness." *International Journal of Tourism Cities* 2(2): 108–124.

Booms, B. H. and M. J. Bitner. 1981. "Marketing Strategies and Organization Structures for Service Firms." In *Marketing of Services,* edited by J. H. Donnelly and W. R. George, 47–51, Chicago, IL: American Marketing Association.

Buhalis, D. 1998. "Strategic Use of Information Technologies in Tourism." *Tourism Management*, 19(1): 409–421.

Buhalis, D. 2003. *eTourism: Information Technology for Strategic Tourism Management.* London: Financial Times Prentice Hall.

Buhalis, D. and K. Kaldis. 2008. "eEnabled Internet Distribution for Small and Medium Sized Hotels: The Case of Athens." *Tourism Recreation Research*, 33(1): 67–81.

Buhalis, D. and R. Law. 2008. "Progress in Tourism Management: Twenty Years on and 10 Years after the Internet: The state of eTourism Research." *Tourism Management*, 29(4): 609–623.

Cabiddu, F. C., T.-W. Lui, and G. Piccoli. 2013. "Managing Value Co-Creation in the Tourism Industry." *Annals of Tourism Research*, 42: 86–107.

Campos, A. C., J. Mendes, P. O. do Valle, and N. Scott. 2018. "Co-Creation of Tourist Experiences: A Literature Review." *Current Issues in Tourism*, 21(4): 369–400.

Dayour, F., S. Park, and A. N. Kimbu. 2019. "Backpackers' Perceived Risks towards Smartphone Usage and Risk Reduction Strategies: A Mixed Methods Study." *Tourism Management*, 72: 52–68.

Gretzel, U., Y. L. Yuan, and D. R. Fesenmaier. 2000. "Preparing for the New Economy: Advertising Strategies and Change in Destination Marketing." *Journal of Travel Research*, 39 (2): 146–56.

Hall, C. M. and S. Page. 2006. *The Geography of Tourism and Recreation: Environment, Place, and Space.* London: Routledge.

Internet World Stats. 2018a. "World Internet Users and 2018 Population Stats." *Internet World Stats.* Accessed September 25, 2018. https://www.internetworldstats.com/stats.htm

Internet World Stats. 2018b. "Internet Users Statistics for Africa." *Internet World Stats.* Accessed September 25, 2018. https://www.Internetworldstats.com/stats1.htm

Kotoua, S. and M. Ilkan. 2017. "Online Tourism Destination Marketing in Kumasi Ghana." *Asia Pacific Journal of Tourism Research*, 22(6): 666–680.

McCarthy, E. J. 1964. *Basic Marketing.* Homewood, IL: Richard D. Irwin.

Migiro, S. O. and D. N. Ocholla. 2005. "Information and Communication Technologies in Small and Medium Scale Tourism Enterprises in Durban, South Africa." *Information Development*, 21(4): 283–294.

Minghetti, V. and D. Buhalis. 2010. "Digital Divide in Tourism." *Journal of Travel Research*, 49(3): 267–281.

Mistilis, N., D. Buhalis, and U. Gretzel. 2014. "eDestination Marketing of the Future: The Perspective of an Australian Tourism Stakeholder Network." *Journal Travel Research*, 53: 1–13.

Mpofu, K. C. and L. Watkins-Mathys. 2011. "Understanding ICT Adoption in the Small Firm Sector in Southern Africa." *Journal of Systems and Information Technology*, 13(2): 179–199.

Nash, R. and A. Martin. 2003. "Tourism in Peripheral Areas – The Challenges for Northeast Scotland." *International Journal of Tourism Research*, 5: 161–181.

Opara, J. A. and E. Onyije. 2013. "Information and Communication Technologies: A Panacea to Achieving Effective Goals in Institutional Administration." *International Journal of Management Sciences*, 1(1): 11–15.

Organization for Economic Cooperation and Development [OECD]. 2001. *Understanding the Digital Divide*. Paris: OECD.

Osei, B. A., I. Mensah, and E. K. Amenumey. 2018. "Utilisation of Social Media by International Tourists to Ghana." *Anatolia*, 29(3): 411–421.

Paraskevas, A. and D. Buhalis. 2002. "Web-Enabled ICT Outsourcing for Small Hotels: Opportunities and Challenges." *Cornell Hotel and Restaurant Administration Quarterly*, 43(2): 27–39.

Parsons, J. J. and D. Oja. 2013. *New Perspectives on Computer Concepts 2013 Comprehensive*. New York: Cengage Learning.

Rihova, I., D. Buhalis, M. B. Gouthro, and M. Moital. 2018. "Customer-to-Customer Co-Creation Practices in Tourism: Lessons from Customer-Dominant Logic." *Tourism Management*, 67: 322–375.

Scott, N., E. Laws, and P. Boksberger. 2009. "The Marketing of Hospitality and Leisure Experiences." *Journal of Hospitality Marketing and Management*, 18(2–3): 99–110.

SecureIDNews. 2017. "Facial Recognition on Cruise Ships Moves Passengers More Quickly." *SecureIDNews*. Accessed July 14, 2019. https://www.secureidnews.com/news-item/facial-recognition-cruise-ships-moves-passengers-quickly/#

Selwyn, N. 2004. "Reconsidering Political and Popular Understandings of the Digital Divide." *New Media Society*, 6(3): 341–362.

Shanker, D. 2008. "ICT and Tourism: Challenges and Opportunities." Paper Presented at the Conference on Tourism in India - Challenges Ahead. Indian Institute of Management, Kozhikode, May 15–17.

Sheldon, P. 1997. *Tourism Information Technologies*. Wallingford, UK: CAB International.

Sigala, M. 2003. "The Information and Communication Technologies Productivity Impact on the UK Hotel Sector." *International Journal of Operations and Production Management*, 23(10): 1224–1245.

Spencer, A., D. Buhalis, and D. Moital. 2012. "A Hierarchical Model of Technology Adoption for Small Owner-Managed Travel Firms: An Organizational Decision-Making and Leadership Perspective." *Tourism Management*, 33: 1195–1208.

Tichaawa, T. M., O. Mhlanga, and S. Sicwebu. 2017. "The Impact of Information Communication Technologies (ICTs) on Tourism Businesses in East London, South Africa." *Acta Universitatis Danubius Economica*, 13(3): 18–29.

Tourism Australia. 2019. "The Best Jobs in the World." Accessed January 13, 2019. http://www.tourism.australia.com/en/about/our-campaigns/past-campaigns/best-jobs.html

United Nations World Tourism Organization [UNWTO]. 2018. *UNWTO Tourism Highlights 2018 Edition*. Hamburg: UNWTO.

Uwamariya, M., S. Cremer, and C. Loebbecke. 2015. "ICT for Economic Development in Rwanda: Fostering E-Commerce Adoption in Tourism SMEs." *Global Development*, 1. Accessed January 17 2019. http://aisel.aisnet.org/globdev2015/1.

van Dijk, J. 2005. *The Deepening Divide. Inequality in the Information Society*. London: Sage.

van Dijk, J. 2006. "Digital Divide Research, Achievements and Shortcomings." *Poetics*, 34: 221–235.

Warschauser, M. 2004. *Technology and Social Inclusion. Rethinking the Digital Divide*. Cambridge, MA: MIT Press.

Werthner, H. and S. Klein. 1999a. *Information Technology and Tourism – A Challenging Relationship*. Wien, New York: Springer.

Werthner, H. and S. Klein. 1999b. "ICT and the Changing Landscape of Global Tourism Distribution." *Electronic Markets*, 9(4): 256–262.

World Travel and Tourism Council [WTTC]. 2018a. "WTTC Calls on Travel Industry to Maximise Power of Technology on World Tourism Day to Create Jobs." *World Travel and Tourism Council Press Releases*. Accessed July 14, 2019. https://www.wttc.org/about/media-centre/press-releases/press-releases/2018/wttc-calls-on-travel-industry-to-maximise-power-of-technology-on-world-tourism-day-to-create-jobs/

WTTC. 2018b. "What You Didn't Know about Tourism in Africa." *Medium*. Accessed July 14, 2019. https://medium.com/@WTTC/what-you-didnt-know-about-tourism-in-africa-4cdf439f9f9e

WTTC. 2018c. "Four Ways Biometrics Are Making Travel Smarter." *Medium*. Accessed July 14, 2019. https://medium.com/@WTTC/four-ways-biometrics-are-making-travel-smarter-47ea99333bf4

WTTC. 2019. "Mobile Payments in Travel & Tourism: Unlocking the Potential." *World Travel and Tourism Council*. Accessed July 14, 2019. https://www.wttc.org/publications/2019/mobile-payments-in-travel-tourism/

4

Heritage and heritage tourism in Africa

Historical overview and contemporary issues

Noel Biseko Lwoga and Emmanuel Akwasi Adu-Ampong

Introduction

Heritage refers to our legacy *inheritance* from the past, what we live with today, and what we pass on to future generations, including the natural and cultural, living and built elements of culture, tangible as well as intangible cultural aspects with cultural significance or value (ICOMOS, 1999; Timothy and Nyaupane, 2009). Heritage has long been a pull and push factor in travel decisions. Heritage tourism is thus one of the largest, prevalent and fastest growing forms of the tourism industry today. This is the act of, and sum of activities involved therein, visiting heritage places away from person's usual residence, for purposes other than the practice of an activity remunerated from within the place visited (Timothy and Nyaupane, 2009; Lwoga, 2011). According to the United Nations World Tourism Organization (UNWTO, 2018), cultural and heritage tourism activities account for about 40% of all international tourist travel activities. Its growth in Africa is reflected in the Cairo Declaration of 1995 adopted under the auspices of the UNWTO and the United Nations Educational, Scientific and Cultural Organization (UNESCO) (Teye et al., 2011). Across the African continent, there are currently 95 heritage sites inscribed onto UNESCO's World Heritage List – 52 World Cultural Heritage Sites, 38 World Natural Heritage Sites and five mixed World Heritage Sites.

It is increasingly acknowledged today that the tourism phenomenon in general, and heritage tourism in specific and its practice and implications in Africa, especially in the sub-Sahara African region, differ from its practice and impacts in the developed economies (Timothy and Nyaupane, 2009). The difference is underscored basically by variations in heritage, cultures, geography, economics, politics, histories such as slavery and colonial epochs, social mores and demographics (Leung, 2001; Timothy and Boyd, 2006; Huybers, 2007; Timothy and Nyaupane, 2009). Despite such differences, the heritage tourism framework used in Africa is influenced by Western-centric models and doctrines as institutionalised by global entities such as UNESCO and global heritage conventions and legislative tools (Winter, 2007). The Western frameworks are often underpinned with the notion that the *East* and *South* are primitive and remote, and perhaps ignorant of appropriate use and treatment of heritage (Timothy and Nyaupane, 2009).

An analysis of tourism issues in Africa that was done by Rogerson (2007) indicates that the economies and development aspects of tourism in Africa have received strong attention using several strands of development theory, including research from the approach of modernisation, dependency or structuralism, neoliberalism and alternative development including sustainable development. Political economy approaches have been utilised by Dieke (2000) to interrogate African tourism governance within the global tourist system. Deliberation of potential, feasibility and developmental role of tourism for the promotion of economic growth and especially poverty alleviation, and of major constraining factors have been major issues of focus (Elliott and Mann, 2005; Gauci et al., 2005). The common issue emerging in this regard is that tourism, in general, and heritage tourism, in specific, are unrealised potential across many parts of Africa (Rogerson, 2007). Several constraining factors have been discussed, these include the limitations imposed by prevailing air transport networks and regulatory frameworks, the lack of skilled labour resources, weak institutional frameworks and the impact of political instability including terrorism (Rogerson, 2007). One of the interesting issues discussed in this chapter, yet with a limited emphasis in the tourism literature, include the weak linkage between African heritage and tourism (Timothy and Nyaupane, 2009), and the way the paradox of local African conception and treatment of their heritage within the realms of the dominant Western heritage doctrines can underscore and exaggerate challenges in realising the potentials of heritage tourism in Africa today.

Heritage tourism in Africa is important just like in the developed world, however, the language of heritage used in tourism and conservation realms often reflects a Western bias and domination (Lowenthal, 1997). Studies have explored this subject using point of view of modernisation, dependency and neoliberalism separately, thus leaving a dearth of consolidated knowledge on the dynamics of heritage tourism. Moreover, the growing interest in this subject has been much on cultural heritage with limited connection to issues of tourism practices (Nyaupane and Budruk, 2009; Teye, 2009; Timothy and Daher, 2009). This knowledge is critical for the development of heritage tourism that recognises and accounts for the local heritage dynamics for its own longevity and sustainability.

This chapter reflects on the paradox of local heritage doctrines and practices within the realms of dominant Western-based heritage models. The chapter then highlights the challenges to the realisation of heritage tourism's potential in Africa. Unlike past research, this chapter integrates historical accounts related to the development of heritage tourism and heritage management in Africa and draws on local heritage concerns to provide an overview of critical issues facing heritage tourism in Africa, including prospects for developing heritage tourism, that appropriately integrate the local heritage narratives and practices. In this endeavour, the chapter draws much from the selected literature review and the experience and observations of the authors in both the heritage tourism industry and in academic research.

Development and treatment of heritage for tourism in Africa: historic outlook

From the global perspective, the origin of tourism, in general, has been wrongly attributed to one region, mainly Europe, during either the Graeco-Roman period or the industrialisation period between the 18th and 20th centuries (Walton, 2009). In Africa, tourism is also wrongly attributed by scholars to have come with colonialists (Salazar, 2009:03). This tendency narrows the scope of understanding the evolution of tourism and neglects the contribution of Africa and Africans to especially when one among key tourism subjects is their own heritage.

As Ehret (2002:03) has argued, "Africans participated integrally in the great transformations of world history, from the first rise of agricultural ways of life to the various inventions
of metal-working to the growth and spread of global networks of commerce". This chapter
shares this sentiment of the pioneering role of Africans in tourism evolution. When looked
at critically, pre-colonial African travels demonstrate features that either partially or fully
resemble some elements of heritage tourism including the temporality feature and visits to
heritage sites for various purposes.

Travel is deeply embedded in the human DNA since the beginning of humankind. Travel
has been an integral part of life on earth even from 8 to 5 million BC to the emergence of
the first ancient civilisations in the 6000/4000 BC (Ehret, 2002). With the sense of home or
rather organised camps, early humans travelled for subsistence and social purposes and turned
back to their shelters of either caves and rocks or branches, grass and stones (Shillington,
1995). Such movements are the foundation for human travel in which tourism is derived from
(Theobald, 1998; Lwoga, 2011).

When our ancestors learned how to domesticate animals and plants in about 10,000 BC,
that was the beginning of a sense of human ownership and settlements whether temporal
(with reference to pastoralists) or permanent settlements (with reference to crop cultivators).
In Africa, this is believed to have happened in the Nile Valley of north-eastern Africa (Shillington, 1995). In contrast to the earlier ancestors who had no permanent settlements, the
ancestors during the time of domestication had real temporal travels or movements as they
had to come back to their permanent settlements. The human society in such early times
became well organised, socially stratified societies and coordinated in urban centres and kept
written records from 3500 to 3000 BC (Chami, 2006). The civilisation saw the construction
of temples, statues and pyramids such as the Great Pyramid for the first pharaoh of the fourth
dynast in about 2600 BC. The Egyptian Great Pyramid of King Khufu, ancient Egyptian art,
architecture, religion, scientific, social, political and cultural achievements, and the Valley of
the Kings at Thebes attracted visitors and vendors of food and drinks, hawkers of souvenirs
and guides, especially during festivities (Lwoga, 2011). The Nile provided appropriate and
convenient means of transport to the pyramids. There is evidence of early Egyptian graffiti
(marks left by visitors on walls) dating back to 2000 BC showing the presence of heritage
visitors in Africa (Holloway, 1998).

During the Graeco-Roman era (7th century BC to 5th century AD), Africa entered a
period of commercial revolution which created direct links of the continent to other parts of
the world (Ehret, 2002). There was the development of pleasure, exploratory and education
tourism. For instance, the Egyptians held many religious festivals that attracted not only the
religious people, but many who came to see the famous architecture, culture and works of art
in the cities for pleasure and education purposes (Lwoga, 2011). Popular international heritage
visitors such as the Greek historian, Herodotus, visited Africa in the 5th century BC and documented the stories recounted to him by tour guides (Shillington, 1995; Holloway, 1998).

Apart from the Egyptian Kingdom, there were other states south of the Sahara which participated in heritage and trade-related travels. There were visitors to the Kingdom of Meroe
in Sudan who were basically attracted by the Meroe's ruins, pyramids, culture and rich fur-
niture (Croegaert, 1999). People in the Kingdom of Aksum in northern Ethiopia, with their
own written script *Ge'ez*, coins of gold, silver and copper, travelled, interacted and traded in
Egypt, the eastern Mediterranean and Arabia (Reader, 1997). On the East African coast, the
notable trading settlement *Rhapta* had commercial links with South Arabian merchants by
the 1st century AD (Ehret, 2002). The early Bantu communities in the African Great Lakes
visited ritual sites within their land and conducted festivals (Ehret, 2002).

During the Medieval era (5th century AD to 14th century AD), there were great travellers such as Al-Masudi and Al-Idrisi who visited places in Africa and narrated on their journeys. For instance, in the late 9th century AD (around 956 AD) Al-Masudi crossed the Persian Gulf to Kilwa, Beira, Sofala and Madagascar (Croegaert, 1999). In the early 11th century AD (between 1100 and 1166 AD) Al-Idrisi voyaged and described the Arab merchant's itinerary (Croegaert, 1999). During this period, the camel had already revolutionised travel across the Sahara Desert and improved the long-distance trading caravans, particularly the trans-Saharan trade (Shillington, 1995). There were also religious movements (pilgrimages) and travels for education such as those conducted by Sanhaja Berber chief who visited the Muslim scholars in North Africa in the 11th century AD (in 1036) (Shillington, 1995). The early African travels also involved parts of East African coast and southern Africa such as the Swahili-city states and Great Zimbabwe.

As Europe entered the Renaissance period in the 14th century AD, heritage-related travel continued to improve in Africa. For example, the ruler of the empire of Mali, Mansa Musa, in the 14th century (in 1324/1325) made pilgrimage travel to Mecca (Shillington, 1995). He also sent Sudanese scholars to the Moroccan university of Fes for educational purposes (Shillington, 1995). Later on, such scholars initiated the centres of learning and Koranic study at Timbuktu which attracted people for academic and religious purposes. In fact, Timbuktu attracted many visitors including the Berber Geographer Ibn Battuta who praised the Malian people's hospitality and love of justice (Shillington, 1995). The popularity of such destinations as the Empire of Mali gained European attention and was became mentioned in the European geographical maps of the world then.

During all these historical periods and for time immemorial, Africans had their own local traditional forms of treating their heritage that were of importance or that communities identify themselves to (Mapunda and Msemwa, 2005). They were responsible for the designation and maintenance of their traditions and their heritage sites such as shrines, sacred huts, graves, royal palaces, city walls, traditional huts and sacred forests (Joffroy, 2009; Hussein and Armitage, 2014; Ichumbaki, 2016; Lwoga, 2018a). Their traditional system of treating heritage was guided by traditional institutions and custodians such as the Chiefs, clan leaders, priests and elders, through spiritual values such as specific beliefs or prohibitions, taboos and customs that ensured the heritage is preserved from any destruction, and guided communities on how to behave and treat the site with respect (Joffroy, 2009). Technical practices in maintaining their heritage involved activities done to repair or construct heritage sites depending on the physical requirements of the site. They were accompanied by collective and symbolic effort to conserve a site and were connected with special events such as traditional ceremonies related to the religion or beliefs of the community that, intentionally or unintentionally, reinforced the social cohesions of the community (Joffroy, 2009). The inhabitants adhered to the spiritual values and technical practices, which were passed on from one generation to another through storytelling and oral traditions (Hussein and Armitage, 2014).

Africans, by then, did not always aim at pure restoration of their heritage assets in terms of returning them to their original state, but rather aimed at adapting to new conditions such as drought or rain seasons, new expectations, or to the changes of beliefs and social organisation (Joffroy, 2009). For instance, in northern Ghana, the community would repair the decorations on their houses regularly by applying entirely new decorations inspired by mood and trend of the moment, rather than the attempt to imitate the original designs (Kankpeyeng, 2009).

During the 17th to 18th centuries AD, Africa experienced massive slave raiding and rising civil warfare and conflicts. The infamous Trans-Atlantic Slave Trade stands as the height of this slave raiding. Although there were elements of slave trading within Africa in the period of the trans-Saharan trade, towards the mid-1600s, there "was a leap upward in the magnitude of the trade in human beings out of sub-Saharan Africa" (Ehret, 2002:407). Consequently, some African states grew to be large and powerful while others broke down in response to the shift in trade and due to "a decline in the relative importance of African manufacturing" (Ehret, 2002:408). All in all, the slave trade continued and involved the European trading forts along especially the West Coast of Africa and principally along the coast of Ghana (then called the *Gold Coast*) until the 19th century AD.

In addition, Africa also saw the incoming of foreign missionaries, explorers and traders from Europe, including the antiquity collectors. The fall of Africa into a massive slave trade, foreign traders and antiquarians, and later into colonialism was the beginning of Africa to assume the subordinate position in the global economic and political order. Specifically, its history of early travel and tourism networks became written out of history. Traditional conception of heritage, the conservation and treatment of this heritage became undermined and dominated by Western influences. Africans were moulded to accept new ways of living, cultural expressions and other Western features. In the process, African countries began to see their longstanding cultural practices to be signs of under-development. This is what Mulokozi (2005) referred to as cultural genocide which happens when one society is conquered and loses part or its entire cultural heritage.

Although cultural genocide in Africa was not total, it did affect traditional conception and treatment of heritage. The Western conservation system with its roots in the early Western restoration and conservation movements of over 200 years and, especially, the Athens Charter of 1931 (see Jokilehto, 1986) entered Africa. The colonial administration introduced Western-based heritage treatment doctrines. First, the Western doctrines and practices appreciated heritage as monument and physical *material* objects. Under the monumentality doctrine, the attention of conservation efforts is directed to heritage with *exceptional* and *architectural* dimensions, while ignoring the traditional vernacular built heritage (Baca and López, 2018). Within this materiality notion, the attention of conservation efforts is directed to tangible heritage assets while ignoring the intangible heritage. This means that the authenticity of the heritage that is the cornerstone of conservation efforts is conceived from the materials of heritage objects, such as its portrayal of ageless feature (oldness), permanence and originality. Second, the Western conservation system conceived values of heritage as being embodied in the historic monument, and limited to its aesthetics, artistic and historic dimensions. The focus here is on the presence of features that express the beautiful artistic skills of the builder as well as the monument being aged and old enough to carry past history of the place and its people. Other consideration including the need for the monument to have been made or designed by a famous figure such as artists and rulers. Third, they emphasised on the *strict custodial protection* of heritage. This means that for appropriate conservation, the sites' treatment and use are restricted to those who are considered to be experts and professionals.

Post-independence period

After independence from the late 1950s onward, most post-colonial African states had agendas of restoring lost cultural heritage that they held with high value and pride. However, they ended up developing centralised institutional frameworks that adopted Western doctrines and legal systems to define and offer treatment of African heritage (Ndoro, 2005). To date, most African heritage institutional, policy and legislative frameworks still put emphasise on *monumentality*, physical object (*materiality authenticity*), its age (*historic aspects*), its beauty and artistic expressions, and its durability (*permanence of materiality*). However, these dimensions do not resolve the challenge of conserving the African traditional heritage as the community legacy (Ndoro, 2005).

This means that most African states today still favour heritage as physical objects and features endowed with historic and aesthetic or artistic value, and still emphasise the *strict custodial protection* of monuments. In fact, in 1937, the Athens Charter's doctrines were introduced in Tanzania mainland through the Colonial Monuments Preservation Ordinance of 1937. Ignoring the role played by local residents in managing the tangible heritage and the intangible – spiritual and social aspects – they valued, the Ordinance gave the Governor power to issue a statutory order listing all monuments or structures, focusing on the tangible features that portrayed their picturesque, artistic and historic value. As a result, residents were denied access to heritage sites to conduct ceremonies and rituals there. They were regarded as vandals destroying the artistic integrity and historic authenticity of the heritage. The colonialists thus prevented local residents from interacting with their heritage (tangible and intangible) in a process of (i) introducing prohibitive laws that restricted their access, ownership and use of sacred places; (ii) introducing religious beliefs that limited traditional management practices including ceremonies and rituals; and (iii) putting fences around the sites (Hussein and Armitage, 2014). After independence, most post-colonial states in Africa adopted the colonial legislations. Although some amendments were done, similar to the Colonial Ordinance, most of the revised legislations focused on the *monumentalism doctrine*, overlooking the surroundings of a monument, the African traditions that gave roots to the intangible aspects of the heritage such as indigenous knowledge and systems, and other cultural landscapes (Kamamba, 2005). Most of newly formulated legislations still gave the Ministers powers to declare any place or structure a monument, and the Commissioners the power to enter and inspect any monument, and fence, repair and otherwise protect or preserve it. Local residents were not considered in the management of cultural heritage as they were assumed to cause most of the destruction and hence the reasons why fences were erected.

In the 21st century, Africa has been a major focus for donor support in developing heritage for tourism (Rogerson, 2007). World Bank's tourism-related lending to Africa reach about 34% of its total tourism-related lending (World Bank, 2006). With support from other international entities such as the International Finance Corporation, the British Department for International Development/Overseas Development Institute and the Netherlands Development Organization (SNV), tourism development in Africa has been encouraged with the goal of contributing effectively to economic and social development, including poverty alleviation (Ashley, 2006; Rogerson, 2006, 2007; World Bank, 2006). More highlights of tourism's potential for contributing to economic and social upliftment in Africa are provided by the New Partnership for Africa's Development (NEPAD). NEPAD Tourism Action Plan of 2004 interpreted tourism as a sector in Africa's transformation and future development, and set basic objectives and strategies for further development of tourism in Africa (NEPAD, 2004). Indeed, much is said about Africa's tourism potential for economic development. However, little is said about its dynamics especially when given the fact that tourism, in most cases, utilises heritage resources that have historically been in the hands of the local communities as natural custodians. These issues become complex when the conception and treatment of heritage for tourism are considered from the point of view of a local community. This is the view taken in the discussion presented in the next section.

Current dilemma in the maintenance of heritage for tourism

The previous section provided a critical understanding of the ways Africans utilised their heritage for various purposes including tourism, and the various internal and external factors that affected the perception and use of this heritage. Indeed, the discussion of critical issues in the use of heritage for tourism in Africa today is framed within the context of African's position in the global system. Reflection is made in this section on African's conception and treatment of heritage for tourism purposes as they have been affected by global forces including neo-colonial heritage policies, legislations and institutional frameworks.

Marginalisation of African heritage and traditions in heritage tourism

Traditional African heritage included both the tangible and especially intangible aspects of culture held in local folklores and passed on orally from generation to generation. The emphasis on materiality, monumentality and permanence brought about through Western-based heritage doctrine tend to be detrimental to the preservation of intangible African heritage. Western-based values of aesthetics, historic and of strict-custodianship in today's conception and treatment of African heritage is therefore an obstacle to the maintenance of heritage for tourism. Under the materiality doctrine, what has conventionally been considered as important heritage is often associated with material traces that are old and have certain aesthetic qualities. Within this point of view, most post-colonial African states and their heritage legislative frameworks have been paying much attention to heritage in their material forms, and have been ascribing, in most cases, the colonial heritage as national heritage. Consequently, national heritage inventories and lists in African states such as Tanzania and Ghana for instance tend to leave out the intangible cultural traditions which form the core essence of African heritage.

Under the monumentality doctrine, the Antiquities authorities in the post-colonial African states focus on the *exceptional* and *architectural* dimensions as a priority of identifying, documenting, safeguarding and developing heritage for tourism. They consider traditional and vernacular built heritage as structures that do not have *monumental* qualities because they are neither designed by prominent craftsmen nor made of luxurious materials with representative styles of certain stages of history (Baca and López, 2018). While Africa is rich in terms of tangible and intangible culture and traditions, most heritage sites considered as national heritage are foreign-oriented. For instance, in the current Tanzanian National Cultural Heritage Register of 2012, more than 90% of heritage that has been considered as national heritage are foreign-oriented sites. This kind of approach has made African states ignore enormous traditional and vernacular built heritage leaving them unidentified, undocumented, un-conserved and under-developed for heritage tourism (Baca and López, 2018). Indeed, although there can be tourists interested to get close to African culture by visiting such heritage places, the African traditional sites often have poor accessibility and are not well organised to receive and serve tourists.

Mistreatment of African heritage for tourism purposes

The Western notion of permanence in treating heritage contradicts with the impermanence nature of African traditional built heritage. Treatment of traditional heritage in Africa conventionally involved regular repair of mud walls and thatched grass roofs (Kankpeyeng, 2009; Kigongo, 2009). It also involved regular repair of the decorations with limited desire to imitate and restore the existing designs but rather to depict new designs that reflect contemporary societal issues. Such an approach is however in contrast to the preferences of the Western doctrines of aesthetics and artistic consistency. Africans would often apply entirely new decorations during repairs and treat their traditional houses and other built heritage as inspired by expression of their mood and trends of the moment (Joffroy, 2009). Indeed, for local Africans, such inspirations and expressions that accompany the processes in the treatment of the built heritage are part and parcel of their authenticity (Joffroy, 2009). This notion of authenticity comes to discord when conservators attempt to introduce modern materials in treating traditional heritage build in order to make them permanent structures.

A prime example is the treatment of traditional houses in the Village Museum in Tanzania. The museum was established in 1967 as an open-air ethnographical museum showcasing traditional huts from more than 16 different Tanzanian ethnic groups in Dar es Salaam city. In repair of some huts, the authority uses permanent materials. Figures 4.1–4.3 show that the iron smelting furnace representing the advancement in technology of people of *Fipa* ethnicity, the *Hehe* and *Ngoni* houses that represent the building traditions of *Hehe* people of the Iringa region and *Ngoni* people of Ruvuma region in Tanzania respectively, are plastered by cement mortar. While the use of cement mortar is thought to achieve durability and permanence of the structures – core principles in the Western treatment of historic heritage – in the point of view of African knowledge, this tendency freezes the traditional processes including the manifestation of change that often accompany the technical conservation practices. It is therefore neither healthy to the preservation of the traditional heritage nor to the authentic expression and experience for heritage tourists.

The tendency of limiting values of heritage in tourism sites to the concepts of beauty or aesthetics, artistic and historic dimensions often lead to the mistreatment of African heritage. Several traditional heritage properties have been drawn from the local communities to be displayed in museums, where they are interpreted and conceived wrongly with unethical elements. An example of this phenomenon is the misrepresentation and mistreatment of the *Mwananyanhiti* – a secret fertility doll from the Kwere tribe – in the National Museum in Tanzania in the 1970s (Minogape, 2018). The *Mwananyanhiti* doll is used as an initiation teaching of girls who, after reaching puberty, are put into seclusion till harvest season when

Figure 4.1 Iron smelting furnace
Source: Author.

Figure 4.2 Hehe traditional house at the village museum
Source: Author.

Figure 4.3 Inside a Ngoni traditional house at the village museum
Source: Author.

initiation into womanhood is performed (Minogape, 2018). Thus, the African traditions and norms consider the *Mwananyanhiti* as a secret object restricted from public viewing such as that performed in the museum for touristic purposes. However, in the museum, the cultural object is simply appreciated for its beauty and artistic expressions without an appreciation of societal relevance. In addition, traditional masks that were visual teaching aids of societal norms are displayed in many African National Museum and interpreted to tourists as simple covers for the face. This tendency of mistreating the traditional heritage is unethical and unfair to the makers, who happen to be the powerless local communities in Africa.

Another example is the Mongomi wa Kolo Site in Kondoa in Tanzania. The local communities such as the Warangi and the Waasi use Mongomi wa Kolo site for traditional and ritual purposes vis-à-vis ancient paintings. However, to the eyes of Westerners and the site managers groomed in Western doctrines, the paintings reflect the beauty and aesthetic expressions by our ancestors and thus neglect the spiritual value that the site carries with it. This tends to create conflict between maintaining the site for tourism and the access rights of the local communities for ritual purposes.

Marginalisation of local communities in the maintenance of heritage tourism sites

The emphasis on the *strict custodial protection* of heritage has even more serious effects, especially to the treatment of African heritage. The Western essence of strict custodianship was to limit unprofessional people from accessing the site as they might intentionally or unintentionally cause destruction or modification. However, before colonialism, Africans had customary laws, taboos and restrictions that governed the treatment of their heritage (Joffroy, 2009). Indeed, the local communities respected the customary laws and taboos more than they do to formal colonial and post-colonial legislations today. Africans also had a traditional institutional framework and social structures for managing and protecting their heritage. These included the family *kaya*, *rika*, clans and priests in a chiefdom that organised and managed the treatment of heritage. They were responsible for ensuring regular maintenance of cultural heritage, formulation and enforcement of customary laws and taboos. For instance, in the Kabaka Kingdom in Buganda (present-day Uganda), the clan members were responsible for ensuring regular maintenance of the site (Kigongo, 2009). At Mongomi wa Kolo rock paintings site in Kondoa district in Tanzania, there were traditional custodians called *mwanese* and *hapaloe* tasked with managing the site. These custodians came from the Warangi and Waasi ethic group (Bwasiri, 2011).

An important element in the local regime of heritage site maintenance was the social process. As guided by the local social institutions such as clans and priests, the conservation and protection of heritage in African traditions had a conscious intention of reinforcing the social cohesion of the community. This manifested through the collective efforts and symbolic and ritual events that accompanied the treatment of heritage. In Tanzania for instance three-day traditional ceremonies and rituals were carried out at Mwongomi wa Kolo and begun at the house of *mwenese* or *hapaloe* to the site and involved the whole community (Bwasiri, 2011). The conservation of heritage in Ghana, especially at the Tongo-Tengzuk site, was accompanied with traditional dances, education to young generations and transmission of indigenous knowledge through oral traditions as held by the elders (Kankpeyeng, 2009).

The emergence of conservation practices that are based solely on Western-based notion of *strict custodianship* has resulted in changes to and a neglect of the local content including the traditional knowledge that was critical for the survival of the African cultural heritage.

In this regard, African states prevent local communities from interacting with their heritage especially at what may be designed as (inter)national heritage sites by (i) introducing prohibitive laws that restrict their access to and ownership and use of their heritage such as sacred places and (ii) putting fences around the sites (Hussein and Armitage, 2014). No wonder, the early colonial heritage legislations in Africa such as the Monument Preservation Ordinance of 1937 in Tanzania, and even the post-colonial states, dislocated people from their local heritage and lands. This *fine* and *fence* approaches separated local communities from their heritage (Pwiti and Ndoro, 1999). Colonial laws restricted the access of communities to their heritage for ritual activities since traditional treatment were considered as inefficient, primitive and destructive to heritage's integrity and authenticity (Hussein and Armitage, 2014). Ethical treatment of historical heritage such as norms, taboos, customary laws which included restrictions and rules that people must adhere to prior to being permitted to visit such areas are neglected. This also include the neglect of local institutions and social processes that were essential for social cohesion and maintenance of heritage sites. This neglect has largely been due to the opinion of expatriate heritage professions taking precedence over local tradition knowledge and know-how in the current post-colonial heritage management system.

In the traditional heritage management system, responsibilities for site maintenance tended to be decentralised to communities. In contrast, the current heritage management system in many African countries tend to be centralised. All mandates and responsibilities of conservation and treatment of the site are centralised to government bodies. In Ghana, the Ghana Museums and Monuments Board (GMMB) through the National Liberation Council Decree 387 of 1969 (now known as Act 387 of 1969 and its further strengthening through Executive Instrument 29 of 1973) is invested as the legal custodian of the country's movable and immovable material cultural heritage. This is similar to the case in Tanzania where the Antiquities Act of 1964 and its amendment (URT, 1979) stipulates that, nobody should excavate or alter the site without permission from the relevant authority, thus effectively alienating local communities who used the site for rituals, religious shrines and even adapted landscape as burial grounds. Communities within or around heritage sites like Kilwa Kisiwani, Bagamoyo Kaole and Kunduchi are restricted in their ritual worship activities at the heritage, while tourism investors are allowed; a situation that leads to never-ending conflicts between the site authorities and the local communities (Masele, 2012; Lwoga, 2018a, 2018b).

The denial of the local content also manifests itself in the selection of heritage by heritage promoters to showcase to visitors. In various sites such as Pangani historic town, the heritage promotion and especially maintenance for tourism concentrates on colonial built heritage while ignoring the traditional mud houses occupied by local residents in the outskirt of the town (Lwoga, 2017). Indeed, the residents and owners of such houses express their concerns and wishes that, at least, the maintenance could have considered their houses. This would have not only improved local settlements but also would direct tourists to visit the houses in special arrangements, and thus instil positive attitude towards traditional houses.

In addition, there is the issue of local community ownership of resources such as land surrounding national heritage sites or *protected areas*. In such situations, their participation in decision making and equity of the distribution of heritage tourism benefits are still problematic (Timothy and Nyaupane, 2009; Chirikure et al., 2010; Lwoga, 2018a, 2018b). A majority of heritage tourism resources across Africa are owned by the state, powerful foreign investors and few local elites. Many local communities who are the natural custodians of such heritage often left to struggle for an insignificant share of tourist expenditure through selling cultural materials or working in such low paying jobs in the tourism and hospitality industry. A recent experience in Kaole Ruins Site in Tanzania shows that even the limited women benefiting from selling cooked mud snails along the beach were expelled on the grounds of hygiene and environmental pollution (Lwoga, 2018b). Currently, poverty is persisting in rural areas surrounding such sites that are embedded within popular and unique heritage attractions, where tourist flows and tourism investment as well as revenues are ever increasing (Melubo and Lovelock, 2019). This situation shows the ambiguity of the concept of sustainability underlying the promotion of heritage tourism. This ambiguity places the notion of development of heritage for sustainable development as a mere myth, particularly to the local communities in Africa.

Ambiguities in the promotion of heritage tourism as a sustainable development option

Tourism approaches and their underlying principles changed from the traditional mass tourism approach in the 1960s to alternative tourism approaches in the 1980s and 1990s. These alternative approaches included principles of sustainable tourism, ecotourism, community-based natural resource management, community-based tourism and recently the pro-poor tourism. These forms of tourism basically utilise natural and cultural heritage resources and, thus, they are inherently heritage tourism. Alternative tourism approaches and their associated themes have been criticised for their conceptual ambiguity, practicability, and their effectiveness in solving core problems of poverty alleviation, community empowerment and development in Africa (Meyer, 2007; Scheyvens, 2007, 2011). Conceptually, one of the common themes used is a sustainable tourism in the sense of tourism that meets the needs of current generation without compromising the capacity of the future generation to meet their own needs. Can we know the real needs of the future generation? It should be noted that the way we perceive the needs of the future generation with inference from the current generation could be wrong. Due to the rapidly advanced technology, changes in local community and tourists demands and the dynamics of tourism sector and the society in general, the needs of future generation might be completely different from the needs of the current generation.

In the context of globalisation, uneven development, and unequal power relations in the international tourism system (Mowforth and Munt, 2009), the use of heritage tourism in achieving key principles of sustainable development in developing countries is still problematic. It is well known that Western countries form the main market and foreign currency source for African tourism. In case they limit their investment, or citizens to travel to a particular African country, or pose economic barriers for such reasons as insecurity, political instability or unhealthy international relationship, tourism sector in such a country will cease. In that context, African countries assume unequal relationships to the Western countries and local elites' interests. Within the globalisation processes, major supranational organisations, mostly dominated by Western countries, take on far-reaching powers that affect tourism development in individual countries.

In the context of heritage tourism for instance, the decisions on heritage tourism development, new approaches for heritage tourism practices and sector organisation are formed mainly through UNESCO World Heritage processes at the supranational level. These decisions are then to be implemented in local communities in Africa in the name of heritage *development projects and programmes* with little local inputs. or *development programme*. Local African communities are therefore drawn and networked into capitalist economic and social systems over which they have little to no control. Consequently, these communities do not get to benefit fully from the heritage development projects implemented. Within this context, the growth and success of local heritage community enterprises in the internationalised and globalised tourism sector are questioned. In many cases it is the international enterprises, mostly originating in the Western world that are most successful. This is because such enterprises are more powerful, well networked and given highly incentivised opportunities to invest in African countries in the name of foreign investment promotion policies. The question of whether the economic globalisation and expansion of Western capitalist relations with the African countries favour and create fair community participation and opportunities to local community heritage enterprises therefore still remains (Chirikure et al., 2011; Lwoga, 2011; Melubo and Lovelock, 2019).

The tourismification of local community and their culture and traditions entails an aestheticisation process. It involves the transformation of local people's life, feelings and experiences into aesthetic objects and experiences for tourists to enjoy. With the consideration of community-based tourism approach, the aesthetic phenomenon is normally focused on traditional and original culture and environment. The ambiguity here is that if such a community is associated with poverty, the sustainability of tourism and tourist experiences would require the maintenance of the community's traditional way of life embedded with poverty (Mowforth and Munt, 2009). But traditions within communities do change and the development of tourism often brings with it material improvements in living conditions. How do can heritage tourism be promoted as an experience of traditional culture when this culture is in flux due to socio-economic changes. The paradox then is that the very development of heritage tourism can lead to the transformation and/or destruction of aesthetic values of culture and authenticity that tourists seek for.

The current emphasis on international heritage tourists centring on leisure and education in the promotional agenda ignores domestic heritage tourists who conventionally flock to African traditional heritage sites for ritual and pilgrimage purposes (Timothy and Nyaupane, 2009). This raises a tension between the expectations and experiences sought by domestic and that of international heritage tourists. In many Sub Saharan African countries, local people have always visited their heritage for social and spiritual purposes. There are a number of domestic visitors visiting traditional heritage sites overtly or covertly for ritual and healing purposes. Indeed, ancestry and spiritual attachment to heritage still form one of the major motivations for domestic heritage visitors (Sing'ambi and Lwoga, 2018). However, most domestic tourism promotion campaigns are designed to communicate visitor's thought benefits related to education and leisure, which are often the needs of international tourists, while ignoring the spiritual and ancestry kind of though beneficial to the African visitors. The dominant *leisure* conception that underpins the way we think of tourism today limit efforts and genuine promotion of domestic tourism to heritage sites. If the ignorance of the domestic heritage tourism market is caused by their local per capita spending, Timothy and Nyaupane (2009) caution heritage tourism managers to never ignore their overall economic contribution.

History shows that tourism in Africa in the past included inter-regional travels within Africa for social, commercial and cultural reasons including pilgrimages. It was expected that the inter-regional tourism market would grow under the current situation where there is regional cooperation in Africa such as the Eastern African Community (EAC), the Southern African Development Community (SADC), and the Economic Community of West African States (ECOWAS). Nevertheless, it seems that tourism in general and heritage tourism, in particular, has not prioritised in this cooperation (Timothy and Nyaupane, 2009). Efforts at both policy and practical levels need to be made in order to further develop and encourage inter-regional travel within the continent.

Conclusion

There is no doubt that heritage tourism is a growing form of tourism in Africa. The potential of heritage tourism to contribute to socio-economic development and cultural and environmental conservation is well appreciated by scholars and practitioners. However, the actual realisation of this potential has been very limited due to a number of reasons as outlined in this chapter. There are inherent paradoxes in the conception and treatment of the core subject of heritage. This is especially so when it is illuminated from local African discourses within the realm of tourism history, globalisation, politics and socio-cultural contexts. This chapter reflected on these paradoxes, and the way they underscore challenges limiting the realisation of potentials of heritage tourism in Africa. It contributes to the growing interest in the subject of heritage tourism (Nyaupane and Budruk, 2009; Teye, 2009; Timothy and Daher, 2009). This chapter broadens the connection between tourism and heritage issues while putting the local versus colonial conceptions and perspectives at the centre of the deliberations.

The chapter shows the use of heritage for tourism in Africa within the paradoxical frameworks that is based on Western doctrines and the inherent problems this has for conceiving what is heritage, its appropriate treatment and preservation. In most cases, this Western doctrine of heritage is the foundation of prevailing marginalisation of African heritage and traditions and local communities – the primary custodians of heritage – in heritage tourism development, the mistreatment of African heritage, and the ambiguities in heritage tourism marketing promotion programmes. It further shows, from the historical perspective, that the current theoretical and practical paradoxes in the treatment of heritage for tourism in Africa were indoctrinated during the era of the slave trade and colonialism, and further amplified through the prevailing neocolonialism agenda. It is this context that is shaping the ideological foundation for today's heritage and tourism policies and strategies. This may have detrimental effect on the African traditions on the one hand, and to the way heritage tourism is perceived, accepted and supported by the local communities on the other. The effect of these issues – often given a shallow deliberation in *tourism impact* literature – are not only detrimental to the sustainability of heritage tourism but also contributes to the waning of African cultural pride and self-esteem.

Heritage tourism policymakers and practitioners should reconsider broader theoretical issues in the decisions made to ascribe sites as national heritage, the focus of tourism plans and development and mechanisms for developing African heritage for tourism. Alternative thinking towards heritage management and tourism practices needs to be structured in a participatory way in order to preserve and sustainably develop African heritage for tourism with the input of local communities. Some practical suggestions include the genuine participation of the local communities in shaping heritage development and preservation goals and directions; sustainable integration of African intangible heritage in the development of heritage tourism products; integrating African conception of heritage and understanding of broader values including spiritual and socio-cultural values they ascribe to their heritage; promoting social events that are key to local communities in fostering their social cohesion and pride; respecting African traditions and heritage in promoting heritage for tourism; considering both monumental and traditional vernacular heritage in tourism development and conservation planning, and; formalising domestic heritage tourism market and products and account to their economic impact.

This chapter has broadly sketched out some of the current issues in heritage tourism facing countries in Sub Saharan Africa. Using the framework set out in this chapter, future studies can focus on specific country and destination contexts for a more detailed examination of the issues.

References

Ashley, C. (2006) *How Can Governments Boost the Local Economic Impacts of Tourism?* The Hague and London: SNV and ODI.

Baca, L.F. and López, F.J. (2018) Traditional architecture and sustainable conservation. *Journal of Cultural Heritage Management and Sustainable Development*, 8 (2), 194–206

Bwasiri, E. (2011) The implication of management of indigenous living heritage: The case study of the Mongomi wa Kolo rock paintings world heritage site, central Tanzania. *South African Archaeological Bulletin*, 66 (193), 60–66

Chami, F.A (2006) *The Unity of African Ancient History: 3000 BC to AD 500*, Dar es Salaam: E & D Limited.

Chirikure, S., Manyanga, M., Ndoro, W. and Pwiti, G. (2010) Unfulfilled promises? Heritage management and community participation at some Africa's cultural heritage sites. *International Journal of Heritage Studies*, 16 (1–2), 30–44.

Croegaert, L. (1999) *The African Continent: An Insight into its Earliest History*, Nairobi: Paulines Publications Africa.

Dieke, P. (2000) *The Political Economy of Tourism Development in Africa*, New York: Cognizant Communication.

Ehret, C. (2002) *The Civilizations of Africa: A History to 1800*, Charlottesville: University of Virginia.

Elliott, S.M. and Mann, S. (2005) *Development, Poverty and Tourism: Perspectives and Influences in Sub-Sahara Africa*. Washington DC: George Washington Center for the Study of Globalization.

Gauci, A., Gerosa, V. and Mwalwanda, C. (2005) *Tourism in Africa and the Multilateral Trading System: Challenges and Opportunities*. Paper prepared for the Economic Commission for Africa, Addis Ababa.

Holloway, J.C. (1998) *The Business of Tourism*, London: Longman.

Hussein, J. and Armitage, L. (2014) *Traditional Heritage Management: The Case of Australia and Tanzania*, Queensland: Faculty of Society and Design Publication.

Huybers, T. (2007) *Tourism in Developing Countries*, London: Edward Elgar.

Ichumbaki, E.B. (2016) A history of conservation of built heritage sites of the Swahili Coast in Tanzania. *African Historical Review*, 48 (2), 43–67.

ICOMOS Australia (1999) *Burra Charter* [Online] Available from: http://australia.icomos.org/?s=burra+charter [accessed 21 January 2019].

Joffroy, T. (2009) *Traditional Conservation Practices in Africa*, Rome: ICCROM.

Jokilehto, J.I. (1986) *A History of Architectural Conservation: Contribution of English, French, German and Italian Thought towards an Approach to the Conservation of Cultural Property*. Unpublished Ph.D. Thesis, York: University of York.

Kamamba, D. (2005) Conservation and management of immovable heritage in Tanzania. In Mapunda, B.B.B. and Msemwa, P. (Eds.), *Salvaging Tanzania's Cultural Heritage*, Dar es Salaam: Dar es Salaam University Press, pp. 262–270.

Kankpeyeng, B.W. (2009) The cultural landscape of Tongo-Tenzuk, Ghana. In Joffroy, T. (Ed.), *Traditional Conservation Practices in Africa*, Rome: ICCROM Conservation Studies, pp. 16–23.

Kigongo, R. (2009) The Kasubi Tombs: Traditional conservation methods and techniques. In Joffroy, T. (Ed.), *Traditional Conservation Practices in Africa*, Rome: ICCROM Conservation Studies, pp. 32–39.

Leung, Y.F. (2001) Environmental impacts of tourism at China's world heritage sites: Huangshan and Chengde. *Tourism Recreation Research*, 26 (1), 117–122.

Lowenthal, D. (1997) *The Heritage Crusade and the Spoils of History*, New York: Viking.

Lwoga, N.B. (2011) *Tourism: Meaning, Practices & History*, Dar es Salaam: Dar es Salaam University Press.

Lwoga, N.B. (2017) Local collaboration network in management of built heritage: A study of Pangani Conservation Task Force (PCTF) in Tanzania. *Journal of Cultural Heritage Management and Sustainable Development*, 7 (3), 226–243.

Lwoga, N. (2018a) Dilemma of local socio-economic perspectives in management of historic ruins in Kilwa Kisiwani World Heritage Site, Tanzania. *International Journal of Heriatge Studies*, 24 (10), 1019-1037

Lwoga, N.B. (2018b) Heritage proximity, attitude to tourism impacts and local residents' support for heritage tourism in Kaole Ruins Site, Tanzania. *Bulletin of Geography: Socio-economic Series*, 42 (4), 163–181.

Mapunda, B. and Msemwa, P. (2005) *Salvaging Tanzania's Cultural Heritage*, Dar es Salaam: Dar es Salaam University Press.

Masele, F. (2012) Private business investments in heritage sites in Tanzania: Recent developments and challenges for heritage management. *African Archaeological Review*, 29, 51–65.

Melubo, K. and Lovelock, B. (2019). Living inside a UNESCO world heritage site: The perspective of the Maasai community in Tanzania. *Tourism Planning & Development*, 16 (2), 197–216.

Meyer, D. (2007) Pro-poor tourism: From leakages to linkages. A conceptual framework for creating linkages between the accommodation sector and "poor" neighbouring communities, *Current Issues in Tourism*, 10 (6), 558–583.

Minogape, C.M. (2018) *The Role of National Museum of Tanzania in Fostering National Identity in Post-Colonial Period: A Pan-African Perspective*. Unpublished Masters Dissertation. Dar es Salaam: University of Dar es Salaam.

Mowforth, M. and Munt, I. (2009) *Tourism and Sustainability: Development, Globalisation and New Tourism in the Third World*, 3rd ed., Abingdon: Routledge.

Mulokozi, M.M. (2005) Management of intangible heritage in Tanzania. In Mapunda, B.B.B. and Msemwa, P. (Eds.), *Salvaging Tanzania's Cultural Heritage*, Dar es Salaam: Dar es Salaam University Press, pp. 279–292.

Ndoro, W. (2005) *Your Monument Our Shrine: The Preservation of Great Zimbabwe*, Rome: ICCROM Conservation Studies.

New Partnership for Africa's Development (NEPAD) (2004) *Tourism Action Plan*. Discussion document prepared for the 41st Meeting of the World Tourism Organization Commission for Africa, 10–13 May, Mahe, Seychelles.

Nyaupane, G.P. and Budruk, M. (2009) South Asian heritage tourism: Conflict, colonialism and cooperation. In Timothy, D.J. and Nyaupane, G.P. (Eds.), *Cultural Heritage and Tourism in the Developing World: A Regional Perspective*, London: Routledge, pp. 127–145.

Pwiti, G. and Ndoro, W. (1999) The legacy of colonialism: Perceptions of the cultural heritage in Southern Africa, with special reference to Zimbabwe. *African Archaeological Review*, 16, 143–153.

Reader, J. (1997) *A Bibliography of the Continent: Africa*, London: Hamish Hamilton Ltd.

Rogerson, C.M. (2006) Pro-poor local economic development in South Africa: The role of pro-poor tourism. *Local Environment*, 11, 37–60.

Rogerson, C.M. (2007) Reviewing Africa in the global tourism economy. *Development Southern Africa*, 24 (3), 361–379.

Salazar, N.B. (2009) A troubled past, a challenging present, and a promising future: Tanzania's tourism development in perspective. *Tourism Review International*, 12, 1–15.

Scheyvens, R. (2007) Exploring the tourism-poverty nexus. *Current Issues in Tourism*, 10 (2–3), 231–254.

Scheyvens, R. (2011) *Tourism and Poverty*, Abingdon: Routledge.

Shillington, K. (1995) *History of Africa*, Oxford: Macmillan Publishers Ltd.

Sing'ambi, E. and Lwoga, N.B. (2018) Heritage attachment and domestic tourists' visits to historic sites. *International Journal of Culture, Tourism and Hospitality Research*, 12 (3), 310–326.

Teye, V.B. (2009) Tourism and Africa's tripartite cultural past. In Timothy, D.J. and Nyaupane, G.P. (Eds.), *Cultural Heritage and Tourism in the Developing World: A Regional Perspective*, London: Routledge, pp. 165–185.

Teye, V.B., Sevil, S. and Sirakaya-Turk, E. (2011) Heritage tourism in Africa: Residents' perceptions of African-American and white tourists. *Tourism Analysis*, 16, 169–185.

Theobald, W.F. (1998) *Global Tourism*, 2nd ed., Oxford: Butterworth-Heinemann.

Timothy, D.J. and Boyd, S.J. (2006) Heritage tourism in the 21st century: Valued traditions and new perspectives. *Journal of Heritage Tourism*, 1 (1), 1–16.

Timothy, D.J. and Daher, R.F. (2009) Heritage tourism in Southwest Asia and North Africa: Contested pasts and veiled realities. In Timothy, D.J. and Nyaupane, G.P. (Eds.), *Cultural Heritage and Tourism in the Developing World: A Regional Perspective*, London: Routledge, pp. 146–164.

Timothy, D.J. and Nyaupane, G.P. (2009) Introduction: Heritage tourism and the less-developed world. In Timothy, D.J. and Nyaupane, G.P. (Eds.), *Cultural Heritage and Tourism in the Developing World: A Regional Perspective*, London: Routledge, pp. 3–19.

United Nations World Tourism Organization [UNWTO] (2018) *Tourism and Culture Synergies*. Madrid: UNWTO.

URT [United Republic of Tanzania] (1979) *Antiquities Act No. 22* (Amendment), An Act to Amend the Antiquities Act, 1964, Dar es Salaam: Ministry of National Education.

Walton, J.K. (2009) Prospects in tourism history: Evolution, state of play and future developments. *Tourism Management*, 30, 783–793.

Winter, T. (2007) Rethinking tourism in Asia. *Annals of Tourism Research*, 34 (1), 27–44.

World Bank. (2006) *The World Bank Annual Report 2006*. Washington DC: World Bank.

5

Adventure tourism in Africa

Julia Kathryn Giddy

Introduction

Adventure tourism encompasses a wide range of tourism experiences and activities (Rantala, Rokenes, & Valkonen, 2018; Swarbrooke et al., 2003). Traditionally, authors have defined adventure tourism by the associated risk, whether real or perceived (Buckley, 2012; Cater, 2006; Swarbrooke et al., 2003). Subsequently, however, the literature focused more on the thrill, fear, or rush-seeking component of adventure, rather than actual risk (Buckley, 2012; Carnicelli-Filho, Schwartz, & Tahara, 2010; Cater, 2006). In addition, other literature has argued that neither risk nor thrill defines adventure but rather some sense of uncertainty while others have argued that it is related to insight-seeking (Rantala et al., 2016; Swarbrooke et al., 2003; Walle, 1997; Weber, 2001). Although there are a number of definitions for adventure tourism, many of which are relatively broad, for the purposes of this chapter it is defined as a touristic activity or experience which involves some level of risk (whether real or perceived) and often takes place outdoors (Hall, 1992, p. 192). The current growth of adventure tourism has been the result of a number of changes that have occurred in recent years. One such change is the increasing desire of tourists to have interesting and unique interactions with nature (Bell & Lyall, 2002; Giddy & Webb, 2018a). This is a divergence from the passive appreciation of nature previously common in nature-based tourism. Therefore, traditional nature-based tourism experiences have evolved to increase stimulation, often incorporating aspects of adventure (Bell & Lyall, 2002). Another change seen in adventure tourism is the advancements in technological innovation which have allowed a larger number of less skilled tourists to engage in a wide range of adventure activities (Cheng et al., 2018; Puchan, 2004). Both changes have led to the commercialization of adventure. One of the primary focus of much adventure tourism research is on the commodification of adventure which is a result of said commercialization (Kane & Tucker, 2004; Prince & Loynes, 2016; Rantala et al., 2018; Rickly & Vidon, 2017; Taylor, Varley, & Johnston, 2013; Varley, 2006).

Perceptions of the impact of this commodification are varied and dynamic; however commercial adventure tourism is clearly an important emerging tourism market (Carnicelli-Filho, 2013; Fluker & Turner, 2000; Giddy, 2018a). Many developing countries have benefited from the commercial adventure tourism market by developing products in the unique and relatively pristine environment found within many of these places (Giddy, 2018a; McKay, 2016). For example, in Costa Rica, extensive ziplining and canopy tour products have emerged throughout the country and now form an integral part of their tourism offerings. In addition, you can now bungee jump-off at the Victoria Falls, skydive over Mount Kilimanjaro, and kayak down the Nile River (Shearwater Bungee, 2017; Tourism on the Edge, 2017; Yogerst, 2017).

Adventure is often synonymous with tourism experiences in Africa, due to perceptions of the continent as relatively rugged and the tourism activities which are typically associated with the continent (e.g. safaris) (Saarinen et al., 2009). In the case of Africa, we see two primary ways in which adventure tourism has developed. One has been the evolution of specific experiences which fall under adventure tourism and have been relevant in Africa for many years. This includes wildlife safaris, mountaineering (particularly in Kilimanjaro), and scuba diving as well as several others. The second way in which adventure tourism has developed in Africa has been in the emergence of commercial adventure tourism products such as those mentioned above (Giddy, 2018a). However, there are many challenges to increased development of adventure tourism in Africa and questions that emerge as to the real economic benefits as well as management concerns (Giddy, 2016a; McKay, 2013a; Rogerson, 2012).

This chapter, therefore, provides a broad overview of adventure tourism on the African continent. It first discusses the evolution of adventure tourism in Africa from early international tourism which would be considered "adventure" experiences to current manifestations of adventure tourism on the continent. This is followed by an overview of the geography of adventure tourism in Africa. Next, specific sectors of adventure tourism which are prevalent on the continent are highlighted followed by a detailed examination of some of the critical issues facing the adventure tourism industry in Africa, namely, marketing management, adventure tourism employment, and environmental concerns. The chapter then concludes with a look at potential future avenues for research as well as things to consider in the future development of adventure tourism in Africa.

Adventure tourism development in Africa

The history of tourism in Africa is vast and became increasingly relevant during the European colonization of the continent when leisure travel from the developed world began to emerge in Africa (Lwonga, 2011). Much of the early forms of leisure travel to Africa would be considered adventure tourism as elements of risk and uncertainty were commonplace among Western visitors and most of the attractions took place outdoors, fulfilling the basic definition of adventure tourism (Wolf, 1991). There are numerous accounts by early European explorers, however, there also exists significant documentation on the experiences of travelers to Africa, particularly Americans who can clearly be differentiated as leisure travelers or tourists (Dugard, 2003; McCabe, 1883; Vivanco & Gordon, 2006; Wolf, 1991). The accounts by Americans often fit more definitively into the tourism discourse as their journeys are specified as leisure travel. These accounts often discuss the role of uncertainty and risk associated with their experiences and the sense of comradery that develops between fellow travelers (e.g., McCabe, 1883) which are common threads in modern analyses of adventure tourism experiences. One interesting historical study contextualized American travel to Southern Africa, highlighting the commonalities between white Americans and settler communities, particularly those in the British colonies in the region (Wolf, 1991).

More recently, the adventure tourism industry has seen the growth in guided commercial products (Buckley, 2010; Pomfret & Bramwell, 2014; Swarbrooke et al., 2003). These products often replace passive forms of traditional nature-based tourism experiences which have been prevalent in Africa for decades (Bell & Lyall, 2002; Giddy, 2018b). In today's high-speed world, people are continuously seeking new, interesting, and exciting ways to interact with landscapes and are no longer satisfied with passive appreciation (Giddy & Webb, 2018a). Therefore, adventure products are increasingly being introduced into many unique landscapes throughout Africa. One important example is that of Livingstone, Zambia, which has emerged as Africa's 'adventure destination' due to the prevalence of several commercial adventure operations such as bungee jumping over Victoria Falls and white water rafting down the Zambezi River (Rogerson, 2004). Victoria Falls has long been an important tourism attraction; however, in recent years, tourism in the area has been transformed to emulate the changes in the way that tourists seek to experience nature. Following suit, the majority of commercial adventure activities found in Africa have emerged due to the presence of specific landscapes in certain areas. For example, white water rafting operations exist near large rivers, abseiling is found down steep cliffs and canyoning through accessible gorges. In many cases, these are activities which have long been practiced in these areas by recreationists but have now been transformed into highly commercialized products accessible to a much larger number of people (Beedie, 2001; Giddy, 2018a, 2018b). Many destinations in Africa are suitable for this kind of tourism development, due to the prevalence of unique landscapes which are relatively pristine. Therefore, adventure tourism can be seen as an important tool for economic development in small towns and rural areas of Africa (Giddy, 2016a; McKay, 2013a; Mograbi & Rogerson, 2007; Rogerson, 2005, 2015).

Existing research on commercial adventure tourism in Africa has covered a few different topics, though most is limited to South Africa. Research has noted that the profile of commercial adventure tourists which found significant transformations in the characteristics of adventure tourism participants (Giddy, 2018a). Some important findings were the increasing number of women participating in adventure tourism particularly "hard" adventure activities such as skydiving (Giddy, 2018a). Furthermore, the results demonstrated a trend of continuous participation in adventure tourism, broadly, but relatively little commitment to specific activities, a significant change from earlier studies which showed efficacy and development of communities as important motivators for continuous engagement in adventure tourism (Ewert, 1985; Shoham, Rose, & Kahle, 2000). The motivations of commercial adventure tourists in South Africa have also been analyzed demonstrating the importance of novelty and the interactions with the environment in their decision to pursue adventure activities (Giddy, 2018b; Giddy & Webb, 2016, 2018a). In another study on white water rafting in South Africa, Giddy, Fitchett and Hoogendoorn (2017a) examined the influence of extreme weather on the industry which found operators particularly vulnerable to the increasing changes in weather patterns which have been experienced throughout the country in recent years and have resulted in changes related to seasonality. McKay (2013b) also found that in the case of white water rafting along the Ash River, issues have arisen between the use of the river for commercial tourism versus as a water resource for the local community.

The geographic distribution of adventure tourism in Africa also needs to be considered when discussing its development. The distribution of adventure tourism experiences is relatively uneven, geographically, with the majority of well-known adventure destinations and experiences located in Southern Africa (McKay, 2014, 2016; Rogerson, 2007). Most wildlife adventure tourism takes place in Sub-Saharan Africa in places such as Kenya/Tanzania, Rwanda/Uganda, and South Africa/Botswana/Namibia. The vast majority of research as has also focused on these areas, primarily on South Africa with some research on specific sites for adventure activities, namely Kilimanjaro (Tanzania) and Victoria Falls (Zambia/

Zimbabwe) and others on sectors in specific locations, for example, scuba diving in Egypt (e.g. Anderson, 2015; Giddy, 2016a; McKay, 2014; Minja, 2015; Prior et al., 1995; Rogerson, 2004). McKay (2016) conducted a study of the geographic distribution of adventure tourism in South Africa which showed that the majority are found in the Western Cape and KwaZulu Natal provinces. Contrary to expectations, McKay (2016) found that adventure tourism operations were not necessarily clustered around specific landscape features, as is the case in other parts of the world and the continent (e.g. around Victoria Falls). In South Africa, adventure tourism operators were most prevalent in proximity to existing tourism destinations, such as Cape Town and Durban. There is, however, great potential for further development of adventure tourism, particularly in rural areas where natural resources are plentiful and economic development is needed (McKay, 2013a). Clearly, adventure tourism development is uneven across the continent with development potential high but currently untapped in many regions.

A typology of adventure tourism in Africa

Most broad types of adventure tourism can be found somewhere on the African continent (Buckley, 2007, 2010). However, there has been significant emphasis, both in the literature and in practice, on specific subsectors of adventure tourism. Some of the most prevalent subsectors of adventure tourism in Africa are wildlife adventure tourism, marine adventure tourism, and overland adventures as well as mountain-based tourism, particularly surrounding Kilimanjaro.

When considering more traditional forms of tourism to Africa, one of the primary focuses is often on exploration. The earliest exploration in Africa by Europeans paved the way for overland adventures, which have become a staple in African adventure tourism offerings, particularly in Southern Africa (Mathers & Hubbard, 2006). As mentioned above, leisure travel within the African continent has a long history, due to the uniqueness of the continent's landscapes and cultures (McCabe, 1883; Wolf, 1991). Overland adventure tourism continues today, though the experience is clearly different. Traditionally, overland adventures were reserved for highly skilled, relatively wealthy travelers who sought exploration into the "unknown" (Mathers & Hubbard, 2006). This has transformed in recent years, into highly organized, packaged trips into areas that would otherwise be difficult to access, merging into a long-duration commercial adventure tourism product (Weber, 2001). Today, packaged overland adventures are offered in many countries throughout the continent, while several companies offer cross-border experiences (e.g. Nomad Africa Adventure Tours, 2018; Overland Africa, 2018). The continued development of overland adventures as a tourism product in Africa exemplifies long-term trends that have persisted in the African tourism context. As for literature on the topic, it is relatively limited. The majority references historical experiences, which is discussed earlier. Some more recent narrative texts have emerged which chronicles specific experiences (Mathers & Hubbard, 2006; Mewshaw, 2010). In addition, broad literature on overland tourism has referenced Africa (Vivanco & Gordon, 2006; Weber, 2001). One interesting study, by Mathers and Hubbard (2006), which examines a more modern analysis of American overland tourism experiences in Africa demonstrates how these experiences are primarily driven by complicated emotions of both a desire to conquer (Africa) and a desire to submit (to the experience).

Another important example of long-term trends in African tourism is the case of wildlife tourism, particularly "safari" experiences. Wildlife-based adventure tourism accounts for a significant proportion of international travel to the continent, particularly Southern Africa

(Saayman & Saayman, 2008). International and regional tourists travel to the area to participate in safari experiences or wildlife interactions. The extent to which safaris and other types
of wildlife interactions can be considered adventure tourism is highly subjective. However,
wildlife interaction, particularly with dangerous animals (i.e. the African "big 5") and/or
in open air vehicles are often classified as adventure tourism (Buckley, 2010; McKay, 2016).
Many of the concerns associated with safari tourism are related to resource allocation and displacement of local populations, which has been problematic in certain regions, particularly
in East Africa (Gardner, 2016). Other research discusses issues concerned with the sustainable
development of safari experiences, including proximity to wildlife and issues around carrying
capacity (Carruthers, 2007; Tarver et al., 2019). In addition, tourism surrounding hunting
falls under the umbrella of wildlife adventure tourism and is a significant market, particularly
in Southern Africa (Buckley, 2010; Lindsey, Roulet, & Romañach, 2007). Sport and trophy
hunting in Southern Africa has fallen into the spotlight, particularly in recent years with the
killing of Cecil the Lion in Zimbabwe and the subsequent media fall out (Macdonald et al.,
2016). A fierce debate has ensued as a result, both in mainstream media and in academic literature (Nelson et al., 2016; Novelli, Barnes, & Humavindu, 2006). Initial reactions showed
strong opposition to sport and trophy hunting, particularly among exotic and endangered
animals (Nelson et al., 2016). However, some evidence has emerged, particularly in recent
academic studies, which demonstrates the potential benefits of trophy hunting, particularly
for local economies (Baker, 1997; Lindsey et al., 2006; Lindsey, Roulet, & Romañach, 2007).
If properly managed, trophy hunting can generate significant income which can be used both
to support conservation efforts and also to benefit local communities (Baker, 1997; Lindsey,
Roulet, & Romañach, 2007; Novelli, Barnes, & Humavindu, 2006).

Mountain-based adventure tourism in Africa is primarily concentrated on expeditions
up and around Mount Kilimanjaro in Tanzania. As the tallest mountain in Africa, there is a
long history of mountaineers attempting to conquer Kilimanjaro (Salkeld, 2002). However,
as is the case with most adventure tourism experiences and highly evidenced in similar tourism sites, such as Mount Everest (Nepal, 2003; Raspaud, 2014), there has been a significant
growth in the number of people trekking up Kilimanjaro in recent years (Minja, 2015).
Organized mountaineering experiences up Kilimanjaro have become prevalent and the parallel development of tourism surrounding the mountain has emerged (Anderson, 2015). As a
result, a number of studies have emerged which examine the effects of this growth in mountaineering tourism around Kilimanjaro. The two primary avenues of research are on the influence of tourism development on economic development in the area and the environmental
impacts of tourism on the mountain ecosystem. In the case of the latter, some work has
focused on the implications of climate change on the mountain ecosystem and subsequently
on tourism (Frömming & Undine, 2009; Mafuru, Wakibara, & Ndesar, 2009; Minja, 2015).
Some have noted the impacts of the melting ice caps on top of the mountain on tourist routes
up the mountain, as well as the safety of tourists (Frömming & Undine, 2009). Others have
discussed broad environmental impacts caused by tourism, common in trekking and mountaineering tourism such as the introduction of alien species, trampling/trail erosion and waste
disposal (Hemp, 2008; Kaseva & Moirana, 2010; Mafuru, Wakibara, & Ndesar, 2009; Minja,
2015). Trail erosion and the introduction of alien species appear to be significant problems
impacting the mountain ecosystem. However, in contrast to research conducted on Mt. Everest, waste disposal appeared to be relatively efficient on Kilimanjaro with estimates of 94%
of waste removed (Kaseva & Moirana, 2010). This is due to the efforts of porters, who carry
the waste of tourists off the mountain in large quantities, which brings up socioeconomic
and employment concerns (Mafuru, Wakibara, & Ndesar, 2009). The other body of research

on socioeconomic implications of tourism around Kilimanjaro demonstrates that significant benefits have emerged for local communities from tourism development in the area (Anderson, 2015; Mitchell, Keane, & Laidlaw, 2009). Packaged tourism experiences on Kilimanjaro and throughout Tanzania have demonstrated particular benefits in terms of extended stays and high expenditure among international tourists (Mitchell, Keane, & Laidlaw, 2009).

Marine adventure tourism is also prominent throughout Africa, related to tourism development and the emergence of commercial adventure tourism products. Scuba diving is one common activity, which can be found in many locations throughout the continent, though is particularly significant in island destinations such as Mauritius, Mozambique and Zanzibar (Lew, 2013). In addition, well-developed diving industries can be found in South Africa and Egypt (Geldenhuys, van der Merwe, & Slabbert, 2014; Giddy & Rogerson, 2018; Hawkins & Roberts, 1993; Lucrezi, Saayman, & van der Merwe, 2013a; Lucrezi, Saayman, & Van Der Merwe, 2013b; Mograbi & Rogerson, 2007; Prior et al., 1995). The majority of research on marine tourism, and diving, in particular, is focused on the environmental impacts of diving, particularly on reef systems (Hasler & Ott, 2008; Lucrezi, Saayman, & Van Der Merwe, 2013b; Prior et al., 1995). In addition, some literature exists on general trends in dive tourism of specific locations and the characteristics of divers (Giddy & Rogerson, 2018). Some important literature exists on the potential benefits of dive tourism to local economies and local economic development. Mograbi and Rogerson (2007) found that in the town of Sodwana Bay, a popular dive destination, although most of the dive companies are white-owned and/or managed, the local community sees significant benefits in terms of job creation. In addition to the dive operators themselves, dive tourists also utilize secondary tourism assets, which again, can drive local economic development.

Critical issues facing adventure tourism in Africa

There are several critical issues facing the adventure tourism industry in Africa (Giddy, 2016a; McKay, 2013a; Rickly & Vidon, 2017; Rogerson, 2007). Two significant issues, which are prevalent throughout the world but are particularly significant in the African context are challenges and concerns surrounding human resource development within the adventure tourism industry and environmental management in the context of adventure tourism development. Africa, clearly, has a long history of adventure "tourism"; however, academic literature only began to emerge on the topic in more recent years. The importance of tourism, more broadly, in Africa has become increasingly apparent as tourism now forms a major component of economic development initiatives in most African countries (Dieke, 2003; Rogerson, 2005, 2012). With respect to adventure tourism, a number of challenges have been highlighted in previous research, three of which are discussed in detail in the section below, namely marketing of adventure tourism destinations/products, adventure tourism employment and environmental management of adventure tourism in Africa (Giddy, 2016a; McKay, 2013a; Rogerson, 2007).

Despite the wide range of adventure experiences offered throughout Africa, and particularly in certain locations, there is a lack of marketing of these places as "adventure destinations" (Rogerson, 2007). The Tsitsikamma region of South Africa and Livingstone in Zambia are two examples of destinations that offer a number of unique adventure activities. However, marketing strategies of the destinations as a whole are limited (Giddy & Webb, 2016; Rogerson, 2004). Research has shown that in the commercial adventure tourism context, tourists increasingly seek out destinations where they are able to participate in different activities (Giddy, 2018b; Giddy & Webb, 2016, 2018a). However, tourism development and marketing often fail in this regard. In some destinations, many activities are offered, but marketing is not cohesive, often neglecting to highlight the number of activities available in specific areas that might be of interest to adventure seekers (Rogerson, 2004). In other cases, one specific adventure sector is well-developed, but there is no initiative to introduce additional activities that might encourage tourists to stay longer and utilize other tourism resources. An example of this is seen in Gansbaai, South Africa, known for its shark cage diving with great white sharks (Dobson, 2007). Although a number of different shark cage diving companies operate in the area, there is almost no other significant tourism development. This means that the town, itself, is not necessarily benefiting from the significant tourism which occurs within it.

Human resource development and management has been listed as a critical issue in adventure tourism more broadly (Giddy, 2019; Williams & Soutar, 2005). Some of the primary issues are related to the standardization of adventure guide qualifications as well as regulation of the minimal existing standards. These concerns are prevalent in Africa as well, though often at a more basic level of lack of adequate training among adventure guides (Giddy, 2016a; McKay, 2013a). This coincides with the lack of regulation of adventure tourism operators in Africa, which can have serious safety implications (McKay, 2013a). Several injuries and fatalities have occurred due to improper management, untrained guides, and faulty equipment (MacGregor, 2000; News24, 2012; NSRI, 2015; Saal, 2017). However, a number of other issues emerge in the African context. A major concern, in terms of employment in Africa specifically, is the demographics and origins of adventure tourism owners and employees and adventure operators' relationships with local communities (Giddy, 2016b; Mograbi & Rogerson, 2007; Rogerson, 2007). Although tourism, particularly adventure tourism, is frequently discussed in terms of its ability to economically uplift poor communities, particularly local communities surrounding tourist attractions, this rarely occurs. Rogerson (2007) has shown that, in the case of South Africa, nearly all owners and managers of adventure tourism operations are white and, for the most part, provide very few employment opportunities for members of the local community. One of the primary issues noted by adventure tourism operators, at least in the Southern African context, is the lack of necessary skills of local populations (Rogerson, 2007). This, then, links to the need for training programs in order to minimize this discrepancy in the adventure tourism workforce.

Some research has shown that the majority of training among adventure tourism operators is done in-house (Giddy, 2016b). Although, in many cases, this approach appears logical, due to the varying nature of different activities and the unique context of local landscapes; some baseline qualifications should be prevalent among anyone operating in an industry where risk is inherent (Williams & Soutar, 2005). For example, the need for basic first-aid qualifications has been noted to be of particular importance in the adventure tourism context, where real dangers are often present (Bentley & Page, 2001). This becomes even more significant in the context of commercial adventure tourism, where participants are ill-equipped to deal with hazards and often rely almost entirely on guides to ensure their own safety (Holyfield, 1999; Mackenzie & Kerr, 2012). Currently, South Africa has existing policies for registering as a tour guide which is guided by the Tourism Act. However, adventure tourism employees are often not qualified tour guides but rather employees of companies that provided specific activities, though there are a few exceptions (Giddy, 2016b). Some training programs have emerged specifically for adventure guides but there is no requirement for basic training for those employed by the aforementioned operators (Adventure Qualifications Network, n.d.). Therefore, adventure tourism employees require significant training by operators, which is largely done in-house and often relatively ad-hoc (Giddy, 2019). Adventure tourism is highly specialized, though wide-spread throughout South Africa with significant potential employment opportunities. Requiring guides, including those employed by operators of specific activities, to engage in a training program, specifically for adventure tourism, which also includes aspects of first aid, would be beneficial, not only to those who seek employment in the industry. Such requirement would also reduce the burden of training by employers as it now falls almost entirely on operators to ensure staff is adequately trained. In addition, instituting training programs would allow for increased regulation and minimum standards for adventure tourism operators, reducing the potential for injuries and/or fatalities.

A third major concern facing adventure tourism in Africa is environmental management. This has been highlighted in some research discussing challenges facing adventure tourism, globally (Rickly & Vidon, 2017; Williams & Soutar, 2005), but has also been substantiated in the case of South Africa specifically (Giddy, 2016b; McKay, 2013a). One of the reasons environmental management is of significant concern in the African context is due to the unique and often fragile environments in which adventure tourism takes place. Research has shown the increasing importance of interactions with nature in the motivations of adventure tourists in Africa (Giddy & Webb, 2016, 2018a). However, the environmental attitudes of both tourists and staff tend to be relatively low (Giddy, 2016b; Giddy & Webb, 2018b). This is problematic and highlights an important issue in the environmental sustainability of many adventure tourism operations. It is of particular concern in the African context due to, one, the importance of the unique features of the natural environment in attracting tourists and two, the lack of regulations and/or enforcement of environmental regulations to assist in sustainable environmental management efforts (Giddy & Webb, 2016; Gossling et al., 2008; Mafuru, Wakibara, & Ndesar, 2009). Currently, however, environmental protection is often neglected in the name of economic development. More urgent steps need to be made in creating environmental legislation that deals, specifically, with tourism development, and also ensuring that legislation is enforced.

Apart from the importance of preserving natural environments, more broadly, the issue, in the adventure tourism context, which has been witnessed in other parts of the world, is that increased development can result in the destruction of the primary attraction of the tourism product (Nepal, 2003; Njoroge, 2014; Spenceley, 2005). Therefore, the implementation of environmental management techniques is necessary to ensure the sustainability of the vast majority of adventure tourism products found in Africa. Already, there is evidence of the degradation of certain attractions such as Kilimanjaro (Hemp, 2008) and many reef systems in which scuba diving occurs (Gossling et al., 2008; Hasler & Ott, 2008). In addition, changing global climate patterns have already had significant impacts on tourism in Africa, more broadly (Giddy, Fitchett, & Hoogendoorn, 2017b; Hoogendoorn & Fitchett, 2016). In the case of adventure tourism, more specifically, changing weather conditions can have severe impacts on operations due to their reliance on specific natural features. Giddy, Fitchett, and Hoogendoorn (2017a) found that the 2015 drought which hit parts of South Africa, significantly impacted the white-water rafting industry, causing the closure of several operations. Therefore, the fragility of the natural environment and the vulnerability of adventure tourism operations to changes in natural features, landscapes, and resources need to be more carefully considered in tourism development strategies which often prioritize economic development.

Conclusions

Adventure travel experiences have a long history in Africa, beginning with early explorers to the continent, seeking out adventure experiences, and the subsequent leisure travelers which followed from the western world (Vivanco & Gordon, 2006). Clear leisure tourism has been documented particularly for American travelers who sought to experience "wild Africa" (McCabe, 1883; Wolf, 1991). Many of the experiences would fall under current definitions of adventure tourism and are therefore the earliest documented evidence of adventure travel on the continent. However, development of adventure tourism across the continent has been relatively uneven since, both geographically and in terms of products offered. The majority of adventure tourism experiences offered still fall under wildlife adventure tourism and related to experiencing and interacting with the unique wildlife prevalent throughout the continent, namely "safari" experiences, particularly in sub-Saharan Africa (Buckley, 2010). There is, however, great potential for adventure tourism development in many parts of the continent due to the unique and varied landscapes, many of which remain relatively pristine, and therefore ideal for adventure tourism experiences. Therefore, adventure tourism should be considered as a potential tool for economic development, particularly in rural areas. In addition, often minimal investment is needed, particularly in terms of infrastructure development, as adventure tourists typically seek "rugged" tourism experiences (Lian Chan & Baum, 2007).

The nature of adventure tourism experiences has, however, changed somewhat since the turn of the 21st century, with the rise of a wide range of adventure tourism products, particularly those which fall under the commercial adventure tourism sector (Giddy, 2018a). The emergence of commercial adventure tourism allows (particularly international) tourists to replicate some of the emotional states experienced by early travelers to the continent (Mathers & Hubbard, 2006). Therefore, this will likely continue to develop as a trend in tourism throughout Africa. It would be interesting if future research could delve into these emotional experiences of the "explorer" in the future to determine whether or not similar emotional states to those of early tourists to the continent can be replicated in today's modern world.

Despite the potential, there are still several barriers to developing adventure tourism in Africa which need to be addressed (Giddy, 2016b; Rogerson, 2007). The first is marketing adventure destinations cohesively and considering a strategic plan for developing compatible tourism products. The second is human resource development and management within adventure tourism, particularly in the promises to benefit local communities. Not only do the training mechanism and standardization need to increase, but also sustainable human resource management practices need to be implemented to deal with this concern. A third concern, which challenges the sustainability of adventure tourism development, is environmental management (Giddy, 2016a; McKay, 2013b). Environmental management has been noted previously as a critical issue facing the industry globally and is often exacerbated in countries of the global South as poor bureaucratic infrastructure exists for creating and managing environmental regulations linked specifically to tourism. Addressing these three concerns will be crucial to ensure the sustainable development of adventure tourism in the region.

Africa is often synonymous with thoughts of excitement, exoticism, and venturing into the unknown, especially for international tourists, all of which are indicators of adventure (Swarbrooke et al., 2003). For this reason, there are a number of adventure tourism opportunities on the continent. Nevertheless, currently they tend to be concentrated and focus on specific sectors. With the growth of tourism on the continent and increasing intracontinental tourism, there is a great deal of potential to further develop adventure tourism, particularly in relatively underdeveloped rural areas. Development of adventure tourism products does, however, need to be carefully planned and consider some of the above concerns particularly in terms of marketing, training, environmental management, and the inclusion of local communities. A great deal of additional research is needed on this important subsector. A broad approach to examining adventure tourism, as an entity, across Africa is of utmost importance in developing a deeper understanding of the phenomenon. In addition, further investigation into adventure tourism linkages with local communities as well as its real economic benefits would contribute significantly to the current academic discourse and assist future development.

References

Adventure Qualification Network. (n.d.). Adventure qualifications network. Retrieved February 17, 2019, from https://www.adventure-qualifications.com/

Anderson, W. (2015). Cultural tourism and poverty alleviation in rural Kilimanjaro, Tanzania. *Journal of Tourism and Cultural Change, 13*(3), 208–224.

Baker, J. E. (1997). Trophy hunting as a sustainable use of wildlife resources in Southern and Eastern Africa. *Journal of Sustainable Tourism, 5*(4), 306–321.

Beedie, P. (2001). Mountain guiding and adventure tourism: Reflections on the choreography of the experience. *Leisure Studies, 22*(2), 147–167.

Bell, C., & Lyall, J. (2002). The accelerated sublime: Thrill-seeking adventure heroes in the commodified landscape. In Coleman and Crang (Eds.) *Tourism: Between Place and Performance* (pp. 21–37). New York: Berghahn Books.

Bentley, T., & Page, S. J. (2001). Scoping the extent of adventure tourism accidents. *Annals of Tourism Research, 28*(3), 705–726.

Buckley, R. (2007). Adventure tourism products: Price, duration, size, skill, remoteness. *Tourism Management, 28*(6), 1428–1433.

Buckley, R. (2010). *Adventure Tourism Management*. Amsterdam: Butterworth-Heinemann.

Buckley, R. (2012). Rush as a key motivation in skilled adventure tourism: Resolving the risk recreation paradox. *Tourism Management, 33*(4), 961–970.

Carnicelli-Filho, S. (2013). The emotional life of adventure guides. *Annals of Tourism Research, 43*, 192–209. https://doi.org/10.1016/j.annals.2013.05.003

Carnicelli-Filho, S., Schwartz, G. M., & Tahara, A. K. (2010). Fear and adventure tourism in Brazil. *Tourism Management, 31*(6), 953–956.

Carruthers, J. (2007). 'South Africa: A world in one country': Land restitution in national parks and protected areas. *Conservation and Society, 5*(3), 292–306.

Cater, C. I. (2006). Playing with risk? Participant perceptions of risk and management implications in adventure tourism. *Tourism Management, 27*(2), 317–325.

Cheng, M., Edwards, D., Darcy, S., & Redfern, K. (2018). A tri-method approach to a review of adventure tourism literature: Bibliometric analysis, content analysis, and a quantitative systematic literature review. *Journal of Hospitality & Tourism Research, 42*(6), 997–1020. https://doi.org/10.1177/1096348016640588

Dieke, P. U. C. (2003). Tourism in Africa's economic development: Policy implications. *Management Decision, 41*(3), 287–295.

Dobson, J. (2007). Shark! A new frontier in tourist demand for marine wildlife. In J. Higham & M. Luck (Eds.), *Marine Wildlife and Tourism Management: Insights from the Natural and Social Sciences* (pp. 49–65). Wallingford: CABI.

Dugard, M. (2003). *Into Africa : The Epic Adventures of Stanley and Livingstone*. Charnwood: Charnwood Series.

Ewert, A. (1985). Why people climb: The relationship of participant motives and experience level to mountaineering. *Journal of Leisure Research, 17*(3), 241–250.

Fluker, M. R., & Turner, L. W. (2000). Needs, motivations, and expectations of a commercial whitewater rafting experience. *Journal of Travel Research, 38*(4), 380–389.

Frömming, U. U., & Undine, U. (2009). Kilimanjaro's melting glaciers: On the colonial and postcolonial perception and appropriation of African nature1. *Etnográfica, 13*(2), 395–416.

Gardner, B. (2016). *Selling the Serengeti: The Cultural Politics of Safari Tourism*. Athens, Georgia: University of Georgia Press.

Geldenhuys, L.-L., van der Merwe, P., & Slabbert, E. (2014). Who is the scuba diver that visits Sodwana Bay and why? *South African Journal for Research in Sport, Physical Education and Recreation, 36*(2), 91–104.

Giddy, J. K. (2016a). Adventure tourism in South Africa: Challenges and prospects. *Tourism*, *64*(4), 451–455

Giddy, J. K. (2016b). Environmental values and behaviours of adventure tourism operators : The case of the Tsitsikamma, South Africa. *African Journal of Hospitality, Tourism and Leisure*, *5*(4), 1–19.

Giddy, J. K. (2018a). A profile of commercial adventure tourism participants in South Africa. *Anatolia*, *29*(1), 40–51.

Giddy, J. K. (2018b). Adventure tourism motivations: A push and pull factor approach. *Bulletin of Geography: Socio-Economic Series*, *42*, 47–58.

Giddy, J. K. (2019). Insight into adventure tourism employment in South Africa. In Ndiuini, A. and Baum, T. (Eds.), *Sustainable Human Resource Management in Tourism in Africa* (pp. 189–204). Cham: Springer Publishing.

Giddy, J. K., Fitchett, J. M., & Hoogendoorn, G. (2017a). A case study into the preparedness of white-water tourism to severe climatic events in Southern Africa. *Tourism Review International*, *21*(2), 213–220.

Giddy, J. K., Fitchett, J. M., & Hoogendoorn, G. (2017b). Insight into American tourists' experiences with weather in South Africa. *Bulletin of Geography: Socio-Economic Series*, *38*, 57–71.

Giddy, J. K., & Rogerson, C. M. (2018). Tracking SCUBA diving adventure tourism in South Africa euroeconomica. *EuroEconomica*, *37*(1), 47–62.

Giddy, J. K., & Webb, N. L. (2016). The influence of the environment on motivations to participate in adventure tourism: The case of the Tsitsikamma. *South African Geographical Journal*, *98*(2), 351–366

Giddy, J. K., & Webb, N. L. (2018a). The influence of the enviornment on adventure tourism: From motivations to experiences. *Current Issues in Tourism*, *21*(18), 2124–2138.

Giddy, J. K., & Webb, N. L. (2018b). Environmental attitudes and adventure tourism motivations. *GeoJournal*, *83*(2), 275–287.

Gossling, S., Linden, O., Helmersson, J., Liljenberg, J., & Quarm, S. (2008). Diving and global environmental change: A Mauritius case study. In B. Garrod & S. Gössling (Eds.), *New Frontiers in Marine Tourism: Diving Experiences, Sustainability, Management* (pp. 67–90). London: Routledge.

Hall, C. (1992). Adventure, sport and health tourism. In C. M. Hall & B. Weiler (Eds.), *Special Interest Tourism*. London: Belhaven Press. (pp. 141–158)

Hasler, H., & Ott, J. A. (2008). Diving down the reefs? Intensive diving tourism threatens the reefs of the northern Red Sea. *Marine Pollution Bulletin*, *56*(10), 1788–1794.

Hawkins, J. P., & Roberts, C. M. (1993). Effects of recreational scuba diving on coral reefs: Trampling on reef-flat communities. *The Journal of Applied Ecology*, *30*(1), 25.

Hemp, A. (2008). Introduced plants on Kilimanjaro: Tourism and its impact. *Plant Ecology*, *197*(1), 17–29.

Holyfield, L. (1999). Manufacturing adventure: The buying and selling of emotions. *Journal of Contemporary Ethnography*, *28*(1), 3–32.

Hoogendoorn, G., & Fitchett, J. M. (2016). Tourism and climate change: A review of threats and adaptation strategies for Africa. *Current Issues in Tourism*, *21*(7), 742–759.

Kane, M. J., & Tucker, H. (2004). Adventure tourism: The freedom to play with reality. *Tourist Studies*, *4*(3), 217–234.

Kaseva, M. E., & Moirana, J. L. (2010). Problems of solid waste management on Mount Kilimanjaro: A challenge to tourism. *Waste Management & Research*, *28*(8), 695–704.

Lew, A. A. (2013). A world geography of recreational scuba diving. In G. Musa & K. Dimmock (Eds.), *Scuba Diving Tourism* (pp. 29–51). New York: Routledge.

Lian Chan, J. K., & Baum, T. (2007). Ecotourists' perception of ecotourism experience in Lower Kinabatangan, Sabah, Malaysia. *Journal of Sustainable Tourism*, *15*(5), 574–590. https://doi.org/10.2167/jost679.0

Lindsey, P. A., Alexander, R., Frank, L. G., Mathieson, A., & Romanach, S. S. (2006). Potential of trophy hunting to create incentives for wildlife conservation in Africa where alternative wildlife-based land uses may not be viable. *Animal Conservation*, *9*(3), 283–291.

Lindsey, P. A., Roulet, P. A., & Romañach, S. S. (2007). Economic and conservation significance of the trophy hunting industry in sub-Saharan Africa. *Biological Conservation*, *134*(4), 455–469.

Lucrezi, S., Saayman, M., & van der Merwe, P. (2013a). Managing diving impacts on reef ecosystems: Analysis of putative influences of motivations, marine life preferences and experience on divers' environmental perceptions. *Ocean & Coastal Management*, *76*, 52–63.

Lucrezi, S., Saayman, M., & Van Der Merwe, P. (2013b). Perceived Diving Impacts and Management Implications at a Popular South African Reef. *Coastal Management*, *41*(5), 381–400.

Lwonga, N. B. (2011). *Tourism: Meaning, Practices and History*. Dar es Salaam, Tanzania: Dar es Salaam University Press.

Macdonald, D., Jacobsen, K., Burnham, D., Johnson, P., & Loveridge, A. (2016). Cecil: A moment or a movement? Analysis of media coverage of the death of a lion, Panthera leo. *Animals*, 6(5), 26.

MacGregor, D. (2000, March 27). Survivor describes storms river horror. *IOL South Africa*. Retrieved from http://www.iol.co.za/news/south-africa/survivor-describes-storms-river-horror-33378 [Accessed on 20 August, 2020]

Mackenzie, S. H., & Kerr, J. H. (2012). A (mis) guided adventure tourism experience : An autoethnographic analysis of mountaineering in Bolivia. *Journal of Sport & Tourism*, 17(2), 125–144.

Mafuru, N., Wakibara, J., & Ndesar, K. (2009). Tourism-related impacts on Mount Kilimanjaro, Tanzania: Implications for tourism management on mountain ecosystems. *Journal of Tourism Challenges and Trends*, 2(1), 111–123.

Mathers, K., & Hubbard, L. (2006). Doing Africa: Travelers, adventurers, and American conquests of Africa. In L. Vivanco & R. Gordon (Eds.), *Tarzan Was an Eco-Tourist:...and Other Tales in the Anthropology of Adventure* (pp. 197–214). New York: Berghahn Books.

McCabe, J. D. (1883). *Our Young Folks in Africa: The Adventures of a Party of Young Americans in Algeria and in South Central Africa*. Philadelphia: J.B. Lippincott & Company, Ed.

McKay, T. (2013a). Adventure tourism: Opportunities and management challenges for SADC destinations. *Acta Academica*, 45(3), 30–62.

McKay, T. (2013b). Development and land use conflicts on the Ash River, South Africa : Energy provision versus adventure tourism, *African Journal for Physical Health Education*, 19(3), 276–293.

McKay, T. (2014). Locating South Africa within the global adventure tourism industry : The case of bungee jumping. *Bulletin of Geography*, 24, 161–176.

McKay, T. (2016). The geography of the South African adventure tourism industry. *African Journal of Hospitality, Tourism and Leisure*, 5(3), 1–21.

Mewshaw, M. (2010). *Between Terror and Tourism : An Overland Journey across North Africa*. Berkley: Counterpoint Press.

Minja, G. S. (2015). Ecological and socioeconomic implications of climate change and variability on tourism in Kilimanjaro Mountain National Park, Tanzania. *European Scientific Journal*, 11(35), 409–423.

Mitchell, J., Keane, J., & Laidlaw, J. (2009). *Making Success Work for the Poor: Package Tourism in Northern Tanzania*. Arusha, Tanzania: SNV Netherlands Development Organisation.

Mograbi, J., & Rogerson, C. M. (2007). Maximising the local pro-poor impacts of dive tourism: Sodwana Bay, South Africa. *Urban Forum*, 18(2), 85–104.

Nelson, M. P., Bruskotter, J. T., Vucetich, J. A., & Chapron, G. (2016). Emotions and the ethics of consequence in conservation decisions: Lessons from cecil the lion. *Conservation Letters*, 9(4), 302–306.

Nepal, S. (2003). *Tourism and the Environment: Perspectives from the Nepal Himalaya*. Wien: Himal.

news24. (2012). Tourist survives vic falls bungee horror. Retrieved September 14, 2018, from https://www.news24.com/World/News/Tourist-survives-Vic-Falls-bungee-horror-20120109

Njoroge, J. M. (2014). An enhanced framework for regional tourism sustainable adaptation to climate change. *Tourism Management Perspectives*, 12(July), 23–30.

Nomad Africa Adventure Tours. (2018). Nomad Africa adventure tours. Retrieved September 14, 2018, from https://nomadtours.co.za/

Novelli, M., Barnes, J. I., & Humavindu, M. (2006). The other side of the ecotourism coin: Consumptive tourism in Southern Africa. *Journal of Ecotourism*, 5(1–2), 62–79.

NSRI. (2015). Belgian dies in flash flood while kloofing. Retrieved September 14, 2018, from http://www.nsri.org.za/2015/03/belgian-man-dies-in-flash-flood-while-kloofing/

Overland Africa. (2018). Travel overland on an adventure holiday. Retrieved September 14, 2018, from https://www.overlandafrica.com/

Pomfret, G., & Bramwell, B. (2014). The characteristics and motivational decisions of outdoor adventure tourists: A review and analysis. *Current Issues in Tourism*, 19(14), 1447–1478.

Prince, H., & Loynes, C. (2016). Adventure, nature and commodification. In Convery, I. and Davis, P. (Eds.), *Changing Perceptions of Nature* (pp. 227–233). Heritage Matters Series, 18. Woodbridge: Boydell & Brewer.

Prior, M., Ormond, R., Hitchen, R., & Wormald, C. (1995). The impact on natural resources of activity tourism: A case study of diving in Egypt. *International Journal of Environmental Studies*, 48(3–4), 201–209.

Puchan, H. (2004). Living ' extreme ': Adventure sports, media and commercialisation. *Journal of Communication Management*, 9(2), 171–178.

Rantala, O., Hallikainen, V., Ilola, H., & Tuulentie, S. (2018). The softening of adventure tourism. *Scandinavian Journal of Hospitality and Tourism*, *18*(4), 343–361. https://doi.org/10.1080/15022250.2 018.1522725

Rantala, O., Rokenes, A., & Valkonen, J. (2018). Is adventure tourism a coherent concept? A review of research approaches on adventure tourism. *Annals of Leisure Research*, *21*(5), 539–552. https://doi. org/10.1080/11745398.2016.1250647

Raspaud, M. (2014). The transformations of values and aspirations by adventure tourism in Nepal : Example through the figures of three Sherpa, *Revista Turismo em Análise*, *25*(2), 373–391.

Rickly, J. M., & Vidon, E. S. (2017). Contesting authentic practice and ethical authority in adventure tourism. *Journal of Sustainable Tourism*, *25*(10), 1418–1433. https://doi.org/10.1080/09669582.2017 .1284856

Rogerson, C. M. (2004). Adventure tourism in Africa : The case of Livingstone, Zambia. *Geography*, *89*(2), 183–188.

Rogerson, C. M. (2005). The emergence of tourism-led local development : The example of Living-stone, Zambia. *Africa Insight*, *35*(4), 112–120.

Rogerson, C. M. (2007). The challenges of developing adventure tourism in South Africa. *Africa Insight*, *37*(2), 228–244.

Rogerson, C. M. (2012). The Tourism – Development Nexus in sub-Saharan Africa, *Africa Insight*, *42*(2), 28–45.

Saal, P. (2017). Injured tourist rescued after 14-hour ordeal in mountain kloof. Retrieved September 14, 2018, from https://www.timeslive.co.za/news/south-africa/2017-08-15-injured-tourist-rescued-after-14-hour-ordeal-in-mountain-kloof/

Saarinen, J., Becker, F., Manwa, H., & Wilson, D. (2009). *Sustainable Tourism in Southern Africa: Local Communities and Natural Resources in Transition*. Bristol: Channel View Publications.

Saayman, A., & Saayman, M. (2008). Determinants of inbound tourism to South Africa. *Tourism Economics*, *14*(1), 81–96.

Salkeld, A. (2002). *Kilimanjaro: To the Roof of Africa*. Washington DC: National Geographic Society.

Shearwater Bungee. (2017). Home - shearwater bungee. Retrieved September 14, 2018, from http:// shearwaterbungee.com/

Shoham, A., Rose, G. M., & Kahle, L. R. (2000). Practitioners of risky Sports : A quantitative examination. *Journal of Business Research*, *47*, 237–251.

Spenceley, A. (2005). Nature-based tourism and environmental sustainability in South Africa. *Journal of Sustainable Tourism*, *13*(2), 136–170.

Swarbrooke, J., Beard, C., Leckie, S., & Pomfret, G. (2003). *Adventure Tourism: A New Frontier*. Oxford: Elsevier.

Tarver, R., Cohen, K., Klyve, D., & Liseki, S. (2019). Sustainable safari practices: Proximity to wild-life, educational intervention, and the quality of experience. *Journal of Outdoor Recreation and Tourism*, *25*, 76–83. https://doi.org/10.1016/J.JORT.2019.01.001

Taylor, S., Varley, P., & Johnston, T. (2013). *Adventure Tourism: Meanings, Experience and Learning*. Abingdon: Routledge.

Tourism on the Edge. (2017). Tandem skydiving over Kilimanjaro. Retrieved September 17, 2018, from https://www.tourismontheedge.com/get-extreme/tandem-sky-diving-over-kilimanjaro

Varley, P. (2006). Confecting adventure and playing with meaning: The adventure commodification continuum. *Journal of Sport & Tourism*, *11*(2), 173–194.

Vivanco, L., & Gordon, R. J. (2006). *Tarzan Was an Eco-Tourist: ...and Other Tales in the Anthropology of Adventure*. New York: Berghahn Books.

Walle, A. H. (1997). Pursuing risk or insight: Marketing adventures. *Annals of Tourism Research*, *24*(2), 265–282.

Weber, K. (2001). Outdoor adventure tourism: A review of research approaches. *Annals of the Association of American Geographers*, *28*(2), 360–377.

Williams, P., & Soutar, G. N. (2005). Close to the "edge": Critical issues for adventure tourism operators. *Asia Pacific Journal of Tourism Research*, *10*(3), 37–41.

Wolf, J. B. (1991). A grand tour: South Africa and American tourists between the wars. *Journal of Popular Culture*, *25*(2), 99–116.

Yogerst, J. (2017). 10 of Africa's best water adventures. Retrieved September 17, 2018, from https:// edition.cnn.com/travel/article/africa-water-adventures/index.html

6

Tourism and climate change in Africa

Wame L. Hambira and Joseph E. Mbaiwa

Introduction

Sustainable tourism is one of the fundamental focus areas in the realisation of the global agenda for sustainable development as outlined in Sustainable Development Goals 8, target 8.9 and 12, target 12b (United Nations, 2015). Subsequently, the United Nations (UN) flagged 2017 as the International Year of Sustainable Tourism for Development. The main aim of the UN was that of promoting a change in policies, business practices and consumer behaviour towards a more sustainable tourism sector. Notwithstanding the foregoing, climate change poses a threat to natural capital, the impetus for nature-based tourism. The Intergovernmental Panel for Climate Change (IPCC, 2014a) accentuates that the evidence of climate change is most pronounced in natural systems. Tourism thus is closely related to the environment and climate itself (Uchegbu & Kanu, 2013). Climate change brings with it challenges associated with temperature increases, sea-level rise and changes in precipitation all of which have a bearing on the natural capital pivotal for tourism.

Projections for an increase in temperature under medium scenarios revealed that some parts of Africa will exceed 2°C towards the end of the century compared to the late 20th century mean annual temperature (United Nations Environment Programme (UNEP) & African Ministerial Conference on Environment (AMCEN), n.d.). Warmer temperatures are a potential source of a rapid shift in ecosystem ranges leading to loss of biodiversity, accelerated woody plant encroachment resulting in limited grazing options. On the other hand, sea-level rise along the Indian and Atlantic oceans is expected to be around 80 cm above 2,000 by 2,100 under the 4°C scenarios (and 40 cm above 2,000 by 2,100 in a below−2°C scenario) putting coastal cities of Mozambique, Tanzania, Cameroon, Egypt, Senegal and Morocco at risk of flooding (UNEP & AMCEN, n.d.). Changing precipitation, melting snow and ice as well as shrinking of glaciers alter hydrological systems, thereby affecting the quality and quantity of water resources (IPCC, 2014a). Consequently, the geographic ranges, seasonal activities, migration patterns and abundance of many terrestrial, freshwater and marine species have shifted (IPCC, 2014a). Climate change also results in increased frequency of extreme weather events characterised by droughts heat waves, floods, cyclones and wildfires the consequences of which have revealed the vulnerability and exposure of some ecosystems and human systems (IPCC, 2014a). Warming makes heat waves longer, stronger and more frequent; droughts more intense by drying out and heating up land that is suffering from reduced precipitation; puts more water vapour in the atmosphere making wet areas of the world wetter and deluges become more intense and more frequent; raises sea levels making devastating storm surges more likely (Romm, 2018). The consequences include extreme summertime temperatures; loss of biodiversity and natural attractions; disruption of food production and water supply; as well as damage to infrastructure (IPCC, 2014a).

Since climate change is actually the change in mean and variability of climatic properties that persists for an extended period of time (IPCC, 2014); response measures may tend to be reactive than proactive. Responses may also be delayed by the continuing uncertainty about the severity and timing of climate change impacts (see IPCC, 2014a). Timely response measures are however imperative given that some impacts if left unchecked may cause severe, pervasive and irreversible harm to unique and threatened species globally and regionally (see IPCC, 2014a). The two response measures comprise efforts geared towards reducing sources of GhG emissions or enhancing sinks and reservoirs (collectively known as mitigation) as well as those aimed at moderating or avoiding harm or exploiting beneficial opportunities with respect to expected climate and its effects (commonly referred to as adaptations) (IPCC, 2014b; Mayer, 2018; United Nations, 1992). Arguments have been made in favour of adaptation especially for developing countries such as those in the African continent. Some of the reasons advanced are that developing countries are the most affected by climate change whereas they contribute the least to global emission and the least able to afford adaptation efforts (see Scott et al., 2012).

Climate change is likely to continue for centuries to come in the process of changing human and animal life patterns (Uchegbu & Kanu, 2013). This makes tourism led economies especially vulnerable and ultimately their sustainability is questionable unless appropriate and timely action is taken by all tourism stakeholders. This chapter therefore reviews the tourism-climate change nexus as it applies to the African continent. The objectives of the review are to determine the following: the focus of tourism-climate change nexus research in Africa; major tourism destinations that have been or in danger of being affected; and existing climate policy responses by various relevant stakeholders.

Geographical distribution of Africa's nature-based tourism attractions and related climate change impacts

Tourism is geographical in nature in that it occurs in places and involves movement and activities across space (Lew et al., 2008). African countries have now become major tourism growth areas (Uchegbu & Kanu, 2013). In the early 2000s, Southern Africa received the most international tourists followed by East Africa, while North Africa's tourism had not evolved into a major economic growth engine compared to other parts of Africa owing to cultural and religious ideologies which view tourism in a bad light (Lew et al., 2008). In recent years, however, international tourism trends highlight a strong recovery of the industry in North Africa especially in Tunisia and Morocco (United Nations World Tourism Organisation (UNWTO), 2018). In sub-Saharan Africa, good performance was realised from Kenya, Cote d'Ivoire, Mauritius and Zimbabwe while South Africa, the sub-region's top destination was reported to have had a slow growth in 2017 (UNWTO, 2018).

Climate change affects the various geographical areas which form the basis for nature-based tourism and hence the effects are already being felt in coastal zones, wildlife areas and fresh-water ecosystems resulting in changes in the ecosystems and natural resources needed to sustain the tourism economy.

Coastal zones and freshwater ecosystems

With current predictions of climate change and sea-level rise, beaches that have become synonymous with tourism are under significant threat of erosion worldwide (Uchegbu & Kanu, 2013). This is also exacerbated by the fact that coral reefs, a source of white sand that prevents beach erosion, are inundated by bleaching, also resulting from climate change (see Ahmed & Hefny, 2007; Wielgus et al., 2010). Rising sea levels, from melting of polar ice caps and frequency of storms cause beach erosion and places like Barbeach in Lagos Nigeria have been affected (Uchegbu & Kanu, 2013). Impacts include beach erosion, saline intrusion, flash floods, landslides and coral reef bleaching (Uchegbu & Kanu, 2013). Coral reefs are highly sensitive to climate change since they can only withstand a narrow temperature range (Ahmed & Hefny, 2007). The coastal town of Mombasa, Kenya for example is already being affected by extreme climatic events such as floods, droughts and strong winds (Awuor et al., 2008). Some of the best beach tourist destinations are found in Kenya, Malawi, Mozambique, Madagascar, Tanzania, South Africa, Egypt, Seychelles, Mauritius, Namibia, Gabon, Ghana, Sao Tome and Principe, Sierra Leone, Senegal, Cape Verde, Morocco and Tunisia.

In terms of freshwater ecosystems, prominent wetlands on the African continent situated between 15°N and 20°S include the Okavango Delta of Botswana, the Sudd in the Upper Nile, Lake Victoria basin and Lake Chad basin, and the floodplains and deltas of the Congo, Niger and Zambezi rivers; riverine systems of the Nile, Niger, Zaire and Zambezi; Rift valley lakes comprising of Victoria, Tanganyika, Nyasa, Turkana, Mweru and Albert (Kabii, n.d.). East Africa is garlanded with the Great Lakes of Africa emanating from the Great Rift Valley. According to CNN Travel (2018a), the most amazing places to visit in Africa include Victoria Falls of Zambia and Zimbabwe, Wonder of the Nile (includes a cruise down the Egyptian Nile), Flamingos Kenya (Lake Nakuru National Park), Zambia's Lower Zambezi, Fish River Canyon of Namibia and Lake Malawi. On-going climate change has resulted in freshwater species (among others), shifting their geographic ranges, seasonal activities, migration patterns, abundances and species interactions (IPCC, 2014a).

Vegetation, wildlife, protected areas and mountainous places

The rate at which climate change occurs impedes the natural ability of living organisms to adapt to the changes hence some species are threatened by extinction (Nakaya, 2017). Vegetation and animals prevalent in a particular place are influenced by the climate (humidity, precipitation, temperature) and the geomorphology thereof (Lew et al., 2008). Hence the bio-geographical distribution of natural vegetation is such that: Irish green vegetation such as that found in tropical rain forests prevails in high humidity and high-temperature areas; while low humidity and high temperatures are associated with arid, desert vegetation; the lowest temperature regions, on the other hand, are adorned with spruce coniferous trees and tundra type of grass; finally in between the three extremes lies a mixture of evergreen trees, deciduous trees and grasslands (Lew et al., 2008). Global warming has resulted in a decline in vegetation causing wildlife to migrate to areas that still have water (Uchegbu & Kanu, 2013).

East Africa is popular for safari tourism which involves viewing big game in the wild with Kenya being the most visited country in this part of Africa (Lew et al., 2008). Most of Africa's wildlife is found in protected areas which many African countries have adopted for in-situ conservation which is becoming more challenging with the advent of climate change resulting in species range dynamics due to possible range shifts (Monzón et al., 2011; Pettorelli et al., 2012; Tanner-McAllister et al., 2017). CNN Travel (2018b) regard the Serengeti National Park of Tanzania, Kidepo Valley National Park of Uganda, Hwange National Park of Zimbabwe, Samburu National Reserve in Kenya, Botswana's Kalahari Desert, Zambia's South Luangwa National Park and Kafue National Park, Etosha National Park of Namibia and the Kruger National Park of South Africa as eight of the best safari destinations in Africa.

Mountain tourism is also important in Africa. In east Africa for example, there is the mountain region of Kenya, Tanzania, Uganda, Rwanda, Burundi and the Democratic Republic of Congo. These mountains are closely linked to the East African Rift system and offer tourist attractions of Kilimanjaro National Park, moorland zone of the Aberdares, the Kenya section of Mount Elgon; Virunga Mountains comprising of the Kigezi Gorilla Game Reserve on the slopes of Mounts Muhavura and Mgahinga on the Ugandan side while the Volcanoes National Park and the Virunga National Park are found on the Rwanda and Congo portions of the Virunga Mountains (Kalinga & Baker, 2018). In southern Africa, the highest mountain range is the Drakensburg, a primary tourist destination in South Africa (Linde & Grab, 2008). Mountain areas are sensitive to climate change which manifests itself in the form of decrease in snow cover, shrinking of glaciers, melting permafrost and increased frequency of extreme events such as landslides; ultimately economic activities such tourism are affected (Bürki et al., 2003; Uchegbu & Kanu, 2013). For example, winter sport activities have also been affected by climate change due to a decrease in snow cover and shrinking of glaciers, which has resulted in altered winter sport seasons and landscape aesthetics (Uchegbu & Kanu, 2013). This has happened in places like Tiffendell, the highest mountain peak in the Cape and a ski resort in South Africa and, Mount Kilimanjaro in Tanzania (Lew et al., 2008; Uchegbu & Kanu, 2013).

Responses: climate change adaptation and mitigation

In order for the tourism sector to survive the vagaries of climate change there is need for appropriate mechanisms aimed at minimising the impacts on the tourism sector or the contribution of the sector to emissions that result in climate change. "Africa is the continent where rapidly changing climate will deviate from "normal" earlier than across any other continent, making adaptation a matter of utmost urgency" (UNEP & AMCEN, n.d., p.V). Adaptation measures are influenced by the type of tourism subsector, activities offered and the destination in question (Hernandez & Ryan, 2011). The measures may be technical, e.g. artificial snow making, access to early warning equipment; managerial, e.g. product and market diversification, impact management plans; policy, e.g. regulatory compliance, building design standards; research, e.g. assessment of business and tourism knowledge gaps; education, e.g. water and energy conservation training for clients and employees; and behavioural, e.g. greenhouse emissions offset programs, good practice in-house (Hernandez & Ryan, 2011; Simpson et al., 2008). However, adaptation costs of African countries are expected to rise under different scenarios. For example, projections predict that costs could rise to USD50 billion per year (less than 1%of GDP) by 2050 under the below 2°C scenario while it could double by 2,100 in the case of a 4°C warming which would amount to 6% of African GDP (UNEP & AMCEN, n.d). Therefore, limiting the rate and magnitude of climate change is one way of reducing the overall risks of climate change impacts and by so doing, reducing the required scale of adaptation (IPCC, 2014b).

Strategies that may be assumed by the tourism sector for climate change mitigation include government economic policies aimed at raising the price of greenhouse gas emissions or subsidising the price of carbon-free energy sources, e.g. carbon tax or cap and trade system, inclusion of air transport in emission trade systems; increasing the use of clean energy or reducing the emissions of GHGs, e.g. fuel economy standards, design aircrafts that with low fuel consumption levels, alternative fuels; modification of operational procedures for landing and take-off; technological (research-based) policies aimed at lowering the cost and improving the performance of low-carbon sources, e.g. LED lighting, solar panels, room keys to operate lights, light sensors, promoting energy consciousness and energy saving behaviour on the part of the tourist and tourism industry employees (Becken 2005; Chapman, 2007; Hernandez & Ryan, 2011; Mendes & Santos, 2008; Romm, 2018; Scheelhaase & Grimme, 2007).

As illustrated earlier, adaptation and mitigation measures overlap and therefore always advisable to adopt both categories of climate change response measures. Scholars have however observed that the capacity of the continent to cope with the challenges posed by climate change is still wanting as domestic resources and current international funding are not sufficient (Kunreuther et al., 2014; Ojekunle et al., 2013; Scott et al., 2012; UNEP & AMCEN, n.d).

Review protocol: methods

The purpose of the review was to determine and synthesise information available in relation to nature-based tourism and climate change nexus in Africa. The systematic literature review method was applied to answer the following questions: what is the focus of tourism-climate change nexus research in Africa; which major tourism destinations have been affected; what climate policy responses exist and what are the gaps? The procedure followed in conducting the narrative review was adapted after Xiao and Watson (2017) and entailed literature search where electronic databases were the main point of reference particularly Google Scholar and Science Direct and Google while recommendations by colleagues were also taken into consideration. The inclusion criteria were based on academic research published in international journals and specifically addressed issues of tourism climate change nexus based on the research questions of the study. The papers were therefore screened based on keywords such as climate change, tourism, impacts, policy and Africa. The keywords informed data extraction which were synthesised and reported with particular reference to the research questions. Ultimately, there were 81 documentary records identified 81; following screening, 8 were removed since there were no full texts; from the 73 that remained, 39 were excluded (24 did not adequately address issues pertaining to the African continent; 11 touched on economic sectors in general and information pertaining to the tourism sector was tacit; 3 addressed climatic issues but not climate change per se; 1 was a review hence excluded to avoid duplication); leaving 35 that met the criterion for assessment.

Findings

The review resulted in 14 papers dealing with perceptions, views, understanding, awareness, knowledge and attitudes of various stakeholders towards climate change-tourism nexus, 12 papers on impacts of climate change on tourism destinations, nine papers dealing with policy responses by tourism stakeholders towards climate change, four on knowledge inquiry and methodological issues surrounding research in tourism-climate change nexus and one paper investigating the vulnerability of a tourism destination. Some of the papers fell in more than one category (see Table 6.1).

Table 6.1 Research focus on tourism climate change-nexus in Africa

Paper	Description
Vulnerability, threats	
1 Hambira (2011)	To determine the extent to which the tourism sector in Botswana is vulnerable to climate change.
Impacts	
1 Dube and Nhamo (2018a)	An examination of the evidence and potential implications of climate variability and change on tourism in the Zambian town of Livingstone.
2 Ahmed and Hefny (2007)	A determination of the impact of climate change on the Sinai (Egypt) environment and the need to take measures to meet the expected changes in order to maintain tourism industry in Sinai?
3 Steyn and Spencer (2012)	A focus on the relationship between climate and tourism, the likely effects of climate change on tourism in general, and highlights the projected impacts on South Africa. The planning implications of the expected impacts are also highlighted.
4 Sagoe-Addy and Addo (2013)	An assessment of the potential impact of enhanced sea-level rise for different IPCC scenarios on tourism facilities along Ghana's Accra coast.
5 Köberl et al. (2016)	This paper assesses the potential impacts of climate change on tourism demand in the case study regions Cap Bon, Tunisia (of Sardinia, Italy).
6 Darkoh et al. (2014)	An investigation of the trends and impacts of climate change as well as coping and adaptation strategies in Malawi, Botswana and Kenya.
7 Marshall et al. (2011)	A test of climate change impacts and tourism operators' awareness in the Red Sea region.
8 Dube and Nhamo (2018b)	An assessment of the evidence of climate variability and change and its potential impact on the global tourist resort of Victoria Falls, Zimbabwe.
9 Njoroge (2015c)	Consolidation of information on climate change impacts and vulnerability of Kenya's tourism industry to climate change. The paper further discusses the implication of climate change on the role of tourism in contributing to Millennium Development Goals.
10 Shaaban and Ramzy (2010)	An examination of the views of Egyptian policymakers and tourism managers on potential climate change impacts on Egypt's tourism industry, and their policies and action plans in response to such impacts.
11 Fitchett et al. (2016a)	An exploration of climate change threats and perceptions of these threats within the tourist sector in South Africa's coastal towns of St Francis and Cape St Francis.
12 Hambira (2017)	A determination of Botswana tourism operators and policymakers' perceptions and responses to the tourism-climate change nexus. Results touch on impacts of climate change as perceived by the policymakers and tourism operators.
Perceptions, views, understanding, awareness, knowledge, attitudes	
1 Becker (1998)	An examination of the way holidaymakers perceives thermal environmental conditions in some South African beach holiday resorts of Alexander Bay, Capetown, Port Elizabeth, East London, Durban and Richards Bay.
2 Gössling et al. (2006)	Perceptions of climate change by tourists visiting the island of Zanzibar in Tanzania.
3 Fitchett et al. (2016a)	An exploration of climate change threats and perceptions of these threats within the tourist sector in South Africa's coastal towns of St Francis and Cape St Francis.

(Continued)

Paper	Description
4 Dillimono and Dickinson (2015)	An analysis of Nigerian tourists' understanding of travel and tourism linkages to climate change.
5 Marshall et al. (2011)	A test of climate change impacts and tourism operators' awareness in the Red Sea region.
6 Saarinen et al. (2013)	A determination of the perceptions and ultimately the preparedness of tourism businesses with regard to the impending climate change impacts their operations in Maun and Tshabong, Botswana.
7 Hambira et al. (2013)	A determination of how the perceptions of the tourism operators have influenced their preparedness and responses to the impending climate change in Maun, Botswana.
8 Saarinen et al. (2012)	A determination of how the perceptions of the tourism operators have influenced their preparedness and responses to the impending climate change in Kgalagadi South District.
9 Hambira and Saarinen (2015)	A determination of the perceptions of policymakers and implications of the climate change tourism phenomenon in Botswana.
10 Shaaban and Ramzy (2010)	An examination of the views of Egyptian policymakers and tourism managers on potential climate change impacts on Egypt's tourism industry, and their policies and action plans in response to such impacts.
11 Njoroge (2015a)	A determination of tourism stakeholders' past account of environmental hazards and among other things perceptions of potential impacts of climate change in the coastal tourism region of Mombasa, Kenya.
12 Dube et al. (2018)	An examination of the understanding, perceptions, knowledge and attitude of the tourism industry's main stakeholders, the tourists, in light of the future of the tourism industry, in the context of climate.
13 Peck and Hedding (2014)	An exploration of the attitudes of domestic tourists in South Africa towards the introduction of a carbon tax, together with their knowledge and perceptions of climate change.
14 Hoogendoorn et al. (2016)	An exploration of the perceptions of tourists and tourist accommodation establishment operators regarding climate change threats to tourism for the towns of St Francis Bay and Cape St Francis.

Knowledge inquiry and knowledge production

1 Pandy (2017)	An examination of key debates in the nexus of tourism and climate change in order to identify research imperatives including for African scholars.
2 Fitchett et al. (2016b)	A determination of a viable approach of applying TCI for locations in which no sunshine hour data is available.
3 Rogerson (2016)	An examination of issues around climate change impacts for South Africa's tourism sector and in particular implications for local economic development.
4 Steyn and Spencer (2012)	A model proposal for the development of adaptive strategies based on existing impacts of climate change on tourism in Western Cape, South Africa and actions that can be taken to mitigate and adapt to the impacts of climate change.

Policy responses

1 Hambira et al. (2013)	A determination of the adaptation strategies that Botswana tourism operators have, or are planning to put in place, in order to cope with or benefit from climate change.
2 Gössling and Schumacher (2010)	An analysis of energy usage and emission levels in the Seychelles' tourism sector. Ways to reduce the emission levels with the aim of making the island state a carbon neutral destination were also explored.

Paper	Description
3 Gössling et al. (2008)	A review of emerging climate policies in major tourism outbound markets that have direct implications for the Aviation sector. The potential consequences for travel costs and tourism demand in ten tourism-dependent less developed island states including Madagascar and Seychelles were also determined.
4 Rogerson and Sims (2012)	A look into the greening of hotels in South Africa as part of the country's policy agenda on responsible tourism and climate change mitigation.
5 Njoroge (2015a)	A determination of tourism stakeholders' past account of environmental hazards and among other things their response strategies for a coastal tourism region of Mombasa, Kenya.
6 Dube and Mhamo (2018a)	An examination of the evidence and potential implications of climate variability and change on tourism in the Zambian town of Livingstone.
7 Shaaban and Ramzy (2010)	An examination of the views of Egyptian policymakers and tourism managers on potential climate change impacts on Egypt's tourism industry, and their policies and action plans in response to such impacts.
8 Saarinen et al. (2012)	A determination of how the perceptions of the tourism operators have influenced their preparedness and responses to the impending climate change in Kgalagadi South District.
9 Hoogendoorn et al. (2016)	An exploration of the perceptions of tourists and tourist accommodation establishment operators regarding climate change threats to tourism for the towns of St Francis Bay and Cape St Francis.
10 Mbaiwa and Mmopelwa (2009)	An assessment of the impact of climate change on tourism activities and their economic benefits in the Okavango Delta.

Source: Authors.

Tourism-climate change nexus research in Africa

Vulnerabilities and threats

The literature search unveiled one paper that attempted to investigate the vulnerability of a tourism destination. A screening of the Okavango Delta's vulnerability to climate change revealed that the delta was indeed vulnerable (Hambira, 2011). The study determined the extent to which the delta was vulnerable to climate change by screening changes in climatic variables; the physical environment and ecosystems; threats to livelihoods and socioeconomic issues; as well as weaknesses in governance structures.

Impacts

The research considered impacts in terms of observed evidence but mostly potential impacts on tourism destination. The impacts considered were about the sector in general, landscapes in which specific attractions were found, the economy of countries in relation to the contribution of tourism, tourism infrastructure, as well as tourism demand and management. The impacts were mostly expected from climate change drivers such as increased rainfall, extreme weather events, change in seasons and sea-level rise. Expected impacts from increased temperatures on the tourism industry comprise of reduced tourist comfort (Dube & Nhamo, 2018a, 2018b); climate-induced gains and losses, e.g. increased energy demand in summer and reduced energy costs in summer (Dube & Nhamo, 2018a; Köberl et al., 2016); reduced quality of tourism activities such as scenic flights/helicopter rides (Dube & Nhamo,

2018b; Hambira, 2017) and dive tourism (Shaaban & Ramzy, 2010). In terms of impacts from rising sea levels, the result showed that it would culminate in bleaching of coral reefs and salt intrusion (Ahmed & Hefny, 2007); and submergence of beaches and associated tourism infrastructure (Darkoh et al., 2014; Fitchett et al., 2016a; Njoroge, 2015c; Sagoe-Addy & Addo, 2013; Shaaban & Ramzy, 2010). Another interesting impact is that operators who are blind to industry perceptions and consequently fail to meet their needs are expected to lose clients to more responsive competitors (Marshall et al., 2011). On the other hand, change in seasons and water flows as a result of climate change is expected to alter tourism peak and off seasons (Dube & Nhamo 2018a). Extreme weather events are expected to increase in frequency and intensity due to climate change and the expected impacts on tourism include redistribution of tourism resources geographically and seasonally (Steyn & Spencer, 2012). Specific impacts on tourism activities, destinations and tourist attractions are detailed in the next main section of this chapter.

Perceptions and awareness of climate change impact on tourism

Studies under this category covered issues pertaining to various tourism stakeholders' perceptions (including attitudes and views) and awareness (including knowledge and understanding) of thermal conditions of tourism destinations as well as climate change impacts on destinations, business operations and the economy in general.

Based on the perceptions of beach holidaymakers, Becker (1998) developed a Beach Comfort Map of South Africa describing the maximum, minimum and average number of beach days per month and the probability of beach days and thus providing critical information on the thermal conditions of selected beach holiday resorts. People desiring to visit Cape Town in January for example can expect an average probability of more than 70% beach days while a winter holiday in Durban holds a 50% chance for beach days. Another study on thermal conditions was by Gössling et al. (2006) who investigated tourist's travel motives influenced by a mixture of climate-related considerations, incommensurate and convenience motives. The study revealed that a set of parameters comprising temperature, rainfall, humidity and storms affect comfort perceptions as opposed to temperature as a single parameter.

Regarding perceptions on climate change impact on destinations and business operations, Shaaban and Ramzy (2010) noted that many industry managers and policymakers shared views to the effect that damage to coastal tourism facilities was very likely due to sea-level rise. The managers however did not see this having an impact on the volume of tourists but rather on tourism patterns. Other disjunct views were found between tourists and tourist accommodation establishment representatives in St Francis Bay and Cape St Francis. The former were more concerned about the risk of flooding, sea-level rise and degeneration of beaches while the latter were more concerned with day-to-day changes in weather and subsequently the comfort of their guests (Hoogendoorn et al., 2016). Still in the adjacent coastal towns of St Francis Bay and Cape St Francis in the Eastern Cape province of South Africa, Fitchett et al. (2016a) further probed climate change perceptions of proprietors of accommodation establishments. Climate change was a cause for concern for 42 of the 53 respondents especially representatives of establishments located close to the coast and more than half of them believed that it would negatively affect the towns themselves due to their experiences with extreme weather events which damages infrastructure and compromised access to some tourism establishments. A low-level concern for the sea-level rise was noted, save for its immediacy and extent. Fitchett et al. (2016a) further posit that the government was perceived to be responsible for the provision of adaptation mechanisms hence they were not yet investing in infrastructural changes to address flooding induced by sea-level rise. Only small-scale adaptations to address the threats had been instituted but mainly focused on climatic suitability.

In terms of awareness and knowledge of climate change as pertains to the tourism sector, Dillimono and Dickinson (2015) targeted tourists who declared awareness of climate change. The results showed a rudimentary knowledge of the topic related to experience or observation such as seasonal changes. There were misconceptions about the causes of climate change with some answers pointing to ozone depletion which was also in some instances used interchangeably with climate change. The climate change concept was also confused with other environmental issues like earthquakes. The tourists did not see any linkages between their travel and climate change and were not willing to change their travel behaviours to reduce their carbon footprint. On the other hand, Marshall et al. (2011) reveal that climate change has an impact on the perceptions and choices of dive tourists as most of them were of the view that the coral reefs in the Egyptian Red Sea were already declining. The industry was not aware of the changes in the tourists' awareness and attitudes towards climate change.

Saarinen et al. (2013) and Hambira et al. (2013) noted in their research that even though the tourism operators in northern Botswana were aware of the general impacts of climate change, the majority of them did not perceive any critical impacts on their operations and the industry in general. This could explain why they barely had any adaptation measures in place. Most operators had observed changes in the physical environment, livelihoods and weather patterns that they linked to climate change. Consequently, operators rendering nature-based outdoor activities deemed their activities vulnerable to climate change as this would lead to loss of quality of attractions and consequently decline in tourist numbers. However, the operators holding this line of thought said they had not experienced any significant impacts on their activities as a result but anticipated the negative effects in the future. In many instances, there were no adaptation measures in place except for air conditioners which are not for climate change per se. Some mitigation efforts were also evident in some establishments, i.e. energy and water saving mechanisms. The lack of proactive stance could be attributed to lack of information and limited awareness on climate change-tourism nexus. Still in Northern Botswana, Dube et al. (2018) reported that the tourists were aware of the general causes of climate change and the implications of their actions on climate change. However, this awareness has not translated into meaningful actions to reduce their carbon footprint. They perceived water flow as well as flora and fauna of the Okavango Delta to have been altered by climate change. Similarly, Saarinen et al. (2012) showed how Tshabong operators in South Western Botswana, alluded to the fact that they were aware of climate change and that it has had effects on their physical environment but has not had an effect on their businesses and the activities they offer. Hence the operators were likely to react to climate change in terms of adaptation as opposed to being proactive due to the slowness of the climate change process and the uncertainties surrounding the nature of the impacts. Hambira and Saarinen (2015) focused on Botswana's policymakers and revealed that even though some were well aware of climate change and its possible impacts on the tourism industry, the following factors are likely to impede effective policy development: uncertainties surrounding climate change, information gaps, inadequate data and poor public awareness, challenges posed by poor coordination and indeed data capture and harmonisation by concerned institutions.

In Mombasa Kenya, Njoroge (2015a) highlighted that the tourism operator's general awareness and understanding of climate change were good even though there was no precise understanding of the scientific basis and few understood the implications of climate change. On the other hand, scientists, researchers, government officials and tourism-related officials were found well informed about climate change. Based on the claims of an alarmist report that Mombasa would sink due to climate change, the operators were not sure or confident about how their business operations would be affected should that materialise. In another study, Peck and Hedding (2014) posited that domestic tourists interviewed at OR Tambo International Airport in South Africa were said to have a good basic understanding of climate change but lacked in-depth knowledge on the natural causes of climate change and greenhouse gases. Many acknowledged aviation to be a major contributor to climate change and indicated they would consider paying a voluntary carbon tax but due to the concept of attitude-behaviour gap, the number of those who agree would in the end be much less. That is, even though the tourists agreed that they were part of the problem, they did not see themselves as part of the solution.

Knowledge inquiry and methodological issues

Some of the research uncovered the prevailing state of affairs regarding suitable methods and frameworks to employ when studying the nature and extent of climate variability and change as it applies to the tourism sector. Fitchett et al. (2016b) for example provided solutions to data challenges in the calculation of the Tourism Climate Index (TCI) scores in South Africa. While Pandy (2017) unravelled research imperatives in the tourism-climate change nexus including research conducted by African scholars and the research imperatives are: tourism enterprises' capacity to adapt to climate change; adaptive pathways need more attention compared to mitigation research whereas adaptation should be seen as complementary to mitigation issues; perceptions of key tourism industry stakeholders were pertinent in determining the extent to which they recognise the implications of climate change for their industry and the level of interests in particular mitigation actions. Rogerson (2016), on the other hand, examined issues around climate change impacts for South Africa's tourism sector and in particular implications for local economic development

Policy responses

In view of the impending effects of climate change on Africa, research has been conducted on what various tourism stakeholders have done in terms of adaptation strategies, adaptation needs, mitigation responses including how to reduce emission levels from energy use in tourism facilities, emerging policies in relation to the aviation sector, greening of hotels and response strategies to environmental hazards in relation to coastal tourism. The adaptation measures were aimed at coping with increased temperatures (see Dube & Nhamo, 2018a; Hambira et al., 2013); increased frequency of droughts (see Mbaiwa & Mmopelwa, 2009; Saarinen et al., 2012); flooding (Mbaiwa & Mmopelwa, 2009; Njoroge, 2015a); unfavourable weather conditions (Hoogendoorn et al., 2016); extreme weather events (Dube & Nhamo, 2018a); changes in tourism peak and off seasons (Dube & Nhamo, 2018a); as well as inadequate awareness of the tourism-climate change nexus (Shaaban & Ramzy, 2010).

On the other hand, mitigation measures were aimed at addressing environmental and carbon footprint (Hoogendoorn and Fitchett, 2018; Gössling & Schumacher, 2010;

Hoogendoorn et al., 2016; Rogerson and Sims, 2012) and the impact thereof on tourism industry in developing countries (Gössling et al., 2008). Detailed policy responses are presented after this next section.

Endangered tourism destinations and associated climate change impacts

This section addresses the question of the major tourism destinations that have been affected by climate change. The destinations in question were identified from the reviewed papers which had a focus on the impacts component of the tourism-climate change nexus. Reasonable evidence is key in determining whether climate change is a concern in a particular place. Some of the affected places and attractions include the tourist town of Livingstone in Zambia, the Sinai environment and the red sea region in Egypt, the coastal towns of South Africa, Kenya and Ghana, and renowned wetlands of Botswana and Zimbabwe.

In Zambia, a study by Dube and Nhamo (2018a), examined the evidence and potential implications of climate variability and change on tourism in the Zambian town of Livingstone and found statistically significant evidence of climate change for annual temperature. The high temperatures are expected to have the following challenges on tourism activities in the tourist town of Livingstone: reduced tourist comfort; increased air conditioning energy demand in summer while on a positive note energy costs would go down in winter; increased insurance premiums due to extreme weather events such as droughts, extreme rainfall and fires; changes in seasons and water flow at the waterfalls might affect the tourism peak and off seasons. Similarly, in Tunisia, subject to various uncertainties and limitations, there is a potential for climate-induced revenue gains in the shoulder seasons while climate-induced losses are expected in the summer months due to increased heat stress (Köberl et al., 2016).

In Egypt, the fauna and flora, coral reefs, wetlands, avifauna and the general landscape of Sinai are expected to be affected by climate change and Ahmed and Hefny (2007) outline the following expected impacts: bleaching of coral reefs, alteration of the velocity of lakes due to reduction of Nile flow given the rate of precipitation patterns on the Ethiopian and equatorial lakes such as Lake Victoria, as well as salt water intrusion emanating from sea-level rise among other factors. The consequent reduction in tourism revenue would result in a significant impact on the country's balance of payments and economic performance. Still in Egypt, Marshall et al. (2011) maintain that while climate change impacts on coral reefs may not be apparent, it is already impacting the perceptions and choices of dive tourists whereas the industry is not aware of this development. Consequently, their clients' climate and environmental interests are not taken into account in business operations hence they risk losing this cohort of clients to more responsive competitors. Marshall et al. (2011) further posit that the fact that the industry in the Red Sea region is unaware of current dive tourists' perceptions surrounding climate change and coral reef condition makes the region's tourism industry vulnerable to climate change. This leads to what the authors term 'awareness and attitudinal impacts' and they further opine that dive tourists who participated in the study were well educated and aware of environmental as well as climate change issues as pertains to coral reefs. Shaaban and Ramzy (2010), on the other hand, postulate that according to Egypt's policymakers, several types of tourism dominating the international tourism market in Egypt, are expected to be affected by climate change as follows:

recreational or beach tourism in the Sinai Peninsula and the red sea coastal zone are likely to be affected by sea-level rise due to their relatively low elevation thus posing a threat to existing tourism investments; while dive tourism prominent in the red sea coral reefs is expected to be affected by high temperatures.

In South Africa, Steyn and Spencer (2012) advance that the impacts on tourism are expected to be severe manifesting in extreme weather conditions, prolonged droughts as well as a rise in temperatures and sea levels leading to a redistribution of tourism resources geographically and seasonally. For example, sea-level rise is a concern for coastal towns of St Francis and Cape St Francis since accommodation facilities in the said towns are situated in the coastline's low-level elevations (Fitchett et al., 2016a). Threats include flooding of the establishments and damage to local infrastructure which impedes access to tourists. The Digital Elevation Model sea-level rise projections suggest that by 2050, there will be a considerable reduction of the beach area with extensive coastal squeeze (especially Sea Vista Area of St Francis Bay). On the other hand, projections for the year 2100 suggest a complete inundation of the beach affecting the primary tourist town and heighten flood risk for the 11 beach front accommodation establishments.

Similarly, in Ghana's coast of Accra, Sagoe-Addy and Addo (2013) posit that 31% of the tourist facilities cannot physically withstand the event of sea-level rise hazard. According to the study, physical analysis of the vulnerability of accommodation facilities showed that 50% of the facilities are highly vulnerable to sea-level rise. The study's field results revealed that over 50% of tourism facilities represented had no measures and plans for protections and or mitigation/adaptation. While Kenya's coastal town of Mombasa is already experiencing extreme weather events particularly floods, droughts and strong winds (Awuor et al., 2008; Njoroge, 2015a). Darkoh et al. (2014) purport that a rise in sea level is likely to lead to the submergence of the town leading to loss of biodiversity and tourist attractions.

With regard to Botswana, tourism facilities located in the middle of the Okavango Delta were deemed most vulnerable to flooding and in the event of high floods, this would result in permanent flooding of the area, and consequently, turnover will be affected due to cancellation of bookings (Mbaiwa and Mmopelwa, 2009). The vulnerability of the delta to climate change was also reiterated by Hambira (2011) as alluded to in the earlier section. Hence Darkoh et al. (2014) identified the tourism sector as one of Botswana's economic arms which has been affected by climate change and variability.

Another famous wetland endangered by climate change is the Victoria Falls shared by Zimbabwe and Zambia. Dube and Nhamo (2018b) provided evidence of climate variability and extreme rainfall patterns with a stronger leaning towards drought years, shift in seasons and winter warming resulting in shorter peak discharge periods. The study further postulates that temperatures increased by 1.4°C between 1976 and 2016 and the paper purports that this would negatively affect flora and fauna, and tourists' comfort. Other expected negative impacts include increased demand for cooling systems, thereby contributing to carbon emissions leading to more global warming, and increase in fire frequency for the area which can disturb the ecology of the area. Dube and Nhamo further postulate that, generally, there has been a warming of winter months with the month of June witnessing a 1°C temperature increase between 1976 and 2016. Helicopter operations were already affected since high temperatures mean that the aircrafts take longer to climb to regulatory levels hence consuming more fuel. On a positive note, increased rainfall could result in increased runoff and river discharge over a short period which would be a desirable turn of events for tourism as high river discharge enhances the aesthetic value of the falls.

Climate change policy responses in the tourism context

The results presented in this section are from the reviewed cohort of papers that were deemed to answer the question pertaining to climate policy responses that exist in Africa's tourism–climate change nexus. The climate policy actions were in response to the following climatic effects on tourism activities: increased temperatures, frequent droughts, coral bleaching, flooding, poor climatic conditions, extreme weather events. The responses covered both adaptation and mitigation measures.

Adaptations geared towards increased temperatures include alteration of activity times (Hambira et al., 2013) and the adoption of climate-friendly facilities (Dube & Nhamo, 2018a). In response to increased drought occurrences, tourism operators in Botswana planned to provide water holes for animals (Mbaiwa & Mmopelwa, 2009; Saarinen et al., 2012). For impacts that reduced the quality of attractions such coral bleaching, diversification of the tourism product was the way to go. For example, in the Red Sea area in Egypt, companies that are predominantly dive operators have diversified their offerings ranging from bird watching, lessons on astronomy and indigenous foods, culture and music (Marshall et al., 2011). To address flooding, responses ranged from moving guests to alternative rooms or locations (Mbaiwa & Mmopelwa, 2009); improvement of drainage systems by hoteliers in Mombasa Kenya, while the resultant cancelation if bookings were compensated by local walk-ins, day trippers and conference makers (Njoroge, 2015a). In the event of poor climatic conditions, tourists engaged in alternative activities that are not weather dependent while beach tourism operators in South Africa's coastal towns provide board games and satellite televisions for their guests (Hoogendoorn et al., 2016). On the other hand, extreme weather events would require revision of pricing models due to increased insurance premiums while changes in tourism peak and off seasons in Livingstone, Zambia would call for business realignments (Dube & Nhamo, 2018a). Shaaban and Ramzy (2010) identified increasing public awareness as the most appropriate policy response to the impacts of climate change on tourism in Egypt and the country has prepared a national action plan on climate change to coordinate its efforts.

In terms of mitigation measures, the climate actions identified during the review include greening of accommodation establishments, that is, implementation of measures for reduced energy and water consumption and minimisation of the hotel's environmental footprint (Hoogendoorn et al., 2016; Rogerson & Sims, 2012). The studies revealed that various hotels in South Africa were at different levels of implementing green initiatives driven mainly by costs, the voluntary nature of the policy in the country and international tourists who opted to stay in green or environmentally friendly establishments. Examples outlined in the studies included a change from high energy demand electric appliances such as stoves to gas powered appliances, heat pumps to reduce energy costs of boilers, renewable energy and smart technologies for all energy inputs, outputs and consumption; and with respect to water conservation, water saving shower heads were installed and grey water used where possible. With regard to carbon-neutral tourism policies, Gössling and Schumacher (2010) found no correlation between income and willingness to pay indicating that even though the Seychelles for instance is an upscale destination, wealthy travellers will not necessarily want to pay more for their travel in order to offset their emissions. The study however highlights that, in the bid to maintain viable economies, it may be wise for small tropical islands to proactively adopt carbon neutral policies, a path which may not be sustainable in the long run should more large economies join efforts to offset emissions resulting in increased costs for carbon reductions or offsets. Furthermore, according to the study, impact of climate policies on developing countries such as Mada-gascar and Seychelles, for example emission trading schemes, may affect ticket prices, e.g. for price elasticities close to −1 and in the event that tourist's price perceptions would focus on the cost of airfares, demand may decline by up to 6% for the Seychelles. The negative growth rates indicate that developing countries depend on international tourism which involves long haul trips.

Discussion and conclusions

Tourism in Africa is mainly nature-based making the chances of escaping the challenges of climate change very limited. It is thus imperative that research on all facets of climate change including the vulnerability of the tourism sector, the impacts thereof on the sector and appropriate response measures to guard the industry be accelerated. Based on this re-view, not much academic research has been done to inform affected stakeholders on what to expect and what to do to avoid the anticipated negative impacts or to take advantage of the positive ones.

The review showed that only one paper, Hambira (2011) made an attempt to investigate the vulnerability of the tourism sector to climate change. There is therefore limited literature and research that has been carried out on the vulnerability of the tourism sector to climate change. It is however important to determine how vulnerable the tourism sector is to climate change in order to prevent or minimise the loss of value of tourist attractions. In terms of im-pacts of climate change on the tourism sector, the review has indicated that even though the studies have shown evidence of the drivers of climate change such as increased temperatures and precipitations, few of them have shown the actual impacts of these on tourism opera-tions. Therefore most of the papers alluded to expected impacts from the drivers of climate change as opposed to the effect that these drivers have had on tourism-related activities. This may be because climate change is a long-term phenomenon whose impacts may also manifest in the long term (Hambira, 2017).

Without adequate information on the extent of vulnerability of tourism attractions to cli-mate change as well as impacts thereof, efforts to put in place appropriate response measures would be futile. Research and provision of relevant information set a platform for appropriate adaptation or mitigation strategies to be devised in order to minimise or eliminate impend-ing climate change impacts on the tourism industry. This would ensure sustainable tourism practices in Africa. The papers reviewed for this chapter either made some recommendations on suitable response strategies depending on the destination under study or revealed the strat-egies currently in use or planned at various tourism destinations and facilities. The strategies were either aimed at reducing emissions associated with the tourism industry or adaptation and coping strategies that the industry could apply to its operations in order to contend with the effects of climate change. Climate adaptation plans require that both the likely positive and negative impacts be considered (Marshall et al., 2011).

Adaptation by all tourism stakeholders especially tourism operators, tourists or policy-makers is key in sustaining the tourism industry against the vagaries of climate change. Research in Africa has shown however that response leans towards reactionary rather than precautionary measures of climate change since often operators do not have adaptation plans in place or planned. This may be exacerbated by the fact that the impacts of climate change are long term and uncertainties surrounding impact predictions make the deter-mination of adaptation needs difficult. Not only should nature-based tourism be protected from climate change, the sector's contribution to emissions should also be considered and dealt with in relation to the reduction of carbon footprint in facilities and aviation. Given the environmental hazards associated with climate change that have a bearing on tourism in terms of possible flooding events, heat stress, disease outbreaks, it is important for relevant stakeholders to have appropriate plans to deal with the emergencies associated with extreme events resulting from climate change. Considering that climate change has no borders, a sub-regional approach to the tourism-climate change issues could strengthen country efforts.

References

Ahmed, M.T. & Hefny, M. (2007). Climate change and tourism–An Egyptian perspective. *Egyptian biodiversity clearing house mechanism.* Retrieved from http://research.fit.edu/sealevelriselibrary/documents/doc_mgr/387/Egypt_Tourism_&_CC_-_Ahmed_&_Hefny.pdf (accessed 23 March 2017).

Awuor, C.B., Orindi, V.A. & Ochieng, A. (2008). Climate change and coastal cities: The case of Mombasa, Kenya. *Environment and Urbanization*, 20(1), 231–242.

Becker, S. (1998). Beach comfort index–a new approach to evaluate the thermal conditions of beach holiday resorts using a South African example. *GeoJournal*, 44(4), 297–307.

Becken, S. (2005). Harmonising climate change adaptation and mitigation: The case of tourist resorts in Fiji, *Global Environmental Change*, 15, 381–393.

Bürki, R., Elsasser, H. & Abegg, B. (2003). Climate change—impacts on the tourism industry in mountain areas. In: UNWTO [United Nations World Tourism Organization] (Ed.), *Climate change and Tourism.* Proceedings of the First International Conference on Climate Change and Tourism, Djerba, Tunisia, 9–11 April 2003. Madrid: UNWTO [United Nations World Tourism Organization].

Chapman, L. (2007), Transport and climate change: A review. *Journal of Transport Geography*, 15, 354–367.

CNN Travel. (2018a). Inside Africa: 25 of Africa's most amazing places to visit. Retrieved from https://edition.cnn.com/travel/article/africa-amazing-places/index.html

CNN Travel. (2018b, Mark Eveleigh). 8 of the best safari destinations in Africa. Retrieved from https://edition.cnn.com/travel/article/africa-safari-national-parks/index.html

Darkoh, M.B.K., Khayesi, M. & Mbaiwa, J.E. (2014). Impacts and responses to climate change at the micro-spatial scale in Malawi, Botswana and Kenya. In M.A.M. Salih (Ed.), *Local climate change and society* (pp. 109–124). London: Routledge.

Dillimono, H.D. & Dickinson, J.E. (2015). Travel, tourism, climate change, and behavioural change: Travellers' perspectives from a developing country, Nigeria. *Journal of Sustainable Tourism*, 23(3), 437–454.

Dube, K., Mearns, K., Mini, S.E. & Chapungu L. (2018). Tourists' knowledge and perceptions on the impact of climate change on tourism in Okavango Delta, Botswana. *African Journal of Hospitality, Tourism and Leisure*, 7(4), 1-18

Dube, K. & Nhamo, G. (2018a). Climate variability, change and potential impacts on tourism: Evidence from the Zambian side of the Victoria Falls. *Environmental Science and Policy*, 84, 113–123.

Dube, K. & Nhamo, G. (2018b) Climate variability, change and potential impacts on tourism: Evidence from the Zimbabwean side of the Victoria Falls. *Environment, Development and Sustainability*, https://doi.org/10.1007/s10668-018-0118-y

Fitchett, J., Grant, B. & Hoogendoorn, G. (2016a). Climate change threats to two low-lying South African coastal towns: Risks versus perceptions. *South African Journal of Science*, 112(5/6), 86–94.

Fitchett, J.M., Hoogendoorn, G. & Robinson, D. (2016b). Data challenges and solutions in the calculation of Tourism Climate Index (TCI) scores in South Africa. *Turizam: znanstveno-stručni časopis*, 64(4), 359–370.

Gössling, S., Bredberg M., Randow A., Sandström E. & Svensoon P. (2006). Tourist perceptions of climate change: A study of international tourists in Zanzibar. *Current Issues in Tourism*, 9(4), 419–435.

Gössling, S., Peeters, P. & Scott, D. (2008). Consequences of climate policy for international tourist arrivals in developing countries. *Third World Quarterly*, 29(5), 873–901.

Gössling, S. & Schumacher, K.P. (2010). Implementing carbon neutral destination policies: Issues from the Seychelles. *Journal of Sustainable Tourism*, 18(3), 377–391.

Hambira, W.L. (2011). Screening for climate change vulnerability in Botswana's tourism sector in the bid to explore suitable adaptation measures and policy implications: A case study of the Okavango Delta. *International Journal of Tourism Policy*, 4(1), 51–65.

Hambira, W.L. (2017). Botswana tourism operators and policy makers' perceptions and responses to the tourism-climate change nexus: Vulnerabilities and adaptations to climate change in Maun and Tshabong area. *Oulu: Nodia Geographical Publications*, 46(2), ISBN 978-952-62-1629-4

Hambira, W.L., Manwa, H., Atlhopheng, J. & Saarinen, J. (2013). Perceptions of tourism operators towards adaptations to climate change in nature-based tourism: The quest for sustainable tourism in Botswana. *Pula*, 27(1), 48, 69–85.

Hambira, W.L. & Saarinen, J. (2015). Policy-makers' perceptions of the tourism–climate change nexus: Policy needs and constraints in Botswana. *Development Southern Africa*, 32(3), 350–362.

Hambira, W.L., Saarinen, J., Manwa, H. & Atlhopheng, J. (2013). Climate change adaptation practices in nature-based tourism in Maun in the Okavango Delta area, Botswana: How prepared are the tourism businesses? *Tourism Review International*, 17, 19–29.

Hernandez, A.B. & Ryan, G. (2011). Coping with climate change in the tourism industry: A review and agenda for future research. *Tourism and Hospitality Management*, 17(1), 79–90.

Hoogendoorn, G. & Fitchett, J.M. (2018) Tourism and climate change: A review of threats and adaptation strategies for Africa. *Current Issues in Tourism*, 21(7), 742–759, doi: 10.1080/13683500.2016.1188893.

Hoogendoorn, G., Grant, B. & Fitchett, J.M. (2016). Disjunct perceptions? Climate change threats in two-low lying South African coastal towns. *Bulletin of Geography Socioeconomic Series*, 31, 59–71.

Inter-governmental Panel on Climate change (IPCC). (2014a). Summary for policy makers. In Climate change 2014: Impacts, adaptation and vulnerability: Part A: Global and Sectoral aspects. Working Group II contribution to the 5th assessment report of the Inter-governmental Panel on Climate change.

IPCC. (2014b). Climate Change 2014: Synthesis Report. Contribution of Working Groups I, II and III to the Fifth Assessment Report of the Intergovernmental Panel on Climate Change [Core Writing Team, R.K. Pachauri and L.A. Meyer (Eds.)]. Geneva: IPCC.

Kabii, T. (n.d). An overview of African wetlands. *Ramsar Bureau*, Switzerland. Retrieved from https://www.oceandocs.org/bitstream/handle/1834/457/Africa_Wetlands_1.pdf?sequence=1

Kalinga, O.J. & Baker, S.J.K (2018). East African Mountains. *Encyclopaedia Britannica*. Retrieved from https://www.britannica.com/place/East-African-mountains

Köberl, J., Prettenthaler, F. & Bird, D.N. (2016). Modelling climate change impacts on tourism demand: A comparative study from Sardinia (Italy) and Cap Bon (Tunisia). *Science of the Total Environment*, doi: 10.1016/j.scitotenv.2015.03.099.

Kunreuther, H., Gupta, S., Bosetti, V., Cooke, R., Dutt, V., Ha-Duong, M., Held, H., Llanes-Regueiro, J., Patt, A., Shittu, E. & Weber, E. (2014). Integrated risk and uncertainty assessment of climate change response policies. In O. Edenhofer, R. Pichs-Madruga, Y. Sokona, E. Farahani, S. Kadner, K. Seyboth, A. Adler, I. Baum, S. Brunner, P. Eickemeier, B. Kriemann, J. Savolainen, S. Schlömer, C. von Stechow, T. Zwickel & J.C. Minx (Eds.), *Climate change 2014: Mitigation of climate change. Contribution of Working Group III to the Fifth Assessment Report of the Intergovernmental Panel on Climate Change* (pp. 151–205). Cambridge: Cambridge University Press.

Linde, J. & Grab, S. (2008). Regional contrasts in mountain tourism development in the Drakensberg, South Africa. International Mountain Society. Retrieved from http://www.bioone.org/doi/full/10.1659/mrd.0937

Lew, A., Hall, C. M., & Timothy, D. J. (2008). *World Geography of Travel and Tourism: A Regional Approach*. Oxford: Butterworth-Heinemann.

Marshall, N.A., Marshall, P.A., Abdulla, A., Rouphael, T. & Ali, A. (2011). Preparing for climate change: Recognising its early impacts through perceptions of dive tourists and dive operators in the Egyptian Red Sea. *Current Issues in Tourism*, 14(6), 507–518.

Mayer, B. (2018). *The international law on climate change*. Cambridge: Cambridge University Press.

Mbaiwa, J.E. & Mmopelwa, G. (2014). Perceived effects of climate change on the tourism business in the Okavango Delta, Botswana. In L. D'Amore & P. Kalifungwa (Eds.), *Meeting the challenges of climate change to tourism: Case studies of best practice* (pp. 417–434). Cambridge: Cambridge Scholars Publishing.

Mendes, L.M.Z. & Santos, G. (2008). Using economic instruments to address emissions from air transport in the European Union, *Environment and Planning A 40*(1), 189–209.

Monzón, J., Moyer-Horner, L. & Palamar M.B. (2011). Climate change and species range dynamics in protected areas. *BioScience*, 61(10), 752–761.

Nakaya, A.C. (2017). *What are the consequences of climate change?* SanDiego, CA: Reference Point Press Inc.

Njoroge, J.M. (2015a). Climate change-perceived impacts, risks, vulnerability, and response strategies: A case study of Mombasa coastal tourism, Kenya. *African Journal of Hospitality, Tourism and Leisure*, 4(1), ISSN: 2223–814X.

Njoroge, J.M. (2015b). Climate change and tourism adaptation: Literature review. *Tourism and Hospitality Management*, 21(1), 95–108.

Njoroge, J.M. (2015c). Tourism millenium development goals and climate change in Kenya. *African Journal of Hospitality Tourism and Leisure*, 4(1), ISSN: 2223–814X.

Ojekunle, Z.O., Amujo, B.T., Ojekunle, V.O., Dada, E.O., Sangowusi, R.O., Nasamu, R.E. & Ojo, O. (2013). Adapting to climate change in developing countries: A review of strategies, constraints and development in Nigeria. *Herald Journal of Geography and Regional Planning*, 2 (2), 89–97.

Pandy, W.R. (2017) Tourism enterprises and climate change: Some research imperatives. *African Journal of Hospitality, Tourism and Leisure*, 6(4), Open Access- Online @ http//: www.ajhtl.com

Peck, L. & Hedding, D.W. (2014). Developing a weather impact index for O. R. Tambo International Airport, South Africa. *American Meteorological Society*, doi.org/10.1175/WAF-D-17-0007.1

Pettorelli, N., Chauvenet, A.L.M., Duffy, J.P., Cornforth, W.A., Meillere, A. & Baillie, J.E.M. (2012). Tracking the effects of climate change on ecosystem function using protected areas: Africa as a case study. *Ecological Indicators*, 20, 269–276.

Rogerson, C.M. (2016). Climate change, tourism and local economic development in South Africa. *Local Economy*, 31(1–2) 322–331.

Rogerson, J.M. & Sims, S.R. (2012). The greening of urban hotels in South Africa: Evidence from Gauteng. *Urban Forum*, 23, 391–407.

Romm, J. (2018). *Climate change: What everyone needs to know* (2nd ed.). New York: Oxford University Press.

Saarinen, J., Hambira, W.L., Atlhopheng, J. & Manwa, H. (2012). Tourism industry reaction to climate change in Kgalagadi South District, Botswana. *Development Southern Africa*, 29(2), 273–285.

Saarinen, J., Hambira, W.L. Atlhopheng, J. & Manwa, H. (2013). Tourism and climate change in Southern Africa: Perceived impacts and adaptation strategies of the tourism industry to changing climate and environment in Botswana. In V. Reddy & K. Wilkes (Eds.), *Tourism, climate change and sustainability* (pp.243–256). London: Routledge.

Sagoe-Addy, K. & Addo, K.A. (2013). Effect of predicted sea level rise on tourism facilities along Ghana's Accra coast. *Journal of Coastal Conservation*, 17, 155–166.

Scheelhaase, J.D. & Grimme, W.G. (2007). Emissions trading for international aviation – An estimation of the economic impact on selected European airlines. *Journal of Air Transport Management*, 13, 253–263.

Scott, D., Hall, C.M. & Gössling, S. (2012). *Tourism and climate change: Impacts, adaptation and mitigation*. London: Routledge.

Shaaban, I. & Ramzy, Y. (2010). The impact of climate change on tourism in Egypt as perceived by both policymakers and tourism managers. *WIT Transactions on Ecology and the Environment*, 139, 241–251.

Simpson, M.C., Gössling, S., Scott, D., Hall, C.M. & Gladin, E. (2008) *Climate change adaptation and mitigation in the tourism sector: Frameworks, tools and practices.* Paris: UNEP, University of Oxford, UNWTO, WMO.

Steyn, J.N. & Spencer, J.P. (2012). Climate change and tourism: Implications for South Africa. *African Journal for Physical, Health Education, Recreation and Dance*, 18(1), 1–19.

Tanner-McAllister, S.L., Rhodes, J. & Hockings, M. (2017). Managing climate change on protected areas: An adaptive management decision making framework. *Journal of Environmental Management*, 204(1), 510–518.

Uchegbu S.N. & Kanu, E. (2013). The impacts of climate change on tourism in Africa. In Louis D' Amore and Patirck Kalifungwa (Eds.) Meeting the Challenges of Climate Change to Tourism: Case Studies of Best Practice. (pp. 370–384) Newcastle upon Tyne: Cambridge Scholars Publishing

United Nations. (2015). Transforming our world: The 2030 Agenda for Sustainable Development. Resolution adopted by the General Assembly on 25 September 2015. Retrieved from http://www.un.org/ga/search/view_doc.asp?symbol=A/RES/70/1&Lang=E

UNEP & AMCEN (n.d.) Africa's adaptation gap 2: Bridging the gap – mobilising sources. Technical report. Retrieved from http://wedocs.unep.org/bitstream/handle/20.500.11822/9092/Africas_adaptation_gap_2.pdf?sequence=1&isAllowed=y

United Nations World Tourism Organisation (UNWTO). (2018). *UNWTO tourism highlights*, 2018 Edition. Madrid: UNWTO, doi: https://doi.org/10.18111/9789284419876.

Wielgus, J., Cooper, E., Torres, R. & Lauretta, B. (2010). Coastal capital: Dominican Republic case studies on the economic value of coastal ecosystems in the Dominican Republic. Working paper. Washington DC: World Resources Institute. Retrieved from http://wri.org/coastal-capital_dominican_republic.pdf

Yu Xiao, Y. & Watson. M. (2017) Guidance on conducting a systematic literature review. *Journal of Planning Education and Research, 39*(1), 93–112

7

Growing Africa's tourism through air transport liberalisation

Continental aspirations and key policy bottlenecks

Rayviscic Mutinda Ndivo

Introduction

The tourism sector in Africa has proven itself to be a dynamic and fast-growing sector, boasting virtually uninterrupted growth between 1995 and 2014. During this period, the region recorded annual average growth of 6% for arrivals and 9% for international tourism receipts and tourism export revenues (UNWTO 2017). In the year 2016, Africa witnessed an 8% increase in visitor arrivals following a weaker performance in 2014 and 2015 occasioned by various health, geopolitical and economic challenges (Novelli et al. 2018). The region welcomed 58 million international tourists in 2016 representing 4.7% of the world total, 4 million more than in 2015.[1] This earned the region US$ 35 billion in international tourism receipts (representing a 2.9% share) (UNWTO 2017). Further, intra-Africa tourist arrivals have continued to form a significant segment of the visitor arrivals into the region accounting for 46% of international tourist arrivals in Africa (UNWTO 2017). Such performance has seen tourism become a leading economic sector and a leading driver for employment creation in the region (World Travel and Tourism Council (WTTC) 2018).

The noted performance notwithstanding, Africa's tourism generally remains uncompetitive on a number of fronts. First, the region's share of international tourism receipts has remained the lowest, accounting for roughly 5% of global international arrivals and about 3% of global tourism receipts (UNWTO 2017). More so, according to the UNWTO average visitor spending statistics, Africa's tourism seems to attract the lowest spenders with an average spending per visitor of USD 600 against a global average of USD 990. This translates to roughly per arrival spending of USD 73 which is about 2.5 times lower that of visitors to the Americas - the leading region with an average per arrival receipt of USD 1570 (see Table 7.1)

In addition, in spite of the region being the world's second largest and second most populous continent, with a market of 1.2 billion people having increasing disposable incomes, Africa's tourism has largely ignored the regional market. Much of the region's tourism industry has traditionally targeted international tourists from outside the region in particular, Europe and North America. Only four out of ten international tourists to Africa originates from Africa in 2010–2013, a far cry compared to global regional arrivals average of four out of five international visitors (ibid.).

Table 7.1 World: international tourism receipts

| | International tourism receipts Local currencies, constant prices (% change) | | | | Market share (%) | Receipts (US$) | | | |
| | | | | | | billion | | | per arrival |
	13/12	**14/13**	**15/14**	**16/15**	**2016**	**2014**	**2015**	**2016**	**2016**
World	5.6	4.3	4.1	2.6	100	1,252	1,196	1,220	990
Europe	4.1	4.4	2.7	0.9	36.7	513.7	449.6	447.3	730
Asia and the Pacific	8.5	1.5	2.5	4.8	30.1	359.0	349.4	366.7	1,190
Americas	6.6	6.7	8.2	2.7	25.7	288.9	305.6	313.2	1,570
Middle East	−3.3	10.2	7.4	−1.6	4.7	53.6	58.2	57.6	1,080
Africa	**2.5**	**3.7**	**0.5**	**8.3**	**2.9**	**36.5**	**32.8**	**34.8**	**600**
North Africa	−2.1	8.3	−8.8	2.6	0.7	11.0	8.9	9.1	490
Sub-Saharan Africa	4.3	1.9	4.5	10.5	2.1	25.5	23.9	25.6	650

Source: UNWTO (2017).

Major constraints to Africa's tourism growth: the air transport dimension

A number of factors may be identified as being responsible for the relatively poor performance of Africa's tourism despite the rich endowment and relative availability of tourism resources. Though the main constraints to the region's tourism development vary by country, similar patterns have been found to affect the continent as a whole. Some of the notable ones include lack of appreciation of the economic and social importance of the sector by a number of countries in Africa, tourist safety and security, the low levels of investment in the tourism sector, fundamental land issues that have proven a challenge to countries that are scaling up their tourism development, the human resource capacity gap in the industry (Novelli and Burns 2009), and price competitiveness particularly on flights and hotel accommodation (Christie et al. 2013; Twining-Ward 2010).

Further to the above limiting factors, the impact of the generally poor performance of Africa's air transport industry cannot be gainsaid. The performance of the region's civil aviation industry though improving continues to lag behind that of the rest of the world accounting for a meagre 3% of the global air transportation in 2014 (Inter*VISTAS* Consulting Ltd 2014). A number of challenges have been noted as contributing to the poor performance of Africa's aviation industry. Such include poor airport infrastructure specifically and lack of general support infrastructures, inadequate physical and human resources, inadequate transit facilities, distance and limited connectivity, high operating costs, poor record of safety and security and ineffective government actions, among others (UNECA 2016).

More significant to the tourism industry, Africa's air transportation is relatively more expensive compared to other regions of the world. This is primarily as a result of relatively high passenger taxes and excessive levies in the form of airport fees, jet fuel taxes and excise duties (Fortin 2013). For instance, an international traveller landing at Ambouli, Djibouti, is expected to pay up to US$85.89 in extra fees, the highest on the continent. In Accra, Ghana, it is US$75, while in Nairobi, Kenya, the fee is US$40 (Fortin 2013). Comparatively, other countries airports' fees around the world are far less. For instance, at Charles de Gaulle in

Paris, taxes and charges are below US$14 while in Singapore, the same amount to about US$11. In Mumbai, the charges are less than US$6 (Fortin 2013). These factors, among others, make it challenging for tourism to easily access a number of African country destinations.

It is important to note that with most of Africa's iconic destinations situated in remote areas, air access is absolutely crucial for tourism development on the continent. Reduced rates and an increase in scheduled flights on competent, trusted air carriers will undoubtedly improve second- or third-tier access to more African countries. Furthermore, the large size of the continent coupled with a number of landlocked countries and the sheer distances between key African cities makes air transport undoubtedly a crucial means of transport for the continent. Further, the poor overland infrastructure in the continent underpins the importance of airline connectivity within the region (Inter*VISTAS* Consulting Ltd 2014).

Overview of Africa's air transportation performance

In the last decade, Africa has witnessed a sustained growth in the air transportation sector, rising by 6.6% and making the continent the second fastest growing region globally after Asia. International air passenger numbers have grown consistently year on year since 2004 except in 2011 where the numbers dipped as a result of political instability in parts of North Africa. From less than 40 million passengers carried in 2004 by African airlines, passenger numbers increased to 73.8 million in 2013. Domestic passenger numbers within the region have also increased significantly reaching 28 million in 2013 (Chingosho 2012). This growth in Africa's aviation industry is projected to continue into the foreseeable future. As Boeing's long term forecast of 2014–2033 indicates, driven by a positive economic outlook, increasing trade links and the growing middle class, traffic to, from and within Africa is projected to grow by about 6% per year for the next 20 years. Moreover, Africa is projected to require about 1,100 new airplanes over the next 20 years, approximately two-thirds of which will expand the region's fleet (Boeing Commercial Airplanes 2014).

The growth of Africa's aviation industry can be attributed to several factors of which the major ones are outlined below;

a   First, the region has for a while made efforts to liberalise the aviation industry/The most important of these efforts is seen in the Yamoussoukro Decision (YD) of 1999 that sought to deregulate Africa's air services and promote regional air markets open to transnational competition. While the implementation of the YD has notably encountered a number of challenges, its net effect on the growth of intra-regional air travel is commendable.

b   Several airlines from the United States, Europe and Africa have continued to expand operations across the continent. This is in addition to the traditionally established airlines from Europe and Asia. Among the notable examples include Ethiopia Airlines that was serving 46 African destinations by 2013; Brussels Airlines (20 African destinations); South African Airways serving 29 African destinations and the second largest trans-Atlantic carrier to Africa. Delta Airlines remains the largest airline operating to Africa from the United States, accounting for 36% of all US-Africa flights as of September 2013. Currently, Delta Airlines serves four African destinations (i.e. Accra, Lagos, Dakar and Johannesburg) (AfDB, NYU and ATA 2014). In addition, a number of African airlines have continued their aggressive network expansion, new markets development and further penetration of their domestic and intra-Africa markets (Chingosho 2012). As a result, passenger numbers have continued to increase in all market segments.

c   Further, the growing alliances with counterpart regions of the world have played an important role in the development of the African aviation industry. The alliances have made it possible for African airline companies to gain access to new long-haul routes, resulting in higher economies of scale and skills exchange.

d   Moreover, the growth of Low-Cost Carriers (LCCs) in Africa has been on the rise in recent years resulting in reduced airfares and traffic. However, these carriers are not widely spread, with the current composition being in six countries (see Table 7.2).

More so, a number of African LCCs have however become defunct mainly due to financial difficulties or safety records. Notable examples include IRS Airlines, Chanchangi Airlines and Sosoliso Airlines (in Nigeria); Antinea Airlines and Ecoair International (Algeria); Atlas Blue and Jet4you (Morocco); 1time and Velvet Sky (South Africa); and Fly Kumba (Zimbabwe).

e   Africa, as a continent, has also been experiencing accelerated economic growth over recent years. For instance, despite the global recession and political unrest in North Africa, the region's GDP has increased at the rate of 4% annually over the past decade, compared with an average of 2.2% rise during the 1990s. This is attributable to the rising demand for natural resources – particularly from emerging economies in Asia and the Middle East. The continued diversification of African economies has seen such sectors as telecommunications, banking and retail flourish; and the emergence of an economy based on rising incomes, consumption, employment and productivity (Boeing 2014). As a result of such economic growth, 25 African countries had attained middle-income status by the close of 2014.

f   Furthermore, the region has witnessed growth in its middle class equal in size to that of India, thus making consumption a major driver of economic growth. This is expected to grow further with growth in the region's labour-force forecast to expand by 122 million people by the year 2020, becoming a total workforce that will surpass that of China or India by 2035 (Boeing Commercial Airplanes 2014).

With the noted current and projected growth in the aviation sector coupled with the positive socio-economic trends, liberalising the industry would be a natural impetus to the continent's further growth. The benefits will not only be experienced by the air transport sector but also among other sectors of the general economy including more importantly, the region's tourism industry. In addition, such would impact the broad economy within the continent including increased GDP, reduction in airfares resulting in more people being able to travel by air and increased creation of employment opportunities.

Table 7.2 Distribution of LCCs in Africa by 2014

Country	Low-Cost Carriers
Egypt	Air Leisure; Aviator Aviation
Morocco	Atlas Blue; Jet4you; Air Arabia Maroc
Tanzania	Fastjet FTZ
Kenya	Air Peace; Jambojet; Five Forty Aviation
South Africa	kulula.com (Low cost subsidiary of Comair Airlines); Mango Airlines (Low cost subsidiary of South African Airways); Namibia Flyafrica; Skywise Airline; Safair

Source: ICAO (2017).

Despite the noted potential of Africa's aviation industry, a number of facts about the region's air transportation stand out:

- First, Africa's share of the global air transport industry is significantly minimal. Although the region is home to 12% of the world's population, it accounts for less than 3% of the global air service market (Kuuchi 2013).
- Second, the sector's performance in terms of profitability remains below the global average. In the year 2013, for instance, the global air transport industry recorded a net post-tax profit of $10.6 billion up from the US$6.1 billion profit made in 2012. This profitability was achieved largely due to increased demand, the positive impact on cash flow of industry restructuring and slightly lower than expected fuel costs. During the same period, African airlines made a combined loss of about US$100 million (Chingosho 2012).
- In addition, there are only a handful of regional carriers operating within the region with non-African airlines accounting for 80% of the intercontinental market share (ibid). The leading Gulf airlines i.e. Qatar, Etihad and Emirates plus Turkish airlines are leading the competition for the African air space. With the benefit from a combination of aviation-friendly investment and regulatory decisions by their local governments, aviation liberalisation efforts, their own aggressive fleet expansion, the rapid growth of Europe- Asia travel and a low-cost base, the three Gulf airlines in particular, present an enduring competitive threat to the growth of Africa's regional airlines.
- Further, the expansion of airline services in the African region is rather uneven (see Figure 7.1). For example, in the year 2011, only 11 countries experienced growth in air passenger numbers above 1%, with South Africa recording the highest growth (about 36%). Overall, though countries situated in the north, southern and eastern parts of Africa may not be sufficiently developed in the aviation field, they however are in a better position compared to the French-speaking, sub-Saharan countries (Arvanitis and Zenelis 2008).

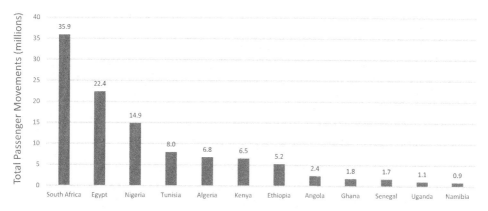

Figure 7.1 Air passenger movements in select African countries, 2011
Source: Airports Council International 2012.

- Poor air connectivity has been noted as one of the key characteristics of the poor performance of not only intra-Africa travel but also intercontinental travel into Africa (Mo Ibrahim Foundation 2014).
- Africa's air transport sector has suffered from challenges of safety and reliability. By 2012 for instance, Africa's aircraft hull-loss accident rate was more than six times higher than those of Asia and Latin America and more than 12 times higher than those of Europe and North America (IATA 2013).

The earlier facts, therefore, underscore the need for fast-tracking intra-regional air transport liberalisation and connectivity noting the potential that the region holds. This would not only open up the region for accelerated growth in intra-regional air travel but also will lead to great international air service connectivity within the region, among a host of many other benefits.

An undying aspiration to liberalise Africa's air transportation

Despite the poor performance of Africa's air transportation sector, it is undeniable that there is a recognition of the potential that liberalising air transportation represents to the continent. As more and more African countries gained independence in the 1950s and 1960s, most African States established their own airlines as national flag carriers. These carriers primarily focused on route development to European capitals mostly focusing on the former colonising regimes as opposed to strengthening intra-African or domestic networks. As a result, domestic, regional, and trans-continental air service markets remained underserved, inefficient and uncompetitive (UN Economic Commission of Africa (UNECA) 2005). Table 7.3 provides a chronology of the major regional aviation industry initiatives in Africa.

From a market liberalisation perspective, the most significant policy initiative was the Yamoussoukro Decision of 1999 that committed its 44 signatory countries to deregulate air services and promote regional air markets open to transnational competition. Moving away from the rigid bilateral air services agreements, the Yamoussoukro Declaration *on a New African Air Transport Policy* (the precursor of the Yamoussoukro Decision) was adopted in 1988 as an important step for a market liberalisation process. Yamoussoukro Decision was adopted out of the recognition that the restrictive and protectionist intra-African regulatory regime based primarily on Bilateral Air Services Agreements hampered the expansion and improvement of air transport in the continent.

The Yamoussoukro Declaration of 1988 committed African States, both individually and collectively, to achieve the phased integration of their airlines within eight years subdivided into three phases: the first phase of two years focusing on maximising capacity usage between carriers. This would entail exchanging of technical and capacity data, preparing for the designation of gateway airports, and promoting cooperation among national carriers in order to eventually merge them into larger and more competitive airlines. The second phase (three years) focused on committing airlines to joint operations on international routes. In addition, certain airline operations were to be conducted jointly to achieve better economies of scale and deeper integration, for example, instituting a common insurance mechanism and computer reservation system, purchasing spare parts and aircraft, undertaking promotion and marketing, providing training and maintaining equipment (UNECA 1988, p. 3). The last phase (three years) was to be used to strive toward achieving the complete integration of airlines by establishing joint airline operations or entities (UNECA 1988, p. 4).

Table 7.3 Chronology of major policy initiatives on Africa's aviation industry liberalisation

Year	Initiative	Main focus
1961	Yaoundé Treaty	• The main provisions of the Treaty covered the creation of *Air Afrique*, the assignment of the international traffic rights of each signatory to Air Afrique and the definition of the relationship between Air Afrique and the national airlines of the signatory states. • Has been blamed as being the main obstacle to efficient and profitable air transport in the region.
May 1963	Adoption of the Charter of OAU	Provided the political umbrella and empowerment Integration and cooperation – underpinning of the history of African civil aviation is the political commitment to cooperate and integrate air transport at the continental level.
November 1964	Conference on Air Transport in Africa	• Organised on the initiatives of the Economic Commission for Africa and the International Civil Aviation Organization (ICAO) • Aimed at examining measures to be taken to develop air transport to, from and within Africa. • Made the first initial attempts at joint collaborative programmes for air transport • Set the stage for three crucial issues for Africa's aero-political policies: (i) creation of a unified African market; (ii) airline integration and cooperation; and (iii) traffic rights issues. • Led to African Civil Aviation Commission (AFCAC) in 1969 • Various integrationist proposals formulated
1978	Launching of the First United Nations Transport and Communication Decade for Africa (UNTACDA) I (1978–1988)	• UNCTADA was to serve as the basis for all of the major air transport initiatives during the following two decades • The air transport component of the programme sought to establish an integrated air transport system by addressing key elements aimed at encouraging African States and airlines to cooperate in air transport in order to be able to create the necessary conditions for the optimum development of air services • Not much was achieved but UNTACDA global objectives and strategy became the de facto African Transport and Communication Policy and fully incorporated into the Lagos Plan of Action
1980	Lagos Plan of Action and Monrovia Strategy	Provided the political and economic basis for air transport development in Africa.
June 1980	General Civil Aviation Policy Declaration	Basis of AFCAC action in the technical, economic and cooperation areas.
1980–	Convention on the Establishment of the African Air Tariff Conference (AFTATC)	• Convention had the main objective of establishing a regional tariff coordination mechanism for all tariffs and act as machinery for negotiating all tariffs. • The Convention was never implemented

(Continued)

Year	Initiative	Main focus
November 1984	Mbabane conference	• Undertook an in-depth examination, for the first time, of the issue of traffic rights • The outcome of the Conference was the adoption of the Mbabane Declaration on the Freedoms of the Air • It led to the adoption of AFCAC Model Multilateral Agreements it set ground for the Yamoussoukro Declaration of 1988
1988–	Yamoussoukro Declaration	Covered three main issues: (i) integration of airlines; (ii) traffic rights; and (iii) costs and tariffs. committed African Governments to achieve the integration of the "airlines within a period of eight years divided into three phases" Not much was achieved
1994–	Mauritius Guidelines on Traffic Rights	Guidelines for the exchange of traffic rights and related issues inadequately covered in the Yamoussoukro Declaration were developed. Adopted proposals on "solutions" for accelerating the implementation of the Declaration.
1999–	Yamoussoukro Decision	• The first Africa-wide legally binding arrangement for the liberalisation of scheduled and non-scheduled air transport services within Africa • The Decision deals only with intra-African air transport leaving domestic air services and relations with third countries to be governed by intergovernmental BASAs
1999 to date	Sub-regional Initiatives	Implementation of YD undertaken under sub-regional level
2007	Third Conference of African Ministers in charge of Air Transport (CAMT) held in Addis Ababa	The Conference adopted a resolution entrusting AFCAC the responsibility of the YD Implementing Agency AFCAC amended its Constitution in 2009 to incorporate the exercise of the powers under Articles 9.4, 9.5 and 9.6 of the Yamoussoukro Decision.
July 2010	Programme for Infrastructure Development in Africa (PIDA) 2010–2040	• Recognises the need for a regionally integrated approach to infrastructure development • Sets Priority Action Plan (PAP) for the transport sector that contains two specific programmes for the regional aviation sector integration: (i) Single African Sky, (ii) Accelerating Yamoussoukro Decision implementation
2014	Agenda 2063	• Recognises the significance of intra-regional travel • Declares a commitment to connect Africa through world-class infrastructure, with a concerted push to finance and implement major PIDA infrastructure projects including improved efficiency and connections of the African aviation sector and implement the Yamoussoukro Declaration
2018	Launch of the Single Air Transport Market for Africa (SATMA)	• The African Union (A.U.) in 2018 launched the Single African Air Transport Market (SAATM) to open Africa's skies and improve intercontinental air connectivity. By the close of 2018, 23 African States had signed up to SATMA

Source: Summarised from ECA (2005, p. 26); AU/AfDB/ECA (2010); AU (2014).

The Yamoussoukro Declaration, however, did not manage to instigate radical changes on the existing status quo concerning privatisation of the national airlines and liberalisation of the air transport in the continent. The stated strategy of cooperation and integration of African carriers seemed to be driven more by the need for pan-African cooperation than by the objective of creating a more competitive market environment (Schlumberger 2010). As such, after the deadline of the scheme in 1996, no important progress was accomplished, thus necessitating further actions to update the decisions and make them realistic and feasible. Traffic rights granting was the most important issue that had to be settled. In the early 90s, there were several regulatory policies across the continent adopted by the African countries and as a result, many aspects of the frameworks established were not compatible with each other. Consequently, the air transport sector was strongly linked and heavily dependent upon fragile political (in)stability. The latter combined with the fact that the majority, if not all, African carriers were (and are still) state-owned led to high regulatory constraints and inflexibility to take strategic decisions.

Resulting from this below par performance, the 1999 meeting of African Ministers in-charge of air transportation was called upon to evaluate the progress of the enforcement of the Yamoussoukro Declaration. The representatives also resolved to adopt the Yamoussoukro Decision committing its 44 signatory countries to deregulate air services and promote regional air markets open to transnational competition. The key policies defined by the Yamoussoukro Decision were:

i   Elimination of limitations concerning frequencies and capacities,
ii Government's approval of free tariff-setting in line with the rules of fair competition,
iii Full liberalisation of intra-African air transport services, both for scheduled and non-scheduled intra-African air transport services in terms of access, capacity, frequency and tariffs;
iv Free exercise of first, second, third, fourth and fifth freedom rights of passenger and freight air services by eligible airlines;
v   Fair competition on a non-discriminatory basis;
vi Compliance with international safety standards.

The Yamoussoukro Decision further recognised Africa's fragmented nature characterised by assorted economic and political organisations. The Decision thus, encouraged sub-regional and regional level implementation of its objectives and programmes. As a result, much of the progress towards liberalisation has been facilitated by regional economic communities (RECs) (Paylor 2015; Schlumberger 2010).

Further to the sub-regional initiatives, region-wide efforts continue to be dedicated to the aspiration of an integrated air transport sector in Africa. For example, the region has in place a Programme for Infrastructure Development in Africa (PIDA), a long-term strategic plan for Africa's regional infrastructure between the period 2010 and 2040 (AU Commission/AfDB/ECA 2010). The programme recognises a regionally integrated approach to infrastructure development as possessing the potential for the formation of large competitive markets in place of small, isolated and inefficient ones, thus, lowering costs across production sectors. Accordingly, PIDA seeks to enable African countries to meet forecast demand for infrastructure services and boost competitiveness by increasing efficiencies, accelerating growth, facilitating integration in the world economy, improving living standards and unleashing intra-African trade. Of particular significance is the PIDA Priority Action Plan

(PAP) for the transport sector that contains two specific programmes for the regional aviation sector integration (AU Commission/AfDB/ECA 2010, p. 18):

- Program no. 2: Single African Sky phase 1 (design and initial implementation). The Single African Sky is a continental programme that will create a high-level, satellite-based air navigation system for the African continent,
- Program no. 3: Yamoussoukro Decision implementation. The program seeks to accelerate the implementation of Yamoussoukro Decision by identifying countries that are ready to fully implement it and discussing and agreeing with both their governments and airlines to launch the voluntary club on a full membership basis.

The other notable initiative is spelt out in the Agenda 2063 for the African Union that among others, recognises the significance of intra-regional travel and declares a commitment to connect Africa through world-class infrastructure including the creation of a Single Air Transport Market in Africa (SATMA) as one of the flagship project through the Yamoussoukro Decision (AU 2014, p. 16). In January 2015, a Conference of Heads of State and Government of the African Union adopted three key instruments towards the implementation of SATMA (AFCAC 2015). These included

a Declaration on the creation of a single air transport market in Africa by 2017;
b Decision on the development of the African Union Agenda 2063; and
c The solemn commitment of the African Union member states with respect to the implementation of the Yamoussoukro Decision on establishing a single air transport market in Africa by 2017.

The Conference also set up a Ministerial Working Group having the responsibility to oversee and guide the implementation of the agreed activities and roadmap for the implementation of SATMA. In addition, a monitoring committee of ambassadors and representatives of the African Union was also formally established to ensure close monitoring and to facilitate the process and effectively liaise between AFCAC and the Member States involved.

Overall, despite the implementation of the Yamoussoukro Decision remaining incomplete or stagnant in many regions of Africa, there is evidence to suggest that progress has been made at the operational level. Some of the most notable impacts of this include (Schlumberger 2010):

- The strengthening of a few stronger African carriers, such as South African, Ethiopian and Kenya Airways, that were able to capitalise on their comparative advantages;
- The consolidation of networks through the elimination of a number of low-density routes and growth of routes to and from the main hubs;
- The development of fifth freedom traffic, especially in regions and country-pairs that lacked strong local carriers;
- The development of sixth freedom traffic fostered by the liberalisation of third and fourth freedom capacities within Africa, and in some cases with the intercontinental counterpart countries.

Drawbacks to the liberalisation of Africa's air transportation: the policy dimension

In spite of the noted progress in the implementation of the Yamoussoukro Decision, its full potential has not been realised to unlock commercial opportunities for African Airlines.

Overall, there remains little practical integration of national airline networks in Africa. Several factors have been noted as hindering the full realisation of the potential represented by air transport liberalisation in Africa as envisioned under the Yamoussoukro Decision such as policy-, Infrastructure- and Non-physical bottlenecks to traffic flow. Nonetheless, policy-based bottlenecks remain the key barriers. Key policy-based challenges to the liberalisation of Africa's air transportation include

1   The question of sovereignty: As in most other countries, the operation of air services in Africa is based on a complex and cumbersome regime of bilateral air service agreements through which decisions on market access and related issues are made in the exercise of sovereignty over their air space. As a result, this in most cases limits the liberal operation of the aviation industry underpinned by free market economy – more often than not, political interests take precedence over commercial ones.

2   Anti-competition and protectionist practices including
    •   Protectionist policies. The desire by most African countries in Africa to have national flag carriers has been noted as a major impediment to liberalisation of air transportation in Africa. This has resulted in a number of countries restricting market access on the grounds that their national airlines are not ready to compete in a liberalised market. Protectionism is often motivated by fear that the national flag carrier will be unable to compete with the continent's larger carriers, for instance from Kenya, Ethiopia and South Africa, as well as intercontinentally. In some instances, change often occurs as part of crisis management. For example, in 2013, it took the collapse of Air Malawi for Kenya Airways to be allowed to operate between Malawi and other countries (Schlumberger and Weisskopf 2014).
    •   Another perceived obstacle to the implementation of the Yamoussoukro Decision is the concern over unfair competitive behaviour. Smaller African carriers in particular fear unfair competitive practices such as price dumping, when competing with larger established airlines. Article 7 of the Decision obligates state parties to "ensure fair opportunity on non-discriminatory basis for the designated African airline to effectively compete in providing air transport services within their respective territory." While this implies that certain common competition rules should be established, the Yamoussoukro Decision falls short of further defining this requirement. It does, nevertheless, refer in Article 8 to arbitration procedures, which are set forth in annex 2 of the decision. The latter primarily defines the duties and responsibilities of the monitoring body, which is established in Article 9. It does not make particular reference to competition rules or arbitration procedures except the duty of the monitoring body to prepare the relevant annexes to the Yamoussoukro Decision for adoption by the Subcommittee on Air Transport. The assumption is therefore that arbitration procedures, still missing from annex 2, are one of the tasks that must be performed by the monitoring body in order to implement the Decision. Another indication in annex 2 (g) is the monitoring body's obligation to state, at the request of state parties, its views on predatory and unfair competition practices.
    •   In addition, cases of countries requiring non-local airlines to pay royalties for the privilege of using additional frequencies beyond what is allowed under the Bilateral Aviation Safety Agreement (BASA) have also been noted. Such royalties and other compensation are at times prohibitive. Other protectionist restrictions include restrictions on frequencies and capacity, type of aircraft operated, volume of traffic to be carried, restrictions on routes to be served and limitations on the number of

designated carriers – usually the designated flag carriers enjoy exclusive and monop-
olistic rights in these markets (Schlumberger and Weisskopf 2014).

- Subsidies to national flag carrier: In addition to restricting competition by limiting
  the number of flights, many countries also provide subsidies to their flag carrier
  thus using scarce resources to prop up inefficient airlines. The situation has also
  acted to prevent the growth of low-cost airlines that have been a major stimulus
  to greater economic efficiency in places where they have been allowed. Similarly, support has been given to large national airports irrespective of the demands
  for their services. Because of political interference, less efficient flag airlines have
  tended to remain in the market preventing a natural hub-and-spoke system being
  developed by African airlines (Heinz and O'Connell 2013). African domicile carriers, in particular, find it difficult to compete with non-African airlines in this
  context.

3 Difficulties and the long process required for exchanging traffic rights, mainly the
  fifth freedom remains a major drawback to the full liberalisation of intra-Africa aviation. For instance, although there were about 560 bilateral air services agreements
  reported to have been signed between African countries covering the intra-African
  routes by 2005, only about 40% of these agreements were actually implemented
  (ECA 2005).

4 Discriminatory practices against African airlines where some African States have re-
  fused to open their skies to each other, preferring to do so to carriers from other continents. This is particularly apparent in West Africa, where non-African airlines tend to
  be given more Third/Fourth and sometimes Fifth freedom traffic rights while African
  carriers are denied (Schlumberger 2010). This has limited the market access for regional
  carriers hence constraining their growth and competitiveness. As a result, it is often more
  convenient and faster to fly from a city in West Africa via London, Paris, Amsterdam, or
  Dubai and back to a neighbouring city in West Africa than to travel directly (Schlumberger 2010).

5 Non-transparent regulations imposed by regulators outside the continent particularly
  on the matter of safety records. Lack of confidence in the safety oversight provided by
  African regulatory authorities has seen a number of airlines, even those with strong
  safety records being prevented from flying to the EU, for instance. These restrictions
  have had detrimental effects on the growth of the air transport sector as the region is
  forced to rely on mainly non-African airlines. Currently, these non-African carriers
  transport about 80% of intercontinental traffic to and from Africa.

Conclusions

Restrictive air service regulations constrain air travel, tourism and business, and as a result,
impact negatively on economic growth and job creation. Liberalisation of air transport is,
therefore, a critical decision that must be taken for the health of the global economy. Notwithstanding the noted challenges, Africa's initiatives towards air transport liberalisation
underscore the significance of the aviation sector to the region's socio-economic growth.
There is the need for intra-African travel, and the integrating and liberalising of the region's
air transportation is an important driver to maximising travel into and within the region.
This fact continues to be well acknowledged in the region.

   This chapter has noted that the air transport industry in Africa can only develop and survive the fierce and competitive environment if the Yamoussoukro Decision is implemented

fully. Going forward, therefore, a number of measures will need to be undertaken to accelerate the implementation of the Decision. There is an urgent need to address the remaining policy bottlenecks that is

Note

1 This excludes Egypt's 5.2 million arrivals reflected under the Middle East region.

References

African Civil Aviation Commission (AFCAC). 2015, 13th Meeting of the AFCAC Air Transport Committee & 16th Meeting of the Technical Committee. Victoria Falls, Zimbabwe: AFCAC https://www.afcac.org/legacy/en/index.php?option=com_content&view=article&id=260:test&catid=57:upcoming-events

Arvanitis, P. and Zenelis, P. 2008, "Destination case studies: Africa", in Graham, A., Papatheodorou, A. & Forsyth, P. (eds), *Aviation and Tourism: Implications for Leisure Travel*. Ashgate Publishing Company, USA, Chapter 23.

AU Commission. 2014, *Evaluation of the Implementation of the Yamoussoukro Decision*, Paper presented during the Africa Wide Air Transport Conference Nairobi, Kenya, 29–31 October 2014.

AU Commission/AfDB/ECA. July 2010, *Programme for Infrastructure Development in Africa (PIDA)*. African Union, Addis Ababa.

Boeing Commercial Airplanes. 2014, *Current Market Outlook, 2014–2033*. Boeing Commercial Airplanes, Seattle.

Chingosho, E. 2012, *Taxes and Charges in African Aviation*. African Airlines Association Dakar, Senegal.

Christie, I., Fernandes, E., Messerli, H., and Twining-Ward, L. 2013, *Tourism in Africa: Harnessing Tourism for Growth and Improved Livelihoods*. Viewed 12 November 2017, http://elibrary.worldbank.org

Fortin, J. 2013, *African Air Travel: Why Are Airlines in Africa So Expensive, Unsafe and Impossible to Navigate*. International Business Times, Viewed 12 November 2017, http://www.ibtimes.com/african-air-travel-why-are-airlines-africa-so-expensive-unsafe-impossible-navigate-1234609

Economic Commission for Africa (ECA) 2005. *Compendium of Air transport Integration and Cooperation Initiatives in Africa*. Addis Ababa: Economic Commission for Africa.

Heinz, S., & O'Connell, J. F. 2013. Air transport in Africa: toward sustainable business models for African airlines. *Journal of Transport Geography, 31*, 72-83.

International Air Transport Association (IATA). 2013, *Using Aviation's Potential to Drive Economic Growth in Africa. Press Release No. 49. Date: 17 September 2013*. Viewed 23 March 2017, http://www.iata.org/pressroom/pr/Pages/2013-09-17-01.aspx.

International Civil Aviation Organisation (ICAO). 2017, *List of Low-Cost Airlines-Africa*, Montreal: ICAO.

InterVISTAS Consulting Ltd. 2014, *Transforming Intra-African Air Connectivity: The Economic Benefits of Implementing the Yamoussoukro Decision*. Prepared for IATA in partnership with AFCAC and AFRAA.

Kuuchi, R. 2013, *An Assessment of African Open Skies*. AFRAA, Algiers, Algeria.

Mo Ibrahim Foundation. 2014, *Regional Integration: Uniting to Compete* London: Mo Ibrahim Foundation

Novelli, M., Burgess, L.G., Jones, A. and Ritchie, B.W. 2018, 'No Ebola... still doomed'-The Ebola-induced tourism crisis. *Annals of Tourism Research*, 70, pp.76–87.

Novelli, M. and Burns, P. 2009, *Restructuring the Gambia Hotel School into a National Tourism Training Institute*, The Gambia Investment Promotion and Free Zone Agency (GIPZA), Banjul.

Paylor, A. 2015, *Indian Ocean airlines unite in Vanilla Alliance initiative*. Air Transport World, 29 May. Viewed on 25 November 2017, http://atwonline.com/airlines/indian-ocean-airlines-unite-vanilla-alliance-initiative

Schlumberger, C.E. 2010, *Open Skies for Africa – Implementing the Yamoussoukro Decision*. World Bank, Washington, DC.

Schlumberger, C. E., and Nora W. 2014. *Ready for Takeoff?: The Potential for Low-cost Carriers in Developing Countries*. Washington DC: The World Bank

Twining-Ward, L. 2010, *Cape Verde's Transformation: Tourism as a Driver of Growth*. World Bank Group, Washington, DC.

United Nations Economic Commission for Africa (UNECA). 1988, *Declaration of Yamoussoukro on a New African Air Transport Policy*. UNECA, Ethiopia.

UNECA. 2005, *Compendium of Air Transport Integration and Cooperation Initiatives in Africa*. UNECA, Ethiopia.

UNECA. 2016, *Fostering Africa's Tourism Growth through Aviation-Tourism Policy Convergence*. UNECA, Ethiopia.

United Nations World Tourism Organization (UNWTO). 2017, *UNWTO Tourism Highlights, 2017 Edition*. UNWTO, Madrid.

World Travel and Tourism Council (WTTC). 2018, *Travel & Tourism Economic Impact 2018*, WTTC, London.

InFocus 1

The role of the United Nations World Tourism Organization (UNWTO) in tourism and sustainable development in Africa

Marie-Alise Elcia Grandcourt

The role of UNWTO in tourism

The 21st century has vividly revealed that continued growth and deepening diversification of the tourism industry have led it to becoming one of the fastest growing economic sectors in the world. Tourism is increasingly recognized as a powerful tool for development and as a key driver for socioeconomic progress. The sector has the potential to address a wide range of global challenges including poverty, employment, climate change and environmental degradation. These challenges should be addressed in a sustainable manner taking into account the current and future economic, social and environmental impacts of tourism, whilst addressing the needs of visitors, the industry, the environment and host communities as simply defined by the World Tourism Organization (UNWTO).

UNWTO is committed to the advancement of global tourism as an essential vehicle for sustainable global development – shifting global focus onto the Post-2015 Agenda for Sustainable Development to an essential promoter of tourism as a direct and indirect contributor to the 2030 Agenda for Sustainable Development and each of its 17 Sustainable Development Goals (SDGs). Tourism has been explicitly identified as targets in the following SDGs:

- **Goal 8;** *Promote sustained, inclusive and sustainable economic growth, full and productive employment and decent work for all*
- **Goal 12**; Ensure *sustainable consumption and production patterns*
- **Goal 14**; *Conserve and sustainably use the oceans, seas and marine resources for sustainable development*

However, due to the transversal nature of the tourism sector, the UNWTO find the transformative power of tourism to be reflected in all of the 17 SDGs. Tourism can and does play a huge part in achieving the SDGs and UNWTO is committed to provide the global tourism community with a space to join forces and contribute to the realization of the 2030 Agenda for Sustainable Development. It is to this end that the UNWTO's *Tourism for SDGs platform* operates as an innovative and unique co-created space developed with the support of the Switzerland State Secretariat of Economic Affairs (SECO), to promote best practices and knowledge exchange to achieve the 2030 Agenda through tourism. This platform allows

Figure IF1.1 Tourism for SDGS
Source: http://tourism4sdgs.org/.

individual travellers, public bodies, international organizations, donors, academic institutions and companies to demonstrate their commitment to advancing the SDGs, both at the national and global level. The *Tourism for SDGs Platform* key features – *Learn, Share* and *Act* is aimed at inspiring stakeholders and contribute to a dialogue for the tourism sector towards 2030, building a smarter, competitive, inclusive and sustainable sector.

Sustainable tourism development in Africa

As the value of the tourism industry continues to gain global respect and appreciation, and therefore momentum, the UNWTO continues to work in close collaboration with its Member States to mainstream tourism in their national agenda. The proclamation of 2017 as the International Year of Sustainable Tourism for Development by the UN General Assembly in its resolution 70/193, thus recognized the important role that sustainable tourism has in the achievement of the SDGs, as a positive instrument towards the eradication of poverty, the protection of the environment, social inclusion and economic empowerment. In tandem, tourism is recognized as a means to foster better understanding among people, leading to a greater awareness of the rich heritage of various civilizations and in bringing about a better appreciation of the inherent values of different cultures, thereby contributing to strengthening peace in the world.

The International Year of Sustainable Tourism for Development in 2017 represented a critical turning point for the global tourism industry in which 1 billion people travelled internationally during that year alone. Africa's share totalled to 62,077 million international tourist arrivals during 2017. The continent's tourist arrivals continue to grow with international arrivals reaching 8% totalling 67 million international tourists arrival at the close of 2018. The UNWTO's forecast that the upward trajectory would continue to reach 134 million tourist arrivals by the year 2030. The sector has clearly proved the enormous role it can play in the economic growth and in local development, as demonstrated by those African economies that depend on this industry as their main source of income. The numbers are impressive, but tourism is much more than the sum of these numbers. The sector does not only play a role in economic growth, it is perhaps most remarkable for its potential to improve the quality of people's lives. Truly sustainable tourism can act as a catalyst for environmental protection, champion diverse cultural heritage and strengthen peace in the continent.

To maximize tourism's contribution, the UNWTO encourages the entire tourism community – from policymakers, private sector and other tourism stakeholders and the development community at large – to take joint actions in a concerted way.

Upon assuming office in 2018, UNWTO Secretary General, Mr. Zurab Pololikashvili consulted and has been working closely with the African Tourism Ministers to map out an agenda for the Africa region. Establishing African tourism development as a priority, this agenda takes into consideration the priorities, challenges and opportunities that are relevant to the region for the development of a more sustainable tourism industry. Through various consultative meetings and brainstorming session, UNWTO has for the first time put together an agenda for the Africa region with an action plan accompanied by key objectives to address the needs of the Member States for the development of a sector that is yet to fulfil its full potential in the continent.

UNWTO agenda for Africa 2030 – tourism for inclusive growth

As the world has set a universal 2030 Agenda for Sustainable Development, UNWTO and its Member States of the Africa region have engaged in collaborative efforts to develop a strategic vision and agenda for the continent. The *UNWTO Agenda for Africa 2030- Tourism for inclusive growth* aims to build a more resilient, sustainable and innovative tourism sector that generate jobs, promote inclusive and low carbon growth in line with all three dimensions of sustainable development, by placing people, the planet and prosperity at its core. The *UNWTO Agenda for Africa 2030- Tourism for inclusive growth*, which has been endorsed at the 110th Executive Council in Baku, Azerbaijan and its subsequent adoption at the 23rd General Assembly, in St. Petersburg, Russia in 2019, will serve as a roadmap to further consolidate the key priority areas for the promotion of the tourism sector in Africa whilst taking into account the SGD targets. The growth and resilience of tourism to external shocks places the sector at the forefront of any country's export strategy and economic diversification, thus playing a decisive role in the achievement of the 2030 Agenda and the Sustainable Development Goals. Investing in people, boosting infrastructure development, shaping better policies and institutions, building resilience, stimulating entrepreneurship, fostering innovation and digitalization and making sustainable use of rich biodiversity and culture, should be at the core of our efforts to unlock and realize the potential of tourism for the continent's economic growth, while mitigating migration and preserving its rich natural and cultural assets. In addition, Member States have been invited to champion core priority areas such as investment promotion, capacity building, branding, biodiversity conservation and destination management among others.

The UNWTO Agenda for Africa 2030- Tourism for inclusive growth encapsulates ten key priority areas that are critical for the advancement of sustainable tourism development on the continent. Each of the priority areas illustrated in Figure C1.2 is linked to corresponding SDG targets.

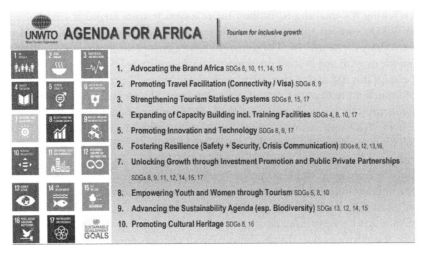

Figure IF1.2 UNWTO Agenda for Africa – Tourism for inclusive growth
Source: UNWTO, 2019.

Advocating the brand Africa – SDGs 8, 10, 11, 14, 15

Tourism, being one of the most promising and growing sectors in Africa, often gets challenged by negative perceptions, stereotypes and generalization associated with crises of specific geographical locations, erroneously attributed to the rest of the continent. It is therefore imperative for the 54 individual African destinations to enhance their image, have adequate capacity to manage their brand, and advance regional coordination and communication as a strong image of an individual destination will reflect into a stronger image of the entire African continent. This is at the basis of the call for a 'Brand Africa', which although often questioned already exists to a lesser or greater extent. Brand Africa is our collective responsibility – it is about narratives, information and imagery that would transmit an inspiring story of the reasons why we should travel to Africa. UNWTO is committed to work with African Member States to generate what is needed to build attractiveness, confidence and credibility for a fast-evolving African tourism sector.

Promoting travel facilitation (connectivity/visa) – SDGs 8, 9

It is without doubt that, over the past decade, Africa has experienced considerable growth in the air transportation sector and visa facilitation, contributing to economic growth through tourism. Despite this, the aviation industry in Africa still lags compared with the rest of the world with less than 3% of the global air service market.

The current state of affairs is characterized by stringent policies that make air travel and visa application procedures and processes cumbersome and costly, hampering both international travel and tourism flows within the region. Engaging in a more connected, easier way to travel throughout the continent is essential to support an inclusive tourism growth.

Strengthening tourism statistics systems – SDGs 8, 15, 17

Tourism is a data-driven business powered by people. Fact-based and data-driven decision making is required to plan policies and execute strategies to enable destinations to become sustainable and competitive. The vast majority of African countries, whether established or emerging tourism destinations, face challenges in gathering, consolidating, analysing and monitoring tourism-related data. As an industry that thrives on information performance, tourism indicators must be based on accurate and reliable information system to better plan and manage the future. Two UN international statistical standards have been developed and adopted to guide countries for the elaboration of tourism statistics:

- the *International Recommendations for Tourism Statistics 2008* for measuring the physical and monetary flows of tourism. In addition to this, UNWTO has issued a companion document to the IRTS 2008: The International Recommendations for Tourism Statistics 2008 Compilation Guide, aimed at providing practical guidance and methods to compile statistics on tourism.
- the *Tourism Satellite Account* (TSA) Recommended Methodological Framework 2008 to measure the economic impact of tourism.

Expanding of capacity building including training facilities – SDGs 4, 8, 10, 17

In tourism, as much as in many other sectors, capacity-building underpins the success or failure of economic transformation, especially for the vitality and sustainability of the tourism sector for inclusive growth and poverty eradication. Africa needs better trained and qualified personnel with marketable skills to address the skills shortages' challenges and meet the requirement of a highly competitive market. To this end the UNWTO Academy was established with the purpose of making training and capacity building more accessible to Member States and is in the process of developing a number of initiatives aimed at strengthening this critical human capital dimension of tourism development for Africa.

Promoting innovation and technology – SDGs 8, 9, 17

In Africa, the tourism industry is in the midst of transformation, with mobile phones' technology and the internet having changed the way we plan and experience travel on the continent. The disruption of the sector allows new opportunities for growth and improved competitiveness where both innovation and technology are instrumental in enhancing cultural tourism development. In general, the tourism sector is gearing more towards new technologies. Not only by how tourists search and receive the information that guides them to the final choice of destination, but also because of how the tourism experience is chosen or lived. Member States acknowledge these facts and highlight the importance of adapting to these new technologies and consumers' behaviour. UNWTO is calling for upgrading the technological capacities of the tourism sectors and encouraging innovation (SDG 9) in the way the sector can be advanced.

Fostering resilience (safety and security, crisis communication) – SDGs 8, 12, 13,16

Any crisis, be it national or international, natural or man-made, may have a strong negative effect and adverse economic impact on any destinations and on consumer travel choices. Crisis' prevention can be as important as effective crisis communication as they are both vital in building a resilient tourism industry. The UNWTO is working with Member States in the African region to build a resilient tourism sector and is encouraging destinations in the region to have the appropriate framework in place to reduce the likelihood of risks, mitigate crisis' effects and support the recovery process.

Unlocking growth through investment promotion by public-private partnerships – SDGs 8, 9, 11, 12, 14, 15, 17

Naturally, investment promotion in the tourism sector must be encouraged as a priority, with the purpose of creating more jobs and developing the sector in a sustainable way. UNWTO recognizes the importance of public-private partnerships as they bring together government and private sector stakeholders to work closer together and raise more funding for tourism and stronger developmental impacts.

Empowering youth and women through tourism – SDGs 5, 8, 10

The importance of gender equality and the empowerment of youth and women through tourism have been at the heart of several African governments and actions have built upon the drive of the 2015 UN Millennium Development Goal (MDG 3), which recommended countries to "promote the total and equitable participation of both men and women" in all areas of the society. The African tourism sector is said to have the highest female workforce rate of all world regions and more women in high-level leadership and management positions than other economic sectors. However, the barriers to entry and progression remain greater for women, with the benefits of tourism being harder to access and retain. Discriminatory social and cultural attitudes intersect with this inherent inequality to severely limit the opportunities tourism can offer to women both in Africa and worldwide. To help tackle this problem UNWTO supports advocacy, awareness-raising and activating supportive activities to sensitize stakeholders and society at large, by encouraging them to create more and decent employment for women. In November 2019, UNWTO with the support of the Government of Ghana through its Ministry of Tourism, Arts & Culture, hosted the first UNWTO Regional Congress on Women Empowerment in the Tourism Sector – Focus on Africa in Accra. During the event, the second edition of the Global Report on Women in Tourism was presented. The Leadership Taskforce Group for Women Empowerment in Africa led by tourism stakeholders from the region endorsed and approved the action plan of the report and also discussed proposals and activities geared towards promoting women empowerment and leadership in the tourism sector in Africa.

Advancing the sustainability agenda (esp. biodiversity) – SDGs 13, 12, 14, 15

For tourism to flourish and to fully benefit local communities and the destinations in the region, sustainability of the sector is a prerequisite in all areas of its value chain to ensure inclusive development for the continent. With the objective to minimize the negative impacts of the sector, sustainable tourism has the potential to be a key driver of wildlife protection and conservation in Africa. Furthermore, the main draw for the outbound market to the region remains its rich natural scenery, culture and biodiversity and unique flora and fauna. UNWTO is committed to support Member States towards the implementation of sound sustainable practices and fostering knowledge sharing. As travellers are becoming more and more aware of the fragility of the environment, with climate change, pollution, poaching, carbon footprints' impacts on the ecosystem, the sector is faced by increasing demands for authentic experiences that not only benefit economically local communities but also respects the natural environment.

Promoting cultural heritage – SDGs 8, 16

Importantly, in Africa, cultural heritage is the lifeblood of the tourism sector. With immeasurable value for communities, it is likely to figure strongly in the tourism product and promotion of most destinations, even those which have traditionally relied on their natural assets for their attractiveness. African heritage and culture paired with the warm hospitality of its people are amongst the most valuable continental assets. Destinations are tapping into cultural and heritage tourism opportunities to increase their attractiveness as a destination. UNWTO will focus on a number of initiatives aimed at enhancing African heritage and culture to support the promotion of the preservation of buildings and open spaces, promoting gastronomy, music, cultural dances and more, which all contribute to sustaining traditional and contemporary cultural values.

Policy frameworks

Further to the significant socio-economic improvement that tourism can bring to a country's economy, it is equally important to highlight the power of this industry to accelerate reform. With the view of increasing the tourist arrivals and consequently the economic flow in a country, governments should have sound policy frameworks for greater political stability, good governance and enabling business environments that lead to tourism growth and progress. UNWTO is committed to facilitating the development of sustainable tourism, making the destination more attractive to tourists and investors, as well as have a more competitive edge among national and international destinations. In so doing, creating a better business environment for tourism, African governments may not only attract more tourists and revenues but may also empower vulnerable groups generating employment and income in the less developed, often peripheral, regions of a country where alternative opportunities for development are more limited.

UNWTO is involved in supporting policy reforms and initiatives aimed at:

- ensuring the availability and sustainable management of water and sanitation for all as tourism can play a critical role in achieving water access and security, as well as hygiene and sanitation;
- building resilient infrastructure, promoting inclusive and sustainable industrialization and fostering innovation as tourism's development relies on good public and privately supplied infrastructure and an innovative environment; and
- protecting, restoring and promoting the sustainable use of terrestrial ecosystems by conserving and preserving biodiversity, respecting terrestrial ecosystems, conservation of native flora and fauna through awareness-raising activities.

African countries' uniqueness and richness allow for a broad tourism offer, unforgettable experiences and unparalleled assortment of national products that need to be provided through an efficient and professionally delivered value chain that is able to attract, sustain and satisfy increasing numbers of tourists. UNWTO is involved in supporting the improvement of countries' tourism value chain and a better management of tourism products and offers.

The UNWTO remains firmly committed to working with its African Member States to ensure that tourism development in Africa is genuinely and sustainably inclusive, inspiring, inviting and innovative. To facilitate and accelerate the sustainable development of tourism in Africa, UNWTO provides a variety of relevant services to its Member States, ranging from advocacy and awareness-raising, to knowledge creation and dissemination, policymaking and capacity-building. Programmes are designed and planned to meet Government's immediate and long-term objectives to improve their respective tourism sectors' competitiveness and to serve as a tool for sustainable development. Unlocking tourism's full potential towards achieving the SDGs, sharing the knowledge and good practices between all stakeholders – governments, businesses, the UN system, the donor community, academia and civil society – will be vital for the long road ahead. For this reason, in line with SDG 17, the UNWTO advocates for more cooperation and for tourism to be integrated into the global agenda.

Bibliography and online links

Christie, Iain, Fernandes, Eneida, Messerli, Hannah, and Twining-Ward, Louise (2014) *Tourism in Africa: Harnessing Tourism for Growth and Improved Livelihoods. Africa Development Forum Series.* Washington, DC: World Bank.

International Labour Organization (2013) *International Perspectives on Women and Work in Hotels, Catering, and Tourism.* Geneva: ILO.

Novelli, M, Gussing-Burgess, L., Jones, A., and Ritchie, W. R. (2018) 'No Ebola…still doomed' – the Ebola-induced Tourism Crisis. *Annals of Tourism Research*, Volume 70, May 2018, 76–87.

Theobald, W. (2005) *Global Tourism* (3rd ed.) Amsterdam: Elsevier Butterworth-Heinemann.

United Nations (2016) *United Nations Demographic Year Book.* New York: UN.

UNWTO (2018) *Report of the Secretary-General, Part I: Current Situation and Activities, (b) Management Vision and Priorities, Towards 2030: Making Tourism Smarter, More Competitive and More Responsible,* Madrid: UNWTO.

World Tourism Organization and United Nations Development Programme (2017), *Tourism and the Sustainable Development Goals – Journey to 2030, Highlights,* Madrid: UNWTO, DOI: https://doi.org/10.18111/9789284419340.

Online links

Observatoire économique et statistique d'Afrique subsaharienne (AFRISTAT) http://www.afristat.org/rcm.unwto.org/es/publication/toolbox-crisis-communications-tourism.

Single African Air Transport Market (SAATM) https://au.int/sites/default/files/newsevents/working-documents/33100-wd-6a-brochure_on_single_african_air_transport_market_english.pdf.

Sustainable Development Knowledge Platform https://sustainabledevelopment.un.org.

Tourism for SDGS http://tourism4sdgs.org/.

United Nations (2017) The Bogota Declaration on Big Data for Statistics https://unstats.un.org/unsd/bigdata/conferences/2017/Bogota%20declaration%20-%20Final%20version.pdf.

UNWTO (n.d) Why Tourism. http://www2.unwto.org/content/why-tourism. www.e-unwto.org/doi/pdf/10.18111/9789284419029.

UNWTO (2011) Tourism Towards 2030 Global Overview. https://www.globalwellnesssummit.com/wp-content/uploads/Industry-Research/Global/2011_UNWTO_Tourism_Towards_2030.pdf.

UNWTO (2017) Measuring Sustainable Tourism: A Call for Action. https://www.e-unwto.org/doi/pdf/10.18111/9789284418954.

UNWTO (2017) Tourism and the Sustainable Development Goals. http://cf.cdn.unwto.org/sites/all/files/pdf/sustainable_development_goals_brochure.pdf.

UNWTO (2018) Abuja Call for Action on the Development of Tourism Statistics in Africa http://cf.cdn.unwto.org/sites/all/files/pdf/abuja_call_for_action-final_rev1-13.06.2018.pdf.

UNWTO (2018) Definitions Committee on Tourism and Competitiveness (CTC). http://cf.cdn.unwto.org/sites/all/files/pdf/ctc_definitions_en_web.pdf

UNWTO (2018) Visa Openness Report http://cf.cdn.unwto.org/sites/all/files/docpdf/2018visaopennessreport.pdf.

UNWTO (2019) Tourism Highlights 2018 Edition. https://www.e-unwto.org/doi/pdf/10.18111/9789284419876.

World Economic Forum (2017) *The Travel & Tourism Competitiveness Report 2017* https://www.weforum.org/reports/the-travel-tourism-competitiveness-report-2017.

InFocus 2

The growth of Meetings, incentive, conferences and exhibition/ events (MICE) industry in Africa

Kwakye Donkor

Meeting, Incentives, Conferences and Exhibitions/Events (MICE) tourism produces the highest daily yield amongst all the sectors in the tourism industry. It stimulates economic growth, as it has a direct knock-on effect only on the tourism industry, but also many other industries and job creation. It also contributes to destination brand building, attract thought leaders, whilst showcasing products, innovation and expertise, and generating media attention. This, in turn showcases a country's level of readiness to do business with the rest of the world. Rwanda is a good example of this despite its challenges of having a skilled workforce, which can fully meet the demands of this fast developing sector (Ndegeya, 2019). Rwanda Convention Bureau reported that in 2018, over 35,000 international delegates were in Rwanda, generating about USD52 million. The amount generated in 2018 is more than the USD42 million generated in 2017 after hosting 192 conferences. Unsurprisingly, in May 2018, 'the International Congress and Convention Association (ICCA) named Rwanda as the third most popular destination in Africa for accommodating international meetings and events' (Ezeana, 2018).

Generally, there is limited understanding of this type of tourism, particularly from public sector's institutions. Equally, venues and destinations on the continent have limited appreciation for the value of MICE or the complexities of what developing this means for a destination. As a result, both public and private sectors have made limited investment into the development of MICE and focused on aggressive marketing and promotion of what they perceive as being their main product. There are also perceived barriers to optimizing tourism assets in Africa to leverage the benefits of the MICE sector. These barriers include high cost of intra-Africa, the level of visa openness, skills and personnel capability issues. These often hinder support, create frustration and consequently hamper destination's success in establishing a robust MICE tourism sector.

Despite the earlier problems, African destinations, such as Ghana, Kenya, Rwanda and South Africa, have stepped up their efforts with innovative approaches, and have established themselves as MICE tourism destinations. The mushrooming international hotel brands all over Africa and roles played by Convention Bureaux across the continent are also contributing positively to plugging the gap between established MICE destinations in Europe, Asia, and Americas and emerging African MICE destinations. This transformation is clearly reflected in the latest International Congress and Convention Association (ICCA) 2018 report, which shows over 40% increase in meetings held on the continent over the past ten years.

In the context of the above, a highly competitive landscape, low economic growth, dwindling global oil economy, and other export resources and the advent of social media, there is a greater need for African destinations to sharpen their efforts and refocus in growing their business and MICE tourism economy as an alternative tourism growth sector to other natural export resources. This, however, requires a totally radical transformative planning and marketing approach to business and MICE tourism and one which is not focused on simplistically 'building another convention centre', but rather working toward an integrated business destination development and management strategy, with the ultimate goal to better capitalize on the opportunities that the 21st-century business tourism presents at national, continental and global levels.

References

Ezeana (2018) Four years after, Rwanda's MICE strategy is yielding impressive results, *The Nerve Africa*, Available at: https://thenerveafrica.com/25406/four-years-after-rwandas-mice-strategy-is-yielding-impressive-results/, Downloaded: 29/09/ 2019.

Ndegeya, C. (2019) MICE tourism paying off, but specialist skills needed to shield growth, *Rwanda Today*, Available at: http://rwandatoday.africa/opinion/MICE-tourism-paying-off/4383220-5000086-3w77opz/index.html, Downloaded: 29/09/2019.

Part II
Tourism in North Africa

8

Tunisian tourism, gender and the contribution of postcolonial feminism

Heather Jeffrey and Nick Rumens

Introduction

Feminist theory in general and postcolonial feminist theory, in particular, has yet to make a significant impact on research that focuses on gender and tourism. Acting in a corrective fashion, this chapter contributes to the paucity of literature on gender and tourism by advocating for and highlighting the utility of postcolonial feminism as a conceptual resource for tourism studies scholars. Pursuing this, we start by outlining the dearth of scholarship on tourism and gender before noting and critiquing the discourse of female empowerment that has come to the fore in academic and policy-making arenas. Next, we discuss the key tenets of postcolonial feminism and demonstrate why and how tourism studies scholars can draw on postcolonial feminism theory to examine the dynamics between gender, cultural difference and tourism. To illustrate its conceptual power, we present a case study of gender and tourism in Tunisia to show how postcolonial feminism can interrogate the European epistemologies that uphold European imperialism (Young, 2001). In this instance, the act of veiling is problematised to challenge assumptions that the veil is synonymous with subordination. We critique tourism's complicity in the creation of neo-colonial relations that exclude visibly Muslim women. In discussing the role of tourism and 'women's rights' to gain political support, postcolonial feminism enables us to highlight how Western norms of women's rights have travelled and been incorporated by local politicians, who continue to construct women who choose to veil as Other (Mohanty, 1988).

Tourism and other women

A significant body of research on tourism and women has emerged since the mid-1990s (Chambers & Rakić, 2018; Cole, 2018; Ferguson, 2011; Figueroa-Domecq et al., 2015; Kinnaird et al., 1994; Marshment, 1997; Pritchard & Morgan, 2005; Small et al., 2017; Vizcaino-Suárez & Díaz-Carrión, 2018), and although seminal author Margaret Swain (1995) described gender as a context-dependent social construct, the geographical scope of gender and tourism research remains narrow. Often researchers neglect geographical contexts in the Third World, and tourism research is yet to lift the voices of women in the Global

South (Chambers & Rakić, 2018; Khoo-Lattimore & Mura, 2016). One reason for this is that gender was placed on the tourism agenda much later than in other disciplines, as well as due to patchy engagement with diverse feminist theories (Chambers & Rakić, 2018; Figueroa-Domecq et al., 2015). In addition, contemporary gender and tourism research is often located within development studies, encouraged by wider initiatives such as the United Nations Millennium and Sustainable Development Goals. For example, the collaboration between UN Women and the United Nations World Tourism Organisation produced the first 'Global Report on Women in Tourism with UN Women' in 2010.

The report primarily focused on the ability of tourism to economically empower women hosts (e.g. women working and living in tourism destinations) in developing contexts, which also underpins academic work on gender and tourism in developing communities (Foley et al., 2018; Scheyvens, 2002). This focal point of research and analysis is founded on the belief that tourism jobs require few skills and so have low entry barriers. However, we argue that the current emphasis on empowerment by academics and policymakers risks reifying discourses that (re)present Third World women as homogenous victims of oppression, not least because those who are empowered must have previously been disempowered (Kabeer, 2005). From a critical perspective, Cole (2018) in the book *Gender Equality and Tourism beyond Empowerment* has taken the first steps to problematise a discourse of empowerment, which it describes as the continuation of a neoliberal agenda. Many societies do not appreciate work that is conceived of as 'women's work' (e.g. cleaning hotel rooms) and as such, women who perform these roles receive low salaries and little opportunity for career progression. Under the banner of economic empowerment, the tourism industry benefits from gender inequality by recruiting flexible low-paid women (Ferguson, 2011), and it is notable that on a global scale up to two-thirds of tourism employees are women (Figueroa-Domecq et al., 2015).

Extant research on women and tourism can be categorised into research with a primary focus on women tourists or women hosts, but Cole (2018) underscores the importance of contextualised, intersectional analyses of women's experiences in tourism. Often women tourists are conceptualised as originating from the Global North and women hosts from the Global South, which overlooks the intersectional nature of gender and limits the potentialities of academic research to explore fully women's experiences in tourism (Jeffrey, 2018). Intersectionality has had little theoretical uptake in the tourism literature but, as its feminist progenitors have argued forcibly (e.g. Crenshaw, 1989), it is a useful conceptual construct to unpack the locational and culturally contingent dynamics between race, gender, religion and class. Indeed, in its earliest manifestation, intersectionality was advocated for and developed by Black feminists (see Hopkins, 2017), who critiqued (white) feminism for theorising woman as a universal category.

Postcolonial feminism

Black feminist critiques of white Western feminist theory and politics have partly shaped the emergence of postcolonial feminism during the 1990s. In contrast to Black feminism, postcolonial feminists such as Chandra Mohanty, Uma Narayan and Gayatri Spivak have sought to expose and interrogate white Western feminism's complicity in (re)producing colonial discourses that have Othered non-Western women (Spivak, 1988). As such, postcolonial feminism converses with but cannot be reduced to postcolonial theory's preoccupation with critiquing and undermining the West/non-West binary that has structured Western understandings of the oriental Other (Said, 1978). In addition, postcolonial feminism has been heavily influenced by a wider postmodern questioning of the humanist concept of the self as stable and fixed. Here, postcolonial feminists have drawn from postmodern and poststructuralist theories to conceptualise the self as a discursive effect, that is constituted by discourse, and to examine how Western discourse has (re)produced and organised cultural difference within a binary formation (e.g. West/non-West). Elaborating this and other aspects of postcolonial feminism, we highlight some of its key tenets as follows.

First, as a starting point, postcolonial feminism understands the postcolonial world as a cultural construction shaped by historical processes of imperialism and colonisation (Mohanty, 2003; Narayan, 2000; Spivak, 1988). Postcolonial feminist scholarship represents a substantial intervention that seeks to rupture Western imperialism (Rajan & Park, 2000), questioning prevailing ontologies and epistemologies of colonialism that have and continue to uphold forms of European imperialism (Young, 2001). One goal is to dislocate the 'motor of world history' from its position in 'Europe', in favour of recognising formations of 'high civilisation outside of Europe' (Kerner, 2017: 854) and their contribution to global power relations. The gendered facets of these debates are numerous and may include undermining a global notion of 'feminist sisterhood', exploring the role of non-Western feminisms within Western feminist theories and acknowledging the contributions of non-Western women in the global campaign for gender equality. Understood as such, postcolonial feminism may be located at the confluence of colonialism and postcolonialism, drawing out its gendered contours but along an axis of cultural difference that considers race, ethnicity, class and sexuality (Rajan and Park, 2000).

Second, postcolonial feminism has paid particular scrutiny to the binary construction of First/Third World Women within Western feminism (Mohanty, 1991, 2003; Narayan, 2000; Spivak, 1988). By bringing different cultural feminism into dialogue with each other, postcolonial feminism has revealed how the category of Third World women is discursively constructed as a homogenous category, where Third World women are characterised as subordinate and victims (Mohanty, 1991, 2003). Scholars of postcolonial feminism argue that Third World women have been robbed of their agency and, ultimately, used as a discursive ploy to legitimise neo-colonial interventions that seek to 'save' Third World women from a perceived life of servitude and victimhood (Spivak, 1988). Put differently, constructed as Third World Women, non-Western women are positioned in a relationship of dependence with their colonisers. Crucially, postcolonial feminism moves beyond simply exposing this binary by seeking to orchestrate its deconstruction. In that capacity, Gayatri Spivak (1988) is well-known for deploying Jacques Derrida's notion of deconstruction as an analytical tool to question the 'truths' that surround the category of 'woman', such as its supposed natural link with femininity, in order to challenge gender binary formations constructed along the axis of cultural difference (e.g. First/Third World Women). For Spivak, deconstruction is a sharp tool for unpicking privilege and destabilising the binaries that cultivate European imperialism.

Third, postcolonial feminism is concerned with how processes of Othering and cultural difference overlap (Sharpe & Spivak, 2003). For example, white Western feminism has been critiqued by postcolonial feminists for its complicity in the (re)production of colonial discourses that have Othered non-Western women (Spivak, 1988). Othering favours the powerful, as Simone de Beauvoir (1949) famously demonstrated in how 'woman' is constructed as Other, sited in opposition and inferior to man. Similarly, Spivak (1988: 75) writes that the Other is invariably understood as being lower down the hierarchy when compared with the self: the Other is 'the self's shadow' (1988: 75). The act of Othering is essentialist in nature because it reduces the difference to narrowly restrictive stereotypes that spark epistemic violence, whereby the complex and sometimes contradictory qualities of the Other remain hidden and are eventually lost (Jack and Westwood, 2009; Spivak, 1988). Postcolonial feminists take to task processes of Othering and cultural difference, but they do not limit this to differences between the coloniser and the colonised Other, but include intra-national differences such as class and education (Sharpe & Spivak, 2003). Related to this, one important outcome of postcolonial feminist interventions is research that is 'politically focused', historically oriented and localised in the cultural contexts of women's lives (Mohanty, 2003: 32), generating empirical insights into issues such as unequal access to education and work, low incomes, female genital mutilation and oppressive marital arrangements.

Postcolonial feminism and tourism studies

As discussed above, gender has often been neglected within tourism studies, and although tourism scholars have started to address this knowledge gap (Chambers & Rakić, 2018; Figueroa-Domecq et al., 2015; Small et al., 2017), research on gender and tourism is a work in progress. It is not altogether surprising that postcolonial feminism is neither a go-to theoretical resource nor an established topic of study within tourism scholarship. While postcolonialism has attracted scholarly attention within tourism studies, with Edward Said's (1978) *Orientalism* cited often by tourism scholars, the scholarship of postcolonial feminists such as Chandra Mohanty and Gayatri Spivak is much less cited. Indeed, a review of gender and tourism scholarship in 2015 revealed that postcolonial feminism is almost non-existent within the already marginal area of gender and tourism (Figueroa-Domecq et al., 2015). This neglect represents the failure of many tourism researchers to account for the gendered consequences of (post)colonial power relationships that have shaped and continue to shape numerous tourist destinations. Our call to more fully embrace the diversity of feminist theory, in particular, postcolonial feminism, aims to address this, as postcolonial feminism demands, for example, that we ask difficult questions about who can speak for who. In other words, one pressing concern for postcolonial feminists is (re)presentation. The (re)presentation of the developing world has often fused together two rather separate ideas: "speaking for" as in political representation and "speaking about" (Spivak, 1988: 70). Within tourism research we must ask who is speaking and who are they speaking for, to critique the classical tourism canon of knowledge that still privileges the voices of white, male academics, and Anglocentric geographical contexts (Chambers & Rakić, 2018; Munar et al., 2015). Furthermore, we must also ask who is speaking about who.

Such questions gain luminosity when we consider that the tourism industry is a dominant image maker, emitting a continuous flow of representations through mass media, advertising, and promotional brochures, which shape tourist expectations when visiting a destination (Kinnaird et al., 1994). These (re)presentations are not 'true' reflections of reality; rather, they are shaped by power relations embedded within neoliberal marketing, racism and neocolonialism. In this vein, the (re)presentation only exists due to the purpose it must serve (e.g.to sell a destination). The politics of (re)presentation demands consideration is given to those 'people that have a stake in representing and reinforcing certain stereotypical gestures, characteristics, or styles do not necessarily operate in the best interests of those represented' (Borgerson & Schroeder, 2002: 579). Tourism as a context is particularly interesting as meanings are created and communicated across cultures, and (re)presentations found in promotional materials perhaps 'speak' both for and about local peoples. The (re)presentations can become normative as they create a self-fulfilling prophecy of what tourists expect to see in the destination (Pritchard & Morgan, 2005).

In light of this, tourism research has not explored fully how women are (re)presented by the tourism industry, and promotional materials have primarily been studied focussing on women tourists or the sexualised women 'hosts' (Alessio & Jóhannsdóttir, 2011; Bandyopadhyay & Nascimento, 2010; Pritchard & Morgan, 2005; Schellhorn & Perkins, 2004). Often hosts lack any form of (re)presentation in brochures as brochures discursively work to sell empty, groomed spaces ready for tourist colonisation (Hunter, 2008). When hosts are (re)presented, it is often done using familiar stereotypes, aimed at selling cultural difference in recognisable formulations (Marshment, 1997). For example, women are often (re)presented alone, portrayed as a submissive Other (Marshment, 1997; Schellhorn & Perkins, 2004). (Re)presentations often discursively merge the feminine and the exotic, effacing individuality and creating a monolithic Other category or, as Pritchard and Morgan (2005: 292) put it, 'each woman represents the essence of her 'exotic' culture'. In tourism contexts where formal processes of colonisation have ended, the legacy of colonisation is such that cultures continue to bear the traces of their colonial (re)construction. Both structural domination and a discursive suppression of the heterogeneous nature of the colonised continues (Mohanty, 1988), as can be identified in tourism promotions.

One resource within postcolonial feminism theory for addressing the issue of representation is Spivak's (1988) essay 'Can the subaltern speak?' Referring to Gramsci's notion of the 'subaltern' (which he applied to those social groups subjugated under the hegemony of the ruling classes), Spivak theorises the conditions of possibility for generating knowledge about the 'female subaltern'. Spivak's complaint concerns how some Western feminists have represented the subaltern woman as a case of 'speaking for the subaltern', rather than letting the subaltern woman speak for herself. Conceived as an act of epistemic violence, Spivak famously ended her essay with the assertion: 'the subaltern cannot speak!' (1988: 312). In so doing, Spivak cast serious doubt on the possibility for the subaltern woman to make a free representation of herself in her own words, arguing that the subaltern is represented and heard through the mediation of the non-subaltern. This is a salient point for tourism scholars and for individuals within the tourism industry because it demands they learn to speak to (rather than listen to or speak for) the subaltern woman. In so doing, a turn of emphasis might be engineered, from simply representing women as alluring figures within exotic tourist destinations to understanding how such representations reproduce the political positions, identities and the interests that lie behind their assumptions and goals. Moreover, postcolonial feminism would seek to interrogate the discourse of empowerment by questioning the position of international organisations who presume to know and speak for Third World women (Spivak, 1988), in particular, how 'they' can empower 'them'.

Notably, Spivak (1988: 189) recast her declaration ('the subaltern cannot speak!') as 'inadvisable' (for potentially robbing subaltern women of agency in being able to speak for themselves), submitting instead that scholars must acknowledge and reflect on their complicity in 'muting' the subaltern subject (1999: 190). This point must be taken up by tourism scholars, both methodologically and analytically. For those seeking to commit methodologically to these principles, Hopeful Tourism, 'a values-based, unfolding transformative perspective' on tourism research (Pritchard et al., 2011: 942) can serve as a point of departure. Epistemologically, scholars must question their own assumptions toward women and further the emerging stream of tourism and gender research (Small et al., 2017). This point is of utmost importance in regard to countries such as Tunisia, hailed as leading the MENA region in gender equality by Western media (Murphy, 1996), which has led to weakened opposition and even support from the West for autocratic regimes viewed as 'liberal' (Dalmasso & Cavatorta, 2010). This discourse has permeated academic work, with some scholars describing the Tunisian dictator Ben Ali as invoking a liberal atmosphere (Sinha, 2011).

The contemporary salience of postcolonial feminism as a theoretical resource for tourism scholars is apparent also in how media and political debate regularly rely on the manufactured image of Muslim women as passive, submissive dupes to a repressive religion (Dabashi, 2012). The use of anachronistic (re)presentations portraying Muslim women as out of place and time, fixed in history and in need of modernising continues to be used as the archetype for (re)presentation (Zine, 2002). Problematising these discursive constructions, postcolonial feminists have intervened in debates around (un)veiling. The veil, an English translation for hijab, has been at the centre of feminist debates on the Middle East. Postcolonial feminist Chandra Mohanty has berated Western feminists for making the analytical jump from the 'veil' to subordination (Mohanty, 1988), but it is not only Western feminists who may be guilty of this conceptual leap. Muslim feminists have also reiterated the dominant construction of veiling as subordination (Ghumkhor, 2012; Mernissi, 1991), perhaps again due to the pervasiveness of the discourse which can be read as a form of epistemic violence, rendering alternative discourses impossible or subordinate. The veil has been discursively (re)presented as a male imposition on Muslim women, which has helped to justify a variety of neo-colonial impositions, such as the war on terror in Afghanistan (Abu-Lughod, 2002), in an effort to rescue her. Yet, the veil in Muslim societies has a variety of meanings, and in many Islamic communities the veil is a symbol of resistance to top down 'de-veiling' (Hoodfar, 1992).

Colonialism within the Muslim world has been characterised by the circulation of dominant discourse pertaining to sexual imaginaries of the harem and conquering the Muslim World (Fanon, 1963). In this frame, Muslim women were (re)presented as an exotic Other, which if to be known had to be uncovered (Zine, 2002). In 1958 during the war of Independence, French soldiers orchestrated a mass unveiling in Algeria to show that the Muslim woman had been conquered, and she and her country had given in to European values (MacMaster, 2012). This (re)presentation has created epistemic (and material) violence towards Muslim women, as the epitome of her 'uncivilised' population and an image of eastern sexual deviance. Travel writers (male and female) of the time were often complicitous in epistemic closure (Hoodfar, 1992; McClintock, 1995). Notably, some postcolonial Muslim, North African States began to re-work these dominant discourses to meet a modernity created by the European colonisers (Said, 1978). The veiled woman was considered to signify all that was 'backwards' and as the denigrated community sought to modernise many initiated processes of unveiling (Fanon, 1963; Ghumkhor, 2012).

The significance of the veil in postcolonial North Africa, especially Algeria, Egypt and Tunisia lie in the transformation of the veil into a symbol of national identity under colonial rule (Fanon, 1963). In Algeria, the French attempted to civilise the colonised by ridding women of the veil, and in Tunisia a return to the veil symbolised Tunisian nationalism, only to be quickly discounted upon gaining independence (Ghumkhor, 2012). The veil in contemporary Muslim societies can have a variety of meanings, but the most important acknowledgement is that many women believe it helps them in their day-to-day lives (Ghumkhor, 2012; Hoodfar, 1992; Zine, 2002). Tunisia is a complex case, as even though the discourse of exotic/backward Other Muslim women is pervasive, the country has been celebrated as a triumph of modernity in the West due to both tourism and unveiling. Yet, this is in part because Tunisia did not question the prevailing epistemologies that have upheld European imperialism, Tunisia has mimicked the West.

The (re)presentation of veiled women in tourism promotions is said to portray the exotic, primitive Other (Jafari & Scott, 2014) and evidence Orientalist discourses (Echtner &

Prasad, 2003; Hoodfar, 1992). Yet, one study of printed brochures and official websites for six countries with a predominantly Muslim population shows that marketers strategically choose to overlook religion, with the exception of aesthetically pleasing mosques (Henderson, 2008). Religion and locals might be replaced by tourists to combat negative Western (re) presentations and the preoccupation with the status of women in Muslim countries. Through Western eyes, the Middle East is often pictured mentally as a place to fear (Morakabati, 2013), and visibly religious Muslim women (those who cover, veil or wear a niqab) have been discursively constructed as the demonised face of Islam in the West, depicted as an inseparable homogenous group, regardless of nationality (Gray & Coonan, 2013).

Illustration: a postcolonial feminist interpretation of Tunisian tourism

A reading of Tunisian tourism through a postcolonial feminist lens can illustrate more vividly how postcolonial feminism can enable tourism scholars to focus closely on the dynamics between gender and cultural difference. By way of context, Tunisia is a small country on the north coast of Africa, home to just over 11 million people of which 99.1% are Muslim and 98% are of Arab ethnicity (CIA, 2018). Despite its small population, since 2010 Tunisia has received much media attention as the country that started the Arab Spring, a revolution that saw the ousting of many Arab dictators. Tunisia has a long history of invasion and colonialism and has been at least a temporary home to the Phoenicians, Punics, Romans, Vandals, Byzantines and more recently Ottomans and the French. In 1574 Tunisia became an Ottoman province, while the Ottoman Empire extended across North Africa, they remained the longest in Tunisia (Rossi, 1967). In 1881 more than a century of authoritarian rule began when France seized Tunisia (Gray & Coonan, 2013).

French colonialists were revered as a symbol of modernity among the local elite (Rossi, 1967), at least in part due to 'an occidental epistemological system imposed by the coloniser' (Barnard, 2013: 74). Tourism was a popular activity among the French elite during the colonial period, forming part of their 'mision civiltrise' which was later continued by the Tunisian elite for the same purposes (Hazbun, 2008). The civilising mission of French colonialism and its abrupt transformation to a modernising neo-colonial endurance (Spivak, 2000) is perhaps nowhere clearer than in Tunisia. Resentment towards the French settlers eventually grew alongside inequality between the two groups. In 1954 the Carthage declaration recognised Tunisian autonomy and in 1956 Tunisia was granted independence (Rossi, 1967). Habib Bourguiba became the first president of this newly independent country.

The 'civilized' Bourguiba had attended a French/Arabic bilingual school which aimed to lead the local elite along a 'modernising' path of assimilation (as was the aim of all schools in the French Protectorate), before further studies in Paris (Salem, 1984). However, in the years prior to independence, Bourguiba drew on the most prominent cultural identity: Islam, to encourage a national identity distinctive to that of the colonialists. Within this project, he vehemently advocated for Tunisian women to cover their hair (Salem, 1984), which could be understood as a move of resistance towards colonial interference (Hoodfar, 1992). However, once Bourguiba was elected President, he introduced a new 'cultural liberation' programme to deliver lessons in morality (Rossi, 1967). Bourguiba wanted to challenge cultural traditions he considered irrational, folkloric and pre-modern, he did this by focussing on both the family and religion. He began to weaken the constraints on women's productive freedom and public participation, in contrast to other North African territories and since this time the veil has been more or less formally banned in public in Tunisia (Marshall & Stokes, 1981). For the most part, this focus targeted Tunisian women and even though Bourguiba was a native Tunisian, his project can most certainly be described as neo-colonialism (Spivak, 2000).

Tourism was ascribed a key role within the 'cultural liberation' programme. Bourguiba relied on tourists to 'train' the local population on what it meant to be modern (Rossi, 1967). Both tourism and a focus on women's rights, which mimicked Western feminist concerns, granted Bourguiba support from the West, leading to his lifetime Presidency (Salem, 1984). Bourguiba's 'modernising' ideology, which excluded many and incarcerated the opposition was the source of his downfall, and, in 1989, an Islamist uprising, concerns about his senility and regarding state intervention, led to his replacement by President Ben Ali (Hazbun, 2008). Ben Ali was to ultimately maintain Bourguiba's modernising project, continuing to focus on tourism as a tool for development and attempting to secularise the nation. Both leaders mobilised a fear of jihadism to legitimise authoritarian rule and secular policies (Dalmasso & Cavatorta, 2010). Human rights abuses, such as torture or a lack of political pluralism, democracy and freedom of expression have been ignored by the West because the Islamist opposition is perceived as being far worse (Dalmasso & Cavatorta, 2010), or because the country is perceived as a liberal tourist safe haven.

This was evidenced in the 1970s when Tunisia became one of the fastest growing tourist destinations in the world (Poirier, 1995). Yet, the success of the tourism industry and Western support for autocratic regimes in Tunisia perhaps says more about the Western tourist self, and a belief that Western women are 'secular, liberated and having control over their own lives' (Mohanty, 1988: 74). As when they look to Tunisia this is the model that they see, at least on the surface. Mutually constitutive, tourism and women's rights have been pivotal in all Tunisia's development plans (Hazbun, 2008). Under Bourguiba tourism and women's rights, traditional notions of the family and religious belief systems were attacked, to achieve a wider goal of 'modernity' (Rossi, 1967). Western tourism has been complicit in Bourguiba's neo-colonial project to modernise Tunisia, as is evidenced by the growing number of European tourist arrivals only ceasing after the 2010 revolution. Tourists were utilised to instil values within the local population, in a similar vein to the civilising missions of the French colonialists. However, in an attempt to move from a simplistic analysis of good and evil (Suleri, 1992), tourism provided much needed foreign exchange, and, in order to attract tourists, Bourguiba had to compete with negative imagery and discourses on Islam. Bourguiba's policies on Women's rights, which were problematically top down, did improve the lives of some women as can be seen from the dramatic shift in the gender gap in education (according to the World Bank, 2016: in 1971 there was 0.6 disparity in favour of boys and in 2011 in 1.01 disparity in favour of girls). However, these policies reproduced two competing discourses on femininity, a modern unveiled secular femininity and a backward veiled religious femininity.

Colonial discursive strategies in (re)presenting the foreign Other have sought to discursively construct the veiled woman as a signifier of all that was 'backwards' (Hoodfar, 1992). Yet, perhaps it is the unveiling of Tunisian woman that is most telling of the perseverance of these discourses. European colonisation of the Muslim world was constituted by and constitutive of a desire to unveil women, who were (re)presented as exotic Others (Zine, 2002). The necessities of certain political discourses shape and give form to (re)presentation (Gianettoni & Roux, 2010) and the political regimes in Tunisia have consistently attempted to repress religious values, primarily the practice of veiling. This privileging of modernity mimics Western discourse on the privileging of modernity (McClintock, 1995). To meet the 'modern' ideal introduced by the colonisers, the local elite worked within the same discursive framework attempting to undo all that had previously been considered 'backward', initiating processes of unveiling (Fanon, 1963).

Postcolonial feminism opens an interrogative space to re-read Tunisian tourism and question prevailing gendered discourses on the cultural practice of veiling that uphold European imperialism. The focus on power relations outside Europe (Kerner, 2017) reveals how tourism and women in Tunisia lie at a complex nexus of local and colonial power relations. Recognising local power relations and situating them within wider colonial power relations enables the probing of both tourism and women within the global order, and in the case of Tunisia, Bourguiba and the discourse of (un)veiling can be read as complicit with European imperialism. For instance, in Tunisia, the Third World woman can be read as the veiled woman who is discursively constructed to garner local support for secular 'modern' regimes. The veiled woman is chastised and made to remain hidden, so Western tourists find Tunisia an attractive tourist destination. Taken together, 'women's rights' and tourism have been utilised to garner Western support for a cultural regime that has been critiqued as a dictatorship (Dalmasso & Cavatorta, 2010). Bourguiba's support for unveiling can be read as problematising the Third World woman category but simultaneously it emulates Western discourse on what constitutes women's rights.

Conclusion

Postcolonial feminism is almost non-existent within tourism scholarship, but, as this chapter highlights, it is an important theoretical resource in the analysis of gendered tourism in previously colonised destinations. Postcolonial feminism urges scholars to view the postcolonial world as a social construct, in order to question the dynamics between gender and cultural difference that sustain a neo-colonial order. Postcolonial feminism can aid tourism researchers in a political project to disrupt European imperialism by challenging Western epistemologies. In addition, it can help us to critique Western feminist scholarship that is complicit in reproducing the First/Third World Woman binary and, for those of us who hail from the West, postcolonial feminism forces thinking on how we position ourselves in relation to non-Western women as Other. As such, tourism researchers must engage in a reflexive project to analyse their own assumptions and account for their results.

Rounding off, this chapter has shown that postcolonial feminism warrants a place in the canon of gender theories drawn on by tourism scholars. In the case of Tunisia, postcolonial feminism demands we question normative understandings of the veil as a symbol of a backward or exotic Other, and its role in upholding European imperialism. The case highlights how veiling was politicised and used locally to (re)present veiled women as a backward, essentialised Other and how, in a tourism context, this strategy was deployed to support autocratic regimes. It is hoped that other tourism studies scholars will follow and extend our efforts to incorporate postcolonial feminism in the study of tourism and gender. In addition to the methodological contributions postcolonial feminism can lend to tourism, as a conceptual resource we see applicability in the questioning of empowerment and problematising of industry (re)presentations.

References

Abu-Lughod, L. (2002). Do Muslim women really need saving? Anthropological reflections on cultural relativism and its others. *American Anthropologist*, 104(3), 783–790.

Alessio, D. and Jóhannsdóttir, A. L. (2011). Geysers and 'girls': Gender, power and colonialism in Icelandic tourist imagery. *European Journal of Women's Studies*, 18(1), 35–50.

Bandyopadhyay, R. and Nascimento, K. (2010). "Where fantasy becomes reality": How tourism forces made Brazil a sexual playground. *Journal of Sustainable Tourism*, 18(8), 933–949.

Barnard, D. (2013). The necessity of having it both ways: Tradition, modernity, and experience in the works of Hélé Béji. In F. Sadiqi (Ed.), *Women and Knowledge in the Mediterranean*. Oxon: Routledge, 73–86.

Bhabha, H. (1994). *The Location of Culture*. London and New York: Routledge.

Borgerson, J. L. and Schroeder, J. E. (2002). Ethical issues of global marketing: Avoiding bad faith in visual representation. *European Journal of Marketing*, 36(5/6), 570–594.

Chambers, D. and Rakić, T. (2018). Critical considerations on gender and tourism: An introduction. *Tourism, Culture and Communication*, 18(1), 1–8.

CIA. (2018). Africa: Tunisia. *The World Factbook*. Retrieved 20/8/2018 from https://www.cia.gov/library/publications/the-world-factbook/geos/ts.html#People

Cole, S. (Ed.) (2018). *Gender Equality and Tourism: Beyond Empowerment*. Wallingford: CABI.

Crenshaw, K. W. (1989). Demarginalizing the intersection of race and sex: A black feminist critique of antidiscrimination doctrine, feminist theory and antiracist politics. *The University of Chicago Legal Forum*, 140, 139–167.

Dabashi, H. (2012). *The Arab Spring: Delayed Defiance and the End of Postcolonialism*. New York: Zed Books.

Dalmasso, E. and Cavatorta, F. (2010). Reforming the family code in Tunisia and Morocco—The struggle between religion, globalisation and democracy. *Totalitarian Movements and Political Religions*, 11(2), pp.213–228.

De Beauvoir, S. (1949). *The Second Sex*. Harmondsworth: Penguin.

Echtner, C. M. and Prasad, P. (2003). The context of third world tourism marketing. *Annals of Tourism Research*, 30(3), 660–682.

Fanon, F. (1963). *The Wretched of the Earth*. (C. Farrington, Trans.). New York: Grove Press.

Ferguson, L. (2011). Promoting gender equality and empowering women? Tourism and the third millennium development goal. *Current Issues in Tourism*, 14(3), 235–249.

Figueroa-Domecq, C., Pritchard, A., Segovia-Pérez, M., Morgan, N. J. and Villacé-Molinero, T. (2015). Tourism gender research: A critical accounting. *Annals of Tourism Research*, 52, 87–103.

Foley, C., Grabowski, S., Small, J. and Wearing, S. (2018). Women of the Kokoda: From poverty to empowerment in sustainable tourism development. *Tourism Culture & Communication*, 18(1), 21–34.

Ghumkhor, S. (2012). The veil and modernity: The case of Tunisia. *Interventions*, 14(4), 493–514.

Gianettoni, L., and Roux, P. (2010). Interconnecting race and gender relations: Racism, sexism and the attribution of sexism to the racialized other. *Sex Roles*, 62(5–6), 374–386.

Gray, D. H. and Coonan, T. (2013). Notes from the field: Silence kills! Women and the transitional justice process in post-revolutionary Tunisia. *International Journal of Transitional Justice*, 7(2), 348–357.

Hazbun, W. (2008). *Beaches, Ruins, Resorts: The Politics of Tourism in the Arab World*. Minneapolis: University of Minnesota Press.

Henderson, J. C. (2008). Representations of Islam in official tourism promotion. *Tourism Culture & Communication*, 8(3), 135–145.

Hoodfar, H. (1992). The veil in their minds and on our heads: The persistence of colonial images of Muslim women. *Resources for Feminist Research*, 22(3/4), 5–18.

Hopkins, P. (2017). Social geography I: Intersectionality. *Progress in Human Geography*, 43(5), 937–947.

Hunter, W. C. (2008). A typology of photographic representations for tourism: Depictions of groomed spaces. *Tourism Management*, 29(2), 354–365.

Jack, G. and Westwood, R. (2009). *International and Cross-Cultural Management Studies*. Basingstoke: Palgrave Macmillan.

Jafari, J. and Scott, N. (2014). Muslim world and its tourisms. *Annals of Tourism Research*, 44, 1–19.

Jeffrey, H. L. (2018). Tourism and gendered hosts and guests. *Tourism Review*, 74(5), 1038–1046.

Kabeer, N. (2005). Gender equality and women's empowerment: A critical analysis of the third millennium development goal 1. *Gender and Development*, 13(1), 13–24.

Kerner, I. (2017). Relations of difference: Power and inequality in intersectional and postcolonial feminist theories. *Current Sociology*, 65(6), 846–866.

Khoo-Lattimore, C. and Mura, P. (Eds.) (2016). *Asian Genders in Tourism*. Bristol: Channel View Publications.

Kinnaird, V., Kothari, U. and Hall, D. R. (1994). Tourism: Gender perspectives. In V. Kinnaird and D. R. Hall (Eds.), *Tourism: A Gender Analysis*. Chichester: John Wiley & Sons Ltd, 1–34.

MacMaster, N. (2012). *Burning the Veil: The Algerian War and the 'Emancipation' of Muslim Women, 1954–62*. Manchester: Manchester University Press.

Marshall, S. E. and Stokes, R. G. (1981). Tradition and the veil: Female status in Tunisia and Algeria. *The Journal of Modern African Studies*, 19(04), 625–646.

Marshment, M. (1997). Gender takes a holiday: Representation in holiday brochures. In M. T. Sinclair (Ed.), *Gender, Work and Tourism*. London: Routledge, 16–34.

McClintock, A. (1995). *Imperial Leather: Gender, Race and Sexuality in the Colonial Context*. New York: Routledge.

Mernissi, F. (1991). *The Veil and the Male Elite. A Feminist Interpretation of Women's Rights in Islam* (M. Lakeland, Trans.). Cambridge, MA: Perseus Books.

Mohanty, C. T. (1988). Under Western eyes: Feminist scholarship and colonial discourses. *Feminist Review*, 30(1), 61–88.

Mohanty, C. T. (1991). Under western eyes: Feminist scholarship and colonial discourses. In C. T. Mohanty, A. Russo and L. Torres (Eds.), *Third World Women and the Politics of Feminism*. Bloomington and Indianapolis: Indiana University Press, 51–80.

Mohanty, C. T. (2003). "Under Western eyes" revisited: Feminist solidarity through anticapitalist struggles. *Signs: Journal of Women in Culture and Society*, 28(2), 499–535.

Morakabati, Y. (2013). Tourism in the Middle East: Conflicts, crises and economic diversification, some critical issues. *International Journal of Tourism Research*, 15(4), 375–387.

Munar, A. M., Biran, A., Budeanu, A., Caton, K., Chambers, D., Dredge, D., Gyimóthy, S., Jamal, T., Larson, M., Nilsson Lindström, K. and Nygaard, L. (2015). *The Gender Gap in Tourism Academy: Statistics and Indicators of Gender Equality*. While Waiting for the Dawn. Report 1. Copenhagen: Tourism Education Futures

Murphy, E.C. (1996). Women in Tunisia: A survey of achievements and challenges. *The Journal of North African Studies*, 1(2), pp.138–156.

Narayan, U. (2000). Essence of culture and a sense of history: A feminist critique of cultural essentialism. In U. Narayan and S. Harding (Eds.), *Decentering the Center: Philosophy for a Multicultural, Postcolonial, and Feminist World*. Bloomington: Indiana University Press, 80–100.

Poirier, R. A. (1995). Tourism and development in Tunisia. *Annals of Tourism Research*, 22(1), 157–171.

Pritchard, A. and Morgan, N. J. (2005). 'On location'Re (viewing) bodies of fashion and places of desire. *Tourist Studies*, 5(3), 283–302.

Pritchard, A., Morgan, N. J. and Ateljevic, I. (2011). Hopeful tourism: A new transformative perspective. *Annals of Tourism Research*, 38(3), 941–963.

Rajan, R. S. and Park, Y. M. (2000). Postcolonial feminism/postcolonialism and feminism. In H. Schwarz and S. Ray (Eds.), *A Companion to Postcolonial Studies*. Malden: John Wiley & Sons, 53–71.

Rossi, P. (1967). *Bourguiba's Tunisia* (R. Matthews, Trans.). Tunis: Kahia.

Said, E. (1978). *Orientalism*. New York: Pantheon.

Salem, N. (1984). *Habib Bourguiba, Islam, and the Creation of Tunisia*. London: Croom Helm.

Schellhorn, M. and Perkins, H. C. (2004). The stuff of which dreams are made: Representations of the South Sea in German-language tourist brochures. *Current Issues in Tourism*, 7(2), 95–133.

Scheyvens, R. (2002). *Tourism for Development: Empowering Communities*. London: Pearson Education.

Sharpe, J. and Spivak, G. C. (2003). A conversation with Gayatri Chakravorty Spivak: Politics and the imagination. *Signs: Journal of Women in Culture and Society*, 28(2), 609–624.

Sinha, S. (2011). Women's rights: Tunisian women in the workplace. *Journal of International Women's Studies*, 12, 185–200.

Small, J., Harris, C. and Wilson, E. (2017). Gender on the agenda? The position of gender in tourism's high ranking journals. *Journal of Hospitality and Tourism Management*, 100(31), 114–117.

Spivak, G. C. (1988). Can the subaltern speak? In P. Williams and L. Chrisman (Eds.), *Colonial Discourse and Post-Colonial Theory*. New York: Columbia University Press, 66–111.

Spivak, G. C. (2000). A moral dilemma. *Theoria*, 47(96), 99–120.

Suleri, S. (1992). Woman skin deep: Feminism and the postcolonial condition. *Critical Inquiry*, 18(4), 756–769.

Swain, M. B. (1995). Gender in tourism. *Annals of Tourism Research*, 22(2), 247–266.

The World Bank. (2016). World Data Bank World Development Indicators. *The World Bank*. Retrieved 29/2/16 from http://databank.worldbank.org/data/reports.aspx?source=2&country=TUN&series=&period=#.

Vizcaino-Suárez, L. P. and Díaz-Carrión, I. (2018). Gender in tourism research: Perspectives from Latin America. *Tourism Review*, 74(5), 1091–1103.

Young, R. (2001). Colonialism and the desiring machine. In G. Castle (Ed.), *Postcolonial Discourses: An Anthology*. Oxford: Wiley-Blackwell, 73–99.

Zine, J. (2002). Muslim women and the politics of representation. *American Journal of Islamic Social Sciences*, 19(4), 1–22.

9

Understanding the complexities of residents' support for cultural heritage preservation through an equity theory lens

The case of World Heritage Sites of Carthage, Tunisia

Huda Abdullah Megeirhi, Manuel Alector Ribeiro and Kyle Maurice Woosnam

Introduction

Throughout the last couple of decades, cultural heritage has found its way into tourism and sustainability strategies. Managing both cultural heritage and tourism effectively and in the frame of sustainability not only boosts the quality of life and pride in a community, but also contributes to the diversification of the local economy and preservation of distinctive cultural heritage features found within the community (especially those possessing a UNESCO World Heritage Site) (Andereck and Nyaupane 2011; Kim et al. 2013; Sirisrisak 2009). Thus, a large number of tourism policies have been designed to link cultural heritage preservation to sustainability criteria.

Considering the preservation of a World Heritage Site (WHS), residents' support is a critical factor for sustainable tourism development (Woosnam et al. 2018; Yung and Chan 2011). Arguably, preservation efforts are only as effective as key stakeholders will allow. Therefore, the progress in cultural heritage preservation is challenging without proper support and contribution from local residents.

Residents' support for cultural heritage tourism preservation processes is a vital prerequisite for a place to be considered for WHS-designated status (Nicholas et al. 2009). In recent years, residents' support is often considered as a tool for preserving the assets of cultural heritage tourism (Ho and McKercher 2004). However, the effective role of resident's support in the practice of tourism and cultural heritage still demands serious and explicit investigation (Hodges and Watson 2000; Landorf 2009; Maruyama and Woosnam 2015).

The preservation of cultural heritage and sustainability is 'two sides' of the proverbial coin. Thus recognizing the complexities of residents' support for cultural heritage preservation can help to promote sustainability principles. The initial idea of sustainability was based on justice and equity; however, few efforts have been made in investigating equity issues within the context of WHS (Mowforth and Munt 2016). This is arguably due to the fact that equity and fairness remain challenging issues facing sustainability and tourism scholars (Jamal and Camargo 2013). As Ryan states "What if sustainability is perceived as a retention of the status quo to protect a cultural or physical environment, but does not recognize the social inequity inherent in those current situations" (2002, p. 22).

A plethora of studies exist examining various factors that influence residents' support for tourism development (e.g. Vargas-Sanchez et al. 2011), with a majority focused on how perceiving positive and negative impacts influences such support (e.g. Sharpley 2014; Vareiro et al. 2013). However, the connection between social equity and fairness to residents' support has been largely neglected. In the context of cultural heritage preservation, the link between perceived equity and local residents' support deserves a closer investigation. Thus, the unique case of WHS of Carthage-Tunisia would make a considerable contribution to the extant literature that addresses focused on cultural heritage preservation through residents' perceptions.

The current study aims to shed light on undiscovered factors potentially influencing the preservation process of WHS. The impact of social class discriminations on supporting culture heritage preservation has not been fully explored. Residents from different social classes may perceive different levels of equity which in turn affect sustainability through their intentions and behavior for supporting cultural heritage preservation. Sustainability scholars have warned of neglecting marginalized groups based on social standing, economic background and educational attainment (Ryan 2002). Therefore, it is crucial to consider a wide spectrum of residents and their perspectives in planning for sustainable tourism.

Based on the above-mentioned arguments, the present study contributes to the field of WHS preservation and residents' behavioral support in two unique capacities. The first of which is to consider cultural heritage preservation among residents focusing on the equity theory. The majority of studies concerning tourism development support, community participation, residents' perceptions, and WHS have relied heavily on the social exchange theory (SET) (e.g. Easterling 2004; Nicholas et al. 2009; Sharpley 2014). Researchers however, have argued that relying highly on SET in order to understand residents' perceptions without taking into account societal considerations might be insufficient (Fairley 2016; Fredline and Faulkner 2000; Pearce et al. 1996). Second, few qualitative studies have been undertaken that analyze potential factors influencing local residents' support for cultural heritage preservation from a philosophical-social point of view (Pearce et al. 1996). Thus, our study attempts to address this gap. Furthermore, the present work provides local residents an opportunity to share their concerns as we begin to understand the complexities involved with the development of perceptions of and intentions to support cultural heritage preservation. Furthermore, theoretical and practical implications along with research recommendations for future studies are also discussed.

Literature review

Local residents' support for cultural heritage preservation

Though the tourism literature is replete with studies involving residents' perspectives surrounding phenomena pertaining to tourism or tourism development (Stylidis 2018; Woosnam et al. 2018), little work has focused on residents' support for cultural heritage preservation in the context of WHS. This is arguably a function of the impending popularization of WHS and the realization that inclusion of residents and their perspectives of support are crucial in ensuring development and visitor management proceeds in a sustainable fashion (World Tourism Organization 2012).

Some tourism researchers have acknowledged the importance of including residents' perspectives concerning support for cultural heritage preservation near WHS. In looking at resident participation in decision making for the Mutianyu Great Wall WHS in Beijing, China, Su and Wall (2014) found that community locals received benefits with minimal participation. The authors further found that local opinions were influenced by different levels of impacts from tourism.

Rasoolimanesh, Jaafar, and colleagues are leading the charge as of late in research including residents' perspectives surrounding WHS and tourism. Rasoolimanesh et al. (2017) recently focused on community participation in WHS conservation and found motivation had the "greatest positive effect on the low level of community participation, whereas opportunity had the greatest effect on high level of participation" (p. 142) among residents. Utilizing stakeholder theory to explain residents' perceptions sustainable tourism development in the midst of a WHS in Malaysia, Rasoolimanesh and Jaafar (2017) revealed differing negative perceptions across demographics such as age, education, and economic involvement in tourism. Further, the authors found that positive perceptions led to a positive effect on support for and participation in tourism development. Focusing on youth residents living near the same WHS in Malaysia, Jaafar et al. (2015) found positive perceptions of conservation programs had a positive effect on involvement in promoting and supporting the WHS. Interestingly enough, the authors reported a positive relationship between negative perceptions and sense of belonging among the youth surveyed.

Much of the extant work pertaining to residents' perception of and support for WHS has not focused on matters of equity in gauging their support for cultural heritage preservation. Timothy (2011) argues that such neglect will only perpetuate a divide and make it difficult to sustainably plan and manage areas adjacent to WHS. Another observation of the existing work pertaining to residents and support for cultural heritage preservation is that the resident population under examination is largely treated as homogenous (with the noted exception of the work by Rasoolimanesh and Jaafar 2017). This implicitly discounts perspectives of disadvantaged residents living adjacent to WHS (Jamal and Camargo 2013). Furthermore, such an oversight downplays any power struggles and consideration of power in determining how a WHS should be preserved or managed. Ultimately, societal and historical context (of how different resident groups interact and their relationships) in many of the reviewed studies is disregarded. One may even go so far as to point out the irony in not acknowledging some of the local power struggles and inequity concerns in the face of trying to "preserve" heritage and history of the place and its structures.

Theory of equity and cultural heritage context

Equity theory, rooted in social psychology, primarily focuses on matters of justice among various stakeholders. Adams (1963), who is credited with introducing the theory in his initial research within an organizational behavior setting, purported that the core assumption of equity theory is equitable resource distribution among all interrelated parties. According to Adams' theory, in order to measure equity, each individual compares the portion of contributions to rewards with others who are involved in the exchange relationship (i.e. ratio of contributions made to outcomes received). Burrai et al. (2014) asserted that equity occurs, "if individuals perceive that there is equity and justice within the exchange relationship, they experience feelings of contentment that results in positive reactions and perceptions" (p. 2). In contrast, inequity occurs if individuals do not perceive their contribution (i.e. inputs) to rewards (i.e. outputs) ratio as similar to others. Comparable to predominant theories of motivation, equity theory admits that one's perception and judgment of equity would be influenced by various factors in the exchange relationship with relative partners (Guerrero et al. 2007).

Within the tourism domain, equity theory has received some attention. For instance, Pearce et al. (1991) concentrated on the social impacts associated with tourism development, while Chang (2008) examined the relationships between tourist consumption and tourists' satisfaction. Coghlan (2005) studied volunteers' experiences shaped by the interface between volunteers and sending organizations. Within a more recent study, Podoshen and Hunt (2011) introduced the concept of equity restoration and its adjacent concepts of discounting and controllability as the theoretical basis in explaining tourists' avoidance behavior.

Also in the context of volunteer tourism, Burrai et al. (2014) focused on how residents perceived the niche form of tourism, highlighting that different stakeholders' support for volunteering was affected by diverse levels of perceived equity. Most recently in a non-host city/host city context, Lovegrove and Fairley (2017) demonstrated how perceived inequity has the potential to influence level of support for a mega-event.

Though equity theory has not been applied in the context of residents' support for cultural heritage within tourism, it has great potential. Employing reasoning that builds off of Adams' (1963) initial work, inputs may be considered as assets or responsibilities (e.g. commitment, tolerance, engagement, skills, trust in authority, support from family and friends, adjustment to heritage managers' decisions and planning, effort, experience). Outputs may take the shape of positive or negative outcomes (e.g. residents' benefits, sense of attainment, reputation, duties, motivations, appreciation, expenditures, community pride and identity, cohesion). Ultimately, if residents have a close ratio of inputs to outputs, that would translate to a higher perceived equity which would lend itself to a greater level of support for cultural heritage preservation.

Justification for applying equity theory for the current study came about from the authors' observed tensions and clashes regarding fairness among residents from divergent social classes in Carthage. Pearce et al. (1996) argued that contextual and societal factors are essential for understanding residents' perceptions, especially within the context of justice, fairness, and equity. As Burrai et al. (2014) have alerted, perceiving inequity may well indeed reflect tensions among stakeholders in a given relationship. Therefore, the current study utilizes equity theory to explore how residents perceive (in)equity, which in turn can influence the level of their support for cultural heritage preservation.

The following assumptions have been applied to the current context of residents' support for cultural heritage preservation as borrowed from equity theory perspectives (see Hatfield et al. 1978) within the business literature:

1   Residents expect a fair return for their contributions/inputs to their support for heritage preservation.
2   Residents decide what the fair return should be after comparing their inputs and outcomes with other residents' inputs and outcomes.
3   Residents who perceive inequity will search for a way to change or modify the inequitable situation by restoring psychological equity, actual equity, or abandoning the relationship.

Methods

Study context

Carthage, located within northeastern Tunisia in North Africa (Figure 9.1), is situated approximately 15 km from Tunisia's capital, stretching roughly 3 km in distance along the country's coastline (Municipality of Carthage 2018). Rich in history, Carthage possesses heritage and artifacts dating back to Ancient Punic Carthage, Roman Christendom, Vandals, Byzantine Empire, and early Arab-Muslim conquerors (see Ennabli 2000; Miles 2011; Soren et al. 1990).

The site of Carthage has a unique variety of remaining historical monuments rich in cultural heritage. As such, the area is comprised of 13 distinct archaeological zones (Table 9.1) dedicated by The United Nations Educational, Scientific and Cultural Organization (UNESCO) as WHS. These sites comprise roughly 4 km² and encompass 63.58% of the total area of Carthage. UNESCO has been able to protect the archaeological and historic WHS through three unique dedications occurring in 1985, 1994, and 1996 (UNESCO 2018).

Carthage is home to nine distinct communities, with a total population of 17,010 residents (Statistical Tunisia 2014). These communities are comprised within two geographical areas:

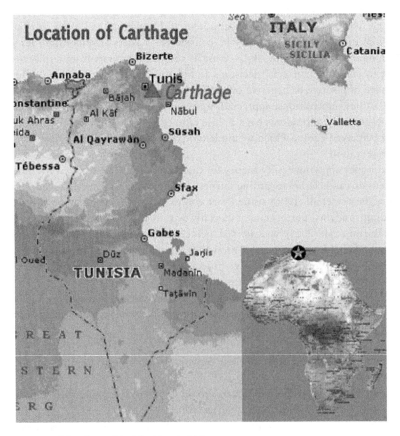

Figure 9.1 Map of Carthage-Tunisia-North Africa
Source: Municipality of Carthage (2018).

Table 9.1 Archaeological sites of Carthage

Name	Property size (ha)
The Area of the Hills	443.48
Land of the "Maison de la chasse au sanglier"	2.31
El Mbazaa Field	1.08
Land of the "Maison de la course des chars"	0.95
Land of the Roman House	0.65
Sector of Bir Messaouda	7.10
Magon District	2.75
Sector of Dermech Basilica	3.42
Sector of Bib Knissia Basilica	7.67
District of the Punic ports and of the Tophet	27.49
Zone of the entrance to the harbors	74.37
Basilica of Saint Cyprien	25.66
Land of the Roman houses of Amilcar	19.09

Source: UNESCO (2018), https://whc.unesco.org/en/list/37/multiple=1&unique_number=41.

Figure 9.2 Map of modern Carthage
Source: Municipality of Carthage (2018).

Area No. 1, which includes Salmppo, Byrsa, Dermech, Hanibal, Presidential, Amilcar, Sidi bou Said, is home to 7,950 residents; Area No. 2, which includes Mohammed Ali and El Yasmina, is home to 9,058 residents. Figure 9.2 shows the map of modern Carthage.

Data collection, sampling, and analysis

Data collection. The present qualitative research study is part of a larger project that investigates residents' behavioral support for cultural heritage preservation of the WHS in Carthage.

The primary form of data for this study took the shape of personal interviews from representatives of entities responsible for the preservation and management of Carthage WHS, namely: Ministry of Culture, Carthage city council, National Heritage Institute, heritage managers and NGOs. In addition, statistical data were gleaned from official webpages of these organizations.

In order to investigate perceptions of residents who live in or around the WHS of Carthage, an interpretivist paradigm was implemented (Thanh and Thanh 2015). Interpretivist paradigm posits that truth is negotiated through dialogue (Angen 2000). Fostering a dialogue between researchers and respondents is critical. Therefore, we chose unstructured interviews to be conversation-like with participants, putting them at ease during data collection (Hannabuss 1996). In addition, given the sensitivity surrounding cultural heritage preservation and sustainability, it was deemed most appropriate to employ an intrepretivist approach to gain insight from the perspectives of residents and knowledge surrounding complex social reality (Qu and Dumay 2011). In our field work, the environment of the interview was unique and yielded various interviewees' perspectives.

Sampling. For diversification reasons, the sampling strategy utilized covered all of the Carthage geographical area—representing individuals from each of the nine communities mentioned prior. In addition, the sample included a cross-section of the community, diverse across gender, profession, and social class (Sood et al. 2017). Respondents were chosen from each community via a blend of two sampling techniques—networking/snowballing and purposive/expert choice (Jimura 2011). Fieldwork yielded a total of 25 in-depth, unstructured interviews with individuals whereby the format was largely conversational. The interviews were conducted in Arabic, analyzed later and translated into English. Of the 25 individuals, 19 were with residents, two with government officials, two with NGO representatives, one was a heritage manager, and one was an academic faculty member. Interviews occurred in-person within public meeting spaces as well as in homes and took place between March and April 2018. This time of the year was deemed ideal given it was during the off-peak tourist season. Each interview lasted between 30 and 70 minutes. The lead researcher utilized results from preceding interviews in selecting potential individuals for subsequent interviews. Data saturation was reached after 25 interviews and hence no additional interviews were needed (Morse 2004). Eight of the participants were female. Participants' ranged in age from 18 to 65 years. In terms of interview question sequencing, we followed similar questions that Kvale (1996) proposed, each meeting distinct purposes. Types of questions including: Introducing questions, follow-up, probing, specifying, direct/indirect, structuring, silence, interpreting and throw away questions.

Analysis. Thematic analysis was undertaken for the current study due to the socio-political complexity and confusion WHS within Carthage. Thematic analysis focused on the explicit description of the content of communication with a limited reflection on its implicit meaning (Ayres et al. 2003; Sandelowski 2010). Its fundamental aspects are the coding systematic process, probing meaning and providing a social reality description via the construction of themes (Berg and Latin 2008).

Analysis of qualitative data was undertaken manually as the lead researcher coded in an inductive style (Glaser and Strauss 1967). Following the transcription of each interview, data were classified thematically into various key elements (Attridge-Stirling 2001), which were explored by concentrating on participants' thoughts regarding support for WHS preservation and related issues (e.g. social class discrimination). The coding identified three primary themes to be discussed in the following section.

Results

Drawing upon equity theory, three themes emerged from analysis that shape perceptions of residents' support which either empower or inhibit the practice of cultural heritage preservation among WHS in Carthage. Each of those will be covered in turn but prior to that, it is worth noting that the nine communities constituting Carthage have not only been geographically classified by the government as Areas No. 1 and 2, but also socially by the residents themselves as upper-class Area No. 1 (Sidi Abu said, presidential, Amilcar, Hanabil, Dermech), middle-class Area No. 1 (Salampo and Byrsa) and lower class/disadvantaged Area No. 2 (Mohammed Ali and El Yasmina).

The history of social class discrimination in Carthage

From speaking with Carthage residents, the history of social class discrimination in areas adjacent to the WHS was clearly observed. The interviews revealed that the discrimination issues among residents had emerged many years ago. For example, a 60-year old resident explained that,

> We are the indigenous of Carthage. Originally we were living in "Almoalka"—modern "Feneix" (one of the Archeological site)—our families used to work as farmers. After Tunisia's independence, the government moved us to "Mohammed Ali" quarter without taken into account our socio-economic needs. We have been marginalized ever since!

Similarly, another respondent from the disadvantaged Area No. 2 agreed that the historic gap between rich and poor has grown wider over time,

> The first high-class building was the presidential palace. The next was the villas belonging to the ministers and rich people, locals or foreigners. This area has become for the wealthy and ours has gotten poorer—they have put us in the bottom.

Still another said:

> Even the official division of Carthage Municipality contributes to social discrimination. The government classified Carthage as two areas—Area No. 1, which includes all lovely classy quarters and Area No. 2, which includes all miserable issues like crowded populations, central points of trash pickup, and ugly buildings.

Several respondents voiced sentiments such as:

> I remember back when I was in school experiencing social discrimination too. Students were mixed from all areas of Carthage. When teachers wanted to punish the class they started with "Mohammed Ali/El Yasmina" students and left the upper class students till the end; they did not punish them!

One respondent went further and argued that, "Injustice among residents of Carthage appears even in death. Those that die from the Mohammed Ali quarter have separate graves and others like Hanibal area get their own!"

When the interviews were carried out with upper-class residents, different opinions were expressed, however discrimination was implicit within their constructed stories. One individual said, "Residents from Area No. 2 created this gap. Look at their behavior on the street and at schools. They are not educated enough to appreciate the WHS of Carthage." It appears that parents from upper-class backgrounds create a sense of discrimination beginning during childhood. One mother from Area No. 1 said that:

> I do not take my children to that park next to Area No. 2. We see families engaging in deviant behavior, with their negative attitudes. I do not want to my children to have contact with those kind of weird kids.

While asking interviewees about discrimination issues, the researchers elicited residents' perspectives regarding preservation matters so as to gain a sense of support for cultural heritage preservation. In so doing, one resident commented that,

> Carthage flows in our blood. We cannot live in any other area. It's like taking fish out of the sea. However, we [residents of Area No. 2] are busy with trying to feed our families; preserving heritage is not a priority here. We are not aware of it and besides, what benefits would the poor receive?

However, at the same time, one activist from Area No. 2 argued, "Awareness does not mean preservation. Some people are educated, rich and a part of heritage protection businesses, but they do wrong things in Carthage such as stealing heritage or keeping it as house decoration in their villa." Contrary to this, residents from Area No. 1 highlighted that, "The key to supporting the preservation of cultural heritage is education and being aware of the values of this WHS—those things are absent in residents who live in Area No. 2." Such perspectives signal concerns of equity among residents of Carthage.

Power relations and authority

(In) equity issues in power relations between various residents were obviously evident among those living adjacent to WHS in Carthage. Respondents from the disadvantage Area No. 2 lamented the lack of local authority support and response. The majority of respondents that were interviewed from Area No. 2 perceived the current authorization system as highly characterized by favoritism. As one angry resident from Area No. 2 claimed:

> Everyone here knows the power of the interpersonal circle that gives rise to law enforcement that won't help us. For example, as Carthage is full of archeological locations, residents are not allowed to build new buildings till they get permission from several related authorities. People who have "under the table" connections can do it where they should not!! When I wanted to build a second floor because my family was getting bigger, I couldn't get bloody permission!

Additional evidence of collusion was found first-hand by the researchers who witnessed an ancient Roman artifact in the backyard of one wealthy resident's villa. UNESCO had also discovered the artifact and placed a placard adjacent to the home. To investigate this further, two residents from different areas and one heritage associate were interviewed to verify opinions. Responses were somewhat mixed. One resident from Area No. 2 explained that,

"Nobody can visit it, the owner of the villa owns this universal value too!!...what can I say, sadly, if those of us [Area No. 2 residents] had any power, this would not be the case." The neighbors from Area No. 1 justified this by claiming, "That is part of the owner's house, he has the right to keep it." While the heritage associate acknowledged the complexity of the situation stating that, "On one hand, there is a lack of law enforcement. On the other hand, regulations and articles about ownership concerns in Carthage remain questionable."

During field work, some of the city council public events were attended by the lead researcher of this study. These opportunities allowed for meeting officials as well as gaining access to potential interviewees. The absence of Area No. 2 residents from these gatherings was clearly noticed. This was confirmed by one resident, as she stated,

> Local authority in Carthage quite often excludes us from city council meetings and our level of participation is limited. Some things they will do are post announcements regarding the meeting late or in places we would not think to look.

A general stereotype of Area No. 2 residents as minimally educated, unskilled and incapable of being part of the decision making process was voiced by Area No. 1 residents. One resident stated that, "If you look at who attends those decision making meetings, second class residents are not there. I call this an overt discrimination." An Area No. 2 residents confirmed such a stereotype, stating:

> We are who come to the government authority rather than being invited. We go to voice our complaints or simply to ask for our rights as citizens who belong in Carthage. They do not consider our existence as important in their official meetings.

This kind of exchangeable relationship that lacks consensus, championed by fruitless communication might serve to threaten the future of WHS within Carthage. One NGO representative warned that,

> The local community suffers from inconsistent and ineffective coordination among various actors within Carthage; like residents, private sector constituents, city council, ministry of heritage, professionals, academics and NGO/government agencies, etc.—each of which pursue their own interests. As a result, we get a lack of consensus and so the situation gets worse.

Perceiving (in) equity and support for cultural heritage preservation

Evidence from the above-mentioned field commentaries (*the history of social class discrimination in Carthage, and power relations and authority*) suggests that inequity, discrimination, marginalized disadvantaged residents, miscommunications with authority, lack of consensus and the dominance of rich and powerful elites, would logically result in negative residents' perceptions that might influence support for heritage preservation. Our field findings uncovered various underlying perceptions grounded in equity theory principles.

One premise of equity theory is that residents would expect a fair return for their contributions/inputs in supporting cultural heritage preservation. One 65-year-old resident stated that:

> The typical scenario is that we live in one of the WHSs. We feel a sense of responsibility toward our site, like engaging in preservation activities with high commitment

and sharing these responsibilities with our family and friends. We do this quite often, in turn, we expect positive outcomes, not necessarily materialistic benefits but rather something more sentimental like respect, or just, community cohesion…

Another resident offered something similar claiming:

I have supported heritage preservation and tourism throughout my whole life living here. I needed to open a small coffee shop close to a roman theater where tourists are usually around, to increase my income. However, the government authority did not allow me to do so. We live in a famous site and we cannot even get benefits from it.

Second, the central feature of equity/justice assessment is social comparisons (Greenberg and Cohen 1982). Thus one's perceived inequity might occur when his/her net outcomes are less than a referent other (Ambrose et al. 1991; Greenberg and Cohen 1982). In other words, residents decide what the fair return should be after comparing their inputs and outcomes with other residents' inputs and outcomes.

In fact, the aforementioned discrimination quotations in sections 4.1 and 4.2 are implicitly considered consequences of social comparison. For instance, residents from the disadvantaged areas shaped their discriminated perceptions and inequitable outcomes in comparison with upper-class residents, not with those of the same class. One resident spoke to this point specifically:

All residents here enjoy the privilege of living in Carthage with the famous WHS. So our duties should be alike in terms of contributing to the preservation of our history and cultural heritage. This is not only a source of pride, but also a source of income from tourism too. However, when I compare my outcomes with people who live in the presidential area, I feel dissatisfied and angry. Here is small example—their streets are clean and ours are the center point of Carthage Trash!!!

Another comparison residents drew concerned getting legal permission for a new building. A resident from Area No. 2 stated that:

I do not mind respecting the law regarding heritage protection, but law enforcement should be for all. For example, I wanted to open a small-scale restaurant but the government would not grant me permission to build it while others who have powerful relationships can do this with no trouble.

In addition, interviewees who live in Area No. 2 felt that the City council has not done a good job empowering or encouraging participation in supporting cultural heritage preservation. One individual stated that, "We do not see people from our area attending local community meetings regarding heritage preservation and tourism planning, compared with residents from upper-class areas. As a result, we have no impact on decision making." In stark contrast to this point of view, one government official argued that:

Our door is open for everyone; we treat residents of Carthage equally. In regards to meetings—we announce them publicly on the city council webpage so those [from Area No. 2] individuals will not perceive any inequity. Preserving heritage or participating in tourism planning has nothing to do with being rich or poor. It is about being a loyal resident and appreciating the value of this ancient city.

The third premise is that residents who perceive inequity will search for a way to change or modify the inequitable situation by restoring psychological equity, actual equity, or abandoning the relationship (Hatfield et al. 1978). According to equity theory, residents (i.e. disadvantaged) who receive inequitable outcomes in exchange relationships with authorities or more wealthy residents would be most unsupportive of cultural heritage preservation. The inequity situations produce distress and tension which will prompt certain behavior as these disadvantaged residents attempt to reduce stress by restoring equity in the exchange relationship. Because every resident experiences a different level of (in) equity, it would stand to reason that tolerance levels for perceived states of inequity would vary.

Some residents choose to change their inputs/outputs ratio until they reach an equitable state. For example, one 70–year-old resident shared that:

> I admire Carthage history. I grew up here and I want to spend the rest of life peacefully here. That's why I strongly advise the young generation not to raise tensions, stop complaining and find a way to increase commitment to our local community instead of trying to compare ourselves with others.

At the same time, some residents choose to increase their inputs to restore equity by establishing a civil society organization that deals with cultural heritage preservation awareness and disadvantaged areas concerns:

> We only have a few NGOs dealing with Carthage's cultural heritage issues, and the few that do exist do not care about disadvantage areas like ours. As a result, we established an organization that specializes in working collectively with the less powerful indigenous residents.

Still, some residents who perceive inequity opt to restore equity negatively by decreasing their inputs to increase outputs to an extent that they would potentially build upon an archeological remains or even steal heritage:

> What would preserving heritage do for my kids? We need to survive. Injustice by the government makes me care less about heritage. If I found any remains I would build upon them, I do not care anymore! At least I would do this for my family's sake, not like wealthy people who steal or keep some statues for house decoration."

The current issues like tensions, power struggles among various stakeholders and weak law enforcement could threaten current and future efforts made in preserving cultural heritage tourism in Carthage. An NGO member warned that:

> Governmental efforts and initiatives are limited in terms of finding a solution for this so called 'social class tensions vs. heritage preservation.' The role of local community in tourism planning is only on paper and as such, many difficulties are encountered in trying to plan sustainably.

Discussion and conclusion

This study utilizes equity theory to better understand residents' perceptions regarding supporting cultural heritage preservation in the WHS of Carthage. As such, the theory offers a framework by which to foster an understanding of the complexity surrounding heterogeneous perspectives among residents from disparate socioeconomic backgrounds. Results revealed that residents' perceptions of supporting cultural heritage preservation were influenced by three primary themes: The emergence of social class discrimination; power relations and authority; and perceived (in) equity. Such findings are consistent with the core principles advanced within Adams' (1965) theory of equity framework.

Unlike previous tourism studies focused on residents' attitudes and support for tourism development (see Easterling 2004; Nicholas et al. 2009; Sharpley 2014), which relied on social exchange theory (SET) to examine costs and benefits concerns, our study employed equity theory to consider a greater context of the societal and historical matters (Pearce et al. 1996) that affect residents' support for cultural heritage preservation. Therefore, research related to residents' perceptions of support for the success of tourism should reflect the contextual and societal factors (Lovegrove and Fairley 2017). The utilization of individual interviews most certainly aided in this approach. This research contributes to the literature concerning cultural heritage preservation and locals' attitudes by focusing on the influence that social class discrimination can have on support for cultural heritage preservation. Attention has been paid to the low income/disadvantaged groups in this research and elsewhere in different contexts (e.g. just destination context, Jamal and Camargo 2013). Research findings focused on WHS has exposed that issues of heritage and indigenous residents' rights have not been fully acknowledged or have been largely dismissed by others in positions of power (Baird 2009, 2013).

As conveyed within other portions of this study, Carthage has been characterized by heterogeneous groups of residents; the prominent group or upper-class residents live in Area No. 1 and the more disadvantaged group or lower-class residents live in Area No. 2. As a result, the level of residents' support varied according to their equity perceptions. Previous research has confirmed that fairness and equity are perceived subjectively and vary depending on social, cultural and historical factors and personal values (Chang 2008). Specifically, within a heritage context, Silverman and Ruggles (2007) discussed that "heritage is generally viewed as positive and shared, but also clearly the site of conflict" (p. 3).

Findings from interviews with respondents exposed that the practice of supporting cultural heritage preservation in Carthage is full of complexities which essentially have been precipitated by a discriminatory background, authority mistrust, power relations and by past failures of existing heritage management to improve a locally applicable practice. This indicates that more often than not, residents' support for such preservation is more easily reached in theory than in practice.

Local authority officials, heritage managers, and tourism decision makers need to cooperate in identifying and implementing more democratic and fair policies for disadvantaged residents (Fainstein 2010). Besides the socio-cultural contribution of heritage assets, the less powerful, poorer residents must be given the chance to benefit economically from heritage sites for tourism to be sustainable. Also to avoid the impact of negative behaviors, "If these impacts are not given sufficient weighting in the overall 'balance,' then the management of heritage attractions will certainly be unsustainable" (Garrod and Fyall 2000, p. 694).

Holding workshops for cultural heritage tourism awareness for youth in the disadvantaged areas would boost future support for WHS preservation. This would be in line with the work by Jaafar et al. (2015) that focused on gauging young local residents' perspectives of WHS. It is evident that active participation by indigenous residents can strengthen the link between an ethic of justice and care, enabling tourism development goals and sustainability principles (Dangi 2018; Dredge and Jenkins 2011; Jamal and Camargo 2013). Thus, it is beneficial for heritage areas managers to further integrate concerns and rights of all respected parties into management and strengthen the link between culture and the heritage environment. Lessons can be learned from ecotourism, where researchers have focused on linking indigenous culture with the environment. In this regard Higgins-Desbiolles (2009) revealed that some indigenous communities are using ecotourism capacity to boost more sustainable lifestyles to teach indigenous values which may ultimately transform attitudes and behaviors among stakeholders.

Furthermore, cultural heritage managers can implement meetings that incorporate indigenous residents from diverse socioeconomic backgrounds whereby team building efforts can be employed. Team building effects can be borrowed from an organizational behavior context. Team gatherings have been found fruitful in mitigating negative feelings by organizing a friendly informal constructive meeting or open, trustful discussion with those who perceive discrimination (Sguera et al. 2016). Working collectively as a team can also help defuse undesirable attitudinal and behavioral outcomes (Megeirhi et al. 2018).

This work raises a number of issues for discussion relevant to tourism development and heritage management through viewpoints of equity and justice. As such, this study provides a new philosophical framework in concerning the support for cultural heritage preservation through the utilization of equity theory. Additional work should consider employing equity theory in ways to better understand the interconnections among various stakeholders surrounding WHS. Areas of research that need to be addressed concern how increased equity may serve to foster greater support for cultural heritage preservation as well as how such support changes over time. Acknowledging the role that equity and power distributions play in fostering sustainable cultural heritage preservation in the wake of conflict will serve paramount to these lines of research. Ultimately, inclusion of all residents living adjacent to WHS will not only foster the most sustainable tourism planning and management for these unique areas (Woosnam et al. 2016), but also give a voice to those who have been silenced for so long.

References

Adams, J.S. 1963. "Toward an Understanding of Inequity." *Journal of Abnormal Psychology* 67 (5): 422–436.

Adams, J.S. 1965. "Inequity in Social Exchange." In *Advances in Experimental Social Psychology*, edited by L Merkowitz, 267–299. New York: Academic Press.

Ambrose, M., L. Harland, and C. Kulik. 1991. "Influence of Social Comparisons on Perceptions of Organizational Fairness." *Journal of Applied Psychology* 76 (2): 239–246.

Andereck, K. and G. Nyaupane. 2011. "Exploring the Nature of Tourism and Quality of Life Perceptions among Residents." *Journal of Travel Research* 50 (3): 248–260.

Angen, M.J. 2000. "Evaluating Interpretive Inquiry: Reviewing the Validity Debate and Opening the Dialogue." *Qualitative Health Research* 10 (3): 378–395.

Attridge-Stirling, J. 2001. "Thematic Networks: An Analytic Tool for Qualitative Research." *Qualitative Research* 1 (3): 385–405.

Ayres L., K. Kavanaugh, and K.A. Knafl. 2003. "Within-Case and Across-Case Approaches to Qualitative Data Analysis." *Qualitative Health Research* 13 (6): 871–883.

Baird, M.F., 2009. *The Politics of Place: Heritage, Identity, and the Epistemologies of Cultural Landscapes.* Thesis (PhD). University of Oregon.

Baird, M.F. 2013. "The Breath of the Mountain Is My Heart: Indigenous Cultural Landscapes and the Politics of Heritage." *International Journal of Heritage Studies* 19 (4): 327–340.

Berg, K.E, and R.W. Latin. 2008. *Research Methods in Health, Physical Education, Exercise Science, and Recreation* (3rd ed.). Baltimore: Lippincott Williams & Wilkins.

Burrai, E., X. Font, and J. Cochrane. 2014. "Destinations Stakeholders' Perceptions of Volunteer Tourism: An Equity Theory Approach." *International Journal of Tourism Research* 17 (5): 451–459.

Coghlan, M., and S. Thomas. 2005. "Deconstructing Volunteer Activities within a Dynamic Environment." In *Niche Tourism*, edited by M. Novelli, 183–200. Oxford: Elsevier, Butterworth and Heinemann.

Chang, J.C. 2008. "Tourists' Satisfaction Judgments: An Investigation of Emotion, Equity, and Attribution." *Journal of Hospitality & Tourism Research* 32: 108–134.

Dangi, T.B. 2018. "Exploring the Intersections of Emotional Solidarity and Ethic of Care: An Analysis of their Synergistic Contributions to Sustainable Community Tourism Development." *Sustainability* 10 (8): 1–20.

Dredge, D. and J. Jenkins (Eds.). 2011. *Stories of Practice: Tourism Policy and Planning.* Ashgate: Surrey & Burlington.

Easterling, D. 2004. "The Residents' Perspective in Tourism Research." *Journal of Travel & Tourism Marketing* 17 (4): 45–62.

Ennabli, A. 2000. "North Africa's Roman art. Its future." September 2000, pp 18–29. UNESCO – San Marcos. Retrieved from http://whc.unesco.org/en/review/. Accessed on May 20, 2018.

Fainstein, S.S. 2010. *The Just City.* Ithaca, NY: Cornell University Press.

Fairley, S., S. Gardiner, and K. Filo. 2016. "The Spirit Lives on: The Legacy of Volunteering at the Sydney 2000 Olympic Games." *Event Management* 20 (2): 201–215.

Fredline, E., and B. Faulkner. 2000. "Host Community Reactions: A Cluster Analysis." *Annals of Tourism Research* 27 (3): 763–784.

Garrod, B. and A. Fyall. 2000. "Managing Heritage Tourism." *Annals of Tourism Research* 27 (3): 682–708.

Glaser, B.S. and A. Strauss. 1967. "The Discovery of Grounded Theory." *Strategies for Qualitative Research.* London: Weidenfeld and Nicolson.

Greenberg, J.K. and R.L. Cohen. 1982. *Equity and Justice in Social Behavior.* New York: Academic Press.

Guerrero, J.K., P.A. Andersen, and W.A. Afifi. 2007. *Close Encounters: Communication in Relationships* (2nd ed.). Thousand Oak, CA: Sage.

Hannabuss, S. 1996. "Research Interviews." *New Library World* 97 (1129): 22–30.

Hatfield, E., G.W. Walster, and E. Berscheid. 1978. *Equity: Theory and Research.* Boston, MA: Allyn and Bacon.

Higgins-Desbiolles, F. 2009. "Indigenous Ecotourism's Role in Transforming Ecological Consciousness." *Journal of Ecotourism:* 8 (2): 144–160

Ho, P. and B. McKercher. 2004. "Managing Heritage Resources as Tourism Products." *Asia Pacific Journal of Tourism Research* 9 (3): 255–266.

Hodges, A. and S. Watson. 2000. "Community-based Heritage Management: A Case Study and Agenda for Research." *International Journal and Heritage Studies* 6 (3): 231–243.

Jaafar, M., S.M. Noor, and S.M. Rasoolimanesh. 2015. "Perception of Young Local Residents toward Sustainable Conservation Programmes: A Case Study of the Lenggong World Cultural Heritage Site." *Tourism Management* 48: 154–163.

Jamal, T. and B.A. Camargo. 2013. "Sustainable Tourism, Justice and an Ethic of Care: Toward the Just Destination." *Journal of Sustainable Tourism* 22 (1): 11–30.

Jimura, T. 2011. "The Impact of World Heritage Site Designation on Local Communities: A Case Study of Ogimachi, Shirakawa–mura, Japan." *Tourism Management* 32: 288–296.

Kim, K., M. Uysal, and M. Sirgy. 2013. "How Does Tourism in a Community Impact the Quality of Life of Community Residents?" *Tourism Management* 36: 527–540.

Kvale, S. 1996. *Interviews: An Introduction to Qualitative Research Interviewing.* Thousand Oaks, CA: Sage.

Landorf, C. 2009. "Managing for Sustainable Tourism: A Review of Six Cultural World Heritage Sites." *Journal of Sustainable Tourism* 17 (1): 53–70.

Lovegrove H., and S. Fairley. 2017. "Using Equity Theory to Understand Non-Host City Residents' Perceptions of a Mega-Event." *Journal of Sport & Tourism* 21 (1): 1–14.

Maruyama, N., and K.M. Woosnam. 2015. "Residents' Ethnic Attitudes and Support for Ethnic Neighborhood Tourism: The Case of a Brazilian Town in Japan." *Tourism Management* 50: 225–237.

Megeirhi, H.A., H. Kılıç, T. Avci, B. Afsar, and A.M. Abubakar. 2018. "Does Team Psychological Capital Moderate the Relationship between Authentic Leadership and Negative Outcomes? An Investigation in the Hospitality Industry." *Economic Research-Ekonomska Istraživanja* 31 (1): 927–945.

Miles, R. 2011. *Carthage Must be Destroyed: The Rise and Fall of an Ancient Civilization.* NY: Penguin Books.

Morse, J.M. 2004. "Theoretical Saturation." In *The Sage Encyclopedia of Social Science Research Methods,* edited by M.S. Lewis-Beck, A. Bryman, and A.F. Liao. Thousand Oaks, CA: Sage (1123–24).

Mowforth, M. and I. Munt. 2016. *Tourism and Sustainability: Development, Globalization and New Tourism in the Third World* (5th Ed) Oxon: Routledge.

Municipality of Carthage. 2018. *The History of Cartage.* Retrieved from http://www.communecarthage.gov.tn/ar/index.php?srub=261&rub=247. Accessed on April 20, 2018.

Nicholas, L., B. Thapa, Y. Ko. 2009. "Residents' Perspectives of a World Heritage Site: The Pitons Management Area, St. Lucia." *Annals of Tourism Research* 36 (3): 390–412.

Pearce, P.L., G. Moscardo, and G.F. Ross. 1991. "Tourism Impact and Community Perception: An Equity-social Representational Perspective." *Australian Psychologist* 26: 147–152.

Pearce, P.L., G. Moscardo, and G.F. Ross. 1996. *Tourism Community Relationships.* Oxford: Pergamon Press.

Podoshen, J.S. and J.M. Hunt. 2011. "Equity Restoration, the Holocaust and Tourism of Sacred Sites." *Tourism Management* 32 (6): 1332–1342.

Qu Q.S., and J. Dumay. 2011. "The Qualitative Research Interview." *Qualitative Research in Accounting & Management* 8 (3): 238–264.

Rasoolimanesh, S.M. and M. Jaafar. 2017. "Sustainable Tourism Development and Residents' Perceptions in World Heritage Site Destinations." *Asia Pacific Journal of Tourism Research* 22 (1): 34–48.

Rasoolimanesh, S.M., M. Jaafar, A.G. Ahmad, and R. Barghi. 2017. "Community Participation in World Heritage Site Conservation and Tourism Development." *Tourism Management* 58: 142–153.

Ryan, C. 2002. "Equity, Management, Power Sharing and Sustainability—Issues of the 'New Tourism'." *Tourism Management* 23 (1): 17–26.

Sandelowski, M. 2010. "What's in a Name? Qualitative Description Revisited." *Research in Nursing & Health* 33 (1): 77–84.

Sguera, F., R.P. Bagozzi, Q.N. Huy, R.W. Boss, and D.S. Boss. (2016). "Curtailing the Harmful Effects of Workplace Incivility: The Role of Structural Demands and Organization-Provided Resources." *Journal of Vocational Behavior* 95–96: 115–127.

Sharpley, R. 2014. "Host Perceptions of Tourism: A Review of the Research." *Tourism Management* 42: 37–49.

Silverman, H. and D.F. Ruggles. 2007. *Cultural Heritage and Human Rights.* Netherlands: Springer.

Sirisrisak, T. (2009). "Conservation of Bangkok Old Town." *Habitat International* 33 (4): 405–411.

Sood, J., P. Lynch, and C. Anastasiadou. 2017. "Community Non-Participation in Homestays in Kullu, Himachal Pradesh, India." *Tourism Management* 60: 332–347.

Soren, D., A.B. Ben Khader, and H. Slim. 1990. *Carthage: Uncovering the Mysteries and Splendors of Ancient Tunisia.* New York: Simon & Schuster.

Statistical Tunisia. 2014. *National Institute of Statistics – Tunisia 2014. General Census of Population and Housing.* Retrieved from http://www.ins.tn/en/themes/population. Accessed on April 1, 2018.

Stylidis, D. 2018. "Residents' Place Image: A Cluster Analysis and Its Links to Place Attachment and Support for Tourism." *Journal of Sustainable Tourism* 26 (6): 1007–1026.

Su, M.M., and G. Wall. 2014. "Community Participation in Tourism at a World Heritage Site: Mutianyu Great Wall, Beijing, China." *International Journal of Tourism Research* 16: 146–156.

Thanh, N.C. and T.T.L Thanh. 2015. "The Interconnection between Interpretivist Paradigm and Qualitative Methods in Education." *American Journal of Educational Science* 1 (2): 24–27.

Timothy, D. 2011. *Cultural Heritage and Tourism.* Bristol, UK: Channel View Publications.

UNESCO. 2018. *Archaeological Site of Carthage.* Retrieved from https://whc.unesco.org/en/list/37/multiple=1&unique_number=41. Accessed on March 30, 2018.

Vareiro, L., P. Remoaldo, and J. Cadima Ribeiro. 2013. "Residents' Perceptions of Tourism Impacts in Guimarães (Portugal): A Cluster Analysis." *Current Issues in Tourism* 16 (6): 535–551.

Vargas-Sanchez, A., N. Porras-Bueno, and M. Plaza-Mejia. 2011. "Explaining Residents' Attitudes to Tourism: Is a Universal Model Possible?" *Annals of Tourism Research* 38 (2): 460–480.

Woosnam, K.M., K.D. Aleshinloye, and N. Maruyama. 2016. "Solidarity at the Osun Osogbo Sacred Grove—A UNESCO World Heritage Site." *Tourism Planning & Development* 13 (3): 274–291.

Woosnam, K.M., K.D. Aleshinloye, M.A. Ribeiro, D. Stylidis, J. Jiang, and E. Erul. 2018. "Social Determinants of Place Attachment at a World Heritage Site." *Tourism Management* 67: 139–146.

Woosnam, K.M., J. Draper, J.K. Jiang, K.D. Aleshinloye, and E. Erul. 2018. "Applying Self-Perception Theory to Explain Residents' Attitudes about Tourism Development through Travel Histories." *Tourism Management* 64: 357–368.

World Tourism Organization. 2012. *Tourism and Intangible Cultural Heritage.* Madrid, Spain: UNWTO.

Yung, E. and E. Chan. 2011. "Problem Issues of Public Participation in Built-Heritage Conservation: Two Controversial Cases in Hong Kong." *Habitat International* 35 (3): 457–466.

10

Current issues of tourism in Morocco[1]

Fernando Almeida-García

Introduction

In this chapter, the evolution of Morocco's tourism sector and its tourism policy is analysed, and the growing role that tourism has played in the country's economic development is shown. This study highlights the role of tourism as an agent of modernisation of the economy and society. These economic and political changes have occurred quite rapidly since 2000. In relation to these aspects, the express support for tourism was a personal decision of the current King Mohammed VI. In the years after independence (1956–1961) the government was not very interested in tourism, since this sector was not considered as a productive and strategic branch. During the long reign of Hassan II (1961–1999), phases of clear support for tourism alternated with others of inaction and carelessness. During the reign of Hassan II, tourism was never a centrepiece of the country's economic development policy, as it happened in other nearby North African countries (Tunisia and Egypt) and European countries specialising in tourism (Spain, Italy and Greece) (Almeida, 2012). In the last decades, tourism has a great importance in the Moroccan economy, in such a way that income from tourism has represented an average of 8.1% between 2012 and 2016 (UNWTO, 2017). In 2016 Morocco was the African country that received the most tourists (10.3 million), followed very closely by South Africa. Other important countries in the tourist field such as Tunisia and Egypt have suffered a significant decrease in income and tourists, which has benefited Morocco.

This study should be understood as an evolutionary analysis of tourism policy in its administrative and economic context. The development of tourism in Morocco has been closely conditioned by public agents, as until recently public agents had a limited role. The remarkable intervention of the State in the Moroccan economy causes that the analysis of the tourist is largely influenced by the public intervention in the tourist sector.

Likewise, the case of Morocco's tourism policy is in accordance with diverse studies that underline the notorious intervention of the government in the development of tourism policy and its strong connection to the economic development process. This subject is receiving increasing attention in the fields of tourism, economics and political science (Hall & Jenkins, 1995). These analyses have been more concerned with highlighting the achievements of economic and tourism policy (Jenkins, 1980; Williams & Shaw, 1988) than with territorial and social imbalances (Lea, 1988). The constraints to generate development conflict with the importance that governments attach to the role of tourism in national and regional economic development (Lamb, 1998). Some authors indicate that tourism has a limited capacity to produce development in developing countries (Britton, 1982), and the income gap between the core countries and developing countries tends to be maintained (Blázquez & Cañada, 2011). The governments of the developing countries consider tourism as one of the few sectors generating employment and foreign income, with a non-complex technology.

Usually, research on tourism policy has focused on countries, as part of national development policy (Lickorish, 1991). Achieving socio-economic development based on tourism depends on a variety of factors that are beyond the control of the tourism sector. A wide assortment of factors plays a key role in this process: the social, economic, political, environment and technological context in which the tourism unfolds. Most studies recognise that the prior level of development of a country at the arrival of tourism, in addition to its geographical size, the rate of growth of tourism, the degree of social adaptation to change, and the existence of tourism planning, are basic factors in determining the future level of development and economic growth (Pablo-Romero & Molina, 2013; Pearce, 1991).

In 2016 arrived at Morocco 10 million tourists, which makes it the most popular destination in Africa. Steady growth has been maintained despite the recent political and terrorist turmoil affecting other tourism-orientated countries in North Africa, particularly Tunisia and Egypt. These countries have suffered a very sharp decline in the number of tourists and income. Nowadays tourism has an important weight in the Moroccan economy. Revenues from tourism accounted for 7.9% of GDP in 2016. Morocco is the African country with the greatest weight in GDP, except for island tourism countries (Cape Verde, Seychelles, Mauritius) (UNWTO, 2017). In the last 15 years, Morocco has experienced significant economic growth based on tourism activity, which has made it a consolidated tourist destination (Table 10.1).

Table 10.1 Basic data of the Moroccan tourist industry

	1991	1995	2000	2005	2010	2016
International tourists	4,162,000	2,602,000	4,278,000	5,843,000	9,228,000	10,046,000
Percentage of tourists from Europe	57.4	81.7	82.7	44.6[a]	44.6[a]	38.0
Average stay (days)	4.0	7.5	6.9	6.3	3.0	2.9
Accommodation (bed places)	116,171	122,956	127,829	124,270	120,039	242,707
Percentage of occupancy by bed places	37.0	45.8	52.0	38.0	35.0	32.0
International tourist spending (billion $)	1.05	1.304	2.039	4.61	6.702	6.850
Tourism as % of GDP	4.0	4.0	6.8	9.1	8.9	7.9

Source: UNWTO (1991–2016); Hillali (2007a)
a Does not include Moroccans resident abroad.

This study is interested in the role played by the government in the tourism policy making-process, together with the analysis of the consequences in the development process, since Morocco is a good example of a developing country that has chosen tourism as a centrepiece of its growth policy. The study includes other secondary objectives such as identifying the role of the Moroccan government in the process of national economic development and examining the main tourism plans related to the tourism sector.

This research organises the analysis of the evolution of tourism in Morocco following three main phases pre-Fordist or artisanal, Fordist and post-Fordist (Fayos-Solá, 1996; Garay & Cánoves, 2011). These phases of the policy are in accordance with the productive cycles of capitalist production and explain well the changes recorded in the tourism sector (Dunford, 1990). These economic changes are well reflected in the phases of arrival of international tourists (Figure 10.1). The political and economic changes are intimately related to the evolutionary process of tourism in Morocco. The first phase corresponds to an elitist tourism, the second phase with mass tourism and the late phase starts with the political and economic changes of Mohammed VI.

This study takes the institutional approach to analyse Morocco's policy (Scott, 2011). The institutional approach views tourism as strongly influenced by the actions of government and is interested in the organisation of power and its relationship to policy, as well as the construction of regulations and incentives. The working method that was adopted begins with a documentary analysis of the main texts and plans related to Morocco's tourism policy and a review of the bibliography applicable to the study's theoretical framework.

Phases of tourism in Morocco

Pre-Fordist and Fordist phase

The first actions related to tourism in Morocco were aimed at a European elite tourism. Both the Spanish and French protectorates carried out measures to welcome these tourists attracted by the oriental environment of Morocco. One of these actions and that is considered as the beginning of tourism in Morocco is the building of the luxurious hotel La Mamounia in Marrakesh (1929) (Chahine, 2010). The colonial administration was interested in the tourist promotion of Morocco, so these governments built more than 240 hotels and 15,000 bed places (Araque, 2015; Berriane, 2009).

In 1956 Morocco gained independence from France and Spain. The State faced numerous problems to organise the country. The main challenge was the creation of a productive structure, which would break economic dependence towards metropolis and generate employment. In the 1960s and 1970s, public investment was mainly directed to agriculture and hydraulic infrastructures and secondarily to industry. These were the sectors considered as productive. Initially, tourism was not considered a true productive sector and received limited investment (Hillali, 2007a, 2007b).

The country received financial assistance from the World Bank and for this purpose, it was recommended to implement development plans following the guidelines of indicative planning (Ramos & Pires, 2008). In such a way, at the end of the 1950s, the first economic development plan began (1958–1959), followed by a quinquennial Plan (1960–1964). In both plans, investment for tourism was scarce and the accommodation capacity remains almost unchanged from 1956 to 1964 (Table 10.2). These resources went towards the historical cities of Morocco (Marrakesh, Fes) and to some tourist complexes in the north. We must emphasise an element that broke this situation and caused more investment in the tourism

Table 10.2 Public investment in the Moroccan tourist industry

Economic plan	Percentage of investment/total budget	Economic plan	Percentage of investment/total budget
1958–1959	0.2	1973–1977	6.5
1960–1964	1.4	1978–1980	3.4
1965–1967	6.4	1981–1985	1.8
1968–1972	6.8	1988–1992	1.2

Source: Hillali (2007a).

sector. This was due to the devastating 1960 Agadir earthquake and the decision to create a new tourist destination. To mitigate the humanitarian and economic crisis, the government turned Agadir into a great seaside destination and unlike the traditional tourism in the Imperial Cities (Fez, Meknes and Marrakech), this new city focused on mass tourism of sun and beach (Hillali, 2007b).

The triennial Social and Economic Development Plan was approved in 1965, assuming a more determined engagement to tourism. Tourism performed various classic functions such as gaining foreign incomes to support development programs, generating employment and attracting foreign investment. On paper, the government expected tourism to be not just an auxiliary sector, but also an industry that would have an active role in development; a Ministry of Tourism was even approved in 1965 in order to aid this Plan. In practice, most of the public investment was allocated to agriculture and hydraulic infrastructure. Moreover, this Plan resulted in a profusion of public agencies regarding tourism that difficult the development process.

The triennial Plan designed a number of regional development areas, named Priority Planning Zones (ZAP). Due to the deficiencies of infrastructures and communication in the country, it was planned to locate the offer in certain areas and that these will count on significant public investment. Seventy-five per cent of the investment went to the Mediterranean area since the plan expected that this region would collect tourist surpluses from Spain.

The spaces with the most suggestive natural and cultural resources with potential for tourism, and located in disadvantaged parts of the north (Tangier, Al Hoceima and the Tetouan) and south (Agadir and the Ouarzazate-Errachidia), were chosen. It continues to support elite tourism, although some concessions are made to mass tourism. Public investment was considerable, as evidenced by the fact that government subsidised 95% of the bed places built in the Mediterranean ZAPs (Hillali, 2007a). Not everything was public investment, the entry of foreign private investment should also be noted, especially the French chain Club Méditerranée, which built six holiday resorts in Morocco. The first was the Club Med in Al Hoceima, which opened in 1964, followed by the one in Agadir in 1965. In 1985, the eight Club Meds achieved an overall of 4,170 bed places (Hillali, 2007a). In 2018 only three Club Med are working: Marrakech, Agadir and Tangier.

To increase the supply of tourist accommodation and tourism promotion, the government created a remarkable set of government agencies and state-run accommodation. During this period, management of it was entrusted to public bodies as the Moroccan National Tourist Board (ONMT), the Deposit and Management Fund (CDG), the Moroccan Society for Tourism Development (SOMADET) and Maroc-Tourist (El Haddadi, 2010). The economic adjustment programme in the 1990s, and the high deficit accumulated by these agencies concluded in their privatisation during this decade.

In the previous plans, the investment was oriented towards a high-quality accommodation. In the 1968–1972 quinquennial Plan, actions focused on mid-range hospitality, according to the new strategy towards mass tourism. Thus, the government carried out large projects to lodge a large number of tourists. These major actions were accompanied by new public agencies for the management of these projects: the National Agency for the Planning of the Bay of Agadir (SONABA) and the National Agency for the Planning of the Bay of Tangier (SNABT). These new administrative bodies joined the previous public agencies (El Haddadi, 2010).

The development plans of 1973–1977 and 1978–1980 were definitely oriented towards mass tourism. Elite tourism has not provided the expected results and neighbouring countries (Spain, Tunisia) are gaining much more income than Morocco. The serious economic and political crisis that affected the country during this period forced to change the objectives (annexation of Western Sahara). On the other hand, the results of public investment were quite limited: only 30% of the planned hotel offer was built in the 1968–1972 plan. The Moroccan administration was quite inefficient. Unlike this situation, the private sector implemented 70% of the planned capacity; destinations with lower public investment are those that showed better performance (Hillali, 2007a). On the other hand, this sector was much more interested in building second tourist homes than hotels.

The retirement of public investment in tourism activities was the pattern in the following plans. One of the most remarkable events was the acute fall in international tourists in 1994, regarding the Marrakech terrorist attack, in addition to the effects of the First Gulf War (Berriane, 2009; Moudoub & Ezaïdi, 2005) (Figure 10.1). In this negative context of falling of demand along with domestic economic problems, Morocco government adopted an economic adjustment programme backed by the World Bank required a major restructuring of the tourist industry, which was already experiencing serious economic difficulties caused by the drop of international demand during the decade of 1990s (Figure 10.1). Most of the most profitable resorts and hotels were sold.

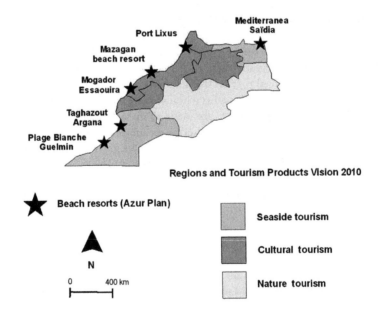

Figure 10.1 Evolution of international tourists in Morocco
Source: Hilalli, 2007a (1960–2000) and UNWTO (2001–2016).

Table 10.3 Milestones in Moroccan tourism policy

1918	Creation of the Central Tourism Committee (current ONMT)
1960	Rebuilding of Agadir
1964	Signing of Tourism Agreement between Governments of Morocco and Spain
1965	Creation of Ministry of Tourism
1965	Triennial Plan (1965–1967). Tourism as a priority
1968	Creation of SONABA and SNABT
1978	Triennial Plan (1978–1980). Sharp fall in state investment in tourism.
1988	Quinquennial Plan (1988–1992). Expanding demand
1990	Approval of the adjustment Plan. Privatisation process begins
1994	Sharp decline in tourism demand
2001	Framework Agreement 2001–2010/Vision 2010
2007	Creation of SMIT
2010	New tourism plan: Vision 2020
2011	Creation of FMDT
2013	Morocco achieve 10 million tourists

Source: Authors.

Due to a lack of initial private capital, tourism is entrusted to the good care of the public sector. The disproportionate importance given to state-owned companies has often depleted the Treasury (senseless expenditure, chronic deficits, confusion between private and public interests). As a result, the liquidation process of the early 1990s was understood as an opportunity by the state and by the private operators (see Table 10.3). The state recovered unprofitable stocks and tourism operators bought at a good price (Hillali, 2005). Thirty-seven hotels were put up for sale and acquired by international and national chains (Ouahidi & Mzidabi, 1994).

As a conclusion of this section, we highlight the intense work carried out by the state between the 1960s and the 1970s with the objective of promoting its own tourism industry. The financial resources were not very abundant and the results were not those expected by the government. In the 1980s and 1990s, tourism lost prominence in the political agenda, investments are reduced more than in past decades and there is a privatisation of public tourism stocks.

Post-fordist phase: the strategic plans of Vision 2010 and Vision 2020

Since the accession of King Mohammed VI to the throne in 1999, there was a noticeable change in Morocco's tourism policy. Tourism was put on the political agenda, and it has remained as one major objective of the sovereign and the government. Since 1999 tourism has become a key element of national economic development. The public authorities carried out actions to achieve this objective: implement strategic plan, attract international capital, international promotion, deregulating administrative rules and in particular building large resorts. Initially, these actions were focused on the European market, fairly close from the geographical point of view (Almeida, 2011; Chahine, 2010). The Moroccan tourist model in this phase has been characterised by a strong international investment, initially by European funds until 2008 and later, by countries of the Persian Gulf. Likewise, the state has continued playing an active role in tourism development, as an investment agent, guarantor of investment, deregulator, particularly in the air sector, and as an infrastructure developer for the tourism sector.

In 2001, the first major strategic plan for tourism in Morocco was approved: the Vision Plan 2010. This plan announces a remarkable change in the orientation of tourism policy. On the one hand, there is real support for the tourism sector that moves to public and private investment, and on the other hand, the country and the tourism sector are integrated into an international and globalised production structure within the post-Fordist production processes. This plan aims that the tourism sector grows in the most intense and fastest way in the shortest possible time. The criteria for sustainable development are forgotten. The main objectives established by the plan were as follow (Chahine, 2016):

a   To attract 10 million tourists in 2010.
b   To host 7 million international tourists in hotels, reaching an accommodation capacity of 230,000 beds.
c   To build six major resorts.
d   To achieve a foreign currency revenue of 8.873 billion dollars.
e   To create 600,000 new direct jobs.
f   To train 72,000 tourism professionals.
g   To increase the percentage of GDP spent on tourism from 6.5% to 8.0%.

The results of the plan were quite satisfactory since most of the objectives were achieved: tourism incomes surpassed 8% of GDP in 2010; 9.3 million international tourists arrived in Morocco in 2010; and tourism receipts were close to its aim ($6.702 billion). Some objectives were clearly not achieved (Traspaderne, 2011). The accommodation offer estimated in the Vision 2010 Plan and its specific plan, the Azur Plan,[2] did not materialise. This Plan was an ambitious scheme to create six large beach resorts, offering 80,000 bed places in a surface of more than 2,500 hectares (Figure 10.2). Only two have opened: Saïdia and Mazagan due to this plan have been deeply affected by the world economic crisis of 2008, which was most intense in Europe (Gil de Arriba, 2011).

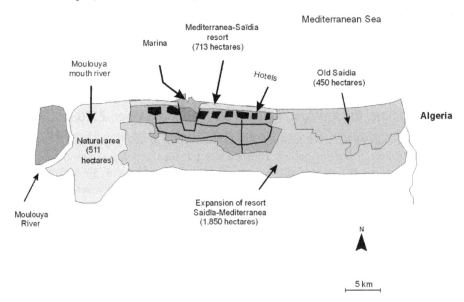

Figure 10.2   Resorts of Vision 2010 and 2020
Source: Author.

The Vision 2020 Plan is a continuation of Vision 2010, although it establishes more ambitious objectives than the 2010 Plan. The main aim is to place Morocco among the top-20 tourist destinations in the world. The major objectives of this strategic instrument are as follows (Ministére du Tourisme, 2013):

a   To double the tourist accommodation capacity with the building of 200,000 new bed places, of which 160,000 are hotel beds and 40,000 are second tourist homes.
b   To double the number of international tourists to 20 million in the horizon of 2020.
c   To multiply by three the number of domestic air passengers.
d   To create 470,000 new direct employees.
e   To increase income from tourism to 15.5 billion dollars in the horizon of 2020.
f   To increase the contribution of tourism GDP to the national GDP by 2 percentage points.
g   Vision 2020 will develop six products through six tourism schemes: Azur 2020 (seaside mega-resorts), Sustainable Eco-Development, Cultural Heritage, Leisure and Sports, Domestic Tourism and Business, Health and Well-Being.

If the previsions of the Vision 2020 Plan are fulfilled, it will suppose a public and private investment of about 16,000,000 million euros, which is equivalent to 18.5 of the Moroccan GDP in nominal terms (CIA, 2015). This figure gives an idea of the enormous economic effort that this plan implies for the country's economy.

Two important changes can be highlighted in the Vision 2020 Plan. First, international funds play a very important role in financing this Plan, and second, we observe a change in the geographical origin of the investment (Shamamba, 2005; Verdaguer, 2005). In the Vision Plan 2010, international capital was linked to large construction companies and international hotel chains, mainly from Europe (Spain, France and Belgium), the United States, South Africa and some Moroccan companies. In addition, the role of international investment funds was secondary. On the contrary, in the 2020 Vision Plan, international funds are predominant, mainly from Persian Gulf countries.

The government approved the creation of a new public agency to facilitate the financing of the Vision 2020 Plan. This new body is the Tourism Development Fund of Morocco (FMDT). It is a public investment fund with 1.66 billion dollars under the control of the Ministry of Tourism of Morocco and the Fund of the Hassan II Foundation. This fund is intended for strategic tourism projects.

The first actions of the FMDT were destined to rescue the Azur Plan resorts. The FMDT has acquired shares in the new allocation of the Saïdia and Taghazout resorts, taking on 30% and 25% of their shareholdings, respectively. Through the FMDT the state has taken over the maintenance of these projects from the Vision 2010 Plan, as well as the completion of those already begun. A quick evaluation of the completed resorts does not show them to be very profitable for the Moroccan state due to the cost of buying the shares, the financial incentives granted to companies and the high expenditure on infrastructure building.

Saïdia: case study of Azur Plan

The Vision Azur Plan is a scheme designed to create a wide range of hotel accommodation and tourism homes, through large resorts (Figure 10.2). Vision 2020 maintains the same objectives and areas of tourism development as Vision 2010.

Saïdia is a small coastal town of 3,338 inhabitants on the Mediterranean coast in the northeast of Morocco, in the province of Berkane and very near the Algerian border. One of the six resorts envisaged in the Vision 2010 Plan is located here. The plans for this project include the construction of nine hotels with a capacity of 17,000 bed places for tourists and 13,000 bed places in second homes. They also include three 18-hole golf courses, a marina, a water park, a heliport, shopping centres, a conference hall. Of these, only the marina and one golf course have been built to date.

The Mediterrania-Saïdia resort was launched in 2003 when the project was allocated by the Moroccan Government to Spanish construction firm Fadesa within a tender linked to the Azur Plan (Vision 2010 Plan). This construction firm was also assigned another Plan Azur resort (Plage Blanque-Guelmin), but did not develop it. To build the Saïdia resort, it partnered with various Spanish hotel chains (Barceló, Iberostar, Oasis and Riu) and the US chain Best Western. Fadesa focused on the real-estate business (sale of tourism housing) and building hotels and infrastructure. The proximity to Spain and Europe promised high residential sales, as tried and tested in Spain (Saad, 2008). Fadesa planned an initial investment of around 2 billion euros. The state provided the land at a very low price, in addition to investing in road building and expanding the airport in the nearby city of Oujda. The official studies predicted that the resort's tourism activity would generate around 5.5 million overnight stays per year, revenue of around 435 million euros and income from levies and taxes of around 240 million euros (Chahine, 2016).

The European economic crisis and the bursting of the property bubble in Spain badly affected Fadesa, forcing it to sell its shares to the Moroccan company Addoha in 2009. Although that year, King Mohammed VI officially inaugurated the resort, with the opening of the 5-star Hotel Barceló Saïdia, with 1,200 bed places (Yrigoy, 2013). The Moroccan Government rescued the Fadesa's project by 125 million euros. In order to move forward, the involvement of Moroccan public enterprises was sought, in such a way that the distribution of shares in the resort was as follows: 60% belong to CDG (the Deposit and Management Fund), 30% are owned by the FMDT (the Moroccan Tourism Development Fund) and 10% are Addoha's. Even the 5-star Hotel Barceló was sold to Atlas Hospitality Morocco, a subsidiary of Royal Air Maroc (Chahine, 2012). Despite the future benefits, this rescue is quite debatable in economic terms. According to the government, the work on the Mediterrania-Saïdia resort has created 1,700 direct jobs and 8,500 indirect jobs, and when it is fully operational it is estimated that it will create 8,000 direct jobs and 40,000 indirect jobs (Yrigoy, 2013). A cost-benefit analysis shows a large deficit for the state, of at least 260 million euros, taking into account the rescue and investments in transport infrastructure, and very low incomes (Chahine, 2016).

The building of this resort caused various environmental impacts. First, the dune system and its vegetation has been destroyed and transformed due to the extraction of aggregates used for the building work. Moreover, the longshore drift has been altered by the construction of the Mediterrania-Saïdia marina, one of the resort's star projects and, in particular, the natural area at the mouth of the River Muluya is under threat. This wetland area is included in the Ramsar Convention (Araque, 2013; Boumeaza et al., 2010; Yrigoy, 2013).

Conclusions

Along the period studied, the tourist activity in Morocco has been closely related to government intervention. This situation must be understood due to the weakness of the private sector and the intense intervention of the government in the regulation of the economy. The entry of international investments has also been connected to the regulatory activities of the Moroccan government.

Morocco's tourism landscape is quite similar to the situation in other developing tourism countries, in which the weakness of private initiative forces government intervention. These direct public interventions tend to generate large projects in which the local community has little participation. Neither large transnational tourism companies are very concerned about community participation.

Morocco's tourism development model has been based on regional policy, developing poles, tourism hubs and spaces, and strategic plans and, on the other hand, international financing. This model is designed almost exclusively to satisfy the large international hotel chains and investment funds. This model is quite fluctuating, since the interests of the international investment funds, which in many cases are not tourist, are very changing. The investments of international funds are exclusively driven by profitability and not by local interests.

As evidenced by the evolution in Moroccan tourism policy, the country has changed significantly in its stance towards tourism. In the first period, during the pre-Fordist phase, the tourism activity was focussed to attract the elite tourist. The oriental exoticism was the main Moroccan charming for these tourists. After independence, public investment for tourism was scarce, since tourism was not considered as a way to development. The development model was different from that of other tourist countries in the Mediterranean basin. Agriculture, mining and basic industry were the sectors that received the investment.

The elite tourism did not provide the expected income, and like other Mediterranean countries, the tourist policy of the 70s, was oriented to mass tourism. This type of tourism was supported despite some rejection of some religious and political authorities. This growth was held back by the 1990 crisis and the clear lack of support from King Hassan II. The government of Hassan II created an extensive network of ineffective public organisms destined to feed a palace elite adept to the regime. This situation explains the inefficiency of tourist agencies, and on the other hand, and some reluctance of the government to increase investment in the tourism sector.

In the third phase, the state once again became the main driver of tourism activity and assumed the majority of investments. The state showed a clear interest in supporting tourism and opening the national tourism market to international investments. The country used recipes already used in other developing countries, such as Spain in the 1960s or some Caribbean islands in the 1990s (Almeida, 2012; Blázquez & Cañada, 2011). The resorts promoted by the Azur Plan show a surprising similarity to the tourism accommodations developed along the Spanish coast from the 1960s to the 1980s (Galiana & Barrado, 2006). Moroccan resorts offer similar incentives and provoke the same environmental impacts as the old resorts Spanish people. The difference is that the Moroccan resorts are much larger and the investment is greater.

In the post-Fordist phase, there are two variables that are important in the case of Morocco: the relationship with international investment funds and the connection with the real estate sector. We have already commented on the close relationship between the development model of Morocco and the international fund role. Regarding the function of the real estate sector, it should be noted that tourism developments rely primarily on tourism second home (García & Tasias, 2007). It seems that resorts will not work if there is no real estate development. On the other hand, the 2010 Vision Plan emerged during the real estate boom in Europe and Spain in particular, thus the Vision 2020 Plan was designed to attract investment for the real estate sector. This plan was part of the expansion of the European and Spanish real estate bubble. It is no coincidence that Fadesa, one of the most important construction companies in the Spanish real estate bubble, took over two of Morocco's tourism mega-projects. Afterwards, the Vision 2020 Plan was linked to the building bubble of the Persian Gulf (Baabood, 2011).

Finally, it is necessary to highlight the questionable economic and social profitability of these plans for the countries receiving the investments. The cases studied in the Caribbean (Britton, 1982; Lea, 1988), North Africa (De Kadt, 1979) and Europe (Almeida, 2012), put into question the results of these models of intensive growth based on tourism. The Moroccan case is no different, being a good example of growth very dependent on foreign investment, strong social and environmental externality and some economic costs assumed by the Moroccan Government, as in the case of Saïdia, question the overall profitability of the applied model.

Notes

1 This study is funded by the project: "Transformations of the historic urban landscape induced by tourism: Contradictions and controversies, governance and governance" (CSO2016-75470-R). Ministry of Economy, Government of Spain; and Malaga University. Andalucía Tech.
2 Creation of new tourism products and new holiday resorts:

- Azur Plan: Proposes the construction of six coastal holiday resorts each targeting a different and specific market segment, focusing on six new development areas. Receives financial support from the Hassan II Fund. Modelled on the big Caribbean and Asian resorts. The resorts put forward are: Mediterrania-Saïdia, Mazagan Beach Resort, Port Lixus, Mogador Essaouira, Taghazout-Argana Bay and Plage Blanche-Guelmin.

References

Almeida, F. (2011) Transformaciones turísticas en el litoral mediterráneo marroquí, in Asociación de Geógrafos Españoles (AGE) (eds), *Espacios y destinos turísticos en tiempos de globalización y crisis*, Madrid: Universidad Carlos III, pp. 67–79.

Almeida, F. (2012) La política turística de España y Portugal, *Cuadernos de Turismo*, 30, 9–34.

Araque, E. (2013) Desarrollo turístico y medio ambiente en la costa norte de Marruecos, *Cuadernos de Turismo*, 31, 13–30.

Araque, E. (2015) Orígenes y desarrollo del turismo en el Protectorado Español del Norte de Marruecos (1912–1956), *Cuadernos de Turismo*, (36), 55–77.

Baabood, A. (2011) *La disminución de las inversiones de los países del Golfo en la región mediterránea*, Barcelona: Instituto Europeo del Mediterráneo (IEMED).

Berriane, M. (2009) *Tourisme des nationaux, tourisme des étrangers: Quelles articulations en Méditerranée?* Rabat: Université Mohamed V, Faculté des Lettres et des Sciences Humaines.

Blázquez, M. and Cañada, E. (eds) (2011) *Turismo placebo. Nueva colonización turística: del Mediterráneo a Mesoamérica y el Caribe. Lógicas espaciales del capital turístico*, Managua: Enlace.

Boumeaza, T., Sbai, A., Salmon, M. and Ozer, A. (2010) Impacts écologiques des aménagements touristiques sur le litoral de Saïdia, Maroc oriental, *Méditerranée*, 115, 95–102.

Britton, S. G. (1982) The political economy of tourism in the third world, *Annals of Tourism Research*, 9(3), 331–358.

Central Intelligence Agency (CIA). (2015) *The World Factbook. Morocco*, https://www.cia.gov/library/publications/the-world-factbook/geos/mo.html, accessed 15 January 2018.

Chahine, S. (2010) *Desarrollo turístico del litoral mediterráneo de Marruecos. Saidia como destino*, Spain: University of Málaga.

Chahine, S. (2012) *Turismo globalizado en Marruecos: el caso de Saïdia*, Working paper "Otras miradas, otros turismos", University of Málaga.

Chahine, S. (2016) *Turismo Globalizado en Marruecos: El caso de Saïdia*, Thesis, University of Malaga, Spain.

Dunford, M. (1990) Theories of regulation, *Society and Space*, 8(3), 297–221.

De Kadt, E. (ed.) (1979) *Tourism: Passport to Development? Perspectives on the Social and Cultural Effects of Tourism in Developing Countries*, New York: Oxford University Press.

El Haddadi, H. (2010) *El turismo interno en la península tingitana. Una aproximación al análisis de la demanda y sus efectos económicos*, Thesis, University of Granada, Spain.

Fayos-Solá, E. (1996) Tourism policy: A midsummer night's dream? *Tourism Management*, 17(6), 405–412.

Galiana, L. and Barrado, D. (2006) Los Centros de Interés Turístico Nacional y el despegue del turismo de masas en España, *Investigaciones Geográficas*, 39, 73–93.

Garay, L. and Cánoves, G. (2011) Life cycles, stages and tourism history: The Catalonia (Spain) experience, *Annals of Tourism Research*, 38(2), 651–671.

García, L. and Tasias, G. (2007) Turismo y promoción inmobiliaria en Marruecos, *Boletín Económico del ICE*, 2(918), 69–75.

Gil de Arriba, C. (2011) Del turismo hotelero al turismo residencial en Marruecos. Entre el negocio inmobiliario y la recreación de imaginarios socioespaciales, *Cuadernos de Turismo*, 27, 471–487.

Hall, C. M. and Jenkins, J. M. (1995) *Tourism and Public Policy*, London and New York: Routledge.

Hillali, M. (2005) Aspects sociogéographiques du développement du tourisme balnéaire au Maroc, *Téoros*, 24(1), 6–11.

Hillali, M. (2007a) *La politique du tourisme au Maroc: diagnostic, bilan et critique*, Paris: Harmattan.

Hillali, M. (2007b) Du tourisme et la géopolitique au Maghreb: Le cas du Maroc, *Hérodote*, 127, 47–63.

Jenkins, C. L. (1980) Tourism policies in developing countries: A critique, *International Journal of Tourism Management*, 1(1), 22-29.

Lamb, A. N. (1998) Tourism development and planning in Australia-the need for a national strategy. *Hospitality Management*, 7(4), 353–361.

Lea, J. (1988) *Tourism and Development in the Third World*. London: Routledge.

Lickorish, L. J. (1991) Developing a single European tourism policy, *Tourism Management*, 12(3), 179–184.

Ministére du Tourisme et l'Artisanat. (2013) *Vision 2020*, http://www.tourisme.gov.ma/francais/2-Vision2020-Avenir/2-chantiers/1-Presentation/presentation.htm, accessed 16 January 2015.

Moudoub, B. and Ezaïdi, A. (2005) Le tourisme national au Maroc: opportunités et limites de développement, *Téoros*, 24, 1–10.

Ouahidi, S. and Mzidabi, S. (1994) *L'impact de la privatisation sur le secteur touristique*, Tanger: Institut Superieur International du Tourisme de Tanger.

Pablo-Romero, M. and Molina J. (2013) Tourism and economic growth: A review of empirical literature, *Tourism Management Perspectives*, 8, 28–41.

Pearce, D. (1991) *Tourist Development*, New York: John Wiley & Sons.

Ramos, J. and Pires, L. (2008) *Los economistas españoles frente a la planificación indicativa del desarrollismo*, IX Congress of AEHE, University of Murcia, Spain.

Saad, Y. (2008) Inversiones españolas por miles de millones en Marruecos: inmobiliario y turismo, sectores claves, *Tendencias Económicas*, Afear/Ideas (2007/2008), 80–81.

Scott, N. (2011). *Tourism Policy: A Strategic Review*, Oxford: Goodfellow.

Shamamba, A. (2005) Marruecos en la vía del turismo industrial, *Tendencias Económicas*, Afear/Ideas (2005), 81–83.

Traspaderne, L. (2011) *El sector del turismo en Marruecos*, Informes sectoriales. Oportunidades de inversión y cooperación empresarial, Embajada de España en Rabat e Instituto Español de Comercio Exterior (ICEX).

United Nations World Tourism Organization (UNWTO). (2017) *Compendium of Tourism Statistics*, Madrid: UNWTO.

Verdaguer, E. (2005) Turismo en Marruecos: retos y oportunidades, *Economía Exterior*, 33, 119–124.

Williams, A. and Shaw, G. (1988) *Tourism and Economic Development. Western European Experiences*, London: Belhaven Press.

Yrigoy, I. (2013) La urbanitzaó turística com a materialització de l' acumulació de capital hoteler, *Treballs de Catalana de Geografia*, 75, 109–131.

11

Tourism in Egypt

The past and the present

Doaa Shohaieb

Introduction

Egypt, the land of civilisation, is one of the most popular touristic destinations in Africa and the world. Egypt possesses numerous types of tourism each of which creates a lifetime experience for those who visit it. Cultural tourism is popular among many others. Having an ancient civilisation that dates back to 7,000 years (Manley and Abdel-Hakim, 2008). Egypt boasts fascinating ruins and monuments from this era. Examples include the Temples of Karnak, the Valley of the Kings, the Step Pyramid, the Pyramids of Giza (the only remaining wonder of the Ancient Seven Wonders of the World), the Sphinx, Abu Simbel Temples, and the Tomb of the Nobles. In addition, there is an interest for visitors to learn about Modern Egypt which includes visits to Salah El-Din Citadel, the High Dam, and Khan el-khahlili bazaar in Cairo where antiques and souvenirs representing the different eras Egypt has been through are sold.

Moreover, religious tourism in Egypt through exploring the rich Islamic and Coptic history symbolised in significant buildings including Al-Azhar Mosque which was founded in 970 (Britannica, 2013) and Mohammed Ali Mosque, monasteries and churches like the Hanging Church. In addition, due to Egypt's location and weather, it possesses well-known resorts and beaches visited by millions every year from around the world. Scuba diving is also popular in Hurghada, Sharm El-Sheikh and El Gouna organised by world-class centres. Enjoying a cruise up the Nile, staying in floating hotels, or eating in floating restaurants in the Nile also form an important aspect in the Egyptian tourism. Furthermore, golf resorts, shopping malls, traditional markets, hot springs and desert oasis for hiking are among the places that tourists also enjoy when visiting Egypt.

As a result of the endless tourism experiences it provides, Egypt's travel and tourism industry is in constant growth. In 2018, Egypt achieved the highest growth in North Africa which reached 16.5% and contributed to 2.5 million jobs by receiving visitors from all over the world especially Germany, Russia and Italy who spent over 29.6 billion dollars (Travel Weekly, 2019).

The next section discusses the most significant events that affected the development of the Egyptian tourism industry since the 19th century when Egypt was first introduced as an important tourist destination to Europe and America and how this development aligned with the development of the international tourism industry.

Section 'The types of tourism in Egypt' then identifies the different types of tourism that existed in Egypt, explaining the most popular in the 19th century along with the changes until the current day. The following section analyses how the Egyptian tourism sector has always played a significant role in the economy, the challenges it has faced over the years, and how it managed to overcome them and regain its strength and retain its position in the global tourism industry.

Section 'The growth of mass tourism in Egypt: the role of Thomas Cook & Son' introduces a case study of a travel agency that played a significant role in facilitating the visitation of hundreds of British tourists to Egypt since the second half of the 19th century until the current day; Thomas Cook. Finally, a conclusion drawing on the topics mentioned earlier is presented.

The evolution of tourism in Egypt

Egypt as a destination has attracted tourists for a long time due to its rich historical past including ruins from different eras. Most especially, the ruins of the ancient Egyptian civilisation era have been a significant attraction for tourists. While there is definitely a long history of tourist visitation, it is probably most relevant to start from the beginning of the 19th century in examining the evolution of tourism in Egypt. Egypt was considered as an important tourism destination in this period of time (Nance, 2007).

The development of tourism in Egypt was influenced by several main factors the first incident being the 19th-century French campaign of Napoleon (1798–1801). This campaign is considered to have planted the seeds of tourism in Egypt thanks to the team of scientists, engineers, and archaeologists that had accompanied the campaign (Kevan, 1993). They reported their discoveries and achievements in books introduced to France and the rest of Europe. In addition to these books, paintings of scenes from Egypt by the artists accompanying the campaign served as advertising brochures when these were presented back in France. The report that made it back with Napoleon and his team brought an awareness among other Europeans about Egypt. It was through this awareness that the dream of visiting Egypt emerged.

The most important achievements of this team was the discovery of the Rosetta Stone (which currently is located at the British Museum) and the publishing of 'Description de l'Egypte' (Hazbun, 2007). The Rosetta Stone, deciphered by Jean-François Champollion, was the main mechanism through which the ancient Egyptian hieroglyphs written on the ruins and in the tombs of ancient Egypt were understood (Robinson, 2011). The 'Description de l'Egypte' contained a description of Egypt in the past and in the time of the campaign. Lyth (2013) claims that for half a century, this book remained the main source of information about Egypt for Europeans leading to an increase in an interest to visit.

The tourism sector after this campaign witnessed continuous developments over time as each ruler in Egypt gave special care and attention to the tourism industry (Hunter, 2004). The number of tourists began to increase during the first half of the 19th century (Ramadan, 1977). Tourism in Egypt in the period 1805–1848 was given a remarkable boost when Muhammad Ali Pasha 'the father of Modern Egypt' ruled the country. He contributed to the tourism industry by constructing the 'Overland Route' in 1840 to deliver mails from London to India through Egypt. This helped promote the transit tourism which depended on the tourists stopping in Egypt. Special facilities were built for those travellers like the 'hammams' (baths) which became very popular over time to the extent that they were later considered as the main travel destinations themselves. In 1845 an institution was specifically established for tourists, mails and trading (Diab, 1994). In addition to this, there was a good level of security which encouraged the arrival of tourists. During this period, Egypt began to be considered as 'a convenient and fashionable tourist destination' (Barrell, 1991).

The number of hotels increased with the growing numbers of tourists to Egypt. They increased from two to five in Alexandria, and from two (Shepheard in 1841 and Monai during the French campaign) to three in Cairo. This increase in tourists was in part aided by the then growing number of guidebooks about Egypt that were published by different travel writers mainly from Europe or America. In 1840, John Murray issued his guidebook that included Egypt as stated by Wilkinson (1847). These guidebooks resulted in attracting more people to visit Egypt and created the desire to 'explore the exotic "other"' as described by these guidebooks (Cobb, 2011). Barrell believes that the period from 1830 to 1860 was 'probably the highpoint of admiration in Europe and the United States of the culture of the Ancient Egyptians' (Barrell, 1991, p. 97).

Tourism continued to develop, and the first regulations regarding the tourists' accommodation were issued in May 1849 to provide security. In March 1857, more regulations were issued in organising everything concerning tourists upon arrival until they leave. During this period, medical tourism developed and its importance increased (Diab, 1994).

Furthermore, tourism in Egypt gained a lot of marketing propaganda as a result of two events, which helped to promote the industry. The first was Egypt's contribution to the Paris exhibition in 1867. This enabled learning more about Egypt through the pictures of several painters who had visited Egypt (Ramadan, 1977). The second incident was the opening of the Suez Canal in November 1869 for which the Khedive Ismail had travelled to Europe to invite kings and rulers to the opening. As part of the opening ceremony, several important sites were built as visitor attraction sites for those who were to attend the opening; The Opera, The Egyptian Museum, Aljazeera Palace and The Zoo. Moreover, there was a special importance given to the restoration of Egyptian monuments that were in a state of disrepair (Diab, 1994).

It has been argued that what had had an impact on tourism in Egypt by the late 19th century, and the early 20th century, was the ease of travelling and rising number of tours (Brendon, 1991). The number of tourists increased from 33,429 in 1856 to 67,772 in 1872 and continued to increase (Ramadan, 1977). Travel firms such as Thomas Cook and Son and Henry Gaze (who was one of the most powerful competitors to Thomas Cook) organised tours for the wealthy and the upper-middle classes (Bryan and Bair, 2009). Egypt then became an international destination for tourists and this affected the development of international tourism. As Hazbun reports, 'the expansion of tourism networks across Egypt and the intensified commodification of Egyptian travel marked a critical era in the international tourism industry's development' (Hazbun, 2007, p. 22). This aligns with what Vitalis noted that 'the global tourist industry began with Thomas Cook and Son's monopoly of Nile steamboat traffic' (Vitalis, 1995, p. 2).

In the 20 century, tourism continued to develop in Egypt with a worldwide reputation stressing the high quality and diversity in its tourism products especially in terms of cultural tourism. As the industry boomed, beach tourism massively developed during this period. The Red Sea coast was transformed from fishing villages to world-class resorts. Wahab (1996) shows that the growth of tourism continued in Egypt despite being interrupted temporarily by the 1952 revolution and the wars in 1976 and 1973. During the second half of the 20 century, the numbers of Arabs and Americans increased after the economic liberalisation policies adopted in Egypt applied by Anwar El Sadat in 1974 (Gray, 1998). Tourism currently is of great importance to Egypt as will be discussed later in section 'The importance of tourism in Egypt'.

The types of tourism in Egypt

In the 19th century, the main kinds of tourism that were developed in Egypt included the following;

- **Transit tourism**: this type of tourism developed after the construction of the Overland Route as passengers going from London to India stopped at Egypt for a tour and then continued their journey (Diab, 1994)
- **Seasonal tourism**: this involved mainly European tourists escaping their winter months by visiting Egypt due to its warm weather during this time (Hazbun, 2007; Nasser, 2007).
- **Bird hunting tourism**: a sport enjoyed by tourists, especially in the winter when birds migrate from Eastern Europe, Russia or Turkey through Egypt to stay in Egypt or head to Chad, Sudan, East Africa and South Africa. During the 19th century, some problems arose from bird hunting as a result of the tourists not only hunting the migrating birds but also hunting birds that belonged to the residents of Damietta where the sport was mostly taking place at that time (Ramadan, 1977).
- **Medical tourism**: Egypt has been long known to have this kind of tourism since ancient times (Magazine, 2010) and the main factor that has helped to develop this type of tourism is the weather and sulphur springs available in the country (Hunter, 2004). Thus medical tourism played an important role in the Egyptian economy at that time (Kevan, 1993).
- **Religious tourism**: with the existence of St. Catherine's Monastery which was built in the year 540 (Diab, 1994), Mount Moses and many other ancient mosques and churches from different eras, pilgrims and followers of different faiths visited Egypt for spiritual experiences.
- **Educational tourism**: for those who were trying to explore the archival documents in St. Catherine's Monastery and also the botanists who were interested in exploring the different kinds of plants in Sinai.
- **Recreational tourism**: this form of tourism developed in Egypt to support the many other forms of tourism activities and to ensure that tourists and visitors alike experience comfortable and safe experience (Gray, 1998).
- **Cultural tourism**: the most ancient type of tourism in Egypt (Wahab, 1996). Egypt possesses numerous monuments and museums from different eras such as the Pharaonic, Greek, Islamic and Roman eras. It is stated that Luxor in Egypt owns nearly one-third of the worldwide discovered monuments (SIS, 2018).

While the old forms of tourism remain (some in evolved forms), new kinds of tourism have emerged in Egypt such as conference tourism, safari tourism, sports tourism and beach tourism. The type of tourism that did not exist in the 19th century is beach tourism, which is currently of great importance to the tourism sector in Egypt. The development of the beach resort tourism started in the 1980s on the Red Sea coast and in Sinai (Gray, 1998). Egypt's popular resorts and beaches mostly visited by tourists are Sharm El-Sheikh and Dahab in Sinai and Hurghada on the Red Sea coast. Sharm El-Sheikh was chosen in 2007 and 2011 as the world's leading dive destination (World Travel Awards, 2011). This has contributed to the growth of leisure tourism in Egypt. Cultural tourism has remained the most important type of tourism and still attracts 1,000 of tourists every year which is reflected by more than 60% of tourists in 2010 who reported their main purpose of visit as being visitation to the historic buildings and museums (Euromonitor, 2012b).

The importance of tourism in Egypt

Tourism has been important to Egypt especially during the 19th century. This is evident in the previous section which explored the evolution of tourism in the 19th century and how consecutive governments contributed to the tourism sector. One of the most important rulers of Egypt who added a lot to the Egyptian tourism sector is the Khedive Ismail who ruled Egypt from 1863 to 1879 (Diab, 1994; Nasser, 2007; Ramadan, 1977). He tried to add to the beauty of Egypt's cities so they would emulate the most beautiful cities around the world at that time such as Paris. Tourism was given great prominence and was considered profitable to work and invest in (Nance, 2007).

Tourism continued to prosper in Egypt, although it was interrupted for a period by the British occupation of Egypt in 1882. The number of tourists increased afterwards in 1886 and so did the number of hotels and improvements in the means of transportation used by tourists especially steamers and 'dahabiyas' (small boats used before the invention of steamers). The number of tourists to Cairo in the winter of the year 1889–1890 was equal to about 11,000, and at the end of the 19th century, the Nile 'had become the favourite winter resort of westerners' (Hunter, 2004).

Tourism to Egypt flourished upon the opening of the tomb of Tutankhamun in 1923 which was considered a great discovery (Brendon, 1991). Tourism was also considered important after Egypt had gained its independence. A country's stability plays a great role in the status of the tourism industry's performance. It is reported that Gamal Abdel Nasser, who was the president in 1956 did not give much importance to the tourism sector (Gray, 1998). The reason was that Egypt after the revolution in 1952 was facing a difficult economic situation and he prioritised the agriculture and industrial sectors to improve citizens' lives and the state of the country. However, the existence of the Suez Canal was still a reason to attract many visitors to Egypt (Gray, 1998).

Tourism flourished after the 'open economy' policy of Anwar El Sadat in 1974. The number of tourists increased gradually starting in 1975 (Wahab and Pigram, 1997). Tourism was also considered important in the period in which Mubarak ruled the country from 1981. The tourism product was diversified, and new types of tourism were developed such as resort tourism and tourism in general received great attention in this period.

Currently, tourism in Egypt plays an important role in shaping the economy. In 2018, Egypt achieved the highest growth rate in North Africa reaching 16.5%. It contributed to 2.5 million jobs by receiving visitors spending over 29.6 billion dollars as stated by Travel Weekly (2019). As a matter of fact, tourism in Egypt is in continuous growth except if interrupted by major events. Egypt has been subject to different challenges that have affected its tourism industry massively. These events include the global financial crisis in 2008, the Egyptian revolution in 2011, the military coup and the Rabaa Massacre in 2013, and the Russian plane crash in 2015 which was claimed to be related to terrorism.

The effect of the revolution on the Egyptian tourism sector was much greater than the impact of the global crisis that had its effect in 2009. As can be seen from Figure 11.1, tourism statistics improved in 2010 as a recovery from the financial crisis but decreased sharply in 2011 and 2013 as a reflection of the circumstances Egypt was undergoing due to the revolution.

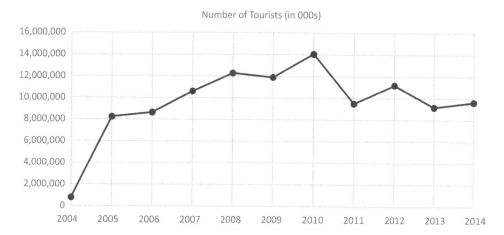

Figure 11.1 Tourist arrivals to Egypt from 2004 to 2014

Source: World Development Indicators (https://datacatalog.worldbank.org/dataset/world-development-indicators, acessed 04/06/2020).

The graph reflects how severe the revolution and the incidents following affected the tourist numbers visiting Egypt. The year 2013 was even worse and was described by the minister of tourism –at that time, Hisham Zazou as 'worst year in modern history' (Kingsley, 2014). During 2012, the country had seen plenty of protests and violent clashes. Therefore, stability had not yet taken place although an increase in the number of tourists can be seen in Figure 11.1. Some researchers have claimed that the increase in the arrival of tourists in 2012 has cost more than what was gained, in the form of tourist revenues due to the vast amount of money spent by the government to attract Arab tourists to visit the country and all the other activities related to promoting tourism to the country.

In 2011, the year the revolution took place, Egypt's travel and tourism sector still managed to contribute to the creation of about 3 million jobs representing about 13.1% of total employment in 2011 and contribute to 14.8% GDP (WTTC, 2012) reflecting the strength and importance of such industry to the country.

Table 11.1 shows the contribution of the tourism sector to the economy and the number of jobs it supported through the years 2012–2017.

It appears from Table 11.1 that the travel and tourism sector does have a great impact on the country's economy. Looking at the figures, it is also noticeable that the figures fluctuate reflecting turbulent times, such as the large protests across the country followed by the military coup, and the Rabaa Massacre taking place in 2013 and the Russian plane crash which had a great impact on tourism in the last two months of 2015 and 2016. Despite these destructive events, it can be seen in Table 11.1 that the industry recovers quickly after each incident which reflects the importance of Egyptian tourism to tourists all over

Table 11.1 The contribution of tourism to GDP and employment in Egypt (2012–2017)

Total contribution[a]	2012	2013	2014	2015	2016	2017
GDP (EGP bn)	199.5	170.6	194.7	212.3	197.8	374.6
Employment ('000)	2,750.5	2,171.3	2,194.7	2,170.5	1,829.2	2,425.4

Source: WTTC (2018).
a Includes the direct, indirect and induced contribution.

Table 11.2 The number of visitors to Egypt from the four biggest markets

	1995	1996	1997	1998	1999	2000	2001	2002	2003	2004
Russia[a]	11,0108	122,546	117,515	–	–	–	210,212	382,536	497,465	785,419
United Kingdom	28,4611	319,229	324,200	230,897	319,226	358,781	324,821	357,546	357,248	546,892
Germany	319,312	436,809	438,372	273,838	547,855	786,336	715,066	730,323	693,445	993,178
Italy	257,272	366,320	389,081	373,067	667,460	752,166	594,549	701,210	795,903	1,010,444

	2005	2006	2007	2008	2009	2010	2011	2012	2013	2014
Russia[a]	777,665	998,149	1,516,561	1,825,312	2,035,330	2,855,723	1,832,388	2,518,275	2,393,908	3,138,958
United Kingdom	837,950	1,033,761	1,055,012	1201859	1,346,724	1,455,906	1,034,413	1,011,775	955,344	905,713
Germany	979,631	966,386	1,085,930	1202509	1,202,339	1328960	964,599	1,164,556	885,479	877,228
Italy	823,199	786,130	983,293	1,073,159	1,047,997	1,144,384	555,246	718,703	504,110	400,356

a The numbers of tourists during the period 1998–2000 are not available.
Source: World Tourism Organization. (2016), *Yearbook of Tourism Statistics dataset* [Electronic], UNWTO, Madrid, data updated on 12/01/2016.

the world and the continuous efforts of the Egyptian government to recuperate from challenges the industry faces.

An important aspect of the evolution of the tourism sector in Egypt is the changing nationality of the visitors that form the highest percentage of tourists. During the 19th century and the first half of the 20th century, the majority of the tourists were from America and Europe especially Britain due to the increasing number of tours to Egypt, books about Egypt and the increasing connection between Britain and Egypt at that time (Barrell, 1991; Diab, 1994; Nance, 2007; Nasser, 2007; Ramadan, 1977; Vitalis, 1995). In 2011, the majority of tourists were from Europe, in particular Russia followed by the British who formed the majority until the year 2006 (Euromonitor, 2012a) as can be seen in Table 11.2. Most Russian tourists visiting Egypt head to Sharm El-Sheikh and Hurghada as they are considered relatively cheap destinations compared to other destinations that offer similar beach resort tourism such as Turkey and Cyprus (Sahoo, 2015).

Beach tourism has contributed to the growth of leisure tourism in Egypt which has had a significant impact on the sector and having a large number of tourists favouring beach tourism, especially Russians and Arabs, has helped to mitigate the severe decrease in tourism receipts in 2011 (Euromonitor, 2012a). As shown in Table 11.2, the Russian tourists form the largest number Egypt receives every year since 2006. The German tourists formed the majority before 2006. The United Kingdom and Italy also are considered main markets for the Egyptian tourism.

The growth of mass tourism in Egypt: the role of Thomas Cook & Son

It has been clear from the previous sections how important tourism is and has always been to Egypt and to tourists. Travel agencies play an essential role in the tourism industry as a result of their experience, the advice they provide, and the planning of trips for which they take responsibility (Hui and Wan, 2006). In this section, one travel agency will be introduced, highlighting the role it played in the early formation of the international tourism industry in Egypt as we now know it. The travel institution is Thomas Cook and Son, has had a significant influence on the Egyptian and international tourism industry since the mid-19th century as stated by Vitalis (1995).

Thomas Cook, the founder, was a British entrepreneur who is considered as one of the main founders of international tourism. He specialised in tours around Europe and North America in the mid-19th century (Wahab and Pigram, 1997). He began his business in Britain by offering tours between British cities in 1841 and afterwards conducted tours to Europe and America. Thomas Cook had a great effect on the international tourism industry in general and to the Egyptian tourism industry in particular (Vitalis, 1995). Hazbun claimed that Thomas Cook was the first person to introduce 'packaged tours', and that Cook was the main reason for 'the expansion' of tourism in Egypt (Hazbun, 2007). This was accomplished by Thomas Cook and Son favourably presenting and describing Egypt in its publications (Hunter, 2004). The main reason for Cook's success in Egypt was his ability to provide middle-class tourists with the opportunity to visit Egypt at affordable prices. In addition, he granted British Victorian women the opportunity to travel alone and feel the freedom they had never experienced before within the rigid Victorian society in Britain at that time (Lyth, 2013).

Thomas Cook made an exploratory tour of Egypt in 1868 to equip him for a proposed group tour in 1869 to witness the opening of the Suez Canal. He was invited by the ruler of Egypt, Khedive Ismail, to attend the opening (Manley and Abdel-Hakim, 2008). As a result of this trip, Egypt was the first place in the Middle East to be considered as a 'tourist destination', as tours before that time only took place in Europe and America (Gray, 1998).

A year later, in 1870, Khedive Ismail gave Thomas Cook & Son exclusive permission to run the Nile traffic between Cairo and Aswan. And afterwards the firm was also appointed to transport official mail (Hunter, 2004). Tourism in Egypt started to flourish, thanks to Thomas Cook's son John Mason Cook's activities and developments in the country (Brendon, 1991). By the year 1872, Egypt and Palestine were considered as the main source of money for the Thomas Cook & Son agency and its first office was opened in Cairo in the same year (Nance, 2007).

Tourism in Egypt faced several crises and so did Thomas Cook and Son respectively. These crises started in 1881 with the revolt led by Colonel Urabi against the bad conditions the country was experiencing and the British interference in Egyptian affairs (Brendon, 1991). This was followed by the British occupation of Egypt in 1882. Tourism was harmfully disrupted (Hazbun, 2007). John Cook's business did not cease in Egypt, but it was no longer tourism that was the main business. Instead of moving tourists on the Nile, he used his steamers to transport soldiers from Britain to Egypt, and between Cairo and Alexandria in Egypt (Hunter, 2003). In 1883 the British government assigned John Mason Cook to undertake an expedition to rescue General Charles Gordon in Sudan. It is reported that he received significant profits and support from the British government for playing this role (Brendon, 1991; Hunter, 2004).

These events and their aftermaths affected the tourism business of Cook. One of the challenges Cook faced was that the steamers were in bad condition due to having used them for the army's activities during the war (Brendon, 1991). Another important challenge was the increasing competition Cook was facing. The major competitors included: Dean & Dawson, John Frames Tours, Quintin Hogg's Polytechnic Tours and Sir Henry Lunn's Tours who were mostly founded in the 1870s and 80s (Brendon, 1991) except for Henry Gaze who had been competing with Cook since the 1850s and had conducted tours to the Holy Land before Thomas Cook (Saad, 2000). It has to be noted that a major contribution to the success of the Thomas Cook and Son firm would not have been achieved without John Mason Cook's close relationship with both the ruling family in Egypt and the British government (Hazbun, 2007).

After the war ended, the number of tourists demanding to visit Egypt increased, especially British tourists who were the major tourists at that time (Hunter, 2004). This led Cook to resume his tourism activities and expand his operations. Cook promoted Egypt as a place with an abundance of historical sites. The covers of Thomas Cook's tourist guides were illustrated with ancient Egyptian symbols, pharaohs, the Nile, and different monuments to be explored. This reflects the type of tourism that prevailed and which was heavily promoted as historical and cultural tourism. Indeed, as mentioned earlier, this type of tourism remains dominant in Egypt today.

Despite the death of both Thomas Cook and John Cook in the 1890s, the firm was managed successfully by John's three sons; Frank Henry, Ernest Edward and Thomas Albert (Thomas Cook, 2018) until the occurrence of the First World War. The tourism industry was disrupted internationally, and in Egypt, the steamers did not operate for tourism from 1914 but were used for the war effort by the British army (Brendon, 1991). This led to the decline of Thomas Cook and Son's agency. And because its power was gained from its successful relationship with both the British government and the ruling family in Egypt (Hazbun, 2007; Hunter, 2003), the firm suffered more. As noted by Hunter, 'when British power weakened, so did Cook's' (Hunter, 2004, p. 50). Another significant event that contributed to weakening the firm's position was the 1919 revolution to gain independence from Britain (Brendon, 1991).

The agency decided to offer the same service – transporting tourists for leisure – but in different geographical areas where there was no war, and peace prevailed (Brendon, 1991). After the war, when the tourism industry was recovering, Thomas Cook and Son benefited and gained remarkable profits (Hunter, 2004).

This continued until the Second World War. Tourism again suffered severely and likewise the Thomas Cook and Son Ltd. In Egypt, the steamers that existed at that time were commandeered for the war (Brendon, 1991). The Second World War was followed by a tourism boom which Cook could not take advantage of due to the attempts of the Egyptian government to control the tourism industry and gain from the tourism profits (Hunter, 2004). Another reason was the nationalists' protests and the 1952 revolution to gain full independence from Britain which was preceded with violence and setting fire to all the British organisations including the Thomas Cook and Son's office in Cairo. Thomas Cook and Son tried to continue their activities from another office in a different area in Egypt, but it failed especially after the invasion in 1956 (Brendon, 1991). The firm was able to reopen in 1960, and at that time, there were a lot of restrictions concerning conducting businesses in Egypt by foreign investors until liberalisation policies were applied in 1974 which resulted in more freedom for companies (Gray, 1998). This led to more tourism companies investing in Egypt, and by 2013 there were about 1192 tourism organisations including Thomas Cook providing tourist services according to the report on the travel agencies and tourism establishments sector.

Conclusion

Tourism in Egypt has a long history and existed before the 19th century due to the presence of the ancients' ruins from different eras. Tourism has always been an important industry in Egypt and the formal development of the Egyptian tourism industry in the 19th century was related to the development of the international tourism industry. The industry has witnessed prosperity since the 1870s due to packaged tours and the ease of travelling in the following decades. The main type of tourism in Egypt was and remains cultural tourism in which tourists are interested in visiting the ruins of ancient Egypt and different eras. Other types of tourism like medical tourism and spiritual tourism still exist but are not as popular as cultural tourism and beach tourism, although the country is rich in the resources it possesses for medical tourism and the numerous buildings and places for spiritual tourism. Some developments and strong campaigns for those two types of tourism can help flourish the number of tourists visiting the country and enhance the country's ranking in the world's top tourist destinations.

Europeans continue to represent the major category of tourists coming to Egypt with the British being the most dominant group in the 19th century and the Russian in the current time. The government of any country has a major role in the development of its tourism sector. Tourism in Egypt was important to the governments in the 19th century and hence witnessed tremendous developments. There have been core developments that have benefited the tourism sector and there is continuous progress in this sector given its economic worth to Egypt which helped Egypt overcome major challenges. The chapter explored how Egypt had been able to survive several crises it faced. Economic crises did not have a tremendous effect on the sector as much as the political ones. This is why Egypt has to try and avoid such events occurring again by ensuring democracy is practiced to avoid protests and violence and also to always work on keeping security tight to avoid any attacks that have a connection to terrorism.

Tourism institutions have existed in Egypt since the mid-19th century. Despite the decrease in the use of travel agencies by many travellers due to the increased dependence on online bookings, travel agencies are still essential to travelling to places like Egypt at least for the first visit to avoid all the ambiguities related to travelling to an unfamiliar place. This is eased by the help of the country considering the safety and security of the tourists as a priority as previously mentioned.

References

Barrell, J. 1991. "Death on the Nile: Fantasy and the literature of tourism 1840–1860." *Essays in Criticism, 41*(2), 97–127.

Brendon, Piers. 1991. *Thomas Cook: 150 Years of Popular Tourism.* Secker (Martin) & Warburg Ltd.

Britannica. 2013. Al-Azhar University. https://www.britannica.com/topic/al-Azhar-University. Accessed 15 January, 2019.

Bryan, M.L.M., & Bair, B. (2009). *The Selected Papers of Jane Addams: Vol. 2: Venturing into Usefulness.* Champaign: University of Illinois Press.

Cobb, E. 2011. "Taking home the pyramids, Andrew. D. White, a tourist in 19th century Egypt." https://rmc.library.cornell.edu/Architourism/exhibition/Taking%20Home%20the%20Pyramids/index.html. Accessed 29 August 2012.

Diab, E.E. 1994. *Alsiyaha fi Misr Khilal Elkarn Eltasie' Ashar, Dirasah fi Tarikh Misr Elektisady wa Elegtema'iy* [Tourism in Egypt during the Nineteenth century: A study in Egypt's economic and social history]. Misr El-Nahda: The General Egyptian Institution for Books.

Euromonitor. 2012a. *Tourism Flows Inbound in Egypt.* https://www.euromonitor.com/tourism-flows-in-egypt/report. Accessed 16 October 2012.

Euromonitor. 2012b. *Tourist Attractions in Egypt.* https://www.euromonitor.com/travel-in-egypt/report. Accessed 16 October 2012.

Gray, M. 1998. "Economic reform, privatization and tourism in Egypt." *Middle Eastern Studies, 34*(2), 91–112.

Hazbun, W. (2007). *The East as an exhibit: Thomas Cook & Son and the origins of the International Tourism Industry in Egypt.* In P. Scranton & J.F. Davidson (Eds.), The business of tourism: Place, faith and history (pp. 3–33). Philadelphia, PA: University of Pennsylvania Press

Hunter, F. R. 2003. "The Thomas Cook archive for the study of tourism in North Africa and the Middle East." *Middle East Studies Association Bulletin, 36*(2), 157–164.

Hunter, F. R. 2004. "Tourism and empire: The Thomas Cook & Son enterprise on the Nile, 1868–1914." *Middle Eastern Studies, 40*(5), 28–54.

Hui, T. K., and Wan, D. 2006. "Factors affecting consumers' choice of a travel agency: The case of Singapore." *Journal of Travel & Tourism Marketing, 19*(4), 1–12.

Kevan, S.M. 1993. "Quests for cures: A history of tourism for climate and health." *International Journal of Biometeorology, 37*(3), 113–124.

Kingsley, P. 2014. "Tourist desert – Egypt desperate to woo back visitors after years of unrest." *The Guardian,* February 10. https://www.theguardian.com/world/2014/feb/10/egypts-tourist-resorts-ghost-towns

Lyth, P. 2013. "Carry on up the Nile: The Tourist gaze and the British experience of Egypt, 1818–1932." In Farr, M. and Guégan, X. (Eds.) *The British Abroad Since the Eighteenth Century, Volume 1* (pp. 176–193). Basingstoke: Palgrave Macmillan.

Magazine, Medical Tourism. 2010. *Egypt, Where It All Begins.* http://www.medicaltourismmag.com/egypt-where-it-all-begins/. Accessed 15 January 2017.

Manley, D., & Abdel-Hakim, S. (Eds.). (2008). *Traveling Through Egypt: From 450 BC to the Twentieth Century* (Vol. 2). Cairo: American University in Cairo Press.

Nance, Susan. 2007. "A facilitated access model and Ottoman Empire tourism." *Annals of Tourism Research, 34*(4), 1056–1077.

Nasser, Noha. 2007. "A historiography of tourism in Cairo: A spatial perspective." In Daher, R. F. (Ed.) *Tourism in the Middle East Continuity, Change and Transformation* (pp. 70–94). Clevedon: Channel View Publications.

Ramadan, S. 1977. *Elhayat Eligtima'iya fi Misr fi Ahd Ismail min 1863–1879* [The Social Life in Egypt in the Era of Ismail from 1863–1879]. Alexandria, Egypt: Monsha'at Al Ma'arif Bilaskandaria.

Robinson, A. 2011. "Styles of decipherment: Thomas Young, Jean-François Champollion and the decipherment of the Egyptian hieroglyphs." *The Hunminjeongeum Society, 3*, 123–132.

Saad, R. 2000. "Travel in the good old days." *Al-Ahram Weekly*, 6–12 January.

Sahoo, S. 2015. "Russian tourists head to more affordable Sharm El Sheikh Instead of Dubai." *The National Newspaper Online,* Available from, https://www.thenational.ae/business/travel-and-tourism/russian-tourists-head-to-more-affordable-sharm-el-sheikh-instead-of-dubai-1.114097. Accessed 25 April 2020.

Thomas Cook. 2018. *Thomas Cook History.* https://www.thomascook.com/thomas-cook-history/

Travel Weekly (2019) Egypt tourism 'fastest growing' in North Africa. https://www.travelweekly.co.uk/articles/326898/egypt-tourism-fastest-growing-in-north-africa. Accessed 22 August, 2020.

Vitalis, R. 1995. "The Middle East on the edge of the pleasure periphery." *Middle East Report,* 196 (Sept.–Oct. 1995), 2–7.

Wahab, S. 1996. "Tourism development in Egypt: Competitive strategies and implications." *Progress in Tourism and Hospitality Research, 2*(3–4), 351–364.

Wahab, S., and Pigram, J. 1997. *Tourism, Development and Growth: The Challenge of Sustainability.* London: Routledge.

World Travel Awards. 2011. *World's Leading Dive Destination 2011.* https://www.worldtravelawards.com/award-worlds-leading-dive-destination-2011. Accessed 12 May 2018.

WTTC. 2012. "Travel & tourism economic impact 2012 Egypt." *Egypt Economic Impact Report.* World Travel and Tourism Council.

InFocus 3

The role of the media in promoting tourism in Africa

Kojo Bentum Williams and Ben Ohene-Ayeh

The media undoubtedly provides powerful communication channels and avenues for disseminating news, information, entertainment, education, or promotional messages to the public. With the advancement of technology today, the media has become even more crucial and virtually inevitable in everyday life as individuals as well as organizations seek to reach the masses with their messages. Its role is so crucial that shirking of its responsibilities in any form would have a detrimental impact on society.

Malcolm X once said, 'The media is the most powerful entity on earth. They have the power to make the innocent guilty and to make the guilty innocent, and that is power because they control the mind of the masses'.

Africa's tourism has in the last decade seen significant growth in terms of infrastructure, product and human resources' development. However, communication remains a challenge, as how small or big the success story, this may have not been communicated well by the media especially by the international news outlet, continuously confining stories about the continent to narratives of crisis, poverty, disasters and despair.

VoyagesAfriq Media's establishment was borne out of the necessity to fill a communication vacuum and help promote Africa's diverse story of tourism success and opportunities to its people and the rest of the world. The objective of the media entity is to offer an avenue for Africa's tourism players and establishments to reach out and promote their unique tourism products and provide compelling news content to change the narratives about the continent.

Our work on the continent has proven that tourism is indeed a sector which can be patronized well by Africans when given adequate information about the different countries and their tourism products. That impression and responses give real meaning to our works and even challenged us further to do more and implore disruptive elements to make it attractive.

VoyagesAfriq having identified some of the challenging ways in which the media communicate news about the continent to the world set up a priority to share the African success story with its flagship publication and also make use of our new social media platforms. Our publication in essence celebrates the achievements, successes and the unique stories of African tourism.

The trend in the tourism sector is fast changing from product development to the introduction of disruptive travel technologies, which seek to make tourism seamless. African

Destinations have introduced different and various forms of ways to make tourism a more sustainable and responsible way of how to enjoy tourism. Highlights of success included that the Kenya Tourism Federation, in conjunction with hotels in the country's coastal areas, banned and introduced a better way of dealing with plastics in the tourism sector. Equally, communication on the Rwanda Development Board deploying an effective way of promoting the gorilla tracking in the volcanoes, also benefitted from the biggest revolution in the industry, the digital revolution which has seen a complete turnaround for the sector.

Effective and better alternatives to the experience have come about with this innovation. The UN World Tourism Organization (UNWTO) in collaboration with the New Partnership for Africa's Development (NEPAD) concluded the 2019 FITUR International Tourism Trade Fair in Spain. Support was given to five African travel tech startups to participate at the tourism tech adventures at the fair, giving them the opportunity to pitch, participate in masterclasses and engage with Ministers of Tourism for their projects.

The above-mentioned examples are only a small attempt to showcase how tourism in Africa is changing for good and as an African media, we ought to not only report but celebrate such successes and achievements. The media has the duty to report on the sterling African stories. Organizations such as Casa Africa, Africa Development Bank (AFDB), Union Economique et Monétaire Ouest Africaine (UEMOA) have all embarked on projects to tell positive and engaging African stories through their respective media entities.

A critical challenge remains in the fact that attention is to be given to the lack of training for media professionals, inadequate funding to embark on PR campaigns and lack of exposure for the media on ways of professionally reporting on the sector. As we seek to bring Africa's tourism to the limelight, many tourism boards and ministries of tourism do not have sufficient capacity to understand that marketing and promotion are not simply confined to the outdated printing of glossy brochures or travel to trade fairs.

The role of the media has become more critical with the rise of social media and at the same time with its growing challenges. In spite of its increasing consumer base, it has led to the 'fake news syndrome', which is on the rise and the need to monitor and address those which may have devastating impacts on a destination. There is a need for a fine balance between traditional ways to give visibility to destinations (i.e. familiarization trips with highly profiled journalists) and the evolution of the new technologies, which require a continuous updating of information to keep readers engaged.

We at VoyagesAfriq Media Limited have made it a core priority to share African stories using numerous media platforms and particularly social media. Our quarterly Travel and Tourism Magazine thus reports the best happenings across the continent and beyond. Our operation is committed to collaborate with different public and private stakeholders to communicate that Africa is on the rise and to create an appealing image to the global tourism and travel market that the African tourism sector is indeed the one to watch!

Part III

Tourism in West Africa

12

"Today is party A, tomorrow is party B"

The Elmina 2015 Strategy and the politics of tourism-led local economic development planning in Ghana[1]

Emmanuel Akwasi Adu-Ampong

Introduction

On 15 April 2002, current King Willem Alexander and Queen Maxima (then Prince and Princess respectively) of the Netherlands were present in Elmina, Ghana to officially open the *Elmina Town Consultation* as part of the Elmina Cultural Heritage Management Programme (ECHMP). This officially opening event was well attended by representatives of Elmina traditional authorities as well as local, regional and national government representatives. Developed by the Komenda-Edina-Eguafo-Abrem Municipal Assembly (KEEA), the ECHMP aimed at leveraging heritage tourism assets within Elmina for local economic development and poverty reduction. An outcome of the consultations under the ECHMP was the development of a set of ambitions plans christened as the Elmina 2015 Strategy.

An underlying ambition of the Elmina 2015 Strategy was to integrate efforts at stimulating local economic development in the city of Elmina "as a means to alleviate poverty an[d] improve the living standard of the Elmina people" (KEEA, 2002:11). The Elmina 2015 Strategy resulted in the development and implementation of a number of tourism, heritage and local economic development-related projects starting from 2002. The ultimate aim of these projects was the achievement of a developmental vision in which by the end of 2015, Elmina would become "the engine of equitable socio-economic development that impacts on the wealth creation, poverty reduction and improved local governance on a sustainable basis" (Arthur and Mensah, 2006:310). This vision was built on the foundation of heritage tourism becoming the central catalyst for all the other efforts for local economic development and poverty reduction.

When the year 2015 ended, however, the outcomes on the ground showed a remarkable difference from the underlying ambitions of the Elmina 2015 Strategy. The expected integration of tourism to foster local economic development could not be fully realised – although some successes were chalked. Collaboration and coordination between various tourism-related and development-related agencies had broken down. A number of the completed infrastructural projects began to fall apart due to a lack of use and maintenance. In some cases, such as the Craft Market, facilities become appropriated for other uses due to a lack of patronage. The tourism products on offer in Elmina were not diversified nor were enough linkages made between potential attractions in the locality to the main attraction of the UNESCO World Heritage Site of the Elmina (St. George's) Castle. The rehabilitated buildings, facilities including tourist signage were left in various stages of disrepair and neglect. Many of the business enterprises that were set up at the start of the ECHMP process to benefit from and attract increased number of tourists into the larger community had closed down because of the failure of institutional collaboration and coordination. The KEEA Municipal Assembly as the highest political and administrative body with responsibility for overall development of the locality appeared to be no longer interested in the Elmina 2015 Strategy. Other institutions that were involved in the planning process seemed to have recoiled back into a narrow focus on their own respective mandates. The governance and management of the Elmina 2015 Strategy appeared to have fallen through the cracks.

Given the wide range of stakeholders involved in the Elmina 2015 Strategy, an examination of the larger context of governance interactions and the institutional structures within which the Elmina 2015 Strategy took place becomes key. This is the focus of this chapter which analyses how institutional setup and political arrangements shaped this tourism-led local economic development planning process. The chapter aims to closely examine the particular ways in which the dynamics of governance interactions shape the use of tourism for local economic development. A strong emphasis in this chapter is placed on the important role of politics in order to address the lacuna in the literature on the tourism-poverty nexus where there is insufficient attention given to the political and governance dimensions of tourism's role in local economic development and poverty reduction (Adu-Ampong, 2019).

After this introduction, the rest of this chapter is organised as follows: first, I briefly sketch out the conceptual ideas around tourism-led local economic development planning and the governance structures in which such process takes place. In particular, I consider how local level political cycles and arrangements shape the use of tourism in local economic development and poverty reduction. Second, I describe the methodology and methods used for data collection and analysis. In the third section, I provide a brief outline of the Elmina 2015 Strategy before moving on to the fourth section that discusses the research findings developed around the political cycles in Ghana. The fifth and final section is the conclusion that draws out implications of this chapter in the wider context of the challenges of leveraging tourism as a tool for local economic development and poverty reduction.

Tourism, local economic development and political cycles

One of the greatest challenges in modern times is the issue of poverty. As such, combating poverty in both "developed" and/or "developing" countries remains one of the main goals of increasing economic development. Within this challenge of global poverty reduction ambitions, tourism is often touted as having the potential to make a significant contribution to the development process (Scheyvens, 2011; Novelli, 2016; Adu-Ampong, 2019). The continuous growth of the tourism sector globally has been the basis on which tourism has come to be regarded as a means to development. This is especially the case in many African countries, where there is an increase in international tourism demand (as also indicated in Chapter 1 of this volume). Many of these African countries possess a wide variety of natural, cultural, and man-made tourism assets like beaches, wildlife parks, cultural festivals and World Heritage Sites. Consequently, tourism has been seen as having the potential to improve livelihoods through foreign exchange earnings, job creation, income generation and biodiversity conservation (Ashley et al., 2000; Meyer, 2007; Christie et al., 2014; Novelli, 2016; Adu-Ampong, 2017). Tourism is therefore expanding rapidly in many developing countries and in context where states struggle to effectively manage development processes at the local level. Questions have therefore been raised as to the ability of tourism to deliver pro-poor economic benefits in such context (Scheyvens, 2007; Spenceley and Meyer, 2012; Adu-Ampong, 2018).

It has been shown that the most effective way of maximising tourism's potential contribution to local economic development and poverty reduction is by embedding tourism policy and planning within place-based strategic initiatives and seen as part of local and regional economic development (Rogerson, 2014:106). Local economic development (LED) is a development strategy that arose out of the disillusionment with mainstream top-down economic development planning and policy to bring about desired outcomes in the 1970s and 1980s (Nel, 2001; Rogerson and Rogerson, 2010). LED planning is undertaken in well-defined territory or locality, with existing resources available in that locality and the process is controlled by local actors and stakeholders (Rodríguez-Pose, 2002; Pike et al., 2006). Thus, for localities with existing tourism resources, the pursuit of LED tends to be built around using tourism as a catalyst for wider socio-economic development goals. The development of strong linkages between tourism and the local economy is fundamental to maximising tourism benefits.

Tourism-led LED planning is therefore about ensuring an integrated development of tourism in a locality, as a means of enhancing the economic base of that area, creating new employment and business opportunities for local people and complementing existing livelihood options. Following Helmsing (2003:69), tourism-led LED is defined as "a process in which partnerships between local governments, community and civic groups and the private sector are established to manage existing [tourism] resources to create jobs and stimulate the economy of a well-defined area". The emphasis here is on local control and the utilisation of an area's existing potential in terms of human, institutional and physical resources. As these resources tend to be controlled by different groups of governors, actors and stakeholders, LED initiatives rely on the mobilisation of actors, organisations and resources in order to develop local systems through building networks of people, institutions and resources in order to bring about local development.

The state needs to play a key role in integrating tourism into local economic development planning processes, in ways that systematically address development and poverty reduction goals. Tourism and development processes are dependent most crucially on state policy directives that span a multitude of institutions across different governance levels. The importance of governance in enhancing tourism's contribution to poverty reduction has been readily highlighted in the literature (Brohman, 1996; Konadu-Agyemang, 2001; Scheyvens, 2007; Holden, 2013; Rogerson, 2014). It has been asserted by Scheyvens (2007:248) that "there is a need for effective governance structures if tourism is to maximise benefits for the poor". More recently, Adu-Ampong (2019:56) has argued that "the issue of governance within the tourism-development nexus has more typically enjoyed only a passing mention, rather than being considered a key explanatory variable in understanding the relationship between tourism and development". Consequently, tourism's role in local economic development needs to be understood from the perspective of the governance structures and interactions at the local level. In particular, it is important to pay attention to the intersection of local governance and local political party cycles.

National and local electoral cycles present both positive and negative incentives that shape the socio-economic and political behaviours of governments. For instance, it has been established that incumbent governments seeking re-election often engage in increased government spending and/or decreased taxation in the year leading up to national, regional and local elections. Such increased government spending close to elections puts the incumbent government in a position to be re-elected (Drazen, 2001; Franzese, 2002; Khemani, 2004; Brender and Drazen, 2005; Keefer and Khemani, 2005; Drazen and Eslava, 2010). This process of political business cycle (PBC) shows that in the run up to elections, incumbents are shown to reallocate the bulk of government expenditure to high visibility projects that make an immediate impression on voters (Rogoff, 1990). Thus, politicians with an eye on re-election take deliberate steps in the allocation and timing of government resources, which is usually in favour of big development projects at key stages of the electoral cycle. The more visible the projects, such as the extension of electricity, road upgrades and other building projects, the more likely electorates are predisposed to vote for the government. In many cases, these projects need only to be started and not be completed by election time.

There is an issue here of project (dis)continuity and what happens to the high visibility projects and programmes once the electoral cycle is over and the incumbent is re-elected? Do the incumbents see these projects through to full implementation or do they let such projects lie idle until the next electoral cycle is on the horizon? Importantly, what happens to the (dis)continuity of projects if and when an incumbent government is voted out of power and a new government is elected? In a highly contested political landscape as in Ghana, what happens to uncompleted projects when a new political party assumes power? Answers to these questions are important in helping to understand how a long-term project like the Elmina 2015 Strategy unfolded within the context of changing party governments.

To fully comprehend what happens to projects after elections, a set of literature on the political economy of public good provision offers a number of insights. Research from this area has shown how national and local electoral cycles impact on project implementation and development outcomes (Lindberg, 2003; Whitfield, 2009; Batley et al., 2012; Kelsall, 2012; Turner, 2012; Hirvi and Whitfield, 2015; Williams, 2016). Thus, while a given government might initiate tourism development policies and projects, the (dis)continuity and full implementation of such projects are dependent on underlying political-economic conditions in a given destination – of which national and local electoral cycles are a prime example. Clearly then, tourism planning and the tourism-poverty nexus projects are bound to be affected by changes in government. The different set of incentives available to politicians and policy-makers in the lead-up to elections may shape their decision to start high visibility projects and to (dis)continue such projects once electoral victory has been sealed. Differing vested interests represents the potential source of stakeholder conflicts that can impede joined-up communication, collaboration and coordination efforts. An awareness of the political nature of tourism-led LED planning initiatives is therefore critical to understanding the process of and enhance the success of such initiatives.

Furthermore, research has shown how, in many instances, politicians especially at the local level tend to devote resources to starting new projects, rather than completing existing ones in order to accumulate electoral goodwill as well as appease distributive pressures from constituents (Williams, 2016). This is especially the case in countries like Ghana, where there is a highly intensive political competition that tends to constrain policy and project continuity (Whitfield, 2011, 2009; Kelsall, 2012). Local governments play an important role in tourism planning and development. As the third tier (after national and regional governments) of the public sector in tourism, they bear the biggest responsibility for ensuring that the tourism product remains competitive (McKercher and Ritchie, 1997). It has also been shown that local governments are key to achieving sustainable tourism development (Dredge, 2006;

Ruhanen, 2013). However, the assessment of local government cycles and capacity in tourism governance and development has been relatively less studied (Churugsa et al., 2007; Slocum and Backman, 2011).

Given that local governments can either facilitate or inhibit tourism-led local economic development planning initiatives, it is important to fully understand their capacity and the political processes of local government management and administration in a destination (Manning, 2001; Crook, 2003; Smoke, 2003; Awortwi, 2010). Thus to understand tourism-led LED policy and implementation like the Elmina 2015 Strategy, one must consider the political and administrative processes – i.e. the national and electoral cycles, within which it was situated. There are key questions to be addressed within such a context: what was the number of electoral cycles over the span of the Elmina 2015 Strategy? In which ways did these electoral cycles lead to administrative changes in local governments? Did electoral cycles coincide with the transfer of key staff on the project and how this affect organisation memory and capacity? Answers to these questions will provide insight into how electoral cycles lead to administrative changes in local governments shaped the Elmina 2015 Strategy.

Methodology and methods

This chapter is based on research carried out as part of the author's PhD project, which took place between 2013 and 2016. While the data collection period appears dated, the findings and implications have contemporary currency. There are new attempts in Ghana in utilising slavery heritage tourism as an avenue for local and national economic development. This is in the context of the "Year of Return 2019" and "Beyond the Return" tourism marketing campaigns. The overall objective of the PhD project was to understand, explain and analyse how governance interactions shape the planning and use of tourism for local economic development. Meeting this objective involved understanding governance interactions between different structures of governance in the tourism sector of Ghana. The research was framed from the philosophical starting point and assumption about the social construction of the governance interactions that give rise to and shape the use of tourism in local economic development planning strategies. Thus, the interaction between actors (both individually and organisationally) is influential in how institutional arrangements are produced and reproduced, which then in turn delineates the processes of future actor interactions. Actors engaged in interactions and social relations they begin to shape institutional processes but then become simultaneously constrained in their choice of actions and strategies by the very institutional processes they shape (Giddens, 1984; Scott, 1995). Nonetheless, actors are considered as being innovative and capable of learning through their interactions and consequently in becoming capable to then change the very structures that guide their interactions in the first place (Healey, 1999, 2003).

Data for this chapter were collected as part of a three-year PhD research period, with a process-based research design focused on examining how (tourism) governance processes influence the role of tourism in local economic development and poverty reduction (Adu-Ampong, 2016). The methodology was built on semi-structured in-depth interviews, policy document analysis and observations. Fieldwork was carried out on two separate occasions (August–November 2014 and July–September 2015). For the whole project, a total of 59 key informant interviews were conducted in addition to 9 community member interviews, three of which ended up becoming a form of focus group with between two and five persons. These individuals included past and present KEEA officers, Directors at the Ministry of Tourism, Culture and Creative Arts (currently Ministry of Tourism, Arts and Culture),

Ghana Museums and Monuments Board, Ghana Heritage Conservation Trust, community members and homeowners who benefitted from the building projects under the Elmina 2015 Strategy, as well as private sector organisations members of the Ghana Tourism Federation. In addition, there were a number of informal conversations with community members and extensive field notes taken that provided background information for this research. These were triangulated with the analysis of national, regional and local level tourism-related development plans, especially the Elmina 2015 Strategy documents including progress reports on project implementation. The interviews were used to confirm evidence from other sources while also opening up new lines of inquiry to the (re)analysis of documents and other pieces of evidence. The iterative process of using document analysis and interviews to confirm, corroborate and highlight differences ensured a robust data collection and analysis process.

The framework approach for qualitative analysis as developed by Ritchie and Spencer (1994) was used to analyse both the primary and secondary data. The five-step process of the approach consisted of familiarisation, identifying a thematic framework, indexing, charting, and mapping and interpretation. An iterative following of these steps enabled the data to be scrutinised for meaning, salience and connections between what interviewees perceived in their governing interactions and what actually pertains to their day-to-day activities. Significantly, this approach to analysis made it easier to identify salience and connections between governing (in)activities and the challenges of implementing the Elmina 2015 Strategy process. Data analysis focused on building up broad sub-themes of commonalities and differences between actors in their views and actions. These themes included "political interfering", "party politics", "forced staff transfer", "project champions", "revenue sharing", "tourism management", "project monitoring", "KEEA politics", "New Patriotic Party role", "National Democratic Congress Party role" among others.

A stylised (tourism development) history of Elmina

There are a number of challenges facing tourism planning in Ghana, especially in terms of project implementation (Adu-Ampong, 2019; see also Chapter 15). The high level of fragmentation in both public and private institutions involved in the tourism sector often hinder effective collaboration and coordination in tourism planning and development (Cobbinah and Darkwah, 2016; Adu-Ampong, 2017). Nonetheless, a number of tourism-related projects have been developed and implemented across the country to varying levels of success. Particularly in the Central Region of Ghana, which is considered as the tourism hub of the country (Adu-Ampong, 2017), a number of projects have been initiated aimed at using a tourism as a catalyst for economic development and poverty reduction (Akyeampong and Asiedu, 2008). This is also the region where Elmina is located.

Given its well-documented extraordinary past, it is impossible to do justice to the complex history of Elmina in a few paragraphs. What follows is therefore a stylised summary of key aspects of this place that are relevant for the current discussion. Imbued with over 700 years of history, the modern city of Elmina traces its roots to the adventures of one Kwaa Amankwaa who gave it the traditional name of Anomansa (Henige, 1974). Elmina was long considered as an independent city-state while the surrounding settlements formed part of the Fante Kingdom. In 1470 Portuguese explorers Juan de Santaran and Pedro d'Escobara landed at the coast of Anomansa which was later christened with the Portuguese name of "La Mina" ("The Mine") in reference to the abundance of gold in the area. Over time the Portuguese name became localised as "Edina" and later anglicised as Elmina. In 1482, a new Portuguese expedition lead by Don Diego d'Azambuja arrived in Elmina and was later leased land by

Figure 12.1   The Elmina Castle (view from the hill of Fort Java)
Source: Author.

the chief of Elmina at the time, Nana Kobina Ansah I for the construction of St. George's Castle (Essah, 2001). The building of the Castle rejuvenated Elmina's development and made it a centre of commerce, with surrounding regions as well as a key node in an international trading network between Africa, Europe and the Americas.

In 1637, the Dutch took over control of the castle from the Portuguese and continued with the booming transatlantic slave trade. It was during this time that Elmina came to be known as the European African city owing to an increased settlement of Dutch merchants in the city. European-styled merchant houses were built and the city layout was reconfigured to Dutch standards. In 1871, the British took over and after the abolition of the slave trade, used the castle as the central administrative centre during colonial rule. In the aftermaths of Ghana's independence in 1957, the castle was used for various purposes including; as an office for the Ghana Education service, as a District Assembly office and as a policy training academy before its inscription unto the UNESCO World Heritage List in 1979 under criteria (iv) – "to be an outstanding example of a type of building, architectural or technological ensemble or landscape which illustrates (a) significant stage(s) in human history". It was only after this time that the Elmina Castle (see Figure 12.1), which remains the oldest European building in Africa, became recognised as a tourist attraction site, and efforts were made to preserve and present it as such (Bruner, 1996).

The population of Elmina currently sits at just over 23,000 (GSS, 2014). Elmina is the biggest settlement in, and the capital of the Komenda-Edina-Eguafo-Abrem (KEEA) Municipality of the Central Region of Ghana, headed by the Municipal Chief Executive. Out of the four major traditional occupations in Elmina – gold prospecting, fishing, salt making and pottery – salt making and fishing with its associated processes remain the most dominant occupation in contemporary times, in addition to the ubiquitous petty trading and commerce. It is estimated that 60% of employment in Elmina is in the informal sector while the remaining 40% of formal sector employment is found in teaching, nursing and government jobs at the KEEA Municipal offices (KEEA, 2002). The informal sector includes activities such as fishing, ship building, fish processing, salt mining, artisanal self-employment, agriculture and petty trading. The poverty incidence in Elmina is widespread as shown

Figure 12.2 A shot of the Elmina Township from the hill of Fort Java
Source: Author.

in a number of indicators such as high rates of unemployment, high school dropout rates, high rates of child delinquency, low school enrolment rates, high rates of teenage pregnancy among others. For instance, the results of the 2010 Ghana Population and Housing Census shows that "at least three in every ten persons [in the KEEA municipality] are economically not active (32.4%)" and that "one key finding of important social and health implication is the poor nature of housing condition in the Municipality which confirms the relative poverty of the residents" (GSS, 2014:70) (Figure 12.2).

As the KEEA Municipal Coordinating Director concedes,

> …yes we have poverty, the bulk of people are poor so to speak and if you go into the hinterland you see people depend on seasonal cropping and they are peasant farmers, from hand to mouth. This is how they've survived all the way.

The Municipal Assembly identifies the key development challenges in Elmina and its environs as found in education, agriculture, WASH (water, sanitation and hygiene), health and local economic development. Improvements in these areas are considered as essential for improving socio-economic development and poverty reduction. It is in this regard that since the mid-1990s, tourism came to be seen as a potential "third sector" growth pole in Elmina – after fishing and salt mining – which could serve as a catalyst for local economic development (Sonne, 2010; Holden et al., 2011).

Elmina is endowed with a number of cultural heritage tourism resources and assets. These include the UNESCO World Heritage Site of Elmina Castle and Fort St. Jago, 18th and 19th century built traditional Asafo Posts, Old Merchant houses, the Old Dutch Cemetery, the Bakatue and Edina Bronya traditional festivals and a number of historical landmarks in addition to a long stretch of beach and the Benya Lagoon. These assets have long been noted as having the potential to attract a large number of both domestic and international tourists to Elmina. The first serious attempt at developing tourism in Elmina as part of a strategy to stimulate regional and local economic development and tackle poverty came under the Central Regional Integrated Development Programme (CERIDEP). CERIDEP, which was funded by the UNDP and USAID, was implemented by the Central Regional Development Commission (CEDECOM) between 1993 and 1998. This project was aimed at developing an integrated tourism programme for the Central Region culminating in the restoration of the Cape Coast and Elmina Castles as well as the development of the Canopy Walkway at the Kakum National Park. Thus in 1995, the Elmina Castle and Fort St. Jago were partly renovated and given fresh painting. Unlike in the case of Cape Coast where a number of historic houses were also renovated through home-owner grants, the project in Elmina was isolated rather than integrated into overall economic development strategy. It was within this context that the Elmina Cultural Heritage Management Programme (ECHMP) was initiated starting from the verge of the new millennium in the year 2000 under the leading auspices of the KEEA Municipal Assembly.

Elmina Cultural Heritage Management Programme and the Elmina 2015 Strategy

The Elmina Cultural Heritage Management Programme (ECHMP) was an attempt to provide a coordinated effort towards existing and ongoing initiatives in order to define and develop an integrated approach to the development of Elmina. The ECHMP aimed at stimulating the development potentials in Elmina through the creation of new local employment opportunities in order to alleviate poverty and improve living standards. With initial funding from the Dutch government, a fundamental aim of the ECHMP was urban heritage conservation and the revitalisation of identified mutual heritage between Ghana and the Netherlands. This mutual heritage consisted of the Elmina Castle, Fort St. Jago, Java Museum, Old Dutch Cemetery, Asafo Posts, St. Joseph's Catholic Church building and museum, the Methodist Church Chapel building, numerous merchant houses and the very layout of the city of Elmina. It was these (potential) tourist assets that underpinned the overall objective of the ECHMP which was to develop a "clear-cut strategy and institutional framework for integrated urban cultural heritage conservation in Elmina town and to revitalise the identified mutual heritage" KEEA (2002:1).

A series of public and stakeholder consultations were held to identify priority areas under the programme. The centrepiece of this process was the Elmina Town Consultation held between 15 and 18 April 2002. The official opening of this was attended by current King Willem Alexander and Queen Maxima (then Prince and Princess respectively) of the Netherlands. At the end of the consultation process, five priority areas were arrived at through a series of community stakeholder consultations. These were: (1) drainage and waste management, (2) fishing and fishing harbor, (3) tourism and local economic development, (4) health and (5) education. The various strategic action plans under each priority area were then aggregated by the core Task Force group of the ECHMP into the Elmina 2015 Strategy.

The Elmina 2015 Strategy mapped out a strategy for the future integrated development of Elmina accompanied by specific action and project plans for all the five priority areas with the tagline of "Building on the Past to Create a Better Future". The overall success of the ECHMP and the resulting Elmina 2015 Strategy was predicated on the effective implementation of priority three – tourism and local economic development. The Elmina 2015 Strategy envisaged heritage tourism as a catalyst for stimulating local economic development. The strategy comprised of three key reports: (1) Sector Strategy and Vision, (2) Project Portfolios and (3) Elmina Profile and Summary Profile. The Elmina Profile was a report on the socio-economic development and political situation of Elmina. This served as basis for developing the Sector Strategy and Vision as well as the Project Portfolios. The Elmina Profile also served as a baseline against which to evaluate its outcomes. Out of the three reports, it is the Sector Strategy and Vision report that offers an insight into how stakeholders arrived at an image of how tourism, local economic development and poverty reduction were related in Elmina. Thus, the Elmina 2015 Strategy set out a tourism-led local economic development planning strategy that went beyond simple heritage conservation. In summary, the argument was this:

> The Elmina 2015 strategy goes beyond restoring monuments. It believes that with improved tourist infrastructure, the revitalisation of the existing monuments and the development of other important cultural sites, tourism can become a major economic activity in Elmina and serve to improve the general standard of living in the town. The strategy identifies tourism as an entry point in facilitating sustainable development through an integrated development approach. Thus mutual cultural heritage and monuments serve as a springboard in working towards improvement of living standards. At the same time, the improvements to the other sectors such as health, education and waste management will enhance the touristic potential of Elmina, thereby allowing for a synergistic development framework.
>
> *KEEA (2002:10)*

In effect, the Elmina 2015 Strategy was positioned as the culmination of a tourism-led local economic development planning process that began in the year 2000 by the KEEA Municipal Assembly in collaboration with the Institute of Housing and Urban Studies of the Erasmus University of Rotterdam in the Netherlands. This process was also initiated in close collaboration with the Ghana Museums and Monuments Board (GMMB), Ghana Institute of Local Government Studies (ILGS) and the Department of International Relations and International Organisations at the University of Groningen in the Netherlands. A number of projects outlined in the Project Portfolio document under the Elmina 2015 Strategy were implemented between 2003 and 2007 (see Table 12.1).

These projects were part of a shared vision mapped out for the future socio-economic development of Elmina, through a series of stakeholder and community consultations lead by the KEEA. These projects ranged from the rehabilitation of St. George's Castle, Fort St. Jago, the Dutch Cemetery, old merchant houses and the dredging of the fishing harbour, as well as training of artisans and the construction of the Elmina Craft Market. The funding sources for these projects included the Dutch Culture Fund, the EU's 9th European Development Fund and Government of Ghana funding through the KEEA Municipal Assembly. The implementation of these and other projects aimed to ensure that by the year 2015 Elmina's socio-economic development fortunes would be flourishing through increased tourism. The ultimate expectation was that by the end of 2015, Elmina would become "the engine of equitable socio-economic development that impacts on the wealth creation, poverty reduction and improved local governance on a sustainable basis" (Arthur and Mensah, 2006:310). It was expected that the implementation of these projects would lead to "…the attainment of longer stays by tourist [which] will contribute to local economic growth and generate employment

Table 12.1 Projects to be implemented the tourism and local economic development with indicative total cost

Project	Total cost (in euros)
Project 41: Erection of signposts at strategic locations in town	€20,000
Project 42: Establishment of an internet café in Elmina	€20,000
Project 43: Upgrading of Kiosks	€30,000
Project 44: Rehabilitation of the historic site adjacent to the Castle	€22,000
Project 45: Developing of community performing arts night theatre	€1,000
Project 46: Providing street lighting in Elmina town and illumination of the Elmina and St. Jago Castles	€43,500
Project 47: Diversify choice of eateries and hotels in Elmina Town and provide alternative services for visitors	€830, 000
Project 48: Redevelopment of Trafalgar Square	€30,000
Project 49: Tree planting	€20,000
Project 50: Skill development and capacity building	€1,000
Project 51: Redevelop the former government garden into a children playground	€50,000
Project 52: Improve the salt industry	€2,900,000 (with € 20,000 for feasibility study)
Project 53: Ironman/Action Elmina Competition: running, cycling, boat races and swimming	Sponsored by the private sector
Project 54: Bike rental and bike taxis for tourists	In co-operation with the private
Project 55: Redevelop the beach along Rawlings high street	€20,000–30,000 in co-operation with the private sector

Source: Compiled from Elmina (2015) Strategy Project Reports.

and income in Elmina. It will thereby contribute to the town's longer-term development goals including its social, economic and heritage revitalisation" (KEEA, 2002:61).

In the conclusion section of the document, the centrality of the tourism and local economic development component to the whole Elmina 2015 Strategy is reiterated. The Elmina 2015 Strategy starts with the restoration and management of existing heritage assets for tourism. It is after this that tourism's potential for local economic development and poverty reduction becomes mutually-reinforcing of the other components of health, sanitation and education. The Strategy document succinctly notes that:

> But this strategy goes beyond restoring monuments. It recognises the importance of taking away the factors that presently prevent visitors from spending more time and money in Elmina Town. Only if the drains will be cleaned, illegal waste dumps are cleared, waste is collected routinely and visitors are not constantly harassed by children, visitors are tempted to further explore the town. Paving the streets of the New Town and upgrading of some strategic sites such as the former Government Garden and the historic site next to the Castle will further improve the town image of Elmina. An increase in tourist numbers can make this sector an important industry to complement the present sources of local employment.
>
> *KEEA (2002:84)*

In the last section of the Strategy document with the title "A Vision for the year 2015" the ultimate vision for Elmina is set out and is worth quoting in part. The vision pointed out that:

> In 2015 we envisage Elmina to be a thriving town in which fishing is still the main economic activity but has significant other sectors of employment in the salt mining, boat building but most importantly the tourist industry. The unique heritage assets and the picturesque harbour make the town Ghana's prime tourist destination. The excellent road conditions allow tourists to reach Elmina by car within 2 hours from Accra, while the building of airstrip is underway. The town is to be visited by over 150,000 tourists annually that spend an average of two nights in the town choosing from a wide range of choices for accommodation. The local population is also benefitting from the tourist boom and consequent economic development.
>
> *KEEA (2002:85)*

This vision for what Elmina will look like in 2015 did not however materialise as originally envisaged. The hope that tourism will serve as a catalyst for local economic development and contribute to poverty reduction turned out to be less real than expected. In the next section, I explore the particular ways in which local governance arrangements and political cycles shaped the outcome of this vision.

Local governance structures and political cycles

The Ghana Museums and Monuments Board (GMMB) is the legal custodian of the Elmina Castle and has management responsibilities for it. Since the Elmina 2015 Strategy went beyond the renovation of the Elmina Castle and expanded to cover overall local economic development of Elmina, there was the need to involve the KEEA Municipal Assembly. The politico-legal backing of the KEEA to the ECHMP rested on the provisions in Ghana's Local Government Act 462 of 1993 and section 5 of the National Development Planning System Act 480 of 1994. Under these legislations the KEEA is a planning authority and the only institution legally mandated to prepare local and/or sub-district development plans either directly or through delegation to lower tiers of government like Town and Urban Councils. The proposals for the ECHMP therefore fell into the category of a sub-district local economic development plan of Elmina and hence the KEEA had to be the leading institution for the project in order to provide the requisite politico-legal instruments. The KEEA had the technocratic mechanism and tools for the planning process as the preparation of District Medium Term Development Plans (MTDP) is one of its key responsibilities.

The KEEA was therefore able to facilitate the Elmina 2015 Strategy which involved a much more detailed planning process than usually accorded to the making of the MTDP. One of the reasons for this was that the financial resources were provided by external parties. The Planning Officer at that time explains that "the Elmina 2015 Strategy, that was, for that one there was a thorough consultation, participation… [T]he resources were not provided by the assembly otherwise there was no [Elmina] 2015". It must also be noted that at this point in time, a new political party had just come into office for the first time and was eager to show that they were bringing the promised development projects to the community. This political context was very instrumental in shaping the enthusiasm and support given to the project in the beginning

Notwithstanding its legal mandate for the overall development of the municipality, the remit of the KEEA did not extend to the management of the Elmina Castle or many of the other tourist assets of the municipality. These areas fell under the responsibility of the GMMB. Thus, while the KEEA came to lead the preparation and implementation of the ECHMP and the Elmina 2015 Strategy plans, it was the GMMB that had the ultimate governing authority over the golden goose upon whose golden eggs all other components of the project hinged. In addition, given the dual governance structure in Elmina (government and traditional authority) it was imperative for the traditional council to give backing to the project. This support consisted largely of the mobilisation of community support for and participation in the projects. During the interviews, an interesting counter perspective as to who should have ultimately been in charge for the project was given by the head of the tourism subcommittee at KEEA, who also serves on the traditional council and is often a spokesperson for the traditional council. He noted that had there been enough capacity within the traditional council, then they should have been the ones to lead the project. In his view, because the land on which the Elmina Castle was built was first given to the Portuguese by the traditional authorities, they have the right to claim the castle as their own. In his own words:

> If the traditional council have the capacity to manage this project I would have been the first person to suggest that what, these help or whatever should have channelled through there. The reason is that any project for the people by the people for the people they handle it very well. But the traditional council weren't in a position to handle such a big project and for that matter assembly came in as the facilitator.

The fragmented nature of stakeholder interactions did not paralyse the project in the beginning due to high levels of cross-sectoral coordination and mobilisation of support. This process was further strengthened by the political support offered by the newly elected government. The implementation of the Elmina 2015 Strategy began earnestly in the context of the New Patriotic Party (NPP) government taking over power from the National Democratic Congress (NDC) party. This context was key in shaping the trajectory and outcomes of the project. In the next sections, I provide an analysis of the evolution of the Elmina 2015 Strategy vis-à-vis the national political (party) cycles in the governance structures of Ghana.

Era of the National Democratic Congress Party: 1992–2000

In the 1980s, Ghana was under the military government of the Provisional National Defence Council (PNDC). Ato Austin, who hailed from Elmina was appointed as the PNDC Regional Secretary (Regional Minister) for the Central Region in this period and sought to remedy the socio-economic decline in the Region – a decline that started once the national government was moved from Cape Coast to Accra in 1877 by the British colonial. Tourism was regarded as a potential catalyst for local economic development and poverty reduction. The Cape Coast Castle and the Elmina Castle, which were in a deplorable state were identified as the key attractions in this scheme. The plan was therefore to restore these Castles and to then market them to African Americans, Afro Caribbean and other Africans in the Diaspora who want to reconnect with their roots. It was thus from this period that a concerted planning and development effort turned the Central Region into the hub of tourism in Ghana (Adu-Ampong, 2017). As one interviewee noted:

> …he [Ato Austin] was looking for a strategy that will stem the economic decline, reverse it and he choose tourism as a catalyst and the proposal, that proposal was to enhance these two Castles, Cape Coast and Elmina, bring them up because they were decaying

very fast. So the proposal's main aim was to restore so that they could be catalyst, important catalyst for African American heritage tourists...

(Interview with Nkunu Akyea, Former Executive Director of Ghana
Heritage Conservation Trust, 08.09.2014)

Following the transition from military rule to democracy in the 1992 national elections, the National Democratic Congress (NDC) party which mutated from the PNDC won the elections and retained control of all Metropolitan, Municipal and District Assemblies (MMDAs). A proposal from the Regional Minister – Ato Austin – known as the Tourism Development Scheme for the Central Region received funding support from UNDP and USAID. The USAID funding for this programme was provided through a so-called Natural Resource Conservation and Historic Preservation Project (NRCHP), which made possible the restoration of the Cape Coast Castle, the Elmina Castle as well as works to stablish Fort St. Jago also in Elmina. In a bid to diversity the tourism products away from only heritage, a visitor reception centre and a canopy walkway were built in the nearby Kakum National Park. It was also realised that this bricks and mortar approach to tourism development in the region was not enough to tap into tourism's full potential for local economic development and poverty reduction. A funded subproject developed an integrated tourism-led town planning and development plan for the Cape Coast metropolis, as well as providing homeowner grants for the renovation of old merchant and colonial buildings with historic value. These buildings were then to be used for commercial activities that generate income for those involved. This initial effort at tourism-led local economic development and poverty reduction did not include Elmina.

At the Komenda-Edina-Eguafo-Abrem District Assembly (KEEA), one Austin Ankumah who was appointed as the District Chief Executive (DCE) was keen on seeing to the restoration of the Elmina Castle for tourism development and to replicate in Elmina the integrated tourism-led local economic development plan that was developed for Cape Coast. Up to the next national electoral cycle in 1996, which was again won by the NDC party, he set about to find external funding. The NDC government at this point had shown strong political will and support to utilise tourism for local economic development and poverty reduction. This resulted in a boom of tourism activities in the region and to Elmina, which the DCE sought to tap into as a catalyst for local economic development and poverty reduction.

The key issue at this point, in the late 1990s, was financing any project. Briggs (2012) notes that, between 1998 and 1999, the NDC government faced a sharp decline in international aid, which limited the government's ability to allocate resources to places like Elmina. Notwithstanding limited government resources, the DCE in Elmina encouraged and was supportive of private initiatives that sought to attract investments for renovating some of the historic buildings for tourism purposes. The point to be made here is that up the year 2000, there was a lot of political support for tourism-led local economic development planning initiatives in Elmina. When the NDC party lost the December 2000 national elections to the New Patriotic Party (NPP) party, much of the ideas that were later to become the Elmina 2015 Strategy were already on the ground.

Era of the New Patriotic Party: 2001–2008

In 2001, the NPP government assumed office and Nana Ato Arthur who hails from Elmina was appointed as the DCE for the KEEA. Keen to get as many high-visibility projects off and running having campaigned on the promise of economic development and poverty reduction, the government committed resources for the Elmina Cultural Heritage Management Programme (ECHMP). The ECHMP was in line with the NPP governments economic development strategy which focused on redistributive policies and poverty-related spending. There was a political incentive for the NPP government to lay full claim to and gain political credit to having implemented the project even if the original ideas were already afloat during the era of the NDC government. As one of the interviewees explained,

> …this project this project was started by Nana, former MCE, he is now died and gone, Nana Ankumah [from the NDC government]. He initiated this 2015 strategy but they were passing through some challenges. It was Nana Ato Arthur's time that we had the funds coming down…
> *(Interview with Ebo Dadzie, Head of Tourism Sub-Committee, KEEA, 31.10.2014)*

The fact that the benefits of the project were realised during the period of the NPP government had a positive impact on standing of the NPP government in general within the locality. The DCE was very committed to the project and endeared himself to both the national government and the people in KEEA. He explains his commitment and dedication to the project as this;

> How we sat day and night to develop this document. I will be here in the afternoon and then J.H. Mensah, the then senior minister will call me to his office in Accra that look, I have been able to get some Ambassadors together and I want you to come and speak with them. It'll be 12midday here, he will tell me I need to be there at 4pm. I need to pick my car and even whether I have said goodbye to my wife or family or not, I will go because I needed to do something for my people. That was the zeal then.
> *(Interview with Nana Ato Arthur, Former MP for KEEA/Former*
> *KEEA MCE/Former Regional Minister, 07.11.2014)*

The NPP government at this time was committed to cross-sectoral collaboration. For instance, while there was no legislative backing, an informal revenue sharing mechanism was established by the NPP government for the proceeds from the Elmina Castle to be split between the GMMB, the KEEA and the Elmina traditional authority. This arrangement greased the wheels of the interactions of stakeholders towards the effective implementation of the Elmina 2015 Strategy. However, after the NDC party returned to power in 2009, the new management of the Ghana Museums and Monuments Board (GMMB) lobbied for this arrangement to be ceased. The argument was that the revenue generated through the Elmina Castle is also used for the preservation and maintenance of the many forts and castles dotted along the Ghanaian coast that do not generate any revenue themselves but are part of the UNESCO World Heritage Status designation. This situation resulted in a dwindling of interest from other stakeholders in working towards the effective implementation of project goals.

The NPP government was returned to power in the December 2004 national elections. A new DCE - Frank Asmah – was appointed for the KEEA to replace Nana Ato Arthur who has been promoted as a Deputy Regional Minister. At this point, a lot of the physical projects were ongoing and near completion with preparations underway to hand over the completed projects to the responsible bodies. Thus the second term of the NPP government coincided with the project implementation and institutionalisation phases of the Elmina 2015 Strategy. However, it is also at this point that the zeal and political commitment shown during the first term of the NPP government began to wane. For the new DCE, there was a little positive incentive to show the same zeal towards the project because the political credits had already being assigned to the previous DCE. Indeed at the national level, the NPP government's commitment to poverty-related spending began to change and this perhaps trickled down to the local level. The Ghana Poverty Reduction Strategy from the government's first term became the Growth and Poverty Reduction Strategy signifying a focus on growth as the main mechanism for poverty reduction. In terms of the Elmina 2015 Strategy, it appears that the new DCE began to privatise certain aspects of the Elmina 2015 Strategy projects and spin-offs like the waste management component. Thus interviewees noted that "It was Frank's time the whole project went off to a private entity. It was Ato Arthur's time we started benefiting. It was Frank Asmah's time this project went off" (Interview with Ebo Dadzie, Head of Tourism Sub-Committee, KEEA and founding member of SEA, 16.07.2015).

The point here is that each political cycle of national elections present a different set of incentives to politicians that shape the extent to which they continue existing projects. Thus after the NPP government had been re-elected, the political commitment and zeal that was associated with the Elmina 2015 Strategy began to wane. Certain aspects of the project did not get the needed attention while other aspects came into private hands. The new DCE did not share the same focus for the project as the predecessor (Interview with Justice Amoah, Former Municipal Planning Officer of KEEA/Former National Project Coordinator of Elmina 2015 Strategy, 17.07.2015). Thus the phase of institutionalising the projects and objectives of the Elmina 2015 Strategy within existing governance structures of the KEEA could not begin in earnest due to the low level of political commitment.

Era of the National Democratic Congress: 2009–2016

Electoral and party politics in Ghana is a highly competitive and intense one. This intensive political competition generates negative incentives for politics in ways that constrain economic progress (Whitfield, 2009, 2011; Kelsall, 2012). This is especially the case when it comes to the project and programme continuity. When a new political party comes into power, there is a negative incentive for them to continue projects already began by the previous government from a different party. At the December 2008 national polls, the National Democratic Congress (NDC) party was elected into power to replace the New Patriotic Party (NPP) government that has been in power between since 2001. This was a keenly contested election that went to a run-off before the NDC was able to secure 50% plus 1 vote of total votes cast. Thus, when the NDC came into office, the positive incentive for them was to initiate and start up their own development projects and programmes even though there were uncompleted programmes and projects of the NPP government. This is simply because the political credits of completing existing projects will be claimed by the NPP party in opposition. Thus, by beginning their own projects, the new government can claim all the political credits available which it is hoped will translate into electoral votes at the next elections. This is exactly what happened in terms of the continuation of the Elmina 2015 Strategy once the NDC party came into power.

The NDC government-appointed one Rev. Veronica Essuman Nelson in 2009 to the position of the Municipal Chief Executive (MCE) for KEE - the KEEA was declared as a municipality in 2007 by the NPP government. This change had a strong shaping role on the trajectory of the final phase of the Elmina 2015 Strategy. This was the institutionalisation phase where the municipality had to ensure, through effective communication, collaboration and communication between stakeholders, that tourism was generating the momentum for local economic development and poverty reduction. It appears that there was not much political commitment to see to this phase of the project. The following quotes from some of the interviewees provide a sense of this situation:

> KEEA, and KEEA keeps on changing with the personnel. Today is party A, tomorrow is party B. Party A does not see anything right with the work started by party A or party B, that itself creates a problem.
>
> *(Interview with Francis Cobbinah, Executive Director, Ghana Heritage Conservation Trust, Cape Coast, 29.09.2014)*

> …paradoxically when this thing started it started with an NDC government, the actual execution was done by an NPP government, an NPP government was succeeded by an NDC government who also wanted to make a niche and did not…now when one party leaves and another party comes, the way it looks at the project differs….
>
> *(Interview with Dr. Anthony Annah-Prah, Head of Implementation of Elmina Cultural Heritage Management Programme, 03.11.2014)*

> …every government, local etc. want to start something that they will be called an initiator and not a person who built upon what the previous person has done and so the Elmina 2015 strategy was unfortunately seen as an NPP achievement, you see and so the NDC had to start on its own.
>
> *(Interview with Dr. Anthony Annah-Prah, Head of Implementation of Elmina Cultural Heritage Management Programme, 03.11.2014)*

The implementation and institutionalisation of the Elmina 2015 Strategy from 2009 onwards began to take a downward turn even as a new political party came into office. As the quotes above makes clear, there was not enough incentive for the new party to continue and make sure that the Strategy is fully institutionalised within the governance structures of the KEEA. While the negative political incentives as discussed above played a role in this downward direction, part of the reason is also closely related to the loss of institutional memory and institutional capacity. For instance, the office room in which the documentations for the Elmina 2015 Strategy were kept at the KEEA were emptied to make room for a German-funded project secured by the NDC government (Interview with Dr. Anthony Annah-Prah, Head of Implementation of Elmina Cultural Heritage Management Programme, 03.11.2014).

The desire to start from scratch therefore meant that there was no incentive to retain institutional memory about the Elmina 2015 Strategy. Moreover, with change in party governments comes a high rate of municipal staff transfers, based on the perception that they may be too loyal to the previous party government and might therefore be a hindrance to agenda of the new government.

Conclusion

This vision for what Elmina would look like in 2015 did not, however, materialise as originally envisaged. The hope that tourism would serve as a catalyst for local economic development and contribute to poverty reduction turned out to be less real than expected. There were a number of reasons that account for the disjuncture between objectives and eventual outcomes. The planning process leading up to the formulation of the Elmina 2015 Strategy, followed a classic stakeholder identification-stakeholder consultation-stakeholder agreed upon action plans process – which is commonly referred to as collaborative/communicative planning (Healey, 1997, 1999; see also Brand and Gaffikin, 2007 for a useful critique). While the planning process to arrive at the Elmina 2015 Strategy might have passed as unproblematic, its implementation was anything but that. This chapter has outlined how the local governance arrangements and political cycles impacted on the eventual outcomes.

This chapter has shown how the temporal dimension of implementing the Elmina 2015 Strategy interacted with and was shaped by the time inconsistency problems that arise from the change of political party in government. The political commitment of successive governments towards the institutionalisation phase of the project declined over the years. This lack of commitment was due to the limited incentives faced by politicians who decide to continue project implementation rather than starting one from scratch. Thus, when the NDC government came into power, they were keen on starting their own new projects rather than continue the Elmina 2015 Strategy. This is because the political credit of this had already been claimed by the opposition NPP government. The Elmina 2015 Strategy was based on a technocratic understanding of governance and the institutional arrangements under which implementation was to take place. This technocratic understanding of governance interactions in the locality meant that the strategy proceeded on the assumption that once the consultations had been completed, plans agreed, and the project had begun, things would fall into place to ensure that tourism leads to local economic development. The inadequate attention given to the political dimensions of governance in the design of the strategy appears to be a key weakness. The fact that the governance system is based on a political cycle that ushers in new political and governance agents through elections conducted every four years was clearly not factored into the design of the strategy and plans for its sustainable implementation.

What is clear is that within the Elmina 2015 Strategy there has been a failure in the governance of tourism planning and hence of creating effective linkages between tourism and local economic development. There is a contemporary implication of this chapter's finding in terms of the current tourism marketing and development campaign of the "Year of Return 2019"and "Beyond the Return". These campaigns seek to use slavery heritage tourism (back-to-your-roots tourism) as a catalyst for national and local economic development. The insights from the implementation trajectory of the Elmina 2015 Strategy in terms of the effects of electoral cycles, should inform these new campaign strategies. Changes in government in a highly competitive political environment like Ghana presents both positive and negative incentives for the level of commitment politicians can make towards existing development projects. It becomes clear that what is needed is a new understanding of the governance of tourism-led local economic development that is sensitive to and grounded in the political context in which it takes place. Such a politically informed understanding of governance can provide a basis for developing a more resilient governance framework for tourism-led local economic development (LED) planning.

Much like any development intervention, tourism-led LED planning initiatives are deeply political. The political underpinnings of tourism-led local economic development initiatives exist at the international, national, regional and local levels. A fundamental reason for this political nature is because at its heart, tourism-led LED involves a wide range of stakeholders and actors with differing vested interests. Tourism tends to be considered as a largely private sector business activity, but research has shown that national government policies play a key role in shaping tourism development in a given destination (Jeffries, 2001; Adu-Ampong, 2015). In terms of the tourism-poverty nexus, Harrison (2008) argues that to maximise the benefits of tourism for economic development and poverty reduction, the state's entire apparatus has to be geared towards this goal. States, however, are not static but are made up of governments that are voted into power in line with a country's national and local electoral cycles. An account of tourism-led local economic development initiatives and their implementation need to be aware of and appreciate the shaping role of underlying electoral cycles and the incentives presented to politicians.

Note

1 This chapter is fully based on the author's PhD thesis which was completed at the Department of Urban Studies and Planning, University of Sheffield, UK in 2017.

References

Adu-Ampong, E. A. (2015). *Tourism Policy and Planning in Ghana: Towards Inclusive Growth?* Paper presented at the Association for Tourism and Leisure Education and Research Africa Conference 2015, Dar es Salaam, Tanzania.

Adu-Ampong, E. A. (2016). *Governing Tourism-Led Local Economic Development Planning: An Interactive Tourism Governance Perspective on the Elmina 2015 Strategy in Ghana.* Unpublished doctoral dissertation, University of Sheffield, Sheffield, UK.

Adu-Ampong, E. A. (2017). Divided we stand: Institutional collaboration in tourism planning and development in the Central Region of Ghana. *Current Issues in Tourism, 20*(3), 295–314.

Adu-Ampong, E. A. (2018). Tourism and national economic development planning in Ghana, 1964–2014. *International Development Planning Review, 40*(1), 75–95.

Adu-Ampong, E. A. (2019). The tourism-development nexus from a governance perspective: A research agenda. In R. Sharpley and D. Harrison (Eds.), *A Research Agenda for Tourism and Development* (pp. 53–70). Cheltenham: Edward Elgar Publishing.

Akyeampong, O. A., & Asiedu, A. (Eds.) (2008). *Tourism in Ghana: A Modern Synthesis.* Accra: Assemblies of God Literature Centre Limited.

Arthur, S. N. A., & Mensah, J. V. (2006). Urban management and heritage tourism for sustainable development: The case of Elmina cultural heritage and management programme in Ghana. *Management of Environmental Quality: An International Journal, 17*(3), 299–312.

Ashley, C., Boyd, C., & Goodwin, H. (2000). Pro-poor tourism: Putting poverty at the heart of the tourism agenda. *Natural Resource Perspectives, 51,* 1–12.

Awortwi, N. (2010). The past, present, and future of decentralisation in Africa: A comparative case study of local government development trajectories of Ghana and Uganda. *International Journal of Public Administration, 33*(12), 620–634.

Batley, R., McCourt, W., & Mcloughlin, C. (2012). Editorial: The politics and governance of public services in developing countries. *Public Management Review, 14*(2), 131–144.

Brand, R., & Gaffikin, F. (2007). Collaborative planning in an uncollaborative world. *Planning Theory, 6*(3), 282–313.

Brender, A., & Drazen, A. (2005). Political budget cycles in new versus established democracies. *Journal of Monetary Economics, 52*(7), 1271–1295.

Briggs, R. C. (2012). Electrifying the base? Aid and incumbent advantage in Ghana. *The Journal of Modern African Studies, 50*(04), 603–624.

Brohman, J. (1996). New directions in tourism for third world development. *Annals of Tourism Research, 23*(1), 48–70.

Bruner, E. M. (1996). Tourism in Ghana: The representation of slavery and the return of the black diaspora. *American Anthropologist, 98*(2), 290–304.

Christie, I., Fernandes, E., Messerli, H., & Twining-Ward, L. (2014). *Tourism in Africa: Harnessing Tourism for Growth and Improved Livelihoods.* Washington, DC: World Bank Publications.

Churugsa, W., McIntosh, A. J., & Simmons, D. (2007). Sustainable tourism planning and development: Understanding the capacity of local government. *Leisure/Loisir, 31*(2), 453–473.

Cobbinah, P. B., & Darkwah, R. M. (2016). Reflections on tourism policies in Ghana. *International Journal of Tourism Sciences, 16,* 170–190.

Crook, R. C. (2003). Decentralisation and poverty reduction in Africa: The politics of local–central relations. *Public Administration and Development, 23*(1), 77–88.

Drazen, A. (2001). The political business cycle after 25 years. *NBER Macroeconomics Annual 2000*, *15*, 75–138.

Drazen, A., & Eslava, M. (2010). Electoral manipulation via voter-friendly spending: Theory and evidence. *Journal of Development Economics*, *92*(1), 39–52.

Dredge, D. (2006). Policy networks and the local organisation of tourism. *Tourism Management*, *27*(2), 269–280.

Essah, P. (2001). Slavery, heritage and tourism in Ghana. *International Journal of Hospitality & Tourism Administration*, *2*(3–4), 31–49.

Franzese, R. J. (2002). Electoral and partisan cycles in economic policies and outcomes. *Annual Review of Political Science*, *5*(1), 369–421.

Ghana Statistical Service. (2014). *2010 Population and Housing Census District Analytical Report: Komenda-Edina-Eguafo-Abrem Municipal*. Accra: Ghana Statistical Service.

Giddens, A. (1984). *The Constitution of Society: Outline of the Theory of Structuration*. Cambridge: Polity Press.

Harrison, D. (2008). Pro-poor tourism: A critique. *Third World Quarterly*, *29*(5), 851–868.

Healey, P. (1997). *Collaborative Planning: Shaping Places in Fragmented Societies*. Vancouver: UBC Press.

Healey, P. (1999). Institutionalist analysis, communicative planning, and shaping places. *Journal of Planning Education and Research*, *19*(2), 111–121.

Healey, P. (2003). Collaborative planning in perspective. *Planning Theory*, *2*(2), 101–123.

Helmsing, A. (2003). Local economic development: New generations of actors, policies and instruments for Africa. *Public Administration and Development*, *23*(1), 67–76.

Henige, D. P. (1974). Kingship in Elmina before 1869: A study in 'Feedback' and the traditional idealization of the past (La royauté à Elmina avant 1869: étude sur le "feedback" et l'idéalisation traditionnelle du passé). *Cahiers d'etudes Africaines*, *14*(55), 499–520.

Hirvi, M., & Whitfield, L. (2015). Public-service provision in Clientelist political settlements: Lessons from Ghana's urban water sector. *Development Policy Review*, *33*(2), 135–158.

Holden, A. (2013). *Tourism, Poverty and Development*. London: Routledge.

Holden, A., Sonne, J., & Novelli, M. (2011). Tourism and poverty reduction: An interpretation by the poor of Elmina, Ghana. *Tourism Planning & Development*, *8*(3), 317–334.

Jeffries, D. (2001). *Governments and Tourism*. Oxford, UK: Butterworth-Heinemann.

KEEA (Komenda-Edina-Eguafo-Abrem Municipal Assembly). (2002). *The Elmina 2015 Strategy: Building on the Past to Create a Better Future*. Elmina: Komenda-Edina-Eguafo-Abrem Municipal Assembly.

Keefer, P., & Khemani, S. (2005). Democracy, public expenditures, and the poor: Understanding political incentives for providing public services. *The World Bank Research Observer*, *20*(1), 1–27.

Kelsall, T. (2012). Neo-patrimonialism, rent-seeking and development: Going with the grain? *New Political Economy*, *17*(5), 677–682.

Khemani, S. (2004). Political cycles in a developing economy: Effect of elections in the Indian states. *Journal of Development Economics*, *73*(1), 125–154.

Konadu-Agyemang, K. (2001). Structural adjustment programmes and the international tourism trade in Ghana, 1983–99: Some socio-spatial implications. *Tourism Geographies*, *3*(2), 187–206.

Lindberg, S. I. (2003). 'It's our time to "chop"': Do elections in Africa feed neo-patrimonialism rather than counter-act it? *Democratization*, *10*(2), 121–140.

Manning, N. (2001). The legacy of new public management in developing countries. *International Review of Administrative Sciences*, *67*(2), 297–312.

Mckercher, B., & Ritchie, M. (1997). The third tier of public sector tourism: A profile of local government tourism officers in Australia. *Journal of Travel Research*, *36*(1), 66–72.

Meyer, D. (2007). Pro-poor tourism: From leakages to linkages. A conceptual framework for creating linkages between the accommodation sector and 'poor' neighbouring communities. *Current Issues in Tourism*, *10*(6), 558–583.

Nel, E. (2001). Local economic development: A review and assessment of its current status in South Africa. *Urban Studies*, *38*(7), 1003–1024.

Novelli, M. (2016). *Tourism and Development in Sub-Saharan Africa: Current Issues and Local Realities*. London: Routledge.

Pike, A., Rodríguez-Pose, A., & Tomaney, J. (2006). *Local and Regional Development*. London: Routledge.

Ritchie, J., & Spencer, L. (1994). Qualitative data analysis for applied policy-research. In A. Bryman & R. G. Burguess (Eds.), *Analysing Qualitative Data* (pp. 173–194). London: Routledge.

Rodríguez-Pose, A. (2002). *The Role of the ILO in Implementing Local Economic Development Strategies in a Globalised World*. Genève: ILO.

Rogerson, C. M. (2014). Strengthening tourism-poverty linkages. In A. A. Lew, C. M. Hall, & A. M. Williams (Eds.), *The Wiley Blackwell Companion to Tourism* (pp. 600–610). Oxford: Wiley Blackwell.

Rogerson, C. M., & Rogerson, J. M. (2010). Local economic development in Africa: Global context and research directions. *Development Southern Africa, 27*(4), 465–480.

Rogoff, K. (1990). Equilibrium political budget cycles. *The American Economic Review, 80*, 21–36.

Ruhanen, L. (2013). Local government: Facilitator or inhibitor of sustainable tourism development? *Journal of Sustainable Tourism, 21*(1), 80–98.

Scheyvens, R. (2007). Exploring the tourism-poverty nexus. *Current Issues in Tourism, 10*(2–3), 231–254.

Scheyvens, R. (2011). *Tourism and Poverty*. London: Routledge.

Scott, R. W. (1995). *Institutions and Organizations. Foundations for Organizational Science*. Thousand Oaks, CA: Sage Publications

Slocum, S. L., & Backman, K. F. (2011). Understanding government capacity in tourism development as a poverty alleviation tool: A case study of Tanzanian policy-makers. *Tourism Planning & Development, 8*(3), 281–296.

Smoke, P. (2003). Decentralisation in Africa: Goals, dimensions, myths and challenges. *Public Administration and Development, 23*(1), 7–16.

Sonne, J. (2010). *The Role of Tourism in Poverty Reduction in Elmina, Ghana*. PhD Dissertation, University of Bedfordshire, Bedfordshire, UK.

Spenceley, A., & Meyer, D. (2012). Tourism and poverty reduction: Theory and practice in less economically developed countries. *Journal of Sustainable Tourism, 20*(3), 297–317.

Turner, M. (2012). Decentralization, politics and service delivery: The introduction of one-stop shops in Mongolia. *Public Management Review, 14*(2), 197–215.

Whitfield, L. (2009). 'Change for a better Ghana': Party competition, institutionalization and alternation in Ghana's 2008 elections. *African Affairs, 108*(433), 621–641.

Whitfield, L. (2011). *Competitive Clientelism, Easy Financing and Weak Capitalists: The Contemporary Political Settlement in Ghana*. DIIS Working Paper 27. Danish Institute for International Studies. Copenhagen.

Williams, M. J. (2016). *The Political Economy of Unfinished Development Projects: Corruption, Clientelism or Collective Choice?* Paper presented at the PacDev Conference, Stanford University.

13

Tourism development in Senegal

Historical overview and new directions for community-based tourism

Aby Sene-Harper

Introduction

Since the 1970s, Senegal has been one of the most popular tourism destinations in West Africa. Within the African continent, Senegal has consistently positioned itself in the top 16 in terms of the share of international arrivals, despite significant downturns over the years. In 2017, the country received 1.37 million tourist arrivals (World Bank, n.d.). Tourism is the second largest contributor to Senegal's economy, behind fisheries (World Trade Organization, 2003). In 2016, travel and tourism directly contributed to 4.8% of the GDP, and directly supported 246,500 jobs (4.1% of total employment) (World Travel and Tourism Council, 2017). As such, Senegal's tourism sector has been at the heart of national social and economic development plans, attracting significant private investments and leading to major financial reforms.

Several development policies have propelled the tourism sector to where it stands today. Principal among these has been the transformation of the coastlines in the regions of Thiès and Dakar into new tropical destinations in the 1970s and 1980s as a response to the global demand for mass tourism. However, there has been little effort from the government to diversify Senegal's tourism products, causing a concentration in tourism activities in these coastal destinations. The littoral region of Senegal alone constitutes, 75% of total tourism revenues (Ministère du Tourisme et des Transports Aériens – MTTA, 2007 quoted in Diombéra, 2012). In 2016, Dakar and La Petite Côte (see Figure 13.1) absorbed, respectively, 41% and 35% of tourism arrivals (Le Journal de L'Economie Sénégalaise, 2017). Behind these numbers are major challenges facing the tourism sector since the beginning of the current decade. Signs of over tourism, including environmental degradation, crowding and sex commerce, have deteriorated the image of Senegal's major destinations (Diagne, 2004). Moreover, local communities have mostly been marginalized from the development process and yet incurred the social costs, including land speculation and loss of traditional livelihoods (Saglio, 1979; Bilsen, 1987; Diagne, 2004). Today, the government is scrambling to rejuvenate the tourism sector and diversity product offerings. Diombéra (2012) argues that in the search for a new identity, greater emphasis should be placed on alternative products such as ecotourism and community participation in line with the sustainable development goals (SDGs).

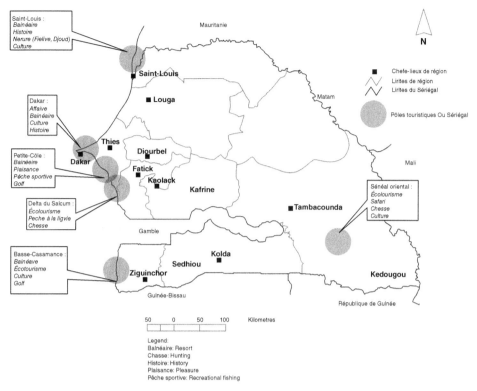

Figure 13.1 Tourism destinations in Senegal
Source: Diombera, 2012.

Community-based tourism (CBT) around national parks has been recognized as a strategy to promote sustainable development at the local level, especially as the government is seeking to further develop ecotourism (MTTA, 2013a). However, the current legal structure of rights allocation places local communities at a disadvantage in the face of private and state entities and ultimately impedes the contribution of CBT. More specifically, the lack of communal land-ownership and concession rights reduce the channels through which communities can benefit from CBT projects. In this chapter, after a brief overview of tourism products, I present the evolution of tourism development in Senegal including a review of major policies, trends and historical context in each period. I then present the development of CBT in the integrated rural tourism program of the Lower Casamance as a counter model of development. Finally, I discuss the critical issues of CBT around national parks as part of Senegal's new tourism identity.

Overview of tourism products

Senegal remains a major vacation hub in Francophone Africa for tourists arriving from Europe and other African countries (see Table 13.1) (Agence Nationale de Statistique et de la Démographie, 2016). Its tourism sector rests upon important environmental and cultural attributes but the main form of tourism in Senegal has been based on the attraction of sea, sun and sand (3S). The 718-km coastal region boasts numerous beach resort towns including those in La Petite Côte, Cap Skirring and the capital city of Dakar, earning Senegal a favorable reputation for winter escapes from Europe. Senegal is also known for its historical

Table 13.1 Tourist arrivals at the Dakar international airport by nationality

Country	2007	2008	2009	2010	2011	2012
France	217,887	212,296	198,978	205,114	194,892	194,609
Belgium	18,788	17,271	14,211	14,400	14,343	15,600
United States	17,216	17,783	18,942	19,958	18,366	17,514
Spain	15,862	14,548	14,032	14,503	13,135	12,572
Italy	11,033	11,482	11,547	11,603	10,960	10,759
Mali	11,348	11,746	10,885	11,919	10,746	9310
Other African countries	59,768	60,676	58,722	56,662	57,975	52,978

Source: Agence Nationale de Statistique et de la Démographie (2016); compiled by author.

landmarks such as Gorée Island and the former colonial town of Saint Louis. Moreover, its biodiversity has gained the interests of tourists, including its rich ornithological diversity, national parks and wildlife reserves (DPN, 2009), and the popular mangroves of Sine Saloum (Ackermann et al., 2006; Dietrich, 2008).

Lastly, but certainly not least, Senegal has a rich and diverse culture made up of over 20 different ethnic groups, which the Serer, Wolof, Toucouleur, Lébou, Jola, Soninké and Malinké counting among the largest ones. The Casamance region in the South of the country has attracted many tourists interested in the local culture (Saglio, 1979; Bilsen, 1987; Sall, 2015). Since the 1970s, the region of Basse Casamance hosts several community-based lodges where tourists can learn about and immerse themselves in the local way of life. Similar projects have been implemented in the early 1990s around national parks. Nonetheless, as visible in Figure 13.2, there is a stark disparity in tourism development across different regions, with Thiès and Dakar absorbing most of tourist arrivals. This is no coincidence, but the result of decades of development policies which has expanded tourism but disproportionately favoring the coastal region over other areas.

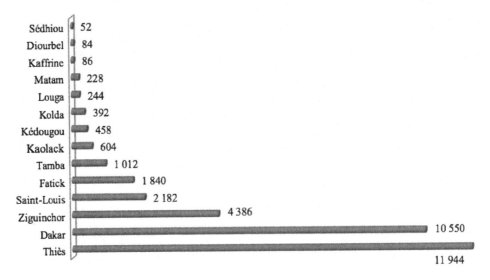

Figure 13.2 Number of beds per region
Source: Ministère du Tourisme et du Transport Aériens, 2013b.

Evolution of tourism development in Senegal

The evolution of tourism development in Senegal can be traced over four major time periods starting in the 1960s. Each of these periods was marked by different tourism trends, policies and strategic plans designed to address issues facing the country at the time and propel the sector into new directions.

Before the 1970s: the embryonic stage

The tourism sector started making its mark on Senegal's economy in the 1970s, but its embryonic stage occurred before that. The capital city of Dakar was also the regional capital of French West Africa during the colonial period. The country's status as the French colonial capital brought in infrastructures to accommodate European visitors who came to the country on administrative duty within the colonial state or for leisure (Tchitou, 2005). However, it wasn't until the 1960s, that government officials started to consider tourism as an economic player for the country. At the time, financial difficulties coupled with the country's capacity to attract private investment compelled the government to include tourism development strategies to the national economic development plan. In 1959, investing in tourism became part of the country's first social and economic development strategic plan (Diombéra, 2012).

In the last development plan of the decade (1965–1969), ambitious provisions were made to move the country from the margins to the ranks of luxury tourism by attracting a clientele with higher economic status. The government saw the highly touted *Festival Mondiale des Arts Nègres*[1] which was taking place in Dakar in 1966, as a unique opportunity to showcase its rich and diverse culture and the different tourism opportunities it offered. In addition to CFA F 180 million (~USD 360,000)[2] in public investment that the government injected in the sector, it actively sought significant private investments to finance the luxury tourism industry. Before 1970, there were 34 hotels of international standing recorded in the country which together employed about 300 people (Schlechten, 1988).

1970s and 1980s: responding to a global demand for mass tourism

Through the 1970s and 1980s, Senegal was preparing itself to gain a greater foothold into the global market, helping to establish a relatively robust tourism economy in the country over the next decade. The development of beach resort towns as a response to the rising global demand for mass tourism was at the heart of this surge and several policies were implemented to support it. The growth of the tourism economy was a change that the nation readily embraced, especially after years of natural disasters that steeped the country into financial uncertainty. When Senegal and the rest of the Sahel region entered the 1970s, it was experiencing a series of droughts spanning from 1968 to 1974. This disaster had devastating impacts on groundnut production, Senegal's main cash crop at the time. In turn, its foreign exchange earnings drastically decreased leading to a search for economic alternatives. For the government, it was the decisive moment leading to a strategic decision to diversify the country's economy by further developing its tourism sector (Tchitou, 2005; Diombéra, 2012).

The decision toward economic diversification happened at an opportune time with the expansion of international tourism into developing countries. The rise of the middle class and the "paid holidays" policies put into effect in industrialized nations in the 1960s and 1970s, contributed to a significant influx of international tourists who spent their vacation time in destinations of newly industrializing countries (Cazes, 1989,; Cazes & Courade, 2004; Diagne, 2004; Diombéra, 2012). Cazes (1989) coined the term "nouvelles colonies de vacances" to refer to the developing world as the new holiday camp of the industrialized world. Africa experienced a 269% rate of increase in international tourist arrivals between 1966 and 1977 (WTO, 1985, quoted in Schlechten, 1988). The government of Senegal sought to gain a bigger share of this growing sector. This led to bolder initiatives in tourism planning and development that are worth noting, including incentives for private investment, structural adjustment plans and an administrative decentralization reform. All these policies were set up to support the growth of the tourism sector that was eagerly expected by the government.

One of the priorities was to increase the capacity to accommodate more tourists by rapidly building and expanding hotels. The objectives were set to have 6,250 rooms, 368,000 arrivals and a revenue of CFA F 22 billion (USD 44 million) by the end of the 1970s. These investments amounted to CFA F 21.34 billion (USD 42.68 million), a significant increase in funding from previous plans. In the face of this colossal amount, several structural adjustment plans were implemented (Schlechten, 1988; Diombéra, 2012; Ly, 2018). In addition, to stimulate the construction of facilities, the government attracted private investment by providing cheap land, low interest rates and financial incentives such as depreciation allowances on tourism accommodation and infrastructure (Diagne, 2004). To support these initiatives, the government drafted a regional development plan with the help of the World Bank (Diagne, 2004). In this plan, four specific tourist areas were targeted to house resort towns, including the Hydrobase in Saint Louis, the coast of Dakar, La Petite Côte in the region of Thiès and Cap Skirring in Basse Casamance. However, La Petite Côte absorbed the largest proportion of the investments (Ciss, 1989; Diagne, 2004).

To gain greater control over the sector, a decentralization reform took effect and resulted in the creation of new agencies in charge of developing and promoting tourism activities. These agencies include Société d'Aménagement de la Petite Côte (SAPCO) Office du Tourisme, which in 2000 became the Agence Nationale de la Promotion du Tourisme (ANPT). SAPCO played a critical role in coordinating the efforts of the projects in La Petite Côte by promoting tourism development more systematically and encouraging private investments (Diagne, 2004; Tchitou, 2005; Diombéra, 2012). To boost tourism arrivals, a reduction of the costs of flying to Senegal and transportations within the country as well as the price of hotel rooms were imposed by the government through the 1980s. This effort was supplemented by marketing campaigns by ANTP to further promote Senegal as a destination and directed at its most important markets, namely Germany, Switzerland, France, Scandinavia, United States and Canada (Schlechten, 1988).

By 1975, Senegal had the seventh largest share of international tourism arrivals in Africa (WTO, 1990, quoted in Tchitou, 2005), yet the country fell short of its initial goals. That year, the Ministry of Tourism recorded 128,578 tourist arrivals. In 1986 and then 1990, there were 271,458 and 246,000 tourist arrivals, respectively, numbers far below the 368,000 target that was initially set (Ministère du Tourisme, 1985, quoted in Schlechten, 1988). The Ministry of Tourism attributed this shortcoming to the global reduction in consumer spending on an international scale due to the oil crisis of 1979 until the mid-1980s. Furthermore, the increase in competition from other beach destinations in Africa, such as Cape Verde and Morocco, was also to blame for this shortcoming (Ly, 2018).

1990–2000: slow growth amid socio-political crisis

During the 1990s, the tourism sector in Senegal continued to record modest numbers of tourist arrivals (see Table 13.2). In the first half of the 1990s, Senegal experienced two turbulent

Table 13.2 International tourism arrivals in Senegal and compared to other West African countries 1995–2000

	Senegal	Ghana	Cabo Verde	Benin
1995	280,000	286,000	28,000	138,000
1996	282,000	305,000	37,000	143,000
1997	314, 000	325,000	45,000	148,000
1998	352,000	348,000	58,000	152,000
1999	369,000	373,000	67,000	80,000
2000	389,000	399,000	115,000	96,000

Source: World Tourism Organization (2018); compiled by the author.

events that tarnished its image as a safe destination. First, years of tensions between Senegal and Mauritania, cumulated in a violent conflict between the two countries and a border closure from leading to the death of thousands and the displacement of around 200,000 people on both sides between 1989 and 1992, (Magistro, 1993; Ly, 2018). Second, socio-political conflicts in the Lower Casamance region reached its climax in 1994, when the riots of the separatists rebel group turned violent and displaced 30,000 people (Marut, 2010). Media coverage of these political crises fueled fear of insecurity among tourists who in turn shortened their stays or canceled their visits (Tchitou, 2005; Ndiaye, 2012).

Nonetheless, other events over the years have helped counter these impacts. In 1994, the devaluation of the Francs CFA currency which hit most West African countries, placed Senegal in a more competitive position, leading to a slow increase in tourism arrivals in 1995 (DeHoorne & Diagne, 2008). Furthermore, the highly anticipated annual rally between Paris and Dakar in 1997 helped restore the image of Senegal. The country recorded a 12.1% rate of increase in tourism arrivals between 1997 and 1998, the highest in that decade (World Bank, n.d.).

The slow growth of the tourism sector didn't discourage the government from setting higher goals. In the 1995 Senegal's tourism development strategic plan, a project called "1.5 million tourists in 2010" was defined. This project placed further emphasis on promotional marketing strategies, redefining financial mechanisms and building human resource capacity. This latter piece was a significant change compared to previous plans. To fulfill this commitment, the government opened three schools specialized in hospitality and tourism and a program in this field was also added to the curriculum of the National School for Applied Economics. As of 2005, Senegal has eight public and one private schools of tourism and hospitality management (Tchitou, 2005). The investment in building human resources laid the ground for the rapid growth of the sector in the next decade.

2000–2010: expansion of the tourism sector

At the beginning of the 2000s, tourism arrivals were affected by the reduction of air access to Senegal due to the terrorists' attacks on US soil of September 11, 2001 and the termination of operations of Air Afrique, Sabena and Swiss Air (Christie, 2004). Yet, Senegal's tourism defied the odds as international arrivals soared in the second half of the decade. Although the goal of 1.5 million by the government hadn't been met, the country reached a record rate of 112% increase in tourism arrivals from 2004 to 2005 (World Bank, n.d.). Compared to other West African countries, Senegal occupied a prominent position in the region (see Table 13.3). The tourism sector is now the second, behind fisheries, the most important source of revenue

Table 13.3 International tourism arrivals in Senegal compared to other West African countries 2001–2010

	Senegal	Ghana	Cabo Verde	Benin	Ivory Coast
2001	396,000	439,000	134,000	88,000	~
2002	427,000	483,000	126,00	72,000	~
2003	354,000	531,000	150,000	175,000	~
2004	363,000	584,000	157000	174,000	~
2005	769,000	429,000	198,000	176,000	~
2006	866,000	497,000	242,000	180,000	~
2007	875,000	587,000	267,000	186,000	182,000
2008	867,000	698,000	285,000	188,000	205,000
2009	810,000	803,000	287,000	190,000	231,000
2010	900,000	931,000	336,000	199,000	252,000

Source: World Tourism Organization (2018); compiled by the author.

for the country. Its share of GDP is around 4.1% over the period of 2000–2008. Despite the slight decline in international arrivals from 2007 to 2009, tourism accounted for 16.3% of the volume of export earnings during this period (World Bank, n.d.). Nevertheless, this rapid expansion was short-lived.

2010- to date: from stagnation to impeding decline

Since 2010, the tourism sector has been stagnant, threading around an average of 992,000 arrivals between 2011 and 2015 (see Table 13.4). The effects of the Ebola epidemic of 2014 in the tourism sector were felt not just in Senegal but also in other West African countries (Ly, 2018; Novelli et al., 2018). The private sector and policy makers have rung the alarm on the deteriorating conditions of the tourism sector. In comparison to other countries in West Africa, Senegal's tourism numbers remain strong, but this belies the crisis facing the sector. Since the mid-2000s, researchers have warned of the risks associated with mass tourism, focusing mostly on La Petite Côte, where close to 75% of tourism revenues for the country are generated (c.f. Crompton & Christie, 2003; Diagne, 2004; DeHoorne & Diagne, 2008; Diombéra, 2012).

Ly (2018) argues that La Petite Côte is going through the stagnation phase of the Butler destination life cycle model (Butler, 1980). Today the symptoms of over-tourism in popular destinations of Senegal are many and contributing to the decline of the sector. Social, economic and

Table 13.4 International tourism arrivals in Senegal compared to other West African countries 2011–2015

	Senegal	Ghana	Cabo Verde	Benin	Ivory Coast
2011	968,000	821,000	428,000	209,000	270,000
2012	962,000	903,000	482,000	220,000	289,000
2013	1,063,000	994,000	503,000	231,000	380,000
2014	963,000	825,000	494,000	242,000	471,000
2015	1,006,600	897,000	520,000	255,000	1,441,000

Source: WTO (2018).

ecological problems have ensued after three decades of rapid tourism expansion, which despite several policies, has mostly been unregulated. A clear manifestation of a lack of planning is the "anarchic" construction of tourism facilities causing land saturation and speculation along the coastal regions expanding from Thiès to Saint Louis (Crompton & Christie, 2003).

The spiral of tourism development and population growth in La Petite Côte has led to the environmental degradation of the area. The increased amounts of human waste, coupled with the inappropriate sewage disposal systems, are increasingly causing beach pollution, posing a serious health hazard for both the residents and the tourists (Diagne, 2004). Furthermore, lack of zoning laws pushed the construction of tourism facilities into ecologically sensitive places. Today, coastal erosion is a growing problem for Senegal, forcing hotels and restaurants located too close to the beach to close (Ministère de l'Environnement et de la Protection de la Nature, 2011). In addition to ecological problems, social ills such as prostitution and pedophilia are rampant, and the medialization of this issue has earned Senegal a poor reputation (Diagne, 2004; Diombéra, 2012; Ndiaye, 2012).

The impacts of tourism expansion are also felt by local communities. Tourism researchers have documented the deterioration of traditional livelihoods, culture and Islamic values of the local communities in La Petite Côte and Cap Skirring. For example, Ciss (1989) denounced the dispossession of locals as they lost access to fishing resources for tourism development. In Casamance, Saglio (1979) observed that the creation of new jobs at the Cap Skirring resort has severely shaken social structures and gave rise to a new hierarchy of values that gives importance to money. It has become clear that tourism development has done little to alleviate poverty especially in local communities (Sonko, 2013). To address these issues, the Ministry of Tourism seeks to further develop CBT in different regions, including around national parks (MTTA, 2013b). CBT projects have been implemented in Senegal since the 1970s, and important lessons can be drawn from this experience in diversifying the current model of mass tourism development.

Community-based tourism, a counter model of development

Integrated rural tourism: the beginnings of community-based tourism in Senegal

Parallel to the development of mass tourism that besieged the sandy beaches of Senegal, rural tourism was also forming in the lower Casamance region of the early 1970s. This model didn't necessarily gain the attention and interest of politicians, but certainly garnered the attention of tourism researchers who considered Casamance as one of the cradles of rural tourism in West Africa (c.f. Saglio, 1979; Bilsen, 1987; Schlechten, 1988). Its early development in Senegal was commensurate with the rise of critical thoughts calling for alternative forms of tourism (Sene-Harper & Seye, 2019).

Christian Saglio, an anthropologist working with the *Agence de Coopération Culturelle et Technique* is credited for creating and spearheading the development of integrated rural tourism in Senegal starting in 1971 (Saglio, 1979; Bilsen, 1987; Schlechten, 1988). Saglio collaborated with Adama Goudiaby, a native of Casamance and at the time the regional coordinator for tourism. With the collaboration of local communities, they opened the first tourist camps in two villages in 1974. Within the next ten years, eight camps with the capacity to accommodate 25–30 tourists opened in different villages throughout the lower Casamance region (Schlechten, 1988). Unlike beach resorts where host-guest interactions are limited, Saglio and Goudiaby envisioned a form of tourism that offers greater opportunities for tourists to learn the local culture and way of life. The effects of integrated rural tourism projects evolved beyond improving guest-host interactions, to become a motor for local development.

The tenets of integrated rural tourism are the same as those of CBT. According to Russell (2000), the three principles of CBT are that:

> it should have the support and participation of local people; as much of its economic benefit as possible should go to the people living at or near the destination; and the act of tourism must protect local people's cultural identity and natural environment.
>
> *(Russell, 2000, p. 1)*

First, in integrated rural tourism projects, the management of the camps is left entirely to the villagers. Cooperatives are formed and made responsible for the operations of the camps. Second, the revenues generated from these projects go toward salaries and the improvement of local community infrastructure such as schools, hospitals and mosques. Third, an important facet of the project is the revival of traditional architecture and arts. The lodges were built using local material and designed to reflect the traditional huts, and guests could enjoy traditional meals. In some cases, craft centers were built where local artists could sell their work (Saglio, 1979; Bilsen, 1987).

These projects didn't contribute significantly to the national economy, but at the village level, the camps have proven to be an important source of income. For example, in 1981 alone, 10,000 tourists visited seven villages for a profit of $43,000 (Bilsen, 1987). In 1990, the camps hosted 20,000 tourists generating $253,000 in tourism revenues (Zeppel, 2006). Because of the political crisis, tourism in Casamance drastically declined throughout the 1990s (Zeppel, 2006; Diombéra, 2012), but has picked up since then. Today, however, CBT projects are facing a different crisis in the face of increased competition from privately owned tourist camps. The success of the integrated rural tourism early on has stimulated the interest among private investors who emulated the program by building similar facilities and offering the same services, but with more comfort for tourists (Bilsen, 1987). In 2008, 17 CBT camps and 29 privately owned ones were recorded. In addition, with resources greater than local communities, private camps can capture a larger share of the market by promoting their products among international tour operators. Sonko (2013) noted that partly for these reasons, CBT camps are struggling to stay open even as the early success in Casamance inspired other similar projects for ecotourism. Since 1994, the government of Senegal has been collaborating with international NGOs and local communities to implement CBT projects in communities around national parks. Today, the government is seeking to further develop ecotourism activities as part of its product diversification strategy. They also regard this as an opportunity to promote sustainable development in local communities by building upon the already existing CBT projects. However, experience from the rural integrated tourism program suggests that critical issues need to be addressed first to level the playing field between local communities and private investors.

Critical issues for community-based tourism around national parks

According to Diombéra (2012), as the tourism sector is seeking a new identity, ecotourism should be at the center of their development plan. The potential for ecotourism development in Senegal is significant. There are six national parks, six nature reserves and five marine protected areas in Senegal. The two largest parks, namely Niokolo-Koba National Park (913,000 hectares) and Djoudj National Park (16,000 hectares) are classified as UNESCO World Heritage Sites. National parks in Senegal received an average of 32,600 visitors and generated revenues of CFA F 67.3 million (USD 134,000) between 2000 and 2010 (Direction des Parcs Nationaux -DPN, 2017). Therefore, they have the potential to contribute to the sustainable development of communities located in their proximity and CBT has been a popular mechanism to channel ecotourism benefits to local communities.

In 1994, communities around Djoudj National Park (Djoudj hereafter) were the first ones to have benefitted from the CBT program with the financial and technical support of the International Union for the Conservation of Nature (IUCN). Djoudj is the most visited park in Senegal, with an average of 8,321 visitors per year between 2005 and 2016 and an estimated average of CFA F 29.2 million in revenues per year between 2000 and 2010 (DPN, 2017). The CBT project at Djoudj provided a tourist lodge (18 beds), three touring canoes, an artisanal boutique, an eco-museum and a Moorish tent to serve traditional refreshments to tourists. The project was supposed to engender employment and income to support 135 households in all seven communities (Zeppel, 2006). Djoudj is often touted as an exemplary CBT model for other communities, yet the revenues generated over the past few years have been minimal and have had limited impacts on poverty alleviation in the surrounding communities (Sène-Harper & Séye, 2019). The effects of CBT around other national parks such as Parc National du Delta du Saloum have also not been perceptible (Dietrich, 2008).

The department of national parks has attributed the shortcoming of CBT projects partly to the decline in visitor numbers (DPN, 2017). There is also a recognition that communities are at a disadvantage in the face of private operators who have access to greater financial and organizational resources, thereby creating an unequal competitive environment (Sène-Harper & Séye, 2019). In 2013, after three days of meetings between community representatives and the ministry of tourism, an agreement was signed between the two parties. In this agreement, CBT principles were reaffirmed placing greater emphasis on the need to increase locals' participation and empowerment. Equitable access to economic opportunities and resources were noted as essential to broaden the positive impacts of tourism activities (MTTA, 2013b). However, reaching this objective is predicated on changing policies that disproportionately puts local communities at a disadvantage in the face of private and state entities, and thereby narrows their revenues streams.

A cornerstone of successful CBT programs in other African countries such as Botswana, Zimbabwe and South Africa is the rights of communities to manage, control and benefits from tourism resources, which is predicated on the restitution of land and concession rights to local communities (Child, 1996; Taylor, 2009; Moswete & Thapa, 2018). In Senegal, however, communities lack communal landownership and have limited concession rights. Senegal's land rights have been a contentious issue between the government and local communities, and this is accentuated by tourism development (Crompton & Christie, 2003). Broadly speaking, land in and around national parks are considered national domain (Diouf, 2010) and communal ownership of land for tourism purpose is not legally supported. It is arguable that this lack of communal landownership impedes the contribution of CBT, especially when competing with private operators. Scheyvens and Russell (2012) maintain that communal land tenure supports the interests of landowners against private investors to ensure communities can receive significant tourism benefits. Communal ownership of land and tourism resources strengthens the community's bargaining power in tourism planning and management on their lands (Ashley & Jones, 2001). In the dominant CBT model in Southern Africa, communities have the authority to negotiate with private business operating on their communal land (Mbaiwa, 2004).

In Senegal, CBT projects face a fierce competition with private and unlicensed tour operators. This is the case in the context of the rural integrated tourism program and one of the reasons community lodges in Casamance have not been as successful. Privately owned hotels and private tour operators are also present at such sites as Djoudj, Niokolo-Koba and Delta du Saloum National Parks. Communities at Djoudj reported that this issue had caused them to lose a significant share of tourism revenues (Sèye & Sene-Harper, 2014). For instance, packages by private tour operators offer daily visits to the park but rarely include a night stay at the community lodge. In 2013, the lodge recorded a revenue of CFA F 2, 147,000 (~USD 4,294) which is relatively small given that the park recorded a revenue of CFA F 30.5 million (~USD 61,000) in permit entry sale in the same year. Yet, the communities are not in a legal position to choose which tour operator can operate in their locality. Neither are tour operators legally bound to negotiate any terms with local communities.

In addition to the lack of communal landownership, limited concession rights over resources in national parks also reduce the channels through which communities can benefit from tourism activities. Unlike private operators, communities in Senegal don't have concession rights for hunting tourism. Besides park visits, hunting within buffer zones constitutes an important source of tourism revenue in protected areas. A study by IUCN in 2006, reported that during the 1999–2000 season, sport hunting firms in Tambacounda and Saint Louis regions, where Niokolo-Koba and Djoudj are located, registered 692 hunters, implying a total revenue of CFA F 450 million (~USD 900,000). Operating costs (e.g. transport and marketing) were estimated at just 3% of total revenues, suggesting a value added to the economy of about CFA F 436 million (USD 872,000) (IUCN, 2006). In 2009, the director of the department of water, forests and hunting reported that the department received total revenues from sale of hunting permits of F CFA 186 million (USD 372,000) from the 2008 to 2009 hunting season (Pana, 2009).

In many Southern African countries hunting is an important source of revenue for communities participating in CBT programs. Communities in those countries receive an important stream of income by leasing their hunting quotas to private operators, which is not the case in Senegal (Child, 1996; Mbaiwa, 2004; Frost & Bond, 2008; Mbaiwa & Stronza, 2010) Realizing the economic value of wildlife resources, including sport hunting is an important aspect of the government's tourism development plan. As a result, private investors are encouraged to develop wildlife-based tourism through temporary concession of exclusive rights for sport hunting and/or animal viewing in designated reserves. Since 1988, the practice of leasing concessions rights by the government was generalized. However, no attempt has been made to decentralize wildlife management for tourism purpose to local communities (IUCN, 2006). This represents an important revenue stream that is not accessible to communities at Djoudj and all other parks, and locals have asked that they be granted the rights to manage hunting areas (Seye & Sene-Harper, 2014).

Conclusions

Tourism remains a major contributor to Senegal's economy. However, development policies have disproportionately focused on three major coastal regions, namely Thiès, Dakar and Saint Louis; and local communities continue to bear the costs of this rapid expansion. Today, the sector is experiencing a serious downturn, forcing the government to diversify its tourism products and redefine its development strategies in ways that align with sustainable development goals. In 2016, the Senegalese president, Mr. Macky Sall reiterated his plan to reinvigorate the tourism sector as a catalyst for sustainable development at the national and local levels. Following his call, the government put in place various policies to incentivize private investment, invest in human capital and attract new tourists. Significantly less emphasis has been put on strengthening the rights and capacity of local communities to manage and benefit from tourism resources. It is critical that in advancing CBT around national parks for national and community development, laws and policies related to land and concession rights are redefined to broaden the impacts of ecotourism. The success and sustainability of the tourism sector don't just depend on investments in its products and human capital. It also requires an appropriate adjustment of the legal structure that mediates the integration of all actors at different levels of the development process, something that the Senegalese government has so far overlooked.

Notes

1 World Festival of Negro Arts.
2 At the time this chapter was written the exchange rate was ay USD 1 = CFA F 500.

References

Ackermann, G., Alexandre, F., Andrieu, J., Mering, C., & Ollivier, C. (2006). Dynamique des paysages et perspectives de développement durable sur la petite cote et dans le delta du Sine–Saloum (Sénégal). *Vertigo-la revue électronique en sciences de l'environnement*, 7(2), 1–9

Agence Nationale de la Statistique et de la Démographie. (2016). *Entréés des tourists par nationalité*. Retrieved from http://senegal.opendataforafrica.org/qbboric/tourisme.

Ashley, C., & Jones, B. (2001). Joint ventures between communities and tourism investors: Experience in Southern Africa. *International Journal of Tourism Research*, 3(5), 407–423.

Butler, R. W. (1980). The concept of a tourist area cycle of evolution: implications for management of resources. *Canadian Geographer/Le Géographe canadien*, 24(1), 5–12.

Cazes, G. (1989). *Les nouvelles colonies de vacances? Le tourisme international à la conquête du Tiers-Monde* (Vol. 1). Editions Harmattan: Paris

Cazes, G., & Courade, G. (2004). Les masques du tourisme. *Revue Tiers Monde*, 2(178), 247–268.

Child, B. (1996). The practice and principles of community-based wildlife management in Zimbabwe: The CAMPFIRE programme. *Biodiversity & Conservation*, 5(3), 369–398.

Ciss, G. (1989). Saly-Portudal, a Senegalese village faced with international tourism.*Cahiers d'Outre-Mer*, 42(165), 53–72.

Christie, I. (2004). Tourism in Senegal. World Bank. Retrieved from https://openknowledge.worldbank.org/bitstream/handle/10986/9701/310480ENGLISH0find235.pdf?sequence=1

Crompton, E., & Christie, I. (2003). Senegal tourism sector study. *Africa Region Working Paper No. 46*, 1–8.

Bilsen, F. (1987). Integrated tourism in Senegal: An alternative. *Tourism Recreation Research*, 12(2), 19–23.

Dehoorne, O., & Khadre Diagne, A. (2008). Tourisme, développement et enjeux politiques: l'exemple de la Petite Côte (Sénégal). *Études caribéennes*, 9–10(2008). https://doi.org/10.4000/etudescaribeennes.1172

Diagne, A. (2004). Tourism development and its impacts in the Senegalese Petite Côte: A geographical case study in centre–periphery relations. *Tourism Geographies*, 6(4), 472–492.

Dietrich, N. (2008). *L'Ecotourisme comme outil de développement local: L'exemple du Sine Saloum* (Unpublished master thesis). Université Paul-Valéry, Montpellier, France.

Diombéra, M. (2012). Le tourisme sénégalais à la recherche d'une nouvelle identité. *Téoros: Revue de Recherche en Tourisme*, 31(2), 21–30.

Diouf, A. (2010). *NEGOS-GRN: Rapport final Etat des lieux du cadre juridique et institutionnel de la gestion des ressources naturelles et foncières au Sénégal*/NEGOS-GRN The Final Report State of the Legal Framework and Institutional Management of Land and Natural Res., Institut de Recherche pour le Development: Dakar Senegal.

Direction des Parc Nationaux. (2009). *Gestion des Parcs, Réserves et Aires Marines Protégées du Sénégal.* Dakar: Sénégal.

Direction des Parc Nationaux. (DPN) (2017). *Plan d'aménagement et de gestion du Parc National des Oiseaux du Djoudj 2017–2021.* Dakar: Sénégal.

Frost, P. G., & Bond, I. (2008). The CAMPFIRE programme in Zimbabwe: Payments for wildlife services. *Ecological Economics*, 65(4), 776–787.

International Union for the Conservation of Nature. (IUCN) (2006). *The economic value of wild resources in Senegal, A preliminary evaluation of non-timber forest products, game and freshwater fisheries.* Gland, Switzerland.

Le Journal de L'Economie Sénégalaise. (2017). *Rapport sur le secteur du tourisme, le Sénégal sur une bonne pente*. Retrieved from https://www.lejecos.com/Rapport-sur-le-secteur-du-tourisme-Le-Senegal-sur-une-bonne-pente_a9966.html.

Ly, M. B. (2018). An application of Butler's (1980) tourist area life cycle to Sally, Senegal. *International Journal for Innovation Education and Research*, 6(1), 47–56.

Magistro, J. V. (1993). Ethnicité et conflit frontalier dans la vallée du fleuve Sénégal. *Cahiers d'études africaines*, 33(130): 201–232.

Marut, J. C. (2010). *Le conflit de Casamance: Ce que disent les armes*. KARTHALA Editions.Paris, France.

Mbaiwa, J. E. (2004). The success and sustainability of community-based natural resource management in the Okavango Delta, Botswana. *South African Geographical Journal*, 86(1), 44–53.

Mbaiwa, J. E., & Stronza, A. L. (2010). The effects of tourism development on rural livelihoods in the Okavango Delta, Botswana. *Journal of Sustainable Tourism*, 18(5), 635–656.

Ministère de l'Environnement et de la Protection de La Nature. (2011). *Etude sur la vulnérabilité du secteur touristique à Saly et de ses implications socioéconomiques sur l'économie locale au niveau de la station touristique*. Dakar: Sénégal.

Ministère du Tourisme et du Transport Aériens du Sénégal. (MTTA) (2013a). *Plan stratégique de développement durable du tourisme au Sénégal 2014–2018*. Dakar: Sénégal.

Ministère du Tourisme et du Transport Aériens du Sénégal. (MTTA) (2013b). *Chartre du Tourisme Responsible et Communautaire*. Dakar: Sénégal.

Moswete, N., & Thapa, B. (2018). Local communities, CBOs/trusts, and people–park relationships: A case study of the Kgalagadi transfrontier park, Botswana. *George Wright Forum*, 35(1), 96–108.

Ndiaye, A. (2012). *Communication, tourisme et développement durable au Sénégal: enjeux et risques* (Doctoral dissertation). Université Michel de Montaigne: Bordeaux III.

Novelli, M., Burgess, L. G., Jones, A., & Ritchie, B. W. (2018). 'No Ebola… still doomed'–The Ebola-induced tourism crisis. *Annals of Tourism Research*, 70, 76–87.

Pana (Nov. 18, 2009). Sénégal: Les recettes pour la saison de chasse 2008-2009. *Kolda News*. Retrieved from https://2009-2013.koldanews.com/2009/11/18/senegal-les-recettes-pour-la-saison-de-chasse-2008-2009/

Russell, P. (2000). Community-based tourism. *Travel & Tourism Analyst*, 5 (2000), 89–116.

Saglio, C. (1979). *Tourism for discovery: A project in Lower Casamance, Senegal* (pp. 321–335). Oxford University Press for World Bank and UNESCO: New York

Sall, M. (2015). Paysages Culturels et Perspectives Touristiques au Sénégal. *Arquitecturas, Multimédia e Turismo: Investimento na aposta Multi-sensorial*, 4(July, 2015), 173–185

Scheyvens, R., & Russell, M. (2012). Tourism, land tenure and poverty alleviation in Fiji. *Tourism Geographies*, 14(1), 1–25.

Schlechten, M. (1988). *Tourisme balnéaire ou tourisme rural intégré?: deux modèles de développement sénégalais* (Vol. 14). Editions universitaires.Fribourg, Suisse

Sène-Harper, A., & Séye, M. (2019). Community-based tourism around national parks in Senegal: The implications of colonial legacies in current management policies. *Tourism Planning & Development*, 16(2), 217–234.

Seye, D. & Sene-Harper, A. (2014). *Vingt ans de gestion integree du Parc National des Oiseaux du Djoudj: Les perceptions et attentes des populations de la peripherie*. Prepared for Department des Parc Nationaux du Senegal, Dakar, Senegal.

Sonko, S. M. (2013). *Le tourisme rural et la réduction de la pauvreté* (Doctoral dissertation). Université Toulouse le Mirail: Toulouse II.

Taylor, R. (2009). Community based natural resource management in Zimbabwe: The experience of CAMPFIRE. *Biodiversity and Conservation*, 18(10), 2563–2583.

Tchitou, J.R. (2005). *Analyse de la politique de promotion touristique au Sénégal*. Retrieved from Memoire Online. https://www.memoireonline.com/06/08/1171/analyse-politique-de-promotion-touristique-au-senegal.html

World Bank (n.d.). *International Tourism, Number of arrivals – Senegal*. Retrieved from https://data.worldbank.org/indicator/ST.INT.ARVL?locations=SN&name_desc=true

World Trade Organization. (2003). *Trade Policy Review: Senegal*. Retrieved from https://www.wto.org/english/tratop_e/tpr_e/s223-02_e.doc

World Travel and Tourism Council. (2017). *Travel and tourism economic impact 2017, Senegal*. London, UK.

Zeppel, H. (2006). *Indigenous ecotourism: Sustainable development and management* (Vol. 3). CABI. Throwbridge, UK.

14

The political economy of tourism development in Cape Verde islands

Manuel Alector Ribeiro, Kyle Maurice Woosnam
and Huda Abdullah Megeirhi

Introduction

Tourism is broadly recognised as a leading industry with key social and economic potential in attracting the attention of local and national governments that promote the development of tourism in their regions as a tool for mitigating economic downturn (Harrill, 2004). Extant literature has demonstrated that economic benefits of tourism not only influence the country but also benefit local residents through employment opportunities and improved public infrastructure (Ko & Stewart, 2002; Lee, 2013; Ribeiro, 2016; Ribeiro, Valle, & Silva, 2013; Sinclair-Maragh, 2017). Concomitantly, tourism development can result in a range of benefits for the environment, local culture, society and local economy (Sharpley, 2014). However, over the last two decades, a growing concern has taken shape concerning the costs that tourism brings to the society, but mostly deeply to the natural environment that has been resulted in an increasing concern surrounding the sustainability of tourism. That being said, it should come as no surprise that sustainability within tourism destinations has become one of the most important topics studied within the tourism research literature (Ribeiro, Pinto, Silva, & Woosnam, 2018; Tubb, 2003), and has been adopted as the concept best matched to address host community residents' needs (Choi & Sirakaya, 2005; Swarbrooke, 1999).

Nevertheless, responding to the growing numbers of people traveling to vulnerable and fragile natural environments (such as those in developing small island countries), it is assumed that sustainability of tourism is largely contingent upon the cooperation of local residents with other stakeholders and their support for the development of sustainable and equitable tourism (Gursoy et al., 2010; Ribeiro et al., 2017, 2018; Twining-Ward and Butler, 2002). As such, beginning the conversation of sustainable and equitable tourism must start with considering residents' attitudes about tourism and what their level of support for tourism development may be—each of which has great implications for how satisfied tourists may be with their experiences, and ultimately, their loyalty to the destination (Alegre & Cladera, 2009; Ribeiro, Woosnam, Pinto, & Silva, 2018; Sheldon & Abenoja, 2001; Swarbrooke, 1993; Valle, Mendes, Guerreiro, & Silva, 2011). In addition, the degree of involvement of residents in planning and managing for tourism is vital for the success of sustainability in any tourism destination (Choi & Sirakaya, 2005; Dredge & Jamal, 2015; Harrill, 2004; Okazaki, 2008; Ribeiro et al., 2018). The extant literature also shows that a fair distribution of the benefits of tourism among all stakeholders is crucial in mitigating any potential conflict between the tourism industry and the resources that tourism depends—satisfying one of the main principles of sustainable tourism development. Chief among these principles are residents' quality-of-life and life satisfaction, citizens' trust in tourism institutions, visitors' quality experiences, and the defence of cultural assets and natural environments for both current and future generations (Bimonte & Faralla, 2016; Choi & Sirakaya, 2005; Gursoy, Chi, & Dyer, 2010; Uysal, Sirgy, Woo, & Kim, 2016).

The challenges faced by developing countries in pursuing sustainable tourism development are widely recognised. Cape Verde, a small island developing state (SIDS), is constrained by its dependence on traditional industries for economic development, its fragile natural environment, its remoteness, its limited economy, and its reliance on imports over exports (Baldacchino & Bertram, 2009; McElroy & Hamma, 2010; Pratt, 2015; Ribeiro et al., 2017). These aspects often lead the country to be highly dependent on international trade and, therefore, vulnerable to external shocks. Hence, tourism development has been identified by successive governments as an effective way to revitalise the Cape Verdean's economy. However, in search of comprehensive sustainable and equitable tourism development and an understanding of the factors that contribute to its growth and development, residents' perceptions of economic benefits, attitudes towards tourism, and trust in tourism institutions have each been identified by scholars as the main predictors residents' support for tourism development (e.g. Boley, McGehee, Perdue, & Long, 2014; Gursoy & Rutherford, 2004; Nunkoo & Gursoy, 2012; Nunkoo & Ramkissoon, 2012; Perdue, Long, & Allen, 1990; Ribeiro et al., 2017; Sinclair-Maragh & Gursoy, 2015; Stylidis & Terzidou, 2014; Woo, Kim, & Uysal, 2015). Needless to say, most of those studies have considered the social exchange theory (SET) as a guiding theoretical framework to explain such residential support (Nunkoo, Smith, & Ramkissoon, 2013; Ribeiro et al., 2017; Sharpley, 2014). SET is a "general sociological theory concerned with an understanding of the exchange of resources between individuals and groups in an interaction situation" (Ap, 1992, p. 668). Nunkoo et al. (2013) highlighted that the widespread popularity of SET within residents' attitudes research is at least partially due to the fact that it acknowledges the heterogeneous nature of local communities with numerous perspectives of tourism among residents.

Community residents' attitudes and support for tourism development are formed by the historical and socioeconomic context of the destination (Fredline & Faulkner, 2000), and these help to establish guiding principles for relating to tourism development. For Lepp (2008), sociocultural, economic, and historical contexts shape significance to social processes like tourism mainly in developing countries. These social processes include residents' trust in tourism institutions which has been considered most recently in residents' research employing the social exchange theory (Gursoy, Yolal, Ribeiro, & Panosso Netto, 2017; Nunkoo, 2015, 2016).

Studies suggest that communities which support tourism development are likely to place a great deal of value in the preservation of natural resources upon which tourism depend (Dyer, Gursoy, Sharma, & Carter, 2007; Lepp, 2007; Ribeiro et al., 2017) and welcome the visitors in a pleasant manner (Valle et al., 2011; Woosnam & Norman, 2010). Some scholars suggest (Lepp, 2007; Ribeiro et al., 2017) that residents who possess positive attitudes towards tourism development will foster pro-tourism development behaviour, and consequently, be more inclined to take part in exchanges with tourists.

Owing to the exponential growth rate of tourism and the resulting economic benefits derived from the industry in Cape Verde throughout the last decade, the government, local authorities, private sector, and host communities widely recognise that tourism is an important vehicle for growth and development. Indeed, in small island developing countries, tourism has become "an important and integral element of their development strategies" (Jenkins, 1991, p. 61), and in many cases "tourism is commonly regarded as the sole option for development" (Ioannides & Holcomb, 2003, p. 40). Likewise, in many developing countries, tourism may represent the only powerful development tool (Brown, 1998). In line with this thinking, the greatest convincing purpose for selecting tourism as a development strategy is its latent influence on national and local economies, predominantly in the balance of payments (Oppermann & Chon, 1997). Generally, tourism is viewed as an important socioeconomic sector, but it is within developing countries that tourism can be seen as a development catalyst. Thus, tourism certainly embodies a possibly attractive means of inspiring socioeconomic development in these countries. However, it can cause significant economic, social and environmental costs to host communities (Gursoy, Jurowski, & Uysal, 2002). With that said, Telfer and Sharpley (2008, p. 4), argued that the "dilemma for many developing countries, therefore, lies in the challenge of accepting or managing such negative consequences for the potential longer-term benefits offered by tourism development".

Rooted in this line of research, numerous scholars argue that residents must cooperate, support and participate in the tourism planning process and trust the institutions responsible for tourism management for the industry to achieve long-term sustainability (Choi & Sirakaya, 2005; Gursoy et al., 2010; Sirakaya, Teye, & Sönmez, 2002). For instance, negative attitudes of residents may cause the loss of destination competitiveness and opposition to support tourism development (Gursoy & Rutherford, 2004; Harrill, Uysal, Cardon, Vong, & Dioko, 2011).

This chapter offers a comprehensive analysis of tourism development in Cape Verde islands supported by the theoretical foundation of social exchange theory (SET) and political economy theory. With that said, it begins with a brief discussion about the political economy and its relationship with the political economy of tourism in the context of developing and emerging island destinations. Thereafter, the remainder part of the chapter discusses the case study of Cape Verde, the implications of the political economy of tourism in this small island developing states (SIDS). The last part of the chapter discusses the analysis of the policies developed in Cape Verde and its consequences on the country's development strategy.

Literature review

Political economy, tourism development and trust in tourism institutions

The concept of political economy is fundamental to the purpose of tourism development and trust in tourism institutions, especially in SIDS where tourism plays a critical developmental role. Political economy theory, a broad social science theory is centred on the understanding of the political nature of decision making and how choices of politics impacts society overall. It encompasses a wide variety of approaches to studying the relationship between "the economy" and its "non-economic" (i.e. political, sociocultural, psychological and geographical) context while providing an understanding of structures and social relations that form societies in order to evoke social change towards more equitable and democratic conditions

(Mosedale, 2011). The political economy provides a useful perspective in examining tourism development and governance processes, yet it has not received significant attention within the tourism research (Bramwell, 2011). Nevertheless, some researchers have successfully applied it to the study of tourism development (e.g. Bianchi, 2009, 2018; Mosedale, 2011; Nunkoo, 2015). Williams (2004) noted that important theoretical developments in the political economy have been largely neglected in tourism studies. Mosedale (2011, p. 7) argued that "political economy (in its various guises and transfigurations) still has much to offer tourism analyses and should not be ignored or indeed written off in favour of a more fashionable approach to studying and analysing tourism".

Political economy sees tourism institutions, mainly the central government as the actor that plays a central role in tourism development and planning (Nunkoo, 2015; Wang & Bramwell, 2012), and its formal intervention in the tourism development process is headed, in some cases, through the minister of tourism and other governmental institutions. However, in some destinations, the responsibility to implement tourism policy and strategies is delegated to the regional government encompassing local municipalities. In this sense, residents' trust in tourism institutions (e.g. federal government, local government, municipalities) is a subjective phenomenon because residents use different criteria to evaluate their level of trust in these institutions (Bouckaert & van de Walle, 2003). For example, residents may trust the institutions differently depending on the context. In this sense, current literature suggests that trust should measure the specific domain of trust and trustworthiness judgements and their impact on general opinion of public trust in institutions (Bouckaert & van de Walle, 2003). The impact of tourism at local level indicates that residents' trust in tourism institutions influences their support for tourism development. With this in mind, and in keeping with the postulates of social exchange theory, we hypothesis the following:

H1: Residents' political trust in tourism institutions positively influences their support for tourism development.

Benefits and costs of tourism development and trust in tourism institutions

The extant literature indicates that residents' trust in tourism institutions and their support for tourism development is highly impacted by their perception about the costs and benefits derived from tourism (Gursoy et al., 2017; Nunkoo, 2015; Nunkoo & Gursoy, 2012). Considering the context of developing islands countries (SIDS), tourism is seen as an industry that is responsible for numerous positive impacts such as the improvement of destinations economies (Gursoy & Rutherford, 2004; Lepp, 2007; Perdue, Long, & Allen, 1990), and favours the creation of new businesses as a great source for direct foreign investment opportunities (Akis, Peristianis, & Warner, 1996; Almeida García, Balbuena Vázquez, & Cortés Macías, 2015; Dyer et al., 2007; Ribeiro et al., 2017). Tourism is also responsible for generating income for local communities and governments (Ribeiro et al., 2017), and is likely to stimulate new investments and foster improvements to destination superstructure and infrastructure (Andereck et al., 2005; Andereck & Vogt, 2000; Belisle & Hoy, 1980; Ribeiro et al., 2013; Yoon et al., 2001). Such development may also result in improvements in local residents' quality-of-life and satisfaction with life (Kim et al., 2013; Woo et al., 2015; Woosnam, Maruyama, Ribeiro, & Joo, 2019). Tourism is also referenced as providing great opportunities to foster host-guest encounters and cultural exchanges (Dyer et al., 2007;

Ribeiro et al., 2017; Woosnam, 2011), enhance host community pride and cultural identity (Andereck et al., 2005; Besculides, Lee, & McCormick, 2002), and help in the preservation of local culture, heritage and natural resources (Akis et al., 1996; Andereck & Nyaupane, 2011; Stronza & Gordillo, 2008).

Although tourism has numerous benefits, its costs to local communities are evident and well documented within the current literature (Ribeiro et al., 2017, 2013). Tourism is often cited as contributing to an increased cost of living for local residents (Liu & Var, 1986; Long, Perdue, & Allen, 1990), economic dependence on the industry (Boissevain, 1979; Mathieson & Wall, 1982), and economic leakage (Pratt, 2015). Several studies show that local residents also recognise tourism has the negative potential to increase delinquency, vandalism and theft (Andereck et al., 2005; Belisle & Hoy, 1980), while also making it easier for residents to be less hospitable towards guests (Liu & Var, 1986). Similarly, tourism can also be responsible for increases in litter and noise pollution (Dyer et al., 2007; McGehee & Andereck, 2004), commodification of local cultures (Akis et al., 1996), and damage to natural and physical resources upon which tourism relies (Ribeiro et al., 2017).

The current literature related to this topic includes many studies which examine and discuss effects of residents' attitudes surrounding benefits and costs of trust in political institutions and support for tourism development (Boley et al., 2014; Gursoy & Rutherford, 2004; Nunkoo & Gursoy, 2012; Ribeiro et al., 2017). Also, considering the political economy, a government that is responsible for its citizens is crucial (Nunkoo, 2015). From this perspective, it is commonly accepted that citizens acknowledge that the government is responsible for tourism planning and making decisions concerning tourism policy (Gursoy et al., 2017; Nunkoo, Ribeiro, Sunnassee, & Gursoy, 2018). Residents see the government as being responsible for the design of tourism policies that increase benefits and decrease the costs for local communities, and in return, the government receives trust from citizens who are satisfied with these policies and disagreement from the dissatisfied ones (Nunkoo, 2015). Rooted in the theoretical underpinnings of SET and the political economy theory, residents who perceive the benefits of tourism tend to trust government and support tourism development of tourism while others are prone to distrust the government and oppose tourism development if they consider that costs outweigh the benefits generated from tourism (Nunkoo & Gursoy, 2012; Ribeiro et al., 2013). Based on the above discussion, the following hypotheses are proposed:

H2: Residents' perceived benefits of tourism positively influence their political trust in tourism institutions.
H3: Residents' perceived benefits of tourism positively influence their support for tourism development.
H4: Residents' perceived costs of tourism negatively influence their political trust in tourism institution.
H5: Residents' perceived costs of tourism negatively influence their support for tourism development.

The state of the local economy, tourism development and political trust in tourism institutions

Some island developing states with scarce natural resources (Twining-Ward & Butler, 2002) face several challenges related to economic development and see tourism as a catalyst for development (Sinclair-Maragh & Gursoy, 2015). This is especially true where jobs are scarce and unemployment rates are high—tourism can be attractive as a means of creating jobs in a burgeoning sector of the economy. As research has revealed concerning island economies, tourism contributes to infrastructure development, direct foreign investments, the balance of payment, and potentially, rejuvenated local economies (Látková & Vogt, 2012; Vargas-Sánchez, Plaza-Mejía, & Porras-Bueno, 2009). Thus, the literature on residents' attitudes of tourism shows how locals perceive the state of the local economy has great implications for how they discern positive and negative impacts of tourism development (Gursoy et al., 2010; Gursoy & Rutherford, 2004; Stylidis & Terzidou, 2014). Thus, in support of the SET, multiple studies (including Dyer et al., 2007) have found a strong relationship between the perceived state of the local economy and residents' support for tourism development. That being said, however, residents in many developing regions are eager to gain increased wages as a result of tourism, so they tend to underestimate associated costs and overestimate economic benefits generated by tourism development (Gursoy et al., 2002; Liu & Var, 1986). As Var, Kendall and Tarakcioglu (1985) observed, residents "are willing to put up with some inconvenience in exchange for tourist money" (p. 654). Of course, this is where the trust in tourism institutions comes into play, where residents will expect government entities to have their best interests in mind so as to help mitigate potential costs they may experience. According to Stylidis and Terzidou (2014) in depressed economies with high unemployment rates, residents that are more concerned about the perceived state of the local economy will tend to have more positive attitudes about tourism impacts, and ultimately, be stronger supporters of the industry. In destinations like Cape Verde (where employment opportunities are limited in other industries), residents tend to maximise economic benefits generated by tourism development and minimise associated costs. Given the above discussion, the following hypotheses are advanced:

H6: Residents' perceptions of the state of the local economy positively influence their perceived benefits of tourism.

H7: Residents' perceptions of the state of the local economy negatively influence their perceived costs of tourism development.

H8: Residents' perceptions of the state of the local economy positively influence their political trust in tourism institutions.

H9: Residents' perceptions of the state of the local economy positively influence their support for tourism development.

Personal economic benefits of tourism, tourism development and political trust in tourism institutions

In many developing regions and local areas, if an economy is struggling, tourism can be viewed as a panacea bringing about much-welcomed opportunities for personal economic benefit (Wang & Pfister, 2008). As such, a host of studies have demonstrated a significant relationship between residents' perceived personal economic benefits from tourism and their attitudes regarding tourism impacts. Within the tourism literature, some studies conclude that residents who financially benefit from tourism tend to have more favourable attitudes of the impacts than those who receive lesser or no benefits (e.g. Boley et al., 2014; McGehee & Andereck, 2004; Nunkoo & So, 2016; Perdue et al., 1990; Vargas-Sánchez, Valle, Mendes, & Silva, 2015). It was Boley et al. (2014), Ko and Steward (2002), and McGehee and Andereck (2004) that each found perceived personal economic benefits from tourism to be the most salient construct in explaining residents' support for tourism development (Boley et al., 2014; Ko & Stewart, 2002; McGehee & Andereck, 2004). Not surprisingly, such finding is supported by logic of the SET, demonstrating that residents who financially benefit from tourism are likely to be the most supportive of tourism and its accompanying development (Ap, 1992; Perdue et al., 1990). However, somewhat contrary to this, Boley et al. (2014) and Vargas-Sánchez et al. (2015) each found the relationship between perceived personal economic benefit and perceived positive/negative impacts of tourism to be insignificant. The authors further found the relationship between perceived personal economic benefit and support for tourism development to be significant and positive. Other studies have demonstrated the inconclusiveness between the constructs, revealing the relationship between perceived economic benefits and the negative impact of tourism was not significant, despite the relationship with positive impact being positive and significant (Andereck et al., 2005; Ko & Stewart, 2002; Vargas-Sánchez et al., 2009). Stylidis and Terzidou (2014) contend that such inconsistencies may be due to the classification of tourism impacts which recent studies have adopted. Therefore, based on tenets of the SET and the above discussion, the following hypotheses are proposed:

H10: Residents' perceived personal economic benefits from tourism positively influence their perceived benefits of tourism development.

H11: Residents' perceived personal economic benefits from tourism negatively influence their perceived costs from tourism development.

H12: Residents' perceived personal economic benefits from tourism positively influence their political trust in tourism institutions.

H13: Residents' perceived personal economic benefits from tourism positively influence their support for tourism development.

Figure 14.1 illustrates the hypothesised model of this study.

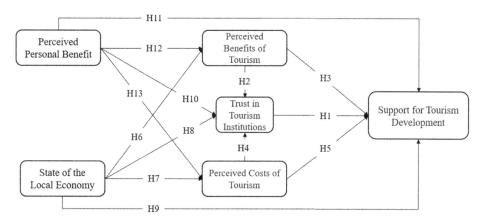

Figure 14.1 Hypothesised model of resident's perceptions, trust and support for tourism development

Source: Author.

Methodology

Study setting

The Republic of Cape Verde is a small island developing state (SIDS) with ten islands (Santo Antão, São Vicente, Santa Luzia, São Nicolau, Sal, Boa Vista, Maio, Santiago, Fogo and Brava) located in the Atlantic Ocean, roughly 550 km off the coast of Western Africa. The Archipelago was discovered and colonised by the Portuguese in 1460–1462 and became a useful point in the Atlantic slave trade to the Caribbean and America. The islands were first populated by European settlers and African slaves in late 1400 and remained a Portuguese Colony until 1975. Recurrent droughts over the second half of the 20th century have brought on massive emigration to the United States, São Tome and Principe, Portugal, France and Angola. For this reason, Cape Verdeans living abroad outnumber those residents living on-island (Åkesson, 2011; Carling, 2014). Currently, the country has an estimated population of 550,000 people across the nine inhabited islands (National Institute of Statistics [NIS], 2019). The white and black sandy beaches, volcanic mountains, and diverse flora and fauna make Cape Verde an attractive and exotic destination for visitors interested in relaxing, arts, culture, and different sports. The economy of Cape Verde is service-oriented, accounting for more than 75% of GDP, with tourism being responsible for 65% of the sector (Bank of Cape Verde, 2019).

Throughout the last 20 years, Cape Verde has received a significant number of international tourists, growing from 145,000 arrivals in 2000 to 765,696 in 2018 (NIS, 2019). Traditionally, tourists are mainly from European countries, such as the United Kingdom (22.7%), Germany (11.8%), France (10.1%), Netherlands/Belgium (10.0%), Portugal (9.3%) and Italy (4.0%) (NIS, 2019). Throughout the years, several Governments of Cape Verde have invested heavily in tourism building infrastructures like roads, international airports (on the islands of Santiago, Boa Vista and more recently, in São Vicente), ports for cruise ships and transport. On the other hand, large hotels and resorts have been built mainly on the islands of Sal and Boa Vista, driven mostly by foreign investors to stimulate tourism. The tourism industry is heavily concentrated within these two islands having welcomed 76.4% of the international tourists in 2018 (NIS, 2019). However, the island of Sal continues to be the preferred destination for international tourists, representing 49.5% of international tourists' arrival and 56% of overnight stays.

Tourism industry is considered as a strategic pillar for the economic and social development of Cape Verde. Tourism is representing major dynamism in terms of economic and social growth by promoting employment and generating income for both residents and the Government. In this sense, the contribution of tourism to the GDP is approximately 22.0% and accounting to 20.1% of employment (Bank of Cape Verde, 2019). In doing so, designing a political policy and strategy to better plan tourism industry in Cape Verde is paramount. Given the importance of tourism for Cape Verdean socioeconomic growth and development, tourism has a dedicated minster responsible for the tourism policy and planning.

Questionnaire design and data collection procedures

Data were collected using a survey design following the recommendations proposed by Churchill (1979) and DeVellis (2012) in developing a reliable instrument. The items were originally developed in English and were translated to Portuguese and then back-translated into English by the researchers. A bilingual speaker (English and Portuguese) then reviewed the translation to guarantee that the translated version reproduced the meanings and content of the original items, following the guidelines recommended by Brislin (1970). A pilot test was conducted on the island of Boa Vista, Cape Verde with 50 participants to assess the validity of the items that were identified from the existing literature.

All items used to measure each factor were adapted from the literature: perceived state of the local economy, perceived personal economic benefits, perceived benefits, perceived costs, trust in tourism institutions, and residents' support for tourism development. Perceived state of the local economy was measured using four items adopted from Choi and Sirakaya (2005), Gursoy, Jurowski, and Uysal (2002), and Gursoy et al. (2010). The construct, perceived personal economic benefits from tourism, was captured through four items adopted from Perdue et al. (1990), McGehee and Andereck (2004), Lindberg and Johnson (1997) and Wang and Pfister (2008).

Perceived benefits and costs of tourism development were each measured by six items adopted from Ribeiro et al. (2013), Gursoy et al. (2002) and Choi and Sirakaya (2005). The construct, trust in tourism institutions was assessed through five items, asking respondents about their level of trust in tourism institutions in Cape Verde. These items were adopted from Nunkoo and Ramkissoon (2012) and Nunkoo (2015). Finally, residents' support for tourism development was assessed by five items, asking respondents about their willingness to support tourism development in Cape Verde. These items were adopted from Nunkoo and Gursoy (2012) and Nunkoo and Ramkissoon (2011). Items used to measure the perceived state of the local economy, perceived personal economic benefits, perception of benefits and costs of tourism and support for tourism development were rated on a five-point Likert-type scale, where 1 = strongly disagree and 5 = strongly agree. The items used to measure residents' perceived trust in tourism institutions were rated on a five-point Likert scale, ranging from 1 = do not trust at all to 5 = trust entirely. In addition, general sociodemographic variables were also included in the instrument to better profile sample respondents.

Results

Demographic profile

The sample profile can be found in Table 14.1. Respondents were split across gender with a great proportion falling between the ages of 18 and 39 (72.7%) and 40 and 64 (23%), married or living with a partner (48.3%), with a secondary education (67.5%) and having some qualification/training in tourism (23.2%). Over half of the participants (51.9%) were either born on other islands or abroad. Nearly 60% of respondents had daily or nearly daily contact with tourists. The sample was split evenly across tourism-related professions, with 49.1% of respondents working in the tourism industry.

Hypotheses testing

Regression analysis was used to test whether residents' perceived personal economic benefits from tourism and the perceived state of the local economy influence their support for tourism development, as well as the influence on perceptions of benefits and costs of tourism and trust in tourism institutions. As presented in Table 14.2, residents' perceived trust in tourism institution, perceived benefits and perceived costs significantly predicted their levels of support for tourism development. Results indicated a significant and positive effect of residents' trust in tourism institutions and support ($\beta = 0.663$, $p < 0.001$), perceived benefits on trust ($\beta = 0.402$, $p < 0.001$) and on support ($\beta = 0.208$, $p < 0.001$) lending support to H1, H2 and H3.

Table 14.1 Sociodemographic profile of the respondents

Demographic	n	%
Gender (n = 418)		
Male	208	49.7
Female	210	50.3
Island of residence		
Boa Vista	200	47.8
Sal	218	52.2
Age (=418, M = 32.3 years of age)		
Young (≤39)	304	72.7
Middle age (40–64)	96	23.0
Old (≥65)	18	4.3
Marital status		
Married/Living with a partner	202	48.3
Single	197	47.1
Divorced/Separated	15	3.6
Widowed	4	1.0
Education (n = 418, median = Secondary Education)		
Elementary education	64	15.3
Secondary education	282	67.5
Higher education	72	17.3
Training/Qualification in tourism (n = 418)		
Yes	97	23.2
No	321	76.8
Job (n = 415)		
Tourism-related job	207	49.1
No tourism-related job	208	50.9
Place of birth (n = 418)		
The same island	201	48.1
Other islands	196	46.9
Abroad	21	5.0
Reasons for change (n = 214)		
Professional	167	78.0
Family	28	13.2
Personal	11	5.1
Educational	8	3.7

Source: Authors.

The negative effect of perceived cost on trust was found to be insignificant ($\beta = -0.060$, $p > 0.05$) rejecting H4. Conversely, the negative effect of perceived cost on support ($\beta = -0.091$, $p < 0.05$) was significant, supporting H5. Additionally, findings indicated a significant positive effect of the state of the local economy on perceived benefits ($\beta = 0.108$, $p < 0.05$), a significant negative effect on perceived cost ($\beta = -0.115$, $p < 0.05$), on support ($\beta = 0.080$, $p < 0.05$) and an insignificant effect on trust ($\beta = 0.065$, $p > 0.05$). These results provided

Table 14.2 Regression analyses

Dependent Variables	Independent Variables	Std. Beta	t-values	Hypotheses
Perceived benefit	Personal economic benefit	0.452***	10.276	H12: (S)
	State of the local economy	0.108*	2.456	H6: (S)
	R^2	0.237	$F_{(2-415)} = 64.354$, $p = 0.000$	
Perceived cost	Personal economic benefit	−0.270***	−5.656	H13: (S)
	State of the local economy	−0.115*	−2.401	H7: (S)
	R^2	0.099	$F_{(2-415)} = 32.918$, $p = 0.000$	
Trust in tourism institutions	Personal economic benefit	0.126**	2.771	H10: (S)
	State of the local economy	0.065^{ns}	1.323	H8: (R)
	Perceived benefit	0.402***	8.858	H2: (S)
	Perceived cost	−0.060^{ns}	−1.213	H4: (R)
	R^2	0.126	$F_{(4-413)} = 33.507$, $p = 0.000$	
Support for tourism development	Personal economic benefit	0.096**	2.956	H11: (S)
	State of the local economy	0.080*	2.291	H9: (S)
	Perceived benefit	0.208***	5.925	H3: (S)
	Perceived cost	−0.091*	−2.585	H5: (S)
	Trust	0.633***	18.141	H1: (S)
	R^2	0.621	$F_{(5-412)} = 135.291$, $p = 0.000$	

*$p < 0.05$; **$p < 0.01$; ***$p < 0.001$.
ns = Not significant; R^2 = Variance explained.

Source: Authors.

support for H6, H7, H9, though not H8. Moreover, results revealed that the perceived personal economic benefits are a significant predictor of support ($\beta = 0.096$, $p < 0.01$), trust in tourism institutions ($\beta = 0.126$, $p < 0.01$), perceived benefits ($\beta = 0.452$, $p < 0.001$) and negatively predicted perceived costs ($\beta = −0.270$, $p < 0.001$). These results provided support for H10, H11, H12 and H13. Overall, 62% of the variance in support for tourism development was explained through the model antecedents.

Conclusions and implications

In seeking to understand attitudes and support for tourism development, a model was conceptualised and empirically tested among Cape Verdean residents. This study has provided findings able to enhance the comprehension of residents' attitudes and support to tourism development considering the political economy of tourism. Specifically, the findings and subsequent discussion provide evidence for the need to challenge existing knowledge to advance theoretical understanding.

As in most studies concerning residents' attitudes, the prevailing theory used was the social exchange theory (SET). A central tenet of SET is that residents will evaluate tourism based upon the costs and benefits incurred to them from tourism (Ap, 1992; McGehee & Andereck, 2004; Nunkoo & Gursoy, 2012). While SET is the main theory within resident attitude research, the literature review revealed criticism aimed at SET for straying away from its original interpretation focusing on the benefits and costs associated with tourism towards more of an emphasis on the economic exchange between residents and tourists (Woosnam, Norman, & Ying, 2009). Other studies suggest that SET is too simplistic in its explanation of residents' attitudes towards tourism and that additional theories need to be incorporated to explain the complexity of attitudes towards tourism (Boley et al., 2014; Látková & Vogt, 2012; Nunkoo & Gursoy, 2016; Nunkoo & So, 2016; Ward & Berno, 2011). Moreover, some researchers find SET to focus much on the economic dimensions of an exchange process, undermining other intangible factors that may influence social relationships (Woosnam et al., 2009). Hence, there have been calls from researchers to study residents' attitudes and support from more than one theoretical perspective in an effort to address limitations of SET (Látková & Vogt, 2012; Nunkoo & Smith, 2013). Consequently, there is a need for studies that not only make a comprehensive use of SET, by considering its core variables such as attitudes but also integrate other less-studied variables such as trust to enhance its theoretical perspective. With this shortcoming in mind, this study included trust as a component of SET to shape residents' support for tourism development, making another contribution to the literature.

Economic variables (perceived economic benefits and the perceived state of the local economy) are among those that influence perceptions about tourism impacts the most, as demonstrated in several other studies (i.e. Nunkoo & So, 2016; Ribeiro et al., 2017). Therefore, these studies postulated that if an individual perceives personal and community economic benefits from tourism it will influence their perception about tourism and consequently support tourism development. In line with SET, residents are likely to support tourism development as long as they believe that its benefits outweigh the costs. However, in some developing countries, residents are likely to permit some negative impacts of tourism if they believe they will get rewards resulting from tourism development (Ribeiro et al., 2017; Teye, Sönmez, & Sirakaya, 2002), such as pollution, traffic congestions, and queues. Other studies conclude that residents who demonstrate a positive attitude about tourism are likely to trust tourism institutions (Nunkoo, 2015) and be more supportive of tourism through the preservation of natural resources upon which tourism depends (Dyer et al., 2007; Lepp, 2007) and develop pleasant interactions with community guests (Valle et al., 2011). This study makes another contribution to the literature since the above-mentioned items were fragmented in previous studies and have never been analysed in a single construct to measure residents' support for tourism development behaviour in developing island countries. Overall, the premise that residents with positive attitudes towards tourism will foster supportive tourism development behaviour was confirmed by this study.

Practical implications

Lankford and Howard (1994, p. 133) describe resident attitudes about tourism as being a "complex and dynamic phenomenon in which a variety of factors exert a differential influence on local residents". Through a more complete understanding of the economic and non-economic factors affecting resident attitudes and support to tourism development, tourism planners, decision-makers and destination managers can work more efficiently to include the voices of local residents into the tourism planning strategy and assure that tourism is developed for and by residents. In addition, it has been shown that residents are key stakeholders in the success or failure of tourism within a destination (Belisle & Hoy, 1980; Gursoy & Rutherford, 2004). Further, this research on residents' attitudes will shed light on how economic factors influence trust in tourism institutions, their perception about the costs and benefits, and support for tourism development. Understanding how residents perceive the economic factors of tourism has the potential to make tourism more successful because of its implications for increasing residents' support for tourism development.

Understanding residents trust in tourism institutions (Government, Minister of Tourism, General Tourism Directorate) is important for policymakers and DMOs to better design tourism policy and tourism strategies. Thus, according to political economy, citizens' trust in their institutions responsible for tourism management is crucial for good governance and sustainability of the industry. The findings of this study showed that residents' perceptions of personal economic benefits derived from tourism and the state of the local economy are important predictors of their trust in tourism institutions and their level of support for tourism development in Cape Verde islands. Supporting this line of reasoning, it is fundamental for the tourism institutions to work efficiently to guarantee that the benefits of tourism development will result in sustainable community development. However, there is some evidence in Cape Verde, mainly on the island of Boa Vista where the political process of tourism development has demonstrated an imbalanced distribution of benefits and created some socioeconomic problems concerning access to decent accommodations, health system, education and safety among residents who work within the tourism industry. These socioeconomic problems may hinder the benefits and outweigh the costs of tourism that will result in citizens' mistrust in tourism institutions. Tourism institutions, particularly the government and local authorities, must work together in an effort to efficiently mitigate the costs of tourism, by providing land for housing construction, improving the health and education system and providing greater security on the island to help residents feel that they are benefiting from tourism development. Such strategies will enhance residents' trust in tourism institutions, as well as their level of support for tourism development.

Study limitation and future study direction

As with all types of research, this study has limitations and as such, the results should be interpreted in light of these limitations. The first of these is the methodological decision to investigate the research objectives of this study solely using a quantitative approach rather than either a qualitative or mixed methods approach.

Second, the hypotheses and the proposed theoretical model was assessed using data gathered only from two Cape Verdean islands–Boa Vista and Sal. Since Cape Verde comprises nine inhabited islands and the data were collected in only two of them, results may not be widespread to residents who are living on other islands. Additionally, findings may indicate the particular conditions on these two islands where the core touristic product is sun-and-sea and offered mostly under the all-inclusive system (López-Guzmán, Orgaz-Agüera, Martín, & Ribeiro, 2016; López-Guzmán, Ribeiro, Orgüera-Orgaz, & Martín, 2015; Ribeiro, 2016), which is quite different from the other islands. Therefore, the findings reflect residents' attitudes about tourism development from these two islands that might further restrict their extrapolation to other islands. Another limitation is that the data were gathered from individuals in the most popular and crowded places on these two islands such as squares, terraces, cafes, shops, offices. However, this approach may not guarantee that all local residents had the opportunity to be involved in the study. Consequently, findings are not appropriate to be used outside the study context. Replication of this research on different islands and destinations with a similar context might still need to check the validity of the results stated here. Thus, these two islands were chosen because of their higher level of tourism development where tourism is the main economic activity and many residents are largely employed within the tourism sector. This can impede the extrapolation of findings to other less touristic islands within Cape Verde. In fact, the low levels of tourism development on other islands may impede some constructs such us perceived personal economic benefits from tourism and the perceived state of the local economy from being significantly related to perceptions of tourism impacts and support for tourism development. It is uncertain whether or not these lower levels of tourism development on other islands may play a factor in testing the proposed hypotheses.

This study utilised data that were collected during the summer time/high season (i.e. in August and September). As suggested in previous studies, while residents' attitudes and behaviours are likely to remain strong over time, individuals tend to become more worried about the costs of tourism over time (Gursoy et al., 2011). As this study did not examine the temporal effects, future research is certainly needed to analyse these proposed constructs with data collected in both low and high seasons because residents' attitudes and behaviours towards tourism are found to be influenced by seasonality (Vargas-Sánchez et al., 2014). Thus, future studies should consider other variables such as place attachment (Eusébio, Vieira, & Lima, 2018; Strzelecka, Boley, & Woosnam, 2017), life satisfaction (Woo et al., 2015) and empowerment (Boley & McGehee, 2014; Boley et al., 2014; Strzelecka et al., 2017) as a predictor of resident trust in tourism institutions and support for tourism development. Moreover, future studies should also consider possible moderator factors, such as residents with tourism-related jobs and non-tourism related jobs to better understand if these relationships vary across groups with different employment statuses.

References

Åkesson, L. (2011). Remittances and relationships: Exchange in Cape Verdean transnational families. *Ethnos, 76*(3), 326–347.

Akis, S., Peristianis, N., & Warner, J. (1996). Residents' attitudes to tourism development: The case of Cyprus. *Tourism Management, 17*(7), 481–494.

Alegre, J., & Cladera, M. (2009). Analysing the effect of satisfaction and previous visits on tourist intentions to return. *European Journal of Marketing, 43*(5/6), 670–685.

Almeida García, F., Balbuena Vázquez, A., & Cortés Macías, R. (2015). Resident's attitudes towards the impacts of tourism. *Tourism Management Perspectives, 13*(0), 33–40.

Andereck K.L., Nyaupane G. 2011. Development of a Tourism and Quality-of-Life Instrument. In: Budruk M., Phillips R. (eds) *Quality-of-Life Community Indicators for Parks, Recreation and Tourism Management*. Social Indicators Research Series, vol 43. Springer, Dordrecht.

Andereck, K. L., Valentine, K. M., Knopf, R. C., & Vogt, C. A. (2005). Residents' perceptions of community tourism impacts. *Annals of Tourism Research, 32*(4), 1056–1076.

Andereck, K. L., & Vogt, C. A. (2000). The relationship between residents' attitudes toward tourism and tourism development options. *Journal of Travel Research, 39*(1), 27–36.

Ap, J. (1992). Residents' perceptions on tourism impacts. *Annals of Tourism Research, 19*(4), 665–690.

Baldacchino, G., & Bertram, G. (2009). The beak of the finch: Insights into the economic development of small economies. *The Round Table, 98*(401), 141–160.

Bank of Cape Verde. (2019). *Relatórios do Conselho de Administração. Relatório e Contas 2018*. City of Praia: Bank of Cape Verde.

Belisle, F. J., & Hoy, D. R. (1980). The perceived impact of tourism by residents a case study in Santa Marta, Colombia. *Annals of Tourism Research, 7*(1), 83–101.

Besculides, A., Lee, M. E., & McCormick, P. J. (2002). Residents' perceptions of the cultural benefits of tourism. *Annals of Tourism Research, 29*(2), 303–319.

Bianchi, R. (2009). The 'critical turn' in tourism studies: A radical critique. *Tourism Geographies, 11*(4), 484–504.

Bianchi, R. (2018). The political economy of tourism development: A critical review. *Annals of Tourism Research, 70*, 88–102.

Bimonte, S., & Faralla, V. (2016). Does residents' perceived life satisfaction vary with tourist season? A two-step survey in a Mediterranean destination. *Tourism Management, 55*, 199–208.

Boissevain, J. (1979). The impact of tourism on a dependent island: Gozo, Malta. *Annals of Tourism Research, 6*(1), 76–90.

Boley, B. B., & McGehee, N. G. (2014). Measuring empowerment: Developing and validating the Resident Empowerment through Tourism Scale (RETS). *Tourism Management, 45*(0), 85–94.

Boley, B. B., McGehee, N. G., Perdue, R. R., & Long, P. (2014). Empowerment and resident attitudes toward tourism: Strengthening the theoretical foundation through a Weberian lens. *Annals of Tourism Research, 49*(1), 33–50.

Bouckaert, G., & van de Walle, S. (2003). Comparing measures of citizen trust and user satisfaction as indicators of 'good governance': Difficulties in linking trust and satisfaction indicators. *International Review of Administrative Sciences, 69*(3), 329–343.

Bramwell, B. (2011). Governance, the state and sustainable tourism: A political economy approach. *Journal of Sustainable Tourism, 19*(4–5), 459–477.

Brislin, R. W. (1970). Back-translation for cross-cultural research. *Journal of Cross-Cultural Psychology, 1*(3), 185–216.

Brown, D. O. (1998). In search of an appropriate form of tourism for Africa: Lessons from the past and suggestions for the future. *Tourism Management, 19*(3), 237–245.

Carling, J. (2014). Scripting remittances: Making sense of money transfers in transnational relationships. *International Migration Review, 48*, S218–S262.

Choi, H. S. C., & Sirakaya, E. (2005). Measuring residents' attitude toward sustainable tourism: Development of sustainable tourism attitude scale. *Journal of Travel Research, 43*(4), 380–394.

Churchill, G. A. (1979). A paradigm for developing better measures of marketing constructs. *Journal of Marketing Research, 16*(1), 64–73.

DeVellis, R. F. (2012). *Scale development: Theory and applications* (3rd ed.). Thousand Oaks: Sage publications.

Dredge, D., & Jamal, T. (2015). Progress in tourism planning and policy: A post-structural perspective on knowledge production. *Tourism Management, 51*, 285–297.

Dyer, P., Gursoy, D., Sharma, B., & Carter, J. (2007). Structural modeling of resident perceptions of tourism and associated development on the Sunshine Coast, Australia. *Tourism Management, 28*(2), 409–422.

Eusébio, C., Vieira, A. L., & Lima, S. (2018). Place attachment, host–tourist interactions, and residents' attitudes towards tourism development: The case of Boa Vista Island in Cape Verde. *Journal of Sustainable Tourism, 26*(6), 890–909.

Fredline, E., & Faulkner, B. (2000). Host community reactions: A cluster analysis. *Annals of Tourism Research, 27*(3), 763–784.

Gursoy, D., Chi, C. G., Ai, J., & Chen, B. T. (2011). Temporal change in resident perceptions of a mega-event: The Beijing 2008 Olympic Games. *Tourism Geographies, 13*(2), 299–324.

Gursoy, D., Chi, C. G., & Dyer, P. (2010). Locals' Attitudes toward mass and alternative tourism: The case of sunshine coast, Australia. *Journal of Travel Research, 49*(3), 381–394.

Gursoy, D., Jurowski, C., & Uysal, M. (2002). Resident attitudes - A structural modeling approach. *Annals of Tourism Research, 29*(1), 79–105.

Gursoy, D., & Rutherford, D. G. (2004). Host attitudes toward tourism: An improved structural model. *Annals of Tourism Research, 31*(3), 495–516.

Gursoy, D., Yolal, M., Ribeiro, M. A., & Panosso Netto, A. (2017). Impact of trust on local residents' mega-event perceptions and their support. *Journal of Travel Research, 56*(3), 393–406.

Harrill, R. (2004). Residents' attitudes toward tourism development: A literature review with implications for tourism planning. *Journal of Planning Literature, 18*(3), 251–266.

Harrill, R., Uysal, M., Cardon, P. W., Vong, F., & Dioko, L. (2011). Resident attitudes towards gaming and tourism development in Macao: Growth machine theory as a context for identifying supporters and opponents. *International Journal of Tourism Research, 13*(1), 41–53.

Ioannides, D., & Holcomb, B. (2003). Misguided policy initiatives in small-island destinations: Why do up-market tourism policies fail? *Tourism Geographies, 5*(1), 39–48.

Jenkins, C. L. (1991). Tourism development strategies. In L. J. Lickorich, A. Jefferson, J. Bodlender, & C. L. Jenkins (Eds.), *Developing tourism destination: Policies and perspectives* (pp. 61–78). London: Longman.

Kim, K., Uysal, M., & Sirgy, M. J. (2013). How does tourism in a community impact the quality of life of community residents? *Tourism Management, 36*, 527–540.

Ko, D.-W., & Stewart, W. P. (2002). A structural equation model of residents' attitudes for tourism development. *Tourism Management, 23*(5), 521–530.

Lankford, S. V., & Howard, D. R. (1994). Developing a tourism impact attitude scale. *Annals of Tourism Research,* 21(1), 121–139.

Látková, P., & Vogt, C. A. (2012). Residents' attitudes toward existing and future tourism development in rural communities. *Journal of Travel Research, 51*(1), 50–67.

Lepp, A. (2007). Residents' attitudes towards tourism in Bigodi village, Uganda. *Tourism Management, 28*(3), 876–885.

Lepp, A. (2008). Tourism and dependency: An analysis of Bigodi village, Uganda. *Tourism Management, 29*(6), 1206–1214.

Lee, T. H. (2013). Influence analysis of community resident support for sustainable tourism development. *Tourism Management, 34*(1), 37–46.

Lindberg, K., & Johnson, R. L. (1997). Modeling resident attitudes toward tourism. *Annals of Tourism Research,* 24(2), 402–424.

Liu, J. C., & Var, T. (1986). Resident attitudes toward tourism impacts in Hawaii. *Annals of Tourism Research,* 13(2), 193–214.

Long, P. T., Perdue, R. R., & Allen, L. (1990). Rural resident tourism perceptions and attitudes by community level of tourism. *Journal of Travel Research, 28*(3), 3–9.

López-Guzmán, T., Orgaz-Agüera, F., Martín, J. A. M., & Ribeiro, M. A. (2016). The all-inclusive tourism system in Cape Verde islands: The tourists' perspective. *Journal of Hospitality and Tourism Management, 29*, 9–16.

López-Guzmán, T., Ribeiro, M. A., Orgüera-Orgaz, F., & Martín, J. A. M. (2015). El turismo en Cabo Verde: Perfil y valoración del viajero. *Estudios y Perspectivas en Turismo, 24*(3), 512–524.

Mathieson, A., & Wall, G. (1982). *Tourism: Economic, physical and social impacts.* London: Longman.

McElroy, J. L., & Hamma, P. E. (2010). SITEs revisited: Socioeconomic and demographic contours of small island tourist economies. *Asia Pacific Viewpoint, 51*(1), 36–46.

McGehee, N. G., & Andereck, K. L. (2004). Factors predicting rural residents' support of tourism. *Journal of Travel Research, 43*(2), 131–140.

Mosedale, J. (2011). *Political economy of tourism: A critical perspective.* London: Routledge.

National Institute of Statistics [NIS]. (2019). *Análise dos principais resultados – movimentação de hóspedes em Cabo Verde em 2018.* City of Praia: National Institute of Statistics.

Nunkoo, R. (2015). Tourism development and trust in local government. *Tourism Management, 46*(0), 623–634.

Nunkoo, R. (2016). Toward a more comprehensive use of social exchange theory to study residents' attitudes to tourism. *Procedia Economics and Finance, 39*, 588–596.

Nunkoo, R., & Gursoy, D. (2012). Residents' support for tourism: An identity perspective. *Annals of Tourism Research, 39*(1), 243–268.

Nunkoo, R., & Gursoy, D. (2016). Political trust and residents' support for alternative and mass tourism: An improved structural model. *Tourism Geographies, 19*(3), 318–339.

Nunkoo, R., & Ramkissoon, H. (2011). Developing a community support model for tourism. *Annals of Tourism Research, 38*(3), 964–988.

Nunkoo, R., & Ramkissoon, H. (2012). Power, trust, social exchange and community support. *Annals of Tourism Research, 39*(2), 997–1023.

Nunkoo, R., Ribeiro, M. A., Sunnassee, V., & Gursoy, D. (2018). Public trust in mega event planning institutions: The role of knowledge, transparency and corruption. *Tourism Management, 66*, 155–166.

Nunkoo, R., & Smith, S. L. J. (2013). Political economy of tourism: Trust in government actors, political support, and their determinants. *Tourism Management, 36*(0), 120–132.

Nunkoo, R., Smith, S. L. J., & Ramkissoon, H. (2013). Residents' attitudes to tourism: A longitudinal study of 140 articles from 1984 to 2010. *Journal of Sustainable Tourism, 21*(1), 5–25.

Nunkoo, R., & So, K. K. F. (2016). Residents' support for tourism: Testing alternative structural models. *Journal of Travel Research, 57*(7), 847–861.

Okazaki, E. (2008). A community-based tourism model: Its conception and use. *Journal of Sustainable Tourism, 16*(5), 511–529.

Oppermann, M., & Chon, K.-S. (1997). *Tourism in developing countries.* London: International Thomson Business Press.

Perdue, R. R., Long, P. T., & Allen, L. (1990). Resident support for tourism development. *Annals of Tourism Research, 17*(4), 586–599.

Pratt, S. (2015). The economic impact of tourism in SIDS. *Annals of Tourism Research, 52*(0), 148–160.

Ribeiro, M. A. (2016). Cape Verde, tourism. In J. Jafari & H. Xiao (Eds.), *Encyclopedia of tourism* (pp. 1–2). Cham: Springer International Publishing.

Ribeiro, M. A., Pinto, P., Silva, J. A., & Woosnam, K. M. (2017). Residents' attitudes and the adoption of pro-tourism behaviours: The case of developing island countries. *Tourism Management, 61*, 523–537.

Ribeiro, M. A., Pinto, P., Silva, J. A., & Woosnam, K. M. (2018). Examining the predictive validity of SUS-TAS with maximum parsimony in developing island countries. *Journal of Sustainable Tourism, 26*(3), 379–398.

Ribeiro, M. A., Valle, P. O., & Silva, J. A. (2013). Residents' attitudes towards tourism development in Cape Verde Islands. *Tourism Geographies, 15*(4), 654–679.

Ribeiro, M. A., Woosnam, K. M., Pinto, P., & Silva, J. A. (2018). Tourists' destination loyalty through emotional solidarity with residents: An integrative moderated mediation model. *Journal of Travel Research, 57*(3), 279–295.

Sharpley, R. (2014). Host perceptions of tourism: A review of the research. *Tourism Management, 42*(0), 37–49.

Sheldon, P. J., & Abenoja, T. (2001). Resident attitudes in a mature destination: The case of Waikiki. *Tourism Management, 22*(5), 435–443.

Sinclair-Maragh, G. (2017). Demographic analysis of residents' support for tourism development in Jamaica. *Journal of Destination Marketing & Management, 6*(1), 5–12.

Sinclair-Maragh, G., & Gursoy, D. (2015). Imperialism and tourism: The case of developing island countries. *Annals of Tourism Research, 50*(0), 143–158.

Sirakaya, E., Teye, V., & Sönmez, S. (2002). Understanding residents' support for tourism development in the central region of Ghana. *Journal of Travel Research, 41*(1), 57–67.

Strzelecka, M., Boley, B. B., & Woosnam, K. M. (2017). Place attachment and empowerment: Do residents need to be attached to be empowered? *Annals of Tourism Research, 66*, 61–73.

Stronza, A., & Gordillo, J. (2008). Community views of ecotourism. *Annals of Tourism Research, 35*(2), 448–468.

Stylidis, D., & Terzidou, M. (2014). Tourism and the economic crisis in Kavala, Greece. *Annals of Tourism Research, 44*, 210–226.

Swarbrooke, J. (1993). Local authorities and destination marketing. *Insights, 5*, A15–A20.

Swarbrooke, J. (1999). *Sustainable tourism management.* Wallingford: CABI Pub.

Telfer, D. J., & Sharpley, R. (2008). *Tourism and development in the developing world.* London: Routledge.

Teye, V., F. Sönmez, S., & Sirakaya, E. (2002). Residents' attitudes toward tourism development. *Annals of Tourism Research, 29*(3), 668–688.

Tubb, K. N. (2003). An evaluation of the effectiveness of interpretation within Dartmoor National Park in reaching the goals of sustainable tourism development. *Journal of Sustainable Tourism, 11*(6), 476–498.

Twining-Ward, L., & Butler, R. (2002). Implementing STD on a small island: Development and use of sustainable tourism development indicators in Samoa. *Journal of Sustainable Tourism, 10*(5), 363–387.

Uysal, M., Sirgy, M. J., Woo, E., & Kim, H. (2016). Quality of life (QOL) and well-being research in tourism. *Tourism Management, 53*, 244–261.

Valle, P. O. D., Mendes, J., Guerreiro, M., & Silva, J. A. (2011). Can welcoming residents increase tourist satisfaction? *Anatolia, 22*(2), 260–277.

Var, T., Kendall, K. W., & Tarakcioglu, E. (1985). Resident attitudes towards tourists in a Turkish resort town. *Annals of Tourism Research, 12*(4), 652–658.

Vargas-Sánchez, A., Plaza-Mejía, M. Á., & Porras-Bueno, N. (2009). Understanding residents' attitudes toward the development of industrial tourism in a former mining community. *Journal of Travel Research, 47*(3), 373–387.

Vargas-Sánchez, A., Porras-Bueno, N., & Plaza-Mejía, M. Á. (2014). Residents' attitude to tourism and seasonality. *Journal of Travel Research, 53*(5), 581–596.

Vargas-Sánchez, A., Valle, P. O., Mendes, J. C., & Silva, J. A. (2015). Residents' attitude and level of destination development: An international comparison. *Tourism Management, 48*(0), 199–210.

Wang, Y., & Bramwell, B. (2012). Heritage protection and tourism development priorities in Hangzhou, China: A political economy and governance perspective. *Tourism Management, 33*(4), 988–998.

Wang, Y., & Pfister, R. E. (2008). Residents' attitudes toward tourism and perceived personal benefits in a rural community. *Journal of Travel Research, 47*(1), 84–93.

Ward, C., & Berno, T. (2011). Beyond social exchange theory: Attitudes toward tourists. *Annals of Tourism Research, 38*(4), 1556–1569.

Williams, S. (2004). *Tourism: Critical concepts in the social sciences.* London: Routledge.

Woo, E., Kim, H., & Uysal, M. (2015). Life satisfaction and support for tourism development. *Annals of Tourism Research, 50*, 84–97.

Woosnam, K. M. (2011). Comparing residents' and tourists' emotional solidarity with one another: An extension of Durkheim's model. *Journal of Travel Research, 50*(6), 615–626.

Woosnam, K. M., Maruyama, N. U., Ribeiro, M. A., & Joo, D. (2019). Explaining minority residents' attitudes of ethnic enclave tourism from general perceptions of tourism impacts. *Journal of Tourism and Cultural Change, 17*(4), 467–484.

Woosnam, K. M., & Norman, W. C. (2010). Measuring residents' emotional solidarity with tourists: Scale development of Durkheim's theoretical constructs. *Journal of Travel Research, 49*(3), 365–380.

Woosnam, K. M., Norman, W. C., & Ying, T. (2009). Exploring the theoretical framework of emotional solidarity between residents and tourists. *Journal of Travel Research, 48*(2), 245–258.

Yoon, Y., Gursoy, D., & Chen, J. S. (2001). Validating a tourism development theory with structural equation modeling. *Tourism Management, 22*(4), 363–372.

15

Backpacking in Ghana

Prospects and challenges

Frederick Dayour

Introduction

Backpacker tourism takes its roots from the Grant Tour in Europe – between the 17th and 18th centuries. This travel style was, in no doubt, epitomised by the activities of drifters and explorers (i.e. the sons and daughters of the English aristocrats) who escaped their mundane and habituated lifestyles (Cohen, 1973) often associated with the cities – to more untouched and culturally rich countryside or countries – to learn and discover themselves. Research has shown that this travel group is predominantly youngsters who are on average aged around 24 years (Pearce, 1990; Hunter-Jones, Jeffs, and Smith, 2008; Paris, 2012a; Adam, 2015; Dayour, Adongo, and Taale, 2016) and motivated by the cultural renditions as well as the ecological and adventure offerings of destinations (Dayour, 2013). This travel segment forms part of the *boomerang generation* or *peter pan generation* that McGlone, Spain and McGlone (2011) mentioned in their study – mostly youth born between 1980 and 2000. Accordingly, they are hypermobile in nature and use various communication technologies to enhance their travel experiences (O' Regan, 2008). This has resulted in the sub-categorisation of the segment into "flashpackers" and "backpackers" – the former being the most digitally savvy and an upscale market (Paris, 2012a; Dayour, 2018). What had become a mere adventure activity and quest to know the world beyond familiarised spaces, started showing signs of economic viability in most developing countries around the 1990. Consequently, a wide stream of academic literature has touted and promoted the backpacker segment as a more sustainable and viable option for emerging destinations (e.g. Scheyvens, 2002). Particularly, backpackers' predilection for locally produced services implies that their expenditure impacts directly on the local economy in comparison to mass tourists who prefer well-known brands and thereby may contribute to the repatriation of money generated from local economies (Dayour, Adongo, and Taale, 2016).

This chapter focuses on backpacking in Ghana, which has become a promising travel market for the last five years. Ghana's tourism industry, since independence in 1957 has witnessed many successes but also failures. While focusing on backpacking as the central subject, this chapter begins by highlighting Ghana's geographical characteristics and tourism development trajectory through an evolutionary lens. It also examines market trends in the industry regarding the contribution of tourism to Gross Domestic Product (GDP) and employment. Significantly, it critically presents and discusses some of the challenges bedevilling the industry especially the backpacker market, as well as its prospects for growth. Suggestions are made as to how to deal with the challenges affecting growth in Ghana's tourism industry and how to leverage prospects for growth in the backpacker segment.

Geographical features of Ghana

The Republic of Ghana is located on Latitude 8°00 N and Longitude 2°00 W of the West African Coast (see Figure 15.1). The country has a total land area of about 238,540 km² and a population of nearly 28,308,301, as well as nearly 100 different ethnic groups (Ghana Statistical Service [GSS], 2016). Ghana's location gives it an advantage as a major trading hub and a gateway to some neighbouring countries in the West African sub-region. Administratively,

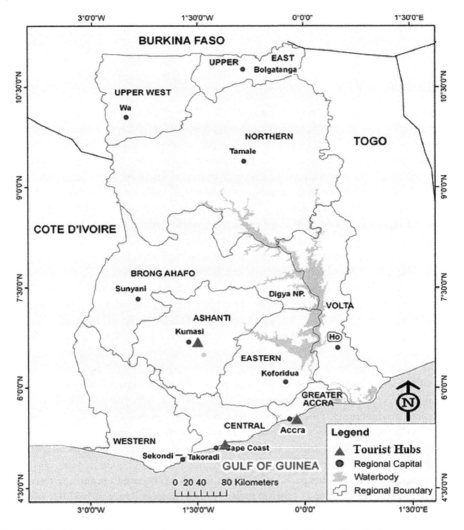

Figure 15.1 Map of Ghana showing regional capitals and major tourism hubs
Source: University of Cape Coast Geographical and Cartographical Unit, Ghana (2016).

the country is subdivided into ten major regions of which three (Greater Accra, Ashanti and Central regions) serve as the major tourism hubs of the country (Boakye, 2010). Topographically, the country is nearly flat with an elevation of 150 m above sea level. However, one outstanding land feature is the famous Mountain Afadja, which is about 885 m high and is found in the Volta Basin of the country. At the South-eastern end of the country is the Volta Lake covering 5% of the country and serves as a major source of hydro-electric power for Ghana. Quite interestingly, all major inland water bodies flow into the Gulf of Guinea except for Lake Bosumtwi which is a natural lake in the Ashanti region.

Climatically, the Southern part of Ghana has two wet seasons each year characterised by double maximal rainfall between April and August, and then September and October. Due to its propinquity to the Sudan-Sahel Sahara Desert, Northern Ghana, however, is typified by a single rainy season starting from April to October (erratically) trailed by a prolonged parched dry season from November to March. The rain and deciduous forests are found in the Southwestern sections while the wooded savannah vegetation is commonly found in the Northern and Central regions of the country. The section hereafter discusses Ghana's tourism development trajectory before and after independence.

Ghana's tourism development pathway

Ghana has a wide range of attractions (such as ecological, historical, cultural attractions as well as pristine beaches), which endear it to a wide range of tourists especially backpackers (Dayour, 2013). The last decade has, indubitably, witnessed quite a significant growth in the tourism industry in terms of arrivals and infrastructure development but not without bottlenecks. Ghana's tourism development has been influenced by successive governments since the pre-independence epoch till date. The political ideologies and manifestos of different administrations affected the growth, structure, resource base and management of the tourism industry in Ghana. I will discuss these different eras and regimes and point out what impacts they have had and are having on the tourism industry hereafter.

Pre-independence era (before 1957)

This period was characterised by the Trans-Atlantic Slave Trade in Ghana, which witnessed the interference of foreign expatriates from Europe – who engaged in slave trade, as well as trade in other merchandise. For tourism, the country's natural resources, such as the hills, beaches and traditional festivals were the major attractions. The industry at that time could be said to be woefully underdeveloped with very few attractions that drew the attention of the expatriate community and other merchants who exhibited their habitual recreational patterns at those attractions as they did back home. Especially, leisure time was spent at the hillsides and beaches in the Volta and Eastern regions of the country and it was along these places that some attempts were initiated at developing leisure-specific facilities in the Gold Coast (Akyeampong and Asiedu, 2008). However, these activities did not involve the patronage of overnight stay accommodation and were solely patronised by the colonial administrators. Later, when a few hotels become part of the industry, they were mostly sited in built-up areas particularly along the banks of water bodies, especially, Lake Bosumtwi. Apparently, these then became overnight accommodation for the colonial community and other merchants as they travelled through some mining and major slave markets. But there was no official public institution or formal sector to control the activities of the industry at the time (Akyeampong and Asiedu, 2008) when compared with the era of state activism.

Era of state activism (1957–1966)

This era represents the period when the state as well as private enterprises developed vested interests in the operations of tourism such as hotels, travel agencies and coach services (Akyeampong and Asiedu, 2008). The development of tourism and its promotion were engendered by the ruling party of the day (led by Dr. Kwame Nkrumah) whose ideology of equality promoted the spread of tourism facilities (especially accommodation facilities) across the length and breadth of Ghana. For instance, between 1957 and 1966, many international class hotels were developed throughout the country's commercial and industrial areas including the Continental Hotel, Volta Hotel, Ambassador Hotel, Meridian Hotel and Elmina Hotel. In addition to these, the state also operated catering rest houses in most regional capitals targeting the lower class in society and itinerant public servants (Akyeampong, 2007). The main tourism products at that time were the beaches and the culture of the Ghanaian people. Additionally, with the end of colonialism, Ghana as an independent nation began attracting inbound tourists (most of whom were British nationals) because of their colonial ties with the country either as ex-administrators or traders. The castles and forts, as well as colonial cemeteries in most coastal areas also became attractions and still are. Regarding transportation, the Ghana Airways and Ghana Transport Corporation were established in 1958 to superintend matters concerning transportation in the country. Accordingly, this era marked the commencement of modern tourism in Ghana in terms of the connection between attractions, accommodation, transportation and other supporting services. Hence, this era could be said to have determinedly supported tourism but thwarted during the era of state passivism – discussed hereafter

Era of state passivism (1966–1981)

This was the most turbulent time in the history of governance in Ghana mainly characterised by coup d'états and general insecurity in not only Ghana but most of Africa (Akyeampong and Asiedu, 2008). Though a modicum of interventions were made regarding tourism, governments attention was focused on resolving the socio-economic difficulties and political instability that confronted the country. Various ruling governments that assumed power became somewhat ambivalent about tourism by allowing the private sector to operate alongside state-owned tourism corporations but also mishandled such state entities eventually. They neither invested in new tourism resources nor refurbished deplorable facilities in the industry thus tourism, without a choice, assumed a back seat in governments' priorities. However, during this time a legislation was passed to formally acknowledge the forts, castles and cemeteries as tourism attractions. The general insecurity in the country and other parts of the continent around the 1970s destroyed the country's appeal to inbound travellers (Teye, 1988). Later, the introduction of economic reforms and democratic processes from the 1980s gave tourism a face-lift when the country inched into the era of laissez-fairism.

Era of laissez-fairism (1982–2001)

This was the era in which Ghana had to rely on the Bretton Wood Institutions to revitalise its ailing economy instigated by political instability and mismanagement. Notably, the International Monetary Fund (IMF) and the World Bank helped Ghana and other affected countries in region to revamp their economies but not without conditionalities. The Structural Adjustment Programmes (SAP), which happened to be the main intervention, required beneficiary states to diversify themselves of state-owned enterprises, cancel subsidies, reduce inflation, increase support for the private sector and obliterate price controls (Boakye, Otibo, and Frempong, 2013). Thus, there was the liberalisation of the economy – mirroring economic laissez-fairism around the globe in the early 1980s. At the instance of these directives as earlier stated, the Provisional National Defence Council [PNDC] (1982–1993) and the National Democratic Congress [NDC] (1993–2001) stripped themselves of direct ownership and control of commercial tourism – giving way for the private sector to flourish, both local and foreign entrepreneurs. More importantly, the liberalisation of the economy saw the blossoming of business travel exemplified by the proliferation of multinational companies particularly in transportation (e.g. British Airways and KLM) but also small and medium-sized enterprises (SMEs) (Ministry of Tourism, 2015). A substantive Ministry of Tourism, for the first time, was established in 1993 to promote tourism and also oversee the development of five-year Tourism Development Action Programme in 1996 (Adu-Ampong, 2018). In relative terms, more focused attention was placed on tourism from 2001 to date heralded by the commitment of state resources and the passing of regulations to support growth in the industry. Next is the era of democratic consolidation in tourism development.

The era of democratic consolidation of tourism development (2001–2019)

The management of the tourism industry during this period toggled between two major political parties: the New Patriotic Party [NPP] (2001–2008), National Democratic Congress [NDC] (2008–2016) and the NPP, which is currently in power since 2016 to date. The ministry in charge of tourism has undergone changes in terms of its nomenclature and now known as the Ministry of Tourism, Culture and Creative Art, but its mandate almost always remains unchanged. The era of democratic consolidation of tourism development marks the "Golden Age of Tourism" (Adu-Ampong, 2018) epitomised by strategic planning and development in the industry.

Private sector investment has become a key priority area and was captured in the Growth and Poverty Reduction Strategy 2006–2009, the first national economic strategy for this period. Especially, the accommodation sub-sector (e.g. Movenpick, Accor, Marriot, Holiday-inn, Kempinski and Novotel), Food and Beverage (e.g. KFC) and transportation (e.g. airlines) are blossoming with multinational companies. One important feature of this period is that tourism planning is strategically linked to national development goals. Especially, the Ministry of Tourism and Diaspora Relations (MOTDR) started the Joseph Project to strategically market and position Ghana not only as an attractive tourist destination but also as a home for African Diasporians who engage in root tourism. Furthermore, several strategic plans such as the Ghana National Tourism Development Plan [GNTDP] (1996–2010) and the Tourism Sector Medium Term Development Plan [TSMTDP] (2010–2013) were implemented. The aim of the TSMTDP was to make Ghana an internationally competitive destination but also to enhance the livelihood of local communities and conserve Ghana's cultural, environmental and cultural heritage (Adu-Ampong, 2018). This was then followed by a 15-year Ghana National Tourism Development Plan (GNTDP) 2013–2027. Important among the aims of this plan is to identify opportunities as well as constraints for the growth of the tourism industry. As part of accomplishing the targets in the plan, the Ministry of Tourism, Culture and Creative Art launched its domestic tourism campaign dubbed "see Ghana, wear Ghana and eat Ghana" to promote domestic tourism and the patronage of locally made clothing. In addition, as 2019 marks 400 years since the first Africans arrived in the Americas as slaves, 2019 has been christened "The Year of Return" for Ghana with the aim of attracting African Americans back to their roots. The ministry has also secured a $40 million dollar grant from the World

Bank to upgrade some selected attractions in the country to international standard. The next section presents travel market trends in Ghana relative to inbound and outbound travels, as well as domestic tourism.

Travel market trends in Ghana

This section discusses market trends in the tourism industry relative to inbound tourism and originating countries, as well as domestic and outbound tourism. It also sheds light on tourism receipts and its contribution to Gross Domestic Product (GDP).

Tourist arrivals, receipts and contribution to GDP

One of the key pillars of Ghana's economy has been the tourism industry, however, the destination is still within the initial phases of the destination lifecycle (between late involvement and early development) as proposed by Butler (1980) modified in 2006. Whereas the stage of involvement is characterised by the domination of local enterprises and largely underdeveloped facilities, the early development stage is typified by the appearance of a formal tourism industry such as packaged tours and foreign businesses, as well as institutions to regulate and manage the process of development. Butler's (1980) model further posits that tourist arrivals at the involvement stage are low in comparison to more developed stages.

As per Table 15.1, tourist arrivals in Ghana have been snowballing from the 1990s but with a few bad growth rates experienced in the early 2000s. This could be ascribed to the

Table 15.1 Tourist arrivals, receipts and contribution to GDP

Year	Arrivals	Change (%)	Receipts ($million)	Contribution to GDP (%)
1999	372,653	7.1	304.1	3.9
2000	456,275	25.1	289.5	7.8
2001	609,822	33.7	335.9	6.4
2002	584,329	−4.2	239.7	3.4
2003	688,970	17.9	452.1	7.9
2004	582,108	−15.5	487.0	7.3
2005	392,454	−32.6	627.1	7.8
2006	508,199	22.7	740.1	4.8
2007	580,895	10.8	879.0	4.8
2008	672,434	13.6	1,052.3	4.9
2009	667,275	−0.7	1,211.4	6.2
2010	746,527	9.9	1,406.3	5.8
2011	827,501	9.7	1,634.3	5.6
2012	903,300	8.3	1,704.7	5.7
2013	993,600	9.1	1,876.9	7.2
2014	1,093,000	9.1	2,066.5	6.7
2015	1,300,000	6.9	3,699.5	6.2
2016	1,316,000	1.2	1,278.4	7.1
*2026	1,913,000	31.2	4,736.0	–

Source: GTA (2015); Ministry of Tourism [MOT] (2015) and World Travel and Tourism Council [WTTC] (2017).
*Estimate.

ill-famed 9/11 terrorist attack on the United States in 2001, which not only reduced the appeal of the destination due to security concerns but also slumped travel globally (Shin, 2005). However, since 2011, international tourist arrivals have been increasing (GTA, 2015; WTTC, 2017). This trend was also reflected in tourists' receipts over the same period. With its current contribution of about 7.1% to GDP ($1,278.40 million) and 5.9% to total employment (693,000 jobs) in 2016, it is projected that by 2026, the sector will inject about $4,736.00 million annually into Ghana's economy (WTTC, 2017).

Ghana's new industry – the oil and gas industry has steadily overtaken the tourism industry as the fourth highest foreign exchange earner for the country (MOT, 2015). On the other hand, the pull exerted by the new oil industry has profited and is still benefiting the tourism industry due to the arrivals of business travellers, who ultimately become latent tourists, mostly during their downtimes. This has witnessed the expansion of more facilities to cater to the thriving business market particularly in and around Takoradi in the Western region of the country.

Tourist originating countries

Table 15.2 shows the geographical spread of the major tourist generating countries who patronise Ghana, which clearly represent the diverse cultures of the world. The top markets for Ghana include the United States, Cote d'Ivoire, Nigeria and the United Kingdom (GTA, 2015).

Ghanaians living abroad who come to Ghana to visit friends and family contribute a significant part of the country's tourists market. The US' position as the leading generating region can be attributed to the activities of Peace Corps – a US volunteer organisation that places its volunteers in the country to work in many areas, including education and health. Also, African Americans engage in root travel to Ghana – another reason for a disproportionately high arrival from the United States.

Table 15.2 International tourist arrivals by generating markets (2012–2014)

Country	2012	2013	2014
United States	118.4	123.5	135.9
United Kingdom	77.6	82.7	91.0
Germany	33.6	37.6	41.4
France	19.9	21.6	23.8
Netherlands	28.2	30.7	33.8
Canada	25.1	26.8	29.5
Switzerland	4.5	5.0	5.5
Scandinavia	18.0	21.1	23.2
Italy	9.1	10.7	11.8
Cote d'Ivoire	40.5	50.5	55.6
Nigeria	102.2	112.4	123.6
Togo	26.5	31.3	34.4
South Africa	25.1	28.2	31.0
Overseas Ghanaians	106.6	113.3	124.6
Others	268.1	298.2	328.0
Total	903.3	993.6	1,093.0

Source: GTA (2015).
Note: Number of Arrivals ('000).

Purpose of visit

Tourist travel to Ghana for varied reasons comprising business, Visiting Friends and Relatives (VFR) and holiday/leisure while a chunk also travels through the country as part of a longer trip in the region (Figure 15.2). The country is, apparently, attractive to business professionals since 2009 because of the petroleum and gas industry but this has been lost to VFR (24.7%) more recently. Likewise, others visit either for holiday and leisure (19%), conferences/meetings (8.9%) or education (7.9%) (GTA, 2015).

Domestic and outbound tourism

Domestic tourism activities in Ghana concentrate mainly around public holiday leisure activities, VFR, naming ceremonies, weddings, festivals, health treatment, conventions, business, pilgrimages and funerals (Ghana Statistical Service [GSS], 2015). The GSS (2015) reported that the most common reason for which Ghanaians travel within the country was to visit friends and relatives (40.5%) followed by funerals (30.6%) and business travels (12.6%). Regarding the domestic travel market, Greater Accra (258,112) recorded the highest in VFR visits followed by the Ashanti (118,332) and Eastern regions. However, the Eastern region appeared to be on top for attending funerals followed by the Volta and Ashanti regions. And for business reasons, the Ashanti region recorded the highest trailed by Greater Accra and Brong Ahafo regions.

Domestic travel expenditure for 2015 was about GH¢ 698.40 million (US$ 183.30 million) constituted by 29.6% of VFR, 24.3% of funerals, 21.6% of business followed by leisure and recreation. Furthermore, the expenditure for transportation was the highest spend (47.8%) followed by shopping (21.3%) and food and beverage (18.9%). Interestingly, domestic tourism appears to be providing a strong support for Ghana's economy than inbound tourism. As at 2016, domestic tourism contributed 56.7% (GH¢ 4,923.10 million; US$ 1,180.60 million) to GDP in comparison to 43.3% (GH¢ 3,252.40 million; US$ 779.90 million) by foreign visitor exports.

Outbound tourism, which represents Ghanaians travelling abroad was mostly to the Economic Community of West African States (ECOWAS). The GSS (2015) report indicated that 83.6% of Ghanaians travelled to member state countries for overnight trips, 6.9% travelled to

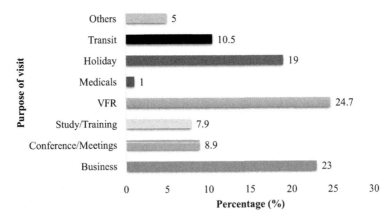

Figure 15.2 Trend of international tourist arrivals by purpose of visit (2012–2014)
Source: GTA (2015).

other African countries outside the ECOWAS while another 9.5% travelled to destinations outside Africa. Accordingly, most Ghanaians embark on outbound trips in November and August each year. The section hereafter examines the backpacker travel market, which has become part of Ghana's tourism industry.

The backpacker segment in Ghana – characteristics, motivations, experiences and risk perceptions

The growing popularity of backpacking as a viable and sustainable market segment is at present not a preserve of the so-called "Banana pancakes" of Asia or the "Gringo trials" of South America' but African destinations (Dayour, 2013). The "breeze" of backpacking is also felt across some African destinations such as Ghana hence researchers and policy-makers have initiated research into the peculiarities of the segment and strategies to exert more pull.

This part of the chapter turns attention to backpackers who have become part and parcel of the inbound travel market of Ghana in the last decade. In particular, the spotlight is on the characteristics, experiences and motivations of this unique market, as well as their risk perceptions in Ghana. Thereafter, a critical discussion about the prospects and challenges of this budding segment followed by some recommendations as to how to address the problems in order to leverage the backpacker market in Ghana is presented.

Still at an early stage of development and with various opportunities for exploration, Ghana endears itself to various types of travellers, especially backpackers (Dayour, 2013). Particularly, the sub-destinations of Accra, Cape Coast, Tamale and Kumasi (see Figure 15.3) have been found as attractive hubs for backpackers due to the spread of budget accommodation facilities in those areas (Dayour, 2013; Adam and Adongo, 2016; Dayour, Adongo, and Taale, 2016). Ghana's attractiveness in all-year-round sunshine, as well as a plethora of attractions: ecological, heritage, rich cultures, pristine beaches and hospitality, attract backpackers the most (Dayour, 2013; Adam and Adongo, 2016).

Most remarkable is the proliferation of budget accommodation facilities (such as hostels) in the cities and towns of the country (Dayour, 2013) that target low budget travellers. Similarly, the homestay phenomenon is also gaining attention as local folks have started cashing in on it by providing beddings and local home experience to tourist at relatively moderate costs. Agyeiwaah (2013) reports that backpackers and volunteers are about the main patrons of the homestay business in Ghana. Consequently, backpacker arrivals have been increasing over the last five years with the major markets being the United States and Ivory Coast (Dayour, Adongo, and Taale, 2016).

After South Africa, Ghana is, seen as one of the destinations that appeal most to backpackers (Dayour, 2013; Adam, 2015). Travel within the country could be described as relatively cheap due to the incessant bad performance of the Ghanaian cedi against major currencies like the Dollar, Euro and Pound. Figure 15.3 shows the routes and areas of backpacking in Ghana.

Characteristics of backpackers

This section provides an overview of the demographic profile and travel characteristics of the backpacker segment in Ghana. Particularly, issues bordering on sex, age, marital status, level of education, occupation, continent of origin, travel budget are discussed. In addition, travel-related characteristics such as familiarity with Ghana, experience with backpacking in general, travel party and size, length of stay, travel arrangement and type of accommodation are highlighted.

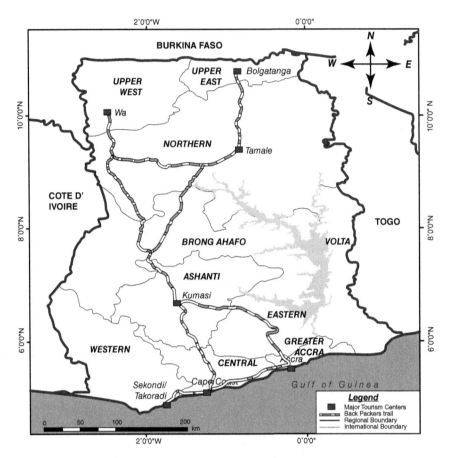

Figure 15.3 Map of Ghana showing backpacker trails
Source: University of Cape Coast Geographical and Cartographical Unit, Ghana (2016).

Since 2013, several academic studies have been conducted to understand the dynamics of the backpacker market in Ghana. Generally, more female backpackers visit Ghana than males. For example, Adam (2015) found that about 74.1% of backpackers were female relative to 25.9% male. This is also in consonance with Adongo, Badu-Baiden and Boakye (2017) who found more female (61.0%) backpackers than males (39.0%) in their study. Relative to age and marital status, most backpackers who travel to Ghana are young and unmarried. For instance, Dayour (2013) found that about three-quarters (75.0%) of backpackers were between the ages of 20 and 29 with the average aged being 23. More recently, Dayour (2018) note that about 59.8% of them were aged 20–29 years and were unmarried (87.5%) corroborating Adongo, Badu-Baiden and Boakye (2017) who found 87.2% of them as being single. In terms of the highest educational qualification and profession, most backpackers have university/college education but are unemployed or still in school. Adam (2015) established that 60.0% of backpackers had attained their university/college education. Dayour, Adongo and Taale (2016) also found that nearly 55.8% were unemployed. As to place of origin, most backpackers to Ghana originate from Europe (Dayour, 2013; Badu-Baiden, Boakye, and Otoo, 2016; Dayour, Adongo, and Taale, 2016; Dayour, 2018) and the minority from Africa (Badu-Baiden, Boakye, and Otoo, 2016; Adongo, Badu-Baiden, and Boakye, 2017; Dayour,

2018). Regarding travel budget, Dayour, Adongo and Taale (2017) reported that most backpackers travelled on an average budget of US$ 1,368.13 while Dayour (2018) showed a travel budget of about US$ 1,609.64.

To their travel characteristics, most backpackers who visit Ghana are first timers (Adam, 2015; Dayour, 2018) but often repeating their backpacking experience in general. For instance, Dayour (2018) in his study found that most had been backpacking for more than five years. It is also interesting to note that most of them travel around the country in the company of others (about three in a group) mostly for security reasons (Dayour, 2018). The majority arrange their travel by themselves (Adam, 2015; Badu-Baiden, Boakye, and Otoo, 2016) and spend only one week to backpack in Ghana (Adongo, Badu-Baiden, and Boakye, 2017). As to the choice of accommodation, evidently, most backpackers use budget accommodation facilities such as hostels (Dayour, 2013). However, more recently Dayour (2018) has found that 1–4 Star hotels are being utilised, as well as homestay though to a small extent.

Motivations and experiences

Backpackers are motivated by a mix of factors to visit Ghana. In one of the first studies that sought to understand the dynamics of this segment in Ghana, Dayour (2013) showed that backpackers were drawn to the country by push factors (such as the quest for escape and adventure) and pull factors (such as service delivery, ecological, historical and cultural attractions). In a related study, Badu-Baiden, Boakye and Otoo (2016) noted that backpackers were motivated by novelty, relaxation, learning, adventure, social contacts and culture in Ghana. More recently, Adongo, Badu-Baiden and Boakye (2017) also found that drivers such as the ecological resources of the country, the need for relaxation, culture and learning were some of the reasons why backpackers came to Ghana. In relation to their experiences, Adongo, Badu-Baiden and Boakye (2017), who examined the effect of experience on their length of stay, noted that backpackers found experiences such as skills acquisition, participation in varied recreational activities and hospitality of the local people as exciting while experiences with poor sanitary conditions, fob offs and unfair pricing were lamented by them.

Risk perceptions

Contrary to past studies (e.g. Cohen, 1973; Elsrud, 2001) that found backpackers as a risk-tolerant group of travellers, a more recent one by Adam (2015) established that backpackers in Ghana get concerned about expectation, physical, health, financial, political and socio-psychological risks. Likewise, Badu-Baiden, Boakye and Otoo (2016) highlighted issues of health risk and financial risk, as well as crime as major concerns of backpackers in the country. In another study by Adam and Adongo (2016), it was noted that backpackers became victims of physical assault, larceny, fraud and verbal assault with more females suffering larceny than males. Recently, Dayour (2018) in examining backpackers' perceptions of risk towards smartphone usage found that backpackers were concerned about destination-infrastructure risk, security risk and destination physical risk.

A critical reflection on the prospects and challenges of backpacker tourism in Ghana

The evidence presented in the previous sections indicates that backpacking can potentially become a large market for Ghana if the right strategies are used to leverage it. It is important to note that the proliferation of budget accommodation facilities in Ghana (Badu-Baiden, Boakye, and Otoo, 2016) creates a relevant prospect for the backpacker market to thrive. The largely youthful nature of this segment suggests many of them travel on constrained budgets – making budget accommodation facilities the most favoured accommodation for backpackers (Dayour, Adongo, and Taale, 2016). Related to that is the emergence of homestay facilities in the informal accommodation subsector. According to Agyeiwaah (2013), homestay facilities are becoming relevant to tourists particularly backpackers who wish to participate in local cultures. However, most of these low scale accommodation facilities especially homestays are unregulated in Ghana. No form of monitoring or inspection is undertaken at such sites which implies that the quality of services rendered could be compromised.

Another potential for growth in the segment is the many unexplored natural tourism resources in the country – most of which are found in the peripheries of the country in especially the Northern and Volta regions of Ghana. Most backpackers seek out the untouched and unexplored destinations of the world (Elsrud, 2001) hence Ghana's richness in several unexplored resources makes it ideal for backpacking especially the adventure seekers. However, it is important to note that poor access roads to some of those attractions could pose undue challenges and risk to potential backpackers to such attractions. Especially, in the Volta region of Ghana, access roads to some attractions are in a very deplorable state, which could pose potential danger to travellers.

Ghana's inimitable and rich cultural diversity provides another opportunity for the backpacker segment to flourish. Particularly, Dayour (2013) intimated that there was the need for destination marketers to leverage the diversity in the Ghanaian culture to attract more backpackers. Thus, adequately packaging and marketing the country's cultural attributes could serve to exert more pull for backpackers who crave such experiences in the country. However, it is regrettable to note that Ghana's cultural attributes have not been being fully harnessed for tourism – especially when it comes to the backpacker market segment. The story around the cultural attractions of the country is a bit uncoordinated and weakly marketed to the rest of the world (Dayour, 2013).

Furthermore, Ghana's biggest sector is the agriculture sector (GSS, 2015), which could also be leveraged to enhance the growth of the backpacker market. For example, countries like Australia have taken advantage of the backpacker market to boost productivity in not just agriculture but other industries. As some backpackers take up temporary jobs at destinations to supplement their budgets, Ghana could equally use farm tourism to entice more visits to the country. Backpackers' experiences could be enhanced through working on farms, which could, in turn, boost productivity in the agriculture sector.

Other challenges bedevilling not only the backpacker segment but the tourism industry in general include the poor transportation network and a lack of relevant statistics on different tourist markets, which makes it difficult to ascertain arrivals and to do forecasting in the industry. There remain risk concerns among backpackers and other tourists about crime against tourists. These challenges need to be addressed in order to benefit from the potentials of the backpacker tourism segment.

Concluding remarks and recommendations

The chapter clearly shows that Ghana's tourism has been evolving since the 1950s and does wield a strong growth potential. The country abounds in a diversity of attractions that serve as a pull for various travel segments including backpackers. Significantly, the country's historical, ecological and cultural attractions endear it to backpackers but also serve as an escape route for those who wish to go off their habitual environment. Nevertheless, the industry is currently confronted with several challenges that could thwart or slow down its growth potentials, especially in relation to the backpacking sector.

First, there is the need for the Ministry of Tourism, Culture and Creative Arts, as well as the Ghana Tourism Authority to put into place mechanisms for the continuous collection and publishing of data on the industry to enable benchmarking, as well as forecasting. There is quite a wide gap in the collection and dissemination of data in the tourism industry, especially data on backpackers, which needs to be bridged. Such data are required by academics and industry practitioners to understand the dynamics of the backpacker segment and to adequately cater for them.

Furthermore, as most backpackers in the country now utilise the services of hostels, as well as homestay accommodation facilities, it is about time the industry's governing institutions licensed all such facilities and put in measures to maintain quality standards. As most backpackers prefer patronising local services and learning about local cultures, improving service quality in such facilities could increase demand – creating a wider multiplier effect on local economies. Moreover, there is a need for destination managers to leverage the cultural diversity of the country by using targeted marketing strategies. This requires careful market segmentation to facilitate the delivery of tailored cultural products to backpackers and other travel segments.

Besides, the government of Ghana needs to improve on the images and appeal of existing attractions by improving access to them. The deplorable nature of roads leading to some attractions especially those in the countryside not only pose risk to road users but could possibly generate negative words of mouth among potential tourists (Nutsugbodo, Amenumey, and Mensah, 2018). Most backpackers prefer to use public transport network because of budgetary constraints but also the desire to interact with the local people (Dayour, 2018). However, most of these services are unsafe due to reckless driving and unplanned schedules (Nutsugbodo, Amenumey, and Mensah, 2018). Thus, there is a need for improvement in the public transport system in the country especially "trotro" (which is the most common and affordable local transport system in the country). Furthermore, more punitive measures need to be enforced to ensure drivers and other road users comply with road traffic regulations in the country. Finally, the security situations at various tourist hubs also need to be improved as visitors especially backpackers are becoming concerned about both violent and nonviolent crimes at some places (Boakye, 2010). Frequent policing and use of CCTV cameras at attractions and public places could reduce this menace.

This chapter has briefly traced the development of the tourism sector in Ghana and has identified the backpacker segment as having a great growth potential. Nonetheless, there remain a number of key challenges facing the sector that need to be addressed in order to enable the tourism sector in general and the backpacking sector more specifically to take off and make significant contribution to local economic activities across the various destinations in Ghana.

References

Adam, I. 2015. "Backpackers' risk perceptions and risk reduction strategies in Ghana." *Tourism Management* 49: 99–108.

Adam, I., and C. A. Adongo, 2016. "Do backpackers suffer crime? Empirical investigation of crime perpetrated against backpackers in Ghana." *Journal of Hospitality and Tourism Management* 27: 60–67.

Adongo, C. A., F. Badu-Baiden, and K. A. A. Boakye. 2017. "The tourism experience-led length of stay hypothesis." *Journal of Outdoor Recreation and Tourism* 18: 65–74.

Adu-Ampong, E. A. 2018. "Historical trajectory of tourism development policies and planning in Ghana, 1957-207." *Tourism Planning and Development. 16*(2), 124-141

Agyeiwaah, E. 2013. "International tourists' motivations for choosing homestay in the Kumasi Metropolis of Ghana". *Anatolia* 24 (3): 405–409.

Akyeampong, O. 2007. *Tourism in Ghana: The accommodation sub-sector.* Accra: Janel Publications

Akyeampong, O., and A. B. Asiedu. eds. 2008. *Tourism in Ghana: A modern synthesis.* Accra: Assemblies of God Literature Centre.

Badu-baiden, F., K. A. Boakye, and F. E. Otoo. 2016. "Backpackers views on risk in the Cape Coast-Elmina area of Ghana." *International Journal of Tourism Sciences* 16 (1–2): 1–14.

Boakye, K. A. 2010. "Studying tourists' suitability as crime targets." *Annals of Tourism Research* 37 (3): 727–743.

Boakye, K. A., F. Otibo, and F. Frempong. 2013. "Assessing Ghana's contemporary tourism development experience." *Journal of Global Initiatives,* 8(1/2): 133–154.

Butler, R. W. 1980. "The concept of a tourist area cycle of evolution: Implications for Management of Resources". *Canadian Geographer* 24: 5–12.

Cohen, E. 1973. "Nomads from affluence: Notes on the phenomenon of drifter-tourism." *International Journal of Comparative Sociology* 14 (1–2): 89–103.

Dayour, F. 2013. "Are backpackers a homogeneous group?" *European Journal of Tourism, Hospitality and Recreation* 4 (3): 69–94.

Dayour, F. 2018. Backpackers perceptions of risk towards smartphone usage, Ghana. Thesis submitted to the University of Surrey for a PhD.

Dayour, F., C. Atanga, and F. Taale. 2016. "Determinants of backpackers' expenditure." *Tourism Management Perspective* 17: 36–43.

Elsrud, T. 2001. "Risk creation in traveling: Backpacker adventure narration." *Annals of Tourism Research,* 28 (3): 597–617.

Ghana Statistical Service [GSS]. 2015. *Statistics for development and progress: Gross gomestic product 2014* (April), 3. Available at: http://www.statsghana.gov.gh/docfiles/GDP/GDP_2014.pdf.

Ghana Statistical Service [GSS]. 2016. *Projected population by sex (2010–2016).* Data Production United. Available at: http://www.statsghana.gov.gh/socio_demo.html.

Ghana Tourism Authority [GTA]. 2015. *Tourism facts sheet on Ghana.* Accra: Ghana Tourism Authority.

Hunter-Jones, P., A. Jeffs., and D. Smith. 2008. "Backpacking your way into crisis: An exploratory study into perceived risk and tourist behaviour amongst young people." *Journal of Travel and Tourism Marketing* 23 (2/4): 237–248.

McGlone, T., J. W. Spain, and, V. McGlone. 2011. "Corporate Social Responsibility, and the Millennials". *Journal of Education for Business,* 86(4): 195-200.

Ministry of Tourism [MOT]. 2015. *National tourism development plan.* Accra: Ministry of tourism.

Nutsugbodo, R. Y., E. K. Amenumey, and C. A. Mensah. 2018. "Public transport mode preferences of international tourists in Ghana: Implications for transport planning." *Travel Behaviour and Society* 11: 1–8.

O' Regan, M. 2008. Hypermobility in backpacker lifestyles: The emergence of the internet café. In Burns, P. M. and Novelli, M. (eds.), *Tourism and mobilities: Local-global connections* (109–132). Trowbridge: Cromwell Press.

Paris, C. M. 2012a. "Flashpackers: An emerging sub-culture?" *Annals of Tourism Research* 39 (2): 1094–1115.

Pearce, P. L. 1990. *The backpacker phenomenon: Preliminary answers to basic questions.* Townsville: James Cook University of North Queensland.

Scheyvens, R. 2002. "Backpacker tourism and Third World development." *Annals of Tourism Research* 29 (1): 144–164.

Shin, Y.-S. 2005. "Safety, security and peace tourism: The case of the DMZ area." *Asia Pacific Journal of Tourism Research* 10 (4): 411–426.

Teye, V. B. 1988. "Coups d'etat and African tourism: A study of Ghana." *Annals of Tourism Research* 15 (3): 329–356.

World Travel and Tourism Council (WTTC). 2017. *Travel and tourism global economic impact and issues 2017.* Available at: https://www.google.co.uk/search.

16

Drivers and opportunities in Nigeria's tourism industry

Towards sustainable growth and development

Ogechi Adeola, Oserere Eigbe and Omotayo Muritala

Introduction

Tourism is generally understood to mean the act of travelling to places outside one's home environment for pleasure or professional purposes for not more than one successive year (Mejabi and Abutu 2015; United Nations World Tourism Organization (UNWTO) (2008). The UNWTO emphasized that the travel itself is not related to employment (e.g. airline personnel, business meetings) and does not result in establishing permanent residence. The World Travel and Tourism Council (WTTC) defines tourism as a commercial activity that is in the business of providing cultural or entertainment attractions, transportation, lodging, retail stores, and meals (Fadipe 2016).

Hospitality is a key component of the tourism system. The role of hospitality is to assure that tourists' expectations of a tourist destination are met (Eja et al. 2011; Ndanusa et al. 2014). While tourism deals with a range of activities that attract tourists to locations such as mountains, beaches, festivals, and monuments, amongst others, hospitality addresses the tourists' needs for goods and services (Fadipe 2016).

Tourism has become one of the fastest growing sectors in most developing and developed countries due to its significant contribution to the nations' economies (Ayeni and Ebohon 2012; Nana 2017; Ndanusa et al. 2014). Tourism contributed close to 9.5% of global GDP and generated about 266 million jobs by 2013 (Nana 2017; World Travel and Tourism Council Report 2014); 10.2% of global GDP and about 292 million jobs by 2016 (World Travel and Tourism Council 2017a, 2017b); and 10.4% of global GDP and about 314 million jobs by 2017. Its total contribution to GDP was projected to rise by 4.0% in 2018 (World Travel and Tourism Council 2018).

Reporting on the economic impact of the global hospitality industry, Vanguard Report estimated that global tourist arrivals had numbered over 1.2 billion people in 2016, projected global tourist arrivals at 1.4 billion in 2020 and 1.8 billion in 2030, and estimated revenues at about $600 billion in 2018 (Okogba 2018). In 2017 the WTTC predicted that the sub-Saharan Africa tourism industry would generate 4 million jobs in 2020. Africa indeed has huge potentials for growth in the tourism industry given its broad range of tourist attractions, which include cultural and historical sites (as discussed later) (Okupe et al. 2018).

Background to Nigeria's tourism industry

According to the WTTC (2017), the direct contribution of travel and tourism to Nigeria's 2016 GDP was estimated to be ₦1,861.4 billion (US $5.17 million); 1.7% of the country's total GDP. This was estimated to rise by 1.1% in 2017. Both the direct and indirect contribution of tourism and travel for 2016 was estimated to be ₦5,124.3 billion (US $14.23 million); 4.7% of GDP. The direct contribution of tourism to job creation was estimated to be 1.6% (649,500 jobs) of total employment in 2016 and was expected to rise to 3.4% in 2017. Both direct and indirect contributions to employment in the industry were calculated to be 4.5% (1,793,000 jobs) in 2016.

The importance of tourism to Nigeria's economic growth and development is directly related to its potential for income generation. The anticipated creation of jobs and opportunities around other economic sectors will be another significant contribution from the tourism industry. Opportunities for wealth creation exist along the value chains of tourism: telecommunications, finance, construction, entertainment, and other complementary sectors of the economy.

Tourism management in Nigeria

The establishment in 1992 of Nigeria's National Tourism Development Corporation Act with Decree No. 82 brought increased attention to the tourism industry as a driver of economic growth and development (Metilelu 2016; Ndanusa et al. 2014). The 2005 National Tourism Policy further provoked the government-led administration to request the United Nations Development Programme (UNDP), in collaboration with UNWTO, to produce a master plan for Nigeria in 2006 (Esu 2012; Metilelu 2016; Nana 2017).

In order to ensure the promotion of Nigeria's rich cultural heritage, the Federal Ministry of Culture and Tourism was established in June 1999 as the apex body responsible for the tourism industry. The ministry's primary mission was to promote culture and tourism in a way that would generate foreign exchange, increase distribution of income, create labour employment opportunities, reduce rural poverty, and promote peace. To perform these roles, the ministry, now known as the Federal Ministry of Information and Culture, currently has eight agencies, known locally as parastatals. The agencies are shown in Table 16.1, along with their key roles and responsibilities.

The roles and responsibilities of the agencies summarized in Table 16.1 differentiate the expectations of each in its approach to fulfilling the country's tourism objectives. Currently, accomplishments of these designated functions have been described as failing to meet those expectations, leaving the tourism industry with many untapped potentials (Eneji et al. 2016; Fadipe 2016; Mejabi and Abutu 2015). For instance, despite the responsibility of the National Institute for Hospitality and Tourism to offer training and postgraduate programmes in hospitality and tourism management, it was reported by UNWTO (2006) that the agency's environment is poorly equipped, employees are unskilled and inexperienced, and budget allocations are inadequate. The UNWTO report also stated that the NTDC, nominally the top regulatory body, suffers from these same challenges coupled with the problem of unreliable data and market information about the sector (Adeola and Ezenwafor 2016; Nwosu 2016). The UNWTO graded the NTDC as an ineffective organization (Nwosu 2016). Consequently, tourism and hospitality sector businesses are left to formulate and implement their own standards of operations (Adeola and Ezenwafor 2016).

Table 16.1 Roles and responsibilities of tourism agencies in Nigeria

Tourism agencies	Key roles and responsibilities
Nigerian Tourism Development Corporation (NTDC)	• Standardize and sensitize the tourism industry through registration, inspection, classification and grading of Hospitality and Tourism Enterprises (HTEs). • Identify, assess, and document tourism sites and attractions for development/investment and promotion purposes. • Provide technical and advisory services to the public. • Publicize and promote Nigeria's tourism endowments. • Provide reliable and up-to-date statistical tourism data through the establishment of the Tourism Data Bank and the implementation of the Tourism Satellite Account. • Serve as liaison with relevant government ministries and agencies to ensure and facilitate the provision of infrastructural facilities at tourism sites.
National Institute for Hospitality and Tourism (NIHOTOUR)	• Provide supervisory management courses for middle and managerial cadres and upgrade courses for junior- and middle-level cadre personnel. • Manage tourism statistics courses for planners, research officers, and statisticians. • Organize Tourism Journalism certificate courses for journalists in the tourism sector. • Organize specialized diplomas and postgraduate programmes in hospitality and tourism management for senior functionaries and trainers. • Provide short-term managerial training for senior managers and principal grade officers in both the public and private sectors.
National Institute for Cultural Orientation (NICO)	• Build up personnel and materials to encourage innovative study and development of Nigeria's history. • Promote the nation's cultural heritage and the continuous movement of Nigeria's cultural policy in line with globalization. • Conduct in-depth research and documentation into Nigerian culture and history.
National Gallery of Arts (NGA)	• Build a variety of galleries (e.g. Portrait Galleries, Galleries of Modern Arts, The National Hall of Fame, Galleries of Contemporary Islamic Arts, Galleries of Contemporary Christian Arts, National Photographic Gallery, National Gallery of Architecture and Designs, and a Special Workshop/Studios Project). • Accept and store gifts of contemporary art, property, money or other assets from individuals and organizations, provided these gifts are not inconsistent with the objectives of the gallery.
National Council for Arts and Culture (NCAC)	• Promote and foster the appreciation, revival, and development of Nigerian arts, crafts, and culture. • Register artists and artiste groups for effective business relationships. • Coordinate inter-state cultural exchange activities. • Organize exhibitions in visual, performing, and literary arts. • Promote the development of traditional dance, drama, opera, photography, folklore, oral tradition, literature, poetry, painting and general arts, woodworks, embroidery, weaving, and similar crafts. • Establish cultural centres, theatre arts galleries, and craft centres for the promotion of arts and culture. • Preserve cultural materials that contribute to the image of personality of Nigeria.

(Continued)

Tourism agencies	Key roles and responsibilities
National Commission for Museums and Monuments (NCMM)	• Administer the National Museum's antiquities and monuments throughout the country. • Construct, maintain, and manage national museums/outlets for or in conjunction with antiquities, science and technology, warfare, Africa and black arts, architecture, national history, and educational services. • Grant approvals for the establishment of private museums.
Centre for Black and African Arts and Civilization (CBAAC)	• Preserve the Festac '77 legacies through public lectures, discussions, symposia, and performances. • Provide indexes, guides, catalogues, and bibliographies to facilitate the utilization of the Centre's resources.
National Troupe/ National Theatre of Nigeria (NT/ NTN)	• Encourage the discovery and development of talents in the arts. • Promote healthy cultural activities and habits in the society. • Efficiently manage the National Theatre. • Provide and manage venues and facilities for the exhibition of fine arts, furniture, building materials, science equipment, computers, and other material objects.

Source: Nigerian Arts & Culture Directory (http://nacd.gov.ng/ministry%20of%20culture%20and%20tourism.htm).

The recent history of international tourist arrivals in Nigeria (see Figure 16.1) reveals some inconsistencies. This can be attributed, to some extent, to the incidence of terrorism during these periods. According to Riti et al. (2017), political instability and terrorism dissuaded tourists from visiting Nigeria. The environment did not guarantee the protection of lives and properties, hence, the tourist visits declined, as expected, and only began to rise when assurance was restored, and tourist perceptions changed.

According to tourism research published by the Official Tourism, Trade & Investment Promotion Agency for Cape Town and the Western Cape (Wesgro 2017), the majority of

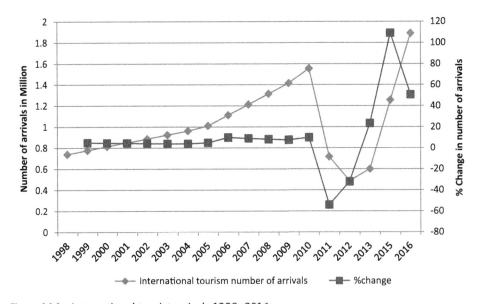

Figure 16.1 International tourist arrivals 1998–2016

Source: Authors; data from World Development Indicators https://datacatalog.worldbank.org/dataset/world-development-indicators).

tourists to Nigeria are from nearby countries – Cameroon, Liberia, Sudan, Benin, Niger, and Chad – because access to Nigeria from these countries is quite easy.

Tourism resources and assets in Nigeria

Nigeria is located entirely within the tropics and is endowed with a moderate climate and numerous attractive ecological resources and captivating natural features such as waterfalls, lakes, mountains, hills, vegetation, and beaches (Eneji et al. 2016; Mejabi and Abutu 2015). Nigeria possesses cultural and heritage assets that are among the most eye-catching and thrilling in the world. These include festivals, historical monuments, museums, and arts and crafts venues (Mejabi and Abutu 2015). These assets place Nigeria at the forefront of tourism paradise in Africa (Eneji et al. 2016). Some of the tourism assets and their development status are presented in Table 16.2.

Sport is another major driver of both domestic and international tourism. Nigeria has achieved some prominence in this area with sporting facilities that include the Abuja (M.K.O. Abiola) stadium complex, Lagos national stadium, IBB international golf course, an international stadium complex in Uyo, and other stadia located across the country. Nigeria has hosted international sporting events, including All African Games, the 1999 World Youth Soccer Championship, and the 1980 and 2000 African Cup of Nations (co-hosted with Ghana) (Fadipe 2016).

According to Mejabi and Abutu (2015), Nigeria's religious tourism sites have attained good development status. Some of these include Osun Oshogbo Grove in Osun state; Canaan land, Ota in Ogun state; National Mosque in Abuja; National Ecumenical Christian Centre in Abuja; Catholic Cathedral in Lagos; and Redemption Camp along Lagos-Ibadan Expressway. There has been a consistent annual influx of tourists into some religious sites. These religious sites have amazing structures and monuments. For instance, the Oduduwa Shrine and Grove is a predominant historical and educational site. A local chief resides at the site and is always willing to tell stories about the days of yore to tourists. Other shrines that attract tourists include Adoro Ero (Alor), Ube Uhunowerre and Api, Opi, located in Nsukka cultural zone of Enugu State (Ele 2017). Tourists travel to these sites for diverse religious pursuits, including oath-taking, sacrifices, reconciliation, and covenant-making (Ele 2017). Recently, the Commissioner of Tourism in Lagos state declared that the Lagos State Government Tourism Master Plan adequately captured the potentials of spiritual or religious tourism (PM News May 2018). This is in a bid to ensure that the necessary infrastructure and enabling the environment are in place to fully sustain development.

Contribution of tourism to the Nigerian economy

WTTC has reported the contribution of tourism to Nigeria's economy in terms of GDP, employment, domestic tourism spending, and visitor exports. Figure 16.2 tracks these contributions over a period of 23 years, 1995–2018.

Figure 16.3 shows that the contribution of the tourism sector to GDP was US $20.2 billion in 2017, an increase from US $13.7 billion in 2012. The recent contributions demonstrated significant growth, in real terms, when compared to the sector contribution of US $5.6 billion in 1995. Domestic tourism spending has closely followed that trend as well. The number of jobs and the value of visitor exports (i.e. international tourists spending) are two areas with stagnant or no growth.

Table 16.2 Nigeria's tourism assets

S/N	Resources	Location	Development status
Natural attraction			
1	Wikki warm spring	Bauchi	Developed
2	Ikogosi warm spring	Ekiti	Developed
3	Assop falls	Plateau	Partially developed
4	Owu falls	Kwara	Partially developed
5	Kwa falls	Cross River	Partially developed
6	Agbokim and Ikom waterfalls	Cross River	Partially developed
7	Gurara falls	Niger	Not developed
8	Erin Ijesha waterfalls	Osun	Not developed
9	Farin Ruwa waterfalls	Nassarawa	Not developed
Mountains, hills, and rock formations			
10	Obudu mountain resort	Cross River	Developed
11	Olumo rock	Ogun	Developed
12	Aso rock	Abuja	Partially developed
13	Ogbunike caves	Anambra	Partially developed
14	Idanre hills	Ondo	Partially developed
15	Mount Patti	Kogi	Not developed
16	Shere hills	Plateau	Not developed
17	Zuma rock	Niger	Not developed
18	Riyom rock	Plateau	Not developed
19	Mambila	Plateau, Taraba, and Adamawa	Not developed
Beach resources			
20	Calabar beach	Cross River	Developed
21	Aiyetoro Maiyegun Coastal resort	Lagos	Developed
22	Lekki Peninsula	Lagos	Developed
23	Takwa Bay beach	Lagos	Developed
24	Eleko beach	Lagos	Developed
25	Tourist beach	Rivers	Developed
26	Lagos bar beach	Lagos	Partially developed
27	Warri beach	Delta	Partially developed
28	River Niger waterfront	Kogi	Partially developed
29	Egga-Idah waterfront	Kogi	Not developed
Eco-tourism resources			
30	Lekki conservation centre	Lagos	Developed
31	Gashaka/Gunti national park	Adamawa, Taraba	Developed
32	Yankari game reserve	Bauchi	Developed
33	Old Oyo national park	Oyo	Developed
34	Cross River national park	Cross River	Developed
35	Kainji lake national park	Niger	Developed
36	Jos wildlife park	Plateau	Partially developed
37	Kamuku national park	Kaduna	Partially developed
38	Chad basin national park	Borno	Partially developed
39	Okomu national park	Edo	Partially developed

Heritage, museum and monuments

40	National Arts Theatre	Lagos	Developed
41	Enugu national museum	Enugu	Developed
42	National war museum	Abia	Developed
43	Esie national museum	Kwara	Developed
44	Owo national museum	Ondo	Developed
45	Jos national museum	Plateau	Developed
46	Benin national museum	Edo	Developed
47	Oba of Benin palace	Edo	Developed
48	Alaafin of Oyo palace	Oyo	Developed
49	Ooni of Ife palace	Osun	Developed
50	Oloibiri oil museum	Bayelsa	Partially developed
51	Gidan Makama	Kano	Partially developed
52	Gobarau Minaret	Katsina	Partially developed
53	Relics of colonial history	Kogi	Partially developed

Cultural festivals

54	Durbar festival	Kano, Kaduna, and Katsina	Developed
55	Adimu Orisa (Eyo) festival	Lagos	Developed
56	Argungu fishing festival	Lagos	Developed
57	Osun Osogbo cultural festival	Osun	Developed
58	Abuja carnival	FCT Abuja	Developed
60	Afan cultural festival	Kaduna	Partially developed
61	Ovia Osese festival	Kogi	Partially developed
62	Igue festival	Edo	Partially developed
63	Mmanwu festival	Anambra and Enugu	Partially developed
64	Kwaghir festival	Benue	Partially developed

Recreation/theme parks

65	Oakland wonderland	Enugu	Developed
66	Wonderland amusement park	Abuja	Developed
67	Water park	Ikeja	Developed
68	Trans amusement park	Ibadan	Developed
69	Frankkid children amusement park	Festac Lagos	Developed
70	Gamji park	Kaduna	Developed
71	Paparanda amusement park	Lokoja	Partially developed

Business/conference tourism assets

72	Tinapa business resort	Cross River	Developed
73	Shehu Musa Yar'Adua conference centre	Abuja	Developed
74	Muson centre	Lagos	Developed
75	International conference centre	Abuja	Developed
76	Ladi Kwali conference centre, Sheraton Hotel	Abuja	Developed
77	Congress Hall, Transcorp Hilton hotel	Abuja	Developed

Source: Mejabi and Abutu (2015); Fadipe (2016).

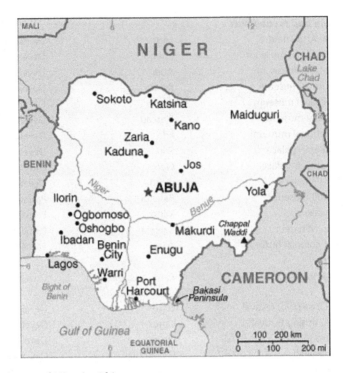

Figure 16.2 A map of Nigeria, Africa

Source: World FactBook (https://www.cia.gov/library/publications/resources/the-world-factbook/geos/ni.html).

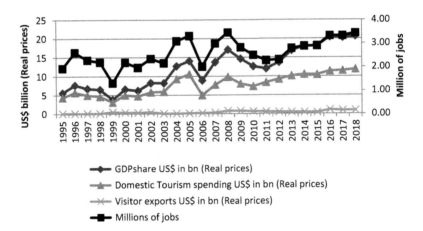

Figure 16.3 Contributions of the tourism sector to the national economy

Source: Authors; data from WTTC https://tools.wttc.org.

Figure 16.4 shows the fluctuations in the percentage share of tourism to GDP, total employment, and domestic tourism spending percentage share, and visitor exports as a percentage of exports. The percentage share of the sector to GDP was 5.1% in 2017 and 5.2% in 2016. The share of the tourism sector to GDP has remained below 7%, with the highest contribution of 6.5% in 2005, and the lowest, 3%, in 1999. Similarly, the percentage share of total

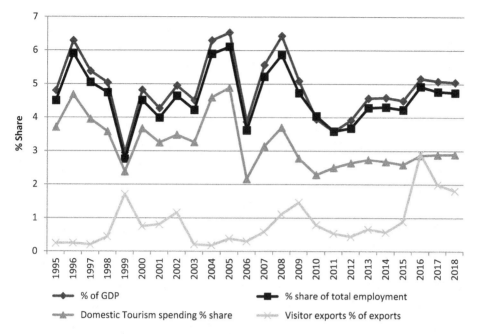

Figure 16.4 Percentage share of tourism sector contribution to national economy
Source: Authors; data from WTTC Data Gateway, https://www.wttc.org/datagateway/.

employment has remained within a 2.8–6.1% band and below 5% since 2009. The domestic tourism sector has experienced consistent spending fluctuations, and this is more apparent in the past decade. Visitor exports as a percentage of total exports performed poorly, generally below domestic tourism spending. Domestic tourist spending offers greater contributions to the economy when compared to visitor exports. Domestic tourism spending closely mirrored trends in the nation's employment sector and GDP.

Tourism should be a source of revenue in the form of positive returns on financial investments and foreign exchange earnings (Eneji et al. 2016). However, tourism's contribution to Nigeria's GDP is generally 5% lower than the average found across the continent (Eneji et al. 2016), job creation is low, and revenue from visitors' exports is very low. Several challenges are standing in the way of tourism becoming a significant contributor to Nigeria's economy: insecurity, inconsistent government policies on tourism, lack of maintenance of monument sites, and poor infrastructures amongst others.

Challenges inhibiting growth in Nigeria's tourism industry

The future of tourism in Nigeria holds great promise, given the presence of unique tourist attractions, but the country has only just begun to tap the potential that the tourism industry has to offer. A number of tourist sites, such as the Niger and Benue rivers, the ancient cities of the north, and the Atlantic Ocean coastal areas are yet to be fully developed. Successive Nigerian governments have not given the tourism sector the attention that it needs to revitalize the tourist industry so that it can contribute meaningfully to socio-economic development. The Nigerian tourism industry is still affected by a poor destination image, corruption and insecurity being a prime concern. The problem of infrastructure (poor electricity, roads, and water access) and the lack of political will on the part of successive governments to take effective policy steps in addressing these concerns (Leadership 2018), has meant that the tourism sector is operating below optimal levels. Numerous challenges are faced by Nigeria's tourism industry:

Security concerns: In recent times, Nigeria has faced diverse cases of unrest, and as a result, most western countries issue warnings to travellers to avoid certain parts of the country, particularly the Niger-Delta and northern parts of Nigeria (Adewale 2016; Ashikodi 2012; Eneji et al. 2016). Rampant cases of armed robbery, kidnapping, suicide bombings, and assassinations make it clear that the security of lives and property is not guaranteed. The Boko Haram menace and the Fulani Herdsmen killings in the northern part of the country make international news and negatively affect the image of Nigeria as a tourist destination. The Niger Delta region is still volatile with repeated kidnappings, and the same is true for the southeastern part of the country. The World Economic Forum's (2017) Travel and Tourism Competitiveness Index (TTCI) indicated that Nigeria ranked 132 out of 136 in global safety and security, a report that clearly marks the country as unsafe for visitors and tourists (Ekundayo 2014), thereby hindering the growth of tourism in the country (Eneji et al. 2016; Fadipe 2016).

Poor infrastructure: Nigeria experiences inadequate or poorly maintained infrastructure (Nana 2017). There are poor means of transportation by road, air or sea (Ekundayo 2014; Eneji et al. 2016). The state of domestic and international airports is inadequate and roads, especially those in rural areas where the majority of tourist sites are located, are in disrepair (Ashikodi 2012). Tourist sites lack tour guides and efficient signs and symbols (Ndanusa et al. 2014). Access to healthcare and sanitation are held in high regard by tourists (Okupe et al. 2018), and according to the TTCI 2017 report, Nigeria ranked 132 out of 136 in global health and hygiene. The country is still far from providing quality healthcare services to all, and this is likely to dissuade tourists.

Neglected monument structures: Most of Nigeria's monument locations lack proper maintenance, and this could inhibit growth in the tourism industry (Adewale 2016; Ashikodi 2012). The Lagos National Theatre and the Badagry Slave Route, for example, are among the nation's most important monument sites, and they are in appalling states as a result of poor maintenance (Adewale 2016). Many rural tourism projects in Nigeria have been abandoned due to inadequate funding (Ndajiya et al. 2014). The Nigerian government appears to be paying lip service to the issue of tourism development when inadequate budget allocations are approved for site maintenance (Fadipe 2016; Ndanusa et al. 2014).

Inconsistent government policies on tourism: The government of a country is responsible for formulating and implementing policies that should enhance the growth of various sectors within the economy, including tourism. Government policies define the nature and extent of tourism development. In Nigeria, high tariffs and taxes have a negative effect on the tourism and hospitality sectors; private businesses are discouraged from investing in the sector. High taxes are seen as evidence of poor decision-making that resulted in high costs of implementing effective tourism (Ekundayo 2014). While a number of brilliant policies have been formulated by the government for the tourism sector, the implementation of these policies continues to be a challenge (Adewale 2016).

Low level of technology access and poor information dissemination: Recent reports have revealed the low uptake of information and communication technologies (ICT) in Nigeria. In the ICT Development Index rankings of 2016 and 2017, Nigeria ranked 143rd of 176 surveyed countries worldwide, and 15th of 38 surveyed countries in Africa (International Telecommunication Union 2017). The application and integration of ICT in the economy, with no exception for the tourism sector, has achieved very little uptake (Ekundayo 2014).

Information dissemination plays an essential role in showcasing tourism opportunities available in any country, and digital technologies support such dissemination (Fadipe 2016). One consequence of inadequate pre-visit information about Nigeria's tourist attractions is that tourists are amazed at the number of interesting places to visit once they arrive in the country (Ndanusa et al. 2014). An uptake of ICT and related applications would boost the tourism sector's contributions to the nation's socio-economic development.

Drivers and opportunities

In 2001, then Lagos State Governor Bola Ahmed Tinubu embarked on a campaign to attract international tourists to Lagos. His plans, however, were scoffed at by a widely read London economist who suggested that the government should "make the place habitable first" (Eneji et al. 2016). Since that time the bottlenecks associated with the development of the tourism sector have been identified, along with certain drivers and opportunities that can be harnessed to make Nigeria habitable for tourists and to attain sustainable development.

Provision of infrastructural amenities: Good roads, access to electricity, and dependable communication systems are essential in any country and should be provided by the government to assure that the country is habitable for its citizens as well as tourists; land, sea, and air transportation must be made safer, affordable, and comfortable (Ekundayo 2014). One such effort to improve infrastructure and enhance tourism is the Lagos-Calabar coastal railway project which took off in 2016 and is expected to be completed in 2019. Similarly, the Eko Atlantic City project, an infrastructural project also known as the Great Wall of Lagos, that flagged off in 2013 (Come to Nigeria, 2016). Completion of these ambitious projects, along with adding and improving the state of infrastructure, generally are viable ways of stimulating growth in the tourism sector.

Promotional tourism policies and incentives: In order to develop the tourism sector, the Nigerian government needs to formulate and fully implement favourable policies. As noted by Ekanayake and Long (2012), tourism will not manifest as a potential source of economic growth in developing countries such as Nigeria until economic policies that would promote tourism become paramount. The government can introduce incentives that would encourage the private sector's investment in the tourism industry. Such incentives include tax holidays, tax rebates, soft loans, and copyright regulations that will attract investors in tourism (Ekundayo 2014).

Anazia (2016) reported in the Guardian Newspaper about Nigeria's state government-sponsored Nigerian Corner, a popular feature of London's Notting Hill Carnival (Europe's biggest and the world's second biggest carnival). During the three-day event, the "Love Lagos Weekend" platform showcased Lagos' powerful brand in arts and entertainment. The event was also used to market the State to potential investors and partners.

Nigeria participates in the United Nation's annual World Tourism Day to propagate the role of tourism within the international community and to demonstrate its global impact on social, cultural, political, and economic values. In September 2018, the Lagos State Ministry of Tourism, Arts and Culture marked the day by launching its Tourism Master Plan, which would anchor the promotion of tourism programmes of the state for the next 20 years (Ezeobi 2018). By so doing, the government created a public-private partnership in investing in the tourism sector.

Safety and security: For Nigeria to develop its tourism industry, the security of lives and properties is crucial, beginning with strict adherence to standards of compliance with security issues such as natural disasters, health hazards, violence and terrorism, fire prevention, and environmental pollution (Fadipe 2016). In addition, there must always be adequate protection of tourist facilities. The government could partner with the private sector to provide general or specific security measures to assist victims of natural or man-made disasters. Ghana established a tourist police force to ensure security and safety at tourist sites (Mawby et al. 2015), a model that Nigeria would do well to emulate. The Institute of Security Studies, a government initiative currently underway, seeks to ensure the training and placement of security personnel and fill the current security gaps in the country.

Showcasing tourism assets: The Nigerian government must take steps to ensure that its tourism assets are well packaged and showcased; promotional campaigns must be carried out to counter the negative image that is being portrayed to the rest of the world (Adewale 2016). Public relations campaigns should spread information about tourist attractions and places of leisure at international events such as the World Tourism Day and the Notting Hill Carnival (Ndanusa et al. 2014).

The ministry of culture and tourism can be further empowered by the government to organize annual festivals where various states can promote their tourist attractions (Ekundayo 2014). Some examples of such festivals include the Festac '77 (also known as the Second World Black and African Festival of Arts and Culture), a major month-long international festival held in Lagos in 1977; the Idoma International Carnival, an annual event in Otukpo, Benue State; the Eyo Festival, which is usually presented by the people of Lagos as a tourist event; the Argungu Fishing Festival, since 1934 an annual festival in north-west Nigeria that attracts over 1 million participants from around the globe. The Lagos Museum project to be sited at the New Eko Court is underway, and the Kanta Museum is a major historical site and tourist attraction in Argungu.

Intentional, purposeful, and international dissemination of information about such events will contribute to the development of Nigeria's tourism sector in the country and the world.

Tourism industry regulation and visa policies: It is important to have laws and regulations that assure that personnel involved in the tourism sector curtail illegal or unethical excesses and conduct themselves in agreement with the industry's objectives (Ekundayo 2014). The government can also provide avenues for training staff in tourism establishments to assure that they have the necessary service delivery skills and expertise (Adewale 2016). A review of tourist entry visa regulations should seek compliance with similar regulations from other parts of the world. A lack of openness in the visa acquisition process has been identified as one of the factors that inhibit tourist visits, particularly within Africa (Okupe et al. 2018). Some African tourism countries such as Kenya, Uganda, and Rwanda have provisions for eVisa or Visa on Arrival (VOA) options. The regulators in Nigeria should establish an online platform that supports visa applications that can be processed without delay (Adewale 2016; Ekundayo 2014).

Technology/ICT readiness: ICT according to the World Economic Forum, is essential in all sectors, tourism inclusive, as it contributes to the enabling environment of a country (Okupe et al. 2018). Technology serves as a driving force to provide effective and efficient tourism service delivery at visitor destinations; ICT tools allow for operational improvement and competitiveness in the industry (Fadipe 2016). In Nigeria, the effective implementation of digital technologies and internet access will enable sales of tourism products, travel services, and hotel reservations, and meet tourists' demands for voice, text, and email communication (Ogbu et al. 2011). Online promotion of tourist sites would enhance tourist experiences with pre-visit planning, housing and travel reservation commitments, and in-country communication. Being ICT-ready implies that the country is aligned with global trends and priorities; a beneficial long-term investment.

Tourism and sustainability in Nigeria

Tourism is a complex endeavour, with diverse services provided at various stages from a traveller's initial contact to the destination of interest. Sustainable tourism development is a process that meets the needs of present tourists and host communities while protecting and enhancing their needs for the future.

UNWTO identified 12 aims of tourism sustainability: economic viability, local prosperity, employment quality, social equity, visitor fulfilment, local control, community wellbeing, cultural richness, physical integrity, biological diversity, resource efficiency, and environmental purity (World Tourism Organization 2013). Coccossis (1996) concluded that sustainable tourism could be understood in four dimensions: "economically sustainable tourism, ecologically sustainable tourism, environmentally sustainable tourism, and finally, tourism as a part of a strategy for sustainable development" (cited in Benson 2014: 652).

The essence of sustainable tourism is to make development a positive experience for local residents, companies, and tourists. Sustainable tourism takes full account of "current and future economic, social and environmental impacts, addressing the needs of visitors, the industry, the environment and host communities" (UNWTO n.d.). Attention to the environment, the economy, and the social aspects of tourism development and the attainment of balance among these dimensions will contribute to the achievement of long-term sustainability. It is as a result of the impact of tourism on all groups of society that it is given special recognition within the UN Sustainable Development Goals and the wider Agenda 2030.

Sustainable tourism development requires the involvement of all stakeholders working with robust political leadership and intergovernmental collaboration to ensure broad participation in meeting strategic goals. Itayemi (2017) emphasized that sustainable tourism can become more effective on the national level with collaboration between the Nigerian Tourism Development Corporation (NTDC), Ministry of Information & Culture, National Orientation Agency (NOA), Ministry of Internal Affairs, Ministry of External Affairs, Ministry of National Planning, National Bureau of Statistics (NBS), Nigerian Immigration Service, Nigerian Police, Ministry of Transport and Aviation, Ministry of Education, Ministry of Trade & Investment, and Nigerian Customs Service.

The attainment of sustainable tourism is a continuous process and monitoring of preventive and corrective measures as needed. Sustainable tourism is also a way of ensuring that economic, social, and aesthetic needs can be fulfilled while balancing cultural integrity, biological diversity and life in totality.

The quality and diversity of Nigeria have always been cited as a strong reason why tourism can be major foreign exchange earnings. With its population of over 180 million people and over 300 ethnic groups, Nigeria is endowed with several tourist sites or attractions. Table 16.2 identifies Nigeria's tourist attractions, most of which are natural sites at locations that require little effort for face-lifting to attract visitors.

The state of Nigeria's tourism development and identified challenges points to the lack of effort that has been made to ensure the sustainability of the sector. Though the status of tourist sites differs across the country, the overall evaluation suggests a disconnect from a sustainable tourism pathway. A review of extant economic, social, and environmental sustainability practices provides some clarity.

Good standards should aim at maximizing social and economic benefits, minimizing negative impacts on cultural heritage and minimizing negative impacts in the environment (Clarkin and Kähler 2011). Sustainable development of tourism sites requires active consultation and partnership relevant stakeholders, including host communities and local governments. Such involvement is too often lacking. Although policies exist to recognize and monitor the responsibilities of local government agencies to play specific roles in their localities, in general, there is little active participation due to the many challenges and limitations that the institutions face, including financial support. Local governments are not included in the decision-making process of national and state projects and tourism sites development. Partnership with the host communities could ensure the long-term sustainability of tourist sites as a high level of trust is built over time. Host communities can take a personal interest in their tourist sites, promoting them in a way that will generate greater interest as a tourist attraction and increase revenues. The current situation – exclusion of host communities in the development of local tourist sites – are in casts a shadow on the importance of sustainability in the tourism sector. Policies and institutional arrangements contribute to these limitations.

In Adebayo and Iweka's 2014 study of Nigeria's tourism sector, they focused on "design for deconstruction" as a way of maximizing infrastructure sustainability and minimizing harmful environmental impacts, costs, and waste. Abebayo and Iweka observed that tourism infrastructure in the country does not adopt sustainability principles – designs cannot be disassembled for re-use, thereby creating unnecessary waste and negative environmental impacts. Imikan and Ekpo (2013) found a positive correlation between infrastructure and tourism development. Fully developed infrastructure – potable water, communication technologies, housing, electricity, and transportation – are necessary catalysts to the development of tourism with attendance benefits and serve as a basis for advancing sustainability discussions.

The abundance of tourism resources in different parts of the country have the potential to become good sources of revenue, but the lack of an entrepreneurial spirit to develop and transform those resources into revenue generation is generally lacking. Cultural tourism resources are a good source of competitiveness for the country in the global tourism market (Ognonna and Igbojekwe 2013). The country can leverage the wealth of these resources to drive earnings and compete in the international market.

Some eco-tourism resources provide environmental balance. For example, the Lekki Conservation Centre is a notable "pearl of ecotourism" situated in the eastern part of Lagos state. Its mission is to preserve the natural and recreational values and biodiversity peculiar to coastal regions. The Lekki initiative was established by the Nigerian Conservation Foundation (NCF 2015), a non-governmental organization that aims to promote conservation of biodiversity and environmental sustainability. The NCF and the involvement of non-governmental organizations, private sectors, and international agencies are committed to ensuring a sustainable tourism sector.

The way forward

In Nigeria's attempt to improve the tourism industry, the Federal Ministry of Information and Culture hosted the 61st UNWTO Regional Commission for Africa and "Tourism Statistics: A Catalyst for Development" Seminar in Abuja in June 2018. Attended by various stakeholders in the tourism industry, including government ministers, agency representatives, and experts from different countries, the event positioned Nigeria on the global tourism map and its relevance in tourism development in Africa. This event focused on the goals of alleviating poverty through tourism projects, sharing innovative ideas for tourism development, and creating and sustaining partnerships to improve tourism.

The UNTWO Secretary-General reported that the seminar in Nigeria created a platform to discuss and chart a path forward to developing tourism in Africa and finding agreement on how to lay out ways the Sustainable Development Goals would align with the UNTWO agenda:

> Advocating the brand Africa; promoting travel facilitation (Connectivity / Visa); strengthening tourism statistics systems; expanding of capacity building including training facilities; promoting innovation and technology; fostering resilience (safety and security, crisis communication); unlocking growth through investment promotion by public-private partnerships; empowering youth and women through tourism; advancing the sustainability agenda (esp. biodiversity); promoting cultural heritage.
>
> *(Leadership 2018)*

Generally, the poor performance of Nigeria's tourism industry is being attributed to lack of attention and underinvestment in the industry. Fadipe (2016) recommended the following actions as remedies:

1 Regular promotion of and increase in awareness of tourism opportunities through the media.
2 Provision of adequate infrastructure at tourism sites.
3 Provision of adequate security at tourist sites.
4 Creation of investment incentives such as tax rebates, subsidies, and quicker investment approvals.
5 Ease of foreign exchange remittances.

Nigeria's tourism industry has great potential. This potential can be reached when the government enacts enduring tourism policies that are capable of protecting investments and encouraging easy flow of tourist traffic to the country (Fadipe 2016). The Nigerian tourism industry offers many opportunities for diversification of the revenue stream away from oil. However, inadequate attention given to the tourism sector has been the major hindrance to the utilization of vast resources throughout the country. To fully harness its potential, the Nigerian government needs to create an enabling environment for tourism to thrive by improving the infrastructure of the industry, attracting investors through enhanced ease of doing business, improving the security system, and addressing other economic, social, and ecological challenges that hinder the tourism industry.

References

Adebayo, A. K. and Iweka, A. C. O., 2014. Optimizing the sustainability of tourism infrastructure in Nigeria through design for deconstruction framework. *American Journal of Tourism Management*, 3(1A). doi: 10.5923/s.tourism.201401.03

Adeola, O., & Ezenwafor, K., 2016. The hospitality business in Nigeria: Issues, challenges and opportunities. *Worldwide Hospitality and Tourism Themes*, 8(2), pp. 182–194. doi:10.1108/whatt-11-2015-0053

Adewale, A. A., 2016. The task, challenges and strategies for the marketing of tourism and relaxation services in Nigeria. *International Journal of Marketing Practices*, 3(1), pp. 24–32.

Anazia, D., September 3, 2016. When Lagos takes Notting Hill Carnival by storm with #LoveLagosWeekend. *Guardian Newspaper*. Accessed on June 25, 2019. Available at: https://guardian.ng/saturday-magazine/when-lagos-takes-notting-hill-carnival-by-storm-with-lovelagosweekend/

Ashikodi, J., 2012. Tourism development in the coastal region of Nigeria: Economics of tourism development, a shift from oil dependence. Paper Presented at the Annual Conference on Tourist Development in Nigeria.

Ayeni, D. A. and Ebohon, O. J., 2012. Exploring sustainable tourism in Nigeria for developmental growth. *European Scientific Journal, ESJ*, 8(20), pp. 126–140.

Benson, E. I., 2014. Cultural tourism and sustainability in Nigeria. *Mediterranean Journal of Social Sciences*, 5(14), pp. 649–655.

Clarkin, T., and Kähler, K. N. 2011. Ecotourism. Encyclopedia of environmental Issues. *Pasadena: Salem Press*, 2, pp. 421–424.

Coccossis, H., 1996. Sustainable tourism? European Experiences *In* Priestley, G. K., Edwards, J. A, and Coccossis, H. (Eds) Tourism and sustainability: Perspectives and implications. pp. 1–21. Wallingford: Cabi.

Come to Nigeria, July 7, 2016. Nigeria infrastructural projects. Accessed on June 21, 2019. Available at: https://www.cometonigeria.com/tag/nigeria-infrastructural-projects/

Eja, E. I., Oto, Y. E., Yaro, M. A., & Inyang, I. O., 2011. Impact of hospitality industry in poverty alleviation in a tourist destination: Cross river state scenario. *Mediterranean Journal of Social Sciences*, 2(3).

Ekanayake, E. and Long, A. E., 2012. Tourism development and economic growth in developing countries. *International Journal of Business and Finance Research*, 6(1), pp. 61–63.

Ekundayo, Y., 2014. Strategic development and sustainability of tourism industry in Nigeria. Bachelor's Thesis, Laurea University of Applied Sciences, Kereva Unit. Accessed on May 31, 2018. Available at: https://www.theseus.fi/bitstream/handle/10024/83702/Strategic%20Development%20and%20Sustainability%20of%20Tourism%20Industry%20in%20Nigeria.pdf?sequence=1.

Ele, C. O., 2017. Religious tourism in Nigeria: The economic perspective. *Online Journal of Arts, Management & Social Sciences* 2(1), pp. 220–232.

Eneji, M. A., Odey, F. A., and Bullus, M. L., 2016. Diversification of Nigeria's economy: Impact of tourism on sustainable development in Nigeria. *International Journal of Research in Humanities and Social Studies*, 3(5), pp. 36–44.

Esu, B.B., 2012. Linking human capital management with tourism development and management for economic survival: The Nigeria experience. *International Journal of Business and Social Science*, 3(11), pp. 276–287

Ezeobi, C., September 27, 2018. Nigeria: Commemorating world tourism day the Lagos way. Accessed on June 25, 2019. Available at: https://allafrica.com/stories/201809270099.html

Fadipe, A. S., 2016. Current and future global trends in hospitality and tourism: A case of Nigeria. International Conference on Food Science and Human Technology, College of Food and Human Science, Federal University of Agriculture, Abeokuta, Ogun State, Nigeria.

Imikan, A. M and Ekpo, K. J., 2013. Infrastructure and tourism development in Nigeria: The case study of rivers state. *International Journal of Economic Development Research and Investment*, 3(2), pp. 53–60.

International Telecommunication Union, 2017. Measuring the information society report, Volume 1. Available at: ttps://www.itu.int/en/ITU-D/Statistics/Documents/publications/misr2017/MISR2017_Volume1.pdf

Itayemi, O., October 7, 2017. The challenges of sustainable tourism in Nigeria. *This Day*. Accessed on June 25, 2019. Available at: https://www.thisdaylive.com/index.php/2017/10/07/the-challenges-of-sustainable-tourism-in-nigeria/

Leadership, 2018. As Nigeria moves to reposition tourism. Accessed on August 17, 2018. Available at: https://leadership.ng/2018/06/14/as-nigeria-moves-to-reposition-tourism/

Mawby, R., Boakye, K. and Jones, C., 2015. Policing tourism: The emergence of specialist units. *Policing and Society*, 25(4), pp. 378–392.

Mejabi, E. I. and Abutu, G. N., 2015. Nigerian Tourism: a catalyst for sustainable national development. *International Journal of Public Administration and Management Research*, 3(1), pp. 37–47.

Metilelu, O. O., 2016. Human capital development trends in the hospitality and tourism industry: A case of southwest Nigeria. *African Journal of Hospitality, Tourism and Leisure*, 5(4), pp. 1–9.

Nana, A. E., 2017. Tourism: A promoter of human development. *UJAH: Unizik Journal of Arts and Humanities*, 18(2), pp. 192–210.

NCF, 2015. *Lekki Conservation Centre*. Accessed on June 30, 2019. Available at: https://www.ncfnigeria.org/about-ncf/support-ncf/item/235-lekki-conservation-centre.

Ndajiya, A., Shehu, M. and Yunusa, H. M., 2014. The possible impact of tourism industry on Nigeria's economy. *Review of Public Administration and Management*, 3(5), pp. 67–75.

Ndanusa, M. M. N., Harada, Y. and Islam, M. A., 2014. Challenges to growth in tourism industry of a developing country: The case of Nigeria. *Asian Social Science* 10(19), pp. 282–290.

Nwosu, B., 2016. A review of the hotel industry in Nigeria: Size, structure and issues. *Worldwide Hospitality and Tourism Themes*, 8(2), pp. 117–133. doi:10.1108/whatt-10–2015–0042

Ogbu, S. E., Idris, S. and Ijagbemi, A. B., 2011. Information and communication technology (ICT): A veritable tool for tourism development in Nigeria. In Nigeria Computer Society (NCS), 10th International Conference, July, pp. 25–29.

Ognonna, C. O and Igbojekwe, P. A., 2013. Local government and responses to sustainable tourism development in Nigeria: A study of local government authorities in Imo State. Accessed on June 24, 2019. Available at: http://www.ijbts-journal.com/images/main_1366796758/0053-Ognonna.pdf

Okogba, E., 2018. Tourism: Nigeria's new economic frontier. Available at: https://www.vanguardngr.com/2018/05/tourism-nigerias-new-economic-frontier/

Okupe, A., Ward, T. and Adeola, O., 2018. Enhancing hospitality and tourism industry competitiveness in sub-Saharan Africa. In Adeleye, I. and Esposito, M. (Eds.) *Africa's Competitiveness in the Global Economy* (pp. 137–167). Palgrave Macmillan, Cham.

PM News, May 7, 2018. Religious tourism captured in Lagos tourism master plan – Ayorinde. Accessed on June 21, 2019. Available at: https://www.pmnewsnigeria.com/2018/05/07/religious-tourism-captured-in-lagos-tourism-master-plan-ayorinde/

Riti, J. S., Song, Y. and Kamah, M., 2017. Terrorism and tourism trend (T3): Empirical evidence from Nigeria. *Procedia Engineering*, 1, pp. 125–136.

UNWTO, 2006. Nigeria tourism development master plan: Institutional capacity strengthening to the tourism sector in Nigeria: Final report executive summary. Accessed on June 25, 2019. Available at: http://www.ibadektyma.com/tourism_masterplan.pdf

UNWTO, 2008. Tourism highlights. Accessed on June 13, 2018. Available at: https://www.e-unwto.org/doi/pdf/10.18111/9789284413560.

UNWTO, n.d. Sustainable development of tourism. Accessed on June 30, 2019. Available at: https://sdt.unwto.org/content/about-us-5.

Wesgro, 2017. Nigeria: Tourism market insights, 2017. Accessed on June 13, 2018. Available at: http://www.wesgro.co.za/pdf_repository/Tourism%20Market%20Insights%20Nigeria%202017.pdf

World Economic Forum, 2017. The travel & tourism competitiveness report 2017. Accessed on June 15, 2018. Available at: https://www.weforum.org/reports/the-travel-tourism-competitiveness-report-2017.

World Tourism Organization, 2013. Sustainable tourism for development: Guidebook: enhancing capacities for sustainable tourism for development in developing countries. UNWTO.

World Travel and Tourism Council, 2017a. Travel & tourism economic impact 2017 world. Accessed on June 12, 2018. Available at: https://www.wttc.org/-/media/files/reports/economic-impact-research/regions-2017/world2017.pdf.

World Travel and Tourism Council, 2017b. Travel & tourism economic impact 2017, Nigeria. Accessed on June 13, 2018. Available at: https://www.wttc.org/-/media/files/reports/economic-impact-research/countries-2017/nigeria2017.pdf.

World Travel and Tourism Council, 2018. The economic impact of travel & tourism. Accessed on June 12, 2018. Available at: https://www.wttc.org/-/media/files/reports/economic-impact-research/regions-2018/world2018.pdf.

WTTC Report, 2014. 44th tourism working group meeting Cusco, Peru. Accessed on June 12, 2018. Available at: http://mddb.apec.org/Documents/2014/TWG/TWG1/14_twg44_021.pdf.

17

Tourism development in Niger

Challenges and opportunities

Sarah Gafarou

Introduction

Despite its contrasting natural landscapes, rich biodiversity and unique cultural mix, Niger is not considered to be a global tourist destination. Tourism has, however, proven to be a lucrative activity for many local communities in Northern Niger from the 1980s until the 1990s. Although the 1980s saw Niger's Northern tourism industry flourishing due to the dessert's appeal and interest surrounding Tuareg communities, waves of instability caused by rebellions between 1991-1995 and in 2007 later negatively impacted the image of the destination, resulting in a reduction in demand and consequent collapse of the industry. Although there have been attempts at restoring tourist activities in several parts of the country, the instability following the Arab Spring of 2011 and more recent terrorist attacks in the region are still preventing the rebirth of an industry that, in the context of Niger, heavily relies on international arrivals. The country is, however, launching new initiatives as an attempt to diversify its tourism industry which is still subject to instability caused by tensions in the North and neighbouring countries.

This chapter seeks to explore the intricacies of tourism in Niger by looking at the interconnection between peace and tourism, the historical evolution of tourism development, its impact on political and social dynamics, the characteristics of the tourism market and recent trends and the opportunities and constraints of tourism in Niger.

Location and tourism attractions

Niger is the sixth largest country in Africa, with an area of 1,267,000 km². It is located in the Sahel region, a transition zone, between the Sahara in the North and the Sudanic Savanna in the South. Niger is a landlocked country surrounded by seven countries (Libya, Chad, Nigeria, Benin, Burkina Faso, Mali and Algeria). The country is covered by the Sahara Desert for 80% of its land areas, whilst the South in contrast is characterised by forests and grassland areas.

The varied geography of the country makes it an interesting place to visit in the region.

Attractive wild and scenic African imagery is ever-present; in the South, fauna-rich savanna lands contrast with the memorable desert plains of the North. The country also boasts

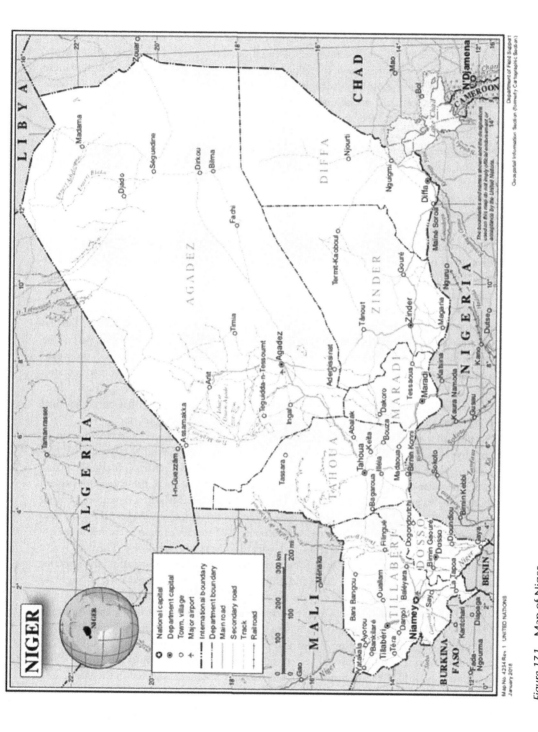

Figure 17.1 Map of Niger
Source: UN (2018).

the largest World Heritage Site in Africa, recognised by UNESCO since 1991 (UNESCO 2018a), the Aïr and Tenere reserve, also called the Alps of the Sahara.

The North, gathers a wide variety of landscapes, from sand dunes of the Sahara to volcanic rock mass of the Tenere. Isolated and mysterious, the site is ideal for excursions and bivouacs in the desert (Grégoire 2006) for tourists in search of adventure. As the point of departure for treks in the desert, tourists have the opportunity to visit Agadez, famous for its Sudanese architecture. Built in the 10th century, it is home to historic monuments, its great Mosque and archaeological remains of the mysterious Tuareg cité of Assodé (Boucksom 2009). Additionally, the desert was, for several years, known for hosting the internationally famous cross-country Dakar rally.

Not only are the geographical features of Northern Niger attractive, but its cultural specificities and differences also make it a unique tourist destination. Home to the largest group of Tuaregs, its cultural differences set Niger apart from its neighbours. Treks in the desert are often sold as a cultural experience with the promise of nomadic adventure and learning about the myths of the blue men of the desert, the Tuaregs, who represent 10% of the overall country's population (Grégoire 2006).

The cultural diversity of Niger allows for a rich set of festivals where different ethnicities celebrate their traditions, promoting cultural tourism in the region. As such, the Festival de l'Aïr, held annually since 2001, gathers Tuaregs from numerous countries to promote their music, dances, handicrafts and rituals such as the camel races. As the largest Tuareg gathering, the three-day festival brings an increasing number of visitors (Dambo et al. 2014). Other traditional ceremonies also promote cultural tourism, such as the Géréwol festival. Each year, at the end of the rainy season and as part of the larger Cure Salee festival, the Woodabee men, part of the Fulani people, perform dances at the Géréwol ceremony. Enchanting and enigmatic, the week-long celebration has become a tourist attraction since notorious magazines and documentaries have covered the festivities (Lassibille 2006). Other festival included the Agadez African Music Festival (Geels 2006) gathering attendees from all over the region which has been cancelled since 2014 due to security reasons, as will be discussed in the following section.

On the other hand, the lush and green Southern end of the country is notorious for its rich biodiversity and wildlife. Located a mere two hours from the capital Niamey, the W National Park is one of the most easily accessed protected areas in West Africa. It takes its name from the meander of the Niger River, which provides scenic views of the riverbank broken by rocky hills. As part of the WAP complex (W-Arly-Pendjari), the largest contiguous region of protected areas in West Africa spread over three countries namely Niger, Burkina Faso and Benin, it houses rich vegetation and approximately 77 species of mammals including endangered elephants, lions, hippopotamus and leopards (Grettenberger 1984). The park is also famous for ornithology with a variety of approximately 300 species (Boucksom 2009) and for housing archaeological sites. The value and importance of the W National Park of Niger for global conservation was recognised in 1996 when it was inscribed as a World Heritage site by UNESCO (2018b). Similarly, the Kouré reserve, 60 km away from Niamey, is the last giraffe refuge in West Africa, increasing to more than 200 giraffes in 2009 (Ciofolo et al. 2009).

Culturally, the Southern region is also full of unexplored potential such as the Prix Dan Gourmou in Tahoua, a music festival celebrating Nigerien artists and music in Niger, which last took place in 2014. Rich in history, the ancient capital, Zinder, situated in the South-East region, is the vestige of the Sultanate of Damagaram, housing its palace and numerous architectural treasures. The area is also famous for its Hausa houses in banco and its handicrafts, popular among tourists. As for the capital, it serves as the crossroads between different ethnicities of the country, gathering historical and cultural facts in the National museum Boubou-Hama.

A historical narrative on tourism in Niger

This section will explore the birth of the tourism industry in Niger, starting with its development in the North of the territory which was punctuated by waves of insecurity affecting the growth of the industry. Also impacted by Northern unrest, the development of the industry in the South followed a different course and approach which will be covered in the second part of this segment.

As the largest desert in the world, the Sahara has, for many years, fascinated scientists and European explorers. By the end of the 19th century, Tuaregs, the nomadic inhabitants of the desert, stood up against colonisation efforts from France, realising they would be losing control over their land. France however, managed to conquer the region by dividing Tuaregs into artificially created cantons. Once the Sahara Desert was under French occupation (which was later split into several states), it became the playground of French administrators, government officials, explorers and rare tourists, avid for adventures across the desert. In 1968, based on various desert expeditions, Louis-Henri Mourèn, a French pharmacist, developed Air Trans Image Niger the first commercial tours of the desert (Grégoire 2006). This was supported by road infrastructure facilitating access, thanks to the uranium boom of the 1970s. French expatriates working in the uranium mines of Arlit created the first demand for these desert expeditions. Initially, the Tuaregs' involvement in tourism was coincidental; expatriates working in the region asked locals for tours to their villages. Due to their knowledge of the region, locals were hired by tour operators as guides and drivers. At the time, the potential for tourism as a tool for economic development was unknown. Tourism was even criticised in traditional Tuareg society, seen as a white western influenced. However, it offered alternative forms of employment to pastoralism, which was struggling after the droughts of the 70s and 80s. Further development occurred and several agencies, all run by Europeans, were created in the early 1970s, to take European tourists particularly French and Italians, on trips and treks into the desert (Scholze 2010).

At the beginning of the 1970s, the Nigerien government started realising tourism's economic potential. As a result, a law to formalise tour agencies was adopted in 1974 and later the Directorate of Tourism and Hospitality (Direction du Tourisme et de l'hôtellerie, DHT) was created in 1977 to support the efforts of the tourism board (Office National du Tourisme) (Boucksom 2009). In 1980, as an effort to promote tourism to local communities, the Nigerien government imposed a law preventing foreigners from owning tour agencies (Grégoire 2006). Consequently, the first local agencies were created that same year, headed by Mano Dayak. Thanks to his experience as a guide for a French company, he created his agency, Temet Voyage in 1988. Using his knowledge of the region and strong European connections, he became a leader of the Tuareg community, not only for tourism but also as a figure of the Tuareg rebellion of 1991 (Boucksom 2009; Scholze 2010). Quickly becoming the largest in the region, his agency offered complete desert and cultural Tuareg experiences, bringing European tourists to local communities. As a friend of Thierry Sabine, the creator of the Dakar rally race, Mano Dayak helped to create routes passing through Agadez when he realised the economic potential it had for the region. The event, which passed through Agadez in 1978, the year of its creation, was a huge contributor to the expansion of the tourism industry, whether directly, through the creation of employment, or indirectly, by promoting the region of Agadez in the European market. For several years from 1978 to 1990, the rally passed through Agadez and occasionally Niamey (Boucksom 2009). At each edition, it was estimated that between 300 and 500 millions of FCFA were injected into the local economy. For over a decade, tourism in northern Niger was thriving and run exclusively by local operators. Although it was on a small scale and targeted a niche market, the tourism industry largely benefitted the local community. From restaurants to hotels, artisans and even hawkers, everyone was benefitting from the growth of the industry (Grégoire 2006).

The town of Agadez, famous for its Sudanese architecture, became the point of departure for treks into the desert (Grégoire and Scholze 2012). Tourism in Agadez was at its peak in 1990, when the city was reachable by direct flights from Paris. Though numbers differ, it was reported that in 1990, approximately 3,000 tourists would visit Agadez (Scholze 2010). While there were tensions between the Tuaregs of the North and the government in the South (Hausa and Zarma communities) for many years due to ethnic rivalries which were intensified by the colonial regime (Youngstedt 2008), they peaked in 1990–1991 after the casualties of the Tchin-Tabaraden incidents. Tourism growth in the region drastically plunged in 1991 after the rebellion led by Tuareg groups. Temet-Voyages run by Mano Dayak, the leader in the region, had to close following orders from the Nigerien Armed Forces (Forces armées nigériennes, FAN) for suspicion of complicity in the rebellion (Grégoire 2006). As tourism in Niger was heavily dependent on international arrivals, the perception of insecurity in the country by the international community had devastating effects on the industry.

During the following three years, tourism in the region was almost non-existent. The incidents not only affected tourism in the North, but in the country as a whole. Even though peace accords were signed in 1995 and new agencies were created in 1996, tourism struggled to regain footing. In an effort to attract tourism, promote the Nigerien fashion industry and create jobs, the United Nations Development Program supported the creation of the FIMA, the Festival International de la Mode Africaine (the International Festival of African Fashion) held in Agadez in 1998 (Cooper 2003). The event received criticism from Islamists groups, which blamed the West for influencing Nigerian culture and values. As a result, violent protests held during the second edition of the FIMA in Niamey in 2000, led to the move of FIMA outside of Niger, before it returned in 2003 (Youngstedt 2008).

In the second phase of tourism development in the 2000s, Tuaregs purposely got involved in tourism, as many knew its economic benefits. Between 2000 and 2006, efforts were made by the Minister of Tourism, Rhissa ag Boula (a Tuareg former leader or rebel factions) to revive the tourism industry by granting licenses to local agencies. The renewal of direct flights between Paris and Agadez boosted the number of tourist arrivals, reaching between 3,500 and 5,000 people by season, between November and January (Grégoire and Scholze 2012). However, the second rebellion of 2007–2009 damaged all chances of tourism growing in the North. Locals previously working as guides used their knowledge of the desert to find a new source of income by smuggling migrants headed to Libya (Raineri 2018). Subsequently the 2011 unrests and civil wars of neighbouring countries Mali and Libya worsened the situation furthermore. The continuous insecurity in the region, linked to hostage situations of terrorist groups (Al Qaïda au Maghreb islamique, AQMI) as well as military attacks and trafficking (drug, weapons) prevented potential tourist activities from recovering (Dambo et al. 2014).

With regard to tourism in the South of Niger, the dynamic was very different. Niamey, the capital, was originally a collection of small fishing villages. During French colonization, it was chosen over Zinder to serve as the new capital in 1926 due to its position on the banks of the Niger River (Youngstedt 2013). As the capital, it developed to become the centre for administrations during and after colonisation. After independence in 1960, expatriates (mostly French) as well as diplomatic and humanitarian missions settled in Niamey. For many years, tourists would only pass through Niamey as a stopover before driving to Agadez to trek in the desert until direct flights were made available in 1988 (Boucksom 2009; Grégoire 2006).

While the North focused on leisure tourism, Niamey's tourism development was centred around the MICE (Meetings, Incentives, Conferences and Exhibitions) segment. To develop tourism in the capital, state-owned hotels the Sahel and the Grand hotel were built in the 1960s. The government attempted to attract tourists by hosting numerous events in the capital. In this regard, the Paris-Dakar Rally passed through Niamey in 1979, 1980 and from 1988 to 1990. Unfortunately, the insecurity situation also affected tourism prospects in the capital, as seen by the cancellation of four stops between Niamey and Sabha (Libya) for the Paris-Dakar Rally in 2000. Similarly, that same year, during the second edition of the FIMA protests and deadly demonstrations further exacerbated the perception of insecurity in the country (Boucksom 2009). In an effort to restore a positive image of Niger and boost the economy, political leaders decided to host the fifth edition of the Jeux de la francophonie or "Francophone Sports and Arts Festival" in Niamey in December 2005. As a founding father of the International Organisation of La Francophonie, Hamani Diori, Niger's first President managed to secure the rights for Niger to host the event which is held every four to five years. By hosting the Jeux, Niamey was able to acquire newly built infrastructure through public-private partnerships and successfully welcome over 4,000 visitors (Youngstedt 2008).

Further South, the potential of leisure tourism had long been minimised. Leisure tourism around Niamey was mostly catering to expatriates living in Niamey desiring to visit the surrounding areas on the weekend such as the Kouré reserve or W National Park of Niger (Boucksom 2009). While the park received the status of reserve in 1926, it was only in 1954 that park and reserve limits started to be enforced by the government, leading to several conflicts over the use of natural resources, such as land encroachment from local farmers, or pastoralists moving south into wetter grasslands where the park is located (Amadou and Boutrais 2012).

The park had been suffering from the encroachment of local communities after the droughts of the 1970s affected the whole country. The potential of the W National Park for tourism had therefore not been explored due to lack of investment and conservation problems. Communities living around the park still heavily rely on the use of natural resources, from agriculture and forestry to raising livestock. Several efforts have been made by local and international organisations to conserve biodiversity, which is the principal reason for visiting the park. As such, a transboundary biosphere reserve was established in 2002, encouraging the three countries of the WAP (W-Arly-Pendjari) complex to work together in order to improve biodiversity conservation (Michelot and Ouedraogo 2009). In 2017, the conservation value of the W National Park as part of the WAP complex was recognised by UNESCO when it was listed as a World Heritage Site. These efforts to protect the conservation and tourism potential of the park reflect the strategy of the government to further develop the tourism industry in the South of the country, as the insecurity in the North hinders further planning.

Composition of the tourism market in Niger

Figure 17.2 provides data about the number of arrivals by air in Niger between 1990 and 2017. While the evolution is not linear and drops may correspond to security incidents in the country (e.g. 1992 and 2007), we can also see that the number of tourists arriving to Niger has continuously increased from 2009 to 2017, despite unrests in the North in 2011–2012.

This increase also proves that efforts by the Nigerien government to grow the tourism industry have been successful. Due to problems in the North, the government has decided to diversify its product offering and provide more accommodation in the capital, in order to grow the business tourism segment as per the National Strategy for Sustainable Development of Tourism (Stratégie National de Développement Durable du Tourisme) for 2011–2015 (PNDS-TARAYYA 2016). Table 17.1 documents the evolution of the number of hotels in Niger (1991–2017), showing a clear increase in Niamey from 11 to 75. In 2010, hotels in Niamey accounted for only 34% of overall hotels in Niger, while the rate has increased to 45% in 2017, highlighting the number of investments in the capital, as well as the importance of Niamey to Niger's tourism strategy.

Figure 17.3 provides the composition of international tourist arrivals between 1990 and 2017.

The data confirms that up to the first rebellion, tourists were coming in majority from Europe (over 50% until 1992). Inevitably, the rebellion elicited a negative perception and had drastic

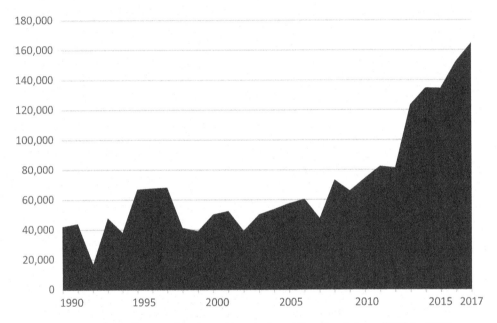

Figure 17.2   Number of international tourist arrivals to Niger by air from 1990 to 2017
Source: Based on various Annual Statistical Reports of Tourism in Niger (Institut National de la Statistique).

Table 17.1   Breakdown of the number of hotels and capacity in Niger from 1991 to 2017 (Niamey and Agadez)

	1991	*1995*	*2000*	*2005*	*2010*	*2015*	*2017*
Niger Hotels	29	38	55	80	94	125	164
Rooms	1,224	1,146	1,304	1,919	2,119	2,690	3,248
Agadez Hotels	6	4	12	16	9	11	15
Rooms	98	66	150	250	170	267	246
Niamey Hotels	11	10	12	23	32	57	75
Rooms	671	559	529	867	982	1,333	1,578

Source: Based on various Annual Statistical Reports of Tourism in Niger (Institut National de la Statistique 2010, 2014, 2016, 2018).

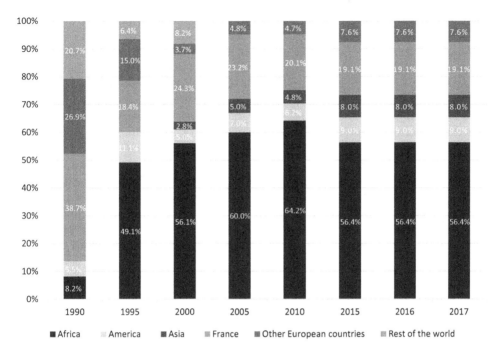

Figure 17.3 Composition of international tourist arrivals by air in Niger from 1990 to 2017 by source market

Source: Based on various annual statistical reports of Tourism in Niger (Institut National de la Statistique).

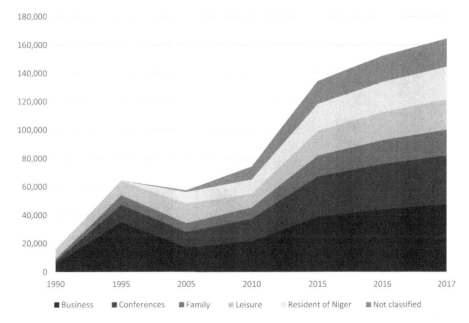

Figure 17.4 Evolution of the number of international tourist arrivals in Niger by air, according to the source market

Source: Based on various annual statistical reports of Tourism in Niger (Institut National de la Statistique).

consequences on the number of European tourists which continuously decreased, to represent less than 26% of arrivals (by air) in 2017. Niger's heavy dependence on western tourists (mainly France) has been replaced by other African tourists, representing over 56% of air arrivals in 2017.

Even though the share of African travellers has decreased between 2010 and 2017, Figure 17.4 demonstrates that this figure has continued to increase, but has been lowered by an increase in Asian tourists. The share was lowered due to the increase of tourists arriving from Asia.

Since the early 2000s, there has been a significant decrease in tourists coming from the segment "rest of the world", from 8.2% arrivals in 2000 to 0 arrival from 2005 to 2015. This data confirms the negative impact the unrest has had on the industry. Interestingly, while there were no tourists coming from Asia until 1995 (or no data), the number has grown to reach 8% of overall arrivals in 2017. The overall composition of international travellers in 2017 is a testimony to the Government's strategy to diversify its source markets.

As confirmed by Figure 17.5, in 2017, only 12% of arrivals by air in 2017 were for leisure purposes compared to over 41% in 1990. As expected by the government's strategy to focus on business tourism in the capital, the share of conference travellers grew from 12% in 1990 to 21% in 2017.

Constraints and challenges

The African continent is one of the least visited regions in the world, accounting for only 5% share of international arrivals (UNWTO 2018). According to the Africa Tourism Monitor (2015), the negative image of Africa (health and insecurity), as well as the lack of transport infrastructure and the high cost of travel and tourism services are some of the main barriers to

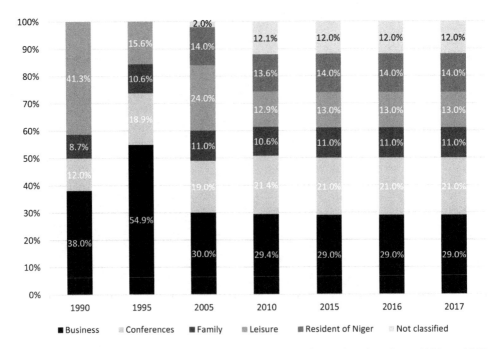

Figure 17.5 Composition of the type of tourists arriving by air in Niger from 1990 to 2017, according to the reason for the trip

Source: Based on various annual statistical reports of Tourism in Niger (Institut National de la Statistique).

the development of the industry. In the case of Niger, the international community's perception of insecurity, coupled with limited access due to a minimal number of airlines servicing the capital as well as high travel costs, is all impeding the expansion of the industry. Insecurity in the North has changed the behaviour and precautions taken by tourists; and as such, tourism has had to be guided by professionals. Adventure travel (driving treks through the desert from Algeria to Niger) which was popular in the 1980s and 1990s, collapsed after the Tuareg rebellion (Scholze 2010). Niger's tourism industry severely suffered several waves of insecurity, deterring western travellers from visiting. With neighbouring countries such as Libya and Mali facing rebellions and political instability, it has proven difficult to position Niger as a safe place to visit (Dambo et al. 2014). Peace and security are often perceived as a requirement for tourism, to not only attract tourists but also investors for the planning and development of the activity and its infrastructures (Causevic and Lynch 2013; Henderson 2007). Furthermore, travel warnings from western countries put an even greater strain on potential international travellers. Within Niger, even European expatriates based in Niamey are deterred from visiting other regions due to the travel warnings and red zones issued by their Foreign Ministries.

While the tourism industry was impacted by insecurity and tensions in the North, the aftermath could have been minimised. Governments have an important role to play in the development and growth of tourism (Akama 2002). Institutional failure, linked to the lack of investment and interest by the government contributes to the deterioration of the quality of the industry (FMI 2013). Though the government has since recognised the contribution of, and role of tourism in development, for many years, the sector lacked support and investment from the government (Boucksom 2009; Scholze 2010) resulting in a lack of competitiveness at the international level.

Focusing on the business segment allowed Niger to recuperate tourism traffic after the crisis of the 1990s and early 2000 however, in the long term; the country needs to diversify its product offering to cater to a wider range of travellers. As such, targeting different segments would benefit a wider range of tourist professionals, from accommodation to catering, while preventing over-reliance on one type of traveller.

Moreover, the quality of tourism products offered may hamper the potential of tourism expansion. Conserving biodiversity is paramount to the quality and success of ecotourism.

At the W National Park, rural communities, as in other countries in Sub Saharan Africa, are heavily reliant on natural resources to survive and have very limited livelihood alternatives (Muller and Albers 2004). In the case of Niger, the scarcity of arable land in the country, coupled with droughts and the level of poverty, explains pressures the park faces and issues with local communities over land use restrictions. Tourism is often chosen as the most appropriate route to sustain conservation initiatives while providing income to local communities (Whande 2010) and Park W is no exception. However, the biggest issue is that currently tourism is not providing substantial revenues to sustain the communities around the park, whether through the entrance fees or through the tourism services created around the park, such as guides, hotels and restaurants. As a result, communities continue to hinder conservation efforts in the park through poaching, agriculture and deforestation. Consequently, failed conservation efforts lead to a decrease in the quality and value of the tourism product offer, preventing the success of tourism and its benefits to locals, ultimately resulting in a vicious cycle.

Numerous conservation projects are run by international organisations; however, many issues arise with such initiatives. Decisions taken internationally are often inconsistent with local realities, focusing on creating theoretical action plans at the international level, far from fieldwork reality (Büscher 2009) ultimately resulting in ineffective management of the area. The appeal of implementing ecotourism projects is the idea of creating self-financing conservation initiatives, which would ultimately not need any further aid or projects. However, as seen with the situation at the W National Park and the numerous projects aiming at improving ecotourism by UNWTO, UNDP and other organisations alike (UNESCO 2018b), tourism is still not allowing for self-financing of conservation efforts and continues to rely on international aid for financing (Miller et al. 2015). In comparison, at the peak of its glory in the early 1990s, the cultural and adventure tourism undertaken in the North of the country was very profitable for local communities (Grégoire 2006).

Opportunities

Strengthening of intra-regional and domestic tourism has been shown to have a positive impact as post-crisis management (Al-Hamarneh and Steiner 2004; Kabii 2018). The potential of intra-Africa travel is being emphasised by new regulations in trade and in the aviation industry which may facilitate exchanges and travel within the continent. Led by the African Union as part of its Agenda 2063 to commemorate the Yamoussoukro decision of 1999, the Single African Air Transport Market (SAATM) was launched in January 2018. The aim of the SAATM is to liberalise civil aviation in Africa by creating a single unified air transport market (African Union 2018) boosting intra-Africa tourism by enhancing air connectivity and inducing competition of air services leading to fare reductions. Parallelly, the African Continental Free Trade Area (AfCFTA) was signed during the tenth Extraordinary Summit of the AU Assembly of Heads of State and Government in 2018, promising to expand intra African trade through the free movement of business persons and investments. Though these agreements have not been implemented yet, the signing marks the beginning of promising exchanges within Africa, facilitating the movement of people, goods and services, providing an opportunity for tourism in Niger to attract intra-regional tourists. In the case of Niger, 56.7% of arrivals by air in 2017 were from Africa while globally, intra-regional tourism represents 80% of international arrivals (UNWTO 2018). This number highlights the potential for Niger to further focus its efforts on targeting other African nations as intra-regional helps to build a more resilient industry as also seen since 1995 in Niger. As such, intra-regional and domestic tourism allows for the tourism industry to stabilise in times of crisis (Al-Hamarneh and Steiner 2004) and external economic shocks (UNWTO and ILO 2013).

While domestic tourism has long been neglected (Scholze 2010), particular efforts should be undertaken to address the various segments of that market, targeting both expatriates based in Niamey and Nigeriens. As mentioned in the 2016 presidential program, the re-elected President Issoufou Mahamadou highlighted the need to develop domestic tourism to strengthen the industry against western dependence for tourism. By diversifying its tourism to target the domestic segment, Niger's tourism industry could be more stable and resilient, preventing potential external shocks. By the same token, the intensification of trade and relations between Niger and China, the first tourism source market in the world (UNWTO 2014), could also create opportunities for Chinese tourism to develop in Niger, as seen by the increase of tourists arriving from Asia. Targeting different source markets and different types of travellers would ultimately encourage Niger to also propose varied tourism products to cater to the needs and interests of the travellers.

The MICE segment continues to be a strong product that Niger wants to develop. The successful hosting of international events such as the 33rd Summit of Heads of State of the African Union which took place in July 2019 can lead to the development of MICE products in the country. The benefits of hosting international event are twofold; on one hand, such international events provide exposure and global prestige to the country further contributing to its rebranding; on the other hand, important budgets are allocated for the hosting of these conferences, providing the opportunity to gather important funds to create new infrastructures. The event, which was expected to welcome more than 4,000 guests, surpassed expectations and gathered more than 5,316 guests (Agence UA 2019). Through this event, Niger was able to promote itself as a global destination and show that it was able to successfully host international events. In preparation for this event, a number of hotel developments were undertaken which helped to increase the hotel capacity of Niamey, leaving a legacy of tourism development in the country (NouvelObs 2019).

Similarly, regional or global sports events may help build a destination's brand, attracting investments in infrastructure development and more visitors. The Paris-Dakar Rally, which last took place on the African continent in 2007, was rumoured to return to the continent in 2020 (Kalfa 2018). While the director of the rally mentioned an interest in countries such as Algeria and Angola, there is the hope that the competition could eventually return to Niger if security conditions permit.

Along the same line, the Nigerien government has also taken the necessary precautions to upgrade its infrastructure as an attempt to revamp its tourism industry. Following the government's tourism strategy of 2011–2015, several construction projects through public-private partnerships, have been undertaken to improve the infrastructure in Niger, including roads and airports. The Diori Hamani road interchange and the express road leading to the international airport of Niamey have been renovated, for safer transit across the city (Lawan 2018), while the renovation of the Diori Hamani International Airport of Niamey is expected to allow for an increase in air traffic (ICAO 2016). Other cities in Niger have also upgraded their infrastructures. Several airports are undergoing renovations such as the airport of Agadez, the extension of a runway landing in Diffa and the modernisation of Zinder airport to become an international airport (Niamey et les 2 jours 2018). Not only are the renovations benefitting the inhabitants of Niger, but they are also providing infrastructure that can contribute to the growth of tourism domestically and internationally.

Other recovery mechanisms to rejuvenate the tourism industry include new campaigns and international marketing strategies to improve the country's image (Al-Hamarneh and Steiner 2004). To successfully attract new markets and counteract the negative image of the country, Niger has to work towards rebranding and repositioning the country on the tourism scene.

However, the lack of online presence of tourism bodies such as the Ministry of Tourism or the National Office of Tourism reflects a missed opportunity to promote tourism and portray the country differently.

Conclusion

The development of the tourism industry in Niger has shown that while peace and security are important components of the expansion of the industry in a country, careful planning and coordination need to be undertaken to recover and rebuild the industry after a crisis. As a transversal sector, tourism has on the one hand the potential to have an impact on all dimensions of sustainable development, but on the other hand, it depends on various industries as it includes complex linkages with all other economic sectors, from transport to infrastructure and agriculture.

Careful considerations need to be given to post-conflict zones, in order to develop a national tourism development strategy encompassing a wide range of cross-sectorial linkages.

While tourism alone cannot solve conflicts, there is an intricate relationship between tourism and peace and security. Managed responsibly, tourism may be used as a powerful tool in post-conflict areas, stimulating economic growth and employment, particularly in areas with high youth unemployment rates, as this segment is more vulnerable to fall prey to violence and extremism.

Bibliography

Africa Tourism Monitor. 2015. "Unlocking Africa's Tourism Potential." *African Development Bank, the Africa House at New York University and the Africa Travel Association.* Accessed 7 June 2018, https://www.afdb.org/fileadmin/uploads/afdb/Documents/Publications/Africa_Tourism_Monitor_-_Unlocking_Africa's_Tourism_Potential_-_Vol_3_-_Issue_1.pdf

African Union. 2018. "Establishment and Launching of a Single African Air Transport Market (SAATM)." October 28. Accessed 13 August 2018, https://au.int/en/newsevents/20180128/establishment-and-launching-single-african-air-transport-market-saatm

Agence UA. 2019. "Détails Événement". *Presidence de la République du Niger,* July 17. Accessed 28 September 2019, https://www.agenceua-niger2019.ne/event-details/247

Akama, John S. 2002. "The role of government in the development of tourism in Kenya." *International Journal of Tourism Research* 4 (1): 1–14.

Al-Hamarneh, Ala, and Christian Steiner. 2004. "Islamic tourism: Rethinking the strategies of tourism development in the Arab world after September 11, 2001." *Comparative Studies of South Asia, Africa and the Middle East* 24 (1): 173–182.

Amadou, Boureima, and Jean Boutrais. 2012. "Logiques pastorales et de conservation de la nature: les transhumances et le Parc du W (Niger, Burkina Faso, Bénin)." *Autrepart* 1(60): 55–75.

Boucksom, Audrey. 2009. "Arts 'touristiques' en Afrique et consommateurs Occidentaux: le cas de l'artisanat d'art au Niger." PhD diss., Université Panthéon-Sorbonne-Paris I.

Büscher, B. E. 2009. "Struggles over consensus, anti-politics and marketing: neoliberalism and transfrontier conservation and development in Southern Africa." PhD diss., Vrije Universiteit.

Causevic, Senija, and Paul Lynch. 2013. "Political (in) stability and its influence on tourism development." *Tourism Management* 34: 145–157.

Ciofolo, Isabelle, Ambouta Karimou, and Le Pendu Yvonnick. 2009. "Les dernières girafes d'Afrique de l'ouest: sauvegarde assurée ou avenir menacé?" *Revue d'écologie* 64 (4): 351–358. http://hdl.handle.net/2042/55797

Cooper, Barbara M. 2003. "Anatomy of a riot: The social imaginary, single women, and religious violence in Niger." *Canadian Journal of African Studies* 37 (2/3): 467–512.

Dambo, Lawali, Maman Waziri Mato, and Elhadji Maman Moutari. 2014. "Insecurity and generalized political crises. A challenge for tourism development in the Aïr massif region of Niger." *Journal of Alpine Research|Revue de géographie alpine* (102-1) doi: 10.4000/rga.2349

FMI (Fonds Monétaire International). 2013. *Niger: Document de stratégie pour la réduction de la pauvreté.* FMI No. 13/105F.

Geels, Jolijn. 2006. *Niger: The Bradt Travel Guide.* Bucks: Bradt Travel Guides.

Grégoire, Emmanuel. 2006. "Tourisme culturel, engagement politique et actions humanitaires dans la région d'Agadès (Niger)." *Autrepart* 4 (40): 95–111.

Grégoire, Emmanuel, and Marko Scholze. 2012. "Identité, imaginaire et tourisme en pays touareg au Niger." *Via. Tourism Review* 2 (2012). https://doi.org/10.4000/viatourism.1102.

Grettenberger, John. 1984. "W National Park in Niger—A case for urgent assistance." *Oryx* 18 (4): 230–236.

Henderson, Joan C. 2007. *Tourism Crises: Causes, Consequences and Management.* Abingdon: Routledge.

ICAO (International Civil Aviation Organization). 2016. "ICAO States Today and Tomorrow". Accessed 5 September 2018, https://www.icao.int/publications/journalsreports/2018/ICAO%20_States_Today_Document.pdf

Institut National de la Statistique. 2010. Annuaire statistique des cinquante ans d'independance du Niger. Accessed 17 July 2018, http://www.stat-niger.org/statistique/file/Annuaires_Statistiques/Annuaire_ins_2010/serie_longue.pdf

Institut National de la Statistique. 2014. Annuaire statistique du Niger 2009–2013. Tourisme et Hôtellerie. Accessed 17 July 2018, http://www.stat-niger.org/statistique/file/Annuaires_Statistiques/INS_2014/AS2009-2013_TOURISME.pdf

Institut National de la Statistique. 2016. Annuaire statistique du Niger 2011–2015. Accessed 17 July 2018, http://www.stat-niger.org/statistique/file/Annuaires_Statistiques/ANNUAIRE_STATISTIQUE_2011-2015.pdf

Institut National de la Statistique. 2018. Annuaire statistique du Niger 2013–2017. Accessed 24 September 2019, http://www.stat-niger.org/statistique/file/Annuaires_Statistiques/Annuaire_Statistique_2013-2017.pdf

Kabii, Francis. 2018. "Terrorism and Tourism: Kenya's Resilient Tourism Industry Survival Strategies." *Global Journal of Human-Social Science: H Interdisciplinary* 18 (3): 15–25.

Kalfa, David. 2018. "Sports mécaniques: un retour du rallye Dakar en Afrique en 2020?" *RFI*, May 18. Accessed 22 July 2018, http://www.rfi.fr/sports/20180518-sports-mecaniques-retour-rallye-raid-dakar-afrique-2020

Lassibille, Mahalia. 2006. "Les danses woDaaBe entre spectacles touristiques et scènes internationales: les coulisses d'une migration chorégraphique." *Autrepart* 4 (40): 113–129.

Lawan. 2018. "La voie express reliant l'Aéroport International Diori Hamani au centre ville de Niamey sera bientôt aménagée et bitumée". *Agence Nigerienne de Presse*, May 18. Accessed 10 August 2018, http://www.anp.ne/?q=article/la-voie-express-reliant-l-aeroport-international-diori-hamani-au-centre-ville-de-niamey-sera

Michelot, A., and B. Ouedraogo. 2009. *"Transboundary protected areas: Legal framework for the W transboundary biosphere reserve (Benin, Burkina Faso, Niger)"* IUCN: Gland, Switzerland.

Miller, Daniel C., Michael Minn, and Brice Sinsin. 2015. "The importance of national political context to the impacts of international conservation aid: Evidence from the W National Parks of Benin and Niger." *Environmental Research Letters* 10 (11): 115001.

Muller, Jeffrey, and Heidi J. Albers. 2004. "Enforcement, payments, and development projects near protected areas: How the market setting determines what works where." *Resource and Energy Economics* 26 (2): 185–204.

Niamey et les 2 jours. 2018. "Les travaux de construction et de réhabilitation de l'aéroport de Zinder ont atteint un taux de réalisation d'environ 15%". Accessed 15 August 2018, https://www.niameyetles2jours.com/l-economie/transports/3008-2756-les-travaux-de-construction-et-de-rehabilitation-de-l-aeroport-de-zinder-ont-atteint-un-taux-de-realisation-d-environ-15

NouvelObs. 2019. "Sommet UA: lancement 'historique' de la zone de libre-échange africaine". Accessed 2 October 2019, https://www.nouvelobs.com/monde/20190707.AFP0016/sommet-ua-lancement-historique-de-la-zone-de-libre-echange-africaine.html

PNDS-TARAYYA (Parti Nigérien pour la démocratie et le socialisme). 2016. "Programme de campagne Renaissance II". Accessed 5 September 2018, https://static1.squarespace.com/static/58a4235717bffc153c6d9a3c/t/5a5f81aac8302548e71db750/1516208576121/programme_de_renaissance_phase_2-2016-2021_2.pdf

Raineri, Luca. 2018. "Human smuggling across Niger: State-sponsored protection rackets and contradictory security imperatives." *The Journal of Modern African Studies* 56 (1): 63–86.

Scholze, Marko. 2010. "Between the worlds: Tuareg as entrepreneurs in tourism." In *Tuareg Society within a Globalized World*, edited by A. Fischer and I. Kohl, 171–188. New York: Thomson Press.

UN (United Nation). 2018. *Niger, Map No. 4234 Rev.1*, January 2018.

UNESCO (The United Nations Educational, Scientific and Cultural Organization). 2018a. *Air and Ténéré Natural Reserves.* Accessed 20 July 2018, https://whc.unesco.org/en/list/573

UNESCO (The United Nations Educational, Scientific and Cultural Organization). 2018b. *W-Arly-Pendjari Complex.* Accessed 20 July 2018, https://whc.unesco.org/en/list/749

UNWTO (World Tourism Organization). 2014. *Chinese Outbound Travel to the Middle East and North Africa.* Madrid: UNWTO.

UNWTO (World Tourism Organization). 2018. *UNWTO Tourism Highlights, 2018 Edition.* Madrid: UNWTO.

UNWTO and ILO (United Nations World Tourism Organization and International Labour Organization). 2013. *Economic Crisis, International Tourism Decline and its Impact on the Poor.* Madrid: UNWTO.

Whande, Webster. 2010. "Windows of opportunity or exclusion? Local communities in the Great Limpopo Transfrontier Conservation Area, South Africa." In *Community Rights, Conservation and Contested Land*, edited by F. Nelson, 159–185. Abingdon: Routledge.

Youngstedt, Scott M. 2008. "The 5th Francophonie sports and arts festival: Niamey, Niger hosts a global community." *African Studies Quarterly* 10 (2–3), 129–151.

Youngstedt, Scott M. 2013. *Surviving with Dignity: Hausa Communities of Niamey, Niger.* Rowman & Littlefield.

18

Tourism development in Sierra Leone

Desmond O. Brown

Brief background and macroeconomic trends

The Republic of Sierra Leone is bordered by the North Atlantic Ocean, Guinea and Liberia. With a population of about 7 million in 2018, it has an area of 71,740 km² (27,700 mi²) with vast natural endowments in land (75% of which is arable); mineral resources including rutile, diamonds and iron ore; water (marine resources) and tourism resources. According to a recent UNCTAD report (2018), from a macroeconomic point of view, the country is ranked as low income with a ranking of 164 in the world development indicator index for 2017 and an average real GDP growth of 5.7% in 2018. Furthermore, the poverty rate of its population earning below US$1.50 per day is conservatively listed at about 60%. The economy is primarily dependent on agriculture (51.5%), industry (14.9%) and services (33.6%) and migrant remittances contributed about $50 million in 2017 (less than 5% of GNI for the same period).

According to the World Bank (2020), the country's 2019 debt stock hovered around an average of 62.3% of GDP while domestic financing remains high. The country remains at a "high risk" of debt stress for external public debt and overall public debt. The current account of the balance of payments remains under pressure to date as the trade deficit has widened, reflecting weak export growth and increased imports of food items, machinery and petroleum. The country has vast natural endowments in land (75% of which is arable); mineral resources including rutile, diamonds and iron ore; water (marine resources) and tourism resources.

The following sections will attempt to provide a discussion of some political, economic and other pertinent issues and challenges pertaining to the country's tourism industry and provide some insights into the way forward.

Current tourism trends

In 2012, Sierra Leone received 60,000 international tourists, an increase of 13.9% from the previous year (UNWTO 2013). Tourism's direct contribution to GDP increased from US$101 million in 2012 to $109 million in 2013, an increase of 4.3% (WTTC 2013). Tourism directly employed 30,000 people or 2.5% in 2011. The latest figures (2011) available from the country's tourist board provide some arrival and other sector indicators shown in Tables 18.1 and 18.2. The dispersion of tourism arrivals and receipts by the various visitor markets

Table 18.1 Monthly visitor arrivals by air by continent of residence, 2011

Month	Africa		Asia	America	Middle-East	Europe	Australia & Oceania	Total
	Ecowas	**Non-Ecowas**						
January	875	857	510	784	319	1,025	322	**4,692**
February	593	283	336	774	215	969	297	**3,467**
March	925	492	536	892	384	1,021	537	**4,790**
April	917	431	578	1,264	292	1,822	492	**5,796**
May	876	381	552	1,037	430	1,066	475	**4,817**
June	856	482	302	1,065	253	1,099	259	**4,316**
July	831	201	357	742	193	994	242	**3,560**
August	854	178	313	458	154	844	167	**2,968**
September	872	261	356	501	170	1,000	211	**3,371**
October	1,033	330	494	715	353	1,088	200	**4,213**
November	1,271	368	586	741	395	1,337	191	**4,889**
December	1,151	331	440	1,501	327	1,542	271	**5,563**
Total	**11,054**	**4,598**	**5,360**	**10,474**	**2,485**	**13,807**	**3,664**	**52,442**

Source: Sierra Leone National Tourist Board.

Table 18.2 Visitor expenditure by purpose of visit (2009–2011)

Type of visitors	Arrivals by air	Visitor expenditure for the year 2011 Estimated average night spent	US dollars Est. Acc. (Exp. $)	FTS ($)	Amount ($)
Holiday	11,146	7	80	200	8,470,960
VFR	9,483	7	40	120	3,793,200
Business	18,480	7	90	250	16,262,400
Conference	5,337	7	70	230	3,842,640
Others	7,996	7	60	150	4,557,720
Total	**52,442**				**36,926,920**
		Visitor expenditure for the year 2010			
Holiday	7,728	7	80	200	5,783,280
VFR	5,156	7	40	120	2,062,400
Business	12,803	7	90	250	11,266,640
Conference	4,208	7	70	230	3,029,760
Others	8,720	7	60	150	4,970,400
Total	**38,615**				**27,112,480**
		Visitor expenditure for the year 2009			
Holiday	8,627	**7**	80	200	6,556,520
VFR	4,635	7	40	120	1,854,000
Business	11,414	7	90	250	10,044,320
Conference	4,577	7	70	230	3,295,440
Others	7,522	7	60	150	4,287,540
Total	**36,775**				**26,037,820**

Source: Sierra Leone National Tourist Board.

for the period in question show fairly significant market growth of tourism and its relative contribution to the economy.

Tourist attractions and regional competitive advantage

Sierra Leone's main attractions are beaches, colonial sites and ecotourism sites (wildlife, woodland savanna, and rare flora and fauna). Given its geographic location in the Western Peninsula and nearby islands, Sierra Leone is renowned for its outstanding white sand and golden beaches with dramatic tropical and mountainous backdrops. Being only a five or six-hour flight from Northern Europe, the country offers a comfortable, tropical dry season precisely during the European winter. With some reports depicting the country's beaches as one of the best beach destinations in West Africa, its tourist appeal includes visitors seeking tranquility, a sense of discovery and cultural stimulation in addition to the usual requirements of beach tourism (i.e. sun, sea and sand) this touristic pull is one of the most important tourism assets for Sierra Leone. Some of the more popular beach attractions have been noted in Table 18.1. In addition to their usual qualities such as climate, surface, ocean temperature and beauty, most of Sierra Leone's beaches have the advantage of being relatively pristine and less crowded compared to its regional rival, The Gambia, which has been a popular European destination for mass tourism (Shakya 2009).

Another significant tourism asset is its nature and wildlife. The country's tropical environment and scenery (mountains, forests, rivers, coastline, islands) and nature (birds, flora and fauna) are again relatively close to Europe. Although its wildlife does not quite match that of those Eastern or Southern Africa, Sierra Leone has interesting wildlife, and potential to tap into the rapidly growing bird-watching tourism market.

Similar to Senegal's Gori Island and Ghana's Cape Coast forts and castles, Sierra Leone's heritage history can be built into an attractive 'story' for European tourists and for potential visitors from the diaspora including the United States. The interpretation of the 'story' has the potential to focus on the return of freed slaves and expanded to include the tribal and colonial European history in the country. Other potential attractions include its diamond mining heritage, which potentially offers a special 'story' for tourists as well as a potential 'buying' opportunity with proper planning (see Table 18.3).

In spite of the relatively impressive economic growth of the sector, poverty levels remain high with a per capita GDP of US$373 and over half of the population living under the poverty line in 2011. The Sierra Leone Integrated 2011 Survey shows that 52.9% of the population still lives in poverty, a decline from the 66.4% recorded in 2003.

During the last decade or so, in an effort to revitalize and rebuild the post-war economy, recent recovery strategy documents as well as government pronouncements indicate the country's desire to rebuild its tourism industry. The government in power also promulgated various Acts and Statutory Instruments to enhance the development of tourism which culminated in the Development of Tourism Act 1990. Among the important issues enshrined in the Act was the establishment of the National Tourist Board (NTB) and several tax reliefs for businesses engaged in tourism development.

Despite these efforts, a concrete tourism policy remains elusive since the sector has failed to put together an overarching policy to capture niches such as natural, cultural/heritage, leisure tourism, etc. Nonetheless, the attractions, which include beaches, natural reserves and mountains, offer a strong platform for tourism and provide a great opportunity to develop special interest tourism. Although several growing market niches have been identified by the government, such as eco-tourism as well as cultural heritage tourism, they have not been

Table 18.3 Selected tourism resources

Attraction type	Examples	Comment
Beaches and islands	• River No. 2 Beach • Black Johnson • Banana Island • Turtle Islands • Lakka Beach • Lumley Beach	Some of the world's most beautiful pristine, white and untouched beaches dotted along the Atlantic Ocean
Nature and wildlife	• Outamba Kilimi National Park • Lake Sonfon • Tiwai Island Wildlife Sanctuary • Gola Forest Reserve • Bumbuna Falls • Kabala Mountains • Lake Sonfon • Mount Bintumani	A wide array of nature and wildlife viewing opportunities that are often miles from the nearest road
Heritage/dark tourism sites	• Gateway to Old King's Yard • Historic Maroon Church • The Historic Cotton Tree • Old Wharf Steps • Slave forts and Castles	A multitude of replicas depicting rich heritage depicting Sierra Leone's dark days as a slave outpost as well as colonial resettlement of liberated slaves.

articulated in a holistic policy direction. Furthermore, even though niche tourism and the acquisition of desired skilled manpower to run the industry has the potential to stimulate growth in Sierra Leone's tourism industry there is the need for more critical analysis of the country's comparative advantage and competitive edge in these market in light of other competing West African markets (such as Ghana, Nigeria, The Gambia, Senegal and Cape Verde).

The discussion that follows will attempt to highlight issues that account for the tourism sector's slow resurgence from the pre-war era of growth and prominence.

Political risk and image

The tourism literature is replete with empirical conclusions that political instability and violence can have considerable impacts on a destination's image, especially on fragile economies in developing nations such as Sierra Leone. For example, Ritchie (2004) argued that in today's interconnected world, tourism is increasingly affected by forces and events in the external environment to the extent that even a small-scale crisis, whether in immediate proximity or not, can have considerable negative effects on a destination's image.

Given this logic, the issue of a negative country image along with other factors has been cited as an important concept in tourism development in Sierra Leone and other African tourist destinations. This has been highlighted by a study conducted in Uganda by Lepp, Gibson and Lane (2011) who concluded that a major negative image affecting the country's tourism was tourists' perception of the destination which was mainly related to perceptions of poverty, war and disease. Similar conclusions have also been drawn by Brown (2000) and Campo and Alvarez (2010) in their research on tourism development in Africa and Turkey's image as a destination respectively.

In the case of Sierra Leone, the period from 1991 to 2002, witnessed an engagement in a bitter civil war over diamonds that spread from the main mining district to Freetown, the capital. After two major peace accords (in Lomé in July 1999 and Abuja in May 2001) and given the massive destruction of infrastructure as well as the human and social capital during the civil war, it can be observed that to date, there has been rapid progress towards recovery mostly aided by the donor community such as the World Bank. However, when compared to the tourism sector growth of the 1980s and early 90s, during which the government heavily invested in hotels and its tourism policy and planning frameworks yielded positive results, the tourism sector today remains in a pre-emergent stage, with promising post-war growth in visitor arrivals and investment cut short by the Ebola crisis of 2013/2014. While the country still possesses substantial mineral, agricultural and fishery resources, the post-Ebola tourism sector is one of the few industries which rapidly flourished, despite the fact that its physical and social infrastructure has not yet fully recovered from the civil war, and serious social disorders continue to hamper tourism development.

Weak institutional frameworks

While opportunities exist for Sierra Leone's tourism sector to reinvent itself and emerge from its post-war crisis, frameworks and processes need to be put into place to enable the sustainable and inclusive development of the sector and for its continuous expansion, as has been the case for international success stories in Laos, Republic of Georgia and Rwanda for example. Although the World Bank is currently funding a project development objective to improve the tourism business environment, enhance market access and improve tourism products and services in Sierra Leone, the following are also immediate issues that need to be tackled for the sustainability of this important re-emerging sector:

Improvement of institutional capacity in policy development and planning

Such improvement must be done by the coordination of tourism development through concerted efforts of the ministry of tourism. The Ministry of Tourism and Cultural Affairs was established in 1973, and in 1975 the previously autonomous Hotels and Tourist Board became an integral part of the Ministry. Among its broad statutory objectives, the ministry's role is to promote sustainable tourism as a means of economic growth and socio-cultural integration as well as promoting Sierra Leone as an environmentally friendly tourist destination. It aims at building the image of Sierra Leone abroad as a country with a glorious past and a vibrant future. It also aims at preserving, protecting and promoting cultural diversity in order to revive and strengthen national consciousness, understanding and appreciation of the cultural heritage and artistic creativity of the Sierra Leonean people. Its specific functions can be summarized as follows:

- Legislation (through parliament) and regulations on tourism development, including investment policies and incentives;
- Policy formulation and programming for the development and promotion of domestic, regional and international tourism;
- Policy formulation of tourism and culture;
- Capacity building of staff to enhance productivity and deliver tourism products and services efficiently;
- Monitoring tourism development.

The current state of public attractions particularly in areas with ecotourism potential, electricity, water, signage, toilets, solid waste and parking facilities which are currently poor or non-existent are among the major challenges currently faced by the ministry of tourism. Since tourism is multi-sectoral, implementation of development plans is the responsibility of various stakeholders, public agencies, the private sector as well as the ministry of tourism.

Improving the poor image through proactive marketing planning utilizing International and Regional partnerships

The primary institution entrusted with this task is the Tourist Board.

Sierra Leone National Tourist Board

Previously called the National Tourist Board, the Sierra Leone National Tourist Board (herein known as SLNTB) was established by Parliament in 1991 as an independent agency of the ministry of tourism. The main functions of the board can be summarized as follows:

- Marketing tourism both domestically and internationally, including participation in tourism trade fairs and exhibitions;
- Conducting research to monitor tourism trends;
- Regulation and control of the tourism industry including registration, classification, licensing and application of standards for accommodation, tourist food service facilities and travel agencies.

Since international tourism is one of the major drivers of international trade in Sierra Leone as in many developing economies, the SLNTB requires certain facilitating mechanisms to properly carry out its statutory responsibilities. Among the means that have been deemed effective by many successful tourist destinations are effective linkages with international and regional organizations. As Sierra Leone is a member of the United Nations World Tourism Organization (UNWTO), participation in UNWTO's regional Commission for Africa's tourism education and training programs on the many topics of relevance to tourism marketing and promotion (such as monitoring and utilizing published statistics on international tourist movements) could be very useful in improving tourist attraction. Other potential benefits could be image building and branding training exercises.

In terms of regional co-operation within West Africa, Sierra Leone and other countries in the region (The Gambia, Ivory Coast, Senegal, Ghana) tend to offer similar and complementary tourist attractions. This could open up corridors and opportunities for combined marketing efforts in promoting, heritage, business and wildlife tourism exchanges for example.

Addressing the critical capacity shortages of human development in the various sectors within the industry

For tourism to be successful in Sierra Leone, education and training at all levels either through direct training activities and/or indirect facilitation through the private sector is necessary. In this vein, establishing and applying industry training standards is of utmost importance. Furthermore, conducting research on marketing and product development through educational institutions is important for broad and long-lasting success in the industry. To date, although small private colleges train tour guides, housekeepers and food service workers, there is a deficit in terms of adequate training facilities in Sierra Leone as well as limited graduate or postgraduate education or research.

Encouragement and promotion of domestic tourism

Domestic or internal tourism promotion in a destination has many advantages, chief among which is political integration and rejuvenation. It helps provide an integrating force that could help strengthen national sentiment (pride in national heritage) among citizens, especially given the circumstances that led to Sierra Leone's 11-year civil war discussed previously.

From a social perspective, domestic tourism can help promote an intermingling of people from diverse social and cultural backgrounds while providing spatial redistribution of spending power within the economy. Moreover, it is an opportunity for locals to benefit from government investment in tourism infrastructures such as national parks and reserves.

Other potential benefits include the compensating for seasonal variations in overseas tourism thereby sustaining tourism demand and employment during off-peak periods.

Further suggestions

- Capitalize on offering and re-launching a more deliberate marketing campaign that would attract the adventure affinity tourist market;
- Facilitating air access, costs and visa procedures;
- Establishment of Historic Preservation Programs through the existing Monuments & Relics Commission;
- Enhanced Tour Guide Training Programs and the number of workers trained in tourism services delivery;
- Tourist Attraction Development Programs through the institution of higher learning;
- Application of land use and zoning regulations to designated tourism development areas;
- Establishment of a Tourism Development fund financed through expenditures at hotels, restaurant and other tourist facilities to enable marketing, product development and training;

Summary and conclusions

Sierra Leone's tourism sector experienced robust growth in the 1980s and early 1990s but was unfortunately interrupted by its 11-year civil war. Prior to that, the government made substantial investments in hotels (such as Cape Sierra, Bintumani, Paramount hotels among others). To a large extent, its tourism policy and planning frameworks yielded positive results as a beach and island-based discovery destination. However, as previously mentioned, postwar Sierra Leone has been experiencing lopsided economic growth, due to the government concentrating heavily on the mining sector – which has also been largely blamed for the violent insurgency that engrossed the country between 1991 and 2001.

A recent change in government has signaled a re-focus on tourism as a viable sector that can help the country recover from previous dependence on minerals to the development of one or more labor-intensive sectors including agriculture, and light manufacturing. It is hoped that this will help rebuild its social fabric and create a sustainable economy that can have a direct impact on the poor through direct employment. Although tourism infrastructure remains poor, despite the government's promise to pay more attention to the industry, nevertheless, with proper planning, well-thought-out policies and a trained workforce, Sierra Leone's tourism sector has substantial potential to be a key economic driver similar to other countries in the sub-region such as Ghana, Senegal and the Gambia.

Among the key challenges highlighted in this chapter are poor image, a difficult enabling environment, weak institutional capacity in policy development, planning and marketing as well as trained human capacity shortages that require proactive marketing planning and increased international, regional and private-sector partnerships. To date, it appears that through government pronouncements, the sector is motivated to recover, and is attracting substantial private sector interest and investment such as the World Bank and other development partners. However, much needs to be done to rebuild the current crumbled post-war infrastructure as well as invest in new ones in order to boost the current low demand levels as well as improve effective market linkages.

References

Brown, D. (2000). Political Risk Factors and other Barriers to Tourism Promotion in Africa: Perceptions of US Based Travel Intermediaries. *Journal of Vacation Marketing*, 6(3), 197–210.

Campo, S., & Alvarez, M. D. (2010). Country versus destination image in a developing country. *Journal of Travel & Tourism Marketing*, 27(7), 749–765.

International Monetary Fund (IMF). (2011). Sierra Leone: Poverty reduction strategy paper: Progress report, 2008–2010. *Country Report* No. 11/195. Washington DC.

Lepp, A., Gibson, H., & Lane, C. (2011). Image and perceived risk: A study of Uganda and its official tourism website. *Tourism Management*, 32(30), 675–684.

Ritchie, B. W. (2004). Chaos, crises and disasters: A strategic approach to crisis management in the tourism industry. *Tourism Management*, 25, 669–683.

Shakya, M. (2009). Competitiveness assessment of tourism in Sierra Leone: A cluster-based approach. The world bank poverty reduction and economic management network international trade department. *Policy Research Working Paper* 5083.

United Nations Conference on Trade and Development (UNCTAD). (2018). *Statistical Tables on the Least Developed Countries*. Geneva: UNCTAD.

United Nations World Tourism Organization. (2013). *Compendium of Tourism Statistics, Data 2007–2011*. Madrid: UNWTO.

World Bank. (2020). *Sierra Leone: Country overview and context*. Available from https://www.worldbank.org/en/country/sierraleone/overview [Accessed on 22 August, 2020].

World Bank. (2006). *Sierra Leone: Adding Value through Trade for Poverty Reduction: A Diagnostic Trade Integration Study*. Washington DC: The World Bank.

World Travel and Tourism Council. (2013). *Travel and Tourism. Economic Impact*. London: WTTC.

InFocus 4

Afrogallonism, yellow brick road and 360La – grassroot contemporary arts in motion

Nana Osei Kwadwo

Serge Attukwei Clottey is a contemporary artist from La (Labadi), a neighbourhood from Accra (Ghana), who works across installation, performance, photography and sculpture to explore personal and political narratives rooted in histories of trade and migration. His work sits at the intersection of making and action, drawing heavily on his immediate and ever-changing environment. Based in La and working internationally, Clottey refers to his work as 'Afrogallonism', a concept that confronts the question of material culture through the utilisation of the Kuffuor gallons, which are yellow containers used to transport cooking oil and reused to transport fuel or store water. Cutting, drilling, stitching and melting these found materials, Clottey's sculptural installations are bold assemblages that function as a means of inquiry into the languages of form and abstraction.

In his wall and floor pieces, he uses flattened Kuffuor gallons, jute sacks, discarded car tires and wooden pieces to make abstract formations onto which he inscribes patterns and text. In doing so, the artist seeks to elevate the material into a powerful symbol of Ghana's informal economic system of trade and re-use. While some surfaces resemble local textile traditions such as 'Kente', a key reference in west African Modernism throughout the 20th century, others refer to barcodes and feature Chinese characters in reference to the emergence of new power structures in Ghana.

The artist's use of these plastic containers in his art, touching on the global issues of plastic waste and access to basic services, but also promoting his greater philosophy of exploring social norms, as well as personal and political narratives rooted in histories of colonialism, trade and migration.

Performance and its potential to engage a broad audience are at the centre of Clottey's practice and are part of the making and displaying of his material works showcasing a dialogue with Ghana's cultural history amongst many other things. In addition to his own studio practice, through his performance collective GoLokal, public art works and performances are co-produced, often functioning as political and/or environmentalist gestures and statements. One of his on-going projects is the *Yellow Brick Road*, which can be sited in Clottey's own Labadi neighbourhood in occasion of his open studio events, such as the 360La. In this occasion, the artist with help from Labadi community members covers the dirt streets with a patchwork of his 'tapestries delineating space in new way', as he puts it. An aerial view of the installation shows brilliant golden lines and dots flowing through a maze of grey and brown homes towards the sea. 'For me, it signifies the history of migration—and home,' Clottey explains.

Through his notable work, *My Mother's Wardrobe*, presented at Accra's Gallery 1957 in 2016, in collaboration with his GoLokal performing collective, the artist used performance to explore traditional gender roles along with notions of family, ancestry and spirituality. Here the artist dressed in the clothes and jewellery of his recently deceased mother both as a tribute to her and other Ghanaian women, who are the collectors and custodians of cloth (and which serve as signifiers of history and memory). Also, by wearing the attire of a woman, as a provocation to the people of Accra in general, and to question typical gender roles in Ghanaian society.

In 2018, Clottey decided to open his La studio to his community, in an attempt to share, showcase, engage and celebrate the culture of La during the Homowo Festivities. On the 25th August 2018, 360La was born as a solo exhibition and GoLokal Performance in the streets of La neighbourhood of Accra (Ghana) – see: https://www.youtube.com/watch?v=A3gm-KNBC98Q&t=27s. Clottey deems La community as key component of his art practices and materials' source, also providing a conducive and inclusive environment for the production of his art works and performances.

The exhibition was undoubtedly a success, not only because of the unexpected number of local and international visitors who turned at Clottey's studio, but most importantly because of the interactions and participation of La community. Much of La community members came out to lend a hand in the setting up of the exhibition and embraced whatever the exhibition embodied. At the end of the event, La's traditional leaders and community elders approached Clottey and the exhibition's curator asking to repeat the event and make it an official part of the annual traditional Homowo festivities.

360La will open its doors to other La-based artists, with the aim of weaving together the narratives of the various artists in a way that effectively shares and preserves local historical and contemporary tales about their neighbourhood and local artists' role in shaping the future of La community.

360La aims at providing an open platform and use the arts as a vehicle to inspire public interaction first between La people and then between them and those that will visit. 360La will be a space for knowledge exchange aimed also at encouraging people to share their aspirations and experiences and ultimately foster a common developmental agenda. This will be achieved through the organisation of workshops, art talks and collaborating with other local and international organisations that will have an interest in actively contributing to 360La. For instance, since 2018, 360La has been actively collaborating with the University of Brighton in identifying a programme of research and capacity building in line with its vision to create a sense of belonging through the arts, by collaborating with traditional leaders, community elders and youth (men and women) from La and other key stakeholders and create an inclusive and enabling environment. This programme has already had considerable impact by using the arts as a vehicle to stimulate La community members' awareness about their own community development needs and better understand how they can actively contribute to it. External participants and visitors have already shown interest giving hope that this can become an example of good practice where grassroot contemporary arts in motion has evolved into a portfolio of community-based activities that may also serve as an alternative and sustainable form of tourism in Accra's urban settings.

InFocus 5

Aviators Africa Academy (AAA) – capacity development in Africa's aviation industry

Toni Ukachukwu and Olayemi Akinoshun

Since the turn of this decade, the view of many aviation industry stakeholders at different fora is that Africa remains the next frontier for aviation and aerospace development. Africa presently has a population of about 1.3 billion people with a median age of 19.4 years, the largest number of young people among the regions of the world (Worldometers, 2019) and the fastest growing population of middle-class in the world (Pandey, 2018). This may suggest that there is a bright future for air transportation on the continent, with skilled workers playing a central role towards delivering efficient service that would bring about high socio-economic effects in Africa.

The reality, however, is that serious efforts are not being put in place by most African governments and stakeholders alike to raise the next generation of aviators able to take over the baton from the aging workforce in the African aviation industry.

Many are the challenges to be faced. Aircraft flight and engineering and other technical training course in aviation are quite expensive for many Africans to pursue. In Nigeria, for example, it takes on the average, about US$30,000 and US$70,000 to complete ab-initio training in aircraft piloting and engineering respectively. Adding the Type Ratings training costs increase the overall investment cost in becoming full-fledged certified pilots and aircraft engineers. The airlines are unwilling to sponsor training of Nigerians because of fear of losing out on their investment to poaching by other airlines. Because of this, those who are passionate about aviation are then left to source huge funds required for aviation course on their own. As such, aviation in Nigeria is generally viewed as a career for the rich and wealthy alone, even when there are other career paths in the field of aviation which may be equally interesting, but more accessible as their training costs relatively more affordable. The lack of initiatives aimed at increasing human capacity development in an affordable manner means that Nigeria, like many other destinations in Africa, stands at the risk of facing technical and managerial aviation personnel shortage and continues to rely on foreign aviation professionals, increasing the sector's overheads bill and in turn slowing down the national travel and tourism development potential.

One model to address this challenge is to first provide African youths with exposure to various career paths in aviation. This may include the creation of aviation clubs in primary, secondary and tertiary schools. Creating awareness is essential and once this is achieved, the next step could involve supporting local youths, who have shown passion in aviation but do not have the needed financial means to undergo aviation training by themselves.

The above model is what Aviators Africa Academy (AAA) is currently adopting to promote aviation careers among Nigerians and Africans at large, yielding gradual results. As a social enterprise, which seeks to inspire and engage the next generation in aviation and aerospace, it is keen to open provide underprivileged African youths at primary, secondary and tertiary school level with the opportunity to learn about different exciting career paths in aviation, through engagements and outreaches. AAA prides itself to be a platform that enables individuals who are passionate about pursuing a career in aviation but financially unable, to do so, making their dreams come true. As part of the engagements, AAA is linking aviation passionate youths across Africa to aviation colleges for partial and/or full scholarships, airlines and aviation organisations (private and government owned) for on-the-job training and absorption, and successful aviation practitioners for mentoring and guidance. AAA has three categories to achieve its aim and objectives. The first is creating aviation-focused clubs in secondary schools. The second is organizing outreaches in universities to expose career projections in the aviation industry and inspire career change and guidance for passionate ones and lastly, to mentor those already in Aviation schools and engage those who have graduated but are not gainfully employed.

Realizing the need for a more robust Africa aviation space that gives room for gender diversity, all-inclusiveness and innovation, they are encouraging more girls to pursue careers in aviation and STEM (Science, Technology, Engineering and Mathematics) through a fixed quota allocation of 30% exclusively reserve for girls in their academy. The plan is to train a minimum of 40 technologically sound aviation personnel annually, from 2020 to 2025, through funding from donor agencies, corporate organisations and interested airlines in Nigeria and across the continent. The products from this initiative are envisaged to form a global pool of talents from which the Africa aviation and aerospace industry could tap from.

Initiatives like the AAA are aimed at focusing on building the local capacity using a social entrepreneurial approach and addressing grassroots needs. The AAA scouts for aviation talents and supports them to become skilled in general aviation and respective core areas of interest in the sector, providing the continent's aviation industry a better chance to improve its capacity to absorb local youths, contribute towards the forecasted growth of the sector by the International Air Transport Association (IATA) and Boeing and Airbus' 2016–2035 market outlooks for Africa and increase locally supported air transport activities that will benefit the African continent over the next 20 years.

References

Pandey, E. (2018) Africa's growing middle class drives capacity, January 2018, Available at: https://www.axios.com/africas-growing-middle-class-is-a-source-of-pros-1516452641-9f257787-0cd6-403c-b7dc-954f078e24f6.html, Accessed: 1/06/2019.

Worldometers (2019) Africa Population, June 2019, Available at: https://www.worldometers.info/world-population/africa-population – June 2019, Accessed: 1/06/2019.

Part IV
Tourism in Middle Africa

19

Eco-tourism in Cameroon's protected areas

Investigating the link between community participation and policy development

Vyasha Harilal and Tembi Tichaawa

Introduction

The tourism industry has been cited many times over as an industry to ignite and spur on growth in countries (Hugo & Nyaupane, 2016; Kimbu & Ngoasong, 2013; Mowforth & Munt, 1998; Tyrrell, Paris & Biaett, 2013), framed by the developmental potential that tourism can bring to economies, especially within the global south context (Saarinen & Rogerson, 2014). This may also be attributed to the resilience of the industry, as evidenced by its out-performance of other industries (such as transport, retail and distribution, manufacturing and financial and business services) for the seventh consecutive year (WTTC, 2017, 2018). Furthermore, it has been noted that the tourism sector is one that enjoys rapid growth globally (Campbell, 1999; Letoluo & Wangombe, 2018) and has experienced above average growth in relation to international tourism arrivals globally, which increased 7% in 2017 (UNWTO, 2017).

Moreover, the eco-tourism sub-sector of the industry has grown at a faster rate that the tourism industry itself (Atieno & Njoroge, 2018). In addition, the tourism industry is known to bring with it many benefits to be leveraged onto local citizens, such as the alleviation or reduction of poverty through the creation of employment and community development, as well as nature and culture conservation (Andereck, Valentine, Knopf & Vogt, 2005; Das & Chatterjee, 2015; Hugo & Nyaupane, 2016; World Bank, 2018). This notion is supported by Buckley (2003: 76) who notes the central principles of eco-tourism as "nature-based product, minimal impact management, environmental education, contribution to conservation and contribution to communities". According to the World Travel and Tourism Council (WTTC, 2017, 2018), the tourism sector accounted for the equivalent of 1 in 10 jobs globally or approximately 292 million jobs, contributing a staggering 10.2% to the global GDP.

Within the African context, tourism has been highlighted as a sector to promote economic growth and development (United Nations, 2017; World Bank, 2018). International tourist arrivals have been forecasted at between 5% and 7% for Africa in 2018 (UNWTO, 2017), with 40.7 million international tourist arrivals in Sub-Saharan Africa in 2017 (UNWTO, 2017). In Cameroon, the tourism sector's direct contribution to GDP was approximately USD 1.2

billion (or 3.7%), with the total contribution of the sector being 8.1% in 2016 (WTTC, 2017). Overall, the contribution of the sector to employment in Cameroon accounted for 289,500 jobs (3.1%) in direct employment and 658,500 jobs (7.1%) in total employment. This is indicative of the potential widespread benefits that the country (and people) could accrue from the sustained growth of the industry. However, to ensure sustained (and sustainable) growth of the tourism sector in Cameroon, suitable forms of tourism should be implemented within the country, with steadfast support from strategic policies to reinforce the industry. Such policies would ensure that the maximum benefits are gained by key stakeholders (Kimbu & Ngoasong, 2013), through the involvement and participation of key stakeholders in the tourism industry including local communities who reside within or in close proximity to where tourism-related activities occur.

In Cameroon, the development of the tourism industry is a key strategic goal set forth by the government (Kimbu & Ngoasong, 2013), with the sub-sector of eco-tourism being an important sector to develop, based on the many protected areas in the country (Tchindjang, Banga, Nankam & Makak, 2005), as well as on the variety of flora and fauna located in the protected areas (Tegha & Sendze, 2016), which has earned the country the title of "Africa in miniature" (Lambi, Kimengsi, Kometa & Tata, 2012; Tichaawa, 2017). One of the main hurdles to development in Cameroon is the lack of participation by the population (African Development Bank, 2015), which could be overcome through the development of eco-tourism, a sub-sector of the tourism industry premised on community participation for sustainable outcomes. Eco-tourism sectors are being or have been developed in many African countries, due to the abundance of natural resources and pristine, ecological areas located on the continent, as well as because of the benefits for local communities (Atieno & Njoroge, 2018; Venkatesh & Gouda, 2016; Wu & Chen, 2018).

However, despite eco-tourism's theoretical basis in environmentally responsible tourism, that is also rooted in community involvement, the theoretical basis does not always translate to practice (Atieno & Njoroge, 2018). Furthermore, the lack of research within the Central and West African context (Kimbu, 2010; United Nations, 2017) has stymied the growth and development of eco-tourism within Cameroon and has not supported the development of strategic policy tools to aid in the development of the industry, despite the aforementioned "Africa in miniature" title. Communities, in particular, have not enjoyed the benefits of having an established eco-tourism sector, despite living either within or adjacent to the protected areas where these activities occur. Therefore, this chapter seeks to investigate why current practices in the eco-tourism sector, specifically within protected areas in Cameroon, are not resulting in sustainable outcomes for local communities.

Literature review

Development of tourism policy in Cameroon

The tourism industry in Cameroon was highlighted as a key area of development in the country in 1981, to encourage economic growth and development (Kimbu & Ngoasong, 2013). The Ministry of Tourism and Leisure (MINTOUR) was born out of this designation as a key area for development in 1989 and was tasked with overseeing and coordinating the intricacies of the development of the tourism industry (Kimbu & Ngoasong, 2013). Post 1994, the ministries were restructured, resulting in the Ministry of Environment and Forestry (MINEF) being created from MINTOUR, with its division, the Department of Wildlife and Protected Areas, taking over the administration of wildlife management, protected areas and community forests (Ezzine de Blas, Ruiz-Pérez & Vermeulen, 2011), resulting in the handover of management responsibilities and control to local communities (Mbatu, 2009). In 1994, a new forestry law was enacted with a threefold purpose of "community involvement in forest management through management decentralisation, sustainable forests management through the multiple-use doctrine and poverty alleviation through financial benefits from forestry taxation" (Mbatu, 2009: 755).

In 2005, the MINEF was divided into two separate ministries: the Ministry of Environment and Nature Protection (MINEP) and the Ministry of Forestry and Wildlife (MINFOF), with these new ministries being responsible for the administration of biodiversity protection and the administration of the protection of flora and fauna respectively (Kimbu & Ngoasong, 2013). Due to the structural changes within and to the various Ministries, MINTOUR's portfolio was further expanded to work collaboratively with these Ministries for the effective and efficient development of tourism. Consequently, the development of tourism in the country, as a key developmental area, is dependent on many parties, each with differing interests and agendas. This highly fragmented approach to the management of tourism in the country could inhibit the ability of MINTOUR to operate efficiently and to develop and implement strategic policies to enhance the tourism sector, if there is an absence of effective communication between key stakeholders. Due to the aforementioned structural changes, the management approach has morphed to a decentralised one, enabling all stakeholders from the different government ministries, non-governmental organisations (NGOs) and civil society to participate in the management (Ezzine de Blas et al., 2011; Mengang, 1998).

Protected areas, eco-tourism and community participation

Protected areas (PAs), established primarily with the aim of biodiversity conservation (Stone & Nyaupane, 2016), are also the areas within which eco-tourism occurs, and where the "attractions" (flora and fauna) of eco-tourism are located. For eco-tourism to thrive, flora, fauna and ecological diversity must be conserved. However, in many cases, PAs are also home to local communities, who live either within or adjacent to the PAs and, more often than not, source their livelihood from the PA. If not well managed, this dynamic may be the cause of much discord between communities and authorities responsible for eco-tourism, thus highlighting the importance of community involvement and participation in eco-tourism activities. There are many studies that note communities who are involved in these activities are more likely to have a positive and supportive attitude towards eco-tourism in their localities, as opposed to those who are uninvolved (Bello, Lovelock & Carr, 2017; Moswete & Thapa, 2018; Saarinen, 2010; World Bank, 2018; Wu & Chen, 2018). Furthermore, as Agüera (2013) states, communities should be the first stakeholders to benefit from the introduction or presence of eco-tourism in an area. This is supported by Goodwin (2002) who highlights that PAs that are associated with tourism activities must serve a dual purpose of community upliftment as well as conservation of the natural environment, as per the 1992 World Congress on National Parks and Protected Areas.

Eco-tourism is a type of tourism that is premised on the involvement of key stakeholders, communities being one of these, as well as on the conservation and sustainable use of natural resources for income generation (Atieno & Njoroge, 2018). However, through this, if not managed properly, resources could be exploited, and community stakeholders could be disadvantaged by the presence of eco-tourism in their localities, leading to exploitation of natural resources (Bello et al., 2017). For example, if communities are not involved in eco-tourism, with eco-tourism related activities instead leveraged to external or private stakeholders, communities may have no choice but to turn to the unsustainable use (exploitation) of natural resources. It is therefore critical for success that communities are involved in eco-tourism activities, to increase the likelihood of "positive social and ecological outcomes" (Redmore, Stronza, Songhurst & McCulloch, 2018: 455), as communities have historically interacted with and traditionally managed natural resources successfully (He, Gallagher, Su, Wang & Cheng, 2018). Furthermore, as Tosun (2000) notes, the implication of community participation is that the communities are the drivers of their own development, thus having a vested interest in the process.

The achievement of community participation is inextricably linked to the notion of sustainable tourism development (Mowforth & Munt, 1998), with a decentralised approach and policy environment supporting this initiative (Chirenje, Giliba & Musamba, 2013). In addition, through sustainable tourism, the participatory aspect of community participation can enhance democracy and transparency within communities (Bramwell, 2010), thereby enhancing social capital within communities (Situmorang, 2018). The involvement and participation of communities in eco-tourism related activities includes participation in the planning process, making communities the drivers of eco-tourism in their areas, with specialists occupying the role of facilitators (Chirenje et al., 2013). Through this approach, communities are empowered to make decisions and implement plans that are suitable to their unique situations, encouraging them to play an active role in the implementation of eco-tourism in their communities and enhancing their livelihood (Mtapuri & Giampiccoli, 2013), as they have first-hand, direct experience and knowledge of the possible impacts of tourism activities. Furthermore, drawing on the pillars of sustainability, community participation may be viewed as an imperative to counterbalance the interests of business and private stakeholders (Bramwell, 2010).

Community participation and policy development

The presence of a policy framework is not all that is required for the successful implementation of tourism, whereby communities are involved and able to reap the benefits of the various associated activities. Policy frameworks need to enable community participation and involvement in the process, to ensure that the input of community members is included in the planning process. One of the main inhibitors to effective community participation, linked to policy development, is the ineffective implementation of policy (that already accounts for community participation in theory) (Njoh, 2002).

This seems to be the case in Cameroon, where communities do not benefit as they should, as per the various policies in place. However, the current policy is structured in a bottom-up, decentralised approach (Kimbu & Ngoasong, 2013) to accommodate for community involvement and participation. For example, with the institution of community forests and forestry taxation, communities should be benefiting from the use of the PAs. However, this is not the case, due to various factors including corruption and incorrect application of the policy (Spratt, Kargbo, Marfo, Ngungoh & Ramcilovik-Suominen, 2018). Furthermore, within the Cameroonian context, the structure of the government is such that many different ministries are related to the dissemination of tourism activities. If there is ineffective and inefficient communication and coordination between these ministries, the implementation of tourism itself, and the participation of communities (and any benefits), will be minimal. In addition, when policies are not implemented correctly, important key stakeholders are eliminated from the process, leading to a lack of involvement and participation of communities (Mbile, Vabi, Meboka, Okon, Arrey-Mbo, Nkongho & Ebong, 2005).

Study setting

Cameroon has been referred to as an "Africa in miniature" (Lambi et al., 2012; Tichaawa, 2017), alluding to the country's immense potential as an eco-tourism destination. The study was set in two of the many protected areas of Cameroon, the Mount Cameroon National Park (MCNP), established in 2009 (Tata & Lambi, 2014), and the Douala Edea Wildlife Reserve (DEWR), established in 1932 (Tchindjang et al., 2005), as indicated in Figure 19.1. These protected areas are located in different provinces in the country, with the MCNP being located in the South-West Region (Tegha & Sendze, 2016) and the DEWR being located in the Littoral Region (Angoni, 2015).

The MCNP and the DEWR were chosen as the case study areas for this study due to their unique eco-tourism potential, owing to factors such as the abundance of flora and fauna

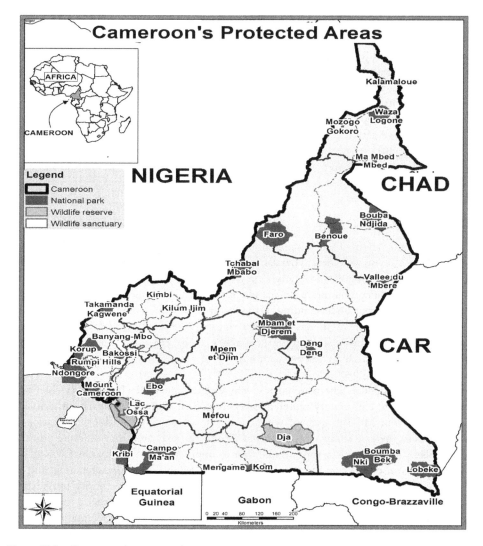

Figure 19.1   Cameroon's protected areas
Source: Authors' own, based on fieldwork.

within each of these protected areas, some of which are critically endangered or endemic species (Ajonina, Ajonina, Jin, Mekongo, Ayissi & Usongo, 2005; Tata & Lambi, 2014; Tegha & Sendze, 2016). These endemic and endangered species, such as the forest mountain elephant, avian and primate species form part of the unique tourist offering in these national parks. In addition, MCNP is home to the highest mountain peak in West and Central Africa, which is also the largest active volcano on the continent of Africa. The MCNP has the facilities of a hotel and restaurant within the park itself, however, eco-tourism infrastructure within the region is under-developed (MINFOF, 2014). Furthermore, the DEWR is located in a unique coastal zone of the country, bringing a further element of attraction to the eco-tourism offering (FAO, 2011).

Moreover, having local communities living either within or adjacent to the protected area borders of the park/reserve will provide a comprehensive overview of community participation in eco-tourism activities, especially given that not all communities reside within the borders of a protected area. The primary local livelihood activities in these protected areas are centred on agriculture, with this accounting for as much as 80% of household income in the MCNP region (MINFOF, 2014). In the DEWR region, fishing is a major agricultural activity that most local community members rely on (FAO, 2011). In addition to agricultural activities, other forms of livelihood activities that locals practice include hunting, logging, artisanal work and producing non-timber forest products (NTFP) and bee-keeping (MINFOF, 2014). With the exception of artisanal work, most of these livelihood activities require access to or resources from the protected areas. This is especially important within the DEWR setting, where communities reside within the borders of the protected area and are therefore heavily reliant on the natural resources contained therein.

Methodology

The current study adopted a qualitative research design and utilised in-depth, face-to-face interviews with key stakeholders as the data collection tool. The qualitative approach enabled an in-depth investigation of the variety in key stakeholder opinions and perceptions (Flick, 2014) on the state of community participation and involvement in eco-tourism activities, as well as to gain a deeper understanding of the factors inhibiting communities from achieving sustainable outcomes from eco-tourism activities. A qualitative research approach was particularly suited in this context given the exploratory nature of this study (Mason, 2017), due to the lack of research carried out within the Central and West African context (Harilal, Tichaawa & Saarinen, 2018).

Five key stakeholders, who were purposively selected, included a community chief from the MCNP region, community representatives from each study area, a park authority and a tour guide from MCNP; each of whom was able to provide valuable information on eco-tourism in the case study areas, within differing contexts and from differing points of view (Cohen, Manion & Morrison, 2002). For example, the community chief was able to provide historical context on the development of the MCNP as a protected area, and the formal establishment of eco-tourism in the MC region. The park authority provided an overview on the rules and regulations (policy) for communities living either within or adjacent to a protected area, and the community representatives and tour guide put forward the perspective of the community in relation to the establishment of eco-tourism in local communities and community participation in eco-tourism related activities (and subsequent outcomes). Within the Cameroonian context, community chiefs are held in high regard within traditional communities such as this, with most major decisions concerning or affecting the community usually being sanctioned by the chief. The community representatives are respected members of the community who are elected by the community to represent their interest. Generally, the community representative works closely with the community chief.

Open-ended interview schedules were used in this study, with questions relating to the development of eco-tourism in the locality, local community participation in eco-tourism, strategies in place to leverage benefits to local communities through eco-tourism, and community consultation on eco-tourism prior to implementation, being posed to the key stakeholders. The use of open-ended interview schedules to facilitate face-to-face interviews as a data collection tool enabled the collection of in-depth and focused data, as well as the opportunity to probe secondary issues that arose during the interview discussion (Kothari, 2004). Data were collected during the period August–September 2017, with each interview being audio-recorded, transcribed and analysed and the data from each transcription analysed and categorised into emerging themes. Key findings from the interviews are discussed below.

Results and discussion

Following content analysis of the interview transcripts, several themes emerged central to the link between community participation in eco-tourism activities and policy development. Table 19.1 details these themes, as well as the associated sub-themes that emerged from the analysis.

Protected area dynamics

Access to resources vs. conservation of resources

The establishment of protected areas serves to conserve the natural resource base, an essential drawcard for a thriving ecotourism sector (Eshun, 2014). However, through the establishment of protected areas, communities who reside in close proximity to (either within or adjacent to) these areas may have their source of livelihood sustenance compromised, if their access to the natural resource base is limited or entirely restricted (Morton & Meadows, 2000; Nkemnyi, De Haas, Etiendem & Ndobegang, 2013). This could, and has in many cases (Stronza & Gordillo, 2008; Wishitemi, Momanyi, Ombati & Okello, 2015; Wu &

Table 19.1 Key theme and sub-theme

Key theme	Sub-theme
Protected area dynamics	- Access to resources vs. conservation of resources
Disinterest and discontent in communities	- Waning trust in government
Community involvement, participation and collaborative planning	- Reality vs. theory of policy
	- Importance of community involvement in eco-tourism related activities
	- Collaborative planning and management
An opportunity ... (lost)	- Lack of benefits to communities
	- Eco-tourism benefiting natural environments
Eco-tourism revenue	- Money matters and community upliftment

Source: Own elaboration.

Chen, 2018), led to discontent amongst communities, with communities' attitudes towards eco-tourism related activities being negative or indifferent. This is illustrated by the case of the MCNP, where a local community chief indicated the discontent of the community, as a result of the establishment of the park as a protected area.

> It was a war between the village and the government…because there, they get their living.
>
> *(MCNP Community Chief)*

> They (the community) are not really involved, they are not really interested.
>
> *(MCNP Community Representative)*

Communities rely on access to protected areas to obtain natural resources from ecosystem services to sustain their livelihoods (Stone & Nyaupane, 2016). The establishment of eco-tourism, which is based on nature conservation as well as community involvement, to enhance conservation within protected areas, as well as improve the socio-economic status communities, could be counter-intuitive in this respect, as communities will not be motivated to participate in an activity that might threaten their livelihood. Hence, eco-tourism is perceived as a threat in some instances due to a lack of community participation and involvement. This has been noted by many (Bello et al., 2017; Stone & Nyaupane, 2016; Wu & Chen, 2018), who note the link between community involvement and support of eco-tourism and their positive (or negative) perception of it, as has proven to be the case in Cameroon, where the community have lost interest and are uninvolved in eco-tourism related activities in MCNP region.

Disinterest and discontent of communities

Waning trust in government

With government being a key stakeholder in tourism, it is imperative that relations of trust are maintained with all stakeholders, including communities (Njoh, 2002). Government is responsible for initiating and driving policy agendas that directly affect communities (Dieke, 2000), especially when the aforementioned protected area dynamics are considered. Furthermore, it is also important that the role of community members in the conservation of biodiversity is considered and incorporated into policy, so as not to trivialise and ultimately lose out on valuable traditional knowledge (Fonjong, 2006; Weladji, Moe & Vedeld, 2003). Communities have long since been implementing traditional conservation measures in current PAs, prior to their establishment, and benefiting from their efforts.

As the MCNP Community Representative and Chief elaborated, prior to the formalisation of eco-tourism in the MCNP region, communities accessed the park and reported to the community chief. All tourists who visited the park were escorted by tour guides and porters from within the community. At the end of each tourism season, all of the community chiefs from the region would meet to calculate the profit generated from tourism in the park and share it equally amongst all the communities in the region. However, following the formalisation of the MCNP in 2009, the operations surrounding the park changed, with the conservator becoming the primary liaison for all visitors entering and exiting the park, as well as for the general management of the park. The chief and community were mostly excluded from the majority of decisions regarding eco-tourism in the region, thereby reducing the benefits that they previously gained. External/private tour companies currently organise tours through the park, bypassing the community completely.

> The communities are not benefiting from eco-tourism and the creation of the park. Before the park, they were.
>
> *(MCNP Community Chief)*

All arrangements are made through the conservator, with none of the proceeds from park fees being filtered to the community either (Egbe, 2001). Communities are also restricted in terms of access to the park, and for example, the species that they can hunt, as noted by the DEWR Community Representative. Whilst these rules are a necessary part of conservation measures, they do impact on the livelihood of the communities, as many people are reliant on the "bushmeat" as a source of food (protein) (Egbe, 2001), oftentimes leading to the illegal poaching of these species (Tata & Lambi, 2014).

Since the creation of the PA and the formal institutionalisation of the park, communities' benefits from various ecosystem services, upon which they are dependent (Bele, Somorin, Sonwa, Nkem & Locatelli, 2011), have been compromised, putting their livelihood at stake. Furthermore, since the formalisation of the MCNP and eco-tourism in the area, the locals are unaware of eco-tourism related activities that occur. The traditional and cultural hierarchy in the communities, with the local chief as the head, has also been disregarded by the government, as the local community chief is not informed about current developments regarding eco-tourism in the area.

> I fought for it, but now they do not know me…without me, there would have been no eco-tourism. I do not see them this time. Since the creation of the park, nothing has been done by the park authority.

This feeling of utter discontent is echoed by a community representative from the DEWR area, who stated that the community feels extremely disheartened at the current state of affairs, as there is a chronic lack of community involvement or consultation in eco-tourism related activities. Consequently, this activity, which is grounded in community participation and involvement, incongruously does not serve to benefit the community at all. Furthermore, the feeling of discontent in the community is perpetuated by the fact that government officials have previously visited the community on several occasions, without any tangible socio-economic or environmental benefits for the community.

> If the government wants to do it, government will do it…The Minister of Tourism has been there a good couple of times, but after he comes and goes, nothing has been done. So, there is no confidence at all, doesn't trust that anything will happen.

The lack of trust in government is a key factor in communities not benefitting from eco-tourism (Weladji et al., 2003), as government is the driver of policy (Dieke, 2000) which does not seem to be inclusive of the wider community. Communities are motivated and interested in taking part in eco-tourism related activities but require authorisation from government to do so. Authorisation of this nature could emanate from an inclusive policy, that is effective and correctly implemented.

Community involvement, participation and collaborative planning

Reality vs. theory of policy

Over the past few decades, the structure of Cameroon's government ministries has changed (Kimbu & Ngoasong, 2013), with different ministerial departments being responsible for different portfolios. As tourism is multi-disciplinary, there are several different ministries involved in the establishment, growth and development of tourism in Cameroon. Focussing on eco-tourism specifically, one of the other ministries concerned (other than MINTOUR) is MINEF, due to the incorporation of protected areas in eco-tourism. Therefore, the policies associated with each of these ministries must be considered in the establishment, development and implementation of the country's eco-tourism industry, to ensure that all key stakeholders are included in the process (Bele et al., 2011).

An integral piece of legislation, Law no. 94/01 of 20 January 1994 was adopted to institute forestry, wildlife and fisheries regulations (MINEF, 1994). Sections of this law pertained to the management of natural resources within the different classification of forests, also detailed within this law. It was through this law that the concept of state forests (i.e. National parks, wildlife reserves and other similar areas) and community forests were conceptualised, thus linking directly to the mandate of MINTOUR (Djeumo, 2001; MINEF, 1994). In addition, there are other management plans and documents relating to the MCNP and DEWR respectively, each underpinned by the fundamental pillars put forward in the law. For the MCNP, the Ministry of Forestry and Wildlife (MINFOF) assembled The Management Plan of the Mount Cameroon National Park and its Peripheral Zone, 2015–2019 (MINFOF, 2014); whilst in the DEWR region, the Food and Agriculture Organisation (FAO) of the United Nations in partnership with the Ministry of Environment and Nature Protection (MINEP) undertook the Sustainable community-based management and conservation of mangrove eco-systems in Cameroon, a project which was based in the Douala Edea Wildlife Reserve and addressed issues related to eco-tourism in the region (FAO, 2011).

One of the common issues that these laws, management plans and projects cited was collaborative management with all stakeholders, including the community. The community forests, provided for in terms of the Law, allocate sections of the forest to communities, to be managed by them in accordance with an agreed upon management plan (Egbe, 2001). All produce emanating from the community forest would belong to the community itself, thereby supporting their local livelihood activities (MINEF, 1994). Other collaborative management activities involving the community in both the MCNP and DEWR regions include surveillance of the protected areas with guards, participation in meetings regarding the protected area and the reporting of prohibited activities such as illegal hunting. These regulations pertaining to the daily management of protected areas are all the responsibility of the park conservator, who is assisted by civil servants, community recruited staff and community-based organisations to achieve the objectives of collaborative management (MINFOF, 2014).

Furthermore, as community chiefs are legally recognised by the Cameroonian government, they also provide further support in the achievement of these objectives, through their authority within their given communities. The management authority in specific situations (such as community forests) are transferred to the local communities, as discussed above. There are also other measures in place which allow for the decentralisation of authority, such as village development measures (VDM) and alternate income generation activities (IGA). Other measures in place include the provision of an annual community bonus (CB), which is an incentive to the community for their collaboration in management (MINFOF, 2014).

Unfortunately, although there are policies in place, and although the restructuring of the Cameroonian ministries has resulted in decentralisation and a bottom-up approach, this is not what is being implemented in reality (Mbatu, 2009). The little community involvement there is, is superficial at best.

> Community involvement is limited to surveillance through NGOs when required.
> *(DEWR Community Representative)*

> No involvement of the community by the park authority since the creation of the park.
> *(MCNP Community Chief)*

The importance of involving communities in the planning process and formulation of plans is another key issue to be highlighted. Communities who live in close proximity to PAs have an intimate knowledge of the area and can therefore give valuable input on the formation of policy and plans (Egbe, 2001; Mbile et al., 2005). When communities are excluded from this process, it can often result in failure of policy or in ineffective policy which is not beneficial to communities, hence the need for community participation has been noted (Poudel, Nyaupane & Budruk, 2016; Wishitemi et al., 2015), evidenced in the MCNP region. Policies are only effective when they are properly implemented, thus resulting in the difference between reality and what should be occurring (community participation and collaboration) as per the policy.

> When the management plan was implemented, it failed. They did not take the community knowledge into consideration.
> *(MCNP Community Representative)*

There also seems to be a pattern of inconsistency with regard to the application of policy, resulting in isolated incidents of community involvement and participation, as opposed to ongoing involvement and participation, which would lead to sustainable outcomes for all stakeholders involved. For example, there was an instance where certain community members were called on to participate in training to become tour guides and porters for eco-tourists who visit the MCNP, but there was no other consultation with the community or the local chief regarding involvement and participation in other areas of eco-tourism.

This seems to be a trend, with a similar situation indicated by the DEWR Community Representative indicating that the community as stakeholders do not benefit from eco-tourism, nor are they consulted on any initiative related to eco-tourism, despite this being provisioned for in the law and management plans for these protected areas (Djeumo, 2001). Hence, reality vs. the theory of policy.

Importance of community involvement in eco-tourism related activities

As eco-tourism often occurs at the place of residence of communities, or in a place where communities source their livelihoods, communities are stakeholders who are fundamental to the success of eco-tourism in an area, without whom the process is likely to fail (Fonjong, 2006; Wisely, Alexander, Mahlaba & Cassidy, 2018). Local members of a community have historical and cultural ties to an area and have intimate knowledge of how to sustain and conserve resources.

> If there is a beneficiary system that does not involve the community, it will fail. If you want to do eco-tourism, call the community.
>
> *(MCNP Community Representative)*

In addition, social capital within communities, between local community members, perpetuated by traditional hierarchy, is an important consideration in community involvement in eco-tourism related activities (Manwa, Saarinen, Atlhopheng & Hambira, 2017; Mura & Tavakoli, 2014). This is illustrated in the case of the MCNP, where although the community remained unconvinced about the formalisation of the park and of eco-tourism, they accepted it because their community chief did. Through these relations, eco-tourism and the protected area was able to be formalised, with buy-in from the community.

However, subsequent to the establishment of the PA and of eco-tourism in the area, community involvement (through consultation with the local chief) halted. Consequently, community members are disinterested in eco-tourism activities. This occurrence is not unique to the MCNP region and has occurred in other regions in the country, including the DEWR region. It should be noted however, that the disinterest on the part of communities is not as a result of not wanting to be involved in eco-tourism in the area, but rather a result of being undermined and ostracised by other stakeholders (government and private).

> The community should be more involved…community would want to organise and develop eco-tourism, but need authority to do so.
>
> *(DEWR Community Representative)*

Collaborative planning and management

In most cases, communities are not opposed to eco-tourism and in fact would like to be involved in the activity to support their own livelihoods (Kimengsi, 2014). This is imperative as it will foster positive attitudes from the communities towards eco-tourism (Park, Nunkoo & Yoon, 2015), motivating them to work together with other stakeholders to achieve the maximum benefits. The need for collaborative planning and management is an integral aspect of eco-tourism (Venkatesh & Gouda, 2016). This has also been incorporated into the management plans for the implementation of eco-tourism in communities but has not materialised in some cases.

> When the management plan was drawn, they said it was participatory. But they drew it without asking the community.
>
> *(MCNP Community Representative)*

> Lack of cohesion and collaboration between the government and the community.
>
> *(DEWR Community Representative)*

Hence, a situation characterised by non-communication between government and communities has arisen, where communities are distanced from the eco-tourism activities that are occurring in their immediate vicinity, a direct result of the lack of involvement and participation.

An opportunity... (lost)

Lack of benefits to communities

Eco-tourism is an activity that can enhance the quality of life of locals in communities through the provision of alternate livelihood strategies (Harilal et al., 2018). As a result of communities' lack of participation, and in most cases, complete non-involvement in eco-tourism activities, communities have lost out on the chance to capitalise on opportunities offered by the presence of eco-tourism in their localities to enhance their livelihoods.

> When there was no park, the community was benefiting.
>
> *(MCNP Community Chief)*

> Eco-tourism is not about us anymore, we don't benefit. It is about the conservator.
>
> *(MCNP Community Chief)*

As a consequence of limited consultation and involvement of communities in eco-tourism by government authorities, there is an uneven, limited spread of benefits from eco-tourism that is circulated within communities. For example, the benefits of eco-tourism in the MCNP area seem to be limited to those who are porters or tour guides only but do not seem to benefit anyone in the DEWR region.

> Since the creation of the park, we have just porters and guides who are benefiting.
>
> *(MCNP Community Chief)*

> Eco-tourism has benefited me personally, to be employed as a tour guide.
>
> *(MCNP Tour Guide)*

> The activity is not beneficial to the community at all.
>
> *(DEWR Community Representative)*

The jobs of porters and tour guides must also be closely examined as a positive, sustainable outcome of eco-tourism for community members, considering the seasonal and temporary nature of these jobs (confined to tourism peak seasons) (Eshun, 2014; Harilal & Tichaawa, 2018). This brings into question the effectiveness of the existing policy on eco-tourism and protected areas, as well as if these policies are being properly implemented to achieve sustainable outcomes for communities, which implies long-term benefit, not just fleeting periods of involvement and subsequent benefit. A deeper and more meaningful approach to community involvement in eco-tourism activities needs to be adopted to ensure that all stakeholders, including communities, benefit alike (Mbile et al., 2005).

Eco-tourism benefiting natural environments

Despite eco-tourism not benefiting communities, it is acknowledged that the policies governing protected areas (related to eco-tourism) serve to conserve the natural environment (Weladji et al., 2003), upon which many rely, and to which most have culturally significant ties (Fonjong, 2006).

> There is conservation there, there is preservation of their heritage, they are happy, but just in that sense.
>
> *(DEWR Community Representative)*

However, whilst communities may be satisfied that culturally significant areas and resources are being conserved, the policies that serve to protect the natural resource base should not serve to exclude and disadvantage communities. Communities have invaluable indigenous knowledge of conservation (Bramwell, 2010), which should be incorporated into the protected area policies to ensure meaningful and sustainable community involvement.

Eco-tourism revenue

Money matters and community upliftment

As an activity that is based in the immediate vicinity of where communities reside, the long-term success of eco-tourism is dependent on community buy-in, with community involvement in eco-tourism related activities being a central theme. If communities are to be involved and remain involved, they must receive benefits from eco-tourism (Eshun, 2014; Ngoran, Xue & Ndah, 2016; Poudel et al., 2016; Wishitemi et al., 2015), especially since one of the primary reasons for eco-tourism being instituted in an area is to generate income (Andereck & Vogt, 2000). However, in the case of both case study areas, the communities do not seem to receive any monetary benefits from eco-tourism, which could be used for community upliftment projects.

> Money from eco-tourism doesn't reach the community.
>
> *(DEWR Community Representative)*

> Eco-tourism money goes to the government treasury. Before the creation of the park, money was shared amongst the villages in the community. We don't know how the money is shared...the Ministry decides.
>
> *(MCNP Community Chief)*

Prior to the creation of the park and the formal establishment of eco-tourism in the MCNP area, there existed a system whereby the community was involved in (non-institutionalised) eco-tourism activities, and the resultant monetary benefits were shared amongst the various villages in the community. Since the establishment and formalisation of eco-tourism, the practice of sharing monetary benefits generated from eco-tourism has ceased, as the money is all directed to the government treasury, in most cases (according to the various stakeholders interviewed), never to be seen by local communities. This is more than a result of failure to implement policy, which provides for a percentage of monetary benefits to be directed back to communities, but rather a symptom of a larger problem in Cameroon. Corruption is a major stumbling block in the country (Mbatu, 2009) and seems to be acknowledged by residents as the norm. As the MCNP Community Representative stated *"it's the nature of Cameroon"*.

Conclusion and recommendations

The foregoing discussion on the link between community participation in eco-tourism and policy development has revealed that there are various factors that inhibit effective and meaningful community participation, as well as poor implementation of existing policies, resulting in communities' disinterest in eco-tourism and consequent resistance to be involved. The deep-seated problem of corruption in Cameroon serves to further deter communities from participating. There are various policies from various ministries related to the implementation of eco-tourism in Cameroon. However, this decentralised approach has not truly been implemented, with the actions of government still very state-centric. The inherent lack of community consultation on matters relating to eco-tourism results in their lack of participation and involvement. In addition, it seems as if the existing policies, in addition to not being implemented properly, do not account for the invaluable indigenous knowledge that locals possess, thereby trivialising the ability of local community members to effectively contribute to the various facets of eco-tourism in the area. This is evidenced by the failure of the management plan in the MCNP area, which was supposed to account for community consultation, but eventually did not.

It has been suggested that there is a greater need for collaboration between the communities and the government (DEWR Community Representative). This collaboration should occur with an umbrella body that is representative of all the communities in each area, ensuring full representation. Through this approach, the central tenets of eco-tourism (community involvement and natural resource conservation) can both be satisfied. The governance structure relating to eco-tourism would need to allow for these collective bodies to be representative of communities, and policies would need to be modified or new policies developed to account for the involvement of these key stakeholders.

References

African Development Bank. (2015). *Cameroon: Strategy and Programme Evaluation 2004–2013 Summary Report.* Retrieved from https://www.oecd.org/derec/afdb/2015-Cameroon-Country-Strategy-Evaluation-Report.pdf.

Agüera, F.O. (2013). Stakeholder theory as a model for sustainable development in ecotourism. *Revista de investigación en turismo y desarrollo local,* 6(15). Retrieved from: http://www.eumed.net/rev/turydes/15/stakeholders.html.

Ajonina, P.U., Ajonina, G.N., Jin, E., Mekongo, F., Ayissi, I. & Usongo, L. (2005). Gender roles and economics of exploitation, processing and marketing of bivalves and impacts on forest resources in the Sanaga Delta region of Douala-Edéa Wildlife Reserve, Cameroon. *International Journal of Sustainable Development & World Ecology,* 12(2), 161–172.

Andereck, K.L. & Vogt, C.A. (2000). The relationship between residents' attitudes toward tourism and tourism development options. *Journal of Travel Research,* 39(1), 27–36.

Andereck, K.L., Valentine, K.M., Knopf, R.C. & Vogt, C.A. (2005). Residents' perceptions of community tourism impacts. *Annals of Tourism Research,* 32(4), 1056–1076.

Angoni, H. (2015). Non-timber forest products and their contributions on the income of local residents in the Douala-Edéa Wildlife Reserve of Cameroon. *Journal of Ecology and the Natural Environment,* 7(10), 263–270.

Atieno, L. & Njoroge, J.M. (2018). The ecotourism metaphor and environmental sustainability in Kenya. *Tourism and Hospitality Research,* 18(1), 49–60.

Bele, M.Y., Somorin, O., Sonwa, D.J., Nkem, J.N. & Locatelli, B. (2011). Forests and climate change adaptation policies in Cameroon. *Mitigation and Adaptation Strategies for Global Change,* 16(3), 369–385.

Bello, F.G., Lovelock, B. & Carr, N. (2017). Constraints of community participation in protected area-based tourism planning: the case of Malawi. *Journal of Ecotourism,* 16(2), 131–151.

Bramwell, B. (2010). Participative planning and governance for sustainable tourism. *Tourism Recreation Research,* 35(3), 239–249.

Buckley, R. (2003). Environmental inputs and outputs in ecotourism: Geotourism with a positive triple bottom line? *Journal of Ecotourism,* 2(1), 76–82.

Campbell, L.M. (1999). Ecotourism in rural developing communities. *Annals of Tourism Research,* 26(3), 534–553.

Chirenje, L.I., Giliba, R.A. & Musamba, E.B. (2013). Local communities' participation in decision-making processes through planning and budgeting in African countries. *Chinese Journal of Population Resources and Environment*, 11(1), 10–16.

Cohen, L., Manion, L. & Morrison, K. (2002). *Research Methods in Education*. London: Routledge.

Das, M. & Chatterjee, B. (2015). Ecotourism: A panacea or a predicament? *Tourism Management Perspectives*, 14, 3–16.

Dieke, P.U. (2000). Developing tourism in Africa: Issues for policy consideration. *Development Policy Management Forum*, 7(1), 25–31.

Djeumo, A. (2001). The development of community forests in Cameroon: Origins, current situation and constraints. Rural Development Forestry Network. Network Paper 25b(i), 1–16. Retrieved from https://www.odi.org/sites/odi.org.uk/files/odi-assets/publications-opinion-files/1208.pdf

Egbe, S.E. (2001). The law, communities and wildlife management in Cameroon. Rural Development Forestry Network. Network Paper 25e(i), 1–12. Retrieved from https://www.odi.org/sites/odi.org.uk/files/odi-assets/publications-opinion-files/1216.pdf

Eshun, G. (2014). Towards the dual mandate of ecotourism in Africa – Comparative evidence from Ghana. *Africa Insight*, 44(3), 164–184.

Ezzine de Blas, D., Ruiz-Pérez, M. & Vermeulen, C. (2011). Management conflicts in Cameroonian community forests. *Ecology and Society*, 16(1), 8. Retrieved from: http://www.ecologyandsociety.org/vol16/iss1/art8/.

FAO (Food and Agriculture Organisation of the United Nations). 2011. *CBSP – Sustainable Community Based Management and Conservation of Mangrove Ecosystems in Cameroon*. Rome: Food and Agriculture Organisation of the United Nations.

Flick, U. (2014). *An Introduction to Qualitative Research* (5th ed.). London: Sage.

Fonjong, L. (2006). Managing deforestation in Anglophone Cameroon: Are NGOs pacesetters? *International Journal of Environmental Studies*, 63(5), 663–679.

Goodwin, H. (2002). Local community involvement in tourism around national parks: Opportunities and constraints. *Current Issues in Tourism*, 5(3–4), 338–360.

Harilal, V. & Tichaawa, T.M. (2018). Ecotourism and alternate livelihood strategies in Cameroon's protected areas. *EuroEconomica*, 37(2), 127–142. Retrieved from http://journals.univ-danubius.ro/index.php/euroeconomica/article/view/5180/4557

Harilal, V., Tichaawa, T.M. & Saarinen, J. (2018). Development without policy: Tourism planning and research needs in Cameroon, Central Africa. *Tourism Planning and Development*, [online], pp. 1–10. Retrieved from https://doi.org/10.1080/21568316.2018.1501732.

He, S., Gallagher, L., Su, Y., Wang, L. & Cheng, H. (2018). Identification and assessment of ecosystem services for protected area planning: A case in rural communities of Wuyishan national park pilot. *Ecosystem Services*, 31, 169–180.

Hugo, N.C. & Nyaupane, G.P. (2016). *Poverty alleviation in Third World countries through tourism development: A comparison study of Costa Rica and Nicaragua*. ScholarWorks@UMass Amherst. University of Massachusetts, Amherst. Tourism Travel and Research Association: Advancing Tourism Research Globally. *2009 ttra International Conference*. Retrieved from http://scholarworks.umass.edu/cgi/viewcontent.cgi?article=1464&context=ttra.

Kimbu, A.N. (2010). The non-prioritization of the tourism industry and its impacts on tourism research, development and management in the Central African sub-region. *Revista Turismo & Desenvolvimento*, 1(13&14), 51–62.

Kimbu, A.N. & Ngoasong, M.Z. (2013). Centralised decentralisation of tourism development: A network perspective. *Annals of Tourism Research*, 40, 235–259.

Kimengsi, J.N. (2014). Threats to ecotourism development and forest conservation in the Lake Barombi Mbo Area (LBMA) of Cameroon. *Journal of International Wildlife Law & Policy*, 17(4), 213–230.

Kothari, C.R. (2004). *Research Methodology: Methods and Techniques*. New Delhi: New Age International.

Lambi, C.M., Kimengsi, J.N., Kometa, C.G. & Tata, E.S. (2012). The management and challenges of protected areas and the sustenance of local livelihoods in Cameroon. *Environment and Natural Resources Research*, 2(3), 10.

Letoluo, M.L. & Wangombe, L. (2018). Exploring the socio-economic effects of the community tourism fund to the local community, Maasai Mara national reserve. *Universal Journal of Management*, 6(2), 51–58.

Manwa, H., Saarinen, J., Atlhopheng, J.R. & Hambira, W.L. (2017). Sustainability management and tourism impacts on communities: Residents' attitudes in Maun and Tshabong, Botswana. *African*

Journal of Hospitality, Tourism and Leisure, 6(3), 1–15. Retrieved from http://www.ajhtl.com/up-loads/7/1/6/3/7163688/article_15_vol_6__3__2017.pdf

Mason, J. (2017). *Qualitative Researching* (3rd ed.). Sage: London.

Mbatu, R.S. (2009). Forest exploitation in Cameroon (1884–1994): An oxymoron of top-down and bottom-up forest management policy approaches. *International Journal of Environmental Studies*, 66(6), 747–763.

Mbile, P., Vabi, M., Meboka, M., Okon, D., Arrey-Mbo, J., Nkongho, F. & Ebong, E. (2005). Link-ing management and livelihood in environmental conservation: Case of the Korup National Park Cameroon. *Journal of Environmental Management*, 76(1), 1–13.

Mengang, J.M. (1998). Evolution of natural resource policy in Cameroon. *Yale Forest & Environmental Science Bulletin*, 102, 239–248.

MINEF. (1994). Forestry, wildlife and fisheries regulations. Law no. 94/01/94. Ministry of Environ-ment and Forestry, Yaoundé, Cameroon.

MINFOF. (2014). The management plan of the Mount Cameroon National Park and its peripheral zone 2015–2019. Ministry of Forestry and Wildlife, Cameroon.

Morton, J. & Meadows, N. (2000). *Pastoralism and Sustainable Livelihoods: An Emerging Agenda*. Gilling-ham: Natural Resources Institute.

Moswete, N. & Thapa, B. (2018). Local communities, CBOs/trusts, and people–park relationships: A case study of the Kgalagadi Transfrontier Park, Botswana. *George Wright Forum*, 35(1), 96–108.

Mowforth, I. & Munt, M. (1998). *Tourism and Sustainability: Development and New Tourism in the Third World*. London: Routledge.

Mtapuri, O. & Giampiccoli, A. (2013). Interrogating the role of the state and nonstate actors in community-based tourism ventures: Toward a model for spreading the benefits to the wider com-munity. *South African Geographical Journal*, 95(1), 1–15.

Mura, P. & Tavakoli, R. (2014). Tourism and social capital in Malaysia. *Current Issues in Tourism*, 17(1), 28–45.

Ngoran, S.D., Xue, X.Z. & Ndah, A.B. (2016). Exploring the challenges of implementing integrated coastal management and achieving sustainability within the Cameroon coastline. *Revista de Gestão Costeira Integrada*, 16(1), 45–56.

Njoh, A.J. (2002). Barriers to community participation in development planning: lessons from the Mutengene (Cameroon) self-help water project. *Community Development Journal*, 37(3), 233–248.

Nkemnyi, M.F., De Haas, A., Etiendem, N.D. & Ndobegang, F. (2013). Making hard choices: bal-ancing indigenous communities livelihood and Cross River gorilla conservation in the Lebialem–Mone Forest landscape, Cameroon. *Environment, Development and Sustainability*, 15(3), 841–857.

Park, D.B., Nunkoo, R. & Yoon, Y.S. (2015). Rural residents' attitudes to tourism and the moderating effects of social capital. *Tourism Geographies*, 17(1), 112–133.

Poudel, S., Nyaupane, G.P. & Budruk, M. (2016). Stakeholders' perspectives of sustainable tourism development: A new approach to measuring outcomes. *Journal of Travel Research*, 55(4), 465–480.

Redmore, L., Stronza, A., Songhurst, A. & McCulloch, G. (2018). Which way forward? Past and new perspectives on community-based conservation in the Anthropocene. *Encyclopedia of the Anthropo-cene*. Retrieved from https://doi.org/10.1016.B978-0-12-809665-9.09838-4.

Saarinen, J. (2010). Local tourism awareness: Community views in Katutura and King Nehale conser-vancy, Namibia. *Development Southern Africa*, 27(5), 713–724.

Saarinen, J. & Rogerson, C.M. (2014). Tourism and the millennium development goals: Perspectives beyond 2015. *Tourism Geographies*, 16(1), 23–30.

Situmorang, R.O. (2018). Social capital in managing mangrove area as ecotourism by Muara Baimbai community. *Indonesian Journal of Forestry Research*, 5(1), 21–34.

Spratt, S., Kargbo, P., Marfo, E., Ngungoh, E. & Ramcilovik-Suominen, S. (2018). Forest taxation and REDD+: An analysis of potential impacts in Cameroon, Ghana and Sierra Leone. Institute of Development Studies. *Working Paper 76*. Retrieved from https://papers.ssrn.com/sol3/papers.cfm?abstract_id=3149491.

Stone, M.T. & Nyaupane, G.P. (2016). Ecotourism influence on community needs and the functions of protected areas: A systems thinking approach. *Journal of Ecotourism*, 16(3), 222–246.

Stronza, A. & Gordillo, J. (2008). Community views of ecotourism. *Annals of Tourism Research*, 35(2), 448–468.

Tata, E.S. & Lambi, C.M. (2014). Challenges and opportunities of the Mount Cameroon Forest Re-gion as a national park. *Journal of International Wildlife Law & Policy*, 17(4), 197–212.

Tchindjang, M., Banga, C.R., Nankam, A. & Makak, J.S. (2005). Mapping of protected areas evolution in Cameroon from the beginning to 2000: Lesson to learn and perspectives. *Proceedings of the 22nd International Cartographic Conference*, pp. 9–16.

Tegha, K.C. & Sendze, Y.G. (2016). Soil organic carbon stocks in Mount Cameroon National Park under different land uses. *Journal of Ecology and the Natural Environment*, 8(3), 20–30.

Tichaawa, T.M. (2017). Business tourism in Africa: The case of Cameroon. *Tourism Review International*, 21(2), 181–192.

Tosun, C. (2000). Limits to community participation in the tourism development process in developing countries. *Tourism Management*, 21(6), 613–633.

Tyrrell, T., Paris, C.M. & Biaett, V. (2013). A quantified triple bottom line for tourism: Experimental results. *Journal of Travel Research*, 52(3), 279–293.

United Nations. (2017). *Economic Development in Africa Report 2017: Tourism for Transformative and Inclusive Growth*. Retrieved from http://unctad.org/en/PublicationsLibrary/aldcafrica2017_en.pdf.

UNWTO (World Tourism Organization). (2017). *Tourism Highlights*, 2017 edition. Madrid: UNWTO.

Venkatesh, R. & Gouda, H. (2016). Eco-tourism – Planning and developmental strategies. *Global Journal for Research Analysis*, 5(12), 420–422.

Weladji, R.B., Moe, S.R. & Vedeld, P. (2003). Stakeholder attitudes towards wildlife policy and the Benoue Wildlife Conservation area, North Cameroon. *Environmental Conservation*, 30(4), 334–343.

Wisely, S.M., Alexander, K., Mahlaba, T. & Cassidy, L. (2018). Linking ecosystem services to livelihoods in southern Africa. *Ecosystem Services*, 30, 330–341.

Wishitemi, B.E., Momanyi, S.O., Ombati, B.G. & Okello, M.M. (2015). The link between poverty, environment and ecotourism development in areas adjacent to Maasai Mara and Amboseli protected areas, Kenya. *Tourism Management Perspectives*, 16, 306–317.

World Bank. (2018). *Supporting Sustainable Livelihoods through Wildlife Tourism*. Washington DC: The World Bank Group.

World Travel & Tourism Council (WTTC). (2017). *Travel and Tourism Economic Impact Cameroon*. Retrieved from https://www.wttc.org/-/media/files/reports/economic-impact-research/countries-2017/cameroon2017.pdf.

World Travel & Tourism Council (WTTC). (2018). *Travel and Tourism Economic Impact Cameroon*. Retrieved from https://www.wttc.org/-/media/files/reports/economic-impact-research/countries-2018/cameroon2018.pdf.

Wu, S.T. & Chen, Y.S. (2018). Local intentions to participate in ecotourism development in Taiwan's Atayal communities. *Journal of Tourism and Cultural Change*, 16(1), 75–96.

20

Tourism development in Gabon
Pioneers operating under adverse conditions

Isabelle Cloquet

Introduction

Situated in Western Central Africa, Gabon is a country of 1.6 million inhabitants with a land area of 267,670 km². Its political system builds upon presidentialism, highly centralized power, and continuity: Léon Mba (1960–1967), Omar Bongo (1967–2009), Ali Bongo (2009–present). Its economy is essentially based on oil, with a poorly developed agricultural sector that represented 5% of the GDP in 2017. These characteristics have enabled the country to maintain its forest, which currently still covers more than 75% of its land area (www.worldbank.org, 2018). With the prospect of a severe decrease in oil reserves, tourism has been considered by the government and tier parties as a sector that could help sustain economic development while protecting the country's forest and endemic species.

It is in this context that a documentary on tourism in Gabon was broadcast on television in 2004. It displayed a whole range of irresistible images for nature lovers: untamed tourist-magnetic elephants, hippopotamuses, and buffalos walking on the beach and bathing in the sea, leatherback turtles, chimpanzees, mandrills, gorillas… and sumptuous white sand beaches on the edge of the rainforest. The documentary also focused on a ground operator whose strategy had influenced that of the whole country, following the principle of "tourism pays for conservation". The documentary was only one of several of the kind, which advertised Gabon, at that time, as one of the most promising upmarket ecotourism destinations.

As was depicted in those documentaries, the tourism strategy adopted by Gabon appeared indeed to be promising. It was in line with market trends, showing a general increase in sustainability awareness and the success of several "ecotourism" destinations, Costa Rica in particular. Moreover, besides its natural resources, Gabon seemed to have several other assets in comparison to other countries in sub-Saharan Africa. The country had been politically stable since the 1960s with an incredibly high GDP per capita[1] and literacy rate[2] (www.worldbank.org, July 2013). Personal observation and conversations with Gabonese who studied in universities in Canada and France also indicated that the number of Gabonese citizens who has for several decades been receiving a high-level education in foreign universities across the world is sizeable.

Despite these assets, Gabon is still not on the "global tourism map". On the contrary, major tourism development projects have been abandoned or are at a standstill. Personal communications with tourism stakeholders in 2012 confirmed a sharp slowdown of the industry compared to 2007, which was often referred to as a year of reference (Personal communications, 2011, 2012). The chapter provides insight into this problem using a structure-agency approach rooted in Jessop's (2008) strategic relational theory. It first gives an overview of tourism development and trends in the country, highlighting the structural inconsistencies that affect the industry. It then discusses the tourism initiatives that were able to emerge, including a close examination of how and why these pioneering undertakings were able to emerge in their specific time-space context, and to what extent tourism providers have been able to operate in such structural environment. The chapter concludes by considering implications for destination development in the future.

Development of tourism in Gabon

In this section, a chronological and political economy approach is adopted in order to highlight variables that have determined, influenced, or shaped tourism development over time in Gabon. Three time periods can be distinguished using this approach: (1) the colonial era, in which tourism was essentially utilized as a means to promote the "benefits" of colonization (1886–1960); (2) the immediate post-independence years (1960–1973/74), during which tourism development was not on the agenda; (3) the oil-rent era (1974-present) with its alternating economic boom and stagnation periods which set the pace for, and shaped, tourism development.

The first evidence of tourism in Gabon dates back just before the colonial era, and more particularly to the second half of the 19th century, with travel accounts of Western explorers, e.g. Paul Du Chaillu, Alfred Marche and Victor (Marquis) de Compiègne, and Savorgnan de Brazza. Travel motives included developing trade but also verifying narratives from Carthaginian manuscripts (5th century BC), and discovering areas, species, or tribes still poorly known by Westerners (Pourtier, 1989). Gabon was accessed from Liverpool as there was no direct shipping line with France (Domergue, 1893). The Ogooué River was a key route to discover hinterland with canoes as a main means of transport (Kingsley, 1993). Accounts from that time period depict an image of a remote, wild, and dangerous area. Domergue (1893, p. 57) writes: "Ever since 1856 [...] Gabon has been regarded as Europeans' grave", mainly due to a combination of humidity, heat, swamps, and insects, causing sicknesses and death (Domergue, 1893; Plais, 1882). The natives were portrayed as solidly-built, intelligent, sly, and clean, though lazy, with some tribes being reported as warriors and even cannibals (Domergue, 1893; Plais, 1882; Pourtier, 1989). The fauna was described as dangerous and abundant although Domergue (1893) reported (already) a decreasing number of elephants. Some of these expeditions led to the establishment of French protectorates, and later to colonization (Pourtier, 1989).

Dulucq (2009b) reports great similarities between the narratives of these explorers and those of the first tourists traveling between 1900 and 1920 in the French territories in tropical Africa, which included both French Equatorial Africa (FEA) and French West Africa (FWA). Driven by adventure and thrill these first leisure tourists—several hundreds of them—traveled independently, had financial means and time. They hired porters, servants, cooks, drivers, and guides, and expected a certain range of services, including hospitality and activities. Hospitality was provided in hotels (in main towns) or by the French administrators or soldiers. Activities mainly consisted of hunting, photography, wildlife watching as well as attending dance or musical shows or visiting local markets.

The years between 1920 and independence in the 1960s saw an institutionalization of tourism in French tropical Africa, with the listing of sites, the creation of tourist itineraries, the provision of information, and promotion. Shipping lines also multiplied in the 1930s (Dulucq, 2009b). The main stakeholders in this institutionalization process were individuals, including French administrators, soldiers or wealthy tourists (Dulucq, 2009a). Promotional narratives praised the benefits of colonization (Dulucq, 2009a, 2009b). In the years between 1940 and 1950, there was a change in the approach to institutionalization with political motivations gradually giving way to economic considerations (Dulucq, 2009a). In the 1930s, observing how the British colonies benefited from tourism, the French administration increased its support to tourism development, and adopted the safari model, together with that of the hunting lodge, leisure homes, and natural park models (Dulucq, 2009b). In Gabon, these policy measures led to the creation of the Lopé national park in 1946 by the FEA administration as well as increased regulation of hunting activities. Although hunting remained a key tourist activity after World War II (WWII), it was progressively replaced by photo safari. Exoticism and "unscathed" nature were amongst the main travel motivations.

There is an indication that tourism in Gabon as well as in other countries of FEA developed later than in FWA. For instance, the first promotional brochure on FEA was published in 1940 compared to 1924 for that on FWA. While first development strategies emerged in the 1950s in FEA with the creation of a first tourist office in 1956, as opposed to 1945 in FWA. It can be suggested that tourism development in Gabon was inhibited by administration problems, a general lack of basic infrastructure, and little economic incentives in what was the most profitable colony of the FEA thanks to the rent-generating export of *okoumé* timber (Aucoumea Klaineana). A brochure published in 1955 described Gabon as "mysterious and impenetrable" and emphasized the poor access of its hinterland and its challenging climate conditions (Mer, 1955).

Soon after WWII, regular airlines started to connect Europe to FEA, and Libreville was served five days a week in 1955 (Mer, 1955). Tour operators such as "Thomas Cook", "Havas", or transport companies such as "Air France" or the "Compagnie Internationale des Wagons-Lits" started to provide cruises of two to four weeks to FEA (Dulucq, 2009b). However, the number of hotels remained low in FEA, with 36 establishments in the 1950s compared to 85 in FWA and 25 in Madagascar (Defert, 1954). Mainly located on the coast, hotels in FEA essentially targeted business tourism. The number of tourists was estimated to be around a few 1,000 in the whole French tropical Africa (Dulucq, 2009a). Based on the fact that FWA was ahead in developing and promoting tourism, it can be assumed that FEA only received a minority of those tourists.

Very few data could be found about tourism in the immediate post-independence years (1960–1973/1974). It may be argued that tourism was not part of the State's priorities which focused on exports of raw materials, including newly discovered oil, uranium, and manganese. In a context in which France sought to preserve its economic interests in Africa, independence was associated with cooperation agreements among which were exemptions from custom duties on Gabonese exports to France and on French imports to Gabon (Yates, 1996). There is no indication of a real tourism development strategy despite evidence showing that there was a Ministry of tourism. In the early 1970s, several decrees and orders were issued with the aim to regulate the hospitality sector—mainly business travel-oriented and concentrated in cities—and the exploitation of the fauna and protected areas as tourist attractions.

The first sizeable leisure-travel oriented tourism initiatives emerged in the 1990s, in the oil-rent era which extended from 1974 to the present day. Between 1974 and 1997 the country benefited from a quasi-permanent boom as bust periods were mitigated with increases in either oil production or crude oil price, and foreign borrowings against future oil revenues (Soares De Oliveira, 2007; Söderling, 2002; Wunder, 2003). In that particular context, there was thus little incentive for the authorities to support the development of inbound and domestic leisure travel. Inbound tourism would have contributed even more to oil-rent induced inflation, whereas the domestic market—i.e. the elites with their conspicuous consumption behaviors and foreign residents, including Western expatriate workers—was characterized by a preference for international travel in addition to being small in size (Cloquet, 2016).

However, since the 1990s, oil production and reserves have continuously decreased, urging the State towards economic diversification and the search for new sources of hard currencies. This is when the first real leisure travel-oriented tourism projects were undertaken. As will be shown in the subsequent section, these initiatives have so far not been conducive to tourism growth; they have been scattered and have faced numerous hindrances related to the country's structural elements (Cloquet, 2016). These structural elements are typical of rentier states. They are deeply rooted in Gabon as they date back to the colonial era and were reinforced with the oil boom which had a catalyzing effect on rent-seeking and rent-seizing behaviors, leading to highly centralized power and institutional breakdown (Barnes, 2003; Ross, 2001).

In such circumstances, as we shall see below, developing tourism seems a considerable challenge regarding interests at stake among the elite and long-lasting, unchanging, and very selective social and political structures. Some of these structures relate to variables known for directly affecting tourism growth (see Breakey, 2005; Butler, 2005; Cohen, 1979; Cole, 2007; Haywood, 1986; Ioannides, 1992; Johnston, 2001; Ma & Hassink, 2013; Miossec, 1977; Plog, 2001; Prideaux, 2000) by shaping the business environment and opposing considerable barriers to the development of the industry. In Gabon structural barriers were found to be:

- unattractive visa policies and limited flight connections, hence relatively high airfares;
- internal accessibility with reduced land, water, and air transport networks;
- limited access to land tenure as land is still mostly owned by the State;
- high cost of living and of business operations;
- low availability of human resources in the industry and most particularly in the hinterland;
- lack of public support to the industry and effective strategy (limited implementation),
- lack of public measures aimed at easing access to finance and limiting risks in business investment (see Cloquet, 2016, for further insight into structural effects of oil-rents on tourism in Gabon).

Tourism trends

As a consequence of these barriers, the number of international tourist arrivals (ITAs) remains particularly low. Table 20.1 provides a compilation of available statistics on ITAs in Gabon and Cameroon, one of its neighboring countries, from 1995 to 2016. Whereas Cameroon has shown signs of growth since 2005, reaching around 800,000 ITAs in 2012, this is not the case of Gabon. ITAs in Gabon never went beyond 270,000 in 2005, a figure—published by the World Bank—the reliability of which can be questioned as it is much higher than that of 151,000 ITAs released by the Gabonese Ministry of Tourism and National Parks for that year.

Table 20.1 International tourism arrivals in Gabon and Cameroon, 1995–2016

		1995	1996	1997	1998	1999	2000	2001	2002	2003	2004	2005
Gabon	TF	125	[145]	[167]	[195]	[178]	[155]	[169]	[208]	[222]	[244]	[269]
											(180)	(151)
Cameroon	THS	100	n.d	n.d	n.d	n.d	277	221	226	n.d.	190	[176]

		2006	2007	2008	2009	2010	2011	2012	2013	2014	2015	2016
Gabon	TF	(149)	(159)	n.d.	186 96*	n.d.	n.d.	n.d.	n.d.	n.d.	n.d.	n.d.
Cameroon	THS	[451]	477	487	498	569	604	812	912 [783]	822	n.d.	n.d.

n.d.: no data available. Data in (…): Ministère du tourisme et des parcs nationaux (2009); data followed by a *:
GEODE (2010).
Sources: UNWTO (2000, 2007, 2013, 2014, 2015, 2016, 2017); Date in [...]: World Bank, online, July 2018, https://
data.worldbank.org.

As can be concluded from Table 20.1, examining tourism trends in Gabon is not an easy task. There are very few reliable data available, and data often vary depending on the source. Not only the UNWTO database on ITAs have gaps as the country has not released its statistics on a regular basis, but concern has also been raised about their reliability. According to key informants involved in setting up a national tourism satellite account in 2009, the data in UNWTO publications include the total number of international passengers arriving at Libreville airport, implying that outbound travelers coming back from their trip abroad are computed in those statistics.

According to the tourism satellite account published in 2010, Libreville airport received in reality 96,149 ITAs in 2009 (inbound travelers), that is, half the number found in UNWTO Tourism Highlights. There were 89,308 (93%) non-resident visitors, and 6,841 Gabonese from the Diaspora (7%). A survey conducted by GEODE in 2009 with 1,686 inbound tourist respondents at Libreville airport showed that Gabon's main outbound markets—all motives included—were France (41%), Cameroon (9%), Great Britain (7%) and the United-States (4%). Even though the number of ITAs in 2009 might have been negatively impacted by the death of the late President Omar Bongo Ondimba, the figures—even those published by the UNWTO—appear negligible when they are compared with other African destinations such as South Africa (7 million ITA in 2009), Kenya (1.4 million), Senegal (810,000), Uganda (807,000) or even Cameroon (498,000) (UNWTO, 2012). To fully appreciate the significance of these figures, it might be worth recalling that Gabon has a population of 1.6 million inhabitants and targets a total number of 100,000 international leisure travelers a year by 2020 (www.presidentalibongo.com, 2012).

Data released by the World Travel and Tourism Council (www.wttc.org, 2018) give an idea of the economic contribution of the tourism industry in the country, and its evolution through the years. It is estimated that the tourism industry directly contributed 147 million USD in 2009, that is, 1.3% of Gabon's GDP (Direct contribution to GDP, real prices). In 2015 this estimated contribution reached USD 161 million, and 1% of the GDP. Foreign spending contributes little, with 10 million USD in 2009 and 2015 (Visitor exports, real prices). As is shown in Figure 20.1, foreign spending was particularly high in the late 1990s, reflecting the tourism development initiatives of the time. It then fell to remain at its lowest

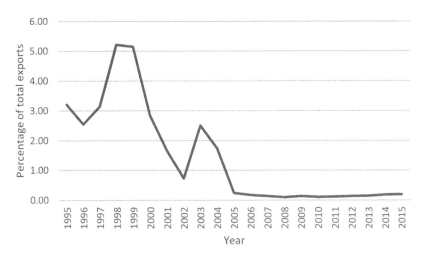

Figure 20.1 Foreign spending in Gabon, 1995–2015
Source: www.wttc.org, 2018.

ever since 2005, contributing an average 0.15% of exports; the organization of the African Cup of Nations football event in 2012 did not do much in stimulating tourism growth either.

Data show that numbers of inbound leisure travelers remain limited, and the leisure-oriented travel industry mainly relies on the domestic market (GEODE, 2010). Indeed, of the 96,149 ITAs, 12.6% were leisure-driven while 59% were business travelers, 8.4% came for meetings and events, and 9.4% were VFR travelers. In 2009 non-resident visitors accounted for 17% of total customers in hotels of all categories, and 28.5% in hotels of middle and higher price categories. Foreign residents accounted for 21% of customers in all types of accommodation establishments (all categories included); they are represented in establishments of all price categories but weigh heavier in the higher price categories. The Gabonese represent the main clientele of luxury hotels (between XAF 100,000 and 300,000[3] a room per night), with 55% of all customers (GEODE, 2010).

Regarding leisure travel, the country's primary tourist attraction is the rainforest and its wildlife, with 13 national parks created in 2002 (Decrees 607–619, August 30, 2002). Although beaches are not particularly promoted in the tourism image of Gabon projected on the international market, these constitute a major attraction for domestic tourism. A general observation is that different types of resources (including culture and sports events) have yet to be valued for their tourism potential across the country and their tourism development remains rudimentary. Table 20.2 shows Gabon's strengths and weaknesses compared with destinations offering similar products.

In 2006 Lecolle reported that the national parks received only 1,500 and 2,000 visitors a year (Lecolle, 2006). Visitors of national parks slightly differ from that of international tourists arriving at Libreville airport. A survey conducted in French with 86 visitors of the Lopé National Park (one of the most visited parks in Gabon) in April–May 2009 recorded 22 Americans, 19 French, 12 British and 12 Swiss (French, 2009). In 2005 Chao noted that half of the 181 respondents surveyed at the Lopé National Park had booked their trip to Lopé through an incoming tour operator based in Libreville, whilst 30% were independent travelers, and 20% had booked directly with the hotel. Half of the respondents had combined their visit with at least two other destinations, among which were Libreville, Loango National Park, Ivindo National Park, Lambaréné, and Sette Cama (Chao, 2005).

Table 20.2 Gabon's current strengths and weaknesses

Tourism products	Strengths	Weaknesses	Some competitors
Safari – Wildlife	• A sense of adventure less present in other destinations, except for Congo; • Other endemic species than in eastern and southern African countries (forest elephant, mandrills)	• Lower quality of animal sightings in the wild; • Higher prices; • Less diversified (other destinations offer horse-safari, balloon trips); • Limited range of accommodation	Botswana Kenya South Africa Tanzania Rwanda Uganda
Gorilla tracking		• Fewer chances to view western lowland gorillas	Uganda Rwanda Congo (Central African Republic. But not politically stable)
Forest-based tourism	• The specificities of African rainforest; • Chances of seeing "big" animals during treks as opposed to Ecuador or Costa Rica	• Limited range of activities; • Limited range of accommodation possibilities; • Lack of destination image • As opposed to Costa Rica, car hire is very expensive in Gabon, and not offered by tour operators • Higher prices	Costa Rica Ecuador (Congo – not developed yet)
Beach tourism	• White sand beaches bordering with forest • Opportunity to see animals close to/on the beach (possibilities of game drives from the hotel/lodge)	• High prices, middle to high comfort (not upmarket though) • Not standardized • Small-size accommodation capacity • Accessibility problems • Lack of destination image	Northern Africa Kenya Mauritius Senegal Seychelles Sao Tome y Principe
Cultural tourism	• Potential (Traditions are still alive, Bwiti, cultural associations) • Fame of Albert Schweitzer in Germany, Switzerland in particular.	• Culture is not much valued in tours, and barely is in official promotion discourse, except for the "Hôpital Schweitzer" • Built heritage is hardly valorized	Kenya, Tanzania (Masai) Namibia (Himba) Botswana (Bushmen…) Cameroon; Senegal; Mali

Source: Authors.

Operating pioneering businesses in adverse conditions

In order to provide further insight into why inbound leisure travel has not developed to a greater extent since the 1990s, this section examines more in-depth a number of initiatives launched since then. It does so by examining (1) their characteristics; (2) how and why the initiatives were able to emerge; and (3) to what extent they have been able to operate within the realm of these constraints and act upon them in order to improve their business environment. These questions are investigated based on 21 case studies which represent most of tourism projects developed throughout the country since the 1990s. Data used in this study were collected in 2011 and 2012 through semi-structured interviews with (former) managers of these businesses or projects as well as documentary research and observation.

Typology of tourism projects and businesses undertaken since the 1990s

A variety of tourism initiatives were able to emerge despite big structural barriers. The projects and businesses greatly differed from one another in terms of the profile of their initiator(s)-manager(s), the tourism products they offered, their target market(s), and their organizational structure. A key distinction was the motives governing their emergence and business-related decision-making: Six cases followed a dynamic that was not centered on tourism; the patterns of their development differed from that of the other cases, which were driven according to tourism interests.

Projects responding to a dynamic not centered on tourism

For six cases tourism was not an end on its own but a means to achieve other goals, including conservation, the preservation of rural villages, cultural heritage, and the promotion of values. These cases related to wildlife watching in the Lopé-Okanda national park and in the Lékédi park in Bakoumba, community-based tourism (CBT) in Makoghé, in the Mondah forest and in Sette Cama, and volunteer tourism at the Hôpital Schweitzer in Lambaréné. These projects were initiated by different types of stakeholders, sometimes jointly: Aid agencies and a development fund (i.e. in Mikongo Conservation Centre in Lopé-Okanda, in Sette-Cama, in Makoghé), non-profit organizations (i.e. in hôpital Schweitzer), a private corporate company (the Lékédi park), and patriarchs of rural villages (i.e. in the Mohdah forest and Makoghé).

These stakeholders chose to invest in tourism—rather than in another industry—for several reasons. Some of them identified opportunities in terms of resources at the local level that had been developed for tourism elsewhere; some perceived tourism as an industry that only requires basic skills and limited initial capital. Tourism was also regarded as an "acceptable" trade-off to conservation. Fewer stakeholders considered evidence of actual demand. None of these projects were viable in economic terms, leading some of them to interrupt their activity (Mikongo Conservation Centre, CBT in Sette Cama and Makoghé).

A key determining factor in the development of these projects was their initiators' values or beliefs. By conditioning access to funding and governing or guiding project objectives and key decisions, those values not only pushed stakeholders to take action and set up their projects but also had significant effects in shaping the projects in terms of:

- their location which cannot be understood using a tourism-oriented rationale (i.e. accessibility, infrastructure, resources);
- the type of resources selected to be commodified for tourism purpose;
- the type of commodification;
- some characteristics of the facilities, including size, building materials, level of comfort;
- their internal employment policies (local workforce);
- their targeted market segments (international market);
- and, for some, their organizational structure (empowerment principles).

Although the key objectives and management decisions of these projects were driven by interests not directly related to tourism, they had considerable implications in terms of tourism performance. Indeed, they dictated market positioning, business models, and operations. Market positioning includes the type of product and location, which were determined independently of any reliable estimation of tourism performance, even very basic objectives such as reaching break-even. The absence of minimal consideration of project viability enhanced risk-taking, and favored lumpy investment associated with project lifecycles, and/or a reactive, "wait and see" type of management behavior. Whilst growth was not a core objective of these projects, achieving a minimum level of economic viability appears a cornerstone if the projects are to meet their primary objectives, that is, economic contribution to environmental and cultural heritage conservation, social and economic arguments likely to convince the local inhabitants to stop encroachment and/or to remain in their villages.

Moreover, these social and environmental objectives were associated with additional expenses that were not necessarily accounted for in business models (e.g. number of employees, training costs, a share in the revenues or profits…). This makes economic viability even more difficult to ensure in an unfamiliar, unsupportive, and not-so-attractive business environment. Additional difficulties encountered in these cases included poorly informed project coordinators, concerning Gabon's social and political frameworks, environmental resources, or in the cases in which initiators were Gabonese, about tourism demand. This is illustrated in the following quote from an ECOFAC[4] report relating to the projects initiated in the Lopé-Okanda national park:

> Nature-based tourism development in Central Africa is like trying to square the circle. That amounts to attempt to develop an industry in an unfavorable context, or a context which is not ready for it, and this, in a short term imposed by the lifetime of a project. When one knows that tourism operators estimate that five to ten years are needed to launch a destination [...] Tourism development in forest areas is hindered by significant constraints in terms of logistics and supervision which increase the cost of guided tours. The hosting capacity remains limited [...] because the project works at its own scale (with limited investment capacities) and not at the scale of a business-driven operator.
>
> *(ECOFAC, 2003, p. 41)*

Values and beliefs also governed decisions regarding human resources and organizational structure, favoring the hiring of local workforce and, in some projects, community involvement, and empowerment. However, project designs did not take enough consideration of the local context and social behavioral patterns in terms of motivation (e.g. absenteeism, reliability) and customer-oriented attitudes. There was also a lack of local tourism knowledge and skills which severely hampered project implementation and made project viability even more difficult to achieve. Training was included in various degrees in the projects, this however was not sufficient to ensure service quality and project continuation once funding ceased.

It can also be surmised that values and beliefs prevented project coordinators to actively look for (transitory) alternative solutions when needed. The cases of the Lékédi park, of Mondah Ecotour and of the Hôpital Schweitzer, which were still in operation at the time of this study in 2012, are particularly interesting in this respect. They tend to show that, at present in Gabon, a hierarchical structure is more viable than a bottom-up or an empowerment approach in the form of associations. Leadership also seems to be a key feature of these three cases. Even though these projects encountered problems with staff, their managers supervised service provision, and actively and patiently addressed problems with a long-term perspective.

Projects driven by tourism interests

Of the fifteen cases responding to a tourism-oriented dynamic, seven essentially targeted the domestic market, four of which opened in the 1990s. The seven hotels were run by private investors and they were all initiated by men who lived in Gabon and had prior experience in business or project management in the country. Most were serial entrepreneurs, profit-making was part of their primary motivations, together with a fondness for nature, calm and the beauty of the site, the urge for challenges, and a desire to slow down. These hoteliers offered recreational activities at a short distance from Libreville and diversified their sources of income in order to keep their businesses afloat and continue their tourism operations, by organizing special events for instance.

For them, targeting the domestic market was a response to their limited power of action on the structural inconsistencies affecting Gabon's competitiveness and attractiveness on the international market, making it beyond their reach. By deliberately opting for a strategy that reduced the influence of constraining factors, they demonstrated their capability of strategic-context analysis. As epitomized in the following quote:

> [...] at the moment, we have no other choice than to target Gabon's domestic market, simply because there is no international tourist inflow. Clients are too few compared to what it is possible [to get], they are really very few, and this is discouraging, honestly, this is discouraging.
>
> *(Hotelier, interview, Libreville, July 2012)*

These hotels essentially offered a product based on relaxation and recreation located on the coast or by the riverside. They were designed as spaces for enjoying the sun (sunbathing, bathing, beach volley), relaxing in a peaceful environment, eating and drinking. Particular attention is given to the quality of the food served by trained chefs. Even though one cannot speak of enclaves, there were limited connections between the hotels and the villages nearby. Because the domestic market in small in size, and the product sold on this market only partly matched the destination image promoted by the authorities on the international market, these hotels contributed little to tourism growth.

Eight hotels focused on the international market; four were initiated under President Omar Bongo's regime in the early 2000s, the other four under President Ali Bongo's regime (i.e. after 2009). Of those eight cases, four had pretension to stimulating tourism growth on a national scale. One, initiated in 2002 by a foreign private investor, was designated "top new tourist destination in the world" by the British Guild of Travel Writes in 2008, and was undoubtedly the most promoted and internationally distributed multi-site lodge-resort in Gabon. It was led to close unexpectedly in 2012 in controversial circumstances (Baron, January 2012; informal conversations, Libreville, July 2012). The three others were not yet in operation at the time of the study; these resort projects were announced to the public in 2011 and were meant to open a few years later in Cape Esterias, Pointe Denis, and Loango National Park.

These three projects included one led by a foreign private investor and two public and private partnerships (PPPs). The former was launched in 2011 but was suspended by the main shareholder in 2013 following a dispute with the Gabonese authorities over road access. When interviewed in 2012, this private investor with solid business experience in Africa pointed out that "[...] It is the first country where I face barriers which are so considerable. [...] tourism is not a priority. The decision-makers are not convinced, or at least part of them or even most of them" (Private investor, interview, Libreville, June 2012). PPPs intend to attract foreign investors despite the deterring effects of the general business environment. This type of partnership is new in Gabon's leisure travel industry; it was introduced under Ali Bongo's regime indicating that the president or—at least—his office (i.e. the president and the people revolving around him, such as his personal advisors) can be considered a core agent in the current tourism system.

The abovementioned cases led by private investors show that, despite their networking abilities, stakeholders who are external to the political system face major difficulties to prompt the structural changes that are needed to develop tourism projects in the long run in Gabon. As PPPs are governed by the president's office, it is likely that the stakeholders involved in the projects have more opportunities of introducing those changes as long as partners are in line with each other and are capable of meeting their commitments. However, the lack of transparency surrounding these projects—notably about the structure of the partnership, the amount invested by the authorities, the amount of shares held by each party, and the content of the concession agreements—does raise questions concerning the governance. One is left to ponder over whether these projects were meant to be a tool for tourism and national development or just a new way to "privatize" rents derived from natural resources. It should be noted that both PPPs were still not in operation in 2018, and there is no indication that these three projects will be implemented in the near future. The oil and political crisis of recent years may have played a part in the failure to implement these projects.

Conclusions

Tourism development in Gabon faces numerous barriers and hindrances which are rooted in the country's structural foundations. These structural elements were reinforced with decades of rent-seeking and rent-seizing behaviors, with little change over time. This creates a macro-environment, which is very rigid and not so attractive for tourism entrepreneurs, providing a first explanation of the inertia of the tourism industry. Indeed, only a handful of stakeholders were motivated enough and had the financial capacities to venture into investing in a tourism business, and even fewer were able to keep theirs afloat.

As has been shown above, any attempt to stimulate tourism growth is strictly linked to the ability of tourism stakeholders to introduce changes in the political, sociocultural, and environmental structures. The political structure, and governance in particular, is central to create a supportive climate to investment and to contribute to the opening up of rural areas. Moreover, if local jobs are to be created, the country's social and cultural structures need to be adapted, through training and incentives to work in the tourism industry and in rural areas for instance. Similarly, if tourism is meant to be based on wildlife watching, changes need to be introduced in Gabon's natural environment (e.g. habituation of wild animals and/ or development of tourism facilities in the tropical forest).

Yet, as has been shown through the examination of this chapter's case studies, there are currently very few stakeholders capable of introducing such changes (for instance, by having influence on visa policies, the official tourism strategy, road construction). Although most tourism providers, independently of their profile, demonstrate they are aware of the strategic context in which they operate, their business activities are still strongly affected by inconsistency in the structural elements over which they have no or little control. In other terms, most stakeholders could act within the realm of structural constraints, but not necessarily upon them.

In such circumstances, more than any form of economic rationality, the investors' values and beliefs are often of most significance when seeking to understand the dynamics governing tourism development and its shaping effects on the destination, notably in terms of project location and employment policy. These values and beliefs also explain why some stakeholders kept going despite considerable difficulties to maintain the business afloat. It can be suggested based on observations of current political and economic trends that prospects of tourism development will continue to be shaped by the vested interests and rent-seeking behaviors of the ruling elites, and the president in particular. The oil and political crisis of recent years makes it difficult to see clearly as to what will be the priorities at this level. However, considering that, compared with the years 1990–2000s, less attention is currently attributed to tourism as a tool for conservation or rural development on the international and national scene, it can be surmised that the internal leisure travel industry will largely depend on small individual entrepreneurial initiatives in forthcoming years.

Notes

1 In 2004: Gabon's GDP per capita was evaluated at 4,602 current USD; at the same period, South Africa's, one of the strongest economies in Africa, was 3,648 current USD; Kenya's, one of the leading tourism destinations on the continent, was of 440 current USD. A high GDP per capita could be an indicator that there is disposable income which could be invested in the tourism sector.
2 Ninety-seven percent of total youth population according to data provided by the World Bank.
3 EUR 150-450.
4 ECOFAC was a conservation and development program funded by the European Union in Central Africa.

References

Barnes, J. F. (2003). The Bongo phenomenon: Power in Gabon. In: Reed, M. C. and Barnes, J. F. (eds), *Culture, Ecology, and Politics in Gabon's Rainforest* (pp.309–331), Lewiston: E. Mellen Press.

Baron, D. (2012, January). Gabon's eco-tourism efforts stumble, *Public Radio International*. Retrieved on May 1, 2015, from http://www.pri.org

Breakey, N. (2005). *Tourism Destination Development – Beyond Butler*, Doctoral dissertation, The University of Queensland.

Butler, R. W. (2005). The concept of a tourist area cycle of evolution: Implications for management of Resources. In: Butler, R. W. (Ed.) *The Tourism Area Life Cycle. Applications and Modifications*, Vol. 1 (pp. 3–12), Clevedon: Channel View Publications.

Chao, N. (Oct. 2005). *Evaluation d'un tourisme au parc national de la Lopé*, Gabon, Unpublished report. Retrieved, on August 2, 2010 from http://fr.calameo.com.

Cloquet, I. (2015). *Tourism Development and the Question of 'Stasis': A Case Study of Internal Leisure Tourism in Gabon*, Doctoral dissertation, Université Libre de Bruxelles, unpublished, 310 pages.

Cloquet, I. (2016). Oil, centralised power and their shaping effects on tourism in Gabon, *International Journal of Tourism Policy*, 6(3/4), 299–320.

Cohen, E. (1979). Rethinking the sociology of tourism, *Annals of Tourism Research*, 6(1), pp. 18–35.

Cole, S. (2007). Beyond the resort life cycle: The micro-dynamics of destination tourism, *The Journal of Regional Analysis and Policy*, 37(3), pp. 266–278.

Defert, A. (1954). L'hôtellerie et le développement du tourisme en Afrique Française, *France Outre-Mer*, février 1954, pp. 44–51.

Domergue, Ad. (1893). Simples notes de voyages. Gabon-Madagascar-Guyane. Paris: Imprimerie Paul Dupont, 101 p. Retrieved on October 15, 2014 from http://gallica.bnf.fr/ark:/12148/bpt6k1058815.

Dulucq, S. (2009a). «Découvrir l'âme africaine». Les temps obscurs du tourisme culturel en Afrique coloniale française (années 1920-années 1950), *Cahiers d'études africaines*, 1(193–194), pp. 27–48.

Dulucq, S. (2009b). L'émergence du tourisme dans les territoires de l'Afrique tropicale française (années 1920–1950). In: Zytnicki, C. and Kazdaghli, H. (eds), *Le tourisme dans l'Empire français. Politiques, pratiques et imaginaires (XIXe-XXe siècles). Un outil de la domination coloniale?* (pp. 61–71), Paris: Publications de la Société française d'histoire d'outre-mer.

ECOFAC. (2003). *Rapport d'activités.* Janvier-Juin 2003. Unpublished report, Libreville: ECOFAC.

French, J. (2009). *Can Western Lowland Gorilla Tourism Become a Viable Tool for Conservation in Gabon?* Masters' thesis, Msc. Conservation Science, Imperial College London, Retrieved on May 9, 2011, from www.iccs.org.uk/thesis/consci/msc09-french, joanna.pdf.

GEODE. (2010). *Système de Statistiques du Tourisme - Compte Satellite du Tourisme de la République gabonaise,* Unpublished workshop presentation.

Haywood, H. M. (1986). Can the tourist-area life cycle be made operational? *Tourism Management,* 7(3), pp. 155–167.

Ioannides, D. (1992). Tourism development agents. The Cypriot resort cycle, *Annals of Tourism Research,* 19(4), pp. 711–731.

Jessop, B. (2008). *State Power,* Cambridge: Polity Press.

Johnston, C. S. (2001). Shoring the foundations of the destination life cycle model, part 1: Ontological and epistemological considerations, *Tourism Geographies,* 3(1), pp. 2–28.

Kingsley, M. (1993). *Une odyssée africaine, translated by Anne Hugon,* Paris: édition de poche, Editions Payot et Rivages.

Lecolle, L. (2006). *Identification d'un circuit d'écotourisme dans le parc national de l'Ivindo (Gabon). Cas d'une liaison Kongou-Djidji-Langoué.* Rapport de stage. Université Montpellier II. Retrieved on August 2, 2010, from http://fr.calameo.com.

Ma, M. and Hassink, R. (2013). An evolutionary perspective on tourism area development, *Annals of Tourism Research,* 41, pp. 89–109.

Mer, J. (1955). Le tourisme en Afrique Equatoriale Française, Encyclopédie Mensuelle d'Outre-Mer, *Le tourisme en Afrique française (Special Issue),* pp. 193–224.

Ministère du Tourisme et des Parcs Nationaux. (2009). *Plan Directeur du développement de l'Ecotourisme 2008–2014.* Libreville: de la République du Gabon.

Miossec, J.-M. (1977). Un modèle de l'espace touristique, *Espace géographique,* 6(1), pp. 41–48.

Plais, E. (1882). *Lettre sur le Gabon. Rouen: Imprimerie de Espérance Cagniard,* 12 p. Retrieved on October 15, 2014, from http://gallica.bnf.fr/ark:/12148/bpt6k5759244q.

Plog, S. C. (2001). Why destination areas rise and fall in popularity. An update of a Cornell classic. *Cornell Hotel, Restaurant & Administration Quarterly,* 42(3), pp. 13–24.

Pourtier, R. (1989). *Le Gabon. Espace, histoire, société,* Paris: L'Harmattan.

Prideaux, B. (2000). The resort development spectrum—a new approach to modeling resort development, *Tourism Management,* 21(3), pp. 225–240.

Ross, M. L. (2001). *Timber Booms and Institutional Breakdown in Southeast Asia,* Cambridge: Cambridge University Press.

Soares De Oliveira, R. (2007). *Oil and Politics in the Gulf of Guinea,* London: Hurst and Company.

Söderling, L. (2002). *Escaping the Curse of Oil? The Case of Gabon,* IMF working Paper, International Monetary Fund.

UNWTO. (2000), *Tourism Highlights,* 2000 Edition, Madrid: UNWTO.

UNWTO. (2007), *Tourism Highlights,* 2007 Edition, Madrid: UNWTO.

UNWTO. (2012), *Tourism Highlights,* 2012 Edition, Madrid: UNWTO.

UNWTO. (2013), *Tourism Highlights,* 2013 Edition, Madrid: UNWTO.

UNWTO. (2014), *Tourism Highlights,* 2014 Edition, Madrid: UNWTO.

UNWTO. (2015), *Tourism Highlights,* 2015 Edition, Madrid: UNWTO.

UNWTO. (2016), *Tourism Highlights,* 2016 Edition, Madrid: UNWTO.

UNWTO. (2017), *Tourism Highlights,* 2017 Edition, Madrid: UNWTO.

Wunder, S. (2003). *Oil Wealth and the Fate of the Forest. A Comparative Study of Eight Tropical Countries,* London: Routledge.

Yates, D. A. (1996). *The Rentier State in Africa. Oil Rent Dependency and Neocolonialism in the Republic of Gabon.* Asmara, Eritrea: Africa World Press, Inc.

21

Tourism and nature in São Tomé and Príncipe

Opportunities for the internationalisation of a Small Island State

Brígida Rocha Brito

Introductory and contextual issues

São Tomé and Príncipe[1] is a small island developing state (SIDS) with an area of 1,001 Km², unevenly distributed across to main islands[2] and a group of islets mostly inhabited with a diversity of biological life. The islands of São Tomé and Príncipe are 150 km³ apart and are influenced from a climatic and geophysical point of view by the geographic location of the Central Africa sub-region, with the Atlantic and equatorial orientation[4] that characterises the Gulf of Guinea, and by the importance of maritime extension in relation to the total territorial area. The geophysical and climatic influence is reflected in the predominance of volcanic soil with high productive potential associated with a hot and humid climate characteristic of this African subregion (Brito, 2015).

The climate in this area is predominantly humid/ tropical,[5] with two main seasons: the rainy season, which occurs between October and June, and the dry season, called *Gravana*, between July and September. However, in January, there is usually a dry climate trend, which the local population refers to as *Gravanito*.

The country is usually considered as the second smallest state in sub-Saharan Africa and is strongly influenced by its insularity, which causes isolation, a factor that contextualises and conditions the development of Small Island States (Turner, 2015; Brito, 2010a, 2010b, 2010c).

SIDS is defined as fragile, isolated and dependent states in regards to international relations, in particular, economic ones.[6] However, from an environmental point of view, distance, isolation from international centres and their small size have contributed to the growing importance given to natural resources, in particular in regards to the maintenance of flora[7] and fauna[8] endemism, preservation of ecosystems and programmes for the conservation of species.

As an archipelagic SIDS, and in view of the size of the territory, the 209 km stretch of coastline (AIDA, ANEMM, n.d.: 4) shows, on the one hand, the environmental relevance that translates into the variety of ecosystems and the biodiversity of endemic flora and fauna and, on the other, the socio-economic importance of the geographical location, defined by the preponderant productive activities that tend to be identified with the main sources of income.

In administrative terms, the country is divided into seven districts[9] – six in São Tomé and one in Príncipe – and, coincidentally, all the districts converge to the sea, having a longer or shorter coastline. Thus, the maritime context has a direct influence on this island territory by uniquely connecting two ecosystems, the oceans and forests, that are defined and characterised by their natural ability to promote atmospheric regulation.[10] Due to being an island, the whole country is influenced by the Atlantic Ocean and, in parallel, about a third of the territory consists of protected forest area, the Obô Natural Park, which is present in the two main islands. The relevance of the environmental context is recognised internally through the creation of specific legislation[11] that regulates protected area management models and the authorised productive activities, such as hunting, extraction and collection of natural resources and deforestation in the buffer zone.

In addition to the connection between the archipelago and the sea having a territorial association, it also contains a historical interpretation and indicates the influence of the regional and international context. These are both centred on countries of geographical and strategic proximity, such as Gabon, Equatorial Guinea and Nigeria, and in countries with which it maintains an ancestral and cultural relation of proximity, namely Portuguese speaking countries like Angola, Cape Verde, Portugal and Brazil.

The continuity of relations with these countries has proved fruitful and advantageous, translating into the creation and implementation of tourism projects,[12] and also in the promotion of an international tourism marketing strategy.[13] Currently, the position of the destination in the international market sees the involvement of multiple tour operators[14] working with São Tomé and Príncipe, including those that focus on natural products.[15]

From an international point of view, the archipelago has received increasingly more recognition as a result of the enhancement of its potential in terms of landscape diversity, ecosystems and biological life. This recognition has also occurred due to the cultural and human elements that illustrate the combination of the ancestry of practices and the desire for a change intended to be both progressive, adapted and appropriate. As a differentiating factor, in 2012 UNESCO awarded the Biosphere Reserve title to the Island of Príncipe, which symbolically acquired the international attribute of the place of excellence[16] for the socio-environmental management models in a protected area context, defined as balanced, integrated and optimised. This factor has led to the revaluation of the island, which has been usually defined by its double insularity and vulnerability stemming from the greater isolation caused by the distance between the country's main point of connection and the capital.

In light of the island's various potential elements – natural, cultural and historical – tourism has been considered as a strategic sector to develop, particularly the segments focusing on nature and community-based activities. It has also been recognised that by promoting international tourism this will attract foreign private investment.

Brief characterisation of an archipelago open to the world

The Democratic Republic of São Tomé and Príncipe is a young nation-state that, despite being discovered by Portuguese navigators[17] in the second half of the 15th century, only reached political independence on the 12 of July 1975. After the discovery of the territory, the settlement phase was slow and miscegenated, involving Portuguese, Spanish, African slaves, particularly from the western coast of the continent and, later on, Cape Verdeans doing agricultural work in the *Roça* plantations.[18]

From a socio-cultural point of view, from the date of discovery[19] to the present day, São Tomé and Príncipe define itself as a Creole country, as a result of the multiple processes of miscegenation, especially among Angolans, Cape Verdeans, Portuguese and Spanish. This creolisation reflects the international influence for opening culture to the outside world and receptivity to new ideas, be it due to African, Portuguese, European, Asian, or American influence, resulting in a mixture of cultural elements that indicate originality.[20]

Complementarily, during the colonial period, in economic terms, the archipelago was dominated by the model of the three productive cycles – sugar, coffee and cocoa – developed at the *Roças* and that have remained until today's agricultural resources of international interest.

From an early age, São Tomean society was marked by creolisation, particularly established in the *Roças*, where the majority resided and worked, and the coastline.[21] This mixed society is a result of a fusion of cultures, combining symbolic elements of diverse origins that have translated into the recreation of cultural practices based on custom and oral tradition, as is the case of traditional medicine, but also gastronomy,[22] the innovation of musical rhythms, dance styles[23] and theatrical representations.[24]

Nowadays, São Tomean society continues to be marked by characteristics of creoleness that are reflected both in everyday life and in the openness and receptivity to the outside world.

Despite the small size of the country, the population is unevenly distributed throughout the territory, being mostly concentrated on the island of São Tomé, which exert greater pressure in the district of Água Grande. Rural population groups move toward the capital and settle in creating new neighbourhoods and new communities around the city centre.

The country has been benefiting from improvements in the Human Development Index, standing in 142nd place (UNDP, 2014), which corresponds to the average level of development. In total, in 2017, the country had 197,700 inhabitants,[25] unequally distributed between the islands, with only 3.5% (7,500) residing in Príncipe.

The majority of the population lives in cities, (67.7%) and is young, with an average age of 20 years and an average life expectancy at birth of 67 years.

Given the cultural characteristics of the archipelago, which are defined by ancestry and tradition, the desire of the young population to establish intercultural contacts with knowledge of new models and integration of different reference and identity elements contributes to socio-cultural recreation (Brito, 2013a, 2013b, 2013c).

A picture of tourism internationalisation for sustainability

The focus on tourism as a development sector is recent and occurred in the transition from the 20th to the 21st century. The country's standing as an international tourism destination has been marked by an uneven evolution, with alternating high and low growth periods. This trend (see Table 21.1) shows an initial growth momentum in international arrivals between 2002 and 2005, after the approval of the first *Strategic Plan for the development of tourism*,[26] which recognised the natural potential for the promotion of the ecological segment.

At the same time, it coincided with the concession of direct air transport from Portugal to a private civil aviation company,[27] temporarily ending the monopoly of the Portuguese air carrier TAP.

The following years, from 2006 to 2010, registered a marked fall in international arrivals, evidencing absence or poor definition of a national strategy for the promotion of the destination abroad. This situation was aggravated by the growing difficulty in ensuring regular and direct transport between Europe and the archipelago, given the increase in tariffs practised by TAP, which once again gained the monopoly of air connections.[28] In 2008, the São

Table 21.1 International arrivals in São Tomé and
Príncipe, 2002–2016

Year	Number
2002	5.757
2003	8.037
2004	10.792
2005	15.746
2006	12.266
2007	7.601
2008	10.474
2009	9.148
2010	7.963
2011	10.319
2012	12.743
2013	13.709
2014	18.187
2015	21.162
2016	28.919

Source: Directorate General for Tourism and Hospitality.

Tomean airline STP Airways was created, which, despite representing a competitive segment for TAP, was faced with a ban on operating in European airspace and had to use EuroAtlantic Airways aircrafts.[29] In regard to air connections between São Tomé and Príncipe, in 2009 STP Airways was granted authorisation for scheduled flights with the dual objective of reducing the characteristic isolation of small island areas and boosting inter-island tourism flows.

At the same time, in 2008, the *Plano Director de Turismo para São Tomé e Príncipe* (Tourism Master Plan for São Tomé and Príncipe) was created,[30] defining 37 lines of action, including territorial planning, the creation of a tourism brand, and the identification of a marketing model geared towards the international market, and taking into account the need to attract foreign investment for the creation, implementation and development of direct and indirect tourism services.

In 2012, with a regular and continuous increase in international arrivals, which reveals a progressive consolidation of the sector associated with the government's investment, the *Plano e Agenda de Desenvolvimento Sustentável da Ilha do Príncipe* (Plan and Agenda for Sustainable Development of the Island of Príncipe) was created,[31] which coincided with the designation of this island as a Biosphere Reserve by UNESCO, an initiative framed by the Man and the Biosphere Programme.[32]

This new context also led to the provision of international transport services, allowing a multiplicity of flights between the two continents, with an increase in arrivals of 263% between 2010 and 2016 (Costa, 2018). Starting in 2012, the boost of the country's tourism was notable, as a result of a number of factors, among which the improvement of accessibility and procedures to welcome foreign tourists[33] stand out, as well as the reduction of bureaucracy for tourism and leisure for travellers from the Schengen Area and the United States of America.

The reduced bureaucracy, in particular, the exemption of tourist visas, explains in part the prevalence of Portuguese, French, American and English tourists visiting the archipelago

Table 21.2 International arrivals by country

São Tomé	Príncipe
Portugal	United States
Angola	United Kingdom
France	Australia
United States	France
United Kingdom	Netherlands
Cape Verde	Portugal
Gabon	Angola

Source: Costa (2018).

(see Table 21.2), entering the country through São Tomé International Airport, but also making the connection to the Island of Príncipe.[34] Thus, with regard to the main origin of tourists, there is a significant variation in those visiting the two main islands, although there is a tendency for the main markets to be present in the two islands.

In 2018, a new Plan was approved, titled *Strategic and Marketing Plan for São Tomé and Príncipe's tourism*, extending the proposal until 2025. Following the guidance of the Director of Tourism and Hospitality, Mirian Daio, it reinforces the archipelago as

> the most preserved island tourism destination in Equatorial Africa, with a unique nature and biodiversity, paradisiacal beaches, and where Santomean hospitality, based on the historical and cultural legacy of the coffee and cocoa plantations, shares its way of life and the colourful way of hosting.
>
> *(Costa, 2018: 5–7)*

This Strategic Plan has five main objectives, namely:

1   to prepare the archipelago for sustainable tourism, although this concern is evidenced in previous plans;
2   to contribute to the preservation of natural and cultural areas;
3   to promote the country as a destination in the international market, achieving a 65.5% increase in international arrivals and a 19.7% increase in the occupancy rate;
4   to qualify human resources and consolidate the quality of the services offered, contributing to a 5.8% increase in employment;
5   to improve performance, promoting the attraction of investment by 81.2% and expected growth of 73.4% in the contribution to the GDP.

Over time, and following the trend of international arrivals, the tourism offer increased (Table 21.3), with a concentration of hotel units in the Água Grande district, where the capital is located (55.7% of beds available), followed by Caué (13.8%), at the southern end of the island, a district that is geographically influenced by the Equator (0° latitude).

The concentration of the majority of the accommodation in these two districts is particularly justified by the implementation of foreign private initiative in the territory, of which the Pestana Group stands out, as it manages two of the main large capacity hotels in the capital.[35] This Group's investment in the archipelago was extended to the Caué district with *Hotel Pestana Equador* at the Rolas islet, allowing the creation of competitive tour packages.

Table 21.3 Accommodation capacity

	Água Grande	*Lobata*	*Caué*	*Lemba*	*Mé Zochi*	*Cantagalo*	*Príncipe*	*Total*
Hotels	21	2	6	2	8	4	12	55
Bedrooms	403	6	100	22	44	64	84	723

Source: Costa (2018).

Table 21.4 Restaurants, bars and similar establishments offer

District	*Number*
Água Grande	84
Lobata	13
Caué	7
Lembá	10
Mé-Zochi	22
Cantagalo	3
Príncipe	11
Total	150

Source: Directorate-General for Tourism and Hospitality.

This strategic procedure facilitated the promotion of the sector and the dissemination of the destination's potential in the international tourism and travel market.

One of the regions that have benefited from a more significant increase in the tourism offer is the island of Príncipe. In this case, both investment and tourism promotion have been taken over by the HBD Group,[36] which also owns a hotel in the capital,[37] allowing the connection between the two islands.

Complementing the analysis of the indicators related to the tourism offer, it seems evident that the restaurants, bars and similar establishments are concentrated in the Água Grande district, with variations in the other district areas. Mé-Zochi district, located in the centre of the island, has experienced increasing dynamism in recent years, which is directly associated with the diversity of natural, heritage, cultural, historical, and social tourism attractions[38] (see Table 21.4). Given the characteristics of the island of Príncipe,[39] the offer of restaurants, bars and similar establishments is limited, focusing on hotel units. Unlike São Tomé city, on the island of Príncipe, the main hotel units, which offer greater reception capacity, are away from the city centre of Santo António, with no regular public transport,[40] which conditions or prevents the movement of tourists, particularly at night.

Natural attractions are usually considered to have direct potential since nature plays a fundamental role in the archipelago. Densely forested landscapes, landscape diversity[41] and biodiversity[42] are the infographic elements most used in tourism promotion and marketing campaigns to attract international tourists and foreign investment.

To a large extent, the archipelago is environmentally characterised by endemism, which reinforces the appreciation of the ecological segment in implementing a tourism strategy.

The cultural potential, which reflects traditional practices and ways of life, is common throughout the country, and in socio-anthropological terms, it is possible to relate, more directly and at some point, a musical rhythm or a typical dance with ancestral roots with one of the districts. However, the differences are not very evident at this level, resulting from the small size of the country and the proximity between the districts.

From a heritage point of view (see Table 21.5), each district is characterised by elements that refer to their historical traditions and that have influenced the local communities. In this sense, there are churches, architectural landmarks and especially *roças* that are currently

Table 21.5 Main natural and historical heritage sites

District	Natural attractions	Historical heritage sites	Accommodation
Água Grande	Emília Beach Ilha Beach	Marcelo da Veiga Cinema Bom Despacho Church Cathedral National Museum People's Palace Pantufo Court Toponymy Colonial Architecture	Pestana São Tomé Miramar by Pestana Omali Lodge Hotel Praia Hotel Agôsto Neto Hotel Cocoa Residence Residencial Avenida São Pedro Guesthouse
Cantagalo	Colónia Beach Micondó Beach Boca do Inferno	Roça Água Izé Roça Bombaím Roça Colónia Açoreana Roça Uba Budo Santana	Roça Bombaim Clube Santana
Caué	Ribeira Peixe Waterfall Rolas Islet Malanza River Lagoon Mangrove Obô Natural Park Cão Grande Peak Angolares Beach Inhame Beach Jalé Beach N´Guembú Beach Piscina Beach Xixi Beach	Lighthouse Islet Ecuador Landmak Roça de Porto Alegre Roça de Ribeira Peixe Roça de São João dos Angolares	Pestana Equador Roça S. João Eco-resort Praia Inhame Jalé Ecolodge Mionga N'Guembu
Lembá	Bay of São Miguel Contador River	Neves Anambô Landmark Roça Diogo Vaz Roça Monte Forte Roça Ponta Figo Santa Catarina	Mucumbli Roça Monte Forte
Lobata	Blue Lagoon Morro Peixe Conchas Beach Governadores Beach Tamarindos Beach	Fernão Dias Roça Agostinho Neto	

District	Natural attractions	Historical heritage sites	Accommodation
Mé-Zochi	Botanical Garden of Bom Sucesso Amélia Lagoon Obô Natural Park	City of Trindade Almada Negreiros House Museum Milagrosa Café Museum Roça Monte Café	
Príncipe	Boné de Jockey Ponta do Sol Waterfall Bom Bom Islet Papagaio Peak Banana Beach Macaco Beach Sundy Beach	Príncipe Cultural Centre City of Santo António Padrão dos Descobrimentos Roça Belo Monte Roça Sundy	Bom Bom Island Resort Roça Belo Monte Roça Sundy Sundy Praia Residencial Apresentação Residencial Palhota Hotel Rural Abade Makaira Lodge Domus Rio Papagaio

Source: Author's own.

Table 21.6 Direct employment in tourism creation by district

District	Number
Água Grande	1033
Lobata	86
Caué	178
Lembá	68
Mé-Zochi	109
Cantagalo	161
Príncipe	199
Total	1834

Source: Costa (2018).

regarded as residential areas. The historical weight of most of the heritage elements, whether in the capital or other districts, results in the strengthening of the identity of local communities.

The creation of direct employment is something that has gone hand in hand with the increase in the hotel and catering offer (Table 21.6). At the same time, the number of vocational and higher education courses has increased, as well as the interest of students who complete high school.

The main creation of direct employment has been, once again, in the Água Grande district, since it encompasses 53.6% of the country's total, followed by Príncipe island and Caué, districts that have received larger investments, particularly foreign and private ones.[43]

Foreign economic interest in the archipelago goes back a long time and has accompanied all phases of implementation and consolidation of the tourism sector. São Tomé and Príncipe is an appealing country, since it is in a climate of tranquillity and social peace, without armed conflicts impacting on the socio-economic and political scenario. The country's image internationally reveals that the business environment has benefited from significant improvements, ranking 169th (World Bank, 2018), 62nd regarding the transparency indicator (Schwab, 2017) and 124th for economic freedom.[44] Foreign investment in the tourism sector has particularly focused on the rehabilitation of historic heritage, especially the *Roças*, or on construction work, as is the case of the new hotels. To a certain extent, this interest is also seen in the private national initiative, although investment capacity is naturally much lower.

Concluding notes

The analysis of the evolution of tourism in São Tomé and Príncipe shows that the development of this sector has been marked by discontinuity, despite the international recognition of the multiple natural and cultural potential attractions. It is true that despite over 20 years of efforts to attract foreign investment, boost the country's image and build a connection between the dynamics of social development, cultural enhancement and environmental preservation, the results still require consolidation.

Sustainable tourism remains an objective and a challenge, although it has been included in the State-approved Strategic Plans since 2001. Continuity seems to be one of the key factors to be improved, although a broader investment in key and complementary areas is necessary to overcome the vulnerability that characterises the country as a Small Island State. The strategic vision that foresees internationalisation requires national entrepreneurship focused on the attributes of hospitality, the quiet and leisurely rhythm characterised by the *leve-leve* (light-light) local expression, safety, natural diversity, and cultural and historical richness.

Notes

1 Democratic Republic of Sao Tome and Principe.
2 The island of São Tomé has 859Km^2 and the island of Príncipe 142 km^2.
3 Cf. National Institute of Statistics, Democratic Republic of São Tomé and Príncipe, accessed at https://ine.st on 06-09-2018.
4 The geographical coordinates of the archipelago are 00°04'N latitude and 06°25'E longitude, viewed at https://ine.st/, 06-09-2018.
5 There are no significant thermal variations during the year, the average temperature is 26°, with high humidity, on average 75%, but reaching 90% in the rainy season.
6 The situation of the SIDS in the international context is defined by the term syndrome of Small Island States, which stems from a set of characteristic features such as insularity, distance and isolation that limit development opportunities both internally and in terms of regional and international relations.
7 Endemisms have become increasingly important in the archipelago, focusing on ornamental plants such as orchids and plants of food value, as is the case of the São Tomé peach tree.
8 With regard to the fauna endemism, the main focus is on bird species, such as the endemic birds of the island of S. Tomé (*Anjolô, Picanço de São Tomé-, Neospiza concolor; Lanius newtoni*) and of Príncipe (*Tordo, Tecelão do Príncipe*- Turdus xanthorhynchus; Ploceus príncepts).
9 According to the Administrative Division Law of 21 November 1980, the districts of Água Grande, Cantagalo, Mé-Zochi, Lembá, Caué, and Lobata are located on the island of São Tomé and Pagué is on Príncipe Island.
10 Regarding the natural mechanisms of atmospheric regulation at world level, the problem is highlighted by climate change and the socio-economic and environmental impacts, which include the legal and administrative (or governmental) aspects, given the influence on the communities' life models on the small islands, with high population concentration close to the coastline, which places increased pressure on vulnerable areas and resources.
11 In São Tomé and Príncipe, the Environment Basic Law was enacted in 1999 (Law no. 10/1999), after which the Obô Natural Parks of São Tomé (Law no. 6/2006, of 2 August) and Príncipe (Law no. 7/2006, of 2 August) were created. There is also environmental legislation, namely the Conservation of Fauna, Flora and Protected Areas Law (Law no. 11/1999, of 31 December) and the Forests Law (Law no. 5/2001).

12 The main tourism projects in the archipelago were the result of foreign private initiative, namely business groups of the sector, such as the Portuguese Pestana or the South African HBD.

13 The international tourism marketing strategy is evidenced by the creation of the "true tranquillity" brand and the logo, the re-creation of the web page, the presence in social networks like Facebook, and participation in international fairs with a stand promoting the main tourism products.

14 Top Atlântico, Soltrópico, Vivrance, Go Voyages, Broadway Travel, Thomas Cook, Expedia, Olimar, Tui and Sep Voyages.

15 Operators such as Responsible Travel, Holdbrooktravel, Undiscovered Destinations, Aliveworld-wide, Ecoompanion, Greenloons, Tribes and Keadventures.

16 The international distinction given by UNESCO stems from the recognition of a set of criteria, including the conjugation between different human activities and nature; the understanding of protected areas as learning spaces in the promotion of sustainable development; and the possibility of using innovative methodological resources to implement guidelines adopted at the World Summit on Sustainable Development and at the Convention on Biological Diversity. Cf. *Man and the Biosphere*, [http://www.unesco.org/new/en/natural-sciences/environment/ecological-sciences/] accessed on 10/07/2018.

17 Discovery of the islands is attributed to Portuguese navigators Pêro da Covilhã and João de Santarém, who landed on 21 December 1470 in the northern area of São Tomé, in Anambô, and a month later on the island of Príncipe. In any case, they found desert islands, and the settlement began at the end of the 15th century (Brito, 2004).

18 The *Roças* were administrative units with profitability productive objectives, being considered *States within the State*, since they had their own organisational structure, and their own judicial system, church, railway and even port.

19 It is noteworthy that on the date of the discovery of the archipelago, São Tomé in 1470 and Príncipe in 1471, the islands were uninhabited and were later populated by settlers and slaves with multiple origins, predominantly Cape Verdeans and Angolans.

20 The cultural elements that evidence creolisation focus on the arts – painting and sculpture – on music and dance, celebrations of festive dates, ritual practices associated with witchcraft, such as the *Djambi*, and on gastronomy.

21 The population of Cape Verdean origin was predominantly concentrated in the *Roças* while the Angolan community was dedicated to fishing and resided in coastal zones.

22 This is the case of the *calulu* of fish, chicken, duck or pork with banana *angu*, commonly defined as the typical national dish, of *cachupa*, of Cape Verdean influence or chicken *cafreal*.

23 Ranging from the more traditional rhythms like *bulaué*, *puíta*, *socopé* or *ússua* to the recent rhythms like *quizomba* or *kuduro*.

24 The main theatrical plays include *Auto de Floripes*, *Tchiloli ou a Tragédia do Marquês de Mantúa e do Imperador Carlos Magno*, and *Danço-Congo*, usually staged during festive seasons.

25 For additional information, check the National Institute of Statistics of the Democratic Republic of São Tomé and Príncipe. Available at https://www.ine.st/index.php/o-pais/indicadores, accessed on 07/09/2018.

26 Plan coordinated in 2001 by a consultant at the service of the UNDP and the World Tourism Organization.

27 The Air Luxor aviation company operated direct flights twice a week offering competitively priced flights because they were lower than TAP's. During this period, there were three direct connections between Lisbon and São Tomé, two operated by Air Luxor and one operated by TAP.

28 The drop in arrivals was in part related to the extinction of flights previously operated by Air Luxor due to the company's bankruptcy, which was part of the Mirpuri Group.

29 With the entry of STP Airways into the civil aviation market, operating twice a week between Lisbon and São Tomé, competition increased again, especially because since 2014 these have become the only direct flights between Europe and the archipelago, as TAP introduced a stop in Accra, capital of Ghana, making the flight longer.

30 This Plan was prepared by a Spanish consulting firm, Koan Consulting SL, hired by the Spanish Agency for International Cooperation for Development, Ministry of Foreign Affairs and Cooperation of the Spanish Government.

31 This Plan was created by a consortium of private companies that sought to promote an island which, in the total territorial area, was internationally classified as having protection status. From

the tourist's point of view, accessibility is limited to a return flight per day with reduced number of seats available and reinforced by the airport's inability to receive large international airplanes.

32 For additional information see http://www.unesco.org/new/en/natural-sciences/environment/ecological-sciences/, accessed on 02/05/2018.

33 São Tomé International Airport was modernised, including the creation of a tourist office delegation on the premises, and an approved project for the extension of the runway.

34 As there are no direct connections between international origins (Europe) and Príncipe Island the tourists travel to São Tomé but a large part make the connection to Príncipe. Since the island was classified as a Biosphere Reserve, the number of tourists has been increased.

35 *Hotel Pestana São Tomé*, the best rated on the island, classified with five stars and offering a standard of international comfort, and *Miramar by Pestana*, which is one of the oldest hotels in the country and has been refurbished several times.

36 The HBD Group– *Here Be Dragons* – began operations on the island with the acquisition of the flagship *Bom Bom Island Resort* by South African Mark Shuttleworth, and later *Roça Sundy* and *Sundy Praia*, making an estimated investment of USD 80 million. Available at https://www.telanon.info/sociedade/2018/01/30/26318/principe-homenageia-investimento-que-protege-o-ambiente/, accessed on 04/03/2018.

37 *Omali Lodge* which, together with the *Bom Bom Island Resort,* were bought from Dutchman Rombougt Swanborn, who acquired them from the South African initial owner Christopher Hellinger. These businesses demonstrate the dimension of internationalisation in the face of the interest and external standing of the archipelago. However, the Dutch entrepreneur maintained his interest in the tourism promotion of the island, acquiring the *Roça Belo Monte* and rehabilitating it, recovering its image in the colonial period. This hotel unit benefits from the geographical point of view of one of the island's most emblematic beaches, Banana Beach, which was once the advertising image of the Bacardi brand.

38 From nature's point of view, this is the district that houses the emblematic S. Nicolau Waterfall, the Bom Sucesso Botanical Garden and the entrance to Obô Natural Park with connection to the Amélia Lagoon, an extinct volcano crater that is possible to visit doing trekking. From a cultural, heritage and historical point of view, in Mê-Zochi one can visit Batepá, marked by the 1952 massacre, Roça Monte Café, one of the most important coffee producers during the colonial period and that currently hosts the Café Museum, and the Almada Negreiros House-Museum, which has a restaurant, and is particularly emblematic for being located in Roça Saudade, where the plastic artist and writer was born.

39 It is a small island, where the capital, the city of Santo António, presents a geometrical toponymy, not yet focused on tourism. Its population is engaged in traditional activities, such as fishing, subsistence agriculture and the use of forest resources. After being classified as a Biosphere Reserve, the policy of the Regional Government has focused on the optimisation of the socio-environmental relationship that was defined as balanced when the international designation was given.

40 The problem of the absence of a public transport network providing scheduled and fixed priced services is common to the whole territory, representing a constraint for tourism promotion. Across the country there are 945 registered taxis and 2,300 motorcycle taxis (Costa, 2018).

41 The landscape's diversity characterises the entire archipelago. There are tropical forests dominated by palm trees and coconut palms, particularly in the South, and also shrub savanna in the north of the island, agricultural plantations with a predominance of cocoa and coffee. The forest is home to water sources, such as rivers, streams and waterfalls that flow into the sea, leading to the emergence of mangroves and coastal zones, some abrupt due to the influence of volcanic soil, and other sandy soils.

42 The biodiversity is strongly influenced by the dominant ecosystems, either those living in the forests, with emphasis on reptiles, birds, lizards, monkeys and rodents, and coastal and marine species, such as seabirds and migratory species, five species of sea turtles, cetaceans such as dolphins and whales, and large pelagic fish such as sharks.

43 In addition to the aforementioned projects, there is proliferation of tourism initiatives from São Tomé and abroad, to a large extent inspired by the sustainability *leitmotiv* focusing on the nature, ecological or environmental segment.

44 These indicators reflect a reduction in the time of obtaining licenses and the elimination of minimum capital for the creation of companies, making it easier to start companies, among other measures implemented to attract foreign investment.

References

AICEP (2017). *São Tomé e Príncipe, síntese país*. Lisbon: AICEP Portugal Global.

AIDA; ANEMM (n.d.). *Estudo de São Tomé e Príncipe. Levantamento e caracterização de empresas industriais*. Aveiro: AIDA e ANEMM.

Alarcão, N; Brito, B; Marques, J. (2009). Turismo, culturas tradicionais e identidades em São Tomé e Príncipe. In Brito, Brígida (coord.) *Desenvolvimento Comunitário: das teorias às práticas. Turismo, Ambiente e Práticas educativas em São Tomé e Príncipe*. Lisbon: Gerpress, pp. 76–82.

Brito, Brígida (2015). Sao Tome and Principe. In Jafari, J. and Xiao, H. (eds.) *Encyclopedia of Tourism*. Switzerland: Springer International Publishing. https://doi.org/10.1007/978-3-319-01669-6_690-2

Brito, Brígida (2013a). *Turismo em área protegida. O caso Biosphere Responsible Tourism, ilha do Príncipe*. Final report. Available at https://www.researchgate.net/publication/328861526_turismo_em_area_protegida_o_caso_de_biosphere_responsible_tourism_a_ilha_do_principe [Accessed on 07/09/2018].

Brito, Brígida (2013b). Fragilidades sócio-ambientais e potencialidades insulares face às alterações climáticas. In Brito, Brígida (coord) *Alterações Climáticas e suas repercussões sócio-Ambientais*. Aveiro: Associação Portuguesa de Educação Ambiental, pp. 6–19.

Brito, Brígida (2013c). *Preservação ambiental e turismo de natureza em área protegida: iniciativas e experiências em contexto africano*. In Nature and Conservation, Aquidabã, v.6, n.1, pp. 6–21.

Brito, Brígida (coord) (2010a). *Turismo em meio insular africano. Potencialidades, constrangimentos e impactos*. Lisbon: Gerpress.

Brito, Brígida (2010b). *Turismo em meio insular africano: análise comparativa de impactos*, in Recursos e Instrumentos, Ambientalmente Sustentable, xullo-decembro, ano V, vol. I, núm. 9–10, páxinas 157–177.

Brito, Brígida (coord) (2010c). *Desenvolvimento Comunitário: das teorias às práticas. Turismo, Ambiente e Práticas Educativas em São Tomé e Príncipe*. Lisbon: Gerpress

Brito, Brígida (2004). *Turismo ecológico: uma via para o desenvolvimento sustentável de São Tomé e Príncipe*. Ph.D. thesis. Lisbon: ISCTE.

Costa, António Jorge (coord) (2018). *Plano estratégico e de marketing para o turismo em São Tomé e Príncipe*. São Tomé e Príncipe: Government of São Tomé and Príncipe.

Economic Freedom Index Essentia (2012). *Plano e agenda de desenvolvimento sustentável da ilha do Príncipe*. Available at https://www.heritage.org/index/ranking, [Accessed on 17/10/2018].

Schwab, Klaus (ed.) (2017). *The Global Competitiveness Report 2017–2018*. Geneva: World Economic Forum

The World Bank (2018). *Doing Business 2018. Reforming to Create Jobs. Comparing Business Regulation for Domestic Firms in 190 Economies*. Washington, DC: International Bank for Reconstruction and Development/The World Bank.

Turner, Rochelle (2015). *Travel and tourism. Economic impact 2015. São Tome and Principe*. London: World Travel and Tourism Council.

UNDP (2014). *Relatório do Fórum dos economistas de S. Tomé e Príncipe*. São Tomé: United Nations Development Programme.

InFocus 6

Diary of a woman in tourism

Bénédicte Joan

Although it is hard to make generalisations about all women from Sub-Saharan Africa (SSA), I would like to share a few personal observations I have made, following from travelling in over 60 countries. My bold statement is that 'African women may lack self-confidence and cultural pride'. Women like me face gender inequality as part of their daily lives. This inequality manifests itself in lack of educational opportunities, barriers to employment, economic marginalisation, among many other things. Young African women are particularly affected, with very little control over the economic and natural resources in their communities. They are generally unable to leverage these resources and promote development and seek better lives for themselves, their families, and the broader community.

In the early 1990s in Congo (where I come from), the country suffered from years of war and hatred between ethnic groups. My mother, a well-educated and travelled Congolese woman, had seven children. She rescued me as I was caught into the Congo war and put me on a plane from Brazzaville to Bordeaux. I lost touch with my place of birth because of war, but I was destined to become an avid traveller. Today I am a young 30 years old African woman and as far I can remember I always had the desire to travel. What was left back in my place of birth was the memory of sexual abuse I had gone through and a persistent reminder that the role of a woman was in the kitchen in a family that had not envisioned me travelling the world, apart from my mother who believed in me.

Being in Bordeaux meant for me that I had the privilege of benefiting from an education, which encouraged me to grow curious and understand the concept of inequality, and even further motivated my mother to finance my trips to summer camps internationally. This built my interest in adventure thus later on, I studied Adventure Tourism Management in Birmingham (UK) in 2009. On the last year of my Bachelor degree, I travelled to Togo for a 1-month expedition, an impactful experience during which I was exposed to and confronted the negative side of volunteer tourism and the related 'white saviour syndrome' (see for example https://afropunk.com/2018/06/white-savior-your-volunteer-trip-to-africa-was-more-beneficial-to-you-than-to-africa/), which is historically linked to the perception of the West saving the poorest in Africa.

Tourism is an industry that can build a positive image of a destination area but SSA countries are still affected by their colonial pasts. Being back on African soil drove me to support women in smaller communities to appreciate tourism and travel as a mean of doing business and be less dependent on handouts and foreign aid. The need for greater and more meaningful interventions in the region to address gender inequality, a sense of cultural pride and economic marginalisation of young women in particular, with a real impact at a grassroots level became my main motivator.

In 2017, I settled in Côte d'Ivoire. There, young women struggle to find employment due to a lack of skills, qualifications and mentoring, ultimately because they have limited access to education and training. In rural areas of the country, only 2% of girls from poor families complete secondary education, compared to 49% of boys from wealthy families in urban areas (French Agency Development, 2018). Country-wide, only 36.6% of girls complete secondary education and just 7.3% go to university, compared to 51% and 11.2% of boys (Oxford Business Group, 2016). This translates into a lack of employment opportunities: according to World Bank figures, less than half of all women in Côte d'Ivoire are formally employed (World Bank, 2019).

These issues all relate back to gender inequality, which is for a large part to blame for the barriers to education and employment faced by young women and girls in Côte d'Ivoire, and in SSA more broadly. For example, families often view girls' education as less important than boys', and the Ivorian Government reportedly banned women for doing jobs that are deemed to 'exceed their abilities' (Club of Mozambique, 2018).

In countries like Côte d'Ivoire, the tourism industry represents an opportunity to promote women's economic participation and give them a stake in the country's natural and economic resources, and thus promote gender equality. Women's empowerment is vital to sustainable development and for the promotion of human rights for all members of society. More particularly, women's participation in the tourism sector has been shown to significantly reduce poverty, particularly in rural communities (Irena, 2018). The tourism sector consistently sees growth rates equal to or higher than global economic growth. According to the Oxford Business Group (2018), the growth figures of recent years indicate that contribution of travel and tourism to employment (% of GDP) for Côte d'Ivoire accounts 7.3%, and so represents a great opportunity.

According to the UNWTO (2018), there is a much higher proportion of 'self-employed' women working in the tourism industry compared to other sectors in Africa. It is common for women to work without pay in home-based tourism businesses as 'contributing family workers'. Unpaid female workers in family businesses are vulnerable to exploitation and, in my experience, empowering women through skills and training gives them the opportunity to actively participate in the local economy in a way that may limit the risk of vulnerability and exploitation. In the long term, this has the potential to help breaking down barriers at all levels of society and change perspectives around women's roles and capabilities.

In 2017, I founded a Non-Profit called *Train & Travel* to work with women aged between 15 and 25 years old and provide them with the skills and knowledge they need to become promoters of sustainable tourism in their community. We empower these women through trainings and mentorship, enabling them to participate in the local economy through tourism-based activities while being in a position to advocate for environmental and political issues in their community.

One of the key challenges at local level includes the fact that in the Lagoon Region of Côte d'Ivoire, young women struggle to find employment due to a lack of skills and qualifications and limited access to education and training, and face economical marginalisation due to root issues of gender inequality. In order to address this, *Train & Travel* aims at empowering young women to overcome these barriers and at creating employment opportunities in the sustainable tourism sector, as well as offering further educational and awareness-raising activities for others in the community.

Over the past 2-years, we have focused on proving that training and employment opportunities for young women within the tourism sector can have a significant impact on the broader community while promoting gender equality. The project has not only offered specific opportunities to local women to become tour guides through a dedicated training and mentorship programs, but it has also provided professional development and entrepreneurship skills to more women, as well as raising awareness on issues related to sustainable tourism and gender equality. Finally, through the participation of foreign volunteers, the project aims to promote mutually beneficial cultural exchanges and international solidarity.

Challenges and opportunities and expected impact

This project aims to train a total of 20 young women to become sustainable tour guides as part of two 1-year mentorship programs. In addition, we have a potential reach of 400 women to become the beneficiary of a training programme in professional development, entrepreneurship, sustainable tourism and gender equality. This will reduce unemployment rates among young women in the region and at the same time will raise awareness around sustainable tourism, gender equality and solidarity in the broader community. At an individual level, participants will be equipped with the personal, professional and entrepreneurial skills necessary to become entrepreneurs within the sustainable tourism sector, greatly increasing their likelihood of securing regular income to support themselves and their families.

References

Club of Mozambique (2018), Ivory Coast bans women from jobs which 'exceed their abilities'. Retrieved March 8, 2018, https://clubofmozambique.com/news/ivory-coast-bans-women-from-jobs-which-exceed-their-abilities/. (p.3).

French Agency of Development. (2018). In Côte D'Ivoire, girls are pushing open doors of school. Retrieved April 30, 2019, https://www.afd.fr/en/cote-divoire-girls-are-pushing-open-doors-school. (p.2).

Irena, A. (2008). *Women empowerment through tourism*. The Netherlands: Wageningen University.

Oxford Business Group. (2016). More education opportunities for students in Côte d'Ivoire. Retrieved May 10, 2019, https://oxfordbusinessgroup.com/overview/access-granted-increased-interest-private-sector-and-continued-efforts-state-level-broaden.

Oxford Business Group. (2018). Government makes tourism priority sector in Côte d'Ivoire. Retrieved June 28, 2019, https://oxfordbusinessgroup.com/overview/turning-corner-government-designates-tourism-priority-sector-following-its-key-contributions-growth.

UNWTO. (2018). Supporting tourism recovery in Africa. Retrieved June 17, 2018, http://www.travel dailynews.com/pages/show_page/25456.

World Bank. (2019). Gender data portal: Côte d'Ivoire. Retrieved May 10, 2019, http://datatopics. worldbank.org/gender/country/cote-d'ivoire.

Part V
Tourism in Eastern Africa

22

The potential of tourism revenue sharing policy to benefit conservation in Rwanda

Ian E. Munanura and Edwin Sabuhoro

Introduction

Some developing countries in sub-Sahara Africa have pursued wildlife tourism to promote sustainable conservation of wildlife. Public and private conservation institutions in the developing countries have initiated programs with the potential to generate social and economic benefits for local residents while maintaining the ecological integrity of natural areas (Stem, Lassoie, Lee, Deshler & Schelhas, 2003). Over the past 20 years, numerous community-based tourism programs have emerged in sub-Sahara Africa to promote sustainable conservation of wildlife. These efforts have led to the advancement of the Tourism Revenue Sharing (TRS) concept. The TRS concept has emerged as a strategy through which livelihoods could be improved, thereby indirectly creating incentives for wildlife conservation among local residents (Archabald & Naughton-Treves, 2001; Blomley, Namara, McNeilage, Franks, Rainer, Donaldson, Malaps, Olupot, Baker, Sandbrook, Bitariho & Infield, 2010). Consequently, TRS has become a popular strategy for integrated conservation and development in most of the sub-Saharan Africa region (Archabald & Naughton-Treves, 2001; Blomley et al., 2010).

In some of the sub-Saharan Africa countries, TRS has been embraced as a strategy through which wildlife conservation can be sustained in highly threatened and human-dominated forest landscapes (Adams and Infield, 2003; Blomley et al., 2010, Ahebwa, van der Duim & Sandbrook, 2012; Munanura, Backman, Hallo & Powell, 2016). In Rwanda, for example, 5% of annual tourism revenue is put in a TRS fund to support community projects in communities adjacent to national parks (Kagarama, Bizoza & Kayigamba, 2012). In Uganda and Tanzania, approximately 20% of tourism revenue is allocated to fund integrated conservation and community development programs (Spenceley et al., 2019). The argument for such substantial tourism revenue investment in communities adjacent to protected areas is to offset the opportunity cost of coexisting with wildlife and to improve livelihoods (Archabald & Naughton-Treves, 2001). The opportunity cost of coexisting with wildlife may include loss of agricultural productivity to animal crop raiding, loss of human life to animal attacks, and loss of access to forest resources (Archabald & Naughton-Treves, 2001).

Evidence from the literature, however, has cast doubt on the potential of TRS to sustain integrated conservation of wildlife in areas where TRS has been applied (Archabald &

Naughton-Treves, 2001; Adams & Infield, 2003; Ahebwa, van der Duim & Nyakana, 2008; Mackenzie, 2012; Ahebwa et al., 2012; Munanura et al., 2016; Spenceley et al., 2019). The TRS limitations documented in the literature has been attributed to policy gaps, policy implementation constraints, and mismanagement of TRS programs (Archabald & Naughton-Treves, 2001; Blomley, et al., 2010; Mackenzie, 2012; Ahebwa et al, 2012; Munanura et al., 2016; Spenceley et al., 2019).

The TRS operates on the premise that resident's access to income through community-based human development programs will incentivize residents to value wildlife and help protect it (Wunder, 2000; Walpole & Thouless, 2005). Achieving this objective is complex because of multiple limitations, some of which are outlined above. For example, it has been suggested that most TRS programs have failed because of poor linkages between tourism benefits and wildlife conservation objectives, and unequal distribution of benefits among local residents (van der Duim & Caalders, 2002; Walpole & Thouless, 2005). Some studies suggest that indirect monetary benefits are not effective in ensuring the sustainability of community support for conservation (Bookbinder et al., 1998; Wunder, 2000; Kiss, 2004; Munanura et al., 2016). It is also noted that the TRS benefits are not substantial enough to offset the cost of coexisting with wildlife (Mackenzie, 2012; Spenceley et al., 2019).

These limitations of TRS demonstrate the complexity of understanding the potential of TRS to sustain forest landscapes in sub-Sahara Africa. The TRS policy implementers could benefit from exploratory case studies to understand and address the complexity associated with the TRS policy. In this chapter, a Sustainable Livelihoods framework is used to conceptually explore the potential of Rwanda's tourism revenue sharing program to achieve Rwanda's wildlife conservation goals. The proponents of the sustainable livelihoods framework argue that wildlife conservation is secure when residents have the capability to access and maintain livelihoods, livelihood producing resources are equitably distributed, and when livelihoods are socially and environmentally responsible (Chambers and Conway, 1992; Scoones, 1998).

Sustainable livelihoods framework

The Sustainable Livelihoods (SL) framework guides the synthesis of Rwanda's TRS in this chapter. Chambers and Conway (1992) defined livelihoods, as the means of making a living consisted of capabilities, assets, and resources used in daily activities. They argued that the sustainability of livelihoods can be realized when a household is able to cope and recover from shocks to satisfy and maintain a decent living without compromising the opportunities for the next generation (Chambers & Conway, 1992). Scoones (1998) further underscored that livelihoods must not threaten the natural resource base to be sustainable. The SL approach integrates capabilities, equity, and sustainability as key determinants of meaningful, decent, and secure livelihoods.

Overall, the Sustainable Livelihoods framework has been extensively used in literature to explore links between livelihoods and wildlife conservation (Reardon & Vosti, 1995; Salsfsky & Woollenburg, 2000; Wunder, 2000; Bhandari & Grant, 2007). However, the SL framework has rarely been applied to assess tourism policies linking human livelihoods and wildlife conservation goals, such as the TRS. In this chapter, we use the SL framework to synthesize the positive impact of Rwanda's TRS policy on human livelihoods and the associated wildlife conservation implications. The SL framework enables us to conceptually explore the potential of Rwanda's TRS to improve livelihood capabilities of beneficiaries, ensure equity in benefit distribution, and maintain the social and environmental sustainability of livelihoods. The SL determinants are briefly introduced in this chapter.

Capability to maintain livelihoods

The ability of a household to access, maintain, and transform basic living conditions demonstrates its livelihood capabilities. From the sustainable livelihood perspective, livelihood capabilities encompass the ability to adequately access the basic needs of life and to take advantage of available resources to transform livelihoods (Chambers & Conway, 1992). Therefore, livelihood capabilities encompass assets, resources, and opportunities available to make a living (Chambers & Conway, 1992). The assets, resources, and opportunities important for livelihood capabilities appear in the form of natural, financial, human, and social capital (Scoones, 1998; Bebbington, 1999). Therefore, the livelihoods capability of a household is determined by its ability to access and transform assets, resources, and opportunities into enhanced livelihoods (Bebbington, 1999; Scoones, 2009).

Most of the above determinants of livelihood capabilities are not mutually exclusive. For example, social capital has the potential to facilitate access and transform the financial capital into desired livelihoods (Munanura et al., 2016). Equally, enhanced financial capability promotes self-esteem and confidence of the socially and economically disadvantaged households, enabling them to be active participants in the community (Scoones, 2009). In addition, limited access to resources among the most disadvantaged has the potential to influence the desperate and illegal use of wildlife resources to sustain livelihoods, which threatens natural capital and erodes livelihood capabilities (Munanura, Backman, Moore, Hallo & Powell, 2014).

Equitable access to livelihoods resources

Equitable access to resources that produce livelihoods occurs when all interested and able members of a community have adequate access to assets, resources, and opportunities needed to produce decent livelihoods (Chambers & Conway, 1992). From the sustainable livelihoods perspective, equitable access to livelihoods resources requires the inclusion and facilitation of the most deprived and vulnerable people in the community to access resources for desired livelihoods (Solesbury, 2003). Therefore, enabling the most socially and economically disadvantaged individuals to have equitable access to social and economic opportunities are important to the sustainability of livelihoods (Norton and Foster, 2001). There are two key elements to equitable access to resources that produce desired livelihoods. For example, households must be enabled to have equitable access to tangible and intangible resources (Guatam, 2009). Additionally, the most disadvantaged members of the community must be empowered and facilitated to participate in the development and natural resource management decisions. Sharing benefits and promoting social equity improves capabilities, and will spur self-esteem, confidence, and local conservation support (Guatam, 2009).

Social and environmental sustainability of livelihoods

Sustainable livelihoods demand consideration of both environmental and social risks in acquiring and maintaining resources that produce livelihoods (Chambers & Conway, 1992). Environmental sustainability consideration calls for attention to livelihoods producing activities, which have the potential to degrade non-renewable resources (Chambers & Conway, 1992). Such livelihood activities may include illegal hunting for wildlife, forestland encroachment for agriculture, as well as the extraction of oil, gas, and minerals from protected natural areas. Communities, whose livelihoods production threatens the functioning of natural systems, must be supported to minimize the negative impacts of their actions on the environment (Solesbury, 2003).

Equally, social sustainability demands households to be in a position to cope with livelihood stress, and be able to transform assets, opportunities, and resources into adequate livelihoods (Chambers & Conway, 1992). A household may experience livelihood stress in form of crop damage from problem animals, famine, drought, civil war, and natural disasters. The individuals and households who are unable to cope with livelihood stress would struggle to maintain livelihoods (Scoones, 1998). One of the essential tools of social sustainability is social capital (Scoones, 1998). The ability of individuals to access and actively participate in social relationships and networks is critical in accessing and maintain sustainable livelihoods. For example, access to social capital has enabled residents in some developing countries to meaningfully engage public and private collaborators (Fox, 1996).

Rwanda's tourism revenue sharing program

Tourism is one of the most important economic sectors of Rwanda. Rwanda has experienced substantial tourism growth since the year 2000 when the country was emerging from years of insecurity and political conflict. For example, in 2017, the direct contribution of tourism to Rwanda's GDP was over USD 460 million according to the World Travel and Tourism Council. The direct contribution of tourism to Rwanda's economy is expected to grow at an annual rate of about 6% in the next ten years (WTTC, 2018). Rwanda's tourism success is largely attributed to the popularity of mountain gorilla tourism at Volcanoes National Park. According to Rwanda Development Board statistics presented in Figures 22.1 and 22.2, Volcanoes National Park, the focus of this chapter, in the year 2017 alone contributed over USD 16 million. The tourist revenue from VNP amounts to about 90% of Rwanda's total annual tourism revenue generated annually (see Figure 22.2).

Due to the success of tourism and potential risk from human communities adjacent to parks, the Government of Rwanda launched the TRS policy in 2004 with an initial investment of approximately USD 84,000 (GOR, 2005). Since the year 2005, Rwanda has invested approximately USD 1.3 million in communities neighboring its three national parks, including Volcanoes, Nyungwe, and Akagera National Park. The TRS policy aims to share 5% of annual tourism revenue from wildlife tourism with neighboring residents (Kagarama et al., 2012). Each year, the Government of Rwanda allocates approximately 40, 30, and 30% of the annual tourism revenue fund to support residents adjacent to Volcanoes, Nyungwe, and

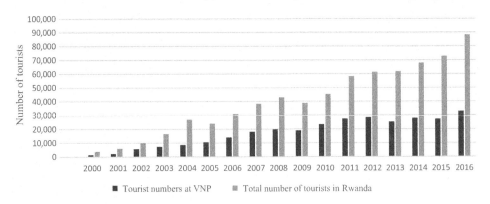

Figure 22.1 Annual tourist numbers for Rwanda and VNP

Source: Data on tourist numbers was obtained from Rwanda Development Board (RDB).

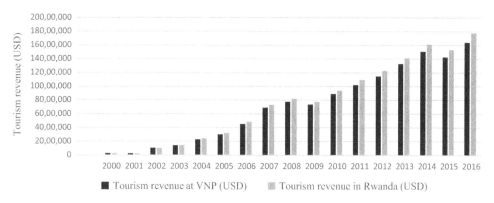

Figure 22.2 Annual tourism revenue for Rwanda and VNP

Source: Data on tourism revenue was obtained from Rwanda Development Board (RDB).

Akagera National Parks respectively (Kagarama et al., 2012). By sharing tourism revenue with residents, the Government of Rwanda aims to provide park adjacent residents with economic incentives to improve livelihoods and, in return, generate resident support for wildlife conservation (Kagarama et al., 2012). For Rwanda, therefore, the TRS policy is a means to sustain the integrity of its wildlife parks.

The TRS policy in Rwanda identified the administrative sectors neighboring three national parks as target areas for TRS benefits distribution. The policy stipulates that a revenue-sharing committee determines TRS benefit allocations. A revenue sharing committee is typically composed of park management officials and local representatives who often are elected local government officials. However, the revenue sharing committee is encouraged to collaborate and seek input from the district community development committees (GOR, 2005). The revenue sharing committee typically invites application for TRS support and selects projects for funding based on conditions such as proximity to the park, the potential impact on conservation and livelihoods, and the applicant's financial contribution (Tusabe & Habyarimana, 2010).

While Rwanda's TRS policy specifically identifies the poor and more disadvantaged residents in communities neighboring the parks as primary beneficiaries of the TRS investment (GOR, 2005), the TRS investment distribution requires beneficiaries to be organized in local cooperatives for accountability and management purposes (Munanura et al., 2016). However, local cooperative membership is typically subject to membership fees ranging between 5 and 20 US dollars per year (Munanura et al., 2016). Consequently, the membership fee requirement has restricted the participant of the most disadvantaged residents, who are clearly identified as the TRS benefit target group by Rwanda's TRS policy.

Overall, Rwanda's TRS was established to improve wildlife conservation, improve human livelihoods, and improve the relationship between local residents and the park management (GOR, 2005). To improve wildlife conservation, Rwanda's TRS policy aims to support programs with the potential to reduce illegal activities, ensure sustainable conservation, and increase community support for conservation (GOR, 2005). To improve human livelihoods, Rwanda's tourism policy aims to reduce poverty, compensate for the loss of wildlife damage, provide alternative livelihoods, and support community-based tourism (GOR, 2005). To improve the relationship between residents and park management, Rwanda's TRS policy aims to build trust, increase resident ownership of wildlife, reduce human-wildlife conflicts, and increase resident participation in wildlife conservation.

The extent to which all the Rwanda's TRS policy objectives are met so far is debatable. Recent research has revealed some discrepancies between the above objectives and funded programs, which may limit the success of Rwanda's TRS as originally conceptualized. In the study at Volcanoes National Park, for example, it was revealed that most of Rwanda's TRS investment at Volcanoes National Park is social in nature and may not enable direct access to TRS benefits for the most disadvantaged residents (Munanura et al., 2016). Spenceley et al. (2019) also noted that the lack of the poor's access to TRS benefits in Rwanda and elsewhere in Africa has limited the conservation impact of the TRS programs. Other scholars have also alluded to limited evidence of conservation impact for Rwanda's TRS policy, attributing the criticism to investing more TRS resources in social infrastructure programs (Sabuhoro, 2006; Nielsen & Spenceley, 2010; Spenceley, Habyalimana, Tusabe & Mariza, 2010).

Synthesizing Rwanda's tourism revenue sharing policy

Rwanda's TRS policy and livelihoods capability

Residents neighboring protected areas in Rwanda experience food security constraints due to poor agricultural productivity attributed to limited economic opportunities, insufficient agricultural land, and animal crop raiding. These constraints have challenged the ability of residents in areas adjacent to protected areas to acquire and maintain desired livelihoods. For example, in a study conducted by Munanura and colleagues (2016), animal crop raiding was found to be one of the main factors responsible for the reduced productivity of the agricultural land near the Volcanoes National Park. Additionally, it was observed that at Volcanoes National Park, the optimal size of the agricultural land available to most residents in adjacent communities is 0.8 hectares (Munanura et al., 2016; 2013). Therefore, food insecurity is arguably one of the main factors responsible for the diminished livelihood capabilities of park adjacent residents in Rwanda.

Over the past 15 years, the Rwandan government, through the TRS policy, has attempted to improve the livelihood capabilities of residents neighboring protected areas. For example, Munanura and colleagues (2016) have indicated that residents in communities adjacent to the Volcanoes National Park draw financial capital from TRS programs. Spenceley and colleagues (2018) indicated that at Sabyinyo Silverback lodge at Volcanoes National Park has contributed about 7.8% of sales to capitalize park-neighboring communities. Nielsen and Spenceley (2010) have also indicated that in three years of its launch, the TRS program contributed about US$ 430,000 toward the community development projects in areas adjacent to Volcanoes National Park.

These examples of TRS investment demonstrate the social and economic opportunities of TRS available to residents in areas adjacent to Rwanda's protected areas. Such opportunities include the establishment of valuable infrastructure projects such as roads, bridges, water supply systems, schools, and health centers. In addition, residents have been empowered to create small and medium enterprises that have created dependable occupations and income. These opportunities have boosted the wellbeing of residents who have access to them either directly or indirectly. Further, these opportunities have also boosted the local economy. For example, TRS programs have created linkages between local and regional markets. Local producers now have access to larger markets in regional trading towns such as Musanze, Rusizi, Nyamagabe, Kibungo, and Kigali. As suggested by Munanura et al. (2016), it appears that residents adjacent to protected areas of Rwanda have been able to transform their livelihoods as a result of opportunities created by Rwanda's TRS policy.

However, Munanura and colleagues (2016) also noted some of the limitations of the TRS policy regarding the improvement of livelihood capability constraints, including, isolation of poor economically disadvantaged residents from direct access to social, cultural, and economic opportunities created by Rwanda's TRS policy. As suggested by Bebbington (1999) enabling improved livelihood capabilities through social, cultural, and economic opportunities empower residents with confidence to engage actively and meaningfully with the rest of the community. Therefore, the inability of the poorest residents to participate in TRS activities not only limits access to important livelihood resources but also suppresses relationship opportunities that could enable access to resources that may improve livelihood capabilities. As Bebbington (1999) noted, relationships in spheres of markets are essential to gain access to resources and improve livelihood opportunities.

Rwanda's TRS policy and equitable livelihoods

Rwanda's TRS policy has arguably been beneficial to residents neighboring national parks. The TRS benefits accessible to residents have been documented (Sabuhoro, 2006; Nielsen & Spenceley, 2010; Spenceley et al., 2010; Munanura et al., 2016). However, it has also been documented that most of the TRS projects in Rwanda are not as beneficial to the socially and economically disadvantaged as much as they are beneficial to the advantaged members of the community. For example, Munanura et al. (2016) indicated that most TRS projects at Volcanoes National Park benefited economically and socially advantaged individuals in the community bordering the park. Contrary to Rwanda's TRS policy guidelines identifying disadvantaged residents as the primary beneficiary of TRS benefits (GOR, 2005), most of the TRS programs offering direct benefits typically exclude disadvantaged residents due to the annual membership fee requirement (Munanura et al., 2016). There is evidence supporting the existence of inequity concerns in tourism benefit distributions, which have disadvantaged some residents with the greatest impact on wildlife (Brandon & Wells, 1992; Archabald & Naughton-Treves, 2001).

Typically, the TRS benefits in Rwanda are distributed through local cooperatives that require annual membership fees. Unfortunately, such a requirement creates and perpetuates inequity in TRS benefit distribution. For example, the membership fee requirement makes it impossible for the economically disadvantaged individual to join a local cooperative and access TRS benefits. Thus some residents in communities adjacent to the Volcanoes National Park perceived the TRS program to be beneficial to the economically powerful members of their community who can afford to pay an annual membership fee. There was the belief that those individuals with access to TRS benefits have been enabled to diversify investments, creating more economic disparity among residents neighboring the park (Munanura et al., 2016). However, the implications for the economic disparity within communities adjacent to the park may not be positive for wildlife conservation in the immediate term. For example, widening the economic gap among residents may create resentment and influence perpetual human–wildlife conflicts.

Rwanda's TRS policy and livelihoods sustainability

Livelihoods capability and equity constraints of Rwanda's TRS policy discussed previously, could negatively impact the social and environmental sustainability of communities adjacent to parks. For example, the alienation of economically and socially disadvantaged residents from direct access to TRS benefits creates perpetual poverty and dependence on forest resources to maintain livelihoods (Dewi et al., 2005; Fisher, 2004; Munanura et al., 2018). At Volcanoes National Park, for example, it has been revealed that residents who are able to pay cooperative membership fees have access to microcredit facilities (Munanura et al., 2016). It is not surprising to find that most of the people with direct access to TRS benefits are some of the socially and economically advantaged members of the community (Munanura et al., 2016).

However, research has revealed that the degradation of natural resources is also influenced by the most disadvantaged residents who typically rely on forest resources to maintain livelihoods (Fisher, 2004; Masozera & Alavalapati, 2004; Tumusiime et al., 2011; Munanura et al., 2018). Therefore, it may be prudent for wildlife management to consider that the TRS policy could have unintended negative social and environmental consequences and needs to be controlled carefully. For example, residents around the Volcanoes National Park revealed that forest resources such as bushmeat and non-timber forest products such as bamboo wood are sold to advantaged members of the community, some of whom could be TRS beneficiaries (Munanura et al., 2016).

Such perceptions support the argument for the consideration of social research to understand the potential links between TRS benefits and the growth of markets of illegal forest resources. In addition, a study to explore the negative influence of TRS benefits on social systems in communities neighboring the park is timely. As Bebbington (1999) suggests, social capital empowers people to have confidence and to engage actively and meaningfully with the rest of the community. At the same time, social capital constraints may also have negative sustainability implications for communities adjacent to parks.

Conclusion

The synthesis in this chapter reveals that the TRS policy has had a substantial positive impact in Rwanda. At the same time, the synthesis has shown that the TRS policy in Rwanda could have some negative social and environmental implications. From the sustainable livelihood perspective, Rwanda's TRS has improved the livelihood capabilities of residents neighboring parks. The TRS policy has enabled residents organized in local cooperatives to access important resources to produce livelihoods. In addition, the TRS policy has also facilitated relationship-building opportunities, which could have helped to improve the hermeneutic and emancipatory capabilities of park neighboring residents. As seen in the literature, relationships are important and provide means to access livelihood resources (Bebbington, 1999). In some cases, relational networks empowered by TRS policy in communities adjacent to Rwanda's parks have enabled the active participation of residents in the conservation and development debate.

The synthesis also revealed that TRS benefit distribution is inequitable. It revealed that TRS benefits are limited to the economically advantaged residents who are able to afford local cooperative annual membership fees. However, and as noted in this chapter, disadvantaged residents also have the potential to threaten wildlife. The TRS policy in Rwanda could also benefit from balancing the distribution of TRS benefits to both advantaged and disadvantaged residents adjacent to parks. When TRS benefit distribution is shared by both groups of residents, the potential for equity in access to livelihood resources and the sustainability of livelihoods in communities adjacent to parks is greater. In fact, research suggests that pressure on wildfire for livelihood resources is reduced when residents have access to alternative livelihood means (Duffy et al., 2016). Further research is needed to understand the potential causes and consequences of inequitable distribution of TRS benefits.

The sustainability implications of Rwanda's TRS policy could be viewed from both short and long-term perspectives. In the long-term, the wildlife conservation implications of TRS benefits, which appear to be collective, are positive. For example, investment in schools will help to educate and change the behavior of future generation, healthcare centers will help to maintain a healthy and productive human population, and investment in the road infrastructure will improve access to markets. In the short-term, however, the conservation implications of such collective benefit programs are not clearly understood. In fact, the positive conservation impact of TRS collective benefit programs has been challenged in the literature (Munanura et al., 2016; Spenceley et al., 2018). To ensure the social and environmental sustainability of programs supported by TRS, Rwanda could aim to directly link TRS benefits to both short-term and long-term conservation goals. For example, the TRS policy implementers could facilitate disadvantaged residents to access TRS benefits. This could be achieved by adjusting the requirements for TRS benefit distribution. For example, TRS benefits could be distributed through community associations that are not restrictive to disadvantaged residents. It is through such inclusive mechanisms of benefit distribution that social and environmental sustainability for TRS investment can be achieved and maintained.

References

Adams, W. M., & Infield, M. (2003). Who is on the gorilla's payroll? Claims on tourist revenue from a Ugandan National Park. *World Development, 31*(1), 177–190.

Ahebwa, W.M., van der Duim, R., & Nyakaana, J. (2008). Tourism, communities and conservation: An analysis of the tourism revenue sharing programme at Lake Mauro conservation area in Uganda. In R. van der Duim & M. E. Kloek (Eds.), *Tourism, nature conservation and wealth creation. Thematic proceedings of Atlas Africa conferences. Volume 4* (pp. 15-26). Arnhem: Atlas

Ahebwa, W. M., van der Duim, R., & Sandbrook, C. (2012). Tourism revenue sharing policy at Bwindi Impenetrable National Park, Uganda: a policy arrangements approach. *Journal of Sustainable Tourism, 20*(3), 377–394.

Archabald, K., & Naughton-Treves, L. (2001). Tourism revenue sharing around national parks in Western Uganda: early efforts to identify and reward local communities. *Environmental Conservation, 28*(02), 135–149.

Bebbington, A. (1999). Capitals and capabilities: a framework for analyzing peasant viability, rural livelihoods and poverty. *World Development, 27*(12), 2021–2044.

Bhandari, B.S., & Grant, M. (2007). Analysis of livelihood security: A case study in the Kali-Khola watershed of Nepal. *Journal of Environmental Management, 85*(1), 17-26

Blomley, T., Namara, A., McNeilage, A., Franks, P., Rainer, H., Donaldson, A., Malpas, R., Olupot, W., Baker, J., Sandbrook, C., & Infield, M. (2010). *Development and gorillas? Assessing fifteen years of integrated conservation and development in southwestern Uganda*, Natural Resources Issues, No. 23. IIED, London.

Bookbinder, M. P., Dinerstein, E., Rijal, A., Cauley, H., & Rajouria, A. (1998). Ecotourism's support of biodiversity conservation. *Conservation Biology, 12*(6), 1399–1404.

Brandon, K.E., & Wells, M. (1992). Planning for people and parks: Design dilemmas. *World Development, 20*(4), 557-570

Chambers, R., & Conway, G. (1992). *Sustainable rural livelihoods: practical concepts for the 21st century*. Sussex: Institute of Development Studies, UK.

Dewi, S., Belcher, B., & Puntodewo, A. (2005). Village economic opportunity, forest dependence, and rural livelihoods in East Kalimantan, Indonesia. *World Development, 33*(9), 1419–1434.

Duffy, R., St John, F. A., Büscher, B., & Brockington, D. (2016). Toward a new understanding of the links between poverty and illegal wildlife hunting. *Conservation Biology, 30*(1), 14–22.

Fisher, M. (2004). Household welfare and forest dependence in Southern Malawi. *Environment and Development Economics, 9*(2), 135–154.

Fox, J. (1996) How does civil society thicken? The political construction of social capital in Mexico. *World Development, 24*(6), 1089–1103.

Guatam, A. P. (2009). Equity and livelihoods in Nepal's community forestry. *International Journal of Social Forestry, 2*(2), 101–122.

GOR (Government of Rwanda) (2015) *Tourism Revenue sharing in Rwanda: policy and Guideline.* Kigali: Rwandan Office of Tourism and National Parks

Kagarama, J., Bizoza, A., & Kayigamba, C. (2012). *Assessment of performance of the revenue sharing implementation during 2005–2010.* Rwanda Development Board, Kigali.

Kiss, A. (2004). Is community-based ecotourism a good use of biodiversity conservation funds? *Trends in Ecology & Evolution, 19*(5), 232–237.

Mackenzie, C. A. (2012). Accruing benefit or loss from a protected area: location matters. *Ecological Economics, 76*, 119–129.

Masozera, M. K., & Alavalapati, J. R. R. (2004). Forest dependency and its implications for protected areas management: a case study from the Nyungwe forest reserve, Rwanda. *Scandinavian Journal of Forest Research, 19*(S4), 85–92.

Munanura, I. E., Backman, K. F., & Sabuhoro, E. (2013). Managing tourism growth in endangered species' habitats of Africa: Volcanoes National Park in Rwanda. *Current Issues in Tourism, 16*(7–8), 700–718.

Munanura, I. E., Backman, K. F., Moore D. D., Hallo, J.C., & Powell, R.B. (2014). Household poverty dimensions influencing forest dependence at Volcanoes National Park, Rwanda. An application of the sustainable livelihoods framework. *Natural Resources, 5*, 1031–1047.

Munanura, I. E., Backman, K. F., Hallo, J. C., & Powell, R. B. (2016). Perceptions of tourism revenue sharing impacts on Volcanoes National Park, Rwanda: a sustainable livelihoods framework. *Journal of Sustainable Tourism, 24*(12), 1709–1726.

Munanura, I. E., Backman, K. F., Sabuhoro, E., Powell, R. B., & Hallo, J. C. (2018). The perceived forms and drivers of forest dependence at Volcanoes National Park, Rwanda. *Environmental Sociology, 4*(3), 343–357.

Nielsen, H., & Spenceley, A. (2010). *The success of tourism in Rwanda – Gorillas and more: Background paper for the African success stories study.* The Hague: World Bank and SNV.

Norton, A., & Foster, M. (2001). *The potential of using sustainable livelihoods approaches in poverty reduction strategy papers.* London: Overseas Development Institute.

Reardon, T., & Vosti, S. A. (1995). Links between rural poverty and the environment in developing countries: Asset categories and investment poverty. *World development, 23*(9), 1495–1506.

Sabuhoro, E. (2006). *Ecotourism as a potential conservation incentive for local communities around Rwanda's Parc National des Volcans.* Durrell Institute for Conservation and the Environment. University of Canterbury, Canterbury, UK.

Salafsky, N., & Wollenberg, E. (2000). Linking livelihoods and conservation: A conceptual framework and scale for assessing the integration of human needs and biodiversity. *World Development, 28*(8), 1421–1438.

Scoones, I. (2009). Livelihoods perspectives and rural development. *The Journal of Peasant Studies, 36*(1), 171–196.

Scoones, I. (1998). *Sustainable rural livelihoods; a framework for analysis.* Vol. 72. Institute of development studies Brighton.

Solesbury, W. (2003). *Sustainable livelihoods: A case study of the evolution of DFID policy.* Overseas Development Institute, London.

Spenceley, A., Snyman, S., & Rylance, A. (2019). Revenue sharing from tourism in terrestrial African protected areas. *Journal of Sustainable Tourism, 27*(6), 720–734.

Spenceley, A., Habyalimana, S., Tusabe, R., & Mariza, D. (2010). Benefits to the poor from gorilla tourism in Rwanda. *Development Southern Africa, 27*(5), 647–662.

Stem, C. J., Lassoie, J. P., Lee, D. R., Deshler, D. D., & Schelhas, J. W. (2003). Community participation in ecotourism benefits: The link to conservation practices and perspectives. *Society & Natural Resources, 16*(5), 387–413.

Tumusiime, D. M., Vedeld, P., & Gombya-Ssembajjwe, W. (2011). Breaking the law? Illegal livelihoods from a protected area in Uganda. *Forest Policy and Economics, 13*(4), 273–283.

Tusabe, R., & Habyalimana, S. (2010). From Poachers to Park Wardens: Revenue Sharing Scheme as an incentive for environment protection in Rwanda. *Mountain Forum Bulletin, 10*(1), 91–93.

van der Duim, R., & Caalders, J. (2002). Biodiversity and Tourism: Impacts and Interventions. *Annals of Tourism Research, 29*(3), 743–761.

Walpole, M., & Thouless, C. (2005). Increasing the value of wildlife through non-consumptive use? Deconstructing the myths of ecotourism and community-based tourism in the tropics. In R. Woodroffe., S. Thirgood & A. Robinowitz (Eds.), *People and wildlife: conflict or co-existence*, Conservation Biology (9) NA, p. 122. Cambridge University Press, Cambridge.

World Travel and Tourism Council (2018). *Travel and Tourism Economic Impact 2018- Rwanda*. World Travel and Tourism Council, London.

Wunder, S. (2000). Ecotourism and economic incentives – an empirical approach. *Ecological Economics, 32*(3), 465–479.

23

Rock art tourism in Ethiopia and cultural heritage management challenges

Dagnachew Leta Senbeto

Introduction

Cultural tourism has been identified as one of the fastest growing segments of tourism in the world by attracting more than 40% out of overall international leisure tourists (Novelli, 2015). Given the rapid growth of visitor demands toward cultural sites, cultural heritage has been seen as the main pillar of cultural tourism development. Thus, the concern for cultural heritage management has been increasing in many countries. There is a high concentration of cultural heritage in Africa (Boswell & O'Kane, 2011; Christie et al., 2013). Take Ethiopia as an example, cultural heritage places are scattered throughout the country, out of nine tangible world heritage sites, eight of them are tangible cultural heritage listed as UNESCO World Heritage Sites (UNESCO-WHS), as highlighted in Figure 23.1. In addition, at least four cultural heritage sites are known to be under the nomination stage (UNESCO, 2018). In addition, Ethiopia is endowed with numerous natural and cultural heritages, with the northern part of the country known for its cultural and historical heritages, while the southern part for natural heritages.

Although such listing normally creates awareness and recognition for the sites and their respective localities, it is axiomatic that such heritage sites have not been fully receptive to visitors due to the inadequate infrastructure and the absence of any integrated community-based tourism development model that would ensure some level of local stakeholders' active involvement. Despite the fact that rock art has been found in all continents except Antarctica, Africa has a relatively larger concentration of rock art sites which is around 200,000 rock art sites widely distributed across the continent (The Economist, May 1, 2008). Out of these 9 rock art sites are listed as UNESCO-WHS (; Trust for African Rock Art (TARA), 2013). Along with other cultural heritage sites, Ethiopia's numerous rock art painting and engravings have been found in several caves and boulders especially in the northern, southern, and south-eastern parts of the country. Wild animals, geometric and human figures, and castles are the main feature of Ethiopia's rock art (Hagos, 2011). Few studies have been conducted to understand the meaning and interpretation of Ethiopia's rock art, though less is known about the main characteristics of Ethiopia's rock art in detail. Existing studies paid much attention to archaeological perspectives of rock art such as food production and domestication of animals

Figure 23.1   World heritage sites in Ethiopia
Source: Author's map 2019.

(Fernández, 2011; Meressa, 2006; Negash, 2001), and somehow from geography (Asrat, 2002) and conservation-related contexts (Nigus, 2005). Yet so far, attention to rock art from a tourism perspective remains in its infancy, and relatively, there is a paucity of targeted actions at using rock art, as a vehicle to socio-economic development through cultural tourism.

Rock art sites in Ethiopia have been facing several challenges. Unlike other cultural heritage sites, rock arts-based ones are responsive and sensitive to several destructive agents. Besides man-made factors, nature-related ones such as weathering, extreme temperature, and rainfall are known to be amongst the main causes of damages to rock art. To cope with these challenges, in their study on African rock art, Little and Borona (2014) emphasize that responsible rock art tourism can be an essential means to boost the preservation of rock art through tourism. In such context, this chapter focuses on assessing rock art tourism and cultural heritage management challenges. The purpose of this chapter is threefold, to (1) outline the overview of cultural heritage management and its importance, (2) assess Ethiopia's rock art sites and their potential for tourism, and (3) to examine challenges which hinder the rock art sites from further tourism development.

Literature review

Overview of cultural heritage management

The term cultural heritage drew from cultural resources, as Skeates (2000) indicates that cultural resources could be transformed into cultural heritage when the way of life of the people became re-utilized and re-assessed. By the end of the 20th century, the scope of cultural heritage has been changed, and internationally agreed distinction was made between tangible and intangible cultural heritage (UNESCO, 1999, 2003). Tangible cultural heritage, identified as a heritage which can be seen and touched, includes crafts, monuments, art, books, coins, traditions, legacies, stories, and archaeological findings. Intangible cultural heritage represents non-physical objects, which cannot be touched and are customs, traditions, beliefs, artistic expression, indigenous knowledge, festivals, local events, spiritual wealth, and exotic practices. A further distinction of tangible cultural heritage is based on the movability of objects, leading to the distinction between movable and immovable heritage (Watt & Colston, 2016). Movable tangible cultural heritage can be portable or moved from place to place without losing their original structure – i.e. coins, cross, books, and crafts. Immovable tangible cultural heritage is non-portable objects attached to the ground or to other surfaces – i.e. frescos, monuments, battlefields, burial places, buildings, historical and pre-historical archaeological remains.

Cultural heritages have historical, aesthetic, scientific, social, evidential, commemorative, socio-political, spiritual, and economic values, often indispensable to uphold the memory of a place and the advantages that such heritage sites may bring for current and future generations in terms of, for example tourism development (Dümcke & Gnedovsky, 2013). With regard to historical values, cultural heritage sites are well placed to remember the past, understand historical transitions, and enable links between past eras and present scenarios (Anheier & Isar, 2011). For instance, battlefields, public statues, and palaces forward a commemorative significance not only to understand what once was, but it also helps placing and measuring the evolutionary status of the human species and the environment in which this operates.

Aesthetically, the value of cultural heritage can be described as an observer and sensational quality of the site. The design, the form, and the overall feature of the heritage could be eye-catching and attractive. Cultural heritages could contribute to scientific development because of its evidential value and source of information. Researchers investigate archaeological sites and historic objects. Given spirit-related aspects, cultural heritages could receive some considerable attention from the religious perspective. For instance, because of veneration or worship, people visit pilgrimage sites. In addition, cultural heritages have contemporary political and socio-economic significances. Politically, cultural heritage plays a crucial role in developing a sense of common understanding, belongingness, and solidarity. With proper tourism planning and development, cultural heritages could enhance socio-economic development which results in job creation, accelerate economic multiplier and diversification, consequently, boosting collective identity and social ties among people (Boswell & O'Kane, 2011). The trade-off between managing heritage and promoting it for tourism gains still remains questionable (Li, Wu, & Cai, 2008; Nuryanti, 1996). Despite the idea that tourism enhances the socio-economic values of cultural heritage (Esfehani & Albrecht, 2018; Smith, 2015; Timothy, 2014), there is a notion that tourism might adversely affect the sustainability of heritage sites (Coccossis, 2016). However, there are views (McKercher, Ho, & Du Cros, 2005) that the amalgamation of cultural heritage and tourism may encourage not only economic development, but it could also enhance the promotion of local tradition and awareness both within and outside the host community. On this basis, a number of destinations have established their tourism on their respective cultural heritage sites – i.e. Egypt's pyramids, the Berlin Wall, the Inca ruins in Mexico, Timbuktu City in Mali. Ethiopian tourism lies in its early stages of growth, and although the country has been endowed with numerous natural and cultural heritage resources, the country is yet to effectively use such immense cultural assets as a vehicle to socio-economic gain, and worse is at risk of undermining the survival of such heritage.

Cultural heritage management and tourism in Ethiopia

Ethiopia is situated in the northeastern part of Africa, near the Red Sea. With a total population of 90,074, 000 (World Population Review, 2017), it possesses some of the oldest historical civilizations and is known for safeguarding its sovereignty against foreign aggression including colonialism. A number of paleontological and archaeological evidence state that the country is the 'cradle of a humankind' (Brunet, 2010; Frost & Shanka, 2002). Ethiopia is known for the origin of coffee, the root for Blue Nile, and its numerous monasteries, art, and architectural features. In connection with religion, the country plays a principal role in the foundation of Christianity and Islam (Erlich, 2010). Religion and cultural diversity are some of the main attributes of cultural heritage in Ethiopia. For example, the country saved the prophet Mohammed and his fellows in times of hardship they faced at home. Ethiopia is known for being 'land of extremes' with its varieties of topographic features (Beyth et al., 2003). In addition, the country has a diversified culture, ethnicity, tradition, and language (Gordon & Carrillet, 2003). Bearing such uniqueness and diversity, Ethiopia owns several natural and cultural attractions of which nine of them are listed as UNESCO WHS. Cultural heritage management in Ethiopia has been influenced by ethnicity, religion, landscape, economy, and people's perception (Nair, 2016). According to the national proclamation No. 209/2000, tangible and intangible cultural heritage should be legally safeguarded. The Authority for Research and Conservation of Cultural Heritage (ARCCH) is responsible for the conservation and management of the country's heritage. More recently, the government has been paying considerable attention to the socio-economic significances of the nation's cultural heritage. Yet, tourism still contributes 6.3% of the country's GDP (World Travel and Tourism Council (WTTC), 2018), which is still incompatible with the country's tourism resource. The country plays an insignificant role in the regional and global tourism market. In response to this, the government attempts to utilize tourism as a pillar to achieve socio-economic development through focusing on diversification of tourism products through the development of several alternative tourist attractions, among which, rock art recently became the most highly regarded one.

Rock art tourism in Africa

The meaning of rock art is primarily related to images, sculpture, or architecture. However, the perspective of rock art varies from discipline to discipline. For example, for archaeologists, rock art symbolizes geometrical figures or art painted by ancient people. Generally, rock art is an art which consists of paintings (pictographs) and engravings (petroglyphs) (Whitley, 2016). In earlier times, rock art was utilized as a means for human communication and signage, which had been supposedly held to provide a source of information and depict ancient people's ways of life and subsistence patterns (Negash, 2018; Willcox, 2018). The theme of rock art represents vegetation, wild and domestic animals, natural and cultural landscapes, rituals, the division of labors, and historical events. Visualizing past people's activities (e.g. hunting and gathering), is another main aesthetic figure of rock art. This indicates rock art explicitly manifests human's irreplaceable record along with other archaeological treasures since it could envisage the past. Equally, it also supports present development, and its value transcends to the future, and it had been widely utilized to practice ritual activities (Lewis-Williams & Challis, 2011; Ross & Davidson, 2006; Turpin, 2001). Rock art is not only known for its unique art forms but also by its fragileness. Therefore, countries develop rock art tourism by supporting several national and international-led conservation strategies. Some of the known rock art sites are Kakadu in Australia, uKhahlamba/Drakens-burg in South Africa, Lascaux caves in France, and Altamira in Spain (Little & Borona, 2014; Sanz & Keenan, 2011). Due to this, a number of rock art sites have been listed as UNESCO WHS (Conway, 2014; Lambert, 2007).

Likewise, the African continent holds a considerable amount of rock art. For example, the Sahara Desert has the biggest volume of rock art followed by the southern, eastern, and central parts of the continent. Previous studies have shown that Africa's rock art aged millions of years with varieties of paintings and engraved arts (Coulson and Campbell, 2001; Willcox, 1984). Nine Africa's rock arts have been registered under a UNESCO-WHS (TARA, 2013). As cited in Little and Borona (2014), Kofi Annan, the former UN-secretary general said that

> Africa's rock art heritage is the common heritage of all Africans and all people. It is a cultural gift from our ancestors [. . .] we must save this cultural heritage before it is too late. Two initiatives are especially critical: educating our children and engaging local communities.
>
> *(p. 184)*

Thus, the potential for rock art tourism development could indeed also be a vehicle to preserve such 'gift' and with proper planning, rock art sites could indeed enhance local socio-economic development, create investment and employment opportunities, and thereby assists with poverty alleviation (Deacon, 2006; Smith, 2006). However, several factors have been accountable for the low level of rock art tourism development in Africa. These include inadequacy of infrastructure; lack of community involvement; poor conservation and preservation of sites; sensitivity of rock art to natural and human-related damaging factors, such as uncontrolled quarrying and vandalism. (Deacon, 2006; Duval & Smith, 2013; Little & Borona, 2014).

General discussion

Rock art tourism in Ethiopia: potentials and challenges

Along with several other attractions, rock art can be the potential for Ethiopia's tourism development. More than 50 rock art sites have been identified in the southeastern, southern, and northern parts of Ethiopia (Hagos, 2011). The majority of rock art is situated in caves, shelters, boulders, limestone, and sandstone caves. Ethiopian rock art can be categorized into three: paintings and engravings mostly found in south-eastern and northern Ethiopia; engravings are situated in the southern part of the country, and carvings found only in south-central Ethiopia (Negash, 2018). Stylistically, the Ethiopian rock art is designated as an 'Ethio-Arabian style'. The style is classified into two stages of development: Surre-Hanakiya and Dahtami. These two rock art styles are mostly found both in eastern Ethiopia and in other Arabian countries; for example, in Yemen, Jordan, and Saudi Arabia. Ethiopia's rock art symbolizes naturalistic, semi-naturalistic, schematic paintings, and engravings figures (Anati, 1972; Cervicek, 1971, 1978; Fernández, 2011; Meressa, 2006; Negash, 2018). The theme of the rock art is predominantly domestic cattle, wild animals, geometric and human figures, and domestic scenes represented with few plant depictions, abstract human figures, hunters with spears, arrows, bows, plowing acts, as well as attacking felines. Negash (2018, p.1) noted that 'Rock art, although restricted to the Later Stone Age/Neolithic (in Ethiopia), and not found everywhere, is an informative source of evidence in reconstruction of the distribution of animals and their habitats, in addition to providing clues to human subsistence

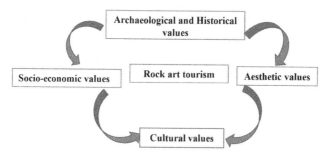

Figure 23.2 Values of rock art for tourism
Source: Author.

patterns'. Figure 23.2 demonstrates that country's rock art has several values such as archaeological, historical, economic, aesthetic, and socio-cultural values.

Given the earlier attributes of rock art exhibited in Figure 23.2, a number of studies examined the socio-economic contribution of rock art tourism. Based on the case of South Africa's rock art sites, Smith (2006) asserts that proper rock art tourism development assists poverty irradiation, enriches the sense of national identity, and creates employment opportunities. Using Huashan rock art area in China as a case study, Gao (2017) argues that rock art tourism could not only contribute to the socio-economic growth of a destination, but it also enhances the emotional attachment of locals and place attachment to rock art heritage. Likewise, in Ethiopia, rock art with its immense potential for history, archaeology, and culture could contribute to the socio-economic development of the country propelled through tourism. Palaeolithic art can expose one to understand ancient people's way of life and Ethiopia's rock art displays primary evidence of the pre-historic period, with an immense historical and archaeological value, revealing important aspects of past human way of life like hunting and gathering, and domestication of animals. In addition, caves and boulder which are home of the paintings could add value to the surrounding scenery as well as for sporting activities like hiking and trekking.

The cultural and socio-economic values of rock art depend on its level of recognition. Visualizing past people's ways of life exhibits the transformative value of rock art; thus, providing a sense of discovery, cross-cultural understanding as well as personal links from the past to the present. Visitors' appreciation of rock art by itself could enhance communities' pride and prestige; especially of those residing in rural and peripheral areas. Rock art tourism has been highlighted as a vehicle to stimulate sustainable tourism development in Ethiopia (Hagos, 2011; Nigus, 2005), with considerable potential to enhance local and regional economic development, the destination attractiveness, tourists' length of stay and expenditure (Conway, 2014; Lambert, 2007), but the rock art sites have been for long neglected, receiving scant attention from both public and private stakeholders.

Cultural heritage management challenges and rock art tourism in Ethiopia

Aim at ensuring longevity, sustainability, and transferability of rock art heritage in Africa, cultural heritage management has been the focus of several stakeholders' attention and on-going conservation and preservation strategies. However, several factors have been hindering such efforts and led to cultural heritages being at risk of depletion. Poor legislation limited human resources and financial constraints have emerged as the main variables working against effective cultural heritage management in Africa (Arazi, 2009). In addition, low levels of awareness of communities residing in proximity of such heritage sites, conflict of interests, and limited sense of belonging and ownership amass into a set of bottlenecks to effective cultural heritage management in Africa (Chirikure et al., 2008, 2010). Such numerous challenges are evident in Ethiopia too, despite recent conservation and preservation efforts by government and concerned stakeholders like ARCCH (Authority of Research and Conservation of Cultural Heritage) in conserving national heritages and identifying unknown public treasures, and UNESCO in conserving registered WHS.

Unlike other cultural heritages, rock art is vulnerable and exposed to damage, because of its sensitivity and fragility to several natural and man-made factors (Agnew et al. 2015). It is uncommon to recognize rock art as a popular tourist destination in most developing countries, mainly in Africa and it is problematic to determine them as valuable a national asset. Thus, issues related to a lack of stakeholder consciousnesses within societies contribute to the destruction of rock art and the loss of potential value and purpose (Bahn, 1998; Cole & Buhrich, 2012; Ross, 2001; Sease, 2002). Although Ethiopia's rock art has a profound contribution to make to national tourism development, several natural and man-made challenges hamper its potential for further development. Natural factors are caused by nature-based risks, since many rock art sites are located in caves and boulders, with some of them being situated in open-air environments. In addition to a low level of awareness and a sense of stakeholders' ownership, natural factors are stand-alone challenges for rock art. Weathering, including fluctuation in temperatures, rainfall, and extreme humidity, as well as landslides, degradation, and soil erosion all may influence the state and survival of the rock art sites. Figure 23.3 shows how rock art sites found in south-eastern Ethiopia have been affected by cracking and washing. reducing their aesthetic value and placing the sites' sustainability under considerable threat.

Additional threats include extreme hot and cold weather conditions during winter and summer leading to fading-up and blurredness of the rock art sites. The formation of algae and lichen is another challenge during the rainy season that can become acidic. In addition to this, the presence of several animals residing or roaming in the proximity of rock arts, bird nests, animal waste, body squeezing on cave and boulders are all factors posing a threat to rock art. Equally, chemical substances wash paintings. As compared to natural factors, man-made challenges have a serious effect on rock art sites and have an alarmingly adverse effect on paintings. Little and Borona (2014) assert that an endeavor to conserve and preserve Africa's rock art is not yet fruitful, with Ethiopia's rock art facing considerable man-made challenges, most of them caused by low levels of awareness, negligence, and recklessness of both host and visitors. Hence, a number of Ethiopia's rock art sites are considered endangered. Figure 23.3 shows Porc-Epic and Olad rock art sites as an example, which has been facing vandalism and encroachment.

Despite some conservation activities carried out by local administrators, as Figure 23.3 exhibits, the sites experience not only residential, visitor, and agricultural encroachment, which is caused by low levels of awareness toward the value of rock art. In addition, vandalism either intentional or unintentional has also tarnished the paintings. According to Howard (1992), intentional vandalism is characterized by a conscious avoidance or removal of the rock art, whereas unintentional vandalism is caused by brushing, writing, and touching the art's fragile part. Ethiopia's rock art faces vandalism that arises by photograph encroachment and intentional vandalism such as writing, picturizing, and erasing on the paintings.

Figure 23.3a

Figure 23.3b Vandalism, cracking, and washing on rock art site of Laga Oda and Porc-Epic caves, south-eastern Ethiopia
Source: Author, 2013.

Conclusion

This chapter aimed at assessing rock art tourism and cultural heritage management challenges in the context of Ethiopia, and it highlights rock art tourism in Ethiopia and in Africa in general. At first, the chapter presents an outline of cultural heritage management in Ethiopia, then it discusses rock art tourism in Africa with emphasis on the potential and challenges of Ethiopia's rock art for tourism. Although cultural heritage has a profound social, economic, political, and cultural values, its contribution to socio-economic development remains in its infancy, especially in developing countries like Ethiopia. As a component of cultural heritage and with its historical, aesthetic, and cultural significances, rock art could elevate the ever-increasing tourist demand for cultural heritage sites. However, to date, little has been known about rock art from the tourism context. In response to this, this chapter focuses on examining the potential and challenges of rock art tourism in Ethiopia, as the country possesses a considerable amount of rock art scattered in and around caves, boulders, and stones found mainly in northern, southern, and south-eastern regions. Despite the cultural, historical, socio-economic, aesthetic values of Ethiopia's rock art, natural and man-made challenges have been destructing its potential, and in some cases, such challenges put the sustainability of rock art sites under question.

Considering challenges that Ethiopia's rock art experiences, this study assumed the premise sustainable tourism development could be an incalculable incentive to safeguard rock art. This requires efforts ranges from awareness creation about the value of rock art tourism to stakeholder collaboration to ensure sustainable rock art tourism development. To achieve this, creating an all-inclusive rock art tourism development plan, assists to minimize such challenges through building cooperation of stakeholders including national and regional tourism and culture departments, local community, tourism enterprises i.e. tour operators, educational institutions, and tourism service providers. To sum up, the chapter has several implications for rock art tourism development in Ethiopia to (1) to understand rock art from the tourism context, (2) to examine the challenges which affect rock art in particular and cultural heritage in general, and (3) to add to the literature in rock art and heritage tourism. In conclusion, the author suggests future studies to focus on various mechanisms such as issues about building and developing ownership. Also, as a sense of proprietorship toward rock art needs fostering in local communities. Besides, future studies could also pay attention to mechanisms to develop and consolidate a public-private partnership with concerned stakeholders.

References

African rock art: The continent's true history. *The Economist*, May 1, 2008. https://www.economist.com/middle-east-and-africa/2008/05/01/the-continents-true-history.

Agnew, Neville, Janette, Deacon, Nicholas, Hall, Terry, Little, Sharon, Sullivan, and Paul, S. C. Taçon. 2015. *Rock Art: A Cultural Treasure at Risk*. Los Angeles: Getty Conservation Institute. http://hdl.handle.net/10020/gci_pubs/rock_art_cultural.

Anati, E. 1972. *Rock-Art in Central Arabia. Corpus of the Rock Engravings*. Louvain: Institut Orientaliste de l'Universite.

Anheier, H., & Isar, Y. R. (eds.) 2011. *Cultures and Globalization: Heritage, Memory and Identity*. London, Los Angeles, New Delhi and Singapore: Sage.

Arazi, N. 2009. Cultural research management in Africa: Challenges, dangers and opportunities. *Azania: Archaeological Research in Africa*, 44(1): 95–106.

Asrat, A. 2002. The rock-hewn churches of central and eastern Tigrai: A geological perspective. Geoarchaeology, 17: 649–663.

Bahn, P. G. 1998. *Prehistoric Rock Art*. Cambridge: Cambridge University Press.

Beyth, M., Avigad, D., Wetzel, H. U., Matthews, A., & Berhe, S. M. 2003. Crustal exhumation and indications for Snowball Earth in the East African Orogen: North Ethiopia and east Eritrea. *Precambrian Research*, 123(2): 187–201.

Boswell, R., & O'Kane, D., 2011. Introduction: Heritage management and tourism in Africa. *Journal of Contemporary African Studies*, 29(4): 361–369.

Brunet, M. 2010. Short note: The track of a new cradle of mankind in Sahelo-Saharan Africa (Chad, Libya, Egypt, Cameroon). *Journal of African Earth Sciences*, 58(4): 680–683.

Cervicek, P. 1971. Rock paintings of Laga Oda (Ethiopia). *Paideuma*, 17: 121–136.

Cervicek, P., 1978. Some African affinities of Arabian rock art. *Rassegna di studi etiopici*, 27: 5–12.

Chirikure, S., Pwiti, G., Damm, C., Folorunso, C. A., Hughes, D. M., Phillips, C., & Pwiti, G. 2008. Community involvement in archaeology and cultural heritage management: An assessment from case studies in Southern Africa and elsewhere. *Current Anthropology*, 49(3): 467–485.

Chirikure, S., Manyanga, M., Ndoro, W., & Pwiti, G., 2010. Unfulfilled promises? Heritage management and community participation at some of Africa's cultural heritage sites. *International Journal of Heritage Studies*, 16(1–2): 30–44.

Christie, I., Fernandes, E., Messerli, H., & Twining-Ward, L. 2013. *Tourism in Africa: Harnessing Tourism for Growth and Improved Livelihoods*. Washington, DC: The World Bank.

Coccossis, H. 2016. "Sustainable development and tourism: Opportunities and threats to cultural heritage from tourism." In *Cultural Tourism and Sustainable Local Development*, edited by Luigi Fusco Girard, Peter Nijkamp, 65–74. London: Routledge.

Cole, N., & Buhrich, A. 2012. Endangered rock art: Forty years of cultural heritage management in the Quinkan region, Cape York Peninsula. *Australian Archaeology*, 75(1): 66–77.

Conway, F. J. 2014. Local and public heritage at a World Heritage site. *Annals of Tourism Research*, 44: 143–155.

Coulson, D., & Campbell, A. 2001. *African Rock Art*. New York: Abrams.

Deacon, J., 2006. Rock art conservation and tourism. *Journal of Archaeological Method and Theory*, 13(4): 376–396.

Dümcke, C., & Gnedovsky, M. 2013. The social and economic value of cultural heritage: Literature review. *EENC paper*, July 2013. Accessed July 11, 2018. http://archive.interarts.net/descargas/interarts2557.pdf.

Duval, M., & Smith, B. 2013. Rock art tourism in the uKhahlamba/Drakensberg World Heritage Site: Obstacles to the development of sustainable tourism. *Journal of Sustainable Tourism*, 21(1): 134–153.

Erlich, H. 2010. *Islam and Christianity in the Horn of Africa: Somalia, Ethiopia, Sudan*. Boulder, CO: Lynne Rienner Publishers.

Esfehani, M. H., & Albrecht, J. N. 2018. Roles of intangible cultural heritage in tourism in natural protected areas. *Journal of Heritage Tourism*, 13(1): 15–29.

Fernández, V. M. 2011. Schematic rock art, rain-making and Islam in the Ethio-Sudanese borderlands. *African Archaeological Review*, 28: 279–300.

Frost, F. A., & Shanka, T. 2002. Regionalism in tourism – the case for Kenya and Ethiopia. *Journal of Travel & Tourism Marketing*, 11(1): 35–58.

Gao, Qian. 2017. Social values and rock art tourism: An ethnographic study of the Huashan rock art area (China). *Conservation and Management of Archaeological Sites*, 19(1): 82–95.

Gordon, F. L., & Carrillet, J. 2003. *Lonely Planet, Ethiopia and Eritrea*. Victoria, AUS: Lonely Planet.

Hagos, T. 2011. *The Ethiopian Rock Arts: The Fragile Resources*. Addis Ababa: Authority for Research and Conservation of Cultural Heritage.

Howard, C. Higgins. 1992. Rock art vandalism: Causes and prevention. In *Vandalism: Research, Prevention, and Social Policy*, edited by Christensen, H. H., Johnson, D. R., & Brookes, M. H., 221–232. Portland, OR: U.S. Department of Agriculture Forest Service Pacific Northwest Research Station.

Lambert, D. 2007. *Introduction to Rock Art Conservation: A Guide to the Preservation of Aboriginal Rock Art*. Sydney: South Press.

Lewis–Williams, D., & Challis, S. 2011. *Deciphering Ancient Minds: The Mystery of San Bushmen Rock Art*. London: Thames and Hudson.

Li, M., Wu, B., & Cai, L. 2008. Tourism development of World Heritage Sites in China: A geographic perspective. *Tourism Management*, 29(2): 308–319.

Little, T., & Borona, G. 2014. Can rock art in Africa reduce poverty? *Public Archaeology*, 13: 178–186.

McKercher, B., Ho, P. S., & Du Cros, H. 2005. Relationship between tourism and cultural heritage management: Evidence from Hong Kong. *Tourism Management*, 26(4): 539–548.

Meressa, G. 2006. "New rock art sites in Northeastern Ethiopia: Their contribution to the development of early food production." MA thesis, Addis Ababa University.

Nair V. S. 2016. Perceptions, legislation, and management of cultural heritage in Ethiopia. *International Journal of Cultural Property*, 23: 99–114.

Negash, A. 2001. *The Holocene Prehistoric Archaeology of the Tembien Region, Northern Ethiopia*. PhD Dissertation., University of Florida.

Negash, A. 2018. Regional variation of the rock art of Ethiopia: A geological perspective. *African Archaeological Review*, 35: 407–416.

Nigus, T. 2005. Conservation of pre-historic rock art in the environ of Harar and Dire Dawa, South Eastern Ethiopia. MA thesis., Addis Ababa University.

Novelli, M. 2015. *Tourism and Development in Sub-Saharan Africa*. Abingdon: Routledge.

Nuryanti, W. 1996. Heritage and postmodern tourism. *Annals of Tourism Research*, 23(2): 249–260.

Ross, M., 2001. Emerging trends in rock-art research: Hunter-gatherer culture, land and landscape. *Antiquity*, 75(289): 543–548.

Ross, J., & Davidson, I., 2006. Rock art and ritual: An archaeological analysis of rock art in arid central Australia. *Journal of Archaeological Method and Theory*, 13(4): 304–340.

Sanz, N., & Keenan, P. eds. 2011. *Human Evolution: Adaptations, Dispersals and Social Developments*. Paris: UNESCO World Heritage Centre.

Sease, C. 2002. *The Conservation of Archaeological Materials*. New Jersey: Pearson education.

Skeates R. 2000. *Debating the Archaeological Heritage*. London: Duckworth.

Smith, B., 2006. Rock art tourism in southern Africa. Problems, possibilities, and poverty relief. In *Of the Past, for the Future. Integrating Archaeology and Conservation*, edited by Agnew, N. & Bridgland, J., 322–330. Los Angeles: Getty Conservation Institute.

Smith, M. K. 2015. *Issues in Cultural Tourism Studies*. London: Routledge.

Trust for African Rock Art (TARA). 2013. Rock art in Africa. Accessed on April 3, 2014. http://africanrockart.org/?option=com_content&view=article&id=86&Itemid =103.

Timothy, D. J., 2014. Contemporary cultural heritage and tourism: Development issues and emerging trends. *Public Archaeology*, 13(1–3): 30–47.

Turpin, S. A. 2001. Archaic North America. In *Handbook of Rock Art Research*, edited by Whitley, D. S, 361–113. California: AltaMira Press.

UNESCO. 1999. *Operational Guidelines for the Implementation of the World Heritage Convention*. Paris: UNESCO.

UNESCO. 2003. The General Conference of the United Nations Educational, Scientific and Cultural Organization (UNESCO) meeting, Paris, 2003, 32nd session. Convention for the Safeguarding of the Intangible Cultural Heritage adopted October 17, 2003. Paris: UNESCO.

UNESCO. 2018. About world heritage. http://whc.unesco.org/en/statesparties/et.

Watt, D., & Colston, B. 2016. *Conservation of Historic Buildings and Their Contents: Addressing the Conflicts*. London and New York: Routledge.

Whitley, D. S. 2016. *Introduction to Rock Art Research*. New York: Routledge.

Willcox, A. R. 1984. *The Drakensberg Bushmen and Their Art: With a Guide to the Rock Painting Sites*. Winterton: Drakensberg Publications.

Willcox, A. R. 2018. *The Rock Art of Africa*. London: Routledge.

World Population Review. 2017. Ethiopian population 2017. http:// http://worldpopulationreview.com/countries/ethiopia-population/.

World Travel and Tourism Council (WTTC). 2018. The economic impact of travel & tourism. https://www.wttc.org/-/media/files/reports/economic-impact- research/countries-2018/ethiopia2018.pdf.

24

Tourism in Mozambique

Historical evolution and future challenges

Mariamo Abdula, Zélia Breda, and Maria Celeste Eusébio

Introduction

Tourism has been one of the fastest-growing sectors over the years, playing an important role in the world economy. Due to the economic role tourism represents, it is the main export sector for many developing countries, creating employment opportunities, reducing poverty and promoting development (WEF, 2011). In 2017, tourism growth was most significant in Africa and Europe (both with 8%), followed by Asia and the Pacific (6%), the Middle East (5%) and the Americas (3%) (UNWTO, 2018). These results reflect the growth of emerging destinations coupled with the recovery of others that have faced security challenges in recent years (UNWTO, 2018).

In the Southern African region, Mozambique is one of the countries that offer a combination of favourable resources to attract tourists and investors with diverse motivations and interests. The warm climate, white sandy beaches, diversity of flora and fauna, cities full of historical monuments and the African-Portuguese-Asian-Arab cultural fusion of its inhabitants offer a sustainable platform for a renowned international tourism destination. In addition, its privileged location, next to one of the most important entry points in Southern Africa – Johannesburg (South Africa) –, makes it possible to connect with regional and international tourism markets. Despite having enormous potential, the contribution of the tourism sector in the country's economy is still incipient. For this reason and because there are a few studies that analyse the profile of tourism in Mozambique, understanding the structure of tourism and its challenges becomes fundamental to guide actions to strengthen the sector.

In this context, this chapter aims to provide a framework for tourism in Mozambique, by presenting its historical evolution, the characterization of tourism and its main challenges. In methodological terms, it is based on secondary data, collected and interpreted from reports of national and international organizations in conjunction with scientific research on Mozambique. Thus, the chapter is divided into five parts, namely: (i) a brief characterization of the country, (ii) the historical evolution of tourism, (iii) current characterization of tourism, (iv) the main challenges of the sector and (v) conclusions.

It is expected that the reflections brought forward in this work may, on the one hand, support public and private tourism stakeholders to advance actions that enable the integrated development of the sector and, on the other hand, provide structured information and add bibliographic sources, on tourism in Mozambique, for the national and international academic community.

Brief characterization of the country

Mozambique became an independent state in 1975 after being colonized by Portugal for about a century, for this reason, Portuguese is considered the official language of the country. The Republic of Mozambique is located on the eastern coast of Southern Africa and covers 799,380 sq. km (of which 98% is land and the remaining 2% is inland waters, including lakes, reservoirs and rivers) (Portal do Governo de Moçambique, 2015). It is bordered by six countries and is bathed by the Indian Ocean along approximately 2,515 km of coastline (Muchangos, 1999) (Figure 24.1).

Administratively the territory is divided into 11 provinces (Figure 24.1) grouped into three geographic regions: (i) the north is composed of the provinces of Cabo Delgado, Nampula and Niassa; (ii) the centre by the provinces of Sofala, Manica, Tete and Zambézia; and (iii) the southern provinces of Maputo City, Maputo province, Gaza and Inhambane. The capital of the country is the city of Maputo (Portal do Governo de Moçambique, 2015).

According to the last population census of 2017, Mozambique has 29 million inhabitants, of which 52% are female. It has a relatively young population, more than half are concentrated in the age group of 15–64 years (52.1%) and with a relatively short life expectancy of 54.1 years, when compared to the world average of 71.4 years (INE, 2017; United Nations Statistics Division, 2018). Social indicators point to a very high infant mortality rate of 77.5%, compared to the regional (62.1%) and worldwide (35%) contexts. The main causes of infant mortality are related to chronic malnutrition, difficult access to health services and clean water, and lack of sanitation, which are responsible for the spread of malaria, cholera and diarrheal diseases (INE, 2017; United Nations Statistics Division, 2018). These indicators place the country in a very low position in the tourism competitiveness ranking, specifically in the "health and hygiene" pillar (WEF, 2007–2017).

In terms of socio-cultural diversity, the Mozambican population is represented by the Bantu people of Central Africa, Arab, Indian and European descendants (MICULTUR, 2014; Portal do Governo de Moçambique, 2015; UNESCO, 2017), which constitute a potential for tourism, translated into unique cultural heritage.

Regarding the economy, data for 2017 indicate that the primary sector (agriculture, fishing and mining) had a GDP contribution of 26.5%, the secondary sector (manufacturing industry) contributed with 13.9% and the tertiary sector (services, including tourism) accounted for 59.6% (INE, 2018). Between 2016 and 2017, the primary and tertiary sectors grew 9% and 3.1%, respectively, while the secondary sector decreased by 3.4%. Mozambique continues to suffer the effects of the hidden debt crisis[1], GDP slowed to 3.7% in 2017, down from 3.8% in 2016 and well below the growth rate of 7% of GDP achieved between 2011 and 2015 (INE, 2018; The World Bank, 2016, 2017). Small and medium-sized enterprises have declined and their capacity to generate jobs has been further reduced. Growth is expected to remain relatively stable at around 3% in the medium term, relatively above sub-Saharan Africa's GDP (2.9%) (INE, 2018; The World Bank, 2016, 2017). Although still incipient, the tourism sector has increasingly contributed to GDP growth (WTTC, 2017), including its social representation within local communities and in fighting poverty, employing women and youth for tasks that do not require specialization.

Figure 24.1 Geographical location and administrative division of Mozambique
Source: Koehne (2007).

Historical evolution of tourism

One of the earliest records on tourism in Mozambique dates back to the 1950s when the country was considered one of the top tourism destinations in Africa. In the second half of the 1950s, the tourism sector began to be regulated and adopted by the colonial government, with the implementation of the first information and tourism centres (MITUR, 2006). At that time, the main tourism attractions were the beaches, the fauna and the dynamic environment offered by the main cities. However, the main attraction in terms of tourist motivation to visit revealed to be the Gorongosa National Park, considered one of the best animal reserves in Southern Africa (MITUR, 2004, 2006). Recognizing the importance of conservation areas for the development of tourism in the then Province of Mozambique, the first generation of tourism legislation began with the approval of legal mechanisms that created the first conservation areas in the 1960s (Table 24.1). However, it was only in the 1970s that the sector grew significantly, receiving around 400,000 tourists in 1973, mostly from

Table 24.1 Main milestones in terms of public policies for the management of the tourism sector

Period	Main milestones and policies in the tourism sector
Colonial period	- Creation of the first information and tourism centres - Definition of tourism zones - Approval of legal mechanisms to create the first conservation areas: o The Decree-Law No. 1993 of 23 July 1960 established the Gorongosa National Park, the Legislative Diploma 47 of 26 June 1962 established the Zinave National Park, and the Legislative Diploma 46 of 25 May 1971 established the Bazaruto National Park.

After the country's independence (1975–1980s)	- The tourism activity suffered a significant decline, due to:
	  o Change of political regimes and dismissal of colonial government technicians;
	  o Lack of qualified human resources to plan and manage the sector;
	  o Difficult political and economic relations with the two main outbound markets in the region (South Africa and Zimbabwe);
	  o The armed conflict (between FRELIMO and RENAMO) that decimated a large part of the fauna resources and prevented access to conservation areas and some tourism destinations in the country.
	- Inbound tourism was based on the stay of international cooperation missions

After the Mozambican 16-Year Civil war (after 1992)	- Restoration of the tourism sector with the Structural Readjustment Program (PRE) - Establishment of the Ministry of Tourism by the Presidential Decree No. 1/2000 of May 23 - Resolution of 14th of April approves "tourism policy and its implementation strategy" - Approval of the Tourism Law and the Strategic Plan for Tourism Development in Mozambique – PEDTM (2004–2013) - Tourism Marketing Strategy in Mozambique (2006–2013) - Closure of the Ministry of Tourism by the Presidential Decree No. 1/2015 of January 16. Art.1 - Creation of the Ministry of Culture and Tourism by the Presidential Decree No. 1/2015 of January 16. Art.2 - Strategic Plan for Tourism Development (2016–2025) approved by the 48th Ordinary Session of the Council of Ministers, December 8, 2015

Source: Elaborated based on Cabrita (2014), MICULTUR (2014, 2017) and Zacarias (2013).

neighbouring countries, such as South Africa and Southern Rhodesia (now Zimbabwe), and employing around 4,000 people (MITUR, 2006). The hotel infrastructure is comprised of around 8,000 beds and was concentrated mainly in the south of the country (formerly Lourenço Marques) (MITUR, 2006), thus following the developmental patterns of the colonial economy, and benefiting from its location and accessibility, both by air and land. This scenario does not differ much from the present time since about 60% of the tourist infrastructure is concentrated in the south of the country, although there are already some resorts in the north (mainly in Cabo Delgado) and in the centre of the country.

After the country's independence in 1975, the tourism sector declined due to the war and economic collapse. Issues such as the difficult political and economic relationship with the two main outbound markets in the region (South Africa and Zimbabwe), the lack of qualified personnel to plan and manage the sector and the armed conflict (between FRELIMO and RENAMO) contributed to weakening the sector, destroying both basic and tourist infrastructures, as well as the flora and the wildlife. In general, the 1980s and early 1990s were characterized by inbound tourism based on the stay of international cooperation missions (MITUR, 2004, 2006). The security issue at that time constituted an obstacle to the development of tourism and other productive sectors of the country, contributing to the reduction of development indicators and providing the emergence of regional asymmetries and a greater gap between social classes.

The revitalization of the tourism sector began in 1992, with the end of the Sixteen-Year war. The country achieved impressive political and economic stability, creating conditions for a substantial renovation of the tourism sector, despite poor infrastructure and widespread poverty (Jones, 2010). A new legislative era of tourism was initiated (Table 24.1), and the positive contribution of tourism was visible in terms of maximizing the entry of foreign exchange, job creation, strengthening regional development and promoting the participation of national entrepreneurs in tourism enterprises (MITUR, 2004, 2006). These actions increased the regulatory capacity of the sector, as well as the quality of tourism products offered. Thus, opportunities were opened to improve the dynamics of the sector in the country, encouraging the entry of tourists and investments and, in the construction and expansion of both general and tourism-specific infrastructures (Azevedo, 2013; Jones, 2010).

The growth trend of international tourism was regular and below 1 million visitors between 2001 and 2008. However, substantial growth was observed between 2009 and 2012, with more than 2 million tourist arrivals being registered (Figure 24.2), which allowed the country to surpass some of the region's main competitors (Table 24.2). It should be noted that

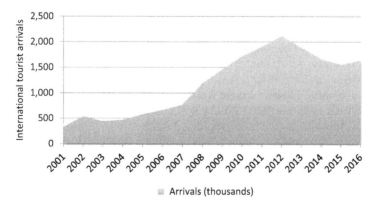

Figure 24.2 Evolution of international tourist arrivals (2001–2016)
Source: UNWTO (2018).

Table 24.2 International arrival in SADC and regional ranking (2009–2013)

Country	2009	RK	2010	RK	2011	RK	2012	RK	2013	RK
Angola	366,000	11	425,000	12	481,000	10	528,000	11	650,000	11
Botswana	1,721,000	3	1,973,000	3			1,614,000	4	1,544,000	4
Congo, Dem. Rep.	53,000	15	81,000	15	186,000	14	167,000	15	191,000	15
Lesotho	344,000	12	426,000	11	398,000	11	423,000	12	433,000	12
Madagascar	163,000	13	196,000	13	225,000	12	256,000	13	196,000	14
Malawi	755,000	8	746,000	10	767,000	9	770,000	10	795,000	10
Mauritius	871,000	7	935,000	6	965,000	5	965,000	7	993,000	7
Mozambique	**1,461,000**	**4**	**1,718,000**	**4**	**1,902,000**	**3**	**2,113,000**	**2**	**1,886,000**	**2**
Namibia	980,000	5	984,000	5	1,027,000	4	1,079,000	5	1,176,000	5
Seychelles	158,000	14	175,000	14	194,000	13	208,000	14	230,000	13
South Africa	7,012,000	1	8,074,000	1	8,339,000	1	9,188,000	1	9,537,000	1
Swaziland	908,000	6	868,000	7	879,000	7	888,000	8	968,000	8
Tanzania	695,000	10	754,000	9	843,000	8	1,043,000	6	1,063,000	6
Zambia	710,000	9	815,000	8	920,000	6	859,000	9	915,000	9
Zimbabwe	2,017,000	2	, 2239,000	2	2,423,000	2	1,794,000	3	1,833,000	3

Source: UNdata- UNTWO, 2018.
Note: RK= Ranking

2009 was the best year in terms of business tourism, which accounted for 22% of the total international arrivals, driven by large investment projects in the country coupled with the preparations for the 2010 FIFA World Cup in South Africa (Industrial Development Corporation, 2012). However, as of 2013, there was a slowdown in this growth caused by various factors, most of them related to the political and economic scenario in the country.

Despite this slowdown in international tourist arrivals, between 2012 and 2013, Mozambique gained prominent positions in the ranking of tourist arrivals in the Southern African Development Community (SADC) region (Table 24.2), reaching second place, a position normally occupied by Zimbabwe. The first position in the regional ranking is dominated by South Africa, which results from the organizational maturity of the sector, the diversity of tourism resources, investments in infrastructure and international marketing (Azevedo, 2013).

In general, the investment and employment generation trend in the sector shows a similar evolution of the country's international tourist arrivals. Mozambique managed to attract significant tourism investment (Table 24.3), with particular growth in 2005 and 2006, representing about ¾ of the total investment in the country. This performance can be attributed to economic recovery, which revitalized business and leisure travel, as well as increasing the interest of foreign investors in large-scale projects, particularly in the central and northern regions of the country. However, there is a slower growth and lower investment weight in the last three years mentioned in Table 24.3. According to Deloitte (2016), the withdrawal of investors in Inhambane province, considered the centre of tourist establishments in the southern region, caused investment to drop from US$ 40 million in 2014 to US$ 10 million in 2015 (Table 24.3). Another peculiarity is related to the composition of the investments. According to Massingue and Muianga (2013), the financing in the country tends to present a pattern in which about 37% corresponds to Foreign Direct Investment (FDI), 6% to National Direct Investment (DNI) and 57% to loans from domestic and foreign banks. Although the composition of the loans is not identified, it can be said that the largest proportion of loans

Table 24.3 Tourism investment

Year	Investment value (US$ million)	Total investment weight (%)	Investment growth (%)
2003	31.50	3.66	
2004	124.80	24.35	74.76
2005	175.60	36.61	28.93
2006	407.30	47.9	56.89
2007	272.20	3.38	−49.63
2008	191.20	18.96	−42.36
2009	264.10	4.59	27.60
2010	134.00	4.34	−97.09
2011	95.10	3.34	−40.90
2012	319.00	10.06	70.19
2013	323.70	10.08	1.45
2014	370.00	8.8	12.51
2015	184.60	8.3	−100.43
2016	199.80	7.3	7.61

Source: CPI (Investment Promotion Centre) cited in INE (2015) and MICULTUR (2015).

corresponds to foreign banks, quite possibly from the countries where FDI is originated. In this sense, the greater participation of FDI increases the flow of values abroad, representing losses in the contribution to the national economy.

With the relative increase in tourist arrivals and prospective investment in the sector, tourism revenues tend to gain a more positive momentum. In this sense, in 2009, the tourism sector generated about US$ 134 million in revenue, representing 6.2% of the total national income and 5.6% of GDP (MICULTUR, 2014). After four years, in 2014, international tourism revenue stood at US$ 206.6 million, representing a growth of 35%. Meanwhile, in 2015, revenues fell by about 7%, to US$ 193 million (WTTC, 2017) (Figure 24.3), indicating

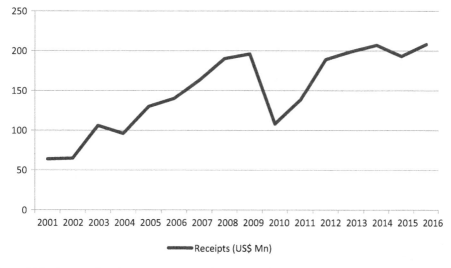

Receipts (US$ Mn)

Figure 24.3   International tourism receipts (2001–2016)
Source: WTTC (2016).

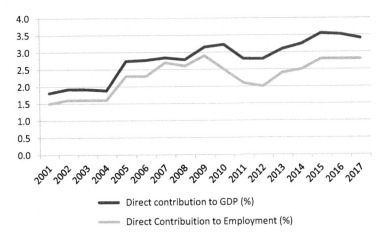

Figure 24.4 Direct contribution of tourism to GDP and employment (2001–2017)
Source: WTTC (2016).

the negative impact of the various aforementioned factors. Analysing Figures 24.2 and 24.3, specifically regarding 2010, the year that Mozambique was supposed to receive a large proportion of tourists who would travel to South Africa to participate in the FIFA World Cup ™, it is visible that there was an increase in the number of international tourist arrivals, but, on the other hand, there was a drastic drop in revenues. The documents analysed do not clarify this inconsistency, for which there could be several reasons, including false statistics.

Overall, the direct contribution of the sector to GDP, as well as to employment, has shown a positive evolution over the 22 years represented in Figure 24.4. However, comparing with the region (Sub-Saharan Africa) and the world, the direct contribution to GDP, as well as to employment, is lower. The average direct contribution to GDP is around 3%, which is below the regional and world averages of 4.2% and 3.8%, respectively (WTTC, 2018b). The level of employability is also below the world average of 3.6%, representing only 2.2% of total jobs created (MICULTUR, 2015; MOZEFO, 2015). However, in relative terms, the direct contribution of the sector to GDP, 3.4% in 2017, exceeds regional (2.7%) and world (3.3%) levels, and employability remains lower (2, 8%) than world (3.8%) and regional (2.3%) levels (WTTC, 2018a).

The evolution of tourism in Mozambique was essentially marked by internal socio-economic and political factors, which have inhibited the more consolidated development of the country in general and the tourism sector in particular. In this context, the current development of tourism in Mozambique faces major challenges, which include altering the image of the destination, restoring the confidence of tourists and investors, improving tourism and related infrastructures, enhancing the country's natural and cultural resources and strengthening relationships between public and private tourism stakeholders. It should be taken into account that tourism in Mozambique has historical importance and remains a strategic priority of the government.

Characterization of tourism in Mozambique

Tourism in Mozambique is mainly developed around beaches, conservation areas, the dynamic business environment in the country's largest urban centres and cultural diversity (MICULTUR, 2017). Natural resources, such as beaches and good climate, are the pillars of tourism, but there are other natural attractions, such as landscapes, inland waters, flora and fauna preserved in specific areas that offer unique experiences to tourists motivated by nature (Table 24.4). The exotic characteristics of the natural resources, as well as their conservation and preservation, placed Mozambique among the 55 best destinations in a group of 139 countries in 2011(WEF, 2017).

The recent introduction of Culture in the Ministry of Tourism (Table 24.1) was, to a certain extent, to value cultural tourism, given that the country counts on material and immaterial cultural heritage, enriched by the ethnic and cultural diversity of its population. It is important to emphasize that Mozambique has at least three important international cultural heritage recognitions: "Ilha de Moçambique" (Mozambique Island) declared as World Cultural Heritage by UNESCO in 1991, the musical instrument "Timbila" also declared as Cultural Heritage and the dance "Nhau-Gule Wankulu" as Intangible Heritage of Humanity (MICULTUR, 2014).

In terms of tourism infrastructure, hotel staff and turnover, it is shown to be very concentrated in the southern region of the country (Maputo, Inhambane and Gaza) (Table 24.5)[2]. For example, in 2016, there were 9,584 beds, 59% of which were concentrated in the southern region, where Maputo itself accounted for 33.3% of the total bed capacity of the country (INE, 2016). In terms of employability, it is also the southern region that employs the most (60%). On the one hand, the direct contribution of the sector in employment is considered minor (3%), on the other hand, according to Azevedo (2013), most of the workers do not have qualifications to carry out the tasks, since they do not have training in the area, which translates into the provision of low-quality services. Indeed, the World Economic Forum (WEF, 2017) assigns a low ranking in terms of the quality of human resources in the sector, placing the country in the 129th position of 136 countries in 2017 (Table 24.5). Regarding the turnover generated by the tourism sector, the pattern is similar to the aforementioned indicators, where the province with the highest participation is Maputo (75.3%).

Apart from the hotels located in the cities (mainly Maputo, Beira, Nampula and Tete), most of the accommodation in the country consists of small-scale beach accommodation, opening up opportunities for the establishment of other types of accommodation, such as country houses, local/rural accommodation and even resorts, exploring the vast natural and cultural tourism resources, both inland and along the north coast.

Due to the proximity to South Africa, Mozambique absorbs a significant part of its share of the international leisure market as an additional destination for visitors to South Africa (Batey, 2014). Portugal, United Kingdom, Germany, Holland, France, Italy, India, Pakistan, China and Brazil are the main incoming countries (MICULTUR, 2015). In regional terms, South Africa, Zimbabwe, Malawi and Swaziland stand out (MICULTUR, 2014, 2015). In terms of representativeness, Africa (80%) is the major region, followed by Europe (13%), the Americas (4%), East Asia and Pacific (2%) and the remaining 1% coming from other regions (MICULTUR, 2014, 2015). About 63% of these international tourists use the roads, 35% air transportation, 1.5% do not identify the type of transportation and only 0.1% use cruises to arrive in the country (MICULTUR, 2015). The geographical proximity, preference on the way to enter into the country, high air transportation costs, among other factors, may justify the aforementioned representativeness of the main tourist markets.

The main purposes of tourist arrivals are personal (90%), including vacations, leisure, visits to family and friends, religion and health. The remaining 10% travel for business and professional purposes (MICULTUR, 2015). Given that business and professional trips are still a small part of the total arrivals in the country, this means that there is still room for improvement, for instance, by creating specific products for this niche market, especially since

Table 24.4 Main tourism attractions by province

Regions/ provinces	Beaches, coastal attractions and freshwater masses			Conservation areas			Culture		
	Sun and beaches	Diving, sport fishing, ocean safaris	Dams, reservoirs and lakes	Mountain tourism, countryside and landscape	Safari	Ecotourism	Built heritage and places of historical-cultural interest	Cultural tourism (ethnographic)	Gastronomy
North									
Niassa	*		**	*	**	**	**	**	
Cabo Delgado	***	**			*	*	**	**	**
Nampula	**	*				*	***	***	
Centre									
Zambézia	**		***	*	*	*	*	*	***
Tete				*	*	**		*	
Manica				**	*	**	*		
Sofala	**				***	***	*		
South									
Inhambane	***	***	*		**	**	**	**	
Gaza	***	**	*		**	*	*		
Maputo Prov.	**	**	**	*	***	*			
Maputo Cidade	*	*				*	**		**

Source: Elaborated based on Cabrita (2014) and MICULTUR (2014).
*low availability/development of attraction in the area
**medium availability/development of attraction in the area
***high availability/development of attraction in the area

Table 24.5 Number of beds, staff and turnover by provinces, 2016

Regions/provinces	Beds		Staff		Turnover	
	Unit	%	Unit	%	Value (Thousand US$)	%
North	**1,482**	**15**	**781**	**15**	**3,473**	**7**
Niassa	306	3.2	126	2.4	541	1.1
Cabo Delgado	547	5.7	361	6.9	1946	3.9
Nampula	629	6.6	294	5.6	986	2.0
Centre	**2,438**	**25**	**1,069**	**20**	**5,189**	**10**
Zambézia	484	5.1	259	4.9	1,378	27
Tete	688	7.2	221	4.2	689	1.4
Manica	458	4.8	314	6.0	1,784	3.5
Sofala	808	8.4	275	5.3	1,338	2.7
South	**5,664**	**59**	**3,387**	**65**	**41,784**	**83**
Inhambane	954	10.0	402	7.7	1,365	2.7
Gaza	905	9.4	473	9.0	1,595	3.2
Maputo Prov.	614	6.4	289	5.5	838	1.7
Maputo Cidade	3,191	33.3	2,223	42.4	37,986	75.3
Total	9,584	100	5,237	100	50,446	100

Source: Elaborated based on survey data (INE, 2016).
Note: Exchange rates for 12/31/2016, 1US$=74Meticais (in https://freecurrencyrates.com/pt/
exchange-rate-history/USD-MZN/2016).

the country is developing projects on the exploitation of energy resources as well as in the development of ports and railways.

Most tourists who choose Mozambique for vacation/recreation are between 25 and 35 years old, being the age group of "65 and over" less representative, whose main reason is related to visiting relatives and friends (MICULTUR, 2015). In terms of travel itineraries, 92% of international tourists prefer to organize their travel independently and the remaining 8% choose package tours (World Tourism Organization, 2018). In this context, opportunities are created to develop specific packages to attract senior tourists, assuming that it is a group with relatively higher purchasing power than the younger tourists.

Foreign tourists tend to stay, on average, 1.5 to 2 nights in commercial accommodation services and between seven to nine days in non-commercial accommodation services. As for daily expenses, the data shows that foreign tourists spend about US$ 130 to 140 per day (World Tourism Organization, 2018). These values are relatively higher compared to the ones of the neighbouring countries, resulting mostly from transportation and accommodation costs. As an example, air transport tariffs from the main origin markets in Europe, Asia and America to Maputo are about 1.8 to 2.2 times more expensive than the cheaper rates for regional competitors in Mozambique (MICULTUR, 2014). In addition, even in land transportation, prices per kilometre from Johannesburg to Maputo are between 2 to 4.6 times higher than the flights from South Africa. The high transportation costs may be reflected in the low bed occupancy rate, which is 25% on average (INE, 2016; MICULTUR, 2014).

Domestic tourism, in turn, is essentially characterized by trips to visit family, especially during festive seasons (Easter and Christmas), but also during extended weekends by public officials and businessmen. In 2016, the number of domestic tourists amounted to 4.1 million, which is more than double of international arrivals (MICULTUR, 2015; MOZEFO, 2015).

Table 24.6 Ranking of tourism competitiveness (selected pillars)

Year	Number of countries	Global position	Safety and security	Health and hygiene	Tourism infrastructure	Human resource	Natural resources	Cultural resources
2007	124	119	100	121	92	124		106
2009	133	124	103	130	117	130	56	113
2011	139	128	125	136	99	135	55	117
2013	140	125	125	136	106	138	64	120
2015	141	130	114	141	111	131	88	121
2017	136	122	105	136	104	129	73	122

Source: WEF (2007–2017).

These figures encourage national government to believe that domestic tourism is a strategic sector to promote social cohesion, defending and consolidating national unity and a culture of peace (Governo de Moçambique, 2015; MOZEFO, 2015). However, there is great difficulty in understanding the dynamics of the domestic tourism sector due to the limitation and inconsistency of existing data (Jones, 2010). This is exacerbated by the lack of studies on the performance of domestic tourism, despite the existence of a comparatively large cohort of expatriates, a growing domestic middle class, and numerous international workshops and conferences occurring in the country. The latter is one of the main motivators for domestic trips of public officials, students and other social groups.

Existing tourism infrastructures, combined with natural and cultural resources, as well as socio-economic characteristics, ranked the country, in 2017, in the 122nd position, of 136 countries, in terms of travel and tourism competitiveness, being considered one of the best positions in the last 10 years (Table 24.6). Due to an increase in the number of protected areas and a greater awareness circa the importance of natural and exceptional resources for tourism, Mozambique reached the 73rd position in the "Natural Resources" pillar. Despite the rise in the ranking, tourism potential remains largely untapped and suffers from imminent sustainability risks, including the lack of water treatment and deforestation caused by illegal logging. Health and hygiene conditions (136th), human resources (129th), cultural resources (122nd), safety and security (105th) and infrastructure (104th) are the areas that most require improvement.

In sum, tourism in Mozambique presents specific characteristics that include little diversified structure, concentration of tourism activities in the coastal zone of the southern region of the country, uncompetitive prices and most tourism investment is foreign. However, there are also a number of external factors, such as political instability and poor social indicators, that negatively affect the advance of tourism, placing the country among the 20 worst countries in the ranking of tourism competitiveness worldwide. In this sense, it is urgent to structure actions to maximize the sustainability of the positive aspects (natural and cultural resources) and minimize the negative aspects (safety, health and hygiene, tourism infrastructures and human resources quality) (Table 24.5).

Tourism challenges and lessons for the future

Tourism in Mozambique is in an emerging phase, presenting solid regulators institutions and is considered one of the pillars for the development of the country (Christie, Fernandes, Messerli, & Twining-Ward, 2013). Despite the sector being part of the sustainable development strategy of the country, it presents specific characteristics that comprise a poorly diversified structure and poles of activity development very concentrated along the southern coast. Thus, in order to reach its tourism potential, Mozambique will have to deal with a number of existing challenges: widespread lack of security, poor public health conditions, difficult investor access to finance, low levels of human resource skills and uncompetitive prices. These obstacles to tourism development mostly depend on the actions of the government and investors. In this context, some of the challenges facing the sector today are described as follows:

Safety and security

The political tension, the outstanding debt, the slowdown of extractive industries and corruption (Aranda, 2013; CIP, CMI, & U4, 2016; Mosca, 2012; MOZEFO, 2015), added to the social problems considered as chronic, such as high infant mortality rates, epidemic diseases and deficient access to basic infrastructures (Astill-Brown & Weimer, 2010), are the main factors for the significant reduction of tourist arrivals in 2014, registering 1.7 million, which represents a decrease of 23% compared to 2012 (United Nations Statistics Division, 2018). This also slowed down the growth of investment in tourism and other sectors of the economy, preventing the effort, of almost 20 years, to build a positive country image, through actions defined in the strategic plans of various sectors of the country in general, and in particular the tourism sector. According to the World Bank (2018), on the one hand, transparent, participatory economic governance and structural reforms could restore investor confidence; on the other hand, the diversification of the current focus of capital intensive and low productivity projects to a more diversified and competitive economy would strengthen the quality of education, provision of basic health services and infrastructures.

Tourism is a sector that sells positive emotions based on experiences acquired in moments of leisure, relaxation, rejuvenation and contact with different cultures. Therefore, its development should, in principle, take place in safe and comfortable environments. The existence of constraints that, due to their characteristics, generate risk perceptions among tourists, investors and other stakeholders in the sector, have a visible impact on the performance and competitiveness of tourism in Mozambique.

Tourism performance

The tourist activity tends to be concentrated in certain regions of the country, more specifically along the southern coast and in the bigger cities of the country. In part, this type of structure is attributed to security and access. On the one hand, cities are considered "safe" for people and good in times of conflict, equipped with basic infrastructure and main points of entry and exit for tourists. On the other hand, the south is more developed in terms of activity and tourist capacity for at least two reasons: (i) Maputo International Airport, in the country's capital, was for many decades the only air access for international flights, and (ii) the main source market for tourists is the neighbouring country South Africa, which has greatly influenced the composition and type of tourist products developed in the country, specifically in the southern coast. However, there is a diversified tourism potential in the rest of the country (Table 24.4) in its different tourist routes and conservation areas, which has not had yet a great impact on the development of tourism.

In general, despite the progress made, with greater emphasis between 2009 and 2012, tourism performance in Mozambique is currently weak. The bed occupancy rate is relatively low, averaging 25%, and the length of stay is only two days. The registration of tourist arrivals, between 2014 and 2016, has a negative annual average growth of −18%. Considering the government's goal of 4 million international arrivals by 2025, the annual growth of tourist arrivals should be 10% per year. These indicators of performance were reflected in the sector's low direct contribution to GDP.

Competitiveness of the sector

In the globalized market, all tourism products compete with each other for their value and price. Although it is the individual traveller who makes the decision, the flow of tourists to a particular destination is largely determined by the world tourism industry, represented by tour operators, travel agents and transport services in outbound countries. Destinations, in turn, can influence the global industry through effective and continuous marketing and promotion campaigns. However, they can only succeed in the competition if they possess high-quality infrastructures, qualified human resources and competitive prices.

The main obstacles to the expansion of the sector in the country include, mainly, poor hotel infrastructure, expensive international/domestic transportation and unskilled human resources. In terms of accommodation, it is estimated that on the African continent only 10% of existing rooms are in line with international standards, of which about half are located in neighbouring South Africa (Christie et al., 2013). In Mozambique, the tourism industry is relatively insignificant when faced with its enormous potential. Apart from the hotels in the main cities (Maputo, Beira, Nampula and Tete), most accommodation consists of small-scale beach accommodation and other types of establishments, namely bed and breakfast and inns (Industrial Development Corporation, 2012), which offer a quality of service below international standards. The supply of higher quality tourism, both to the general market and to specific segments, as well as developed in a sustainable context, could be a way to stand out amongst direct competitors.

Air and road transportation are the main ways of entry into the country and for domestic connections. However, access to different tourism destinations obliges travellers to make a prior assessment of the costs and benefits of scheduled visits, as the high cost of air tickets coupled with a poor road network makes tourism less competitive in Mozambique than in the countries of the region (MOZEFO, 2015). Long-distance air connections are dominated by foreign operators; the only national airline in cooperation with foreign operators offers limited international connections. In terms of domestic flight connections, the national carrier continues to dominate its operation. In both cases, the cost of airfare is high, equivalent to at least two minimum wages for a trip within 500 km, and in international flights, this value can reach 15 times the national minimum wage. The entry of private airlines for domestic flights is still incipient and therefore has little impact on the domestic market. In this context, road transportation becomes the most common mode of travel to and from the Mozambican territory, representing 63% of total international arrivals, of which 93% use their own car (MICULTUR, 2015). This is an opportunity to diversify the product by offering tourist itineraries along the main tourist routes. However, the general conditions of national roads (lack of signage and maintenance) provide precedents to road accidents (Azevedo, 2013). All these aspects end up making tourism more expensive in Mozambique and can contribute to a perception of high financial and physical risks.

In a context of increasing reliance on information technologies and the globalization of the economy, organizations have to stand out from their competitors by relying on customer loyalty strategies. Due to the nature of the tourism product, the qualification of human resources has a direct implication on the overall quality of tourism services, since tourism experience results largely from the relationship between the tourism professional and the visitor. In general, the number of hotel establishments in Mozambique has been increasing, requiring specific skills of the staff to meet the visitor quality standard (Azevedo, 2013), especially when the country's competitiveness index for quality of human resources in tourism is one of the lowest, placing the country in the 129th position among 136 countries (WEF, 2017). The challenge in this context includes the improvement in the delivery of the service to the consumer, which, in part, results in regular training programs in innovative techniques in order to create skills and ensure the competitiveness of the sector.

Recovery marketing

Similar to Mozambique, there are many tourism destinations associated with negative factors that determine them as insecure, and consequently present a negative image that prevents them from attracting tourists and developing local tourism, even though they are rich in tourism attractions. According to Avraham and Ketter (2008a), there are, at least, two types of negative tourist destination images: (i) caused by unexpected crises, such as terrorism, natural disasters or sudden epidemics, and (ii) caused by long-term problems such as economic crises, high crime rates, wars and political instability. In both cases, the image restoration and maintenance exercise are challenging as it is a resource-consuming, long-term process and in many cases, local decision-makers do not know how to act to convince potential tourists and investors that the destination is safe again (Avraham & Ketter, 2008a; Benoit & Drew, 1997). In this way, it is important to work on the set of characteristics related to the image and the physical reality of the destination, which must be improved in order to change the negative image.

Assuming that the perception of Mozambique's image is negative, modifying this perception through image restoration strategies can be vital to position the country as an international tourism destination. Investment in the promotion of tourism potential, domestic tourism and the national private sector would be some of the challenges in this field. Mozambique has high-value natural resources, but there is a weak capacity to exploit this potential in order to promote a positive image. This fragility results, in part, from the lack of articulation and an integrated communication strategy between public and private sector organizations (IESE, 2017; MOZEFO, 2015). Lack of investment in domestic tourism, as well as the capitalization of local investors, creates a set of challenges. A domestic tourist, who has a deeper knowledge of the physical characteristics of the country, would be more able to perceive the real image of the country and appreciate its existing potentialities. Approximately 90% of investment in tourism corresponds to FDI (including loans from foreign banks), which promotes the flow of revenues abroad. In this sense, promoting the involvement of the national private sector becomes indispensable for the growth of tourism, since it will promote the country from the inside out and will contribute to increasing the revenue retention in the country.

Conclusions

Mozambique has the potential to develop its tourism activity, taking into account the existence of natural resources relevant to tourism, the historical importance of tourism in the country and the fact that tourism remains one of the strategic priorities of the government. However, the indicators analysed in this study show that tourism is still incipient in the country, with no significant economic contribution and quite dependent on the region's tourism markets. Tourism activity presents specific characteristics that comprise a poorly diversified structure, high costs and poles of development of tourism very concentrated in the southern region of the country.

The evolution of tourism was marked by events that inhibited the consolidation of the sector. The political instability that the country is facing today has brought the country a step backward to the growth of tourism that was still recovering from the effects caused by the Sixteen-Year war. In fact, a discouraged demand (due to the negative country image), a reduction of investment (due to the low quality of tourism and complementary infrastructures), a poor sector competence (due to low skilled labour and weak public-private cooperation) and the difficulty to access the country (due to expensive and irregular transportation), are part of the sector's main constraints. In this context, in the medium to long term, the challenge will be a broad structural reform to restore the investors' confidence, as well as capitalization of the investment that has been made, in order to generate more revenue through a more integrated intervention on the sectors in the value chain of tourism.

Finally, the limitation and inconsistency of statistical data, especially on domestic tourism, has made it difficult to understand the dynamics of the sector in greater detail. Moreover, of the few published studies on tourism in Mozambique, none have considered the role of domestic tourism in the country's economy. In this sense, it is considered pertinent that future studies address the issue of domestic tourism in Mozambique, specifically on its evolution, characterization and relevance to society and to the country's economy.

Notes

1 The hidden debts results from loans of more than US$ 2 billion borrowed from the European banks Credit Suisse and VTB of Russia in 2013 and 2014 by security-related companies – Ematum (Mozambique Tuna Company), Proindicus and MAM (Mozambique Asset Management) – with guarantees issued by the government at the time (Kroll, 2017).
2 The data in table 3 result from a survey carried out in 2016 (INE, 2016), representing a sample. These results are presented to illustrate the trend of the distribution of mentioned indicators.

References

Aranda, M. (2013). *Moçambique: Paz ameaçada?* Maputo: IMVF.

Astill-Brown, J., & Weimer, M. (2010). Moçambique: Equilibrando o Desenvolvimento, a Política e a Segurança. London: Chatham Hous.

Avraham, E., & Ketter, E. (2008a). *Media strategies for marketing places in crisis: Improving the images of cities, countries and tourist destination.* Oxford: Elsevier Ltd.

Avraham, E., & Ketter, E. (2008b). Will we be safe there? Analysing strategies for altering unsafe place images. *Place Branding and Public Diplomacy, 4*(3), 196–204. https://doi.org/10.1057/pb.2008.10

Azevedo, H. (2013). Turismo em Moçambique: Trajectórias, tendências e desafios. *Revista Internacional em Língua Portuguesa: Turismo, III*(26), 149–162.

Batey, E. (2014). Custo económico do conflito em moçambique: Avaliação do impacto económico do conflito no sector do turismo. *USAID-Moçambique- Programa de Apoio Para O Desenvolvimento Económico,* 78. Retrieved July 18, 2018, from http://www.speed-program.com/wp-content/uploads/2014/05/2014-SPEED-Report-005- Economic-cost-of-renewed-conflict-in-Mozambique-Tourism-value-chains-PT.pdf.

Benoit, W. L., & Drew, S. (1997). Appropriateness and effectiveness of image repair strategies. *Communication Reports, 10*(2), 153–163. https://doi.org/10.1080/08934219709367671.

Cabrita, S. (2014). Moçambique: A emergência de um destino turístico. In C. Costa, F. Brandão, R. Costa, & Z. Breda (Eds.), *Turismo nos países lusófonos: Conhecimento, estratégia e territorios* (Vol. I, pp. 229–346). Lisboa: Escolar Editora.

Christie, I., Fernandes, E., Messerli, H., & Twining-ward, L. (2013). Tourism in Africa: Harnessing tourism for growth and improved livelihoods. *World Bank*. Retrieved August 12, 2018, from https://doi.org/10.1596/978-1-4648-0190-7.

CIP, CMI, & U4. (2016). *Os custos da corrupção para a economia moçambicana: Porquê é que é importante combater a corrupção num clima de fragilidade fiscal*. Maputo: Centro de Integridade Pública (CIP).

Deloitte. (2016). *Mozambique' s economic outlook: Governance challenges holding back economic potential*. Retrieved August 4, 2018 from https://www2.deloitte.com/content/dam/Deloitte/za/Documents/africa/ZA_Mozambique country_report_25012017.pdf.

Governo de Moçambique. (2015). *Plano Quinquenal do Governo 2015–2019*. Maputo: Governo de Moçambique.

IESE. (2017). Desafios para Moçambique 2016. *Instituto de Estudos Sociais E Económicos, nº7*(April 2017), 218. Retrieved May 30, 2018 from www.iese.ac.mz.

Industrial Development Corporation. (2012). Tourism report: The business hotel industry in select East and West African countries. *Department of Research and Information* (May), 14–15.

INE. (2015). *Anuário Estatístico 2015- Moçambique*. Maputo: Instituto Nacional de Estatística, Republica de Moçambique.

INE. (2016). Estatísticas do Turismo 2014–2016. *Instituto Nacional de Estatística, Republica de Moçambique*.

INE. (2017). Divulgacao dos resultados preliminares do IV RGPH 2017. *Instituto Nacional de Estatística, Republica de Moçambique*, 4. Retrieved June 12, 2018 from http://www.ine.gov.mz/operacoes-estatisticas/censos/censo-2007/censo-2017/divulgacao-de-resultados-preliminares-do-iv-rgph-2017.pdf.

INE. (2018). Contas Nacionais de Moçambique : IV Trimestre 2017. *Instituto Nacional de Estatística, República de Moçambique*. Retrieved August 4, 2018 from www.ine.gov.mz.

Jones, S. (2010). The economic contribution of tourism in mozambique: Insights from a social accounting matrix. *Development Southern Africa, 27*(5), 679–696. https://doi.org/10.1080/0376835X.2010.522831.

Koehne, A. (2007). File:Mozambique map cities.png – Wikimedia Commons. Retrieved September 20, 2018, from https://commons.wikimedia.org/wiki/File:Mozambique_map_cities.png.

Kroll. (2017). Auditoria independente relativa aos empréstimos contraídos pela ProIndicus S. A., EMATUM S. A. e Mozambique Asset e Management S.A. *Portal Do Governo de Moçambique*. Retrieved August 29, 2018 from http://www.portaldogoverno.gov.mz/por/Governo/Documentos.

Massingue, N., & Muianga, C. (2013). *Tendências e padrões de investimento privado em Moçambique: Questões para análise desafios para Moçambique*. Retrieved August 7, 2018 from http://www.iese.ac.mz/lib/publication/livros/des2013/IESE_Des2013_5.PadInvPriv.pdf.

MICULTUR. (2014). *Plano Estratégico para o Desenvolvimento do Turismo em Moçambique (2016–2025)*. Maputo: Ministério da Cultrura e Turismo, República de Moçambique.

MICULTUR. (2015). *Indicadores de referência na área do turismo*. Maputo: Ministério da Cultrura e Turismo, República de Moçambique.

MICULTUR. (2017). *Estratégia de Marketing (2017–2021)*. Maputo: Ministério da Cultrura e Turismo, República de Moçambique.

MITUR. (2004*). Plano Estratégico para o Desenvolvimento do Turismo em Moçambique*. Maputo: Ministério de Turismo, República de Moçambique.

MITUR. (2006). *Estratégia de Marketing Turístico 2006–2013*. Maputo: Ministério de Turismo, República de Moçambique.

Mosca, J. (2012). *Economia Moçambicana 2001–2010: Um mix de populismo económico e mercado selvagem* (No. 114/2012). Lisboa.

MOZEFO. (2015). Os desafios do turismo em Moçambique: Crescimento, Inovação e diversificação. *MOZEFO – Fórum Económico E Social de Moçambique*. Retrieved July 18, 2018, from http://www.mozefo.com/biblioteca_online.php.

Muchangos, A. dos. (1999). *Moçambique: Paisagens e regiões naturais*. (A. dos Muchangos, Ed.). Retrieved Jun 06, 2018, from https://doi.org/01048/FBM/93.

Portal do Governo de Moçambique. (2015). Geografia de Moçambique. Retrieved July 18, 2018, from http://www.portaldogoverno.gov.mz/por/Mocambique/Geografia-de-Mocambique.

The World Bank. (2016). *Actualidade económica de Moçambique – Navegando preços baixos. Mozambique Economic Update*. Washington, DC: World Bank Group.

The World Bank. (2017). *Mozambique economic uptade: Making the most of demographic change*. Retrieved July 18, 2018, from http://documents.worldbank.org/curated/pt/386461513950634764/pdf/122234-REVISED-Mozambique-Economic-Update-December-2017-EN.pdf.

The World Bank. (2018). Moçambique: Aspectos gerais. Retrieved July 18, 2018, from http://www.worldbank.org/pt/country/mozambique/overview.

UNESCO. (2017). *UNESCO Moçambique: relatório anual 2016; 2017*. Maputo. Retrieved July 18, 2018, from http://unesdoc.unesco.org/images/0026/002603/260351POR.pdf.

United Nations Statistics Division. (2018). UNdata. Retrieved August 5, 2018, from http://data.un.org/.

UNWTO. (2018). *2017 International tourism results: The highest in seven years. UNWTO World Tourism Barometer* (Vol. 16). Retrieved March 14, 2018, from http://cf.cdn.unwto.org/sites/all/files/pdf/unwto_barom17_03_june_excerpt_1.pdf.

WEF. (2011). *The travel & tourism competitiveness report 2011. Tourism*. Geneva. https://doi.org/10.5585/podium.v5i1.156.

WEF. (2017). *The travel & competitiviness report 2017: Paving the way for a more sustainable and inclusive future*. Geneva. Retrieved March 15,2018, from https://doi.org/ISBN-13: 978-1-944835-08-8.

World Tourism Organization. (2018). Mozambique. Retrieved from World Tourism Organization (2018), Compendium of tourism statistics dataset [Electronic], UNWTO, Madrid, data updated on 12/01/2018. Conceptual references and technical notes are available in the Methodological Notes http://statistics.unwto.org/news/2017.

WTTC. (2017). Travel & tourism economic impact 2017 Mozambique, 24.

WTTC. (2018a). Travel & tourism economic impact 2018 Mozambique. Retrieved August 4, 2018, from https://www.wttc.org/-/media/files/reports/economic-impact-research/countries-2018/malaysia2018.pdf.

WTTC. (2018b). *Travel & tourism economic impact 2018 Sub Saharan Africa*. London. Retrieved August 8, 2018, from https://www.wttc.org/-/media/files/reports.

Zacarias, D. A. (2013). Políticas públicas de desenvolvimento do turismo em Moçambique: Da panaceia à prática. In F. F. Azevedo, S. L. Figueiredo, W. Nóbrega, & C. H. Maranhão (Eds.), *Turismo em foco* (pp. 229–247). Belém: NAEA.

25

Development of tourism in Tanzania

Strengthening agriculture – tourism linkages

John Thomas Mgonja

Introduction

In the recent past, Tanzania has become one of sub-Saharan Africa's most popular and rapidly growing tourist destinations. The country is endowed with abundant natural resources including beautiful, spacious beaches and overflowing wildlife in protected areas. The country is also gifted with a myriad of adventurous landscapes as well as extensive cultural resources (the country has more than 150 ethnic tribes) making it a multicultural country with high cultural diversity.

In the last five years Tanzania has been voted the best safari country in Africa due to the quality and abundance of its natural and cultural resources (Mgonja, Sirima & Mkumbo, 2015; URT, 2013). The county has four notable safari circuits/zones each one making Tanzania a top wildlife destination. The popular Northern circuit with the Serengeti and Ngorongoro crater offers one of the best classical safaris in the World, especially if timed with the annual wildebeest migration (Safari Bookings, 2018). The country is applauded for possessing unmatched wildlife populations and wilderness scenery, with around 30% of the country's total land area set aside in exclusive state-protected areas (Brockington, 2008; Nelson, 2012), making Tanzania as one of the fastest growing global nature-based tourism destinations. The Government of Tanzania views tourism as a significant industry in terms of poverty alleviation, foreign exchange earnings and offering employment opportunities either directly or indirectly through its multiplier effects. The sector directly accounts for about 18% of the GDP and directly supports the estimated 500,000 jobs (2016) and 1,389,000 jobs (direct, indirect and induced). Foreign exchange receipts from tourism grew from US$ 259.44 million in 1995 to $ 2.1 billion in 2016. Over the past ten years, the annual increase in tourist arrivals has been around 9% while the receipts have been around 6.2% (WTTC, 2017).

Due to benefits obtained from tourism, governments in developing countries are becoming increasingly aware of the need to support the tourism sector; unfortunately in many cases policy development, regulations and legal frameworks are still at the planning or infancy stage (Newsome, Moore & Dowling, 2002), and in some cases acting as an obstacle for sustainable tourism development (Krutwaysho & Bramwell, 2010). This chapter analyses the social and economic context under which tourism development in Tanzania has been taking place over time and provides some critique of the potentials it has in enhancing economic development and well-being of Tanzania citizens. Specifically, the chapter focuses on tourism development trajectory following the 1990s institutional reforms. It also focuses on tourism trends (i.e. number of tourists and receipts) over time. The chapter also focuses on agriculture-tourism linkages as an area that has received less attention when it comes to tourism development in Tanzania.

Development of tourism in Tanzania: the historical perspectives

In recent years, Tanzania has experienced a remarkable growth in its tourism sector following major transformations in its tourism policies in the 1990s (Wade, Mwasaga, & Eagles, 2001). To fully understand tourism development trajectory in Tanzania, one needs to understand the political and economic history of the country as a whole. Tanzania attained its independence in 1961 from Britain. Six years later (i.e. 1967) the country adopted a socialist ideology, 'ujamaa'. Ujamaa is a Swahili word which means 'extended family', 'brotherhood', 'family hood' or 'socialism'. As a political concept, it asserts that a person becomes a person *through the people* or community. Ujamaa was centred on collective agriculture, under a process called villagization. It also called for the nationalization of banks and industry (including tourism), and an increased level of self-reliance at both an individual and at the national level (Nyerere, 1970). Socialism as a political framework advocated for a system of collective or government ownership and management of the means of production and distribution of goods and services (Hansen, 2012; Makulilo, 2012). The purpose of socialism in Tanzania was to create a classless society where individual citizens enjoy equally the resources of the country. The ujamaa policy did not succeed as envisaged due to a number of reasons including the oil crisis of the 1770s, the collapse of export commodity prices and consecutive droughts. The economic crisis of the 1970s swung Tanzania to adopt Structural Adjustment Programmes (SAPs) which were primarily grounded in liberalism (Mohan, 2013). This situation led Tanzania to the dilemma of having liberalism and socialism at the same time.

Ujamaa policy did not favour private sector and so tourism industry development at that time occurred at a much slower pace compared to neighbouring countries such as Kenya where the private sector led the economy. Wade et al. (2001) make the case that after independence, the tourism industry in Tanzania was characterized by poor transportations, poor accommodations and information facilities, weak internal tourism education and poorly funded tourism institutional frameworks. Because of these negative enabling environments, the tourism industry performance in Tanzania for much of the first 30 years after independence (1961–1990) had been poor and unsatisfactory. Supporters of neoliberal policies agree with this contention by arguing that tourism development in Tanzania prior to the mid-1980s was hindered by the ujamaa policy, which promoted the state-led economy at the detriment of the private sector (Chambua, 2007).

The government of Tanzania started implementing institutional reforms in the early 1990s, marking a major shift from the government-led economy to a private sector-led economy (MNRT, 2002). Since then there have been significant improvements in the performance of the economy and the tourism industry in particular. Many scholars seem to agree that tourism in Tanzania began to pick up at the beginning of the 1990s because of the economic liberalization policies (Kulindwa et al., 2001; Luvanga & Shitundu, 2003; Ranja, 2002).

The 1990s institutional reform entailed a number of initiatives including the formation of TTB. In 1992, the Tanganyika National Tourist Board Act of 1962 was repealed with the introduction of the Tanzania Tourist Board Act 1992, which subsequently led to the establishment of the Tanzania Tourist Board (TTB). The Board is mandated with the promotion and development of all the aspects of the tourism industry in Tanzania (MNRT, 2002). In terms of promoting the tourism industry (which is one of the main roles of TTB), the country has been participating in various international and national tourist trade fairs. For instance, between 2004 and 2018, Tanzania participated in trade fairs in the United Arab Emirates, India, France, China, Canada, Unites States, Japan, Spain, Russia, the United Kingdom and South Africa at the international level. At the local level, TTB participates annually at Karibu/Kili Travel Fair in Arusha and the Dar es Salaam International Trade Fair (Saba Saba). Karibu/Kili fair provides an excellent opportunity for participants and the general public to network and makes new contacts with partners of the tourism industry in Tanzania in addition to learning about local tourist attractions (Kilifair, 2018).

Another important milestone reached under the 1990's institutional reform is the development of the integrated Tourism Master Plan of 1996 which was reviewed in 2002. One of the strengths of the 1996 Tourism Master Plan is that it advocated for developing Community-Based Tourism (CBT) on village lands in the country, in an attempt to promote tourism outside protected areas for the 'benefit of the local communities' (MNRT, 2002). CBT is a tourism niche in which local people are directly involved in designing, organizing tours and showing tourists some aspects of their lives (Dangi & Jamal, 2016; Mtapuri & Giampiccoli, 2016; URT, 2010). Currently, there are about 50 CBTs (also known as Cultural Tourism Programmes – CTPs) in the country (Nelson, 2004; Salazar, 2012).

Another significant milestone reached under the institutional reform is a revision of the National Tourism Policy in 1999 which was subsequently followed by the setting up of the Tourism Confederation of Tanzania (TCT) to represent the interests of the private sector. TCT is a private sector body that was intended to be the representative, voice of the tourism private sector interests. TCT regulates about 12 private sector associations such as tour operators, travel agencies, hotel associations and all others in the value chain. The push behind policy revision has been towards stimulating more active engagement of the private sector in tourism business, in parallel with the disengagement of the Government from the sole ownership and operation of tourist facilities. The overarching objective of the policy review was to promote the economy and livelihood of the people, essentially poverty alleviation through encouraging the development of sustainable and quality tourism that is culturally and socially acceptable, ecologically friendly, environmentally sustainable and economically viable. The review also came into force as a result of the government recognizing that the private sector plays a major role in the tourism industry development (Melubo, 2017; Musa, 2011)

The hospitality industry in the country has also made a significant change as a result of the 1990s institutional reform. Before the 1990s reform, most hotels and lodges were in a state of decay, and only a handful of international standard hotels existed within the country. Currently, there are 174 registered tourist hotels in the country with a total capacity of approximately 21,929 branded rooms enough to carter for 1,140,156 tourists (URT, 2016a). However, according to Hotel Partners Africa (HPA), this figure leaves the country with a rate of 63 branded rooms per million populations, which is below the Sub Saharan Region and Africa's average at 76 and 106 branded rooms per million populations respectively. These statistics show also that in general Tanzania is even further away from 365 branded bedrooms per million populations recommended by HPA for countries in the SSA (Tanzaniainvest, 2016).

The country has also made some significant changes in human resources development in tourism and hospitality in the past three decades. At the moment, there are 65 tourism training programmes that are offered at different levels including one Master's degree programme,

Table 25.1 Tourism attractions and activities in national parks/protected areas in Tanzania

National park/protected area	Visitors In 2013	Park size (km²)	Tourism activities	Best time to visit
Serengeti (Northern zone)	452,485	14,750 km² (5695mi²)	Hot air balloon safaris, walking safaris, picnicking, game drives, Maasai rock paintings and musical rocks.	Any time of the year, though the dry season (from late June to October) offers the best wildlife viewing in general
Ngorongoro Conservation area (Northern zone)	350,970	8,292 km² (3,202 mi²)	Walking safaris, picnicking, game drives, sightseeing (e.g. Ngorongoro Crater, Olduvai Gorge, Ol Doinyo Lengai volcano and Lake Natron's flamingos.	The scenery is lush and spectacular in the Wet season (November to May). General wildlife viewing (June to September)
Lake Manyara (Northern zone)	187,773	648.7 km² (402 mi²)	Game drives, canoeing, cultural tours, picnicking, mountain bike tours, abseiling and forest walks.	Throughout the year. However, June to October is the best time for large mammals and November to July is ideal time for bird watching.
Tarangire (Northern zone)	165,949	2,850 km² (1100 mi²)	Walking safaris, day trips to Maasai and Barabaig villages, ancient rock paintings in the vicinity of Kolo on the Dodoma Road.	Year round though Late June to October is the best time for large mammals
Arusha (Northern zone)	71,930	552 km² (212 mi²)	Forest walks, bird watching, numerous picnic sites, Mt. Meru climbing.	June-Feb. Although it may rain in Nov. Best views of Kilimanjaro December–February.
Mt. Kilimanjaro (Northern zone)	53,254	1,668 km² (644 mi²)	Mt. Kilimanjaro climbing, hiking Shira plateau, nature trails on the lower reaches, Trout fishing, visit the Chala crater lake on the mountain's southeastern slopes and bird watching	Mountain climbing can be done throughout the year. However, the best time is mid-June– October and December–mid March.
Mikumi (Southern zone)	45,888	3,230 km² (1247 mi²)	Game drives and guided walks.	The dry season (May- October). However, the Northern part of the park is accessible throughout the year.
Ruaha (Southern zone)	21,766	20,226 km² (7809 mi²)	Bird watching, game drives, sightseeing including cultural and historical sites.	May–October (dry season) and November–April (wet season)

Park (zone)	Number	Area	Activities	Best time to visit
Saadani (Eastern zone)	14,709	1,100 km² (425mi²)	Boat safari, watching green turtle breeding site, snorkeling in the caves with colorful fish and green turtles, lunch and sunbathing, walking safari on natural trails of Saadani, game drives, relax on the cleanest beach	Throughout the year
Udzungwa (Southern zone)	7,131	1990 km² (768 mi²)	Hiking to the waterfalls, camping safaris, sightseeing, bird watching	Dry season (June–September) and wet season (November–March)
Saanane (Western zone)	5,150	2.18 km² (0.84 mi²)	Game viewing, bird watching, rock hiking, boat cruise, walking, picnics, bush lunch, meditation photographing/filming and sport fishing. Ideal place for wedding, engagement, team building, family day and birthdays	All year round is possible: birdlife is most varied and scenery greenest over Nov-March. June-August is the dry season and great for iconic, game viewing and rock hiking.
Mahale (Western zone)	1,094	1,650 km² (637 mi²)	Chimp tracking, walking safaris, kayaking, hiking to the sacred peek, camping safaris, snorkeling, sports fishing, water sports activities	The dry season (May–Nov.) but can be visited also in the wet season (Dec– April)
Katavi (Western zone)	4,275	4,471 km² (1726 mi²)	Walking safari, driving and camping safaris, visiting the tamarind tree inhabited by the spirit of the legendary hunter Katabi (for whom the park is named) – offerings are still left here by locals seeking the spirit's blessing.	May to October and mid-December.
Gombe (Western zone)	1,771	56 km² (22 mi²)	Chimpanzee trekking, hiking, bird watching, swimming and snorkeling; sightseeing including dhow building	Year-round. However, for plants/insects and better chimpanzee spotting, the best time is (Nov to mid-May) and for the best photo taking (May–October).
Mkomazi (Northern zone)	1,806	3,245 km² (1253 mi²)	Game drives, camping, sightseeing, bird watching, walking safari and hiking (uphill). Learn more about conservation and rhinoceros at Mkomazi rhino sanctuary.	June–January.
Rubondo (Western zone)	908	457 km² (176 mi²)	Game drives, bird watching, walking safaris.	May–October and mid-December.
Kitulo (Southern zone)	433	413 km² (159 mi²)	Hiking, open walking across grasslands to watch birds and wildflowers, Matema Beach on Lake Nyasa. There are documented 350 species of wild flowers including lilies and fields of daisies.	The park is carpeted in wildflowers for six months of the year, from November to April.

Source: Adapted from TANAPA, 2018.

eight Bachelor's degree programme, six Diploma programmes, 14 Technical certificate programmes and 36 Basic vocational certificate programmes (Anderson, 2015). While this is a success story, as a whole the tourism and hospitality industries in Tanzania is still lagging behind in terms of providing quality products and services and thus, the government in collaboration with the private sector need to put more efforts in strengthening human resources training institutions to cope up with the ever-increasing demand.

As for the infrastructure development (roads, utilities, telecommunications and transport), the country has also made some significant changes as a result of the 1990s institutional reform. For instance, the road from Arusha en-route Lake Manyara and Serengeti National Parks which was so dilapidated in the 1980s and 1990s is now in a good order and is accessible throughout the year. Similarly, road infrastructures in main town areas and areas with major tourism potentials (Table 25.1) have been improved, making traveling conducive, safe and efficient. Other significant changes that have been made in infrastructure development include formulation of air access transport policy and plan, attraction of more international carriers, development of Kilimanjaro International Airport (KIA) and expansion of Julius Nyerere International Airport (JNIA) to facilitate tourism movement. As for the national carrier, in 2016 the government decided to develop a specific programme for revamping its national carrier which included purchasing of six new aircraft between 2016 and 2018, paying off debts, provision of startup capital, improvement and modernization of business system (Citizen, 2016). Improvement of infrastructure such as roads and air transport is critically important as it gives tourists easy access to wildlife sanctuaries (Table 25.1). Although significant changes have been made in infrastructure improvement, there are still more challenges in infrastructure development particularly in the southern and western tourism corridors.

Tourism trends in Tanzania: from 1950 to 2016

According to WEF (2017), Tanzania's wildlife resources are considered among the finest in the world (8th position globally). These include the famous Serengeti ecosystem which hosts the largest terrestrial mammal migration in the world, the Ngorongoro Crater, the world's largest intact volcanic caldera and home to the highest density of big game in Africa, and Africa's highest mountain Kilimanjaro. Tanzania contains approximately 20% of the species of Africa's large mammal population, found across its reserves, conservation areas, marine parks and national parks, spread over an area of more than 42,000 square kilometres (16,000 sq mi) and forming approximately 38% of the country's land (Tegegn, 2014). The Diversity and abundance of flora and fauna in these areas makes a game drive one of the most interesting tourism activities in the country (Figure 25.1). The 2016 International Visitors' Exit Survey shows that wildlife watching (game drive) continues to be one of the main tourism activities in Tanzania (Figure 25.1).

In terms of Travel and Tourism Competitiveness Index (Table 25.2), Tanzania ranks at 91st position in the world (TTCR, 2017 ranking), with Spain leading in the list (WEF, 2017). Although there have been some improvements geared towards attracting more tourists, Tanzania's business environment (102nd) is still considered to be slow and costly particularly in starting a business or obtaining construction permits (WEF, 2017).

On the same note, safety and security (92nd), health and hygiene conditions (125th) and the uptake of ICTs (121st) are still considered to be improving at a slower pace compared to other countries in the region (Table 25.2). Overall it can be argued that despite its immense potential, Tanzania still has important gaps to fill in order to fully leverage the T&T sector as a means to improve the living conditions of Tanzania citizens (WEF, 2017).

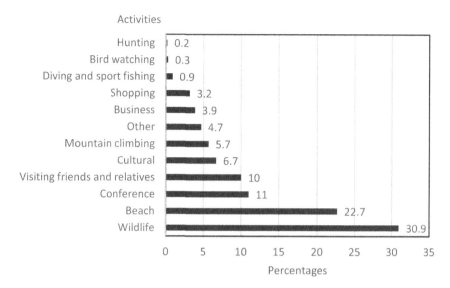

Figure 25.1 Tourism activities in Tanzania
Source: The 2016 International Visitors' Exit Survey.

Despite slow pace in improvement in a business environment, safety and security, health and hygiene, human resources development and ICT readiness, the tourism industry has shown a remarkable growth over the past two decades in Tanzania (Table 25.3) and has continued to be among the key sectors in generating foreign exchange in the country. For instance, in 2016, the tourism industry continued to grow, with the number of tourist arrivals increasing by 12.9% to 1,284,279 from 1,137,182 recorded in 2015. Subsequently, the county's tourism earnings rose by 12.1% to USD 2,131.6 million in 2016 from USD 1,902.0 million recorded in 2015. In 1996 the country received 326,188 international visitors corresponding with USD 322.37 million, while in 1995 the country received 295,312 international tourists corresponding with USD 259.44 million (WTTC, 2017). This is a remarkable growth in the tourism industry in two decades period. This increase is arguably the result of the Tanzanian government strategies and policies that were introduced in 1990s to reform the tourism sector so as to establish Tanzania as a prime safari and beach destination in Africa. However, the number of international tourists is still low compared to the potentials that the country has. In 2020 the inbound tourist arrivals are expected to reach 2 million and by 2025, Tanzania's tourism sector is expected to record about 3 million inbound tourists, growing at a rate of 6.2% per annum, against an expected world average growth of 3.7% (MNRT, 2014).

According to the 2016 International Visitors' Exit survey report, in 2016 the majority of tourists in Tanzania arrived from Kenya, accounting for 18.2% of all international tourists (Figure 25.2). This is an increase of 18.3% to 233,730 compared with 197,562 visitors recorded in 2015 (Table 25.4). Most likely this was due to improved infrastructure particularly telecommunications and transport as well as due to increasing socio-economic interactions in the region. The United State of America was the second largest source market, followed by India and the United Kingdom. It is argued that the sharp increase in the number of visitors from India in 2016 is largely contributed by Dawoodi Bohra's Milad-un-Nabi celebrations that took place in Dar es Salaam in October 2016 (URT, 2016b).

Table 25.2 Travel and Tourism Competitiveness Index 2017: sub-Saharan Africa

| | | Enabling environment (Score ranging from 0 to 7): | | | | | | | | | |
| Country | Global rank/ 136 countries | Business environment | | Safety and security | | Health and hygiene | | Human resources and labor market | | ICT readiness | |
		Score	Rank	Score	Rank	Score	Rank	Score	Rank	Score	Rank
South Africa	53	5.3	21	3.9	120	3.8	113	4.6	63	4.4	68
Namibia	82	4.9	38	5.2	82	3.5	117	4.1	106	3.9	90
Botswana	85	5.1	30	5.3	77	3.5	118	4.5	72	4.1	83
Zambia	108	4.6	52	5.4	73	2.7	131	4.1	109	2.8	118
Zimbabwe	114	3.0	134	5.5	60	2.9	128	3.6	127	2.9	117
Lesotho	128	4.2	93	5.4	71	2.9	124	3.6	128	3.2	113
SA average		4.5		5.1		3.2		4.1		3.5	
Mauritius	55	5.2	24	5.9	33	5.3	69	4.8	48	4.5	65
Kenya	80	4.4	70	3.4	129	3.2	120	4.5	76	3.4	106
Tanzania	91	4.1	102	5.1	92	2.9	125	3.6	131	2.7	121
Rwanda	97	5.1	29	6.4	9	3.8	112	4.7	58	3.3	109
Uganda	106	4.3	87	4.6	104	2.8	130	4.0	115	2.8	119
Burundi	134	3.9	122	4.2	111	3.8	111	3.9	119	1.6	136
Ethiopia	116	4.0	118	4.9	99	4.5	102	3.7	125	2.6	125
Madagascar	121	3.6	126	5.0	93	3.3	119	3.8	122	2.1	133
Mozambique	122	4.2	94	4.6	105	1.8	136	3.6	129	2.6	123
Malawi	123	4.2	99	5.4	74	3.0	123	4.2	97	2.5	127
Congo, DR	133	4.1	107	4.0	117	2.8	129	3.9	118	1.6	135
EA average		4.3		4.9		3.4		4.0		2.7	

Source: Adapted from WEF, 2017: SA= Southern Africa, EA= Eastern Africa.

Table 25.3 Tourist arrivals and receipts in Tanzania from 1950 to 2018

Year	Number of tourists	Receipts (USD millions)	Year	Number of tourists	Receipts (USD millions)
1950	3,720	NA	1985	81,821	10.30
1951	5,120	NA	1986	103,361	20.00
1952	5,830	NA	1987	130,851	31.05
1953	6,700	NA	1988	130,343	40.40
1954	6,210	NA	1989	137,889	60.00
1955	7,930	NA	1990	153,000	65.00
1956	9,500	NA	1991	186,800	94.73
1957	10,600	NA	1992	201,744	120.04
1958	7,630	NA	1993	230,166	146.84
1959	7,880	NA	1994	261,595	192.10
1960	7,530	NA	1995	295,312	259.44
1961	7,350	NA	1996	326,188	322.37
1962	9,260	NA	1997	359,096	392.39
1963	9,880	NA	1998	482,331	570.00
1964	7,140	NA	1999	627,325	733.28
1965	8,280	NA	2000	501,669	739.06
1966	13,460	NA	2001	525,000	725.00
1967	20,180	NA	2002	575,000	730.00
1968	NA	NA	2003	576,000	731.00
1969	NA	NA	2004	582,807	746.06
1970	58,819	13.39	2005	612,754	823.05
1971	68,400	13.65	2006	644,124	950.00
1972	199,200	27.66	2007	719,031	1,198.76
1973	143,500	20.50	2008	770,376	1,288.69
1974	175,500	12.81	2009	714,367	1,159.82
1975	155,412	9.89	2010	782,699	1,254.50
1976	165,839	10.52	2011	867,994	1,353.29
1977	118,000	9.00	2012	1,077,058	1,712.75
1978	148,500	12.73	2013	1,095,884	1,853.28
1979	78,000	16.94	2014	1,140,156	2,006.32
1980	NA	NA	2015	1,137,182	1,902.00
1981	92,000	21.61	2016	1,284,279	2,131.57
1982	71,290	15.22	2017	1,327,143	2,258.96
1983	54,000	12.81	2018	1,505,702	2,412.30
1984	64,000	9.38			

Source: Ouma, 1970; Vojislav, 1972; UNWTO, 2017, 2019; NBS, 2016; URT, 2016b. URT, 2019. NA= Not Available.

According to the World Tourism and Travel Council (WTTC, 2017), the direct contribution of Travel & Tourism to GDP in 2016 in Tanzania was TZS 4, 585.5bn (4.7% of GDP). This primarily reflects the economic activity generated by industries such as hotels, travel agents, airlines and other passenger transportation services (excluding commuter services). It also includes various activities of the restaurant and leisure industries directly supported by tourists. The direct contribution of Travel & Tourism to GDP is expected to grow by 6.8%

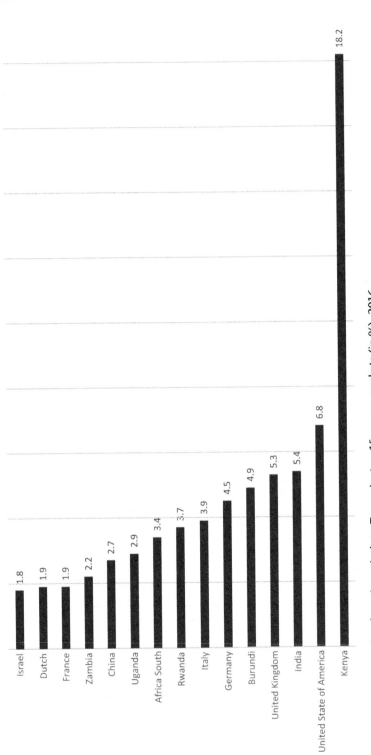

Figure 25.2 International tourist arrivals to Tanzania, top 15 source markets (in %), 2016
Source: Immigration Services Department, 2016.

pa to TZS 9,192.3bn (4.7% of GDP) by 2027. In terms of job creation, Travel & Tourism generated 446,000 jobs directly in 2017 (3.3% of total employment) excluding commuter services but including, employment by hotels, travel agents, airlines and other passenger transportation services (Figure 25.3). The figure also includes, for example, the activities of

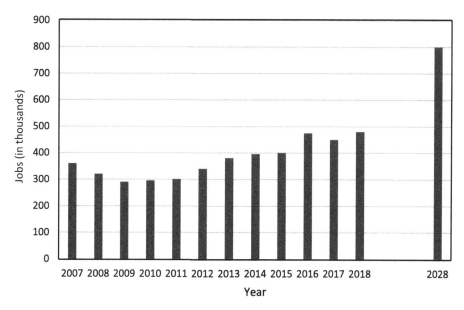

Figure 25.3 Tanzania: direct contribution of Travel & Tourism to employment
Source: (WTTC, 2018).

Table 25.4 Nationality of visitors arriving to Tanzania from 2013 to 2016

Country/territory	2016	2015	2014	2013
Kenya	233,730	197,562	188,214	193,078
United States	86,860	66,394	80,489	69,671
India	69,876	32,608	27,327	27,334
United Kingdom	67,742	54,599	70,379	59,279
Burundi	63,530	48,210	51,553	34,873
Germany	57,643	52,236	47,262	53,951
Italy	50,715	53,742	49,518	57,372
Rwanda	47,056	45,216	50,038	46,637
South Africa	43,468	30,288	26,614	31,144
Uganda	37,870	37,253	36,420	39,488
China	34,472	25,444	N/A	N/A
Zambia	28,836	32,694	36,679	64,825
France	24,611	28,683	33,585	33,335
Netherlands	24,197	20,150	23,710	20,633
Israel	22,967	N/A	N/A	N/A
Zimbabwe	22,148	30,533	36,497	30,765
Mozambique	N/A	27,323	N/A	N/A

Source: NBS, 2018; The 2016 International Visitors' Exit survey report, 2016.

the restaurant and leisure industries directly supported by tourists. By 2028, Travel & Tourism is expected to account for 795,000 jobs directly, an increase of 5.2% pa over the next ten years (WTTC, 2018).

Strengthening agriculture-tourism linkages: a strategy to enhance sustainable tourism in Tanzania

There is no doubt that Travel & Tourism and agriculture sectors are of paramount importance to the economy and welfare of many people in Tanzania, both in urban and rural areas (Amani, 2005; Sarris, Savastano & Christiaensen, 2006; URT, 2016b; WEF, 2017; WTTC, 2017). The majority (almost 70%) of the Tanzanian population live in rural areas (World Bank, 2018), and almost all of them are involved in the agricultural and/or livestock sector. In many rural areas, agriculture is the sole source of income and represents a significant source of livelihood to about 80% of the population in Tanzania. Regrettably, there is a weak linkage (both backward and forward) between these two sectors despite their importance in reducing rural poverty in the country. Agriculture and Tourism Linkages are generally subscribed to as a means of distributing tourism benefits to host communities in tourism dependent developing countries and that supply of local food to hotels is one channel in which these linkages can be facilitated (Mgonja, 2015; Thomas-Francois, Von Massow & Joppe, 2017). Linkages are defined as 'the ability to develop productive relationships through the exchange of information and resources' (Larson & Shaw, 2001, p. 204).

Many scholars agree that there are a myriad of benefits to strengthening agriculture and tourism linkages. Such benefits include; reducing financial leakages and increasing multiplier effects (Cohen, 1982), increasing local ownership and involvement (Milne, 1987; Nyaupane et al., 2006; Sims, 2009; Stynes, 1997), boosting the development of sustainable agriculture and help conserve traditional farming landscapes (Buller & Morris, 2004; Ilbery et al., 2007), improving the local identity of a destination community, and hence bringing about more community participation and inclusion (Quan & Wang, 2004; UNWTO, 2017), promoting sustainable food production (Buller & Morris's, 2004), promoting food authenticity through locally produced foods (Sims, 2009) and reducing greenhouse gas emissions since local food travel minimal distances compared to imported foods (Gössling et al., 2011).

A good number of scholars in food and tourism linkages make the case that weak relationships between local food producers-hotel supply chain [agriculture - tourism] may potentially lead to economic leakages due to high food importation to support the tourism sector particularly in less developed economies such as Tanzania (Belisle, 1983; Henderson, 2009; Mgonja, 2015; Telfer & Wall, 1996; Torres, 2003). Similar sentiment has been echoed by other scholars arguing that the lack of strong linkages between agriculture and tourism sectors normally results in the high dependence on imported food to meet the food needs of the visiting populations (Clayton & Karagiannis, 2008; Meyer, 2007), leading into leakages. Economic leakages occur 'when revenue leaves the local destination as profits to non-local businesses or for the purchase of external goods and services' (Sandbrook, 2010, p. 21).

Further, research expounds that approximately one-third of tourism expenditure is spent on food. Therefore, strengthening linkages between the tourism and agricultural sectors through promoting the use of local foods is crucial and critical to many host destinations in realizing the full benefits of tourism development (Torres, 2003). A study conducted by Tourism confederation of Tanzania in 2009 about tourism value chain revealed that over 60% of all the revenue generated through tourism, goes outside the country through various routes such as airport taxes fuel surcharges (6.7%), foreign operators (15%), foreign airlines

(20%) and expert salaries and food and drinks imports (over 17.3%). The study showed that only 40% of the revenue is what is retained in the country (TCT, 2009).

As discussed earlier, the majority of Tanzanians are farmers, living in rural areas, therefore, solving the problem of weak farmer-hotel supply chain relationships is considered to be necessary for facilitating agriculture and tourism linkages and in reducing exacerbated rural poverty (Ramroth, 2006). The more rural communities (farmers) benefit from tourism through improved agriculture – tourism linkages, the more they are likely to support various conservation initiatives and vice versa, especially rural communities living adjacent to protected areas. The concept of strengthening inter-sectoral linkages such as agriculture – tourism linkages is not a new one. It has been promoted for many years as a viable means of economic development by World Bank affiliated economists (Linden & Mahmood, 2007).

In many parts of the world, agritourism has been highly promoted as an important strategy for diversifying rural livelihoods (Jęczmyk et al., 2014; Marsat et al., 2013). Some of the leading destinations in agritourism in the world include the United States, France, Italy, Australia, Greece, Canada and Austria (Amanor-Boadu, 2013; Rogerson & Rogerson, 2014). For instance, in Austria, Embacher (1994) makes the case that farmers represent approximately one-sixth of the total supply of tourism beds. This is a significant achievement in agritourism development. In Africa, the advantages of agritourism development have also been acknowledged for tourism economic growth and diversification. Some of the leading countries in Africa include Ghana and South Africa (Eshun &Tettey, 2014; Rogerson & Rogerson, 2014). In South Africa, the leading agritourism destinations include the attractions of the wine farms in the environs of Stellenbosch, Montagu, Tulbagh, Paarl and Worcester. Other areas that offer a highly diverse range of agritourism activities in South Africa include; George, Citrusdal, Knysna and Dullstroom in Mpumalanga (Rogerson & Rogerson, 2014). However, compared to Europe and the United States, agritourism in Africa, is still at the infant stage, with little contribution to rural livelihoods.

As for Tanzania, although the country is largely rural and heavily dependent on agriculture, at present there is very little documented concrete evidence of agritourism. Some accommodation establishments and tour companies offer agritourism (mostly coffee) linked activities in the northern tourist circuits. These include Wild tracks of Usa River, Haleluya Tours & safaris, Materuni waterfalls & coffee tour, Budget safari of Tanzania, Elewana collection, Timbuktu travel, Kahawa shambani coffee tours, Farms of dreams and Gibbs farm. Outside of the Northern zone, the two most notable agritourism destinations are Utengule coffee lodge in the Mbeya region and Irente farm lodge in Tanga region. Utengule lodge has remarkable terraced coffee gardens and offers guests a calm oasis with spectacular views across the East African Rift Valley. Irente farm lodge and biodiversity reserve offer a highly diverse range of attractions and it incorporates both environmental conservation and sustainable organic agriculture. Some of the potential areas for agritourism particularly wine tourism in the country include Dodoma and Singida regions in central Tanzania.

Agriculture and tourism linkages have a number of problems that are complex in nature and thus solving them requires government interventions to a large extent. Literature shows that in many cases, these problems are related to; absence of appropriate government policies, demand and supply issues, marketing issues as well as poor infrastructure such as communication and roads, poor food quality and safety along the entire food supply chain (Cohen & Avieli, 2004; Ko, 2010; Meyer, 2007; Pillay & Rogerson, 2013; Torres, 2003; Torres & Momsen, 2004).

Looking at the current national agriculture policy of 2013 and the national tourism policy of 1999 in Tanzania, one realizes that the question of agriculture-tourism linkages is not adequately addressed in these policies. Therefore, the government should review its agriculture and tourism policies to re-address the question of agriculture-tourism linkages. Agriculture and tourism sectors together play a significant role in reducing rural poverty and enhancing the economic well-being of local communities in Tanzania since the majority of Tanzania citizens live in rural areas where agriculture is the main employer. Torres (2003) argues that converting farmers and rural inhabitants into economic stakeholders and beneficiaries of tourism represents an important opportunity to improve the quality of life for the poorest and most marginalized populations, particularly in developing countries.

Conclusions

The position of the Travel & Tourism sector in 2017 remains robust and will most probably continue to be at the forefront of economic development and job creation in Tanzania, despite the ongoing challenges discussed in this chapter. The overall trend shows that the direct Travel & Tourism GDP growth is expected to accelerate in subsequent years despite these challenges. The growth of the Travel & Tourism sector in the country will continue to improve significantly so long as the government of Tanzania promotes public-private partnership through which tourism investment and development initiatives can take place in an open and sustainable manner. The government should be more pro-active in playing the catalytic role in providing a more conducive climate for the private sector to invest in the tourism industry business.

As exemplified by World Travel & Tourism Council in its 2017 report, enacting pro-growth travel policies that share benefits more equitably can foster a talent and business environment necessary to enable Travel & Tourism to realize its full potential. In doing so, Travel &Tourism will continue to provide the rationale for the further protection of natural resources and biodiversity in the country. This is necessary to address because, Tanzania's economy is largely driven by its natural resource, which forms the necessary base for the development of key sectors of the economy including tourism, mining and agriculture. However, as pointed out by other researchers, a viable tourism industry requires more than a range of natural and cultural attractions. A sound infrastructure along with a well-developed superstructure of facilities and amenities are also needed. The majority of tourism stakeholders in the country feel that Tanzania can command a premium price in its tourism products if the deficiencies in relation to the infrastructure, facilities and service standards are considerably improved.

Looking at the Travel & Tourism Competitiveness Index (2017), it is obvious that Tanzania still needs to put more effort to strengthen its competitiveness in the global market. For instance, out of 136 countries involved in the competitiveness ranking in the world, Tanzania ranks 91st (overall rank), Business Environment (102nd), Safety and Security (92nd), Health and Hygiene (125th), Human Resources and Labour Market (131st), ICT Readiness (121st), Prioritization of Travel & Tourism (45th), International Openness (64th), Price Competitiveness (34th), Environmental Sustainability (58th), Air Transport Infrastructure (106th), Ground and Port Infrastructure (102nd), Tourist Service Infrastructure (103rd), Natural Resources (8th), Cultural Resources and Business Travel (86th), Hotel reception capacity, remain low (119th). As indicated in the 2017 index, Tanzania has enormous untapped potential and that it has many important gaps to fill to leverage the full potential of Travel and Tourism. Although significant improvements are currently taking place in some areas (e.g. road, rail, water, telecommunication and air transport, human resource training), further improvements are still required so as to enable tourists to access various attractions in a quick, comfortable, and safe manner.

Tourism and agriculture are significantly important sectors to the economy and welfare of many people in Tanzania. Regrettably, there is a weak linkage between these two sectors despite their importance in reducing rural poverty in the country. The government and the private sector (which is at the forefront of the tourism industry) should formulate appropriate strategies to strengthen Tourism and agriculture linkages so that the tourism industry can significantly increase its impacts on local economic development. Such strategies should pay attention to common problems of sourcing products locally such as inadequate quality and safety, reliability issues, volume of produces, poor transport and weak information communication between local producers and purchasers, e.g. hotels.

References

Amani, H.K.R., 2005. *Making agriculture impact on poverty in Tanzania: The case on non-traditional export crops.* Paper Presented at a Policy Dialogue for Accelerating Growth and Poverty Reduction in Tanzania, ESRF, Dar-Es-Salaam, May, 2005.

Amanor-Boadu, V. (2013). Diversification decisions in agriculture: the case of agritourism in Kansas. *International Food and Agribusiness Management Review, 16*(1030–2016–82820), 57–74.

Anderson, W., 2015. *Human resource needs and skill gaps in the tourism and hospitality sector in Tanzania.* Tanzania: Consultancy Report submitted to The Ministry of Education and Vocational Training.

Belisle, F. J., 1983. Tourism and food production in the Caribbean. *Annals of Tourism Research, 10*(4), 497–513.

Brockington, D., 2008. Preserving the New Tanzania: Conservation and land use change. *The International Journal of African Historical Studies, 41*(3), 557–579.

Buller, H., & Morris, C., 2004. Growing goods: The market, state and sustainable food production. *Environment and Planning, 36*, 1065–1084.

Chambua, G., 2007. *Tourism and development in Tanzania: Myths and realities.* Paper presented at the 4th IIPT African Confrence "Building Strategic Alliances for Sustainable Tourism Development, Peace and Reconciliation on the African Continent", Kampala, Uganda.

Citizen, 2016. Revival of Air Tanzania on course with delivery of dreamliner plane. Retrieved on 22nd August, 2018 from http://www.thecitizen.co.tz/News/1840340-4639824-1nbjx8z/index.html.

Clayton, A., & Karagiannis, N., 2008. Sustainable tourism in the Caribbean: Alternative policy considerations. *Tourism and Hospitality Planning & Development, 5*(3), 185–201.

Cohen, E., 1982. Marginal paradises: Bungalow tourism on the islands of Southern Thailand. *Annals of Tourism Research, 9*(2), 189–228.

Cohen, E., & Avieli, N., 2004. Food in tourism: Attraction and impediment. *Annals of Tourism Research, 31*(4), 755–778.

Dangi, T., & Jamal, T., 2016. An integrated approach to 'sustainable community-based tourism'. *Sustainability, 8*(5), 475.

Embacher, H. 1994. Marketing for Agri-tourism in Austria: Strategy and realisation in a highly developed tourist destination. *Journal of Sustainable Tourism, 2*(1–2), 61–76.

Eshun, G., & Tettey, C., 2014. Agrotourism development in Ghana: A study of its prospects and challenges at Adjeikrom cocoa tour facility. *Bulletin of Geography. Socio-economic Series, 25*(25), 81–99.

Gössling, S., Garrod, B., Aall, C., Hille, J., & Peeters, J., 2011. Food management in tourism: Reducing tourism's carbon 'foodprint'. *Tourism Management, 32*, 534–543.

Hansen, P., 2012. Revisiting the remittance mantra: A study of migration–development policy formation in Tanzania. *International Migration, 50*(3), 77–91.

Henderson, J.C., 2009. Food tourism reviewed. *British Food Journal, 111*(4), 317–326.

Ilbery, B., Saxena, G., & Kneafsey, M., 2007. Exploring tourists and gatekeepers' attitudes towards integrated rural tourism in the England-Wales border region. *Tourism Geographies, 9*, 441–468.

Jęczmyk, A., Uglis, J., Graja-Zwolińska, S., Maćkowiak, M., Spychała, A., & Sikora, J., 2015. Research note: Economic benefits of agritourism development in Poland – An empirical study. *Tourism Economics, 21*(5), 1120–1126.

Kilifair, 2018. Kilimanjaro tourism & industry fair. Retrieved on 11 August, from https://www.trade-fairdates.com/KILIFAIR-M5149/Moshi.html.

Ko, W.H., 2010. Evaluating food safety perceptions and practices for agricultural food handler. *Food Control, 21*(4), 450–455.

Krutwaysho, O., & Bramwell, B., 2010. Tourism policy implementation and society. *Annals of Tourism Research, 37*(3), 670–691.

Kulindwa, K., Sosovele, H., & Mashindano, O., 2001. *Tourism growth for sustainable development in Tanzania.* Dar es Salaam: Dar es Salaam University Press.

Larson, D. W., & Shaw, T. K., 2001. Issues of microenterprise and agricultural growth: Do opportunities exist through forward and backward linkages? *Journal of Developmental Entrepreneurship, 6*(3), 203.

Linden, M., & Mahmood, T., 2007. *Long run relationships between sector shares and economic growth–A panel data analysis of the schengen region.* Finland: Economics and Business administration University of Joensuu.

Luvanga, N., & Shitundu, J., 2003. *The role of tourism in poverty alleviation in Tanzania.* Tanzania: Dar es Salaam.

Makulilo, V.B., 2012. Where is socialism in Tanzania? *Elixir Social Science, 46*, 8170–8180.

Marsat, J. B., Menegazzi, P., Monin, C., Bonniot, A., & Bouchaud, M., 2013. Designing a regional policy of agrotourism–the case of Auvergne region (France). *European Countryside, 5*(4), 308–321.

Melubo, K., 2017. Tanzania tourism policy review conference: 11–12 April 2017, Arusha, Tanzania. *Anatolia, 28*(4), 595–597.

Meyer, D., 2007. Pro-poor tourism: From leakages to linkages. A conceptual framework for creating linkages between the accommodation sector and 'poor'neighbouring communities. *Current Issues in Tourism,* 10(6), 558–583.

Mgonja, J.T., 2015. *Evaluating local food-tourism linkages as a strategy for promoting sustainable tourism and economic development: A case for Tanzania.* Unpblished PhD Dissertation, Parks, Recreation, and Tourism Management Department, University of Clemson, Clemson, USA.

Mgonja, J.T., Sirima, A., & Mkumbo, P.J., 2015. A review of ecotourism in Tanzania: Magnitude, challenges, and prospects for sustainability. *Journal of Ecotourism, 14*(2–3), 264–277.

Milne, S.S., 1987. Differential multipliers. *Annals of Tourism Research, 14*(4), 499–515.

MNRT, 2002. *'Tourism in Tanzania: Investment for Growth and Diversification', Washington multilateral investment guarantee agency/world bank group.* Tanzania: Dar es Salaam.

MNRT, 2014. *Ministry of natural resources and tourism. Tourism statistical bulletin, tourism division.* Tanzania: Dar es Salaam.

Mohan, G., 2013. Contested sovereignty and democratic contradictions: The political impacts of adjustment. In Brown, E., Milward, B., Mohan, G., & Zack-Williams, A. (Eds.) *Structural Adjustment: theory, practie and impacts* (pp. 95–114). London: Routledge.

Mtapuri, O., & Giampiccoli, A., 2016. Towards a comprehensive model of community-based tourism development. *South African Geographical Journal, 98*(1), 154–168.

Musa, I. A., 2011. An overview of tourism policy and plans for tourism development in Tanzania. A paper presented at the UNWTO regional seminar on tourism policy and strategies (Dar es salaam, Tanzania, 12nd–16th September 2011).

NBS, 2016. Tanzania national bureau of statistics. Publications. Hotel and tourism statistics. Retrieved on 12th August 2018 from http://www.nbs.go.tz/.

NBS, 2018. Tanzania national bureau of statistics. Publications. Hotel and tourism statistics. Retrieved on 10th August 2018 from http://www.nbs.go.tz/.

Nelson, F., 2004. *The evolution and impacts of community-based ecotourism in northern Tanzania* (Issue Paper No. 131). London: IIED.

Nelson, F., 2012. Blessing or curse? The political economy of tourism development in Tanzania. *Journal of Sustainable Tourism, 20*(3), 359–375.

Newsome, D., Moore, S. A., & Dowling, R. K., 2002. Natural area tourism: Ecology, impacts and management. Clevedon: Channel View Publications.

Nyaupane, G.P., Morais, D.B., & Dowler, L., 2006. The role of community involvement and number/type of visitors on tourism impacts: A controlled comparison of Annapurna, Nepal and Northwest Yunnan. *China, Tourism Management, 27*(6), 1373–1385.

Nyerere, J.K., 1970. *Ujamaa: The basis of African socialism.* Tanzania: Jihad Productions. Dar es Salaam.

Ouma, J.P.B.M., 1970. *Evolution of tourism in East Africa: 1900–2000.* Nairobi: East African Literature Bureau.

Pillay, M., & Rogerson, C. M., 2013. Agriculture-tourism linkages and pro-poor impacts: The accommodation sector of urban coastal KwaZulu-Natal, South Africa. *Applied Geography, 36*, 49–58.

Quan, S., & Wang, N., 2004. Towards a structural model of the tourist experience: An illustration from food experiences in tourism. *Tourism Management, 25*(3), 297–305.

Ramroth, W. G., 2006. *Pragmatism and modern architecture.* Jefferson, NC: McFarland.

Ranja, T., 2002. *Development of National Entrepreneurship in East Africa: The Case of Tourism and Petroleum Marketing Industry* Paper delivered as Paper 2 of the ESRF Globalisation Seminar Series. Dar es Salaam: Economic and Social Research Foundation

Rogerson, C. M., & Rogerson, J. M., 2014. Agritourism and local economic development in South Africa. *Bulletin of Geography. Socio-economic Series, 26*(26), 93–106.

Safari Bookings, 2018. Africa's best safari country. Retrieved on 11th August from https://www.safaribookings.com/countries-parks.

Salazar, NB, 2012. Community-based cultural tourism: Issues, threats and opportunities. *Journal of Sustainable Tourism, 20*(1), 9–22.

Sandbrook, C.G., 2010. Putting leakage in its place: The significance of retained tourism revenue in the local context in rural Uganda. *Journal of International Development: The Journal of the Development Studies Association, 22*(1), 124–136.

Sarris, A., Savastano, S., & Christiaensen, L., 2006. The role of agriculture in reducing poverty in Tanzania: A household perspective from rural Kilimanjaro and Ruvuma. *FAO Commodity and Trade Policy Research Working Paper Series, Number 19.* Rome: UN-Food and Agricultural Organisation. Available from http://www.fao.org/3/a-ah468e.pdf.

Sims, R., 2009. Food, place and authenticity: Local food and the sustainable tourism experience. *Journal of Sustainable Tourism, 17*(3), 321–336.

Stynes, D. J., 1997. Economic impacts of tourism, a handbook for tourism professionals, Illinois bureau of tourism, Illinois department of commerce and community affairs, prepared by the tourism research laboratory at the university of Illinois at Urbana-Champaign, IL, USA.

TANAPA (Tanzania National Parks), 2018. Sustainable conservation for development. Retrieved on 7th June, 2018 from http://www.tanzaniaparks.go.tz/#.

Tanzaniainvest, 2016. Tanzania seeks investments in hospitality industry to raise tourism competitiveness. Retrieved on 21st August, 2018 from https://www.tanzaniainvest.com/tourism/tanzania-seeks-investments-in-hospitality-industry-to-raise-tourism-competitiveness.

TCT (Tourism Confederation of Tanzania), 2009. *Tanzania tourism value chain study, Final Report.* Tanzania: Dar es Salaam.

Tegegn, M., 2014. The impact of dominant environment policies on indigenous peoples in Africa. In R. Laher & K. Sing'Oei (eds.), *Indigenous peoples in Africa: Contestations, empowerment and group rights* (pp. 45–63). Pretoria: Africa Institute of South Africa.

Telfer, D.J., & Wall, G., 1996. Linkages between tourism and food production. *Annals of tourism Research, 23*(3), 635–653.

Thomas-Francois, K., Von Massow, M., & Joppe, M., 2017. Strengthening farmers–hotel supply chain relationships: A service management approach. *Tourism Planning & Development, 14*(2), 198–219.

Torres, R., 2003. Linkages between tourism and agriculture in Mexico. *Annals of Tourism Research, 30*(3), 546–566.

Torres, R., & Momsen, J. H., 2004. Challenges and potential for linking tourism and agriculture to achieve pro-poor tourism objectives. *Progress in Development Studies, 4*(4), 294–318.

TTCR (The Travel & Tourism Competitiveness Report), 2017. Paving the way for a more sustainable and inclusive future. Retrieved on 10th August, 2018 from https://www.weforum.org/reports/the-travel-tourism-competitiveness-report-2017.

UNWTO (United Nations World Tourism Organization), 2017. World Tourism Barometer; Volume 13, May 2017.

UNWTO (United Nations World Tourism Organization), 2019. International Tourism Highlights. Retrieved on 24th September, 2019 from https://www.e-unwto.org/doi/pdf/10.18111/9789284421152.

URT (United Republic of Tanzania), 2010. Tanzania cultural tourism program. Retrieved on 21st January, 2014 from http://tanzaniaculturaltourism.go.tz/.

URT (United Republic of Tanzania), 2013. Ministry of Natural Resources and Tourism, Tanzania Tourist Board. Retrieved on 4th February, 2014 from http://www.tanzaniatouristboard.com.

URT (United Republic of Tanzania), 2016a. Investment in Hospitality Industry. Retrieved on 20th August, 2017 from http://www.mnrt.go.tz/.

URT (United Republic of Tanzania), 2016b. International visitors' exit survey report-2016. *International Tourist Arrivals*, 73. Retrieved on 12th August, 2018 from http://www.nbs.go.tz/nbs/takwimu/trade/The2016_International%20_Visitors'_Exit_Survey_Report.pdf.

URT (United Republic of Tanzania), 2019. *Ministry of natural resources & tourism. The 2018 tourism statistical bulletin*. Tanzania: Dar-Es-Salaam.

Vojislav, P., 1972. *Tourism in Eastern Africa*. München: Welt forum-Verlag.

Wade, D.J., Mwasaga, B.C., & Eagles, P.F., 2001. A history and market analysis of tourism in Tanzania. *Tourism Management, 22*(1), 93–101.

WEF (World Economic Forum), 2017. Insight report. The travel & tourism competitiveness report 2017. Paving the way for a more sustainable and inclusive future. Retrieved on 10th August 2018 from http://www3.weforum.org/docs/WEF_TTCR_2017_web_0401.pdf.

World Bank, 2018. Rural population (% of total population). Retrieved on 15th September 2018 from https://data.worldbank.org/indicator/SP.RUR.TOTL.ZS?locations=TZ.

WTTC (World Travel and Tourism Council), 2017. Travel & tourism economic impact 2017 Tanzania. Retrieved on 14th August, 2018 from https://www.wttc.org/-/media/files/reports/economic-impact-research/countries-2017/tanzania2017.pdf.

WTTC (World Travel and Tourism Council), 2018. Travel & tourism economic impact 2017 Tanzania. Retrieved on 24th August, 2018 from https://www.wttc.org/-/media/files/reports/economic-impact-research/countries-2018/tanzania2018.pdf.

26

Local community support in tourism in Mauritius – the case of Ray of Light by LUX*

Haywantee Ramkissoon and Vishnee Sowamber

Introduction

Tourism is an important sector for developing countries, especially for Small Island Developing States (SIDS), as it helps to improve the local economy (Kotler, Bowen & Makens, 2014; Al-Badi & Al-Sawaei, 2017). Tourism contributes towards upgrading the standard of living of residents through increased revenue, employment and investment (Ramkissoon, Mavondo & Uysal, 2018) and contributes to an improved quality of life (Rukuižienė, 2014). If tourism is managed in a sustainable manner, it has the potential to create positive value for stakeholders (Tyrrell, Paris & Biaett, 2013; Sowamber, Ramkissoon & Mavondo, 2018). However, tourism also brings negative impacts and social issues within the local community (Woo, Kim & Uysal, 2015) such as an increased cost of living for the locals especially with a rise in prices of properties (Tosun, 2002). The employment in tourism is often low paid and implies working odd hours, weekends and public holidays, which can heavily impact on residents' quality of life (Kim, 2008; Andereck & Nyaupane, 2011; Min, Kim & Lee, 2015).

Research suggests that there is opportunity for tourism operators and hoteliers to demonstrate concrete support to the local community within the destination where they are present through trainings and development (Ramkissoon & Sowamber, 2018). They can do so through their Corporate Social Responsibility (CSR) strategy, actions and stakeholder inclusiveness (Sowamber, Ramkissoon & Mavondo, 2018). Tourism operators can mitigate these impacts through robust CSR projects and initiatives by encouraging a stakeholder inclusive model. Tourism operators have the opportunity to engage in social sustainability to mitigate the negative social impacts. The social factor is considered to be a key area in management level decision-making in responsible business strategy (Dreyer, Hauschild & Schierbeck, 2010). This at the same time helps to maximise positive long-term financial objectives (Buser & Koch, 2014).

Local community's support is crucial for sustainable tourism development (Lee, Kang, Long & Reisinger, 2010; Nunkoo & Ramkissoon, 2010a, 2010b, 2011a; Lee, 2013). Sustainable development helps to enhance brand image, reduce cost and increase employee loyalty (Graci & Dodds, 2008) and also enhances value creation (Ramkissoon & Uysal, 2014). Sustainable tourism development can contribute to an improved quality of life (Nunkoo &

Ramkissoon, 2017). Stakeholder engagement can help to ensure sustainable growth through increased trust, informed decision making and reduced conflicts (Rodgers & Gago, 2004; Byrd, Cardenas & Greenwood, 2008; Nunkoo & Ramkissoon, 2012). LUX★ Resorts and Hotels has implemented a CSR platform 'Ray of Light' to address the social sustainability requirements in the destinations where it is operating. The hotel group is present in Mauritius, La Réunion, Maldives, China and Turkey. LUX★ works with the local stakeholders to optimise positive impacts at the destinations and the company.

Tourism impacts

International arrivals globally for 2018 was 1.4 billion, with an increase of +6% compared to 2017. Arrivals for Africa represents 67.1 million with 7% growth (UNWTO World Tourism Barometer, 2019). Tourism keeps on experiencing innovation and expansion, demonstrating the sector's strength and resilience. International tourism receipts represented US$ 1,448 billion in 2018 (UNWTO, 2018), contributing to a rise in income of locals, creation of jobs and enterprises, export revenues and infrastructure development (Kotler et al., 2014).

Tourism also contributes towards improved service facilities, a higher standard of living and economic development (Ramkissoon et al., 2018). Tourism is essential for income generation in developing countries (Dewnarain, Ramkissoon & Mavondo, 2019). Tourism development helps in the creation of employment opportunities for the local community. It also helps to stimulate entrepreneurship and investment opportunities (Dyer, Gursoy, Sharma & Carter, 2007; Nunkoo & Ramkissoon, 2011a). If tourism is developed in a sustainable manner it can enhance the community well-being or quality of life. It may at the same time add value to human, social and environmental capitals along with financial capitals. The direct contribution of the tourism sector to world GDP represents 9.8% (World Travel and Tourism Council (WTTC). Due to globalisation and increasing contribution towards disposable incomes, tourism has over the last few decades become one of the fastest growing industry (Al-Badi & Al-Sawaei, 2017).

However, at the same time tourism has negative impacts on local residents, such as reduced residents' life satisfaction, decreased health and safety, negative environmental impacts, rising land and property price, crime and substance abuse (Sirgy, Efraty, Siegel & Lee, 2001; Stronza & Gordillo, 2008; Woo et al., 2015). Tourism jobs are often low paid and unskilled (Tosun, 2002). Often local residents in SIDS are merely working for survival in an increasingly competitive market and as the price of property and goods inflates, they struggle with their finances (Weaver & Lawton, 2001). Very often employees in the tourism sector experience job burnout due to work overload and no work-life balance (Kim, 2008; Karatepe, Babakus & Yavas, 2012; Min et al., 2015). Maslach, Jackson and Leiter (1996, p. 20), defines job burnout as 'a state of exhaustion in which one is cynical about the value of one's occupation and doubtful of one's capacity to perform'. This, in turn, reduces job satisfaction (Chalkiti & Sigala, 2010; Lee & Ok, 2012), impacting on the company's sustainability (Lu & Gursoy, 2016).

Island tourism requires a considerable amount of resources for operations and production of high-quality services. This has a negative impact on the local community with regards to access to these resources (Khizindar, 2012) and raises questions about the long-term sustainability of tourism in SIDS (Ramkissoon, Uysal & Brown, 2011). The increasing need for resources and tourists' consumption patterns results in the depletion of the world's natural resources (Ramkissoon, Weiler & Smith, 2012; Ramkissoon, Smith & Weiler, 2013; Melissen, Cavagnaro & Damen & Düweke, 2016). While tourist resource consumption and residents' well-being need to be further explored, it is essential to involve the local community in tourism policy-making.

Local community support

The host community is one of the key stakeholders who help in the success of the tourism activity; their involvement is crucial in sustainable tourism development (Byrd, 2007; Moyle, Croy & Weiler, 2010). Community involvement is very beneficial for tourism operators and their participation and inclusion helps to reduce conflicts (Swarbrooke, 1999; Aas, Ladkin & Fletcher, 2005; Hwang, Chi & Lee, 2013). Sustainable development requires that there is a balance between economic growth, environmental protection and social progress (McKenzie, 2004; Malena, Marcial, Rubinos & Elin, 2016). Sustainability of all operations is the key element of long-term success (Husgafvel, Pajunen, Virtanen, Päävola, Paallysaho, Inkinen & Ekroos, 2015).

Companies are important societal actors, they have the responsibility to ensure social sustainability performance (Baumgartner, 2008). It is recognised that the social part of sustainable development is a more challenging area of business management (Dillard, Dujon & King, 2012). Tourism is a people and service industry; the social dimension of sustainability needs to be further addressed. There are however challenges in terminologies, approaches and notions of the social dimensions of sustainability. The social dimension of the triple bottom line has not received as much attention as the economic and environmental pillars (Colantonio & Dixon, 2010; Vavik & Keitsch, 2010; Dempsey, Bramley, Power & Brown, 2011). Researchers have increasingly sought to address this gap as key stakeholders expect that companies take into great consideration their social impacts (Koc & Durmaz, 2015). This includes good governance, equal opportunity, human rights, diversity and access to basic needs (Western Australian Council of Social Services, 2013).

Social projects can help alleviate the difficult situations of less privileged locals or vulnerable groups (Rachelle, Amekudzi-Kennedy, Sarah, Benya & Cliff, 2016). A business cannot be a sustainable model if the triple bottom line, which also includes the social sustainability dimension, is not addressed (Casula & Soneryd, 2012). Social sustainability at destinations is key; the increasing expectations from key stakeholders within the host destinations are pushing businesses to address negative social tourism impacts (Weingaertner & Moberg, 2014). Organisations are being required to report on their sustainability key performance indicators (KPIs) around the 3 Ps (People, Planet, Profit) (Dewulf & Van Langenhove, 2006). A share of the local community and people are represented by the employees in the tourism business. By having a positive impact on the employees, tourism employers can create a positive image and positive value within the local community (Tongchaiprasit & Ariyabuddhiphongs, 2016; Bufquin, DiPietro, Orlowski & Partlow, 2017). Employees play a very important role, especially frontline staff who have direct contact with the guests (Ustrov, Valverde & Ryan, 2016). The support of the employees as part of the local community remains key in sustainable tourism development.

Responsible business: stakeholders' expectations

The perceived social concerns are pushing companies to take actions to mitigate negative impacts and, in turn, encouraging businesses to be committed to reporting on their sustainability performance (Labuschagne & Brent, 2008). Companies are required to show more ethical behaviours and shareholders are expecting that businesses show transparency and efficiency in their activities (Pava & Krausz, 1996). Stakeholders are seeing how corporate performance fit with their expectations (Woodcraft, Bacon, Caistor-Arendar & Hackett, 2011). Businesses are required to use sustainability indicators to provide information on corporate performance (Singh, Murty, Gupta & Dikshit, 2009) and create sustainable value (Laszlo, 2003). Businesses which embrace good code of ethics and taking into consideration both internal and external stakeholders have social responsibility as part of their management processes which are value-driven (Rendtorff, 2009).

The local community's support to tourism development is influenced by well-being benefits brought to them (Woo, Kim & Uysal, 2015). The residents who receive more economic benefits from tourism are more likely to support its development (Lee et al., 2010). This has also been confirmed by Gursoy, Jurowski and Uysal (2002) who found that perceived benefits along with perceived costs had significant effects on locals' support for tourism development. Employees also form part of the local community. Employees perceive their employers value them when they are supported (Eisenberger, Huntington, Hutchison & Sowa, 1986). The good work practices help to enhance relationships in the organisation (Hur, Moon & Jun, 2013; Cheng, Yen, Chen & Teng, 2016; Han, Bonn & Cho, 2016). When employees are given adequate resources to accomplish their tasks, it enhances positive support towards the organisation (Hochwarter et al., 2006; Karatepe, 2015).

Hence, businesses are recognising the need to identify the social expectations and concerns of their key stakeholders, they are also exploring how they can operate in a manner which addresses those expectations. Organisations are acknowledging the significance of responsible business, which makes their operations consistent with the morals and values of society. Social Sustainability has become the strategic core of many leading businesses (Eccles et al., 2012). The World Commission on Environment and Development (WCED, 1987, p. 43) defines sustainable development (SD) as 'development that meets the needs of the present without compromising the ability of future generations to meet their own needs'. To be able to operate in a sustainable manner, tourism operators need to ensure that they are not compromising the needs of the future generations and also that of our present communities. The organisations are expected to be engaged in voluntary activities such as philanthropic donations, health care, childcare and educational opportunities (Carroll, 1991). Responsible businesses also ensure the safeguarding of the environment, economic development and social justice (Casula, Vifell & Soneryd, 2012). Businesses are increasingly seeking to operate in a socially responsible manner which caters for the interests of the key stakeholders. The LUX* case study gives insights on a concrete social initiative implemented to address these stakeholders' needs and expectations and showcase sustainable tourism development in practice.

LUX* 'Ray of Light' CSR initiative

LUX* Resorts and Hotels is a hotel group operating in Mauritius, La Réunion, Maldives, China and Turkey. It has several projects coming up in the near future in Vietnam, Italy and United Arab Emirates. This chapter focuses on 'Ray of Light' initiative in the Mauritian context, though the CSR platform is also present in all the other destinations. Mauritius is a small tropical island located in the Indian Ocean, about 2,000 kilometres off the southeast coast of the African continent. Mauritius is part of the Small Island Developing States (SIDS). It is very famous for its beautiful sandy beaches, pristine oceans and very comfortable temperature all year round. With 1.3 million inhabitants, the island is a fast-developing country with multiple sectors including agriculture, finance, ICT and tourism. The tourism sector plays an important role as it is a source of income for the inhabitants (Nunkoo & Ramkissoon, 2010a, 2010b; Nunkoo, Ramkissoon & Gursoy, 2012). There are around 111 hotels on the island and the total tourist arrivals in 2017 was 1.3 million, with an increase of 5.2% compared to 2016. As at August 2018, the LUX★ group operates five resorts in Mauritius, namely LUX★ Belle Mare, LUX★ Le Morne, LUX★ Grand Gaube, Tamassa and Merville Beach hotel. Its head office is based in Mauritius and it is listed on the Stock Exchange of Mauritius. The present case study shows how LUX★ group works with the local stakeholders to maximise positive impacts in the destination. The Ray of Light platform enhances dialogues with stakeholders to find solutions to key issues faced by underprivileged ones in the host communities where the hotel group is operating. It at the same time aligns with the local and international objectives such as the Sustainable Development Goals (SDGs) and Mauritius Vision 2020.

The role of key stakeholders is essential for sustainability in destinations (Stumpf & Swanger, 2015; Hristov, Minocha & Ramkissoon, 2018), each stakeholder has its own objectives which should align with the development process (Telfer & Sharpley, 2014). The social initiative 'Ray of Light' was introduced by LUX★ in 2013 as part of its sustainable tourism development strategy to cater for social projects and the needs of the local community. Part of the initiative is funded by the Corporate Social Responsibility (CSR) compliance fund while part of the initiative is funded through voluntary contribution by the company, its employees and guests, to support different projects such as poverty alleviation, education for the marginalised, healthcare provisions, support for disabled persons, provision of sports facilities and other key areas needing attention within the local community. These social projects enhance efforts for sustainable development (Lee et al., 2010).

The 'Ray of Light' platform is comprised various stakeholders including top management, general managers, department heads, front-liners, Non-Government Organisations (NGOs), guests and the respective resorts' sustainability representatives. The participatory approach undertaken by the 'Ray of Light' team helps in creating trust within the local community (Gursoy et al., 2002; Nunkoo & Ramkissoon, 2017). The platform encourages stakeholder engagement, without which it is impossible to identify the key issues faced by the host community. Once the key issues are identified, the stakeholders work together to find solutions with positive impacts. For example, if a community needs sanitary facilities and clean water, the NGOs have the opportunity to communicate about it to the company through the Ray of Light platform. The company can help sponsor the projects which are solutions to these issues, encouraging employees and guests to collaborate to support the locals. Another example is the Pack for a Purpose project, which is communicated through the Ray of Light platform. The NGOs and schools have the opportunity to inform the company about their needs and the information is communicated to guests who are travelling to the destination. The guests make space in their luggage to pack for a purpose in form of school materials and supplies for local children. Once the supplies reach the hotels, the respective teams distribute them to the beneficiaries, schools and NGOs. A third example is, if the blood bank at the destination has a low supply of blood, it communicates to the hotels to have a blood donation day. This helps to save lives and also support patients suffering from Thalassemia.

To ensure results, sustained support is offered to projects of poverty alleviation through quality education from a young age, healthcare for the needy, capacity building for the disabled through IT courses and sports, youth empowerment projects, gender equality through women empowerment/entrepreneurship courses, among others. Beyond legal compliance of CSR fund disbursements, LUX★ offers other forms of donations and sponsorships which support its goals. The selected projects meet international (SDGs), national (National CSR Foundation, Mauritius Revenue Authority, National Empowerment Foundation, Ministry of Social Security) and LUX★ management objectives. LUX★ thus demonstrates its commitment as a responsible business and promotes sustainable tourism (Casula, Vifell & Soneryd, 2012).

Team members generously support calls to participate by volunteering or making donations during periods when natural disaster occur such as cyclones or floods, as well as organising end of year festivities for children. LUX★ is also a member of The Code of Conduct against child trafficking in travel and tourism. In line with the LUX★ Child Protection Policy, LUX★ has taken a public stance against child trafficking in travel and tourism by contributing to the launch of The Code Symposium in Mauritius. The Corporate policy details the correct procedure to tackle any situation, which may arise at the resort or in the local community, showing how LUX★ caters for the interests of the key stakeholders (Hristov & Ramkissoon, 2018). For Mauritius, LUX★ partners with more than 10 NGOs every year, fighting for causes like poverty alleviation through education, gender equality, health and social projects. It also supports the 'Foundation Joseph Lagesse' which covers projects within the ten priority areas of intervention in Mauritius: Poverty, Education, Social Housing, Disabilities, Health, Family, Sports, Environment, Peace & nation building, Road safety & security. LUX★ contributes to the support of the 'Small Step Matters' crowdfunding platform for social, health and other projects. During end of year celebrations, the resorts open their doors to beneficiaries of NGOs applying principles of fairness for the poor and disadvantaged within the society (Sharpley, 2009).

LUX★ works with the Thalassemia Society of Mauritius to help patients suffering from Thalassemia. The NGO has successfully inaugurated a Day care ward at one of the major local hospital (Victoria Hospital) for thalassemia patients who require a safe space for transfusions and treatments. The hotel group also helps during blood donation events and provision of equipment for the day care ward and continues to support the development of the ward. For example, LUX★ Grand Gaube situated on the North coast of Mauritius, is a regular supporter of the national blood bank. It organises a blood donation day, a lifesaving event, where several pints of blood are donated by Team Members. It is a tangible way of showing the benefits of sustainable tourism in an equitable manner (Telfer & Sharpley, 2014). In collaboration with the Joseph Lagesse Foundation, LUX★ collaborates on sensitisation campaign on paediatric health and assist in environmental and social housing projects. Another example is working with various stakeholders e.g. professionals, NGOs, social workers, the Ministry of Health and inhabitants of the area to address substance abuse. Under CADCA's (Coalition Communautaires Anti-Drogue d'Amérique) guidance, the coalition engages in dialogue with the local community. CADCA provides training, technical assistance (across countries) assisting local communities with evidence-based strategies to achieve population-level reductions in substance abuse rates.

LUX★ through the 'Ray of Light' platform helps in poverty alleviation through quality education from a young age and food and healthcare for the needy. Academic as well as creative classes are provided to the disadvantaged children to provide them with a fair chance at succeeding in primary school. Through such sustainable tourism practices, LUX★ contributes to community well-being and quality of life (Moscardo & Murphy, 2014). Social sustainability has thus become the strategic core of the LUX★ business model (Eccles et al., 2012). LUX★ assists NGOs in providing quality education to teenagers from disadvantaged backgrounds of the northern and southern regions providing balanced meals, extracurricular activities such as music and art to encourage holistic development of the youth. LUX★ supports the holistic development of children and teenagers and university students, through quality education, art, music and outdoor activities. The 'Ray of Light' platform supports NGOs engaged in catering for the needs of the disabled. LUX★ supports empowerment through the provision of a computer room and IT classes for beneficiaries, contributes to the capacity building of the physically handicapped who want to try out sports such as swimming and international tennis tournaments. LUX★ also engages in women empowerment through the NGO Gender Links providing entrepreneurship courses to encourage independence/self-sufficiency, challenging the status quo through public sensitisation against Gender Based Violence (GBV) and providing a reliable structure protecting young women from trafficking, substance abuse or from becoming homeless. These are some contributions to the well-being of the local community which may have a positive influence on support for tourism development (Ramkissoon & Nunkoo, 2011; Woo, Kim & Uysal, 2015). LUX★ collaborates with community working groups (under the aegis of the Ministry of Social Integration, for poverty alleviation nation-wide), NGOs, beneficiaries, social workers and private sector representatives, involving all stakeholders (Sowamber & Ramkissoon, 2019) in tackling poverty via agreed action plans. The social legitimacy of the organisation is enhanced through such engagements for the highest good.

Implications and conclusion

The case study of LUX★ shows clearly how responsible tourism is essential in tourism development. Social responsibility is an essential activity of the business (Andriotis, 2005). For the implementation of tangible initiatives, LUX★ has received in 2018 the Sustainable Tourism award from Ministry of Tourism of Mauritius. LUX★ received this award for its voluntary commitment to invest in sustainable tourism projects with flagship projects Tread Lightly by LUX★ and Ray of Light by LUX★ where it goes beyond legal compliance to protect the environment and uplift the communities that host LUX★ as its performance climbs. LUX★ was also recognised for its leadership in sustainable development with international certifications such as Travelife and Green Globe. LUX★ is a member of GRI Community shaping the standards of integrated reporting and is the first hotel group to be listed on SEM Sustainability Index. This Mauritian group of resorts and hotels supports the UN SDGs on all fronts by working with experts, consultants, NGOs and the local community. LUX★ initiatives are acknowledged by policymakers, accreditation bodies and key stakeholders in the value chain which enhances support for development.

This chapter informs academics, practitioners and policymakers on opportunities provided by implementations of tangible social initiatives such as Ray of Light in tourism development. To be successful in destination development, tourism operators are encouraged to advocate social and responsible actions which help improve local residents' quality of life (Ramkissoon et al., 2018). Tourism operators in SIDS can draw on the 'Ray of Light' initiative to further contribute to the betterment of the societies they operate in by bringing real value and making a difference to the locals' quality of life (Lee et al., 2010; Nunkoo & Ramkissoon, 2010a, 2010b, 2011a; McCabe & Johnson, 2013). It is also seen that the tourism development has the opportunity to enhance quality of life of the local residents (Andereck & Nyaupane, 2011). Such actions show that there is intention to have an equitable society, which is one with no exclusionary or prejudiced practices and which does not hinder individuals from participating economically and socially to optimise their job opportunities, health and safety, training and learning and professional growth (Bramley & Power 2009).

Sustainable actions should be at the core of an organisation's business strategy which can, in turn, make it a leader in inclusive business model, which is what a country needs (Eccles et al., 2012). Stakeholders require transparency and efficiency from businesses, they are expected to show continuity, which, in turn, enhance support. This can only be possible through stakeholder inclusiveness. The future of businesses could be threatened if they do not take into consideration the increasing demand for them to support a social cause and hence engaging in sustainable practices can only be beneficial. Sustainability lead to value creation for stakeholders involved and should be a key factor to be considered in decision-making process (Cavagnaro & Curiel, 2012; Cavagnaro, 2018) to bring further benefits to the company such as improved reputation, cost reduction and employee and customer loyalty (Graci & Dodds, 2008).

Hence, social projects and responsible tourism development should be encouraged in tourism organisations in SIDS. The business model needs to ensure that development plans are aiming at the well-being benefits for local residents. Island tourism management needs to ensure that policies also focus on both host and tourist benefits addressing issues of accessibility to and management of resources and well-being benefits from tourism development in addition to profitability of the business. It is crucial to understand that stakeholder engagement and dialogues with stakeholders are key factors for positive impacts in the host destinations. The chapter reveals that more research is needed in stakeholder engagement in social corporate responsibility in small island developing states. Measuring and monitoring of the well-being benefits also need to be addressed by future researchers.

References

Aas, C., Ladkin, A., and Fletcher, J. (2005). Stakeholder collaboration and heritage management. *Annals of Tourism Research*, 32, 28–48.

Al-Badi, A., and Al-Sawaei, S. (2017). Utilizing social media to encourage domestic tourism in Oman. *International Journal of Business and Management*, 12(4), 84–94.

Andereck, K. L., and Nyaupane, G. P. (2011). Exploring the nature of tourism and QOL perceptions among residents. *Journal of Travel Research*, 50, 248–260.

Andriotis, K. (2005). Community groups' perceptions of and preferences for tourism development: Evidence from Crete. *Journal of Hospitality & Tourism Research*, 29, 67–90.

Baumgartner R. (2008). Corporate sustainability performance: Methods and illustrative examples. *International Journal of Sustainable Development and Planning*, 3(2), 117.

Bramley G., and Power, S. (2009). Urban form and social sustainability: The role of density and housing type. Environmental Planning B, 36(1), 30–48.

Bufquin, D., DiPietro, R., Orlowski, M., and Partlow, C. (2017). The influence of restaurant coworkers' perceived warmth and competence on employees' turnover intentions: The mediating role of job attitudes. *International Journal of Hospitality Management*, 60, 13–22.

Buser M., and Koch C. (2014). Is this none of the contractor's business? Social sustainability challenges informed by literary accounts. *Construction Management Economics*, 32(7–8), 749–759.

Byrd, E. T. (2007). Stakeholders in sustainable tourism development and their roles: Applying stakeholder theory to sustainable tourism development. *Tourism Review*, 62, 6–13.

Byrd, E. T., Cardenas, D. A., and Greenwood, J. B. (2008). Factors of stakeholder understanding of sustainable tourism. *Hospitality and Tourism Research*, 8(3), 192–204.

Carroll, A. B. (1991). The pyramid of corporate social responsibility: Toward the moral management of organizational stakeholders. *Business horizons*, 34(4), 39–48.

Casula V. A., Soneryd L. (2012). Organizing matters: How 'the social dimension' gets lost in sustainability projects. *Sustainable Development*, 20(1), 18–27.

Cavagnaro, E. (2018) The Sustainable Hospitality Value Chain. In: Cavagnaro, E. (Ed.) *Sustainable Value Creation in Hospitality: Guests on Earth*. pp. 11-26. Oxford: Goodfellow Publishers

Chalkiti, K., and Sigala, M. (2010). Staff turnover in the Greek tourism industry: A comparison between insular and peninsular regions. *International Journal of Contemporary Hospitality Management*, 22(3), 335–359.

Cheng, J. C., Yen, C. H., Chen, C. Y., and Teng, H. Y. (2016). Tour leaders' job crafting and job outcomes: The moderating role of perceived organizational support. *Tourism Management Perspective*, 20(5), 19–29.

Colantonio A, and Dixon T. (2010). *Urban regeneration and social sustainability: Best practice from European cities*. New Jersey: John Wiley & Sons, Inc.

Dempsey N., Bramley, G., Power, S., and Brown C. (2011). The social dimension of sustainable development: Defining urban social sustainability. Sustainable Development, 19(5), 289–300.

Dewnarain, S., Ramkissoon, H., and Mavondo, F. (2019). Social customer relationship management: An integrated conceptual framework. *Journal of Hospitality Marketing & Management*, 28(2), 172–188.

Dewulf, J., and Van Langenhove, H. (2006). *Renewables-based technology: Sustainability assessment.* New Jersey: John.

Dillard, D., Dujon, V., and King M. (2012). *Understanding the social dimension of sustainability.* New York: Routledge.

Dreyer, L. C., Hauschild, M. Z., and Schierbeck, J. 2010. Characterisation of social impacts in LCA. *International Journal of Life Cycle Assessment*, 15(3), 247–259.

Dyer, P., Gursoy, D., Sharma, B., and Carter, J. (2007). Structural modeling of resident perceptions of tourism and associated development on the Sunshine Coast, Australia. *Tourism Management*, 28, 409–422.

Eccles, R. G., Miller Perkins, K., and Serafeim, G. (2012). How to become a sustainable company. *MIT Sloan Management Review*, 53(4), 43–50.

Eisenberger, R., Huntington, R., Hutchison, S., and Sowa, D. (1986). Perceived organizational support. *Journal of Applied Psychology*, 71(3), 500–507.

Graci, S., and Dodds, R. (2008). Why go green? The business case for environmental commitment in the Canadian hotel industry. *Anatolia: An International Journal of Tourism and Hospitality Research*, 19(2), 251–70.

Gursoy, D., Jurowski, C., and Uysal, M. (2002). Resident attitudes: A structural modeling approach. *Annals of Tourism Research*, 29, 79–105.

Han, S. J., Bonn, M. A., and Cho, M. (2016). The relationship between customer incivility, restaurant frontline service employee burnout and turnover intention. *International Journal of Hospitality Management*, 52(1), 97–106.

Hochwarter, W. A., Witt, L. A., Treadway, D. C., and Ferris, G. R. (2006). The interaction of social skill and organizational support on job performance. *Journal of Applied Psychology*, 91(2), 482–489.

Hristov, D., Minocha, S., and Ramkissoon, H. (2018). Transformation of destination leadership networks. *Tourism Management Perspectives*, 28, 239–250.

Hristov, D., and Ramkissoon, H. (2018). Bringing cross-disciplinarity to the fore: A methodological framework for leadership in destination management organisations. In Nunkoo, R. (Ed.) *Handbook of Research Methods for Tourism and Hospitality Management* (pp. 450–461). Edward Elgar Publishing, Cheltenham, UK

Hur, W. M., Moon, T. W., and Jun, J. K. (2013). The role of perceived organizational support on emotional labor in the airline industry. *International Journal of Contemporary Hospitality Management*, 25(1), 105–123.

Husgafvel R., Pajunen, N., Virtanen, K., Paavola, I., Päällysaho, M., Inkinen, V., and Ekroos A. (2015). Social sustainability performance indicators–experiences from process industry. *International Journal of Sustainable Engineering*, 8(1), 14–25.

Hwang, D., Chi, S-H, and Lee, B. (2013). Collective action that influences tourism: Social structural approach to community involvement. *Journal of Hospitality & Tourism Research*, 1–19. Advance online publication. doi:10.1177/1096348013933999.

Karatepe, O. M. (2015). Do personal resources mediate the effect of perceived organizational support on emotional exhaustion and job outcomes? *International Journal of Contemporary Hospitality Management*, 27(1), 4–26.

Karatepe, O. M., Babakus, E., and Yavas, U. (2012). Affectivity and organizational politics as antecedents of burnout among frontline hotel employees. *International Journal of Hospitality Management*, 31(1), 66–75.

Khizindar, T. M. (2012). Effects of tourism on residents' quality of life in Saudi Arabia: An empirical study. *Journal of Hospitality Marketing & Management*, 21, 617–637.

Kim, H. J. (2008). Hotel service providers' emotional labor: The antecedents and effects on burnout. *International Journal of Hospitality Management*, 27(2), 151–161.

Kim, K., Uysal, M., and Sirgy, J. (2013). How does tourism in a community impact the quality of life of community residents? *Tourism Management*, 36, 527–540.

Koc, S., and Durmaz, V. (2015). Airport corporate sustainability: An analysis of indicators reported in the sustainability practices. *Procedia Social and Behavioral Sciences*, 181, 158–170.

Kotler, P., Bowen, J. T., and Makens, J. (2014). *Marketing for Hospitality and Tourism*. Pearson Education: Harlow, UK

Labuschagne, C., and Brent, A. C. (2008). An industry perspective of the completeness and relevance of a social assessment framework for project and technology management in the manufacturing sector. *Journal of Cleaner Production*, 16(3), 253–262.

Laszlo, C. (2003). *The sustainable company: How to create lasting value through social and environmental performance*. Washington, DC: Island Press.

Lee, C., Kang, S. K., Long, P., and Reisinger, Y. (2010). Residents' perceptions of casino impacts: A comparative study. *Tourism Management*, 31, 189–201.

Lee, J. J., and Ok, C. (2012). Reducing burnout and enhancing job satisfaction: Critical role of hotel employees' emotional intelligence and emotional labor. *International Journal of Hospitality Management*, 31(4), 1101–1112.

Lee, T. H. (2013). Influence analysis of community resident support for sustainable tourism development. *Tourism Management*, 34, 37–46.

Lu, A. C. C., and Gursoy, D. (2016). Impact of job burnout on satisfaction and turnover intention: Do generational differences matter? *Journal of Hospitality and Tourism Research*, 40 (2), 210–235.

Malena, S., Marcial, B., Rubinos, A., and Elin, M. (2016). Sustainable dissemination of earthquake resistant construction in the Peruvian Andes. *Sustainability Science Practice Policy*, 12(1), 22–33.

Maslach, C., Jackson, S. E., and Leiter, M.P. (1996). *MBI: The Maslach burnout inventory: Manual*. Palo Alto, CA: Consulting Psychologists Press.

McCabe, S., and Johnson, S. (2013). The happiness factor in tourism: Subjective wellbeing and social tourism. *Annals of Tourism Research*, 41, 42–65.

McKenzie S. (2004). Social sustainability: Towards some definitions. In Hawke Research Institute Working Paper Series, No 27. Magill (South Australia): Hawke Research Institute, University of South Australia.

Melissen, F., Cavagnaro, E., Damen, M., and Düweke, A. (2016). Is the hotel industry prepared to face the challenge of sustainable development? *Journal of Vacation Marketing*, 22(3), 227–238.

Min, H., Kim, H. J., and Lee, S. B. (2015). Extending the challenge-hindrance stressor framework: The role of psychological capital. *International Journal of Hospitality Management*, 50, 105–114.

Moscardo, G., and Murphy, L. (2014). There is no such thing as sustainable tourism: Re-conceptualising tourism as a tool for sustainability. *Sustainability*, 6(5), 2538–2561. doi:10.3390/su6052538.

Moyle, B., Croy G. W., and Weiler, B. (2010). Community perceptions of tourism: Bruny and Magnetic islands, Australia. *Asia Pacific Journal of Tourism Research*, 15(3), 353–366.

Nunkoo, R., and Ramkissoon, H. (2010a). Gendered theory of planned behaviour and residents' support for tourism. *Current Issues in Tourism*, 13(6), 525–540.

Nunkoo, R., and Ramkissoon, H. (2010b). Modeling community support for a proposed integrated resort project. *Journal of Sustainable Tourism*, 18, 257–277.

Nunkoo, R., and Ramkissoon, H. (2011a). Developing a community support model for tourism. *Annals of Tourism Research*, 38, 964–988.

Nunkoo, R., and Ramkissoon, H. (2011b). Residents' satisfaction with community attributes and support for tourism. *Journal of Hospitality & Tourism Research*, 35, 171–190.

Nunkoo, R., and Ramkissoon, H. (2013). Travelers' E-purchase intent of tourism products and services. *Journal of Hospitality Marketing & Management*, 22(5), 505–529.

Nunkoo, R., and Ramkissoon, H. (2012). Power, trust social exchange and community support. *Annals of Tourism Research*, 39(2), 997–1023.

Nunkoo, R., and Ramkissoon, H. (2017). Stakeholders' views of enclave tourism: A Grounded theory approach. *Journal of Hospitality & Tourism Research*. doi: 10.1177.

Pack for a Purpose – https://www.packforapurpose.org/ (Accessed on 16 Jul 2019).

Pava, M. L., and Krausz, J. (1996). The association between corporate social-responsibility and financial performance: the paradox of social cost. *Journal of Business Ethics*, 15(3), 321–356.

Rachelle, H., Amekudzi-Kennedy, A., Sarah, B., Benya, F., and Cliff, D. (2016). Network priorities for social sustainability research and education: Memorandum of the integrated network on social sustainability research group. *Sustainability Science Practice Policy*, 12(1), 1–7.

Ramkissoon, H., and Durbarry, R. (2009). The Environmental Impacts of Tourism at the Casela Nature and Leisure Park, Mauritius. *The International Journal of Environmental, Cultural, Economic and Social Sustainability*, 5(2), 201–211.

Ramkissoon, H., Mavondo, F., and Uysal, M. (2018). Social involvement and park citizenship as moderators for quality-of-life in a national park. *Journal of Sustainable Tourism*, 26(3), 341–361.

Ramkissoon, H., and Nunkoo, R. (2011). City image and perceived tourism impact: Evidence from Port Louis, Mauritius. *International Journal of Hospitality & Tourism Administration*, 12(2), 123–143.

Ramkissoon, H., Smith, L. D. G., and Weiler, B. (2013). Testing the dimensionality of place attachment and its relationships with place satisfaction and pro-environmental behaviours: A structural equation modelling approach. *Tourism Management*, 36, 552–566.

Ramkissoon, H., and Sowamber, V. (2018). *Environmentally and Financially Sustainable Tourism*, ICHRIE Research report (pp. 1–4), ICHRIE Research reports, Translating Research Implications: Industry's commentary..

Ramkissoon, H., and Uysal, M. S. (2011). The effects of perceived authenticity, information search behaviour, motivation and destination imagery on cultural behavioural intentions of tourists. *Current Issues in Tourism*, 14(6), 537–562.

Ramkissoon, H., and Uysal, M. (2014). Authenticity as a value co-creator of tourism experiences. *Creating experience value in tourism*, 113–124.

Ramkissoon, H., and Uysal, M. (2018). Authenticity as a value co-creator of tourism experiences. In N. K. Prebensen, J. S. Chen, and M. Uysal (Eds.), *Creating experience value in tourism* (2nd ed., pp. 98–109). Wallingford: CABI.

Ramkissoon, H., Uysal, M., and Brown, K. (2011). Relationship between destination image and behavioral intentions of tourists to consume cultural attractions. *Journal of Hospitality Marketing & Management*, 20(5), 575–595.

Ramkissoon, H., Weiler, B., and Smith, L. D. G. (2012). Place attachment and pro-environmental behaviour in national parks: The development of a conceptual framework. *Journal of Sustainable Tourism*, 20(2), 257–276.

Rendtorff, J. D. (2009). *Responsibility, ethics and legitimacy of corporations*. Copenhagen: Copenhagen Business School Press DK.

Rodgers, W., and Gago, S. (2004). Stakeholder influence on corporate strategies over time. *Journal of Business Ethics*, 52, 349–363.

Rukuižienė, R. (2014). Sustainable tourism development implications to local economy. *Regional Formation and Development Studies*, 3(14), 170–177.

Sharpley, R. (2009). *Tourism development and the environment: Beyond sustainability?* London: Earthscan.

Seetaram, N. E. E. L. U., and Joubert, B. (2018). Tourism in the Seychelles: Trends and experiences. *Tourism Management in Warm-water Island Destinations*, 6, 131.

Singh, R. K., Murty, H. R., Gupta, S. K., and Dikshit, A. K. 2009. An overview of sustainability assessment methodologies. *Ecological Indicators*, 9(2), 189–212.

Sirgy, M. J., Efraty, D., Siegel, P., and Lee, D. J. (2001). A new measure of quality of work life (QWL) based on based on need satisfaction and spillover theories. *Social Indictors Research*, 55, 241–302.

Sowamber, V., and Ramkissoon, H. (2019). Sustainable tourism as a catalyst for positive environmental change: A case of LUX★ resorts & hotels. In R. Nunkoo and D. Gursoy (Eds.), *Routledge Handbook of Tourism Impacts*. Abingdon, UK: Routledge, pp. 338–350.

Sowamber, V., Ramkissoon, H., and Mavondo, F. (2018). Impact of sustainability practices on hospitality consumers' behaviors and attitudes. The case of LUX★ resorts & hotels. In Dorgan, G. (Ed.) *Routledge Handbook of Hospitality Marketing*. New York: Routledge, pp. 384–396

Stronza, A., and Gordillo, J. (2008). Community views of ecotourism. *Annals of Tourism Research*, 35, 448–468.

Stumpf, T. S., and Swanger N. (2015). Tourism involvement-conformance theory: A grounded theory concerning the latent consequences of sustainable tourism policy shifts, *Journal of Sustainable Tourism*, 23(4), 618–637, doi: 10.1080/09669582.2014.959967.

Swarbrooke, J. (1999). *Sustainable tourism management*. Wallingford: CABI.

Telfer, D., and Sharpley S. (2014). *Tourism and development: Concepts and issues*, 2nd ed., Channel View Publications: Bristol, UK.

Tongchaiprasit, P., and Ariyabuddhiphongs, V. (2016). Creativity and turnover intention among hotel chefs: The mediating effects of job satisfaction and job stress. *International Journal of Hospitality Management*, 55, 33–40.

Tosun, C. (2002). Host perceptions of impacts: A comparative tourism study. *Annals of Tourism Research*, 29, 231–253.

Tyrrell, T., Paris, C. M., and Biaett, V. (2013). A quantified triple bottom line for tourism: Experimental results. *Journal of Travel Research*, 52(3), 279–293.

World Commission on Environment and Development (WCED) (1987). *Our Common Future*. London: Oxford University Press.

UNWTO (2018). https://www.e-unwto.org/doi/pdf/10.18111/9789284419029 (Accessed on 23 Aug 2018).

UNWTO World Tourism Barometer (2019). https://www.ttr.tirol/sites/default/files/2019-02/UNWTO%20Barometer%20Vol.%2017%20%28J%C3%A4nner%202019%29.pdf (Accessed on 15 July 2019).

Ustrov, Y., Valverde, M., and Ryan, G. (2016). Insights into emotional contagion and its effects at the hotel front desk. *International Journal of Contemporary Hospitality Management*, 28(10), 2285–2309.

Vavik, T., and Keitsch, M. M. (2010). Exploring relationships between universal design and social sustainable development: Some methodological aspects to the debate on the sciences of sustainability. *Sustainable Development*, 18(5), 295. http://ww.wacoss.org.au/Libraries/State_ Election_2013_Documents/WACOSS_Model_of_ Sustainability.sflb.ashx.

Weaver, D. B., and Lawton, L. J. (2001). Resident perceptions in the urban-rural fringe. *Annals of Tourism Research*, 28, 439–458.

Weingaertner, C., and Moberg, A. (2014). Exploring social sustainability: Learning from perspectives on urban development and companies and products. *Sustainable Development*. 22(2), 122–133.

Western Australian Council of Social Services (WACSS) (2013). Model of social sustainability. http://www.wacoss.org.au/Libraries/State_Election_2013_Documents/WACOSS_Model_of_Social_Sustainability.sflb.ashx

Woo, E., Kim, H., and Uysal, M. (2015). Life satisfaction and support for tourism development. *Annals of Tourism Research*, 50, 84–97.

Woodcraft, S., Bacon, N., Caistor-Arendar, L., and Hackett, T. (2011). *Design for social sustainability: A framework for creating thriving new communities, social life*. London. The Young Foundation.

27

Pastoral women participation in community conservancies in Maasai Mara, Kenya

Judy Kepher Gona and Lucy Atieno

Introduction

> In order to promote social participation in conservation and sustainable use processes, it is necessary to recognize, develop, and revisit the concept of "the community" as a homogenous group.
>
> *(Aguilar et al., 2002)*

> Our thinking in the twenty first century must find a way to escape pastoral nostalgia, in order to embrace a post sustainability, that is also, of course, post pastoral.
>
> *(Nardizzi, 2016)*

Community-based tourism narratives, in the parlance of conservancies, are committed to local community inclusion in tourism initiatives. However, this commitment is hinged on a narrowly construed mode of inclusion, which may imply some form of dispossession from traditional livelihood systems, as well as reinforce inequities held within communities, when opportunities presented are viewed from the perspective of gender. Research findings by Keane et al. (2016), criticize community-based conservation for taking a simplistic view of the community and consequently failing to recognize the heterogeneity in community members, especially based on gendered dimensions. Gender equality is a viable indicator for socio-cultural sustainability of destinations (Jamhawi et al., 2015), and the United Nations Sustainable Development Goal number ten emphasizes that achieving a status of reduced inequalities is paramount for various aspects of development.

Franks et al. (2018), argue that development strategies in protected areas should redirect their focus to enhancing equity, rather than improving livelihoods, in order to realize the meaningful impact to conservation and well-being of communities. Feminist perspectives, like the ecofeminist theory (see Merchant, 1983; Berman, 1994, 2001), can be employed to enhance equity and secure a common ground between parties involved in a conservation agenda (see Kanhiya, 2016; Lundberg, 2018; Carter, 2019). Ecofeminism combines principles of ecology with feminism concepts while acknowledging that humans are part of a larger community shared with all life and other living systems. Yet, initiatives for improving livelihoods for communities overlook dimensions of equality in the livelihood system being improved. This hints that conservancy approaches to equity through community inclusion, stem from a position that is interested. In Gosh's (2016) words, most ideas of equality are grotesque fictions designed to secure exactly the opposite of those professed ends. Inclusion strategies are yet to attain impactful participation of community members involved. A community-based project has multiple stakeholders and this requires strong bonding among the different players. Conservancies have also multiple stakeholders, including local communities, tourism investors, government representatives, environmental NGOs, among others. Collaboration of stakeholders in tourism doesn't yield an optimum impact to address sustainable development challenges facing the industry.

The Maasai Mara pastoral landscape, in south-west Kenya, hosts a number of conservancies, whose inception was bargained on a community inclusion front. Nonetheless, scholars have often argued that wildlife conservancies in Maasai Mara in Kenya, most of which are community-owned, fail to deliver benefits to community and elite stakeholders in equal measure (see Akama et al., 2011). Communities are disadvantaged with low compensations for land leases, and punitive measures in forms of fines for trespassing to fenced conservancy property. Conservancies in Maasai Mara form the main wildlife dispersal area for Maasai Mara National Reserve (MMNR). This reserve has the highest density of wildlife in Kenya and benefits the country in wildlife tourism revenue.

In their pursuit of conservation goals, conservancies use tourism as a market tool, and value derived from tourism markets are expected to benefit community livelihoods. Tourism investments in conservancies create multiple avenues through which local communities can be engaged in conservancy projects, e.g. through employment, access to value chain benefits, and promotion of local culture. Nonetheless, engagement in tourism fails to respect gender diversities. According to Foley et al. (2018), there is evidence linking tourism in practice to the disempowerment of women and the sector urgently needs reforms to impact on inequality. Reforms on inequality in the context of conservancy development need to first acknowledge the heterogeneity of a community, whose members are targeted for land leases. This is especially necessary at a time when dissatisfied community members feel excluded from their traditional rights, at the expense of conservancy benefits for a few.

In Kenya, it is commendable that community conservancy projects acknowledge the need to uphold livelihood systems of host communities and place much emphasis on pastoral lifestyles that are dominant in Kenya's rangelands. Initially, market-based instruments for community conservancies, e.g. ecotourism projects, implied pastoral alienation, imposing fence and fines restrictions for herders in search of grazing pasture for their livestock. This alienation that was previously common to conservation initiatives is slowly fading away, as conservancies aim to be more inclusive. In remote geographies of conservancies sutured by patriarchal societies, the pastoral frame exists with correlative disposal of feminist perspectives. The fact is there is always an *us* and *them*, in the language of community tourism focus on pastoralism, and this is men versus women. Community conservancies filter community membership criteria based on land ownership, where the majority of land owners in the pastoral Maasai Mara are men and non-land owners are women. The requirement of land ownership to merit conservancy membership locks out many pastoral women, many of whom missed out land allocations during group ranch sub-divisions. Very few women who are conservancy members own inherited land, mostly from husbands who passed on. Ideas of participation in conservancies are borrowed from masculine understandings of development for the entire community and therefore women have no direct involvement in conservancies.

Loftsdottir (2001) takes the theoretical orientation of Women in Development (WID) to criticize pastoral development as gender-biased, where women's bargaining powers are reduced to be confined within household contexts. Such developments reinforce stereotypes about women's domestic roles (ibid), showing that pastoral women have subordinate roles in livestock production.

Ecofeminists agree that the oppression of women and the domination of nature in a patriarchal society are interconnected and mutually reinforcing (Fill and Muhlhausler, 2001). Patriarchal bias exists in the foundations of pastoralism in the Maasai Mara range lands. In this specific context, a pastoral livelihood implies an idealization of male triumph in the control of key resources supporting rural lives, i.e. land and livestock, obscuring the realities of women existence, and the extent of their rights to ownership over such resources. The bias exists also in man's dominance over nature, where pastoral assumption is that "idea of nature as a stable enduring counterpoint to the disruptive energy and change of human societies" (Garrard, 2004, pp. 56–57), and pastoral landscapes will remain unaltered for generations to come, to support grazing requirement of community livestock. Pastoral settings are therefore dismissive of nature and women. Noting the dismissive sense of pastoral representations, Nardizzi (2016, pp. 564–565) advises that "Our thinking in the twenty first century must find a way to escape pastoral nostalgia, in order to embrace a postsustainability, that is also, of course, postpastoral".

Based on the aforementioned arguments, the language of pastoral development in community conservancies exhibits gender bias in disfavouring women. Ecofeminists, Daly (1980) and Berman (1994) call for the castration of such language, i.e. the metaphorical "cutting away of phallocentric value systems imposed by patriarchy" (Berman, 2001, p. 267). The Maasai culture for example, is highly patriarchal and exhibits salience of pastoralism as a traditionally male role. Since women are unequal in developing countries in terms of opportunities available to them, the situation can be made worse by such patriarchal cultures. Where pastoralism is a gendered activity, entitlements over pastoral property are solely given to men. Grazing land is a vital resource for pastoralists, and in some cultures, the right to own, use, or access land is exclusively given to men. Men additionally get income to support their families from the fee paid for land lease in conservancies. While men own livestock, women can only have control overuse of livestock products, like milk and hides. Through the practice of pastoralism tradition, gender inequities occur, hierarchies are built and maintained, and decisions made based on the gender on who controls what. The pace of community tourism development will not accelerate well without the involvement of all community members, given the possible oversight of women exclusion in compliance to dominant patriarchal systems. Thus, the significance of gender and power, as they influence the experiences of women in tourism is important for research (Hall et al., 2003), especially in the contexts of community conservancies set up in rural gendered societies.

Pastoral women are doubly marginalized, first by being members of rural communities at the margins of national economic and political life, and second, by living in remote, under serviced areas, leading a lifestyle that is misunderstood by decision makers (Watson, 2010). Thus, imperative and worth asking is whether or not, neoliberal community conservancy approaches are gender just, with their strong consideration for improving livelihood systems that exhibit gender bias.

This chapter advances gender-based research in tourism, where according to Pritchard and Morgan (2007), scholarship is dominated by "Malestream" knowledge traditions. To break the silences which break women in community tourism, the chapter explores the factors that encourage women to be involved constantly in community conservancies, as well as to uphold their motivations in engaging in conservancy projects, and the roles that women play when participating in community projects. Content was built from personal observations, data from conservancy governance documents, scholarly publications, and interviews with women in conservancies where community-based tourism initiatives had been set up.

Conservancies in Maasai Mara

Maasai Mara National Reserve is Kenya's leading destination for wildlife tourism. Narok County, where the reserve is domiciled is one of the richest Counties in Kenya. A significant portion of the County's wealth is associated with wildlife tourism. Maasai Mara National Reserve, owes its existence to dispersal areas around the reserve that provide for migration corridors for wildlife between Serengeti and the Reserve. These dispersal areas are community lands that were held under a communal land tenure system known as Group Ranch. The Group Ranches were introduced by Kenya's colonial administration to contain the pastoralist lifestyle. Similar land tenures exist in other parts of Kenya, including Amboseli, and much of Northern Kenya. For decades, pastoralism was the predominant land use in communal land held under the Group Ranch Act.

In the last 20 years much of the Groups ranches have been subdivided, and private titles issued to members of the Group Ranches in Maasai Mara. These communities have roc-consolidated these private parcels to form community conservation areas known as conservancies. Today the predominant land use in the conservancies is tourism, with pastoralism redefined through managed grazing in select areas in the conservancies.

In Maasai Mara, 15 community conservancies have so far been set up, and they cover 64% of the total area (see Figure 27.1). These conservancies support livelihoods of about 14,500 households, or approximately 100,000 people. Each year, land lease fees to the tune of million dollars is paid to conservancy land owners but the benefits of such will not map neatly in equal measure for diversities observed in community members.

Formation of these conservancies requires that households within local communities lease out land, or sections of it for conservation purposes. Since conservancies occupy extensive land areas, some households whose land fall within conservancy boundaries have to be relocated to areas demarcated outside conservancy boundaries. They are resettled temporarily to host parcels of land outside conservancy boundaries. Those whose parcel of land lies within the conservancy boundary may be required to lease only some section of it and retain sections which fall outside conservancy boundary for their livelihood benefits. The opportunity costs of settling in host parcel burden women more. The lifestyle of Maasai women is anchored on social networks with close familial ties. When families are resettled in host parcels, the lives of women change significantly in new neighbourhoods where they have to build new social networks. The Maasai Mara region lies on semi-arid and arid lands. It may have little or no rain, implying periodic scarcity of some resources like water. There are instances where resettlement to host parcels of land puts households in places that are quite some distance from natural water points. In such scenarios, it is women who have to bear the burden of walking long distances to access water for use at home.

Local communities within the Maasai Mara area have strong values of attachment to their land. Primarily, land provides ready pasture for their livestock, since they are pastoralists. With land and livestock, households can be food secure, because they can get milk, blood, and meat from their livestock. In addition, they may trade livestock products and get a monetary exchange for it. But for those resettled in host parcel resettlement, getting access to grazing pastures for their livestock can be problematic. First, conservancies have restricted

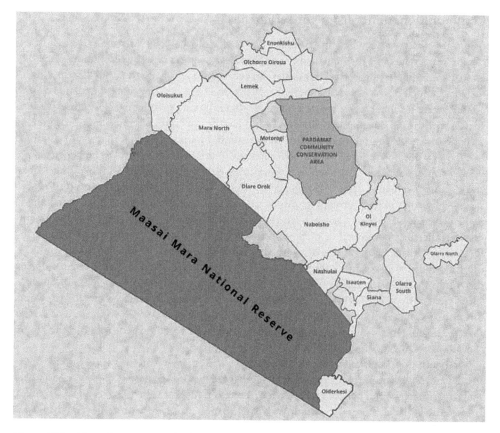

Figure 27.1   Map of conservancies in Maasai Mara
Source: http://maraconservancies.org.

access for livestock grazing. Second, there are bound to be competing needs for livestock grazing between the resettled household and the owner household of the host parcel of land. Those resettled are thus at the mercies of the host parcel owners to guarantee free full-time access to the grazing area. As a result, those who have been resettled in host parcels of land may get low productivity from their livestock. The effects of low productivity from livestock rearing leads to low household income, which can spill over to strain motherhood duties. This complicates women's tasks in providing food for their families, and they have to worry about fending for their families.

Women remain invisible in conservancies for reasons like culture. Typically, a number of women are married young due to customary practice. They may lack vocational skills to access alternative livelihoods. They may also lack life skills, for survival when exposed to risks like droughts and diseases.

Land lease benefits from conservancies do not factor in household size, but rather the size of land leased out for conservation. Given the costs of conservancies to traditional livelihood systems, bigger households are more vulnerable to worries about meeting their basic needs. A majority of local people in the Maasai Mara are have maintained their traditional livelihood systems, which draw much value from access to land resources than income from land lease fee. Studies show that income from livestock remains the highest source of income for most households whereas lease fees from land leased to conservancies are the most regular.

Community benefits from conservancies

The issue of community benefits from conservancies is debatable. Colonial practices of exclusion are pertinent in the management of conservation areas in Kenya (Akama et al., 2011), and this marginalizes local communities in decision making overuse and distribution of benefits accrued from rich natural heritage. When the right of entry to pastoral land is lost to conservation, local herders who are restricted from accessing grazing fields feel displaced. As part of the pastoral community, they agreed to changes in land use from traditional grazing activities to exclusive green agendas for conservation, on understanding that their traditional livelihood would be secured as would be their need to always have land. The benefit of accessing conservancy grazing reserves, conservancy employment in tourism investments, and conservancy payments, are solely enjoyed by conservancy members, yet vulnerabilities occasioned by conservancy set up, e.g. displacements, affect both members and non-members.

Perceived values for conservancy land benefits are divergent for male and female community members. As compared to men, women place less value on access to conservancy land for grazing (Keane et al., 2016). Men are affected more by restrictions on grazing land, having cost implications for fines of up to Ksh. 10,000, (Bedelian, 2014), while women compare the cost to food insecurity, in terms of the reduced number of livestock, lack of milk, (Talle, 1990, cited in Bedelian, 2014), and not being able to access resources like water and firewood. Since such vulnerabilities vary for different community members, there is a need to recognize the heterogeneity of community members, especially based on gendered dimensions, in the context of conservancy benefits.

Community conservancies in the Maasai Mara have great conviction in the dominant neoliberal conservation rhetoric, which attaches market values to nature's resources, in bid to secure partnerships and collaborations to its protection. Market value is attached to resources, to incentivize local pastoral community's participation in conservation. Market-based instruments, e.g. payment for ecosystem services (PES), ecotourism, and biodiversity offsets, give valuation standards to solve conservation problems. In PES, pastoral households forego some land for conservation purposes and are in turn paid an agreed rate per acre under conservation. Households are moved to areas near conservancy boundaries, either within or outside the boundaries. Silvestri et al. (2012), however, caution that PES lacks sensitivities to the gendered nature of resource use, and existing inequalities in access to land resources for pastoral communities disfavour women. According to Beledian (2014), wildlife conservancies in Maasai Mara are set up on lands whose owners benefited from the previously inequitable system of land distribution and pose considerable inequity implications. Pastoral women in the Maasai Mara, therefore, do not get direct benefits of income from PES, which is routed to landowner conservancy members. A few women have access to lease fees through secondment by their spouses or families.

The market value benefits in conservancies, streams down a previously inequitable beneficiary network, as structured by the patriarchal pastoral framework. In monetizing nature, the value of nature transforms into service benefiting genders inequitably. When resources are commodified in community conservancies, men and women do not stand equal chances of benefits. Community conservancy allows for greater participation, but ownership over resources based on a previously inequitable system, e.g. of land distribution, locks out many pastoral women. Participation in community conservancies is based on stewardship rights over resources. Rights to own, use, access, modify pastoral resources, are skewed in favour of men for pastoral communities.

Women involvement in conservation

In most community meetings attended by one of our chapter authors as a guest observer, the local community is represented by a male. For a long time, Maasai women have been side-lined in the management of and benefits derived from Maasai Mara's rich natural resources. Pastoral women in Maasai Mara are inactive in community affairs due to socio-cultural constraints. In Maasai livelihoods, where conservancies are developed, it is men who manage interactions with governments and outsiders such as tourism investors and take political and economic decisions on behalf of the households, including decisions around land use for grazing and conservation (Homewood et al., 2009).

Fortunately, conservancies acknowledge and are addressing challenges of ineffective participation of relevant actors in decision making, as well as unfair benefit-sharing criteria. Listed here, are women-specific issues, which are recurrent in conservancy documents (Sustainable Travel and Tourism Agenda, 2016; Maasai Mara Wildlife Conservancies Association, 2017)

- Few employment options for women by conservancy stakeholders
- Restricted information sharing about conservancy decision making with women
- Limited involvement of women in conservancy decision making
- Lack of women representatives in conservancy sub-committees, e.g. on bursaries
- Women not having the opportunity to explain their needs for development projects
- Women lacking basic information regarding what their rights are, relating to leases and conservancies.
- Slow information flow to women, regarding opportunities in tourism investments set up in conservancies.

Conservancies now have affirmative action to increase women's employment in tourism investments set up within community conservancies. Maasai Mara Wildlife Conservancies Association has a mandate of mainstreaming gender in the management of natural resources. By 2018, some conservancies had achieved their goal of including women in conservancy committees. By April 2018, Maasai Mara conservancies had enjoined a total of 50 women in conservancy boards. Their inclusion has unearthed steadfast conservation champions, as women are able to engage community members, and give feedback from conservancy board meetings, consequently transforming the community's views about conservancies (Maasai Mara Wildlife Conservancies Association, 2017). Other planned actions for conservancies to ensure effective participation of women actors in decision making include information sharing and empowerment programs and encouraging more women to attend Annual General Meetings.

Indeed, opportunities for women in tourism abound in project leadership, entrepreneurship, and employment. Conversely, the involvement of rural women in the tourism business is socially contested (Foley et al., 2018), with a burden to meet traditional gendered expectations in their communities. In rural communities where tourism projects are set up, as well as for most developing countries, the participation of women in tourism initiatives, especially through employment is usually marred with the dilemma of violent erasure of their traditional roles in motherhood and caregiving for families. Gains for women in tourism employment are burdened with pressing practical needs like negotiating domestic tasks with partners, double workload, and tensions resulting from employment (Duffy et al.,

2015). Furthermore, according to Women First (2010), some employment practices abuse precarious workers, and in tourism, women are over-represented in low paid occupations, and underrepresented in decision making roles. Overall, the participation of women in the tourism sector is constrained (Nyaruwata and Ntyyaruwata, 2013; Bazazo et al., 2017). This may result in a biased representation of the female workforce in tourism workspaces and may consequently normalize their marginalization in stakeholder input in community tourism projects. Conservancies, being in rural setups, have possibilities to exhibit aforementioned constraining characteristics to women's involvement in tourism.

On conservancy formation, research findings by Bedelian, (2014, p 102), show that women had no input, and were unaware of the onset of conservancy development. Pastoral women are entrenched in their cultural traditions and are oblivious of the need to be incorporated into community projects.

> we don't know anything, because it was formed abruptly, it was not much discussed, and we were never told. We heard there were meetings, and we heard that the land was given out, but we were never informed.
>
> we don't know because we are women and we are not in control. We have just heard that the contract needs to be increased but we don't know how it will be done... Even when the meetings are held, we are not included.
>
> myself I don't know, it is only men who know ... about conservancies. I told you before I only know about our cattle, but anything concerning about the land, its only men who know.

Aware that their power should be confined to domestic domains, the majority of pastoral women do not negotiate their participation in community conservancies. They are involved in securing family food systems and caregiving. Socio-cultural factors normalize their exclusion from conservancy activities. When their exclusion is viewed as normal, they see no need for activism or protest for their inclusion. Pastoral women within conservancy setups do not necessarily understand the structural inequalities that lead to their subordination. Adjustment in the socio-political environment of local communities is required to accept changes in gender relations caused by women's participation in tourism (Foley et al., 2018). The few avenues that have championed for pastoral women inclusion in conservancy activities in the Maasai Mara, largely originate from outsider push, e.g. regulations, and rarely from the women themselves.

Women's benefit from neoliberal conservation strategies in community conservancies is minimal. Pastoral women in Maasai Mara believe in gendered work spheres, i.e. some work is purely to be done by men, and others by women, and they should not interfere with each other. Introducing the bias of western feminism may be a challenge in such contexts. Nonetheless, conservancies are realizing the need for inclusion of women in their projects and have incorporated processes to enable their participation in conservancy matters. Pioneer conservancies for women inclusion in conservancy activities were Olare Orok Conservancy (OOC), and Naboisho Conservancy, both in Koiyaki. These two have succeeded in most of their goals of women empowerment. Naboisho Conservancy, set up in Koiyaki in 2010, has tourism investments set up on a 20946-ha land, on a 15-year lease period.

While community conservation in pastoral rangelands has great potential for environmental benefits, its impact on livelihood improvement remains debatable, as inequities in gender involvement taint developmental gains.

Motivations for women involvement in community conservancies

Women involvement in community-based tourism initiatives is highly influenced by their recognition of initiatives for environmental protection values in a project (Basecamp Foundation, 2018). Majority of those interviewed were contented that conservancies would put measures for the protection of ecosystems on which they depend on for resource availability. They were also happy that projects initiated, e.g. the use of solar lamps, are environmentally friendly and would contribute to positive adaptation to social and other changes resultant from conservancies.

The conservancies would also uphold pastoral livelihoods, which would be beneficial to their communities in terms of preserving cultures and traditions. Long term tourism leases ensured land remained available for future generations. And livestock rearing project preserved the pastoralist lifestyle while opening a market economy through trade in livestock and livestock products.

Entrepreneurship opportunities for women to sell beaded Maasai jewellery through tourist facilities in the conservancies shaped women's attitudes towards conservancies. In an open evaluation of one conservancy on Maasai Mara, women mentioned a lack of access to camps and lodges to sell beadwork as one of the unmet promises.

Roles played by women in community conservancies

Pastoral women are represented on conservancy boards and are assumed to participate in decision making by virtue of presence. This visibility allows women to voice. For instance, at Naboisho conservancy, the women representative board members have pushed agenda on access to clean water and earning a living from beadwork. Women also have informal networks to share information with other community members on important messages passed by the boards.

Pastoral women are elected to conservancy boards based on the constitutional requirement to have women representatives in all governing bodies at all levels of society organization. This need overlooks their indigenous knowledge and skills on natural resource management and environmental conservation. Their use of firewood, water, and wild fruits requires that they manage forests sustainably, and most pastoral women have mastered this skill. Conservancies, therefore, to some extent, fail to recognize knowledge capacities that women have on environmental matters, and may not give women duties related to such roles. This could be a limiting factor in pastoral women's participation in conservancy boards, through input in decision making.

Other roles played by women in conservancy projects include: mentoring and guiding girls in the community, contribution to the welfare of landowners, spearheading conflict resolution and peace-building, and lobbying for women access to employment and business opportunities.

Links for participation

There is a shift for pastoral women, from non-participation in community tourism projects, towards their inclusion in conservancy roles. Nonetheless, links for women participation in community-based tourism need to be strengthened, especially in remote conservancies situated in gendered societies. The current participation rate is not powerful enough, with women representation in decision making lacking. The inclusion of women in community-based tourism projects overlooks their skills that relate to conservation values and focuses only on the representative capacity of the female gender. This equals to tokenism, where their comments on decisions relating to conservation matters may be silenced. Community-based tourism projects may be missing out on stewardship benefits that would be advanced by pastoral women, who are equipped with knowledge and skills on resource management. Indeed, companies with greater female representation in their boardrooms often outperform their rivals (Catalyst, 2007).

The few women in leadership and boardrooms in conservancies are the first of their kind. In community conservancies in the Maasai Mara, there is a continuous lack of senior women role models for other pastoral women in the community.

Since mid-2016, conservancies in the Mara are conscious to integrate gender issues in all their activities. Their training programs help women overcome societal challenges, and the Women Leadership Forum aims to enhance leadership skills among women in conservancies.

Conclusion

Neoliberal structures of community conservancies in the Maasai Mara are dominated by patriarchal interests in their set up. However, the interests of women are now accommodated, with a realization that the developmental impacts of conservancy operations are gendered. Community conservancies inherit exclusion patterns from prevailing patriarchal systems, as well as previous unjust practices that disfavour women rights over resources. Male regimes of power are evident in community conservancies, creating conditions for exclusion from economic benefits for pastoral women.

The pastoral community in Maasai Mara is not a homogeneous group. Gendered differences are notable within the diversity of this pastoral community. One notable gender-blind assumption in community-based tourism initiatives is that pastoral livelihoods benefit men and women in equal measure. Unfortunately, the over-emphasis on pastoralism serves to blind focus on local women's income-generating activities, e.g. beadwork.

The second assumption is on terms under which women get elected to conservancy boards. Women serve best in boards as representatives of fellow women, and not in skilled capacities to offer any other knowledge related to conservancy benefits to the environment. For more women to assume participating roles in community tourism initiatives, the pastoral frame that largely defines livelihood systems of local communities has to be redefined. The reality of community conservancy is "man-made" construed from a patriarchal view of the salient male role of pastoralism and provides fertile context to flourish the idea of equity first, as advanced by Franks et al. (2018). Conservancies need to embrace a post pastoral outlook, to filter out inequalities that disfavour women participation in projects.

References

Aguilar, L., Itza, C., and Hilda, S. (2002). In search of the lost gender equity in protected areas. IUCN. Social program. MesoAmerican office. World Commission on Protected areas. Absoluto, SA.

Akama, J.S., Maingi, S., and Blanca, A.C.(2011). Wildlife conservation, Safari Tourism, and the role of tourism certification in Kenya: A post-colonial critique. *Tourism Recreation Research. Vol 36(3), pp 281–291.*

Basecamp Foundation Kenya (2018). *Report of Assessment of Status of Landowner Rights in Conservancies in Maasai Mara.* Basecamp Foundation. Narok.

Bazazo, I., Nasseef, M.A., Mukattesh, B., Kastero, D., and Al–Hallaq, M. (2017). Assessing the glass ceiling effect for women in tourism and hospitality. *Journal of management and strategy. Vol 8(3), pp 51–68.*

Bedelian, C. (2014). Conservation, tourism and pastoral livelihoods: Wildlife conservancies in the Maasai Mara, Kenya. PhD thesis submitted to University College of London.

Berman, T. (2001). The rape of Mother Nature? Women in the language of environmental discourse, In Fill, A. and Mühlhäusler (Eds.) *The Ecolinguists Reader: Language, Ecology and Environment*, pp 258–269. London: Continuum.

Berman, T. (1994). The rape of Mother Nature? Women in the language of environmental discourse, *Trumpeter. Vol 11 (4), pp 173–178*.

Carter, A. (2019). "We don't equal just even one man": Gender and social control on conservation adoption. *Society and Natural Resources. Vol 32(8), pp 893–910*.

Catalyst. (2007). *The Bottom-line: Corporate Performance and Women's Representations on Boards*. New York: Catalyst.

Daly, M. (1980). *Gyn/Ecology. The Meta Ethics of Radical Feminism*. Boston, MA: Beacon Press.

Duffy, L.N., Kline, C.S., Mowatt, R.A., and Chancellor, H.C. (2015). Women in tourism: Shifting gender ideology in the DR. *Annals of Tourism Research. Vol 52, pp 72–86*.

Fill, A., and Muhlhausler, P. (2001). *The Ecolinguistics Reader: Language, Ecology and Environment*. London and New York: Continuum.

Foley, C., Grabowski, S., Small, J., and Wearing, S. (2018). Women of the Kokoda: From poverty to empowerment in sustainable tourism development. *Tourism, Culture and Communication. Vol 18, pp 1–15*.

Franks, P., Booker, F., and Roe, D. (2018). Understanding and assessing equity in protected area conservation: A matter of governance, rights, social impacts and human well-being. IIED Issue Paper. IIED, London.

Garrard, G. (2004). *Ecocriticism*. London: Routledge.

Gosh, A. (2016). *The Great Derangement: Climate Change and the Unthinkable*. Chicago: University of Chicago Press.

Hall, D., Swain, M.B., and Kinnaird, V. (2003). Tourism and gender: An evolving agenda. *Tourism Recreation Research. Vol 28(2), pp 7–11*.

Homewood, K., Kristjanson, P., and Chenevix, T.P. (2009). *Staying Maasai? Livelihoods, Conservation and Development in East African Rangelands*. New York: Springer.

Jamhawi, M., Al-Shorman, A., Hajahjah, A., Okour, Y., and Alkhalidi, M. (2015). Gender equality in tourism industry: A case study from Madaba, Jordan. *Journal of Global Research in Education and Social Science. Vol 4(4), pp 225–234*.

Kanhiya, M. (2016). Role of women in environment conservation. *Journal of Advanced Laboratory Research in Biology. Vol 7(1), pp 17–26*.

Keane, A., Gurd, H., Kaelo, D., Siad, M.Y., de Leeuw, J., Rowcliffe, J.M., and Homewood, K. (2016). Gender differentiated preferences for a community based conservation initiative. *PLoS One. Vol 11 (3), pp e0152432*.

Loftsdottir, K. (2001). Women in pastoral societies: Applying WID, eco-feminist, and postmodernist perspectives. *Arizona Anthropologist. Vol 14, pp 81–98*.

Lundberg, A. (2018). Gender equality in conservation management: Reproducing or transforming gender differences through local participation. *Society and Natural Resources. Vol 31(11), pp 1266–1282*.

Maasai Mara Wildlife Conservancies Association. (2018). *Voice of the Mara*. Retrieved from Maasai Mara Wildlife Conservancies Association: https://www.flipsnack.com/MMWCA/voice-of-the-mara-4th-edition.html

Maasai Mara Wildlife Conservancies Association. (2017, May). *Voice of the Mara*. Retrieved from Maasai Mara Wildlife Conservancies Association: https://www.maraconservancies.org/wp-content/uploads/2017/05/MMWCA-Quarterly-Newsletter1.pdf

Merchant, C. (1983). *The Death of Nature: Women, Ecology and the Scientific Revolution*. San Francisco: Harper Collins.

Nardizzi, V. (2016). Shakespeare's queer pastoral ecology: Alienation around Arden. *Interdisciplinary Studies in Literature and Environment. Vol 23(3), pp 564–582*.

Nyaruwata, S., and Ntyyaruwata, L.T. (2013). Gender equity and executive management in tourism: Challenges in Southern Africa Development Community Region. *African Journal of Business Management, Vol 7(21), pp 2059–2070*.

Pritchard, A., and Morgan, N. (2007). De-centring tourism's intellectual universe or the dialectic between change and tradition. In Ateljevic, I., Pritchard, A., and Morgan, N. (Eds.), *The Critical Turning in Tourism Studies*, pp 12–28. Oxford: Elsevier.

Silvestri, S., Osano, P., De Leeuw, J., Herrero, M., Ericksen, P., Kariuki, J., Njuki, J., Bedelian, C., and Notenbaert, A. (2012). *Greening Livestock: Assessing the Potential of Payment for Environmental Services in Livestock Inclusive Agricultural Production Systems in Developing Countries.* Nairobi, Kenya: International Livestock Research Institute.

Sustainable Travel and Tourism Agenda, (2016). *Mara Naboisho Conservancy Ecostorm Report.* Nairobi: Sustainable Travel and Tourism Agenda.

Talle, A. (1990). Ways of meat and milk among the Maasai. In Palsson, G. (Ed.), *From Water to World Making.* African Models and Arid Lands, pp 73–93. Uppsala, Sweden: Scandinavian Institute of African Studies.

Women First (2010). *The case for change: Women working in hospitality, leisure, travel and tourism.* Available online from: https://www.slideshare.net/Emoturismo/women-working-in-hospitality. Accessed on 20 August, 2020.

InFocus 7
Red Rocks Initiatives for Sustainable Development

Greg Bakunzi

Red Rocks Initiatives for Sustainable Development (RRISD) is the brainchild of Greg Bakunzi, as an initiative that started operating in Nyakinama Village, 8 kilometres from Musanze town (Rwanda) in 2013. RRISD is an African non-profit organization that supports sustainable development in Africa by engaging in sustainable tourism and community driven environmental conservation initiatives that are meant to benefit local communities. RRISD initiatives were initiated on the principle that sustainable tourism and community driven environmental conservation are effective tools for poverty eradication when done correctly and in an inclusive manner. By placing aside wistful thinking and self-driven profit-making motifs, RRISD evolved into a partnership with ten ecotourism ventures, one charitable NGO, and five volunteers to fulfil a diverse programme of activities. In this way, RRISD has been able to change the narrative about individualism and self-driven interests by establishing a number of local and international partnerships, which have led to a number of successes. For instance, Red Rocks' ecotourism program continues to provide environmentally sensitive employment to approximately 50 local community members, mostly youth and women, leading to local socio-economic development. RRISD has scaled up their conservationist approach by engaging and forging mutually beneficial partnerships with conservation professionals and community development organizations to provide specialist input required to operate in a truly impactful way. This approach has enabled RRISD to effectively utilize external donors' funds leading to examples of best practices and greater confidence by visiting tourists who can verify how 'their dollars are actually making the profound local differences'.

The model employed by RRISD is based on a 'pragmatic ripple effect approach', aimed at generating a beneficial multiplier effect in the 30 communities in which it operates. For instance, surplus income, produced through its ecotourism operations, enables workers and/or their family members to start up their own small businesses or pass on income to other community members by buying local goods, paying for child care and other services. The value chain generated through RRISD's operation has become stronger year on year with approximately 30 communities' members being directly and indirectly positively impacted upon. In addition to this, RRISD's partnership with the Igihoho Support Cooperative Program promotes sustainable forest management, balancing social, environmental and economic concerns to meet today's needs (i.e. agricultural and logging), while guaranteeing the survival of local forests for future generations. Another example includes RRISD's collaborations with local visual artists and an art gallery in Kinigi, which has become a hub for Musanze's tourism industry and Rwanda in general by sensitizing audiences about conservation and tourism through art classes and artists' artwork aimed at promoting environmental protection for the survival of endangered animal and plant species. Of similar importance is the work of RRISD with the Botanical Gardens around Volcanoes National Parks, where RRISD is involved in protecting indigenous plant species, particularly those involved in traditional medicine and healing. In addition to this, RRISD is involved in encouraging and supporting families to grow nutritious foods in their backyards, sensitizing the local community about the benefits of nutritious foods, providing them with vegetable seeds to grow as well as small livestock's, such as sheep, goat and local chicken.

In 2017, RRISD joined forces with Kahuzi-Biega Community Conservation Trust in the eastern Democratic Republic of Congo (DRC) to identify mutually beneficial and inclusive ways to harness tourism, conservation and sustainable community development in and around Kahuzi-Biega National Park. Under the Karibu Community Conservation Trust Fund, the partnership brings together conservationists, conservation lovers and other environmental management patrons to progress research on the primates found in the park, which include the Lowland gorillas as well as other primates. Through these initiatives and a host of innovative programs established by RRISD, tourism and conservation have been brought together as a conduit to sustainable development around the Volcanoes National Park and the wider Virunga massif, which expands across three countries – Uganda, Rwanda and DRC.

Figure IF7.1 Award of a Sustainable Top Destination in Africa to the Kahuzi-Biega National Park, D.R. Congo at ITB 2019

Source: Author.

Figure IF7.2   Red Rocks Art Gallery in Kinigi, Rwanda
Source: Author.

Figure IF7.3   A tourist on one of the agritourism activities organised by Red Rocks Initiative
with community partners
Source: Author.

RRISD strongly believe in the paramount importance of empowering local communities through education and entrepreneurship, which have proved to go hand in hand with the conservation of the natural environment. RRISD's experience has proved that where and when local communities have been enabled to gain (directly or indirectly) from thriving tourism in their backyards, they become key in protecting their environment and move away from illegal activities like poaching or logging in protected areas, which are activities deeply rooted in histories of rural poverty and marginalization, often leading to irreversible threats to many species, including the iconic mountain gorillas.

RRISD has been highly commended by Rwanda based organizations for its efforts in promoting responsible tourism and for its community development agenda. Its many successes have become also the recipient of a number of national and international awards, including the 2012/2013 Rwanda Development Board (RDB) Business Excellence Award for being amongst the TOP 100 mid-sized company; the 2015 inclusion in the A-Team for Wildlife 'Wall of Fame' for its contribution during the Giving Grid Fundraiser. In January 2016, at the International Tourism Fair of Madrid (FITUR), RRISD received an award by the United Nations World Tourism Organization (UNWTO), FITUR and Casa Africa in recognition of its role as African best responsible travel company. In January 2019, at FITUR, RRISD received another award by the UNWTO, FITUR and Casa Africa in recognition of its activities promoting tourism, conservation and community development in and around the Volcanoes National Park in northern Rwanda. Receiving these awards have had a substantial impact on local communities' sense of pride and belonging as well as a further push for all parties involved in continuing with its challenging, but rewarding mission aimed at enhancing mutual coexistence between human beings and wildlife and to preserve endangered flora and fauna so that the park remains at its pristine state.

Part VI
Tourism in Southern Africa

28

City tourism in Southern Africa

Progress and issues

Christian M. Rogerson and Jayne M. Rogerson

Introduction

Debates about tourism development in sub-Saharan Africa traditionally focus around the region's big five wildlife products, its iconic attractions of natural beauty (e.g. Victoria Falls) as well as the newer growth points in the landscape of African tourism such as cultural heritage tourism products, adventure tourism or volunteer tourism (Rogerson & Rogerson 2018a). With certain exceptions, the geographical location of the vast majority of these tourism attractions is in rural areas. Not surprisingly, therefore, the mainstream tourism scholarship for sub-Saharan Africa concentrates on interrogating issues concerning the impacts of tourism development for local communities in rural environments (Rogerson & Rogerson 2011; Novelli 2015). What is sometimes overlooked, however, is that Africa's cities are important and vibrant tourism destinations. Indeed, for several African countries, particularly those where leisure travel remains undeveloped, cities – and especially capital cities – are the core tourism destinations. In the global North there has appeared a vibrant literature around city tourism and in particular discussions on its multiple ramifications for post-Fordist urban development (Ashworth & Page 2011 for review). The task in this chapter is to provide an overview of scholarship on city tourism in the sub-region of Southern Africa, the most urbanised part of sub-Saharan Africa as well as the most well-documented region in terms of city tourism research.

At the outset, it must be appreciated that across sub-Saharan Africa the phenomenon of city tourism is not new. From the birth of urban settlements, people with the discretionary means and inclination to travel became tourists in order to experience these spaces as melting pots of culture, art, music, literature, architecture and design (Cohen & Cohen 2015). In addition, because of the accumulation of economic and political power in cities and of their command role in national settlement systems, urban settlements become vital destinations for tourism visits for non-leisure purposes, most notably for business travel (Rogerson & Rogerson 2018a). In particular, during the colonial period, African cities as administrative centres emerged as significant focal points for government officials and often functioned as the initial trigger for the growth of a rudimentary accommodation services sector (Magombo et al. 2017).

At present, with the advance of globalisation, the rise of post-independence African economies and the growth of the middle class, cities are key destinations for tourism across the continent. People visit cities for several purposes (and frequently for more than one reason) including for leisure and entertainment, for business, to visit friends and relatives or to undertake personal business which can include shopping or health visits (Rogerson & Rogerson 2017). However, African city tourism is not simply the domain of the wealthy or middle-income strata. Indeed, it is evident that with improved transportation mobilities the poor are also becoming tourists (Rogerson & Mthombeni 2015; Rogerson & Saarinen 2018). For the poor, leisure is not the primary reason for travel instead they become tourists primarily for the reasons of visiting friends and relatives staying in cities, for business purposes or sometimes to secure much-needed health services which are unavailable in small towns or rural areas (Crush et al. 2012; Crush & Chikanda 2015; C.M. Rogerson 2015a, 2017a, b). Arguably, unlike the situation of leisure-dominated nature tourism localities in rural areas or of beach resort destinations, cities across Africa must be understood as multi-motivated or multi-purpose travel destinations.

This survey of the 'state of the art' of city tourism in Southern Africa is informed by the viewpoint that 'a review of past research efforts is an important endeavour in all academic research areas' (Nunkoo et al. 2013: 5). Among its advantages are to identify knowledge gaps where additional research is required as well as potentially to facilitate theoretical advances.

Key research foci in city tourism research

A search for relevant literature on city tourism in Southern Africa was undertaken (June 2018) for the post-2000 period using the contents of leading serials of tourism and hospitality research as well as other significant outlets for African tourism research. For the purposes of this investigation, the Southern African region was defined as including cities in Angola, Botswana, Lesotho, Malawi, Mozambique, Namibia, South Africa, Swaziland, Zambia and Zimbabwe.

Motivating the search beyond the mainstream of tourism and hospitality journals was the observation made in previous reviews that much tourism research about Africa appears outside of the leading international tourism serials. Instead, it is in newer journals, most notably the *African Journal of Hospitality Tourism and Leisure,* which presently publishes the greatest volume of papers (mainly case studies) on African tourism (Rogerson & Rogerson 2011, 2013, 2019a). In addition to tourism journals it has been recorded in previous surveys of African tourism scholarship that a significant amount of tourism research is available in non-tourism journals such as those of urban or development studies, African studies and human geography (Rogerson & Visser 2011; Rogerson & Rogerson 2013; Rogerson & Visser 2014; Visser & Rogerson 2014). In the context of this survey examples of such journals which carry a number of articles on city tourism are *Development Southern Africa, Urban Forum, Urbani izziv, Bulletin of Geography: Socio-Economic Series* and the *South African Geographical Journal.*

The results of the search disclosed over 100 published articles, book chapters or monographs which directly address core research issues about city tourism in Southern Africa. Within this body of scholarship, the largest volume of writings is produced by geographers. Overall, the greatest share of this literature relates to South Africa where since the 1994 democratic transition tourism has emerged as a leading topic for urban researchers in response partially to the new importance attached by national and local governments for tourism promotion (Rogerson & Visser 2005; Nel & Rogerson 2016). Outside South Africa, a smaller number of studies concerning different aspects of city tourism are available for several countries including Botswana (Mbaiwa et al. 2007; Sigwele et al. 2018), Lesotho (Rogerson & Letsie 2013), Malawi (Magombo & Rogerson 2012; Magombo et al. 2017), Mozambique (Vignati & Laumans 2010), Namibia (Buning & Grunau 2014), Swaziland (Ginindza & Tichaawa 2017) and Zimbabwe (Makoni & Tichaawa 2017). The most neglected countries for city tourism research are Angola and Mozambique.

In terms of thematic foci, several research clusters can be isolated albeit these are not discreet. Six clusters are identified relating to (1) African cities as business tourist destinations, (2) the emergence of cities as tourism destinations, (3) tourism and urban economic restructuring associated with the establishment of new leisure tourism products, (4) slum tourism, (5) the growth of accommodation services and (6) informal sector tourism. Key themes and relevant contributions in each of these clusters of work are now briefly outlined.

Exploring six themes in city tourism research

Coles and Mitchell (2009: 3) assert that contemporary Africa is 'the only continent where the number of business tourists consistently exceeds leisure tourists'. Indeed, within the world tourism economy, one of the most distinguishing characteristics of Africa is that business tourism accounts for a higher proportion of overall tourism receipts than for other global regions (C.M. Rogerson 2014a, 2015b, c). According to Daly (2017), business travel accounts for 31 percent of total tourism spending in Africa as compared to 23 percent in Europe or 20 percent in Asia-Pacific. In addition, 18 of the top 20 countries in the world with the largest proportions of business travel in their overall tourism portfolio are from sub-Saharan Africa (Daly 2017). Among that list of countries five are in the region of Southern Africa, namely Lesotho, Swaziland, Malawi, Mozambique and Zambia. Overwhelmingly the activity of business travel is focussed on cities, especially large economic centres and/or capital cities, which are the location of economic and political power. Cities such as Johannesburg, Harare, Lusaka, Maputo, Maseru, Pretoria, or Windhoek are the sites for meetings for private sector businesses at headquarter offices as well as meetings with government, NGOs and international development agencies. The construction of convention centres situated in large cities or national capitals (such as Lilongwe) has been a vital catalyst for conference business travel, much of which is by regional (African) or domestic travellers as well as a smaller flow of long-haul international business travellers. One sign of the expansion of business travel in Africa is the recent boom in upmarket hotel accommodation operated by or branded by major Northern based hotel chains such as Marriott, Hilton or Accor as well as – in the case of Southern Africa – by the expansion of South African-based hotel chains (J.M. Rogerson 2016a). The most economically vibrant cities in the region are the major geographical foci for business tourists with Johannesburg, Cape Town and Pretoria of particular note. The vital significance of formal sector business tourism in these cities is documented in several research investigations (C.M. Rogerson 2005, 2011b; Donaldson 2013; C.M. Rogerson 2014a, b, 2015c).

As earlier indicated, tourism flows to African cities can be tracked from the origins of urban settlements and of colonial expansion with business travel one of the initial triggers for tourism in cities. This said, the beginnings of modern city tourism in Southern Africa are found in the improved context for mobilities which occurred with transportation improvements during the 20th century. In common with trends in global scholarship on urban tourism, however, most research remains overwhelmingly 'present-minded'. Across the entire region of Southern Africa, historical scholarship on city tourism is undeveloped. The only exceptions are studies on South Africa and Malawi. For Cape Town, Bickford-Smith (2009) interrogates how different tourism sites and particular tourism gazes were constructed. Contemporary developments in urban tourism are situated 'within a historical analysis of the place-selling of this city from the late 19th century onwards' (Bickford-Smith 2009: 1765). Another historical study is that of the early development of tourism in Johannesburg for the period from 1920 when the first tourism promotional activities were initiated to 1950 when the national government enacted the Group Areas Act which began the radical remaking of tourism under the influence of apartheid legislation (Rogerson & Rogerson 2019b). City tourism under apartheid is scrutinised both by Jayne Rogerson (2016b, 2017), who analyses the rise and fall of racial segregation of beaches across South Africa's major coastal leisure destinations, and by Christian Rogerson (2019) in terms of the beginnings of conference tourism in the country's major urban centres. For Malawi, Magombo et al. (2017) trace the formative years of tourism in both the colonial and post-independence periods highlighting its particular significance for the major administrative centres.

In terms of contemporary tourism issues, urban economic restructuring emerges as a central theme in much city tourism scholarship for Southern Africa. This thread of scholarly endeavour mirrors that in the global North where tourism 'has become an essential tool for economic regeneration and employment creation, for place promotion, for re-imaging cities and helping to create identity in the new global system' (Williams 2009: 208). Specifically, this topic is strongly evidenced in South Africa where local governments have a developmental mandate to promote place-based development initiatives and tourism is viewed as a tool of economic diversification (C.M. Rogerson 2014b; Nel & Rogerson 2016). With high levels of unemployment and stagnation in manufacturing employment, city governments have sought to leverage tourism as a driver for local economic growth, employment creation and small business development. The significance of innovation for building competitive city destinations is reinforced by findings from South Africa's Western Cape province (Booyens & Rogerson 2016, 2017a, b).

Divergent trajectories of urban tourism development are disclosed in the experience of South Africa's major cities with the coastal centres of Cape Town and Durban leveraging a different set of tourism products to that of Johannesburg, a 'non-traditional' tourism destination (C.M. Rogerson 2002a, 2003; Rogerson & Visser 2006, 2007; Rogerson & Rogerson 2014a; Rogerson & Wolfaardt 2016). This said, all the country's major cities are involved in active initiatives for job creation and inclusive economic growth using tourism (C.M. Rogerson 2002b, 2008, 2013; Nel & Rogerson 2016). The target markets are both international and domestic tourists (C.M. Rogerson 2013, 2015d). In Ekurhuleni, one distinctive pathway of planning for tourism is associated with the unfolding aerotropolis development which is taking root around O.R. Tambo International Airport, South Africa's major gateway (C.M. Rogerson 2018a). As a reflection of the broader phenomenon of cultural commodification, the leading focus of tourism promotion in South African cities is the production of new experiences for leisure consumption. Waterfront re-developments (most notably in Cape Town and Durban), the hosting of festivals and sports events (including the FIFA World Cup), the building of casinos, new shopping and leisure complexes (especially Sandton City and The Mall of Africa) and the creation of cultural heritage products have been at the forefront of city tourism boosterism in South Africa (Ferreira 2011; van der Merwe 2013; Nyakana et al. 2014; Rogerson & Harmer 2015; Rogerson & Rogerson 2017; Boucher et al. 2018; Roux 2018; van der Merwe & Rogerson 2018). Moreover, a number of niche forms of tourism are promoted including backpacker tourism, gay tourism, volunteer tourism and even adventure tourism (Visser 2002, 2003; Rogerson & Visser 2006, 2007, 2011; McKay 2013; Van der Merwe 2013; Rogerson & Slater 2014; Harmer & Rogerson 2017a). Considerable attention currently focuses around opportunities for innovation in terms of new products in creative tourism (C.M. Rogerson 2006; Booyens & Rogerson 2015, 2018), food tourism (Ferreira & de Villiers 2014; Naicker & Rogerson 2017) and 'off the beaten track' inner-city walking tours (Hoogendoorn & Giddy 2017).

The challenges of building city tourism destinations for image enhancement, employment expansion, economic growth and the physical regeneration of declining areas through new leisure products have been investigated in South Africa's leading metropolitan areas (Rogerson 2002a, 2003; Rogerson & Kaplan 2005; Ferreira & Visser 2007: Rogerson & Visser 2007; Ferreira 2011; Rogerson & Visser 2011; C.M. Rogerson 2013; Ferreira & de Villiers 2014). In addition, work also has been undertaken in the next tier of the settlement hierarchy, namely secondary cities, where a different set of leisure tourism attractions are at centre-stage, including agritourism, avitourism, festivals, food and wine tourism, golf as well as heritage tourism (Ramukumba 2012; Ramukumba et al. 2012; Ferreira & Muller 2013; Van der Merwe & Rogerson 2013; Rogerson & Rogerson 2014b; Harmer & Rogerson 2017b). A new research focus in city tourism scholarship concerns resident perceptions of tourism products in Southern African cities, including Zimbabwe's capital city of Harare (Makoni & Tichaawa 2017; Tichaawa & Moyo 2019) and of Buffalo City and Port Elizabeth in South Africa (Tichaawa et al. 2015; Apleni 2017). In Botswana's capital city, Gaborone, the search for a competitive brand for tourism development has been investigated (Sigwele et al. 2018).

The appearance during the 1990s and subsequent rise of slum tourism as a leisure product targeted at Northern tourists visiting African cities is one of the most distinctive facets of city tourism in Southern Africa. Slum tourism represents the touristic valorisation of poverty and is a new niche in international tourism, primarily focused on destinations in the urban global South (Frenzel et al. 2012, 2015; Frenzel 2016). At the heart of slum tourism is organised tours to deprived areas or concentrated locations of poverty in cities (Frenzel 2012; Steinbrink et al. 2012). One of the global origins for slum tourism is South Africa where organised tours began for tourists to 'gaze' at poverty in the country's apartheid created 'townships', most notably Soweto which is the cradle of the anti-apartheid struggle. The popularity of such tours in South Africa has escalated such that visits to slums are increasingly a 'must do' item on the bucket list of Western tourists (Rogerson & Saarinen 2018). Over the past two decades, the geographical spread of slum tourism has occurred with its launch in several other cities of South Africa (especially Cape Town and Durban) and elsewhere across the region of Southern Africa, including Harare and Windhoek (Rolfes et al. 2009; Buning & Grunau 2014).

Accompanying this growth, slum tourism scholarship has expanded to become what Burgold et al. (2013: 101) views 'an established field' in tourism research. Much attention concentrates on whether this form of tourism has pro-poor impacts and thereby contributes to ameliorate poverty conditions in destination slum areas (Booyens 2010; Koens 2012; Frenzel 2013; Koens & Thomas 2015, 2016). Issues relating to empowerment, entrepreneurship and small enterprise development, of residents' perceptions of slum tourists, safety and security, as well as representation and authenticity in the narratives and practices of slum tour operators; and, the potential impacts of slum tours for re-imaging slum areas have been investigated as distinctive contributions to slum tourism scholarship (C.M. Rogerson 2004a, b; Nemasetoni & Rogerson 2005; C.M. Rogerson 2008; Koens 2012; Burgold & Rolfes 2013; Burgold et al. 2013; George & Booyens 2014; Frenzel 2016; Roux 2018). Recent attention centres on the potential for innovation in product development and of opportunities for diversifying the poverty tour to include new creative tourism offerings (Booyens & Rogerson 2019a, b).

The evolution of a vibrant commercial accommodation services sector is both a consequence of the growth of a formal leisure and business tourism economy as well as a prerequisite for further expansion in terms of city competitiveness (Magombo et al. 2017; Rogerson & Rogerson 2018a). Over the past decade, the commercial accommodation sector has emerged as a significant research topic both for South African cities and others in the region. The growth and restructuring of the hotel industry have attracted most attention particularly in South African cities. Themes of investigation have included *inter alia*, the role of liquor in shaping the character of accommodation services (C.M. Rogerson 2011a), the segmentation and appearance of different forms of hotel (J.M. Rogerson 2010, 2011a, b, 2013a; Ferreira & Boshoff 2014), hotels as a property asset class (J.M. Rogerson 2012a), the greening of hotels and responsible tourism practices (Frey & George 2010; Rogerson & Sims 2012; Ismail & Rogerson 2016), food sourcing arrangements (Pillay & Rogerson 2013), the changing location of hotels both at the inter-urban and intra-urban scales of investigation (J.M. Rogerson 2012b, 2013b, c, d, e, 2014a, b, 2018; Rogerson & Rogerson 2018b); and, the expansion of South African hotel chains into other parts of Africa (J.M. Rogerson 2016a). Beyond the hotel sector, other kinds of accommodation have gathered attention. Research has appeared variously on backpacker hostels, bed and breakfasts (including in townships), guest houses as well as serviced apartments (for business tourists) (C.M. Rogerson 2004a, b, 2007; Greenberg & Rogerson 2015, 2018). Such forms of commercial accommodation occur widely across major cities. More spatially concentrated is timeshare accommodation which is primarily focused on coastal destinations (Pandy & Rogerson 2013, 2014a, b). Most recently, research has evolved on the sharing economy with Airbnb accommodation under scrutiny both in South Africa (Visser et al. 2017) and Swaziland (Ginindza & Tichaawa 2017).

The last major theme of city tourism research concerning Southern Africa is informal sector tourism. Informality is the most distinctive characteristic of the economic landscape of cities in the global South. Nevertheless, only recently is there recognition by tourism scholars that much (if perhaps even the majority) of travel and tourism in the global South is of an informal sector character (Gladstone 2005). Tourism scholars 'discovered' and began applying the concept of the informal sector several years after the term was first introduced into the lexicon of development studies by the ILO (1972) and Hart's (1973) seminal study. Although usually overlooked in tourism planning support for the activities of informal tourism entrepreneurs is important in terms of promoting more inclusive forms of tourism development. The existence of a substantial informal sector of tourism encompasses mobilities for the purposes of leisure, business, VFR, health and sometimes for religious purposes (Cohen & Cohen 2015).

In cities, an informal sector of leisure tourism is manifest in activities of beachfront vendors, unlicensed tour guides or handicraft sellers. Across cities in Southern Africa, however, by far the major element in informal sector tourism is the activities of informal sector shopper traders. Johannesburg in particular has been a magnet for informal cross-border shopper/traders from surrounding countries in the region (C.M. Rogerson 2011b, 2015b, c, 2018b). Beyond the activities of international cross-border shoppers, there is also a less well-documented economy of domestic informal sector business tourism. Once again shoppers/traders are a major component (Rogerson & Mthombeni 2015). However, from Maseru there is evidence also that this informal business economy of domestic travellers also includes farmers as well as vendors of traditional medicine (Rogerson & Letsie 2013). Finally, within the informal sector of travel must be considered also the mobilities of large numbers of mainly poor VFR travellers coming into cities for short periods of time from small towns or rural areas (Rogerson 2017a, b). Given its size, the oversight by tourism scholars of the informal sector of city tourism needs to be corrected.

Conclusions

Urban tourism must be recognised as a critical and growing component of the African tourism economy. From the experience of Southern Africa, it is evident that whilst certain parallels are observable with developments taking place in city tourism across the global North, there are certain highly distinctive facets of tourism in African cities. For most African cities it must be acknowledged that tourism is growing mainly because of non-leisure forms of tourism. Arguably, the most notable features of African city tourism are the relative strength of cities as non-leisure destinations (most especially for business tourism), the rise of slum tourism and of the existence of an extensive informal economy of city tourism. Tourism scholars of Africa need to engage further with the extensive research agenda around city tourism.

Acknowledgement

The University of Johannesburg is thanked for financial support of our research.

References

Apleni, L. (2017) 'Residents' perceptions on urban tourism as a catalyst for economic development: a case study of Buffalo City, South Africa', *African Journal of Hospitality, Tourism and Leisure*, 6 (3): 1–16.

Ashworth, G. and Page, S. (2011) 'Urban tourism research: recent progress and current paradoxes', *Tourism Management*, 32: 1–15.

Bickford-Smith, V. (2009) 'Creating a city of the tourist imagination: the case of Cape Town, "The Fairest Cape of all"', *Urban Studies*, 46 (9): 1763–1785.

Booyens, I. (2010) 'Rethinking township tourism: towards responsible tourism development in South African townships', *Development Southern Africa*, 27 (2): 273–287.

Booyens, I. and Rogerson, C.M. (2015) 'Creative tourism in Cape Town: an innovation perspective', *Urban Forum*, 26: 405–424.

Booyens, I. and Rogerson, C.M. (2016) 'Unpacking the geography of tourism innovation in the Western Cape Province of South Africa', *Bulletin of Geography: Socio-Economic Series*, 31: 19–36.

Booyens, I. and Rogerson, C.M. (2017a) 'Tourism networking, learning and innovation: evidence from the Western Cape, South Africa', *Tourism Geographies*, 19 (3): 340–361.

Booyens, I. and Rogerson, C.M. (2017b) 'Managing tourism firms in South Africa for competitiveness: an innovation perspective', *Tourism Review International*, 21 (1): 49–61.

Booyens, I. and Rogerson, C.M. (2019a) 'Recreating slum tourism: perspectives from South Africa', *Urbani izziv*, 30 (Supplement): 52–63.

Booyens, I. and Rogerson, C.M. (2019b) 'Creative tourism: South African township explorations', *Tourism Review*, 74 (2): 256–267.

Boucher, S., Cullen, M. and Calitz, A. (2018) 'Factors influencing cultural event tourism in Nelson Mandela Bay, South Africa', *Journal of Tourism and Cultural Change*, 16 (5): 539–551.

Buning, M. and Grunau, T. (2014) 'Touring Katutura!: developments, structures and representations in township tourism in Windhoek (Namibia)', Paper presented at the Destination Slum! 2 Conference, University of Potsdam, Potsdam, Germany, 14–16 May.

Burgold, J., Frenzel, F. and Rolfes, M. (2013) 'Observations on slums and their touristification', *Die Erde*, 144 (2): 99–104.

Burgold, J. and Rolfes, M., (2013) 'Of voyeuristic safari tours and responsible tourism with educational value: Observing moral communication in slum and township tourism in Cape Town and Mumbai', *Die Erde*, 144 (2): 161–174.

Cohen, E. and Cohen, S.A. (2015) 'A mobilities approach to tourism from emerging world regions', *Current Issues in Tourism*, 18 (1): 11–43.

Coles, C. and Mitchell, J. (2009) *Pro Poor Analysis of the Business and Conference Value Chain in Accra: Final Report*, London: Overseas Development Institute.

Crush, J. and Chikanda, A. (2015) 'South-South medical tourism and the quest for health in southern Africa', *Social Science and Medicine*, 124: 313–320.

Crush, J., Chikanda, A. and Maswika, B. (2012) *Patients without Borders: Medical Tourism and Medical Migration in Southern Africa*, Cape Town: Southern African Migration Programme.

Daly, J. (2017) *Key Characteristics of African Tourism GVCs*, London: Commonwealth Secretariat International Trade Working Paper 2017/03.

Donaldson, R. (2013) 'Conference tourism: What do we know about the business tourist in South Africa?', *African Journal for Physical, Health Education, Recreation and Dance*, 19 (Supplement 2): 24–38.

Ferreira, S. (2011) 'South African tourism road to recovery: 2010 FIFA soccer world cup as a vehicle', *Tourism Review International*, 15 (1/2): 91–106.

Ferreira, S. and Boshoff, A. (2014) 'Post-2010 FIFA soccer world cup: Oversupply and location of luxury hotel rooms in Cape Town', *Current Issues in Tourism*, 17 (2): 180–198.

Ferreira, S. and de Villiers, R. (2014) 'The Victoria and Alfred Waterfront as a playground for Capetonians', *Urbani izziv*, 25 (Supplement): S64–S81.

Ferreira, S. and Muller, R. (2013) 'Innovating the wine tourism product: food-and-wine pairing in Stellenbosch wine routes', *African Journal for Physical, Health Education, Recreation and Dance*, 19 (Supplement 2): 72–85.

Ferreira, S. and Visser, G. (2007) 'Creating an African Riviera: revisiting the impact of the Victoria and Alfred Waterfront development in Cape Town', *Urban Forum*, 18 (3): 227–246.

Frenzel, F. (2012) Beyond 'othering': the political roots of slum tourism, in F. Frenzel, K. Koens and M. Steinbrink (eds.), *Slum Tourism: Poverty, Power and Ethics*, London: Routledge, pp. 49–65.

Frenzel, F. (2013) 'Slum tourism in the context of the tourism and poverty (relief) debate', *Die Erde*, 144 (2): 117–128.

Frenzel, F. (2016) *Slumming It: The Tourist Valorization of Urban Poverty*, London: Zed.

Frenzel, F., Koens, K. and Steinbrink, M. (eds.) (2012) *Slum Tourism: Poverty, Power and Ethics*, London: Routledge.

Frenzel, F., Koens, K., Steinbrink, M. and Rogerson, C.M. (2015) 'Slum tourism: State of the art', *Tourism Review International*, 18: 237–252.

Frey, N. and George, R. (2010) 'Responsible tourism management: The missing link between business owners' attitudes and behaviour in the Cape Town tourism industry', *Tourism Management*, 31: 621–628.

George, R. and Booyens, I. (2014) 'Township tourism demand: Tourists' perceptions of safety and security', *Urban Forum*, 25(4): 449–467.

Ginindza, S. and Tichaawa, T. (2017) 'The impact of sharing accommodation on the hotel occupancy rate in the Kingdom of Swaziland', *Current Issues in Tourism*, 22 (16): 1975–1991.

Gladstone, D. (2005) *From Pilgrimage to Package Tour: Travel and Tourism in the Third World*, Abingdon: Taylor & Francis.

Greenberg, D. and Rogerson, J.M. (2015) 'The serviced apartment industry of South Africa: A new phenomenon in urban tourism', *Urban Forum*, 26 (4): 467–482.

Greenberg, D. and Rogerson, J.M. (2018) 'Accommodating business travellers: the organisation and spaces of serviced apartments in Cape Town, South Africa', *Bulletin of Geography*, 42: 83–97.

Harmer, D. and Rogerson, J.M. (2017a) 'Gap year tourism: international debates, South African issues', *African Journal of Hospitality, Tourism and Leisure*, 6 (1): 1–11.

Harmer, D. and Rogerson, J.M. (2017b) 'Festival processes, innovation and locality response: evidence from South Africa's Rage youth festival', *Tourism Review International*, 21 (2): 169–179.

Hart, K., (1973) 'Informal income opportunities and urban employment in Ghana', *Journal of Modern African Studies*, 11: 61–89.

Hoogendoorn, G. and Giddy, J.K. (2017) ''Does this look like a slum?' Walking tours in the Johannesburg inner city', *Urban Forum*, 28(3): 315–328.

International Labour Office, (1972), *Employment, Incomes and Equality: A Strategy for Increasing Productive Employment in Kenya*, Geneva: International Labour Office.

Ismail, S. and Rogerson, J.M. (2016) 'Retrofitting hotels: evidence from the Protea Hospitality Group of hotels within Gauteng, South Africa', *African Journal of Hospitality, Tourism and Leisure*, 5(1): 1–14.

Koens, K. (2012) Competition, cooperation and collaboration: business relations and power in township tourism, in F. Frenzel, K. Koens and M. Steinbrink (eds.), *Slum Tourism: Poverty, Power and Ethics*, London: Routledge, pp. 83–103.

Koens, K. and Thomas, R. (2015) 'Is small beautiful?: Understanding the contribution of small businesses in township tourism to economic development', *Development Southern Africa*, 32(3), 320–332.

Koens, K. and Thomas, R. (2016) '"You know that's a rip off": policies and practices surrounding micro-enterprises and poverty alleviation in South African township tourism', *Journal of Sustainable Tourism*, 24(12): 1641–1654.

Magombo, A. and Rogerson, C.M. (2012) 'The evolution of the tourism sector in Malawi', *Africa Insight*, 42 (2): 46–65.

Magombo, A., Rogerson, C.M. and Rogerson, J.M. (2017) 'Accommodation services for competitive tourism in sub-Saharan Africa: historical evidence from Malawi', *Bulletin of Geography: Socio-Economic Series*, 38: 73–92.

Makoni, L. and Tichaawa, T.M (2017) 'Residents' perceptions and attitudes towards urban tourism product offerings in Harare, Zimbabwe', *African Journal of Hospitality, Tourism and Leisure*, 6 (4): 1–15

Mbaiwa, J.E., Toteng, E.N. and Moswete, N. (2007) 'Problems and prospects for the development of urban tourism in Gaborone and Maun', *Development Southern Africa*, 24: 725–739.

McKay, T. (2013) 'Leaping into urban adventure: Orlando bungee, Soweto, South Africa', *African Journal for Physical, Health Education, Recreation and Dance*, 18 (Supplement): 55–71.

Naicker, S. and Rogerson, J.M. (2017) 'Urban food markets: a new leisure phenomenon in South Africa', *African Journal of Hospitality, Tourism and Leisure*, 6 (3), 1–17.

Nel, E. and Rogerson, C.M. (2016) 'The contested trajectory of applied local economic development in South Africa', *Local Economy*, 31(1–2): 109–123.

Nemasetoni, I. and Rogerson, C.M. (2005) 'Developing small firms in township tourism: Emerging tour operators in Gauteng, South Africa', *Urban Forum*, 16: 196–213.

Novelli, M. (2015) *Tourism and Development in Sub-Saharan Africa*, Abingdon: Routledge.

Nunkoo, R., Smith, S.L.J. and Ramkissoon, H. (2013) 'Residents' attitudes to tourism: a longitudinal study of 140 articles from 1984 to 2010', *Journal of Sustainable Tourism*, 21: 5–25.

Nyakana, S., Tichaawa, T. and Swart, K. (2014) 'Sport, tourism and mega-event impacts on host cities: a case study of the 2010 FIFA World Cup in Port Elizabeth', *African Journal for Physical Health Education, Recreation and Dance*, 21: 548–556.

Pandy, W. and Rogerson, C.M. (2013) 'The timeshare industry of Africa: a study in tourism geography', *Bulletin of Geography: Socio-Economic Series*, 21: 97–109.

Pandy, W. and Rogerson, C.M. (2014a) 'The making of the South African timeshare industry: spatial structure and development challenges', *Bulletin of Geography: Socio-Economic Series*, 26: 183–201.

Pandy, W. and Rogerson, C.M., (2014b) 'The evolution and consolidation of the timeshare industry in a developing economy: the South African experience', *Urbani izziv*, 25 (Supplement): S162–S175.

Pillay, M. and Rogerson, C.M. (2013) 'Agriculture-tourism linkages and pro-poor impacts: the accommodation sector of coastal Kwa-Zulu-Natal, South Africa', *Applied Geography*, 36: 49–58.

Ramukumba, T. (2012) 'The local economic development in the Eden District municipality, Western Cape Province, South Africa: A case study of emerging entrepreneurs in tourism industry', *American Journal of Tourism Research*, 1 (2): 9–15.

Ramukumba, T., Mmbengwa V.M., Mwamayi, K.A. and Groenewald, J.A. (2012) 'Analysis of local economic development (LED) initiated partnership and support services for emerging tourism entrepreneurs in George municipality, Western Cape Province, RSA', *Tourism Management Perspectives*, 2–3 (April–July): 7–12.

Rogerson, C.M. (2002a) 'Urban tourism in the developing world: The case of Johannesburg', *Development Southern Africa*, 19: 169–190.

Rogerson, C.M. (2002b) 'Tourism-led local economic development: the South African experience', *Urban Forum*, 13(1): 95–119.

Rogerson, C.M. (2003) 'Tourism planning and the economic revitalization of Johannesburg', *Africa Insight*, 33 (1/2): 130–135.

Rogerson, C.M. (2004a) 'Transforming the South African tourism industry: the emerging black-owned bed and breakfast economy', *GeoJournal*, 60: 273–281.

Rogerson, C.M. (2004b) 'Urban tourism and small tourism enterprise development in Johannesburg: the case of township tourism', *GeoJournal*, 60: 249–257.

Rogerson, C.M. (2005) 'Conference and exhibition tourism in the developing world: the South African experience', *Urban Forum*, 16: 176–195.

Rogerson, C.M. (2006) 'Creative industries and urban tourism: South African perspectives', *Urban Forum*, 17: 149–166.

Rogerson, C.M. (2007) 'The challenge of developing backpacker tourism in South Africa: an enterprise perspective', *Development Southern Africa*, 24: 425–444.

Rogerson, C.M. (2008) 'Shared growth and urban tourism: evidence from Soweto', *Urban Forum*, 19: 395–411.

Rogerson, C.M. (2011a) 'From liquor to leisure: the changing South African hotel industry 1928–1968', *Urban Forum*, 22: 379–394.

Rogerson, C.M. (2011b) 'Urban tourism and regional tourists: shopping in Johannesburg, South Africa', *Tijdschrift voor Economische en Sociale Geografie*, 102 (3): 316–330.

Rogerson, C.M. (2013) 'Urban tourism, economic regeneration and inclusion: evidence from South Africa', *Local Economy*, 28 (2): 186–200.

Rogerson, C.M. (2014a) 'How pro-poor is business tourism in the global South?', *International Development Planning Review*, 36: 391–400.

Rogerson, C.M. (2014b) 'Reframing place-based economic development in South Africa: the example of local economic development', *Bulletin of Geography: Socio-Economic Series*, 24: 203–218.

Rogerson, C.M. (2015a) 'Revisiting VFR tourism in South Africa', *South African Geographical Journal*, 97 (2): 139–157.

Rogerson, C.M. (2015b) 'Unpacking business tourism mobilities in sub-Saharan Africa', *Current Issues in Tourism*, 18 (1) 44–56.

Rogerson, C.M. (2015c) 'The uneven geography of business tourism in South Africa', *South African Geographical Journal*, 97 (2): 183–202.

Rogerson, C.M. (2015d) 'Restructuring the geography of domestic tourism in South Africa', *Bulletin of Geography: Socio-Economic Series*, 29: 119–135.

Rogerson, C.M. (2017a) 'Visiting friends and relatives matters in sub-Saharan Africa', *African Journal of Hospitality, Tourism and Leisure*, 6 (3): 1–10.

Rogerson, C.M. (2017b) 'Unpacking directions and spatial patterns of VFR travel mobilities in the global South: insights from South Africa', *International Journal of Tourism Research*, 19: 466–475.

Rogerson, C.M. (2018a) 'Aerotropolis planning and urban tourism: Ekurhuleni and O.R. Tambo International Airport, South Africa', *Miscellanea Geographica – Regional Studies on Development*, 22 (3): 123–129.

Rogerson, C.M. (2018b) 'Informal sector city tourism: cross border shoppers in Johannesburg', *GeoJournal of Tourism and Geosites*, 22 (2): 372–387.

Rogerson, C.M. (2019) 'Business tourism under apartheid: the historical development of South Africa's conference industry', *Urbani izziv*, 30 (Supplement): 82–95.

Rogerson, C.M. and Kaplan, L. (2005) 'Tourism promotion in "difficult areas": the experience of Johannesburg inner city', *Urban Forum*, 16: 214–243.

Rogerson, C.M. and Letsie, T. (2013) 'Informal sector business tourism in the global South: evidence from Maseru, Lesotho', *Urban Forum*, 24: 485–502.

Rogerson, C.M. and Mthombeni, T. (2015) 'From slum tourism to slum tourists: township resident mobilities in South Africa', *Nordic Journal of African Studies*, 24(3–4): 319–338.

Rogerson, C.M. and Rogerson, J.M. (2011) 'Tourism research within the Southern African Development Community: production and consumption in academic journals, 2000–2010', *Tourism Review International*, 15 (1/2): 213–222.

Rogerson, C.M. and Rogerson, J.M. (2013) 'African tourism scholarship: trends in academic journal publishing', *African Journal for Physical, Health Education, Recreation and Dance*, 19 (Supplement 2), 1–8.

Rogerson, C.M. and Rogerson, J.M. (2014a) 'Urban tourism destinations in South Africa: divergent trajectories, 2001–2012', *Urbani izziv*, 25 (Supplement): S189–S203.

Rogerson, C.M. and Rogerson, J.M. (2014b) 'Agritourism and local economic development in South Africa', *Bulletin of Geography: Socio-Economic Series*, 26, 93–106.

Rogerson, C.M. and Rogerson, J.M. (2017) 'City tourism in South Africa: diversity and change', *Tourism Review International*, 21(2): 193–211.

Rogerson, C.M. and Rogerson, J.M. (2018a) 'Africa's tourism economy: uneven progress and challenges', in T. Binns, K. Lynch and E. Nel (eds.), *The Routledge Handbook of African Development*, Abingdon: Routledge, pp. 545–560.

Rogerson, C.M. and Rogerson, J.M. (2018b) 'The evolution of hotels in Johannesburg 1890–1948: a case of historical urban tourism', *GeoJournal of Tourism and Geosites*, 23 (3): 738–747.

Rogerson, C.M. and Rogerson, J.M. (2019a) 'How African is the *African Journal of Hospitality, Tourism and Leisure*?: an analysis of publishing trends 2011–2018', *African Journal of Hospitality, Tourism and Leisure*, 8 (2): 1–17.

Rogerson, C.M. and Rogerson, J.M. (2019b) 'Historical urban tourism: developmental challenges in Johannesburg 1920–1950', *Urbani izziv*, 30 (Supplement): 112–128.

Rogerson, C.M. and Saarinen, J. (2018) 'Tourism for poverty alleviation: issues and debates in the global South', in C. Cooper, S. Volo, B. Gartner and N. Scott (eds.), *The SAGE Handbook of Tourism Management: Applications of Theories and Concepts to Tourism*, London: Sage, pp. 22–37.

Rogerson, C.M. and Visser, G. (2005) 'Tourism in urban Africa: the South African experience', *Urban Forum*, 16(2–3): 63–87.

Rogerson, C.M. and Visser, G. (2006) 'International tourist flows and urban tourism in South Africa', *Urban Forum*, 17: 199–213.

Rogerson, C.M. and Visser, G. (eds.) (2007) *Urban Tourism in the Developing World: The South African Experience*, New Brunswick, NJ: Transaction Press.

Rogerson, C.M. and Visser, G. (2011) 'Rethinking South African urban tourism research', *Tourism Review International*, 15 (1/2): 77–90.

Rogerson, C.M. and Visser, G. (2014) 'A decade of progress in African urban tourism scholarship', *Urban Forum*, 25 (4): 407–418.

Rogerson, J.M. (2010) 'The boutique hotel industry in South Africa: definition, scope and organisation', *Urban Forum*, 21(4): 425–439.

Rogerson, J.M. (2011a) 'The limited services hotel in South Africa: the growth of City Lodge', *Urban Forum*, 22(4): 343–361.

Rogerson, J.M. (2011b) 'The changing all-suite hotel in South Africa: from "extended stay" to African condo hotel', *Tourism Review International*, 15 (1/2): 107–121.

Rogerson, J.M. (2012a) 'Hotels as a property asset class: international and South African trends', *Africa Insight*, 42: 200–211.

Rogerson, J.M. (2012b) 'The changing location of hotels in South Africa's coastal cities 1990–2010', *Urban Forum*, 23(1): 73–91.

Rogerson, J.M. (2013a) 'Market segmentation and the changing budget hotel industry in South Africa', *Urbani izziv*, 24 (2): 112–123.

Rogerson, J.M. (2013b) 'Reconfiguring South Africa's hotel industry 1990–2010: structure, segmentation, and spatial transformation', *Applied Geography*, 36, 59–68.

Rogerson, J.M. (2013c) 'The economic geography of South Africa's hotel industry 1990 to 2010', *Urban Forum*, 24 (3), 425–446.

Rogerson, J.M. (2013d) 'Urban tourism and the changing structure of the hotel economy in South Africa', *African Journal for Physical, Health Education, Recreation and Dance*, 18 (Supplement): 39–54.

Rogerson, J.M. (2013e) 'Size matters in the African hotel industry: the case of South Africa', *African Journal for Physical, Health Education, Recreation and Dance*, 19 (Supplement 2): 217–233.

Rogerson, J.M. (2014a) 'Hotel location in Africa's world class city: The case of Johannesburg, South Africa', *Bulletin of Geography: Socio-Economic Series*, 25: 181–196.

Rogerson, J.M. (2014b) 'Changing hotel location patterns in Ekurhuleni, South Africa's industrial workshop', *Urbani izziv*, 25 (Supplement): S82–S96.

Rogerson, J.M. (2016a) 'Hotel chains of the global South: the internationalization of South African hotel brands', *Tourism – An International Interdisciplinary Journal*, 64 (4): 445–450.

Rogerson, J.M. (2016b) 'Tourism geographies of the past: The uneven rise and fall of beach apartheid in South Africa', in R. Donaldson, G. Visser, J. Kemp and J. de Waal (eds.), *#Celebrateacenturyofgeography: Proceedings of the Centenary Conference of the Society of South African Geographers*, Stellenbosch: Society of South African Geographers, pp. 212–218.

Rogerson, J.M. (2017) '"Kicking sand in the face of apartheid": Segregated beaches in South Africa', *Bulletin of Geography: Socio-Economic Series*, 35: 93–109.

Rogerson, J.M. (2018) 'The early development of hotels in Johannesburg ca 1928–1963', *African Journal of Hospitality, Tourism and Leisure*, 7 (4): 1–16.

Rogerson, J.M. and Harmer, D. (2015) 'A "rite of passage" youth festival in South Africa: the origins, attendees and organization of matric vac'. *Nordic Journal of African Studies*, 24 (3–4): 221–240.

Rogerson, J.M. and Sims, S.R. (2012) 'The greening of urban hotels in South Africa: evidence from Gauteng', *Urban Forum*, 23(3): 391–407.

Rogerson, J.M. and Slater, D. (2014) 'Urban volunteer tourism: orphanages in Johannesburg', *Urban Forum*, 25, 483–499.

Rogerson, J.M. and Wolfaardt, Z. (2016) 'Wedding tourism in South Africa: an exploratory analysis', *African Journal of Hospitality, Tourism and Leisure*, 4 (2), 1–6.

Rolfes, M., Steinbrink, M. and Uhl, C. (2009) *Townships as Attraction: An Empirical Study of Township Tourism in Cape Town*, Potsdam: University of Potsdam.

Roux, N. (2018) "A house for dead people': memory and spatial transformation in Red Location, South Africa', *Social and Cultural Geography*, 19 (4): 407–428.

Sigwele, L., Prinsloo, J.J. and Pelser, T.G. (2018) 'Strategies for branding the city of Gaborone as a tourist destination', *African Journal of Hospitality, Tourism and Leisure*, 7 (2): 1–19.

Steinbrink, M., Frenzel, F. and Koens, K. (2012) 'Development and globalization of a new trend in tourism', in F. Frenzel, K. Koens and M. Steinbrink (eds.), *Slum Tourism: Poverty, Power and Ethics*, London: Routledge, pp. 1–17.

Tichaawa, T., Bama, H. and Swart, K. (2015) 'Community perceptions of the socio-economic legacies of the 2010 FIFA World Cup in Nelson Mandela Bay, Port Elizabeth: a four-year post-event analysis', *African Journal for Physical, Health Education, Recreation and Dance*, 21 (4: 2): 1383–1395.

Tichaawa, T. and Moyo, S. (2019) 'Urban residents' perceptions of the impacts of tourism development in Zimbabwe', *Bulletin of Geography: Socio-Economic Series*, 43: 25–44.

Van der Merwe, C.D. (2013) 'The limits of urban heritage tourism in South Africa: the case of Constitution Hill, Johannesburg', *Urban Forum*, 24: 573–588.

Van der Merwe, C.D. and Rogerson, C.M. (2013) 'Industrial heritage tourism at 'The big hole', Kimberley, South Africa', *African Journal for Physical, Health Education, Recreation and Dance*, 19 (Supplement 2): 155–171.

Van der Merwe, C.D. and Rogerson, C.M. (2018) 'The local development challenges of industrial heritage tourism in the developing world: evidence from Cullinan, South Africa', *GeoJournal of Tourism and Geosites*, 21 (1): 186–199.

Vignati, F. and Laumans, Q. (2010) 'Value chain analysis as a kick off for tourism destination development in Maputo city', Paper presented at the 2ndnd International Conference on Sustainable Tourism in Developing Countries, Tanzania 10–11 August.

Visser, G. (2002) 'Gay tourism in South Africa: issues from the Cape Town experience', *Urban Forum*, 13(1): 85–94.

Visser, G. (2003) 'Gay men, tourism and urban space: reflections on Africa's "gay capital"', *Tourism Geographies*, 5(2): 168–189.

Visser, G., Erasmus, I. and Miller, M. (2017) 'Airbnb: the emergence of a new accommodation type in Cape Town, South Africa', *Tourism Review International*, 21 (2): 151–168.

Visser, G. and Rogerson, C.M. (2014) 'Reflections on 25 years of *Urban Forum*', *Urban Forum*, 25 (1): 1–11.

Williams, S. (2009) *Tourism Geography: A New Synthesis*, Abingdon: Routledge.

29

Wildlife tourism, conservation and community benefits in Zimbabwe

Chiedza Ngonidzashe Mutanga, Oliver Chikuta, Never Muboko, Edson Gandiwa, Forbes Kabote and Tatenda W. Kaswaurere

Introduction

Tourism embraces all movement of people outside their community for not more than one consecutive year for all purposes except migration or regular daily work (Goeldner and Ritchie 2012). Mostly people travel for holidaying, attending conferences and business (Gjorgievski et al. 2013). In many countries such as Indonesia, the Philippines, Fiji, Kenya, Tanzania and the United States, establishing protected areas (PAs) for tourism is bringing fundamental changes to the local communities, such as increasing the proportion of employment, enhancing wildlife conservation and increasing the economic value of natural resources (Franks et al. 2018; Higginbottom 2004).

Tourism as an industry focuses on facilities and services designed to meet the needs of tourists (Dixit and Sheela 2001). The tourism product comprises the country's tourist attractions, transport and accommodation, all of which influence customer satisfaction (Dixit and Sheela 2001). Of these three basic components of a tourist product, attractions are very important as they motivate tourists to visit a particular destination (Bhatia 2006) Attractions are product elements that determine destination choice by tourists to visit, one rather than another (McKercher 2017). The attractions could be natural or man-made (Ngwira and Kankhuni 2018; Bhatia 2006). Natural resources are frequently the key elements in a destination's attraction. These include natural beauty like landforms, hills, rocks, gorges and terrain; flora and fauna; beaches; islands; spas; and scenic attractions.

Wildlife tourism is a form of nature-based tourism dependent on encounters with non-domesticated animals in either the animals' natural environment or in captivity (Kuenzi and McNeely 2008). It includes both non-consumptive activities such as viewing, photography and feeding the animals and consumptive which involve killing or capturing animals (Reynolds and Braithwaite 2001). In Zimbabwe, wildlife resources are a major draw card for tourists which makes wildlife tourism (Zimbabwe Tourism Authority [ZTA] 2017), making wildlife one of the pillars for Zimbabwe's tourism. As such it is part of the national tourism brand, 'Zimbabwe, a world of wonders', pronounced by the ZTA. The national tourism brand is underpinned by the country's unique people and culture, rich history and heritage, majestic Victoria Falls, Great Zimbabwe ruins, wildlife and nature, mystique Eastern

Highlands, mythical Kariba Dam and the mighty Zambezi River (ZTA 2015). Wildlife is thus an important national asset, which, if well managed, will maximise the return for the population in income and wealth creation, employment creation and enhancing the reputation of the country, thus driving tourism and related activities (Belicia and Islam 2018).

Biodiversity conservation and wildlife tourism are interdependent (Liburd and Becken 2017). PAs and tourism thus have a close relationship (Bushell et al. 2007) which offers mutual benefits that include a desirable tourism product, revenue for authorities that can assist in biodiversity conservation and benefits for surrounding communities which are however sometimes associated with costs (Strickland-Munro et al. 2010). The objectives of the study were to (i) trace the development of wildlife tourism, (ii) report on international and domestic tourism trends from 1990 to 2017, (iii) assess how wildlife tourism is contributing to conservation and community development and (iv) outline the challenges associated with wildlife tourism, conservation and community development.

Methods

Secondary data were used in this study where data were collected using a meta-synthesis of academic literature. The literature reviewed mainly included peer-reviewed journal articles, books and reports related to wildlife tourism primarily focussing on Zimbabwe (Machena et al. 2017). Keywords and phrases such as wildlife tourism, conservation, community/ communities and Communal Areas Management Programme for Indigenous Resources (CAMPFIRE) were used to retrieve literature using various search engines such as Google Scholar and Scopus. To trace the development of tourism and to assess the impact of wildlife tourism on conservation and community development and the associated challenges, data were analysed using an inductive qualitative data analysis approach where sub-themes were derived from interpreting each article and later grouping these into each of the identified themes (Mutanga et al. 2015a, 2015b). For the international and domestic trends, a trend analysis was by compiling tourist arrivals and receipts from 1990 to 2017.

Results and discussion

Development of wildlife tourism in Zimbabwe

In Zimbabwe, colonialism replaced the traditional African wildlife management systems with European models in which large tracks of land were taken and designated as PAs (Mhlanga 2001). The allocation of land in Zimbabwe was facilitated through the Land Apportionment Act of 1931 which legalised the allocation of 198,539 km^2 to 50,000 foreign settlers, 117,602 km^2 to 1,080,000 indigenous people while the remaining 74,859 km^2 was set aside for national parks, forestry and other forms of state landownership (Mombeshora and Le Bel 2009). The Game and Fish Preservation Act of 1929 saw the establishment of the first PAs in Zimbabwe (Whande et al. 2003). This was followed by the National Parks Act of 1949 and the Parks and Wildlife Act of 1975 that was amended in 1996. Various levels of PAs were established as state owned PAs of which were 11 national parks, six sanctuaries, 14 recreational parks, 16 safari areas (Figure 29.1), and 16 botanical reserves and gardens.

During the 1950s the wildlife facilities started to improve but only in major attractions. While PAs were managed for many different purposes, the importance of tourism and recreation in PAs is evident as they are permitted in most International Union for Conservation of Nature (IUCN) PA categories (Table 29.1).

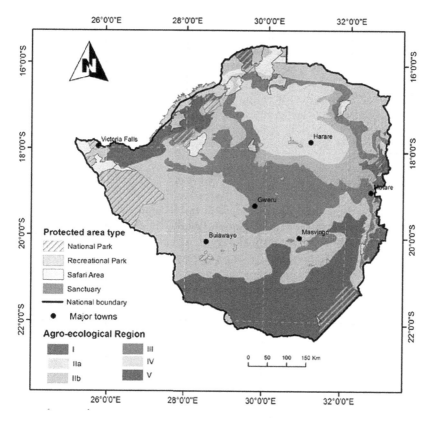

Figure 29.1   Location of major PAs in Zimbabwe
Source: Authors.

Table 29.1   PAs in Zimbabwe and the corresponding IUCN management categories

PA category	Corresponding IUCN category	Purpose	Level of use for tourism and recreation
National Parks	II	Ecosystem protection and recreation	Primary objective
National Parks with natural monuments	III – e.g. Victoria Falls National Park, Matobo National Park, Nyanga National Park	Conservation of specific natural features	Primary objective
Botanical reserves and gardens and sanctuaries	IV	Habitat/species conservation through management intervention	Potentially applicable
Recreational Parks	V	Landscape conservation and recreation	Primary objective
Safari Areas	V1	Mainly for the sustainable use of natural ecosystems	Potentially applicable

Source: Authors.

Of importance to wildlife tourism is the Environmental Management Act (Chapter 20:27) which provides for the sustainable management of Natural resources and protection of the environment, establishment of an Environmental Management Agency and an Environmental Fund. On the other hand, the Tourism Act (Chapter 14:20) provides for the setting up of the Zimbabwe Tourism Authority and its functions, and the designation, registration and grading of tourist facilities, licensing of service providers connected with tourism and imposition and collection of levies in respect of designated facilities (Machena et al. 2017).

Tourism trends

Global travel and tourism trends

Modern tourism is closely linked to development and encompasses growing a number of new destinations. According to the United Nations World Tourism Organization (UNWTO), tourism has become a key driver for socio-economic progress whose business contribution in volume equals or even surpasses that of oil exports, food products or automobiles (UNWTO 2016). Tourism has become one of the major players in international commerce and represents one of the main income sources for many developing countries (Christie et al. 2014). Worldwide, the tourism industry has experienced steady growth almost every year. International tourist arrivals increased from 439 million in 1990 to 1.322 billion in 2017 with total receipts of over US$1.3 trillion in 2017 from US$423 billion in 1990 (UNWTO 2018). The sector generated exports worth USD1.6 trillion in 2017, making it the world's 3rd largest export sector. It also supported about 3.6% of global Gross Domestic Product (GDP), up from 3.2% in 2015 (UNWTO 2018). These figures show the economic importance of tourism globally.

Travel and tourism is an important economic activity in most countries around the world contributing significantly to GDP and employment. Besides its direct economic impact, the sector has significant indirect and induced impacts (World Travel and Tourism Council [WTTC] 2016). The direct contribution of travel and tourism to GDP reflects the 'internal' spending on travel and tourism by residents and non-residents for business and leisure purposes as well as government 'individual' spending on travel and tourism services directly linked to visitors, such as museums or national parks. The total contribution of travel and tourism includes its 'wider impacts', i.e. the indirect and induced impacts on the economy (WTTC 2018). The 'indirect' contribution includes the GDP and jobs supported by (i) travel and tourism investment spending, (ii) government 'collective' spending, which helps travel and tourism activity in many different ways, e.g. tourism marketing and promotion, resort area security services, resort area sanitation services and (iii) domestic purchases of goods and services by the sectors dealing directly with tourists, e.g. purchases of food and cleaning services by hotels, fuel and catering services by airlines, and IT services by travel promoters. By the end of 2017, tourism had contributed over 380 million jobs globally, which is over 9% of total global employment (WTTC 2018).

Tourism has remained strong in spite of a number of factors threatening to disrupt a steady trend of growth like economic instability, security concerns and natural disasters. Natural disasters have a significant effect on tourism, as people shun away from any destination that is in a recovery phase (UNWTO 2016). Shocking events such as earthquakes and tsunami have significant impacts on tourism because the clean-up process can take years. However, despite world encompassing challenges, global travel is still managing to record strong growth statistics. Reasons for this growth include technological advancement, lower oil prices, and that over the years; people have become relatively wealthier with more disposable income, and more leisure time in the form of paid leave, allowing them greater freedom with their money and time (UNWTO 2016)

Regional tourism trends

Tourism in Africa is generally growing in terms of receipts and arrivals. For example, in 1990, the African region recorded about 15 million tourists and in 2016, the number rose to 57.8 million (Regional Tourism Organisation of Southern Africa [RETOSA] 2017, Table 29.2). Africa in 2017 held a 5% share in worldwide tourism arrivals and a 2.9% share of worldwide tourism receipts (UNWTO 2017; ZTA 2016). At Southern African Development Community (SADC) level tourism is supported by a number of agreements, protocols and programmes which are backed by the SADC Declaration Treaty and Protocol of 1992 which calls for inter-sector co-operation and economic integration between member countries (Muboko 2017). These protocols include the 1998 SADC Protocol on the Development of Tourism, which intends to promote equitable distribution of tourism development within the region and establish a conducive environment for tourism growth and the Protocol on Wildlife Conservation and Law Enforcement of 1999, which gave a legal standing to the transfrontier conservation area (TFCA) initiative. The TFCA initiative promotes regional tourism among other objectives, hence the establishment of TFCAs in the SADC region signals positive signs towards tourism growth and development.

Zimbabwe tourism trends

From 1990 there was a noticeable increase in Zimbabwe's tourist arrivals from 582,602 to 2.2 million in 1999 due to the peace in the country and stable economic environment (Figure 29.2) (ZTA 2000). This was followed by a decline in tourist numbers following the fast track land reform program that started in 2000 (ZTA 2015). Tourist numbers have been fluctuating from 1999 to 2008, after which tourist numbers began to increase slowly following the adoption of the multi-currency regime in 2009. In 2015, Zimbabwe was one of the destinations with the strongest growth in international arrivals in Africa (UNWTO 2016). Tourist arrivals in Zimbabwe increased to 2.4 million in 2017, 20% up from 2.2million in 2016 (ZTA 2015).

The tourism sector achieved a significant growth in tourism receipts from 60 million in 1990 to 202 million in 1999. However, like tourist arrivals, receipts have been low since 2000 (US$ 124 million) to US$ 99 million in 2005. Since 2006 tourism receipts have been

Table 29.2 International, regional and national tourist arrivals trends in millions

Year	World	Africa	SADC	Zimbabwe
1990	438	14.8	2.6	0.552
2000	674	26.5	12.6	1.967
2010	953	49	20.378	2.239
2015	1,189	53.4	21.162	2.057
2016	1,235	57.8	23.713	2.168
2017	1,322	62	N.a	2.423

Source: RETOSA (2017). N.a means data were not available.

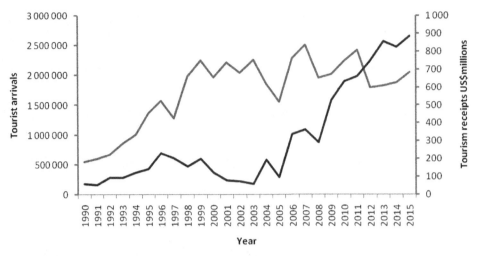

Figure 29.2   Foreign tourist arrival trend, 1990–2015
Source: ZTA (2000, 2007, 2010, 2016).

Table 29.3 The economic impact of tourism in Zimbabwe (%), 2011–2015

Economic indicator	2011	2012	2013	2014	2015
Tourism direct contribution to GDP	5.6	5.7	5.5	5.6	5.2
Total tourism contribution to GDP	11.3	11.7	11.3	11.4	11.0
Tourism direct contribution to employment	4.1	4.0	3.6	3.5	3.0
Tourism total contribution to employment	8.7	8.8	8.2	7.8	7.7
Tourism contribution to capital investment	6.2	6.3	5.9	5.5	6.3
Tourism contribution to export	8.9	10.7	10	9.5	9.0

Source: ZTA (2015).

increasing steadily. About US$886 million was recorded in 2015 with the bulk coming from accommodation and restaurant sub-sectors (Figure 29.2) (ZTA 2000, 2007, 2010, 2016). Although both arrivals and receipts have fluctuated since 1997, tourism receipts have been steadily increasing since 2008 which is, perhaps indicative of low volume, high value tourism. In Zimbabwe, tourism's contribution to GDP has been steady over the years (around 5.6%). However, contribution to employment has been slightly decreasing since 2014 (Table 29.3; ZTA 2016).

Today wildlife tourism is a growing form of tourism that is becoming a big international industry with major economic, social and environmental effects on local and global scale (Buckley 2003). PAs, whose main mandate is wildlife conservation, are therefore important for wildlife tourism. However, trends in tourists' visits to the world's PAs are much less publicised (Jones and Ohsawa 2016) and Zimbabwe is no exception. The Zimbabwe Tourism Authority often publishes trends in tourists' visits to state owned PAs but not much is known about trends in tourists' visits to non-state PAs. In an attempt to fill this gap, Mutanga et al. (2017a) studied tourist trends in northern Gonarezhou National Park, Zimbabwe, 1991– 2014. However, that too, only covered one out of many PAs in the country.

Zimbabwe's PAs with a total of about 656,222 tourist arrivals in 2015, contributed significantly to the national arrivals (32%) (ZTA 2016) making wildlife tourism an important form of tourism in the country. Of the 656,222 arrivals into the national parks around the country, more than half visited the National Parks and Wildlife Management Authority run Victoria Falls and the Zambezi National Parks which leverage on the Victoria Falls (*Mosi-oa-Tunya*), which is the prime tourist attraction in Zimbabwe (ZTA 2016). Unlike the Rainforest, Zambezi and Hwange, other national parks are frequented by local people, mostly individuals, churches and schools (ZTA 2016).

Wildlife tourism's contribution to conservation and community development

The impact of wildlife tourism on conservation

The impact of wildlife tourism on conservation is an interplay of the balance between the negative impacts of tourism-related activities on biodiversity and the positive contribution to their conservation (Higginbottom 2004). However, the specific contribution of wildlife tourism to conservation has rarely been investigated (Balmford et al. 2015). A part of the income from PAs is used to fund wildlife management efforts which include payment of staff salaries, anti-poaching activities and research. However, as Adams and Infield (2003) point out, revenues from tourism in many PAs is barely enough to cover their operating costs and very little funds, if any, can be availed for conservation. Zimbabwe has a number of private conservancies and game ranches such as Save Valley Conservancy, Bubye Valley Conservancy, Malilangwe Wildlife Reserve and Cawston Ranch which also contribute to conservation.

Communities can minimise or eliminate dependence on activities that exploit natural resources like agriculture by opening up business opportunities in tourism. Moreover, UN-WTO (2008) highlighted that to ensure there is poverty reduction in communities there should be a direct sale of goods and services to visitors by the community as this is an effective way of minimising leakages and increasing linkages. This also ensures that the poor are not only employed as a source of cheap labour, but as local entrepreneurs whereby the supply of goods and services to the tourism organisations should be from the locals (UNTWO 2008). Community involvement in wildlife tourism, therefore, helps through the provision of socio-economic incentives for conservation. Communities are also involved through the CAMPFIRE, other ecotourism projects like wildlife viewing, and selling artifacts to tourists visiting the PAs (Machena et al. 2017; Mutanga et al. 2017).

However, in some areas, community benefits from wildlife tourism are low and this contributes to negative attitudes by the communities (Mutanga et al. 2017) This can actually derail conservation efforts. Other studies by Mutanga et al. (2013) and Mutanga et al. (2015) attributed communities' negative perceptions of tourism to lack of financial benefits. This illuminates the importance of economic incentives in conservation. Furthermore, Mutanga et al. (2015)'s study of communities around four PAs in Zimbabwe found out that communities had mixed perceptions of wildlife conservation and concluded that the communities generally understood the importance of wildlife conservation. This indicates that if motivated, communities may significantly contribute to conservation.

Wildlife tourism can also help support conservation through education of tourists or through encouraging them to make voluntary donations towards conservation. In Zimbabwe, this is mainly done through different forms of interpretation which include the use of tour guides and interpretative signs and brochures. However, Hurombo (2016) argues that the syllabi that is used to train tour guides in Zimbabwe does not offer much content and as such leads to the production of insufficiently competent tour guides.

The impact of wildlife tourism on community development

At the SADC level, wildlife-based tourism impacts on community development mainly through community-based conservation projects under the banner of Community Based Natural Resources Management (CBNRM). SADC countries like Botswana, Mozambique, Namibia, Zambia and Zimbabwe embarked on various programmes such as Botswana's conservancy system, Zambia's Administrative Design and Management (ADMADE) programme, Mozambiques' Tchuma tchato programme and Zimbabwe's CAMPFIRE (Murombedzi 2001), all designed to benefit communities through tourism-based activities. These programmes promote the ideals of CBNRM. For example, focusing on CAMPFIRE in Zimbabwe, which was instituted in the late 1980s to promote CBNRM concepts in its rural districts, some lessons can be drawn. The then Zimbabwe's Department of National Parks and Wildlife Management (DNPWM), now the Zimbabwe Parks and Wildlife Management Authority (ZPWMA) conceived the CAMPFIRE program as a policy response to potential threats to wildlife within and outside PAs (Martin 1986). CAMPFIRE is built on the assumption that involving local people in economic benefits and management of wildlife will help ensure the long-term sustainability of the resource and its habitat and enhance rural livelihoods and rural development (Tchakatumba et al. 2019). The accepted but non-binding guideline was that at least 50% of the wildlife revenues was to be paid to the communities (or wards). The CAMPFIRE Association (which represents all CAMPFIRE district councils) receives 4% of gross revenue as a levy. District councils receive a maximum of 15% of gross revenue as a levy. The remaining percentage is allocated to wildlife management, such as habitat management, fire control, monitoring, or hiring of game scouts (Tchakatumba et al. 2019). Over the first decade of its existence, CAMPFIRE garnered positive reviews and served as a model for similar efforts in other countries (Jones and Murphree 2001). More recently, CAMPFIRE has attracted critical scrutiny. Disappointing social, economic and ecological outcomes observed in the field have diluted the initial enthusiasm (Mashinya 2007).

While some Zimbabwean districts did benefit from income at household level, in others no sustainable tangible benefits were provided to the local people (Dressler et al. 2010). Murombedzi (2001) argued that there were challenges with community complexities emanating from the fact that the institutional forms adopted in CAMPFIRE tended to be outgrowths of higher-level government agencies and did not originate within less formal institutions at the community level. More commonly, the absence of well-defined property rights and rights to manage wildlife at community level resulted in limited incentives to conserve (Machena et al. 2017).

A study by Zunza (2012) on local benefits of CAMPFIRE in Mahenye community concluded that the income received by local communities was little and was declining mainly due to corruption and lack of accountability by the elite; there were limited employment opportunities mainly for local community members in CAMPFIRE projects; agriculture had been negatively impacted by crop destruction by wildlife and disease transfer from wildlife to domestic animals, and there was competition for pastures between wild animals and domestic animals. These conclusions indicate that the communities in Mahenye could not have been happy with the CAMPFIRE project especially considering that they were benefiting very little and at the same time suffering costs from wildlife depredation.

Mashinya (2007) in her study on participation and devolution in Zimbabwe's CAMPFIRE program recorded that in communities under Nyaminyami Rural District Council, revenues were still sufficient to support local development efforts but were, however, not equitably shared. Families had not received direct payments for participating in CAMPFIRE since the mid-1990s because it would be more beneficial to use the money for general community infrastructure improvements. However, despite continuing strong revenues there have been no new investments in community projects since 2001, i.e. there was no school construction underway, no road improvements, no maintenance for community grinding mills and no meaningful effects to mitigate human-animal conflicts.

One of the most obvious and immediate benefits of wildlife tourism to local communities is the creation of employment opportunities in hospitality and tourism services. There is also a generation of local entrepreneurial activities amongst the local communities. A number of community members get employment opportunities from wildlife tourism with some being employed on full time basis, while others are employed as part time workers as tourism attracts both skilled and unskilled labour (Beeton 2006). Ashley (2000) suggested that although casual earnings per person maybe very small, their effects are widely spread for instance to cover up children's school fees and sustain a basic living. Wildlife tourism thus helps provide an alternative source of income to the families of those employed thereby reducing community dependence on wildlife resources.

Framework for wildlife tourism, conservation and community benefits

A framework for wildlife tourism, conservation and community benefits is proposed which denotes the inter-relationship between wildlife tourism, community benefits and conservation as indicated by the arrows (Figure 29.3).

The framework shows that wildlife tourism brings in revenue through user fees from, for example, park entrance fees, trophy fees from consumptive tourism, and levies and taxes which are paid by tour operators. Wildlife tourism is enabled by different factors which include capacity building and policy instruments. These are the main efforts by wildlife authorities and the government to improve conservation, community livelihoods, and

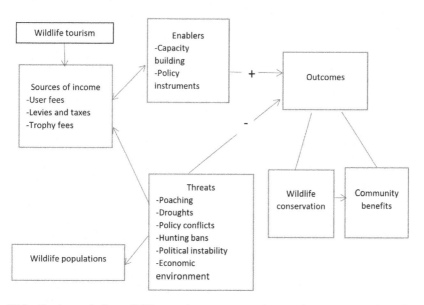

Figure 29.3 Framework for wildlife tourism, conservation and community benefits. The direction of lines indicates interconnectedness of the components

Source: Author.

ultimately wildlife tourism. Policy instruments such as Zimbabwe's National Environmental Policy and Strategies 2009 are instrumental in guiding resource allocation planning and reduction of anti-conservation activities by the communities. Incentives for communities like revenue generating projects and capacity building are important in providing alternative sources of income for the communities and reducing their dependency on wildlife resources. Enablers provide a positive environment to enhance wildlife tourism resulting in both improved wildlife conservation and community livelihoods. In this case, enablers are capabilities, forces or resources that contribute to the success of wildlife tourism which includes capacity building among communities as well as appropriate policy or statutory instruments. On the other hand, wildlife tourism is also threatened by factors like poaching, droughts, policy conflicts, hunting bans, political instability and unconducive economic environment which all affect wildlife populations. Contrastingly, these threats negatively affect both wildlife conservation and community livelihoods. Finally, if communities benefit from wildlife tourism they can be motivated to conserve wildlife. Similarly, if there is improved wildlife conservation, communities can benefit more from improved tourism.

Challenges associated with wildlife tourism, conservation and community development

The recent CAMPFIRE review reported that the direct household benefits have reduced over the years in most producer communities with most benefits being communal (Machena et al. 2017). To support this, a recent study found out that the direct economic benefits from CAMPFIRE in southeast Zimbabwe were small but the households appreciated the infrastructural facilities from CAMPFIRE (Tchakatumba et al. 2019). Furthermore, opportunities for community participation in wildlife tourism are limited, the few available are related to photographic tourism, tour guiding services and selling curios to tourists. Although in principle they are not forbidden to sell curios and artefacts, in most cases they are not allowed to do that in the parks or at the park entrances, and as such, they have limited access to the tourists.

Although some community members benefit from employment in the PAs, the level of employment is limited because most of the community members do not have the necessary educational qualifications or technical skills for them to be employable in higher positions in the tourism industry. Chiutsi et al. (2011) highlighted the essential elements communities need to survive in the tourism industry. These include customer care, language and understanding tourist expectations and more than local skills and knowledge to compete in a complex sector not appropriate for communities with few business competencies.

Another challenge that communities face is their low level of participation in the management of CAMPFIRE and/or wildlife tourism (Mutanga et al. 2017; Gandiwa et al. 2013). Some communities do not participate in collaborative management of wildlife tourism in adjacent PAs. However, some communities adjacent to PAs such as Matusadona and Gonarezhou, have limited participation in collaborative management of CAMPFIRE. Mutanga et al. (2017) commented that this limited participation in CAMPFIRE management meant that community members had no power to influence decisions.

There has been a decline in CAMPFIRE revenue accruing to the communities in the past years (Machena et al. 2017). Moreover, CAMPFIRE depends on the international market which is highly volatile. This is worsened by the fact that the CAMPFIRE proceeds, mostly from trophy hunting activities, are dwindling due to a variety of factors including a limited product range amidst an increasing human population due to in migration and high reproductive rates (Gandiwa et al. 2013). This limits the amount of revenue the communities get from wildlife tourism. Moreover, the CAMPFIRE programme also depends on migratory animals. This poses a challenge in that if animal populations are reduced in PAs; there will be less revenue accruing to communities since hunting will be less viable in CAMPFIRE areas.

In Zimbabwe, the situation with human-wildlife costs negatively affects wildlife tourism. This situation is worsened by the fact that the Government is yet to develop a national policy on compensation for community losses due to wildlife depredation. Conflicts between human and wildlife have become one of the biggest obstacles for CBNRM, a situation which has been aggravated by the 1999 Land Reform which resulted in the indigenous people settling on private game reserves, game safari land and sections of state owned PAs (Chaumba et al. 2003). In Zimbabwe, between 2002 and 2006, more than 5,000 cases of human-elephant conflicts (HEC) were recorded which included crop destruction, livestock predation and human casualties (Le Bel et al. 2010). The subsequent problem-animal-control operations also resulted in many elephants being killed (Le Bel et al. 2011). Communities in Mbire, Chiredzi and Hwange districts generally perceived wildlife as a threat to both people and domestic animals although their perceptions differ as to whether disease transmission, destruction of crops and human and livestock predation were the key threats (Machena et al. 2017; Le Bel et al. 2011).

Community members also reflected negativity in relation to responses by responsible authorities to problem animals across. In Omay communal lands adjacent to Matusadona National Park, Muboko et al. (2014) recorded cases of crop raiding and loss of human life caused by elephants. Loss of human life included the records of 26 people killed by elephants between 2008 and 2012. In another related study, Matema and Andersson (2015) examined human-wildlife conflict in Mbire District in Zimbabwe and pointed to an upsurge in lion attacks on livestock and people, and the complex human-wildlife conflicts about access to, and governance of, wildlife resources.

Similarly, Gandiwa et al. (2013) reported that some communities bordering Gonarezhou National Park experienced conflicts with wildlife inform of crop damage and livestock depredation by large carnivores. In another study on conflict between wildlife and people in Kariba town, Mhlanga (2001) recorded conflicts between wildlife and people in which elephants and buffaloes damaged and destroyed property and frightened or killed people and baboons vandalised homes. Despite encountering these losses, residents were not compensated for death, injury or property damaged by animals.

Emerton (2001) posited that even when the people in wildlife abundant areas are furnished with community development benefits from wildlife revenues, they still lose out in economic terms from the presence of wildlife. In response, people drive elephants away from residential areas using stones and burning fire logs, injure or kill the wild animals. For example, in Zimbabwe, about 728 elephants were poached between 2011 and 2013 and this includes 105 elephants poisoned with cyanide in Hwange National Park in 2013 (Machena et al. 2017). This has got negative consequences on conservation and wildlife tourism. Thus, the survival of wildlife in PAs depends on whether it is an asset or liability to the communities living adjacent to the PAs (Muchapondwa et al. 2009). In spite of genuine efforts in some cases to recruit members of the host communities as stakeholders to participate in biodiversity conservation programmes, some members of these communities view the establishment of PAs as insensitive to their needs (Berkes 2004) since the rights to most of their land is not retained. Even though the local communities do enter into agreements with park authorities to promote biodiversity conservation by sustainable utilisation of available natural resources in the PAs, they usually go back on these agreements as they actively collaborate and participate in habitat destruction, game poaching, illegal tree logging and unsustainable exploitation of other wildlife products (Machena et al. 2017).

Conclusion and the way forward

Wildlife tourism in Zimbabwe started with the development of PAs which was facilitated by European models which came through colonialism, e.g. the Land Apportionment Act of 1931 and the National Parks Act of 1949. Wildlife tourism is enabled by a number of legal frameworks that structure the way in which wildlife tourism grows, e.g. The Environmental Management Act (Chapter 20:27) and the Tourism Act (Chapter 14:20). Both internationally and in Africa, the tourism industry has experienced steady growth in terms of receipts and arrivals. At the SADC level tourism is supported by a number of agreements, protocols and programmes which include the SADC Protocol on the Development of Tourism (1998) and the Protocol on Wildlife Conservation and Law Enforcement of 1999. However, in Zimbabwe tourist arrivals have been fluctuating over the years. While trends in tourists' visits to the country's PAs are much less publicised, Zimbabwe's PAs contribute significantly to the national arrivals making wildlife tourism an important form of tourism in the country.

Wildlife tourism contributes to conservation through (i) financial resources that assist in funding conservation-related activities like anti-poaching activities and research, (ii) provision of socio-economic incentives for conservation to the communities and (iii) educating tourists and/or encouraging them to make voluntary donations towards conservation. On the other hand, wildlife tourism contributes to community development through (i) community-based conservation especially CAMPFIRE, (ii) the creation of employment opportunities in hospitality and tourism services and (iii) generation of local entrepreneurial activities amongst the local communities. It is clear that communities are a key element in natural resource conservation and, if they are treated with respect and benefit from the resource in their backyard, they can contribute significantly to wildlife conservation. It is only unfortunate that in Zimbabwe, most communities, despite the fact that they have been promised an incentive for their conservation efforts, have been short-changed. This has worked against the cause for conservation and subsequently, wildlife tourism which highly depends on the natural resources.

The CBNRM can be made more beneficial by introducing more eco-friendly projects, such as cultural centres, where local historians, community storytellers and traditional music and dance are promoted, to diversify CAMPIFIRE activities. Again, the CAMPFIRE programme can be improved through the establishment of community game ranches to ensure the presence of resident animals in CAMPFIRE areas as opposed to the current system of migratory animals (Mutanga et al. 2017). This can be facilitated through Command Wildlife Farming advanced by the Government of Zimbabwe, which has recently been trending in the local media. This is whereby the communities are funded to start wildlife farming projects and they will pay up the loan when they start to harvest. Product diversification can offer opportunities to enhance community benefits. With support from PAs and Non-Governmental Organisations (NGOs), communities may venture into overnight accommodation provision such as campsites and chalets, cultural centres, crafts and curio shops, bird watching activities, walking safaris, sport fishing and photographic safaris. Some communities such as in Chimanimani, Muzarabani and Uzumba Maramba Pfungwe have benefited from such projects. This can be a valuable lesson to other communities in wildlife areas. PA managements and the government at large need to capacity build the communities especially in terms of technical and financial skills training.

References

Adams, W. M., and M. Infield, M. 2003. Who is on the gorilla's payroll? Claims on tourist revenue from a Ugandan National Park. *World development* 31(1): 177–190.

Ashley, C. 2000. *Applying livelihood approaches to natural resource management initiatives: experiences in Namibia and Kenya.* London: Overseas Development Institute.

Balmford, A., J. M. Green, M. Anderson, J. Beresford, C. Huang, R. Naidoo, M. Walpole, and A. Manica. 2015. Walk on the wild side: estimating the global magnitude of visits to protected areas. *PLoS Biology* 13(2): e1002074.

Beeton, S. 2006. *Community development through tourism.* Landlinks Press.

Belicia, T., and M. Islam. 2018. Towards a Decommodified wildlife tourism: why market environmentalism is not enough for conservation. *Societies* 8(3): 59.

Berkes, F. 2004. Rethinking community based conservation. *Conservation Biology* 18(3): 621–630.

Bhatia, A. K. 2006. *The business of tourism: concepts and strategies.* New Delhi: Sterling Publishers Pvt. Ltd.

Buckley, R. 2003. Environmental inputs and outputs in ecotourism: geotourism with a positive triple bottom line? *Journal of Ecotourism* 2(1): 76–82.

Bushell, R., R. Staiff, and P. F. Eagles. 2007. *Tourism and protected areas: Benefits beyond boundaries.* Presented at the Vth IUCN World Parks Congress. Durban: South Africa

Chaumba, J., I. Scoones, and W. Wolmer. 2003. From jambanja to planning: the reassertion of technocracy in land reform in south-eastern Zimbabwe? *The Journal of Modern African Studies* 41(4): 533–554.

Chiutsi, S., M. Mukoroverwa, P. Karigambe, and B. K. Mudzengi. 2011. The theory and practice of ecotourism in Southern Africa. *Journal of Hospitality Management and Tourism* 2(2): 14–21.

Christie, I., E. Fernandes, H. Messerli, and L. Twining-Ward. 2014. *Tourism in Africa: harnessing tourism for growth and improved livelihoods.* Washington, DC: The World Bank.

Dixit, M., and C. Sheela. 2001. *Tourism products, India.* Lucknow: New Royal Book Company.

Dressler, W., B. Büscher, M. Schoon, D. A. N. Brockington, T. Hayes, C. A. Kull, J. McCarthy, and K. Shrestha. 2010. From hope to crisis and back again? A critical history of the global CBNRM narrative. *Environmental Conservation* 37(1): 5–15.

Emerton, L. 2001. The nature of benefits and benefits of nature: why wildlife conservation has not economically benefited communities in Africa. In D. Hulme, and M. Muphree (Eds.) *African wildlife and livelihoods: the promise and performance of community conservation*, Harare: Weaver Press.

Franks, P., F. Booker, and D. Roe. 2018. *Understanding and assessing equity in protected area conservation.* IIED Issue Paper. London: IIED

Gandiwa, E., I. M. Heitkönig, A. M. Lokhorst, H. H. Prins, and C. Leeuwis. 2013. CAMPFIRE and human-wildlife conflicts in local communities bordering northern Gonarezhou National Park, Zimbabwe. *Ecology and Society* 18(4), 1–15.

Gjorgievski, M., S. Kozuharov, and D. Nakovski. 2013. Typology of recreational-tourism resources as an important element of the tourist offer. *UTMS Journal of Economics* 4(1): 53–60.

Goeldner, C. R., and J. B. Ritchie. 2012. *Tourism principles, practices, philosophies.* Hoboken: John Wiley & Sons.

Higginbottom, K. 2004. Wildlife tourism: an introduction. In K. Higginbottom (Ed.) *Wildlife tourism: Impacts, management and planning*, pp. 1–14. Gold Coast: Common Ground Publishing.

Hurombo, B. 2016. Assessing key tour guide competences to co-create memorable tourism experiences. Doctoral dissertation, North-West University (South Africa), Potchefstroom Campus).

Jones, B., and M. Murphree. 2001. *The evolution of policy on community conservation in Namibia and Zimbabwe. African wildlife and livelihoods: the promise and performance of community conservation.* Oxford: James Currey.

Jones, T., and T. Ohsawa. 2016. Monitoring nature-based tourism trends in Japan's national parks: Mixed messages from domestic and inbound visitors. *Parks* 22(1): 25–36.

Kuenzi, C., and J. McNeely. 2008. Nature-based tourism. In Renn, O. and Walker, K. (Eds.) *Global risk governance: Concept and practice using the IRGC*, pp. 155–178. Dordrecht: Springer.

Le Bel, S., R. Taylor, M. Lagrange, O. Ndoro, M. Barra, and H. Madzikanda. 2010. An easy-to-use capsicum delivery system for crop-raiding elephants in Zimbabwe: preliminary results of a field test in Hwange National Park. *Pachyderm* 47: 80–89.

Le Bel, S., A. Murwira, B. Mukamuri, R. Czudek, R. Taylor, and M. La Grange. 2011. Human wildlife conflicts in southern Africa: riding the whirl wind in Mozambique and in Zimbabwe. In

López-Pujol, J. (Ed.) *The importance of biological interactions in the study of biodiversity*, pp. 283–322. London: IntechOpen.

Liburd, J. J., and S. Becken. 2017. Values in nature conservation, tourism and UNESCO World Heritage Site stewardship. *Journal of Sustainable Tourism* 25(12): 1719–1735.

Machena, C., E. Mwakiwa, and E. Gandiwa. 2017. *Review of the communal areas management programme for indigenous resources (CAMPFIRE) and community based natural resources management (CBNRM) models*. Harare: GoZ and EU.

Martin, R. B. 1986. *Communal areas management programme for indigenous resources (CAMPFIRE)*. Revised Version. Harare (Zimbabwe): Branch of Terrestrial Ecology, Department of National Parks and Wild Life Management. CAMPFIRE Working Document No. 1/86.

Mashinya, J. 2007. Participation and devolution in Zimbabwe's CAMPFIRE program: findings from local projects in Mahenye and Nyaminyami. Doctoral dissertation.

Matema, S. and Andersson, J.A., 2015. Why are lions killing us? Human–wildlife conflict and social discontent in Mbire District, northern Zimbabwe. *The Journal of Modern African Studies* 53(1): 93–120.

McKercher, B. 2017. Do attractions attract tourists? A framework to assess the importance of attractions in driving demand. *International Journal of Tourism Research* 19(1): 120–125.

Mhlanga, L. 2001. Conflict between wildlife and people in Kariba town, Zimbabwe. *Zambezia* 28(1): 39–52.

Mombeshora, S., and S. Le Bel. 2009. Parks-people conflicts: the case of Gonarezhou National Park and the Chitsa community in south-east Zimbabwe. *Biodiversity and Conservation* 18(10): 2601–2623.

Muboko, N., E. Gandiwa, and J. T. Mapuranga. 2014. *Human-elephant conflict in local communities living adjacent to the Southern Boarder of Matusadona National Park, Zimbabwe*. RP-PCP/AHEAD Conference, Painted Dog Conservation Centre, Dete, Hwange, Zimbabwe.

Muboko, N. 2017. The role of transfrontier conservation areas and their institutional framework in natural resource-based conflict management: A review. *Journal of sustainable forestry* 36: 583–603.

Muchapondwa, E., F. Carlsson, and G. Kohlin. 2009. *Can local communities in Zimbabwe be trusted with wildlife management?: evidence from contingent valuation of elephants*. Working Papers in Economics 395. University of Gothenburg, Department of Economics.

Murombedzi, J., 2001. *Committees, rights, costs and benefits: natural resource stewardship and community benefits in Zimbabwe's CAMPFIRE programme. African wildlife and livelihoods. The promise and performance of community conservation*. Oxford: James Currey.

Mutanga, C. N., S. Vengesayi, G. Kwanisai, K. Mirimi, and C. C. Chipotereke. 2013. Tourism development and host communities' perceptions: The case of Mana Pools National Park, Zimbabwe. *Asian Journal of Research in Social Sciences and Humanities* 3(11): 1–15.

Mutanga, C. N., S. Vengesayi, E. Gandiwa, and N. Muboko. 2015a. Community perceptions of wildlife conservation and tourism: a case study of communities adjacent to four protected areas in Zimbabwe. *Tropical Conservation Science*, 8(2): 564–582.

Mutanga, C. N., S. Vengesayi, E. Gandiwa, and N. Muboko. 2015b. Towards harmonious conservation relationships: a framework for understanding protected area staff-local community relationships in developing countries. *Journal for Nature Conservation* 25: 8–16.

Mutanga, C. N., E. Gandiwa, and N. Muboko. 2017a. An analysis of tourist trends in northern Gonarezhou National Park, Zimbabwe, 1991–2014. *Cogent Social Sciences* 3(1): 1392921.

Mutanga, C. N., N. Muboko, and E. Gandiwa. 2017b. Protected area staff and local community viewpoints: a qualitative assessment of conservation relationships in Zimbabwe. *PloS ONE* 12(5): e0177153.

Ngwira, C., and Z. Kankhuni. 2018. What attracts tourists to a destination? Is it attractions? *African Journal of Hospitality, Tourism and Leisure*. 7(1): 1–19.

Reynolds, P. C., and D. Braithwaite. 2001. Towards a conceptual framework for wildlife tourism. *Tourism Management* 22(1): 31–42.

Regional Tourism Organisation of Southern Africa (RETOSA). 2017. *SADC travel and tourism Barometer, "Measuring the impacts of tourism to the economic development of the Southern African Development Community (SADC) member states"*. Johannesburg: RETOSA.

Strickland-Munro, J. K., S. A. Moore, and S. Freitag-Ronaldson. 2010. The impacts of tourism on two communities adjacent to the Kruger National Park, South Africa. *Development Southern Africa* 27(5): 663–678.

Tchakatumba, P. K., E. Gandiwa, E. Mwakiwa, B. Clegg, and S. Nyasha. 2019. Does the CAMPFIRE programme ensure economic benefits from wildlife to households in Zimbabwe? *Ecosystems and People* 15(1): 119–135.

United Nations World Tourism Organisation (UNWTO). 2008. *Tourism highlights, 2008 Edition.*

United Nations World Tourism Organisation (UNWTO). 2016. *World tourism barometer (volume 14).*

United Nations World Tourism Organisation (UNWTO). 2017. *Tourism highlights, 2017 Edition.*

United Nations World Tourism Organisation (UNWTO). 2018. *Tourism highlights, 2018 Edition.*

Whande, W., T. Kepe, and M. Murphree. 2003. *Local communities, equity and conservation in southern Africa.* Programme for Land and Agrarian Studies (PLAAS), School of Government, University of the Western Cape.

World Travel & Tourism Council (WTTC). 2016. *Travel & tourism economic impact 2016*: World Travel and Tourism Council.

World Travel & Tourism Council (WTTC). 2018. *Travel & tourism economic impact 2018*: World Travel and Tourism Council.

Zimbabwe Tourism Athourity (ZTA). 2000. *Tourism trends and statistics report*: Zimbabwe Tourism Authority. Harare.

Zimbabwe Tourism Athourity (ZTA). 2007. *Tourism trends and statistics report.* Harare: Zimbabwe Tourism Authority.

Zimbabwe Tourism Athourity (ZTA). 2010. *Tourism trends and statistics report.* Harare: Zimbabwe Tourism Authority.

Zimbabwe Tourism Athourity (ZTA). 2015. *Tourism trends and statistics report.* Harare: Zimbabwe Tourism Authority.

Zimbabwe Tourism Athourity (ZTA). 2016. *Tourism trends and statistics report.* Harare: Zimbabwe Tourism Authority.

Zimbabwe Tourism Athourity (ZTA). 2017. *Tourism trends and statistics report.* Harare: Zimbabwe Tourism Authority.

Zunza, E. 2012. Local level benefits of CBNRM: the case of Mahenye Ward CAMPFIRE, Zimbabwe. Doctoral dissertation. University of Zimbabwe, Harare.

InFocus 8

South African Airways and corporate social responsibility (CSR) initiatives

Jon Danks

South African Airways (UK&I)

Throughout 2018 the world celebrated 100 years since the birth of Nelson Mandela. The celebration was the latest in a long line of corporate social initiatives (CSR) supported by South African Airways, United Kingdom and Ireland (SSA-UK&I) within a clear framework that supports organisations and initiatives across sub-Saharan Africa. This case study takes a look into this framework and helps explain the purpose that lies behind the complex set of decisions within the airline's CSR program of engagements.

Purpose, digital brand alignment and timing, with clear outputs and outcomes, are an essential aspect of the axis of how decisions are taken. Mandela inspired the world with a message of freedom and unity that spanned generations. Following his release from captivity, he took this message to the world and he often flew with South African Airways (SAA) on these missions. Mandela founded three charities in his name, of which the Nelson Mandela Children's Fund strives to change the way society treats children and youth. Its long-term vision captures the central role that society plays in shaping children's lives. Throughout 2018, the Fund celebrated Mandela's legacy and the impact he continues to have transforming the lives of children, youth and communities around the world. A set of unique activities were organised in the United Kingdom, including bringing together 100 runners to participate in the London's Virgin Sport British 10KM in July 2018. The event had scale, timing and gravitas and took place just three days before the annual Nelson Mandela International Day, which is celebrated annually on July 18, on the occasion of his birthday, following the official institution of the UN Mandela Day in 2010. Mandela Day is a global call to action that celebrates the idea that each individual has the power to transform the world and the ability to make an impact. The day honours the legacy of Mandela and his values. Individuals and teams are asked to donate 67 minutes of their time (67 are the years that Mandela fought for social justice) and engage through volunteering, community service or supporting a cause.

For Mandela's legacy to continue, the support of large corporations and like-minded decision makers are required. Aside from a marketing stunt, with the airline's logo being carried on the jerseys of runners, there was something deeply rooted in the partnership that spoke to the foundation of the SAA brand. As a national carrier, SAA's vision is to play as an enabler of growth within the African continent, with a mission to "Bring the world to Africa and take Africa to the World". The message of making Africa accessible to the world carries a greater purpose, desire and willingness for global citizens, aimed at inspiring individuals to explore the people, beliefs and cultures of sub-Saharan Africa.

The Fund's mantra "A Mandela in every generation" is underpinned by bringing together a movement of great individuals running in the United Kingdom, with inspiration from South Africa. The UK runners were joined by Ipeleng Khunou, a young South African man from a Soweto Township. Khunou was born with a rare brain deformity called Septo-Optic Dysplasia – essentially born without balance and problems with eyesight. Ipeleng was a South African making history. In 2018, he completed the Two Oceans Half Marathon in South Africa as the first ever runner on crutches. Prior to the run, he explained "I'm really excited about this. What makes it special for me is that I'm going to be raising money for the Nelson Mandela Children's Fund. A lot of people tell me that I am an inspirational person because I run on crutches but I haven't felt the same. Now I actually have a purpose to run, and I am driven to finish with a medal. I can't let the children down", says Khunou (Haden, 2018).

The airline's support of an initiative taking place in London, benefitting organisations in Africa, is generally mirrored by initiatives taking place in South Africa, benefitting organisations in the United Kingdom. UK charities supported by SAA included Help for Heroes in April 2016. Then, a team of nearly 20 wounded, sick and injured veterans, supported by rugby legend, Will Greenwood, completed a gruelling six-day cycle ride across South Africa, to raise funds for the "Help for Heroes" Phoenix House Recovery Centre, Catterick Garrison, North Yorkshire. The ride included seven mountain passes and over 18,000 ft of climbs between Franschhoek and Knysna. It tested riders both mentally and physically and was particularly gruelling for wounded veterans riding adapted bicycles. Alongside the riders wearing SAA branded shirts, the team at SAA offered a ticket and digital support and enlisted the fundraising help of its nearby commercial partner, AFC Sunderland, then of the English Premier League. Local fundraising initiatives during the ride showcased the warmth and generosity of the South African people, broadcast digitally and raised £315,000 for the "Help for Heroes" Centre.

Within the framework of supporting organisations across sub-Saharan Africa, SAA struck a clear balance between its commercial aims and the positioning of its brand, alongside its charitable goals, with strong governance around the frequency, the outputs and outcomes of the organisations it supports. From its United Kingdom and Ireland "territory" it carries much commercial expectation as the United Kingdom is South Africa's largest international source market for tourism with nearly half a million visitors each year. SAA's commercial footprint extends geographically over 4,000 km from Tanzania to Cape Point, therefore the volume of requests the airline receives for tickets and support is extensive.

Recognising this, it has used digital channels to transform and extend the distance and reach of the activations it supports. Its 2014 partnership with Lesotho charity Sentebale saw SAA fly R&B artist Joss Stone into Maseru, with strong PR later showcased alongside HRH Prince Harry in Hello magazine. In 2015, SAA's partnership with Sir Ian Botham saw him complete an epic 120-mile walk across South Africa supporting the UK and African organisations. The initiative showcased the airline's network strength and was broadcast via social media and e-CRM channels. In the same year, the partnership with the Mandela Children's Fund supporting the release of the Long Walk to Freedom (Mandela movie), was accompanied by support from Idris Elba via social media platforms.

In all cases SAA's CSR partners hold significant creditability, with sustainable outputs and outcomes. However, implementing a programme of this kind requires accessibility, trust, strong networks, belief and a corporate culture, underpinned by strong commercial and digital DNA, and critically a strong sense of giving.

References

Haden, A. (2018) *Two Oceans Marathon: Meet the Absolutely Incredible Ipeleng Khunou*, Available at: https://www.thesouthafrican.com/lifestyle/two-oceans-marathon-meet-the-absolutely-incredible-ipeleng-khunou/Accessed: 02/07/2019.

Help for Heroes (2016) *Blood, Sweat & Gears Are Coming to Knysna, Available at: https://www.helpforheroes.org.uk/news/2016/april/blood-sweat-gears-are-coming-to-knysna/, Accessed: 02/07/2019.*

InFocus 9

Hatika Adult Education Centre supports community tourism development in Windhoek, Namibia

Sisco Auala

Adult education and training is an important tool for poverty reduction and economic development in Namibia. A young Namibian teacher from Katutura, Windhoek, Wilfried Mbamba, had a dream to make a change in his community. He established an adult education centre in May 2019 called the Hatika Adult Education Centre, thanks to the generous support, by means of a small grant, of the US Embassy in Namibia.

His dream was to bring education to the less fortunate members of his community. As a teacher himself, he believed that by educating adults in his community and using the power of education to inform, enrich and transform lives, the initiative would impact his community positively.

The centre caters to adults in the Katutura informal settlement, in the north-west of the capital Windhoek, who are unemployed and have not had an opportunity for further education. The students acquire skills in art, English and Afrikaans for beginners, business skills, computer skills and financial literacy.

A total of 68 students received training through the centre in 2019. Students ranged in age from 18 to 45 years old, with the majority being young, unemployed women from Katutura.

The centre further introduced art classes for children living within the vicinity of the centre during the school holidays and is managed through a four-member advisory board appointed to serve voluntarily for one year.

The centre runs a volunteer programme for tutors who wish to teach, motivate and contribute to community empowerment through skills acquisition, and by hosting training and motivational talks.

Community tourism awareness was introduced in July 2019, as an extra volunteer activity at the centre on Saturday afternoons, to bring awareness to opportunities available in the tourism sector for community members in Katutura. Urban poverty in Namibia is currently a challenge and tourism is known to provide a unique opportunity for poverty reduction in Namibia. The tourism awareness sessions are one hour long and involve the tutor motivating, teaching and encouraging the students to learn new skills and create employment through participation in the tourism industry.

Students are taught about tourism product development, marketing and sales. Practical demonstrations are offered to students on how to use recycled materials to create products to

477

sell to tourists. The aim is to create a ripple effect, effecting change by ensuring the students share their new skills with other community members and encouraging them to make a living from selling their products. The language, computer and business skills they learn from the centre equips them to become self-reliant and successful business owners who positively impact their communities.

Guest speakers from the tourism sector, who themselves are from the Katutura community, are invited to share their experiences of how they started their community tourism businesses in Katutura. This further motivates participants to push through the poverty barriers and create employment for themselves or to strive to become employable members of the community. The tourism awareness sessions further educate the students on how the tourism sector functions and how they can participate in various ways to benefit from a growing tourism sector in Namibia.

The centre has grown from one classroom session to two within the span of one year, and support from various organisations and individuals is highly beneficial for the further growth of the centre, with the aim of branching out to other towns, ultimately increasing the number of community members living in informal settlements to be able to benefit from this great initiative. For further details about Hatika Adult Education Centre, please contact the Managing Director, Mr. Wilfried Mbamba, on +264 81 3248057 or email: hatikaadult-educationcentre@gmail.com

InFocus 10

The future of tourism in Africa – keeping more tourism spend in destinations for sustainable tourism development through digitalised marketing

Thomas Muller

The global travel, tourism and hospitality industry is changing at an ever-fast pace. The internet has completely transformed the way people book travel experiences. Many new market players, business models and value chains have surfaced, thanks to thousands of new digital systems apps and platforms. Yet many disruptor startups retain most of the profits, costing the little guy 60–80% of their profit. The future of tourism – especially tourism in Africa – depends on yet another shift: one that keeps more tourism spend in destinations for sustainable tourism development.

According to Phocuswright offline bookings continue to decline as European consumers, a large source market for Africa – seek out websites and booking platforms both to plan and purchase their leisure trips. For the first time, more than half of all European travel bookings were made online in 2019. Led by Europe's two largest markets—the United Kingdom and Germany—online bookings are projected to continue to climb. By 2021, Europe will surpass the United States to have the highest online penetration of any other region.

The History of Tourism in Africa

The day-to-day business of hospitality and tourism companies and authorities has become insanely and overwhelmingly complex. Five to seven years ago doing business for Lodges, Guesthouses, Guest Farms and Activity Providers was rather easy. They only needed to work with a hand full of inbound tour operators (DMC) in order to get their and their overseas wholesale operators' business. However, that has changed because of the change of travel behaviour in the respective source markets, where a shift from group travel to individual and self-drive travel (FIT) has taken place, and at the same time, hundreds of potential platforms have been added to provide the potential traveller an easy way to dream, plan and book a destination.

But at the same time, certain areas of the hospitality and tourism industry have gotten stuck in the past, refusing to adapt to new technology. Before the disruption through now market-dominating platforms and Online Travel Agents, the travel industry wasn't an innovative one and instead, focused most of its resources on customer experience.

Hospitality and activity providers (particularly emerging, small, medium and independent ones) as well as small independent tour operators in destinations, are often completely overwhelmed and unable to cope with these fast technological changes and the increased complexity.

In Africa, only 10% of the current 200,000-plus hospitality and tourism providers have a digital presence, while only 15% of them are using any technology to operate and manage their business. This puts them at a huge disadvantage while they operate on either pen-and-paper, Excel or Outlook.

If these hospitality and tourism providers can't embrace the future of tourism in Africa to partake in the digital paradigm shift, it will continue to prevent them from creating sustainable occupancy, revenue and profit. This in consequence also has a negative impact on the entire destination and its people.

Tourism today

As a result, local businesses have become totally dependent on either the traditional and no longer sustainable value chain (such as Thomas Cook who just filed for insolvency) or global market digital value chains (such as booking.com) that now dominate the market.

Meanwhile, traveller behaviour has changed entirely; their demands, wants and desires are very different today from what they were even five years ago.

The move from organised group tours to individual (FIT) travel has had a huge impact on the future of tourism for the value chain. The availability of information on the internet has had an even bigger impact, catering to the traveller's mental model – dreaming, planning, booking, paying, experiencing and sharing.

Furthermore, the majority of travellers no longer travel for one three-to-four-week period for their annual holiday. Instead, they're travelling three-to-five times per year on theme trips (such as wellness, golf or city vacations).

Tourism in Africa

Many African destinations still promote what they have provided for the last 10+ years. They have not changed their offering, presentation, visibility, reputation management and distribution to adapt to market and consumer changes. For them, the future of tourism is stuck in the past.

Today's travellers scour the internet for months, visiting hundreds of websites, social media platforms, review platforms, online travel agents and so forth. In this dreaming and planning phase, they are in no rush. Yet when they have made their decisions and have planned their trip, their mindset shifts.

Travellers demand instant gratification when booking and paying for the trip.

This is where 85% of the providers in African destinations fail. The customer is ready to make their booking, but the in-destination hospitality and tourism providers are not ready. They do not enable the customer to do business with them conveniently. When the customer shifts to "instant gratification" mode, they do not want to email, send enquiry forms or even call the hospitality or tourism provider.

They want to book and pay for the trip immediately in an easy and seamless process. And if they can't book with the provider, they'll do so with a third-party platform or worst case, stuff the trip altogether.

The growing popularity of third-party platforms has also shifted the mindset of the traveller. Third-party platforms offer brand recognition, reviews and an (albeit sometimes a false) sense of security. Should something fall through with the trip, they know exactly how to get their money refunded (as opposed to wiring money to an African tourism provider with no online presence). Many consumers also falsely believe that these platforms offer cheaper prices than booking directly with the local provider.

The future of tourism in Africa and third-party vendors

This results in three types of losses for the destination and its hospitality and tourism businesses.

1   The customer decides to give up on the Destination altogether as it is too complicated to book and opts for another destination entirely. The Cruise Line industry might be our biggest competitor in that case as it is easy, convenient and very diverse.
2   The customer takes the self-planned itinerary and details and asks a high street travel agent to make the booking. As a result, the supplier in the destination pays 60–80% of their profit for those bookings – usually for no good reason as the customer is not genuine to this value chain and only used the travel agent out of frustration and desperation.
3   The customer makes use of online travel agents. Again, the destination supplier unnecessarily pays 60–80% of their profit for those bookings as the customer is not genuine to this value chain either and only used the online travel agent out of frustration and desperation.

The market power of large online travel agents with a strong vision, exposure and offerings place the traditional suppliers under heavy pressure.

The monopolisation of consumer-focused products

Consumer-focused products are also entering the market, hunting for travellers. Large wholesale operators (such as TUI) in major source markets are utilising a strategy of vertical integration.

Some have done this already on the consumer and traveller site; the next step is the supplier and the destination. This will forever change the business of the traditional value chain, DMCs or inbound tour operators. Since the DMC as we know it is no longer needed in such scenarios, they either will go out of business as long as they try to manifest a no longer sustainable business model and run this on the account and to the disadvantage of the hospitality and tourism businesses and the entire destination, or they need to change their business model altogether becoming a service provider for the vertically integrated operators in a completely different way and format.

Hospitality and Tourism Suppliers in African destinations receive more and more pressure from DMCs and traditional value chains to offer lower rates and higher commissions. They are often asked for extra payments for brochure contributions, exhibitions and FAM-trips for travel companies, increasing the cost of distribution even more.

In many cases, DMCs make block bookings at large to keep out other market players by quasi-monopolising the inventory.

Rooms not sold will often be released 30 days prior to arrival with no compensation. This is inventory that is hard to sell, as African destinations are not known as last-minute destinations.

It gets even worse when DMCs now flood the highly discounted unsold inventory to bed banks who sell them to OTAs and other distribution platforms. Without any influence from the hospitality and tourism supplier, they suddenly might appear cheaper on those platforms than the Hotel offers them directly, creating a rate imparity issue that is entirely out of the supplier's control. Again, this harms the hospitality and tourism businesses and the entire destination.

Future of tourism in Africa and sustainable hospitality

In order to create and develop a sustainable hospitality and tourism industry in Africa, it is of utmost importance to enable hospitality and tourism providers to partake in the digital world of travel.

The future of tourism in Africa needs to provide them with digital transformation strategy initiatives, enabling them to make use of technology to conveniently and seamlessly reach potential customers in their respective source markets and market segments addressed.

Education, training, awareness and growth in African destinations are crucial for the future of sustainable tourism. This capacity-building not only affects the market and technology side; it also transforms the economic, social and ecological sustainability of hospitality and tourism in a destination.

Rainmaker digital's Mission

As a social enterprise or a so-called Zebra company, it is rainmaker's passion to democratise technology that previously only large organisations could afford. To rainmaker, the future of tourism is empowering African destinations and their emerging, small, medium and independent hospitality and tourism businesses, enabling them to partake in the digital paradigm shift for sustainable tourism development.

Rainmaker's VISTA Destination Network Open Platform and Ecosystem technology does exactly this. The Public-Private Partnership Model for Destinations and Tourism Authorities and the Freemium business model builds the basis of an inclusive and pervasive Digital Transformation Initiative for the entire destination, aligned to the UNWTO Digital Transformation Strategy. Rainmaker and its partners in the destination develop local capacity building programs, consisting of masterclasses and training programs on visibility, reputation, marketing and communication and distribution management. This inclusive enablement of technical and capacity-building is of utmost importance for a destination, its businesses and people.

The future of tourism is all about keeping more tourism spend in the destination. It also allows for its businesses to move toward an economically, socially and ecologically sustainable tourism development as well as local prosperity, according to the UNWTO Tourism Sustainability Goals.

What has been achieved in other Africa destinations

rainmaker as a social enterprise or nowadays called Zebra company has invented and developed the Award Winning VISTA Destination Network Open Platform and Ecosystem which seamlessly integrates all respective stakeholders such as Accommodation Providers, Activity Providers, Tour Operators, Car Rental Operators, Hospitality and Tourism Authorities and Associations with each other in terms of all rich content and business transactions such as availability, rates, bookings and payments amongst others.

VISTA destination network open platform and ecosystem for destinations

The VISTA Destination Network is provided in a public-private partnership model to Tourism Authorities in order to create an inclusive and pervasive destination wide digital transformation initiative, fully aligned with the UNWTO Digital Transformation Initiative and contributing to the Tourism Sustainability Goals. The core applications are offered in a Freemium business model to especially integrating all emerging, small, medium and independent hospitality and tourism businesses in a destination.

The VISTA Destination Network is also the technology driver and enabler for the Award Winning 5 Stages of Success holistic methodology and managed service for hospitality and tourism providers.

Integrated and interdependent 5 stages of success

Rainmaker has invented the Award-Winning 5 Stages of Success for the last 4 years. The 5 Stages of Success are a holistic methodology and a fully managed service for destinations and the hospitality and tourism sector.

The 5 Stages of Success follow the traveller's mental model and are aimed to gain back control of the visibility, digital presence website, reputation, marketing communication and distribution. Each and any of the 5 Stages depend on each other. The entire approach is aimed to keep more tourism spend in the destination for sustainable tourism development.

Stage 1 | visibility – get found in the first place | dreaming, planning

Ninety-five per cent of all searches happen on Google. Sixty-three per cent of all those searches are done from Smartphones. If a hospitality and tourism business can't be found instantly and on the first page of the results, they will gain no or few visitors to their WebSite. They would be losing hundreds of thousands of potential revenue. Voice Search which is more and more coming up will change this landscape again significantly.

As a Google trusted verifier and Google Business Technology Partner rainmaker set up and verify the hospitality and tourism business on "Google My Business" at first and make sure that all content and details with a great level of attention to detail and accuracy are well managed. We also create a stunning Google Street View Trusted 360° Virtual Tour of the hospitality properties.

Travellers no longer believe "Still Images"

Do you know the saying "A picture is worth more than a thousand words?" Well, the same is true today as we say "A 360° virtual tour is worth more than a thousand pictures". Travellers are 48% more likely to book when walking a virtual tour instead of only having still images.

Why is this? Everyone has experienced it. Gorgeous Images, a Ballroom of a Bedroom with a Fruit Basket, Bottle of Wine and nice and warm light. However, when you come into the room it somehow is not what the photo made you dream of, right? So, travellers don't easily trust those images anymore.

However, having a Google Street View Trusted 360° virtual tour, you give full control to the traveller who can now walk through your property at its own pace and actually see what they want to see and not only what the Hotel wants to show. It is also realistic since the footage can't be staged as per Google guidelines. This simply creates trust and trust creates more direct bookings.

Achievements (2016–2019)

- 11.6 million searches of Google for Hospitality and Tourism Businesses in Namibia
- 23.1 million views of the respective Google Business Cards in Search or Maps
- 1.1 million conversions for Directions, WebSite Clicks or Phone Calls
- 42 million 360° Virtual Tour Image Views for the Destination Namibia

Stage 2 | digital presence WebSite – convert bookings and create leads | dreaming, planning, booking

Even when most questions can be answered already at the first Touchpoint, there is still a reason a Hospitality and Tourism business should have a perfect, stunning and foremost fast loading website.

Even when many potential travellers search on Google, there are plenty of potential travellers that use Online Travel Agents such as booking.com, expedia.com or others or the so-called Meta-Engines such as Tripadvisor or Trivago.

However, it is in the nature of the human being that one always looks for a bargain or sometimes the information on those platforms is not sufficient. This is when potential travellers look for the exact brand name and it is very likely, in case your website performs perfectly in terms of Search Engine Optimisation, they will see your website high up and click on it as they are looking for it.

Since most travellers research for weeks and months and build their itinerary, especially in an itinerary destination with five or more different attractions and locations, they first look at the attractions they want to see. When this itinerary has been compiled, the potential travellers look for accommodation nearby that fits their style, ambiance and budget.

Therefore such a website has two objectives. (1) To create a direct booking or make the "looker" become a "booker" and (2) If that can't be achieved to get the contact details to follow up getting the booking. In that case, such a Hotel, Guesthouse or Lodge WebSite doesn't need to inform the traveller about all the beauty of the region and what to do as they probably know this already – it would rather site track them – and the potential of losing this traveller is very likely.

Such a website needs to load in three seconds, be perfect with all OnPage SEO and needs to fulfil the Dreaming – Planning and Booking Stage of the Travellers Mental Model to improve on direct bookings. It needs to enable the potential traveller to get in contact with the business as easy and seamless as possible and in many ways such as Phone, eMail, Enquiry Form, Live Chat and obviously the ability to check for rates, check for availability and do a booking. These are three different intents and a BOOK NOW button at the top is not good enough.

With data and experience from hundreds of Hospitality websites in itinerary destinations, we have created a best practice model for such Hospitality Websites. If you run a local Tour Operator, the challenges are completely different and are mainly based on so-called customer acquisition. But I will handle this in a separate article.

Achievements 2016–2019

* Generated more than N$ 20 million in Direct Booking Revenue in Namibia
* Generated more than 9.000 Direct Enquiries in Namibia

Stage 3 | reputation – understand where to improve and respond to your reviews | dreaming, planning

Another aspect that is often not really looked at is the reputation and the management of the reputation. Also here the world has changed. When Tripadvisor has been the place to go five years ago, this is no longer the case. Again, The Google Business Review section has become the most looked at right on the Google Search or Google Maps Page. So it is important to actively manage this.

However, there are more than 200 review platforms including the Online Travel Agents, Tripadvisor, Facebook, Google, that it is almost impossible to oversee this complexity.

In our Stage three, rainmaker reads most of those review platforms in 20 languages and through an artificial intelligence semantic analysis, we are able to detect a positive, neutral or negative comment in a written review. We can furthermore segment the comment made to a certain department such as Frontdesk, Housekeeping, Food & Beverage.

So at first, it tells you exactly where you might overperform, where you are OK and where you underperform based on data and not opinion. This will then be benchmarked against your peer group and competitors so that you have a 360° view on your reputation compared to your peer group or competitors. Using this as management or an incentive tool in the day to day operation can certainly improve your reputation.

Every guest that checks out should be enabled to provide you with a review. To gain more reviews and publish them where most needed. However, The Google Review section becomes ever more important to travellers and, even though it is not officially confirmed, can have an impact on your ranking with Google.

Having a huge number of reviews is not good enough. You need to respond to them. To all of them. Here at rainmaker we really much like the negative reviews our customers receive. Why? The potential traveller first looks at the negative reviews. If there are no responses, the traveller understands that the business owner doesn't care about their guests and won't even look at the good ones but instead might no longer consider this Hotel any further.

But, a negative review can be worth much more than a very positive review. It just depends on the way and detail the Hotel is responding to the review and how the issue is being addressed. When the potential traveller can see that the concerns are taken seriously and are addressed adequately and with a decent response to the guest, they value this more than a good review.

Over a period of 18 months, we could manage a Hotel being on 15 of 33 on Tripadvisor to move to 10, 5 and 3 of 33 listings on Tripadvisor. The move from 15 to 10 did not create a big difference in bookings. The move from 10 to 5 doubled the bookings and the move from 5 to 3 almost again doubled the bookings. Here the value for money issue comes into play and if you are #3 you can't be bad. But if your rate is intelligently managed and your Hotel is a bit more affordable then #1 and #2, they simply book #3 as the best option.

Achievements (2016–2019)

* 4% better reputation than the countries average in Namibia

Stage 4 | marketing communication – content-, social- and eMail marketing | dreaming, planning, sharing

As mentioned in Part 1 of the article, just having a WebSite is not making a large difference. Like in the traditional marketing where there was no free advertising on Billboards, in Magazines or on Radio, the same becomes more and more true on the internet.

This Stage 4 is about customer acquisition through content marketing, social media marketing, email marketing and advertising whether on Google or Facebook or other respective platforms targeting your source market and market segments addressed.

This also includes the so-called retargeting to play out adverts to only those who have visited your website but have not concluded on a booking. In that case, you would show adverts to only those visitors who already showed interest in your property.

This Stage is also one that demands constant work on a daily basis as new content is to be posted on various platforms such as Facebook, Instagram, LinkedIn, to attract potential travellers frequently.

For a Hotel or Guesthouse, this might sound impossible in the first place. But how about you post content, stories, images, little things that happen around you? For a Safari Lodge, you have content every day from your Game Drives. You can also think of stories about your team, a kitchen and food story or such. Or how your once housekeeper growth to be a receptionist or such.

Posting those stories and content looks like for free, but remember on Facebook for example that only about 5% of your audience (fans, likes) will actually see your post unless you boost it or create an advert from it which you need to pay for.

Then you have Google Adwords and Facebook Travel Ads where you can create advertising campaigns on various keywords or phrases targeting your source markets and market segments addressed very specifically.

The research and design of such campaigns will take a couple of weeks including testing. For these adverts, you pay for example for every click to your website and depending on the competitive landscape that can vary between like US$ 0.05 and US$5 or even much more. So those campaigns need to be carefully managed on a daily basis from an experienced team.

However, advertising creates paid traffic to your website but it still needs to convert into a booking in order to have any value for your business. It must, therefore, be carefully watched on whether the return in bookings is worth the cost and here is where Stage 2 comes in again.

Again, these are two very specialised fields that require a lot of experience in order to efficiently set up, run and manage your content marketing and advertising.

Key Takeaway | While organic traffic might no longer be sufficient, content marketing, social media marketing, email marketing, retargeting and digital advertising are alternatives to generate significant traffic. However, this comes at a cost and needs to be carefully managed on a daily basis.

Stage 5 | distribution – revenue and yield management | planning, booking

Finally, Stage 5 is where your business takes the revenue and the profits home. It is about the distribution, the revenue and yield management of your rooms inventory.

Some of our customers don't sell their rooms anywhere but on their website, some only through DMCs and others have connected their inventory to every single platform they could connect to.

None of the above "strategies" is perfect or would provide the needed results. The crux like always is in the right mix and whether or not a channel addresses the source markets and market segments your business and the destination addresses. If Japan, for example, is not your source market for the destination, it makes little sense to be present on platforms serving the Japanese market.

The other aspect is the more platforms such as booking.com, expedia.com and others you connect to, the more possibility to dilute your brand. OTA's are using machine learning and algorithms to place adverts on Google and elsewhere with your Brand Name and your location.

That means when someone looks for your Hotel, Lodge or Guesthouse, all of them who have to spend advertising money will come first. It is therefore very likely that they simply click on the first match and off they went to the OTA. If that traveller decides to book there, you pay 60–80% of your profit plus the ownership of the customer. Your Hotel or Guesthouse has become a commodity where the OTA makes more money with the booking and owns the customer and all its meta-data. This is not sustainable.

However, just disconnect from all such platforms is also no solution as the actual value they provide is global exposure. The trick is the right mix and the respective day to day management of all your various sales channels. This is where the complexity comes in. Five years ago it was easy to just work with a few DMC and Tour Operators at a fixed STO-Rate, but those times are gone and no one can run a sustainable business on just this one channel.

The OTA provides all sorts of so-called opportunities. But if you read carefully they are meant to be more opportunities for the OTA to make more money with your product. One needs to be very careful when selecting those. Some enable customers to book with no credit card, others provide an additional discount. In any case, it is all about making it easier and less binding for their customers to book through them with the ability to even cancel on the day of arrival with no compensation and since you have no credit card details, you can't do anything. Their loyalty programs are also operated on your account as it is the Hotel or Guesthouse who pays the extra 10% discount.

The entire distribution management is therefore all about to connect only to those platforms that are addressing your source markets and market segments and produce sustainable revenue and profit. Platforms that don't produce room nights should be disconnected, especially when they use your business for their advertising.

Despite all the platforms, the ultimate goal is to get bookings directly on your own website booking engine. This is another discipline and complexity to provide and make very visible what are the benefits to book directly vs. book on any such platform. If you have an ocean-facing Hotel, you could give all Garden View Rooms to the platforms but the Sea View Rooms can be booked only on the WebSite. There are many other opportunities to show the potential traveller the benefit of booking direct.

Key Takeaway | It takes a lot of research, insights and analysis to find out the best sales mix. If connected to OTA's make sure the "opportunities" are managed on a daily basis as they are changed often. Also, use your rates, amenities, value adds, room types to differentiate your offering on any platform vs. your website where you can gain a direct booking.

Conclusion

30

Prospects and futures for tourism in Africa

Marina Novelli, Emmanuel Akwasi Adu-Ampong and Manuel Alector Ribeiro

This *Handbook* has offered a varied and far-reaching set of insights into the workings of tourism in Africa. Nonetheless, the range of themes, geographical locations and issues covered in here only scratches the surface of all that is evident on the continent in terms of the potentials, challenges and success of tourism development in Africa is facing. We have produced this *Handbook* to showcase and celebrate the richness and diversity of the tourism sector in Africa. In this final chapter, we provide some reflections on the prospects and futures for tourism in Africa and advance suggestions about possible directions for forthcoming research opportunities on tourism 'in' and 'for' Africa.

The direct and indirect potential role of tourism as a vehicle for economic growth and development in Africa is a well traversed discussion across existing literature and to a certain extent in this volume. What has once more emerged is that 'these can be at times be sporadic and tokenistic' (Novelli, 2016: 198). In 2000, Peter U.C. Dieke concluded his volume *The Political Economy of Tourism Development in Africa*, by listing a set of necessary strategic tourism development measure for Africa and the new millennium that had just started, these being:

- well-conceived and well-articulated but realistic tourism policy objectives;
- local involvement and control over tourism development;
- forging private-public sector partnerships for tourism development;
- raising gender awareness to enhance women's participation in the tourism sector;
- promoting regional tourism cooperation and integration;
- availability and allocation of appropriate resources (e.g. financial, human, product);
- developing equity in tourism benefits sharing;
- promoting community tourism awareness campaigns;
- availability of appropriate legal framework for tourism;
- building image of a destination through a marketing and promotional campaign;
- expanding tourism entrepreneurial initiative/investment opportunities.
  Dieke (2000: 312)

Twenty years later, his suggestions are still of much relevance, and issues of policy, planning and implementation remain still amongst the key challenging factors and priorities in tourism for development in Africa. Subsequently, while the need to facilitate an intricate transition from international interventionism to a more localised sustainable approach to development was identified by Novelli (2016), today, the complexities and contradictions complicating tourism and development matters at continental level appear to be unshifted, if not worsened, with only a few exceptions.

This *Handbook* has also evidenced that the national political economy determines the way tourism evolves differently in various locations. In Africa, like anywhere else in the world:

> [p]olitical stability, good governance, enabling business environments, coherent prioritisation and adequate funding of tourism remain fundamental ingredients for the sector to flourish, yield substantial economic gains and stimulate 'good change' at local level. Investment in infrastructures and tourism training, service standards' improvement, access to resources and markets, preservation of physical and cultural assets and destination accessibility remain amongst the most important topics to address the current tourism sector's shortfalls in both established and emerging destinations.
>
> *(Novelli, 2016: 199)*

In 2015, the launch of the United Nations *Agenda 2030 for Sustainable Development* and its 17 *Sustainable Development Goal* (SDGs) provided a new set of indicators and targets for sustainable development. While strongly perpetuating the idea that progress in sustainable development is private sector driven, compared to the earlier UN Millennium Development Goals (MDGs) project, which was mainly governments and development agencies driven, the SDGs' discourse still fails to fully address local challenges, particularly in the African context.

In Africa, as in most parts of the world, governments have widely provided endorsement to adopt the SDGs, which have been incorporated into government policies and national strategies. However, for several African countries to achieve the SDGs by 2030, strong economic growth is deemed paramount but remains problematic. Despite being specifically named in relation to only three SDGs – SDG 8 on 'Decent Work and Economic Growth', SDG 12 on 'Responsible Consumption and Production' and SDG 14 on 'Life below Water', the tourism sector and its value chain linkages make it potentially eligible to *de facto* contribute towards the entire set of SDGs as much as to the required economic growth. African countries need to take the initiative and develop important alliances and linkages that can help them achieve these goals and promote prosperity and sustainable livelihood.

Indeed, one of the crucial challenges for African countries to achieve the SDGs by 2030 will be their capacity to mobilise funds to finance them. In doing so, according to the Brookings Institution (2019), sub-Saharan Africa will need 574 billion dollars per year until 2030 to finance the SDGs. In July 2019, Begashaw also reported that:

> With 11 1/2 years to go, Africa is relatively on track to meet three goals: SDG 5 (gender equality), SDG 13 (climate action), and SDG 15 (life on land). In fact, the SDG Center's forecasts (for the SDGs for which we have sufficient data: poverty, malnutrition, maternal mortality, net school enrollment, access to electricity, and access to drinking water) show that all African regions except North Africa are unlikely to meet the SDGs. The struggle is more pronounced for Central Africa across all the goals.

Although tourism has been recognised as an essential sector to help countries to achieve the SDGs, some African countries still struggle to fully embrace tourism as one of the critical players in their development strategy. To achieve these goals, all stakeholders involved in the tourism industry should stand ready to embrace the cause and ultimately deliver on sustainable development. Those in the public and private sectors are encouraged to use their power to create conditions for investment in the tourism sector, which brings social and economic benefits for the local people and protection to the environment. However, the reality is that what still counts is the return on investment that tourism can bring with the main challenge remaining in its limited immediacy.

What is more is that operating in the era of a 'climate emergency', filled with pledges to reduce air travel flocking from all corners of the globe, the message is confusing at best, contradictory at worse. After promoting tourism as the promise for development in Africa for over 30 years, and having recurrently denounced the lack of intra-Africa air connectivity as one of the major hindering factors to the success of the sector, now that this is being addressed, the avalanche of 'calls to save the world by not flying', may potentially have devastating implications for some of the most tourism dependent and remote locations. That climate emergency focused solutions are urgent is a given fact, that taking climate sensitive actions on a personal level is needed is a reality, but there is some caution needed in the way the path must be laid. There is a need to bring to these debates, the issue of equity in terms of reducing carbon emissions. Given that more developed countries emit more than African countries, for instance, it is important that emission reduction targets are designed in an equitable *pro-rata* basis. The aviation industry has a responsibility more than ever to act to address the climate emergency, as much as anybody else in the private sector, by embracing more sustainable business models and operations, in line with what the SDGs have set as a global ambition. But these responses to the climate emergency should not come at the expense of development efforts in Africa.

There are global leading businesses today that still do not have an environmental policy and are not even thinking about the impacts that they have on the environment and society. Increasingly, tourism companies in Africa are designing environmental policies and practices, much more than in other parts of the world, since environmental protection is essential to their business competitiveness and contribution to the sustainable advancement of African economies. The view that 'being sustainable makes business sense' is increasingly encouraged as the ethos of many companies embracing 'sustaibility as the new luxury' (Kepher-Gona, 2018).

Throughout this *Handbook*, tourism has been portrayed as a sector able to activate socioeconomic progress and gender equality and prone to generate income for some of the most remote destinations. The demand for new tourism products and services gives way to the creation of new jobs, hence potentially contributing to poverty alleviation and reducing inequalities through entrepreneurship. In some countries, tourism has been the seed of collaborative approaches leading to funds fully dedicated to the conservation of wildlife and biodiversity, the regeneration of local assets and the boost of skills across the entire value chain. The purpose of the remainder of this concluding chapter is to provide summaries of all chapters and present some selected questions to stimulate further ideas, debates and research topics about the prospects and futures of tourism development in Africa for students, researchers and practitioners.

Part I: Africa and tourism

Part I comprises six chapters and one InFocus, and discusses in a broader sense, some of the main topics related to tourism in Africa. In this sense, in Chapter 2, Saayman, Saayman and Viljoen identify the determinants that foster a greater understanding of the factors that contribute to the development and appeal of Africa as a competitive tourism player. They also provide several recommendations on how to achieve this goal and to transform Africa into a competitive tourism destination. In Chapter 3, Ayeh discusses the role of Information Communication Technology (ICT) in tourism in Africa. He notes that many African countries are yet to fully exploit the potential of ICT to maximise tourism gains. The continent continues to remain at the heart of the 'digital divide'. He further elaborates on how technology could be harnessed to strategically market Africa's tourism potentials within the framework of the extended marketing mix paradigm and examines the critical issues challenging the adoption of ICT in Africa's tourism sector. This is also a theme that is covered in the InFocus 3 on the role of the media in promoting tourism in Africa. In Chapter 4, Lwoga and Adu-Ampong reflect on the paradox of local heritage doctrines and practices within the realms of dominant western-based heritage models. They provide an overview of critical issues facing heritage tourism in Africa highlighting the challenges that hinder the full realisation of heritage tourism's potential in Africa. In Chapter 5, Giddy highlights that although the growth of adventure tourism in Africa is seen positively by many, there are several challenges to adventure tourism development and concerns that emerge as development increases. She reviews the literature on some of the primary adventure tourism subsectors, delves deeper into some of the primary concerns surrounding adventure tourism development in Africa and suggests recommendations for addressing these. Hambira and Mbaiwa in Chapter 6 review the tourism-climate change nexus as it applies to tourism development in the African continent. The chapter reiterates that some important tourist destinations in Africa, such as wetlands and coastal towns, have already shown signs of negative climatic impacts. In the context of ongoing discussion of 'flight shame' and climate change mitigation through less flying, Chapter 7 by Mutinda discusses the challenges of tourism and aviation in Africa. In explores the efforts undertaken to open up Africa's airspace and the challenges that have stood in the way of such efforts. He also highlights that air travel continues to be the dominant mode of travel in international tourism, emphasising that effective connectivity within the vast continent is key to unlocking Africa's tourism potential. This part of the *Handbook* concludes with two *InFocus* contributions on the role of the UNWTO in tourism and sustainable development in Africa, authored by Grandcourt and on the MICE in Africa authored by Donkor. Questions need to be asked as to how the low level of ICT adoption can be scaled-up through tourism entrepreneurship. How would the emerging discourse on 'flight shame' affect international tourist arrivals in African destinations? How can intra- and inter African domestic tourism be encouraged to secure the sustainability of tourism businesses? If tourism in Africa is to contribute to local economic development and community resilience then it is important to focus on appropriate policy formulation and implementation.

Part II: tourism in North Africa

Part II is dedicated to tourism in North Africa and consists of four chapters and one *InFocus*. In Chapter 8 by Jeffrey and Rumens advocate for the incorporation of a postcolonial feminist perspective in scholarly research on gender and tourism in Tunisia. They show how introducing and mobilising postcolonial feminism provides insights into how tourism shapes what it means to be a woman in Tunisia. In Chapter 9, Megeirhi, Ribeiro and Woosnam examine the ways in which the variation in equity perceptions among various social classes can either trigger or halt the process of cultural heritage preservation. The chapter further expounds the factors that, through the lens of equity theory, explain the perceptions of residents concerning their intentions to support cultural heritage preservation in the World Heritage Site of Carthage, Tunisia. Almeida-Garcia in Chapter 10 touches on current issues of tourism development in Morocco. The chapter analyses the development model based on tourism through the use of the institutional approach to describe the evolution of tourism policy in Morocco and uses Saidïa as a case study. In Chapter 11, Shohaieb provides an overview of the evolution and the importance of the tourism industry in Egypt. She also identifies and explains periods of expansion and recession, the different tourism institutions that developed over time, and the role of the government in the development of the tourism industry in Egypt. This part of *Handbook* concludes with an *InFocus* authored by Williams and Ohene on the tole of the media in promoting tourism in Africa. Key questions that are raised in this section include: how can different theoretical perspectives provide new ways of understanding, explaining and resolving tourism development challenges? What are the impacts of persistent political instability on tourism development? Can tourism-led cultural heritage conservation process deliver equitable benefits within communities? These are critical issues that when addressed can provide the tools needed for effective tourism development.

Part III: tourism in West Africa

Part III covers tourism development in the Western Africa region and it comprises seven chapters and two *InFocus* contributions. The use of tourism as a catalyst for local economic development and poverty reduction is the focus of Chapter 12. Using the case of the Elmina 2015 Strategy in Ghana, Adu-Ampong sets out arguments about the particular ways in which institutions, particularly political party structures, shape the extent to which tourism can be used as a tool for development. In Chapter 13 which focuses on tourism development in Senegal, Sene-Harper presents an evolution of tourism development in this country, including a review of major policies, trends and historical context in each period. She also discusses the development of community-based tourism (CBT) in the integrated rural tourism program of the Lower Casamance as a counter model of development. Thus, she also presents the critical issues of CBT around national parks as part of Senegal's new tourism identity. In Chapter 14, Ribeiro, Woosnam and Megeirhi discuss the realm of the political economy of tourism development in Cape Verde islands. The chapter furthers understandings of the factors that influence public trust in tourism institutions and their support for tourism development within the island context. In Chapter 15, by Dayour, the emphasis is on the opportunities and challenges of backpacking in Ghana. In this chapter, Dayour presents an overview of Ghana's tourism industry, focussing on the dynamics of the backpacker segment, as well as the challenges and issues affecting its growth in the country. Adeola, Eigbe and Muritala in Chapter 16 explore the drivers and opportunities in Nigeria's tourism industry, with a focus on sustainable growth and development. The chapter further explores the challenges inhibiting growth in Nigeria's tourism and hospitality sector and then identify opportunities and growth drivers for the industry. In Chapter 17, Gafarou offers an overview of conservation and tourism in transborder protected areas through the case study of regional parks. She also provides an outlook on the interrelation of security and tourism expansion, with an emphasis on the necessity for strategic tourism planning and diversification of the industry, particularly in post-crisis areas in Niger. The process of tourism development is the focus of Chapter 18 by Brown. The chapter further highlights the country's tourism attractions and its regional competitive advantage and attempts to enumerate the main growth-inhibiting factors that account for the sector's slow resurgence from the pre-civil war era of growth. This part concludes with two *InFocus* contributions, one by Kwadwo on Afrogallonism and the 360La festival, and the other by Ukachukwu and Akinoshun presenting their perspectives on the Aviators Africa Academy. One of the key question raised from this section and which future research need to address as a matter of urgency is the question of politics and local governance in tourism development. Does tourism development under a particular political regime and local governance structure have the potential to contribute more to development than other political organisations? How can tourism development be fully embedded in local political government structures to ensure long terms sustainability of tourism projects? In many Africa countries, tourism development and policy are using driven from the national level with little involvement from local government institutions. It is important that we understand the ways in which local-level politics and governance practices can inhibit and enable new forms of tourism to emerge. Given that tourism is successful in a context of political and economic stability, research should focus on how tourism may help to contribute to political stability and more resilient forms of local governance structures.

Part IV: tourism in Middle Africa

Part IV is devoted to the intricacies of tourism development in the Middle Africa region. This part is composed of three chapters and one InFocus. In Chapter 19, Tichaawa and Harilal endeavour to investigate the link between community participation and eco-tourism policy development in Cameroon's protected areas. Further, the chapter examines why the current practices in the eco-tourism sector, specifically within protected areas in Cameroon, are not resulting in sustainable outcomes for local communities. Gabon is the focus of Chapter 20 in which Cloquet explores the tourism development process in that country using a structure-agency approach. The chapter provides insight into the capacity of some initiatives to stimulate destination growth and development in Gabon and the challenges in this process. Moving to an island context, in Chapter 21, Brito discusses the impacts of tourism in São Tomé and Principe. The chapter explores some comparative advantage of this Archipelago that favour the emergence and implementation of tourism segments, such as nature tourism and the cultural particularities resulting from a miscegenated and Creole society, that can reinforce the relevance of tourism in national development. This part concludes with an *InFocus*, where Joan presents a particularly touching diary of her professional life as a woman in tourism. Key questions that emerge from this part include: how can African cultural practices be maintained in as tourism develops around these cultures? How can the promise of eco-tourism be fully realised for sustainable local development? It is also important to question how existing local power structures enable and constrain the process of tourism development in new areas. In such instances, research needs to address the issue of how best to leverage the community participation process to be more than simple lip-service.

Part V: tourism in Eastern Africa

Part V deals with tourism in the Eastern Africa region and comprises five chapters and one InFocus. In Chapter 22, Munanura and Sabuhoro present an overview of the potential of tourism revenue sharing policy to benefit conservation in Rwanda. This is explained through the use of a sustainable livelihoods framework that synthesises constraints in Rwanda's proposed tourism revenue program with the opportunities available. The chapter also discusses residents' capability to access and maintain livelihoods, equity in livelihoods distribution and sustainability of livelihoods. Chapter 23 by Senbeto enlightens readers about the Rock Art tourism in Ethiopia and cultural heritage management challenges. Additionally, this chapter outlines an overview of cultural heritage management and its importance by assessing Ethiopia's rock art sites and their potential for tourism and examines the challenges which hinder the rock art sites from further tourism development. In Chapter 24, Abdula, Breda and

Eusébio present the historical evolution and future challenges of tourism in Mozambique. The chapter also addresses Mozambique's tourism profile and identifies the main challenges the sector is facing such as political instability, lack of price competitiveness and an image stained by socioeconomic problems which altogether hinders Mozambique from becoming a competitive international tourism destination. In Chapter 25, Mgonja discusses the significance of tourism in Tanzania and highlights the need to recognise the links between tourism and rural livelihoods. He also highlights the importance of strengthening agriculture and tourism linkages as a way of increasing rural inclusiveness and enhancing economic wellbeing in Tanzania's rural areas.

Mauritius is the focus of Chapter 26 where Ramkissoon and Sowamber offer an overview of the tourism and sustainable development in the country. They focus on the case study of Mauritian hotel group LUX★ Resorts and Hotels to address the issues around implementing sustainable tourism development initiatives, which involve stakeholder engagement and participation in the tourism development process. In Chapter 27 by Gona and Atieno deals with the evaluation of the participation of pastoral women in community conservancies in the Maasai Mara, Kenya. They argue that to attain impactful levels of livelihood improvement programmes, community conservancies should first do away with their simplistic view of a community and acknowledge that gendered dimensions of the pastoral frame can disenfranchise local women empowerment. They also propose that community conservancies should focus on strategies for reducing inequalities within diverse positions held by community members. This part of the Handbook concludes with an InFocus, where Bakunz discusses his Red Rocks initiatives for sustainable tourism development in Rwanda. There are a number of key questions here including, how can the capabilities of local communities be developed so that they can benefit from tourism development? What is the role of government and business in strengthening the tourism-agriculture linkages in ways that support rural development? How can communities maintain control over tourism projects that are developed through external agencies?

Part VI: tourism in Southern Africa

Part VI comprises two chapters and three InFocus contributions addressing tourism development issues in the Southern Africa region. C. Rogerson and J. Rogerson in Chapter 28 provide an overview of the extant scholarship relating to city tourism in the sub-region of Southern Africa. They conclude that the most notable features of city tourism in Africa are the relative strength of cities as non-leisure destinations, most notably for business tourism, the rise of slum tourism and the existence of an extensive informal economy of city tourism. In the penultimate Chapter 29, Mutanga and her colleagues portray a positive relationship between wildlife tourism, conservation and community benefits in Zimbabwe. The chapter traces the development of tourism, reports on international and domestic tourism trends and assesses how wildlife tourism is contributing to conservation and community development in Zimbabwe and the challenges involved. The three *InFocus* included here are those of Danks who discusses South African Airways and their Corporate Social Responsibility; Auala who addresses Hatika Adult Education Centre's supports to Community Tourism Development in Windhoek, Namibia; and Muller's making the case for how best to keep more tourism spend within destination as an avenue for sustainable tourism development. Within these contexts, questions need to be asked about the most appropriate ways of sustaining wildlife tourism in Southern African given the increasing impact of climate change (droughts, flooding) on wildlife population. The extensive nature of informal business tourism in many African cities, offers an avenue for future research.

How can informal business tourism be conceptualised and highlighted as a significant contributor to tourism and economic development in Africa?

Conclusion

This final chapter has provided some further reflections on challenges and opportunities for tourism in Africa. The future of tourism in Africa is undoubtedly linked to environmental management actions. Pollution and waste (particularly plastic) are the root cause of environmental degradation, that remain amongst one of the major challenges particularly in urban and coastal areas, where consumption patterns by a fast increasing population is having devastating effects on human quality-of-life and wellbeing. These negative impacts are also the result of the modernisation process, which have led to shifting from more traditional to Western lifestyles, often out of sync with the context in which they are adopted.

The 'Africa rising' narrative is increasingly becoming a reality that many still like to ignore, with stories of successes, buried into neo-colonial tales often fomented by global powers fearing what could really happen if the continent moved to the next stage of development. Moreover, travel and tourism can play the lens through which the changing story becomes more visible and accessible to a wider set of spectators. It is for this reason that we truly believe that Africa is the future of tourism and tourism can provide a promising future for the continent. Travellers will be able to witness the multifaceted nature of a fast evolving sector and look beyond the curtains of stereotypically distressing imagery of striking poverty, by finally experiencing first hand (and hopefully learn from) stories of progress, business achievement and environmental stewardship.

While the future of tourism in Africa includes many challenges and issues, there are also exciting opportunities ahead. The chapters collected in this *Handbook* indicate a keen growing interest in researching the tourism phenomenon in Africa from different perspectives. The interdisciplinary nature of tourism provides the ground for future studies of the sector, as an increasingly recognised force for social, economic and environmental change. There is every reason to believe that at the intersection of the world's most exciting post-industrial and post-colonial industries, tourism provides many opportunities for innovation and disruption of traditional systems and models. We hope that the chapters included in this *Handbook* will be a source of inspiration for tourism scholars, students, industry expert and decision-makers to strive to make Africa a better place to live in and visit for all.

References

Begashaw, B. (2019) *Africa and the Sustainable Development Goals: A long way to go.* Available at: https://www.brookings.edu/blog/africa-in-focus/2019/07/29/africa-and-the-sustainable-development-goals-a-long-way-to-go/, downloaded 30/01/2020.

Brookings Institution (2019). *Building the SDG Economy: Needs, Spending, and Financing for Universal Achievement of the Sustainable Development Goals.* Washington, DC: Brookings Institution.

Dieke, P.U.C. (2000) *The Political Economy of Tourism Development in Africa.* Elmsford: CABI.

Kepher-Gona, J (2018) *Interview with Judy Kepher-Gona on Africa Tourism Business, Destinations and Sustainability.* Available at: https://sustainability-leaders.com/judy-kepher-gona-interview/, Downloaded 30/01/2020.

Novelli, M. (2016) *Tourism and Development in sub-Sahara Africa: Contemporary Issues and Local Realities.* Oxford: Routledge.

Index

Note: Page numbers followed by "n" refer to notes.

Printed in the United States
By Bookmasters